ACC 305

INTERMEDIATE ACCOUNTING

Chapters 17-24

2010 Custom Edition

STRAYER.
UNIVERSITY
1892

WILEY *Custom*
LEARNING SOLUTIONS

ACC 305: INTERMEDIATE ACCOUNTING
2010 Custom Edition

To order books or for customer service, please call 1(800)-CALL-WILEY (225-5945).

Printed in the United States of America.

ISBN 978-0-470-57564-2
Printed and bound by J&M Reproducion Corp.

10 9 8 7 6 5 4 3 2

BRIEF CONTENTS

INTERNATIONAL ACCOUNTING STANDARDS

Relevant and reliable financial information is a necessity for viable capital markets. Unfortunately, companies outside the United States often prepare financial statements using standards different from U.S. GAAP. As a result, international companies such as **Coca-Cola**, **Microsoft**, and **IBM** have to develop financial information in different ways. Beyond the additional costs these companies incur, users of the financial statements often must understand at least two sets of GAAP (understanding one set is hard enough!). It is not surprising, therefore, that there is a growing demand for one set of high-quality international standards.

Presently, there are two sets of rules accepted for international use—**U.S. GAAP** and the **International Financial Reporting Standards (IFRS)**. Also known as iGAAP, these standards are issued by the London-based International Accounting Standards Board (IASB). U.S. companies that list overseas are still permitted to use U.S. GAAP, and foreign companies listed on U.S. exchanges are permitted to use iGAAP. As you will learn, there are many similarities between U.S. GAAP and iGAAP.

Already over 100 countries have adopted iGAAP, plus the European Union now requires all listed companies in Europe (over 7,000 companies) to use it. Recently, the U.S. SEC proposed that it will allow some U.S. companies to adopt iGAAP as early as 2009.

CONVERGENCE OF U.S. GAAP AND INTERNATIONAL GAAP (iGAAP)

We agree that the most important innovation shaping our capital markets was the idea of U.S. GAAP. It might be said that it would be even better if we had one common set of accounting rules for the whole world, which will make it easier for international investors to compare the financial results of companies from different countries. That is happening quickly as U.S. GAAP and iGAAP are converging toward one set of international accounting standards (International Financial Reporting Standards, IFRS or iGAAP) to be used by all companies. And you have the chance to be on the ground floor as we develop for you the similarities and differences in the two systems that ultimately will be one.

Because convergence is such an important issue, we provide throughout this textbook a summary page on international accounting called **Convergence Corner**. This feature will help you to understand the changes that are taking place in the financial reporting arena (related to the chapter topics) as we move toward one set of international GAAP. Each Convergence Corner, as shown here, consists of four sections: (1) An introduction, which typically lists the international accounting pronouncements related to the chapter topic; (2) "Relevant Facts," which explains similarities and differences of U.S. GAAP and international GAAP (referred to as iGAAP); (3) "About the Numbers," which generally provides an example of application of iGAAP (in many cases, using real international companies); and (4) "On the Horizon," which discusses convergence progress and plans related to that topic. Each chapter also has assignment material related to international accounting.

Having a basic understanding of international accounting is becoming ever more important as the profession moves toward convergence of GAAP and international standards. Thus, in addition to the **Convergence Corner** pages discussed above, we continue to include marginal **International Insights**, marked with the icon shown here, which we updated throughout to reflect changes in international accounting. These notes describe or compare iGAAP standards and accounting practices in other countries with U.S. GAAP. This feature helps you to understand that other countries sometimes use different recognition and measurement principles to report financial information. We use this same icon to designate the new international Questions that we added to many of the chapters.

OTHER INTERNATIONAL COVERAGE

INTERNATIONAL
INSIGHT

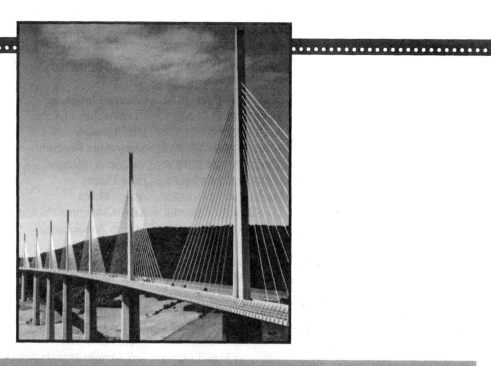

THIRTEENTH EDITION

INTERMEDIATE ACCOUNTING

DONALD E. KIESO PH.D., C.P.A.
Northern Illinois University
DeKalb, Illinois

JERRY J. WEYGANDT PH.D., C.P.A.
University of Wisconsin
Madison, Wisconsin

TERRY D. WARFIELD PH.D.
University of Wisconsin
Madison, Wisconsin

WILEY

JOHN WILEY & SONS

Dedicated to our wives, Donna, Enid, and Mary, for their love, support, and encouragement

PUBLISHER	George Hoffman
ASSOCIATE PUBLISHER	Christopher DeJohn
SENIOR ACQUISITIONS EDITOR	Jeff Howard
DEVELOPMENT EDITOR	Terry Ann Kremer
SENIOR PRODUCTION EDITOR	Valerie A. Vargas
SENIOR MARKETING MANAGER	Julia Flohr
EXECUTIVE MARKETING MANAGER	Amy Scholz
SENIOR DESIGNER	Kevin Murphy
PRODUCTION MANAGEMENT SERVICES	Ingrao Associates
CREATIVE DIRECTOR	Harry Nolan
SENIOR ILLUSTRATION EDITOR	Anna Melhorn
MEDIA EDITOR	Allie K. Morris
PROJECT EDITOR	Ed Brislin
SENIOR PHOTO EDITOR	Elle Wagner
EDITORIAL ASSISTANT	Kara Taylor
PRODUCTION ASSISTANT	Matt Winslow
COVER PHOTO	Jon Arnold Images/SuperStock, Inc.
CHAPTER OPENER PHOTO	Paul Fawcett/iStockphoto

This book was set in Palatino by Aptara®, Inc. and printed and bound by RRD-JC. The cover was printed by RRD-JC.

This book is printed on acid-free paper. ∞

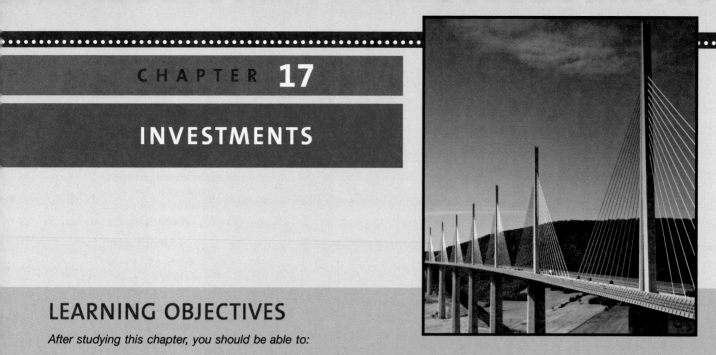

CHAPTER 17

INVESTMENTS

LEARNING OBJECTIVES

After studying this chapter, you should be able to:

- **•1** Identify the three categories of debt securities and describe the accounting and reporting treatment for each category.

- **•2** Understand the procedures for discount and premium amortization on bond investments.

- **•3** Identify the categories of equity securities and describe the accounting and reporting treatment for each category.

- **•4** Explain the equity method of accounting and compare it to the fair value method for equity securities.

- **•5** Describe the accounting for the fair value option.

- **•6** Discuss the accounting for impairments of debt and equity investments.

- **•7** Explain why companies report reclassification adjustments.

- **•8** Describe the accounting for transfer of investment securities between categories.

WHO'S IN CONTROL HERE?

The Coca-Cola Company (Coke) owns 36 percent of the shares of Coca-Cola Enterprises (a U.S. bottling business); PepsiCo Inc. owns 46 percent of The Pepsi Bottling Group (PBG) and 41 percent of PepsiAmericas. These bottling businesses are very important to Coca-Cola and PepsiCo because they are the primary distributors of Coke and Pepsi products. In return, these companies depend on Coca-Cola and PepsiCo to provide significant marketing and distribution development support. Indeed, it can be said that Coca-Cola and PepsiCo control the bottling companies, who would not exist without their support.

However, because The Coca-Cola Company and PepsiCo own less than 50 percent of the shares in these companies, they do not prepare consolidated financial statements. Instead, Coca-Cola and PepsiCo account for these investments using the *equity method*. Under the equity method, for example, Coca-Cola reports a single income item for its profits from the bottlers, and only the net amount of its investment in the balance sheet.

Equity-method accounting gives Coca-Cola and PepsiCo pristine balance sheets and income statements, by separating the assets and liabilities and the profit margins of these bottlers from its beverage-making business. What's more, the International Accounting Standards Board (IASB) has issued *IAS No. 28,* which requires that companies use the equity method. Previously, many international companies were permitted to use either the equity method or proportional consolidation for investments similar to Coke's and Pepsi's. It is good news that both U.S. and international companies are following the same rules. (On the negative side, however, some of these companies should be consolidated but are not.)

A final point: In response to a recent FASB pronouncement, companies are now starting to consolidate more of their 20 to 50 percent–owned investments. Consolidation of entities, such as the Coke and Pepsi bottlers, may be required if the risks and rewards of those investments accrue primarily to Coke and Pepsi. [1] In fact, Coke has consolidated some of its bottling companies, which should result in the reporting of more complete information on these affiliated companies.

PREVIEW OF CHAPTER 17

As our opening story indicates, U.S. and international standard-setters are studying the measurement, recognition, and disclosure for certain investments. In this chapter we address the accounting for debt and equity investments. Appendices to this chapter discuss the accounting for derivative instruments, variable-interest entities, and fair value disclosures. The content and organization of this chapter are as follows.

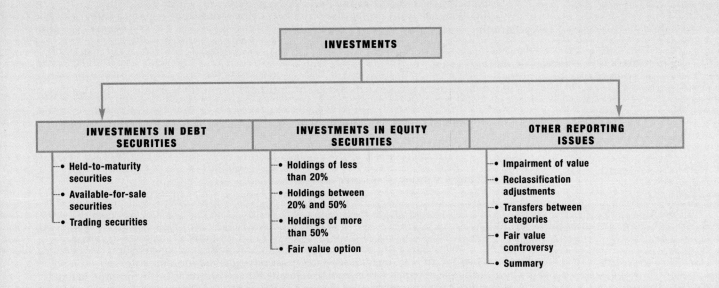

INVESTMENTS		
INVESTMENTS IN DEBT SECURITIES	**INVESTMENTS IN EQUITY SECURITIES**	**OTHER REPORTING ISSUES**
• Held-to-maturity securities • Available-for-sale securities • Trading securities	• Holdings of less than 20% • Holdings between 20% and 50% • Holdings of more than 50% • Fair value option	• Impairment of value • Reclassification adjustments • Transfers between categories • Fair value controversy • Summary

INVESTMENT ACCOUNTING APPROACHES

Companies have different motivations for investing in securities issued by other companies.[1] **One motivation is to earn a high rate of return.** For example, companies like **Coca-Cola** and **PepsiCo** can receive interest revenue from a debt investment or dividend revenue from an equity investment. In addition, they can realize capital gains on both types of securities. **Another motivation for investing (in equity securities) is to secure certain operating or financing arrangements with another company.** As in the opening story, **Coca-Cola** and **PepsiCo** are able to exercise some control over bottler companies based on their significant (but not controlling) equity investments.

To provide useful information, companies account for investments based on the type of security (debt or equity) and their intent with respect to the investment. As indicated in Illustration 17-1, we organize our study of investments by type of security. Within each section, we explain how the accounting for investments in debt and equity securities varies according to management intent.

ILLUSTRATION 17-1
Summary of Investment
Accounting Approaches

Types of Security	Management Intent	Valuation Approach
Debt (Section 1)	No plans to sell	Amortized cost
	Plan to sell	Fair value
Equity (Section 2)	Plan to sell	Fair value
	Exercise some control	Equity method

SECTION 1 · INVESTMENTS IN DEBT SECURITIES

Debt securities represent a creditor relationship with another entity. Debt securities include U.S. government securities, municipal securities, corporate bonds, convertible debt, and commercial paper. Trade accounts receivable and loans receivable are not debt securities because they do not meet the definition of a security.

Companies group investments in debt securities into three separate categories for accounting and reporting purposes:

Objective·1

Identify the three categories of debt securities and describe the accounting and reporting treatment for each category.

- **Held-to-maturity**: Debt securities that the company has the positive intent and ability to hold to maturity.
- **Trading**: Debt securities bought and held primarily for sale in the near term to generate income on short-term price differences.
- **Available-for-sale**: Debt securities not classified as held-to-maturity or trading securities.

Illustration 17-2 (on page 859) identifies these categories, along with the accounting and reporting treatments required for each.

---

[1]A security is a share, participation, or other interest in property or in an enterprise of the issuer or an obligation of the issuer that has the following three characteristics: (a) It either is represented by an instrument issued in bearer or registered form or, if not represented by an instrument, is registered in books maintained to record transfers by or on behalf of the issuer. (b) It is of a type commonly traded on securities exchanges or markets or, when represented by an instrument, is commonly recognized in any area in which it is issued or dealt in as a medium for investment. (c) It either is one of a class or series or by its terms is divisible into a class or series of shares, participations, interests, or obligations. [2]

See the FASB
Codification section
(page 908).

Category	Valuation	Unrealized Holding Gains or Losses	Other Income Effects
Held-to-maturity	Amortized cost	Not recognized	Interest when earned; gains and losses from sale.
Trading securities	Fair value	Recognized in net income	Interest when earned; gains and losses from sale.
Available-for-sale	Fair value	Recognized as other comprehensive income and as separate component of stockholders' equity	Interest when earned; gains and losses from sale.

ILLUSTRATION 17-2
Accounting for Debt Securities by Category

Amortized cost is the acquisition cost adjusted for the amortization of discount or premium, if appropriate. **Fair value** is the price that would be received to sell an asset or paid to transfer a liability in an orderly transaction between market participants at the measurement date. [3]

Underlying Concepts

Companies report some debt securities at fair value not only because the information is relevant but also because it is reliable.

HELD-TO-MATURITY SECURITIES

Only debt securities can be classified as held-to-maturity. By definition, equity securities have no maturity date. A company like **Starbucks** should classify a debt security as **held-to-maturity** only if it has **both (1) the positive intent** and **(2) the ability to hold those securities to maturity**. It should not classify a debt security as held-to-maturity if it intends to hold the security for an indefinite period of time. Likewise, if Starbucks anticipates that a sale may be necessary due to changes in interest rates, foreign currency risk, liquidity needs, or other asset-liability management reasons, it should not classify the security as held-to-maturity.[2]

Companies account for held-to-maturity securities **at amortized cost**, not fair value. If management intends to hold certain investment securities to maturity and has no plans to sell them, fair values (selling prices) are not relevant for measuring and evaluating the cash flows associated with these securities. Finally, because companies do not adjust held-to-maturity securities to fair value, these securities do not increase the volatility of either reported earnings or reported capital as do trading securities and available-for-sale securities.

To illustrate the accounting for held-to-maturity debt securities, assume that Robinson Company purchased $100,000 of 8 percent bonds of Evermaster Corporation on January 1, 2009, at a discount, paying $92,278. The bonds mature January 1,

Objective·2

Understand the procedures for discount and premium amortization on bond investments.

Calculator Solution for Bond Price

	Inputs	Answer
N	10	
I	5	
PV	?	–92,278
PMT	4,000	
FV	100,000	

[2]The FASB defines situations where, even though a company sells a security before maturity, it has constructively held the security to maturity, and thus does not violate the held-to-maturity requirement. These include selling a security close enough to maturity (such as three months) so that interest rate risk is no longer an important pricing factor.

However, companies must be extremely careful with debt securities held to maturity. If a company prematurely sells a debt security in this category, the sale may "taint" the entire held-to-maturity portfolio. That is, a management's statement regarding "intent" is no longer credible. Therefore the company may have to reclassify the securities. This could lead to unfortunate consequences. An interesting by-product of this situation is that companies that wish to retire their debt securities early are finding it difficult to do so. The holder will not sell because the securities are classified as held-to-maturity.

2014 and yield 10%; interest is payable each July 1 and January 1. Robinson records the investment as follows:

January 1, 2009

purchase —

Held-to-Maturity Securities	92,278	
Cash		92,278

Robinson uses a Held-to-Maturity Securities account to indicate the type of debt security purchased.

As indicated in Chapter 14, companies must amortize premium or discount using the **effective-interest method** unless some other method—such as the straight-line method—yields a similar result. They apply the effective-interest method to bond investments in a way similar to that for bonds payable. To compute interest revenue, companies compute the effective-interest rate or yield at the time of investment and apply that rate to the beginning carrying amount (book value) for each interest period. The investment carrying amount is increased by the amortized discount or decreased by the amortized premium in each period.

Illustration 17-3 shows the effect of the discount amortization on the interest revenue that Robinson records each period for its investment in Evermaster bonds.

Underlying Concepts

The use of some simpler method that yields results similar to the effective-interest method is an application of the materiality concept.

ILLUSTRATION 17-3
Schedule of Interest
Revenue and Bond
Discount Amortization—
Effective-Interest Method

			8% BONDS PURCHASED TO YIELD 10%	
Date	Cash Received	Interest Revenue	Bond Discount Amortization	Carrying Amount of Bonds
1/1/09				$ 92,278
7/1/09	$ 4,000[a]	$ 4,614[b]	$ 614[c]	92,892[d]
1/1/10	4,000	4,645	645	93,537
7/1/10	4,000	4,677	677	94,214
1/1/11	4,000	4,711	711	94,925
7/1/11	4,000	4,746	746	95,671
1/1/12	4,000	4,783	783	96,454
7/1/12	4,000	4,823	823	97,277
1/1/13	4,000	4,864	864	98,141
7/1/13	4,000	4,907	907	99,048
1/1/14	4,000	4,952	952	100,000
	$40,000	$47,722	$7,722	

[a]$4,000 = \$100,000 \times .08 \times \frac{6}{12}$
[b]$4,614 = \$92,278 \times .10 \times \frac{6}{12}$
[c]$614 = \$4,614 - \$4,000$
[d]$92,892 = \$92,278 + \$614$

Robinson records the receipt of the first semiannual interest payment on July 1, 2009 (using the data in Illustration 17-3), as follows:

July 1, 2009

Cash	4,000	
Held-to-Maturity Securities	614	
Interest Revenue		4,614

Because Robinson is on a calendar-year basis, it accrues interest and amortizes the discount at December 31, 2009, as follows.

December 31, 2009

Interest Receivable	4,000	
Held-to-Maturity Securities	645	
Interest Revenue		4,645

Again, Illustration 17-3 shows the interest and amortization amounts.

Robinson reports its investment in Evermaster bonds in its December 31, 2009, financial statements, as follows.

ILLUSTRATION 17-4
Reporting of Held-to-
Maturity Securities

Balance Sheet	
Current assets	
Interest receivable	$ 4,000
Long-term investments	
Held-to-maturity securities, at amortized cost	$93,537
Income Statement	
Other revenues and gains	
Interest revenue	$ 9,259

Sometimes a company sells a held-to-maturity debt security so close to its maturity date that a change in the market interest rate would not significantly affect the security's fair value. Such a sale may be considered a sale at maturity and would not call into question the company's original intent to hold the investment to maturity. Let's assume, as an example, that Robinson Company sells its investment in Evermaster bonds on November 1, 2013, at 99¾ plus accrued interest. The discount amortization from July 1, 2013, to November 1, 2013, is $635 (⅔ × $952). Robinson records this discount amortization as follows.

November 1, 2013

Held-to-Maturity Securities	635	
Interest Revenue		635

Illustration 17-5 shows the computation of the realized gain on the sale.

ILLUSTRATION 17-5
Computation of Gain on
Sale of Bonds

Selling price of bonds (exclusive of accrued interest)		$99,750
Less: Book value of bonds on November 1, 2013:		
Amortized cost, July 1, 2013	$99,048	
Add: Discount amortized for the period July 1, 2013, to November 1, 2013	635	
		99,683
Gain on sale of bonds		$ 67

Robinson records the sale of the bonds as:

November 1, 2013

Cash	102,417	
Interest Revenue (4/6 × $4,000)		2,667
Held-to-Maturity Securities		99,683
Gain on Sale of Securities		67

The credit to Interest Revenue represents accrued interest for four months, for which the purchaser pays cash. The debit to Cash represents the selling price of the bonds plus accrued interest ($99,750 + $2,667). The credit to Held-to-Maturity Securities represents the book value of the bonds on the date of sale. The credit to Gain on Sale of Securities represents the excess of the selling price over the book value of the bonds.

AVAILABLE-FOR-SALE SECURITIES

Companies, like **Amazon.com**, report **available-for-sale** securities at fair value. It records the unrealized gains and losses related to changes in the fair value of available-for-sale debt securities in an unrealized holding gain or loss account. Amazon adds (subtracts) this amount to other comprehensive income for the period. Other comprehensive income is then added to (subtracted from) accumulated other comprehensive income, which is shown as a separate component of

Underlying Concepts

Recognizing unrealized gains and losses is an application of the concept of comprehensive income.

Calculator Solution for Bond Price

	Inputs	Answer
N	10	
I	4	
PV	?	−108,111
PMT	5,000	
FV	100,000	

ILLUSTRATION 17-6
Schedule of Interest Revenue and Bond Premium Amortization— Effective-Interest Method

stockholders' equity until realized. Thus, **companies report available-for-sale securities at fair value on the balance sheet, but do not report changes in fair value as part of net income until after selling the security.** This approach reduces the volatility of net income.

Example: Single Security

To illustrate the accounting for available-for-sale securities, assume that Graff Corporation purchases $100,000, 10 percent, five-year bonds on January 1, 2009, with interest payable on July 1 and January 1. The bonds sell for $108,111, which results in a bond premium of $8,111 and an effective interest rate of 8 percent.

Graff records the purchase of the bonds as follows.[3]

January 1, 2009

Available-for-Sale Securities	108,111	
Cash		108,111

Illustration 17-6 discloses the effect of the premium amortization on the interest revenue Graff records each period using the effective-interest method.

10% BONDS PURCHASED TO YIELD 8%				
Date	Cash Received	Interest Revenue	Bond Premium Amortization	Carrying Amount of Bonds
1/1/09				$108,111
7/1/09	$ 5,000[a]	$ 4,324[b]	$ 676[c]	107,435[d]
1/1/10	5,000	4,297	703	106,732
7/1/10	5,000	4,269	731	106,001
1/1/11	5,000	4,240	760	105,241
7/1/11	5,000	4,210	790	104,451
1/1/12	5,000	4,178	822	103,629
7/1/12	5,000	4,145	855	102,774
1/1/13	5,000	4,111	889	101,885
7/1/13	5,000	4,075	925	100,960
1/1/14	5,000	4,040	960	100,000
	$50,000	$41,889	$8,111	

[a]$5,000 = $100,000 × .10 × ½
[b]$4,324 = $108,111 × .08 × ½
[c]$676 = $5,000 − $4,324
[d]$107,435 = $108,111 − $676

The entry to record interest revenue on July 1, 2009, is as follows.

July 1, 2009

Cash	5,000	
Available-for-Sale Securities		676
Interest Revenue		4,324

At December 31, 2009, Graff makes the following entry to recognize interest revenue.

December 31, 2009

Interest Receivable	5,000	
Available-for-Sale Securities		703
Interest Revenue		4,297

As a result, Graff reports revenue for 2009 of $8,621 ($4,324 + $4,297).

---

[3]Companies generally record investments acquired at par, at a discount, or at a premium in the accounts at cost, including brokerage and other fees but excluding the accrued interest. They generally do not record investments at maturity value. The use of a separate discount or premium account as a valuation account is acceptable procedure for investments, but in practice companies do not widely use it.

To apply the fair value method to these debt securities, assume that at year-end the fair value of the bonds is $105,000 and that the carrying amount of the investments is $106,732. Comparing this fair value with the carrying amount (amortized cost) of the bonds at December 31, 2009, Graff recognizes an unrealized holding loss of $1,732 ($106,732 − $105,000). It reports this loss as other comprehensive income. Graff makes the following entry.

December 31, 2009

Unrealized Holding Gain or Loss—Equity	1,732	
Securities Fair Value Adjustment (Available-for-Sale)		1,732

Graff uses a valuation account instead of crediting the Available-for-Sale Securities account. The use of the **Securities Fair Value Adjustment (Available-for-Sale) account** enables the company to maintain a record of its amortized cost. Because the adjustment account has a credit balance in this case, Graff subtracts it from the balance of the Available-for-Sale Securities account to determine fair value. Graff reports this fair value amount on the balance sheet. At each reporting date, Graff reports the bonds at fair value with an adjustment to the Unrealized Holding Gain or Loss—Equity account.

Example: Portfolio of Securities

To illustrate the accounting for a portfolio of securities, assume that Webb Corporation has two debt securities classified as available-for-sale. Illustration 17-7 identifies the amortized cost, fair value, and the amount of the unrealized gain or loss.

AVAILABLE-FOR-SALE DEBT SECURITY PORTFOLIO DECEMBER 31, 2010			
Investments	Amortized Cost	Fair Value	Unrealized Gain (Loss)
Watson Corporation 8% bonds	$ 93,537	$103,600	$ 10,063
Anacomp Corporation 10% bonds	200,000	180,400	(19,600)
Total of portfolio	$293,537	$284,000	(9,537)
Previous securities fair value adjustment balance			–0–
Securities fair value adjustment—Cr.			$ (9,537)

ILLUSTRATION 17-7
Computation of Securities Fair Value Adjustment—Available-for-Sale Securities (2010)

The fair value of Webb's available-for-sale portfolio totals $284,000. The gross unrealized gains are $10,063, and the gross unrealized losses are $19,600, resulting in a net unrealized loss of $9,537. That is, the fair value of available-for-sale securities is $9,537 lower than its amortized cost. Webb makes an adjusting entry to a valuation allowance to record the decrease in value and to record the loss as follows.

December 31, 2010

Unrealized Holding Gain or Loss—Equity	9,537	
Securities Fair Value Adjustment (Available-for-Sale)		9,537

Webb reports the unrealized holding loss of $9,537 as other comprehensive income and a reduction of stockholders' equity. Recall that companies exclude from net income any unrealized holding gains and losses related to available-for-sale securities.

Sale of Available-for-Sale Securities

If a company sells bonds carried as investments in available-for-sale securities before the maturity date, it must make entries to remove from the Available-for-Sale Securities account the amortized cost of bonds sold. To illustrate, assume that Webb Corporation sold the Watson bonds (from Illustration 17-7) on July 1, 2011, for $90,000, at which time it had an amortized cost of $94,214. Illustration 17-8 (on page 864) shows the computation of the realized loss.

ILLUSTRATION 17-8
Computation of Loss on
Sale of Bonds

Amortized cost (Watson bonds)	$94,214
Less: Selling price of bonds	90,000
Loss on sale of bonds	$ 4,214

Webb records the sale of the Watson bonds as follows.

July 1, 2011

Cash	90,000	
Loss on Sale of Securities	4,214	
Available-for-Sale Securities		94,214

Webb reports this realized loss in the "Other expenses and losses" section of the income statement. Assuming no other purchases and sales of bonds in 2011, Webb on December 31, 2011, prepares the information shown in Illustration 17-9.

ILLUSTRATION 17-9
Computation of Securities
Fair Value Adjustment—
Available-for-Sale (2011)

AVAILABLE-FOR-SALE DEBT SECURITY PORTFOLIO **DECEMBER 31, 2011**			
Investments	Amortized Cost	Fair Value	Unrealized Gain (Loss)
Anacomp Corporation 10% bonds (total portfolio)	$200,000	$195,000	$(5,000)
Previous securities fair value adjustment balance—Cr.			(9,537)
Securities fair value adjustment—Dr.			$ 4,537

Webb has an unrealized holding loss of $5,000. However, the Securities Fair Value Adjustment account already has a credit balance of $9,537. To reduce the adjustment account balance to $5,000, Webb debits it for $4,537, as follows.

December 31, 2011

Securities Fair Value Adjustment (Available-for-Sale)	4,537	
Unrealized Holding Gain or Loss—Equity		4,537

Financial Statement Presentation

Webb's December 31, 2011, balance sheet and the 2011 income statement include the following items and amounts (the Anacomp bonds are long-term investments but are not intended to be held to maturity).

ILLUSTRATION 17-10
Reporting of Available-for-
Sale Securities

Balance Sheet	
Current assets	
Interest receivable	$ xxx
Investments	
Available-for-sale securities, at fair value	$195,000
Stockholders' equity	
Accumulated other comprehensive loss	$ 5,000
Income Statement	
Other revenues and gains	
Interest revenue	$ xxx
Other expenses and losses	
Loss on sale of securities	$ 4,214

Some favor including the unrealized holding gain or loss in net income rather than showing it as other comprehensive income.[4] However, some companies, particularly financial institutions, note that recognizing gains and losses on assets, but not liabilities, introduces substantial volatility in net income. They argue that hedges often exist between assets and liabilities so that gains in assets are offset by losses in liabilities, and vice versa. In short, to recognize gains and losses only on the asset side is unfair and not representative of the economic activities of the company.

This argument convinced the FASB. As a result, companies **do not include in net income** these unrealized gains and losses. [4] However, even this approach solves only some of the problems, because **volatility of capital** still results. This is of concern to financial institutions because regulators restrict financial institutions' operations based on their level of capital. In addition, companies can still manage their net income by engaging in **gains trading** (i.e., selling the winners and holding the losers).

WHAT IS FAIR VALUE?

In the fall of 2000, Wall Street brokerage firm **Morgan Stanley** told investors that rumor of big losses in its bond portfolio were "greatly exaggerated." As it turns out, Morgan Stanley also was exaggerating.

As a result, the SEC accused Morgan Stanley of violating securities laws by overstating the value of certain bonds by $75 million. The overvaluations stemmed more from wishful thinking than reality, in violation of generally accepted accounting principles, the SEC said. "In effect, Morgan Stanley valued its positions at the price at which it thought a willing buyer and seller should enter into an exchange, rather than at a price at which a willing buyer and a willing seller would enter into a current exchange," the SEC wrote.

What do the numbers mean?

Especially egregious, stated one accounting expert, were the SEC's findings that Morgan Stanley in some instances used its own more optimistic assumptions as a substitute for external pricing sources. "What that is saying is: 'Fair value is what you want the value to be. Pick a number . . .' That's especially troublesome."

As indicated in the text, the FASB is assessing what is fair and what isn't when it comes to assigning valuations. Concerns over the issue caught fire after the collapses of **Enron Corp.** and other energy traders that abused the wide discretion given them under fair value accounting. Investors recently have expressed similar worries about some financial companies, which use internal—and subjectively designed—mathematical models to come up with valuations when market quotes aren't available.

Source: Adapted from Susanne Craig and Jonathan Weil, "SEC Targets Morgan Stanley Values," *Wall Street Journal* (November 8, 2004), p. C3.

TRADING SECURITIES

Companies hold **trading securities** with the intention of selling them in a short period of time. "Trading" in this context means frequent buying and selling. Companies thus use trading securities to generate profits from short-term differences in price. Companies generally hold these securities for less than three months, some for merely days or hours.

Companies report trading securities at fair value, with unrealized holding gains and losses reported as part of net income. Similar to held-to-maturity or available-for-sale investments, they are required to amortize any discount or premium. A **holding gain or loss** is the net change in the fair value of a security from one period to another, exclusive of dividend or interest revenue recognized but not received. In short, the FASB says to adjust the trading securities to fair value, at each reporting date. In addition, companies report the change in value as part of net income, not other comprehensive income.

[4]In Chapter 4, we discussed the reporting of other comprehensive income and the concept of comprehensive income.

To illustrate, assume that on December 31, 2010, Western Publishing Corporation determined its trading securities portfolio to be as shown in Illustration 17-11. (Assume that 2010 is the first year that Western Publishing held trading securities.) At the date of acquisition, Western Publishing recorded these trading securities at cost, including brokerage commissions and taxes, in the account entitled Trading Securities. This is the first valuation of this recently purchased portfolio.

ILLUSTRATION 17-11
Computation of Securities Fair Value Adjustment— Trading Securities Portfolio (2010)

TRADING DEBT SECURITY PORTFOLIO DECEMBER 31, 2010			
Investments	Cost	Fair Value	Unrealized Gain (Loss)
Burlington Northern 10% bonds	$ 43,860	$ 51,500	$7,640
GM Corporation 11% bonds	184,230	175,200	(9,030)
Time Warner 8% bonds	86,360	91,500	5,140
Total of portfolio	$314,450	$318,200	3,750
Previous securities fair value adjustment balance			–0–
Securities fair value adjustment—Dr.			$3,750

INTERNATIONAL INSIGHT

iGAAP provides for classification as trading, available-for-sale, or held-to-maturity for all types of financial assets. U.S. GAAP applies these classifications only to securities.

The total cost of Western Publishing's trading portfolio is $314,450. The gross unrealized gains are $12,780 ($7,640 + $5,140), and the gross unrealized losses are $9,030, resulting in a net unrealized gain of $3,750. The fair value of trading securities is $3,750 greater than its cost.

At December 31, Western Publishing makes an adjusting entry to a valuation allowance, referred to as Securities Fair Value Adjustment (Trading), to record the increase in value and to record the unrealized holding gain.

December 31, 2010

| Securities Fair Value Adjustment (Trading) | 3,750 | |
| Unrealized Holding Gain or Loss—Income | | 3,750 |

Because the Securities Fair Value Adjustment account balance is a debit, Western Publishing adds it to the cost of the Trading Securities account to arrive at a fair value for the trading securities. Western Publishing reports this fair value amount on the balance sheet.

When securities are actively traded, the FASB believes that the investments should be reported at fair value on the balance sheet. In addition, changes in fair value (unrealized gains and losses) should be reported in income. Such reporting on trading securities provides more relevant information to existing and prospective stockholders.

SECTION 2 • INVESTMENTS IN EQUITY SECURITIES

Equity securities represent ownership interests such as common, preferred, or other capital stock. They also include rights to acquire or dispose of ownership interests at an agreed-upon or determinable price, such as in warrants, rights, and call or put options.

Companies do not treat convertible debt securities as equity securities. Nor do they treat as equity securities redeemable preferred stock (which must be redeemed for common stock). The cost of equity securities includes the purchase price of the security plus broker's commissions and other fees incidental to the purchase.

The degree to which one corporation (**investor**) acquires an interest in the common stock of another corporation (**investee**) generally determines the accounting treatment for the investment subsequent to acquisition. The classification of

Objective•3
Identify the categories of equity securities and describe the accounting and reporting treatment for each category.

such investments depends on the percentage of the investee voting stock that is held by the investor:

1. Holdings of less than 20 percent (**fair value method**)—investor has passive interest.
2. Holdings between 20 percent and 50 percent (**equity method**)—investor has significant influence.
3. Holdings of more than 50 percent (**consolidated statements**)—investor has controlling interest.

Illustration 17-12 lists these levels of interest or influence and the corresponding valuation and reporting method that companies must apply to the investment.

ILLUSTRATION 17-12
Levels of Influence Determine Accounting Methods

The accounting and reporting for equity securities therefore depend on the level of influence and the type of security involved, as shown in Illustration 17-13.

ILLUSTRATION 17-13
Accounting and Reporting for Equity Securities by Category

Category	Valuation	Unrealized Holding Gains or Losses	Other Income Effects
Holdings less than 20%			
1. Available-for-sale	Fair value	Recognized in "Other comprehensive income" and as separate component of stockholders' equity	Dividends declared; gains and losses from sale.
2. Trading	Fair value	Recognized in net income	Dividends declared; gains and losses from sale.
Holdings between 20% and 50%	Equity	Not recognized	Proportionate share of investee's net income.
Holdings more than 50%	Consolidation	Not recognized	Not applicable.

HOLDINGS OF LESS THAN 20%

When an investor has an interest of less than 20 percent, it is presumed that the investor has little or no influence over the investee. In such cases, if market prices are available subsequent to acquisition, the company values and reports the investment using the fair value method.[5] The fair value method requires that companies classify equity securities at acquisition as **available-for-sale securities** or **trading securities**. Because equity securities have no maturity date, companies cannot classify them as held-to-maturity.

[5]If an equity investment is not publicly traded, a company values the investment and reports it at cost in periods subsequent to acquisition. This approach is often referred to as the **cost method.** Companies recognize dividends when received. They value the portfolio and report it at acquisition cost. Companies only recognize gains or losses after selling the securities.

Available-for-Sale Securities

Upon acquisition, companies record available-for-sale securities at cost.[6] To illustrate, assume that on November 3, 2010 Republic Corporation purchased common stock of three companies, each investment representing less than a 20 percent interest.

	Cost
Northwest Industries, Inc.	$259,700
Campbell Soup Co.	317,500
St. Regis Pulp Co.	141,350
Total cost	$718,550

Republic records these investments as follows.

November 3, 2010

Available-for-Sale Securities	718,550	
Cash		718,550

On December 6, 2010, Republic receives a cash dividend of $4,200 on its investment in the common stock of Campbell Soup Co. It records the cash dividend as follows.

December 6, 2010

Cash	4,200	
Dividend Revenue		4,200

All three of the investee companies reported net income for the year, but only Campbell Soup declared and paid a dividend to Republic. But, recall that when an investor owns less than 20 percent of the common stock of another corporation, it is presumed that the investor has relatively little influence on the investee. As a result, **net income earned by the investee is not a proper basis for recognizing income from the investment by the investor**. Why? Because the increased net assets resulting from profitable operations may be permanently retained for use in the investee's business. Therefore, **the investor earns net income only when the investee declares cash dividends**.

At December 31, 2010, Republic's available-for-sale equity security portfolio has the cost and fair value shown in Illustration 17-14.

ILLUSTRATION 17-14
Computation of Securities
Fair Value Adjustment—
Available-for-Sale Equity
Security Portfolio (2010)

AVAILABLE-FOR-SALE EQUITY SECURITY PORTFOLIO DECEMBER 31, 2010			
Investments	Cost	Fair Value	Unrealized Gain (Loss)
Northwest Industries, Inc.	$259,700	$275,000	$ 15,300
Campbell Soup Co.	317,500	304,000	(13,500)
St. Regis Pulp Co.	141,350	104,000	(37,350)
Total of portfolio	$718,550	$683,000	(35,550)
Previous securities fair value adjustment balance			–0–
Securities fair value adjustment—Cr.			$(35,550)

[6]Companies should record equity securities acquired in exchange for noncash consideration (property or services) at (1) the fair value of the consideration given, or (2) the fair value of the security received, whichever is more clearly determinable. Accounting for numerous purchases of securities requires the preservation of information regarding the cost of individual purchases, as well as the dates of purchases and sales. If **specific identification** is not possible, companies may use an **average cost** for multiple purchases of the same class of security. The **first-in, first-out method** (FIFO) of assigning costs to investments at the time of sale is also acceptable and normally employed.

For Republic's available-for-sale equity securities portfolio, the gross unrealized gains are $15,300, and the gross unrealized losses are $50,850 ($13,500 + $37,350), resulting in a net unrealized loss of $35,550. The fair value of the available-for-sale securities portfolio is below cost by $35,550.

As with available-for-sale **debt** securities, Republic records the net unrealized gains and losses related to changes in the fair value of available-for-sale **equity** securities in an Unrealized Holding Gain or Loss—Equity account. Republic reports this amount as **a part of other comprehensive income and as a component of other accumulated comprehensive income (reported in stockholders' equity) until realized**. In this case, Republic prepares an adjusting entry debiting the Unrealized Holding Gain or Loss—Equity account and crediting the Securities Fair Value Adjustment account to record the decrease in fair value and to record the loss as follows.

December 31, 2010

Unrealized Holding Gain or Loss—Equity	35,550	
Securities Fair Value Adjustment (Available-for-Sale)		35,550

On January 23, 2011, Republic sold all of its Northwest Industries, Inc. common stock receiving net proceeds of $287,220. Illustration 17-15 shows the computation of the realized gain on the sale.

Net proceeds from sale	$287,220
Cost of **Northwest** shares	259,700
Gain on sale of stock	$ 27,520

ILLUSTRATION 17-15
Computation of Gain on Sale of Stock

Republic records the sale as follows.

January 23, 2011

Cash	287,220	
Available-for-Sale Securities		259,700 ← original cost
Gain on Sale of Stock		27,520

In addition, assume that on February 10, 2011, Republic purchased 20,000 shares of Continental Trucking at a market price of $12.75 per share plus brokerage commissions of $1,850 (total cost, $256,850).

Illustration 17-16 lists Republic's portfolio of available-for-sale securities, as of December 31, 2011.

ILLUSTRATION 17-16
Computation of Securities Fair Value Adjustment— Available-for-Sale Equity Security Portfolio (2011)

AVAILABLE-FOR-SALE EQUITY SECURITY PORTFOLIO
DECEMBER 31, 2011

Investments	Cost	Fair Value	Unrealized Gain (Loss)
Continental Trucking	$256,850	$278,350	$21,500
Campbell Soup Co.	317,500	362,550	45,050
St. Regis Pulp Co.	141,350	139,050	(2,300)
Total of portfolio	$715,700	$779,950	64,250
Previous securities fair value adjustment balance—Cr.			(35,550)
Securities fair value adjustment—Dr.			$99,800

At December 31, 2011, the fair value of Republic's available-for-sale equity securities portfolio exceeds cost by $64,250 (unrealized gain). The Securities Fair Value Adjustment account had a credit balance of $35,550 at December 31, 2011. To adjust its December 31, 2011, available-for-sale portfolio to fair value, the company debits the

Securities Fair Value Adjustment account for $99,800 ($35,550 + $64,250). Republic records this adjustment as follows.

[handwritten: Differences between Cost & FV]

December 31, 2011

Securities Fair Value Adjustment (Available-for-Sale)	99,800	
Unrealized Holding Gain or Loss—Equity		99,800

Trading Securities

The accounting entries to record trading equity securities are the same as for available-for-sale equity securities, except for recording the unrealized holding gain or loss. For trading equity securities, companies **report the unrealized holding gain or loss as part of net income**. Thus, the account titled Unrealized Holding Gain or Loss—Income is used.

HOLDINGS BETWEEN 20% AND 50%

An investor corporation may hold an interest of less than 50 percent in an investee corporation and thus not possess legal control. However, as shown in our opening story about **Coca-Cola**, an investment in voting stock of less than 50 percent can still give Coke (the investor) the ability to exercise significant influence over the operating and financial policies of its bottlers. [5] **Significant influence** may be indicated in several ways. Examples include representation on the board of directors, participation in policy-making processes, material intercompany transactions, interchange of managerial personnel, or technological dependency.

Another important consideration is the extent of ownership by an investor in relation to the concentration of other shareholdings. To achieve a reasonable degree of uniformity in application of the "significant influence" criterion, the profession concluded that an investment (direct or indirect) of 20 percent or more of the voting stock of an investee should lead to a presumption that in the absence of evidence to the contrary, an investor has the ability to exercise significant influence over an investee.[7]

In instances of "significant influence" (generally an investment of 20 percent or more), the investor must account for the investment using the **equity method**.

Equity Method

Objective•4

Explain the equity method of accounting and compare it to the fair value method for equity securities.

Under the **equity method**, the investor and the investee acknowledge a substantive economic relationship. The company originally records the investment at the cost of the shares acquired but subsequently adjusts the amount each period for changes in the investee's net assets. That is, **the investor's proportionate share of the earnings (losses) of the investee periodically increases (decreases) the investment's carrying amount. All dividends received by the investor from the investee also decrease the investment's carrying amount.** The equity method recognizes that investee's earnings increase investee's net assets, and that investee's losses and dividends decrease these net assets.

[7]Cases in which an investment of 20 percent or more might not enable an investor to exercise significant influence include:
  (1) The investee opposes the investor's acquisition of its stock.
  (2) The investor and investee sign an agreement under which the investor surrenders significant shareholder rights.
  (3) The investor's ownership share does not result in "significant influence" because majority ownership of the investee is concentrated among a small group of shareholders who operate the investee without regard to the views of the investor.
  (4) The investor tries and fails to obtain representation on the investee's board of directors. [6]

To illustrate the equity method and compare it with the fair value method, assume that Maxi Company purchases a 20 percent interest in Mini Company. To apply the fair value method in this example, assume that Maxi does not have the ability to exercise significant influence, and classifies the securities as available-for-sale. Where this example applies the equity method, assume that the 20 percent interest permits Maxi to exercise significant influence. Illustration 17-17 shows the entries.

ILLUSTRATION 17-17
Comparison of Fair Value
Method and Equity
Method

ENTRIES BY MAXI COMPANY

Fair Value Method		Equity Method	
On January 2, 2010, Maxi Company acquired 48,000 shares (20% of Mini Company common stock) at a cost of $10 a share.			
Available-for-Sale-Securities 480,000		Investment in Mini Stock 480,000	
Cash	480,000	Cash	480,000
For the year 2010, Mini Company reported net income of $200,000; Maxi Company's share is 20%, or $40,000.			
No entry		Investment in Mini Stock 40,000	
		Revenue from Investment	40,000
At December 31, 2010, the 48,000 shares of Mini Company have a fair value (market price) of $12 a share, or $576,000.			
Securities Fair Value Adjustment		No entry	
(Available-for-Sale)	96,000		
Unrealized Holding Gain			
or Loss—Equity	96,000		
On January 28, 2011, Mini Company announced and paid a cash dividend of $100,000; Maxi Company received 20%, or $20,000.			
Cash	20,000	Cash	20,000
Dividend Revenue	20,000	Investment in Mini Stock	20,000
For the year 2011, Mini reported a net loss of $50,000; Maxi Company's share is 20%, or $10,000.			
No entry		Loss on Investment 10,000	
		Investment in Mini Stock	10,000
At December 31, 2011, the Mini Company 48,000 shares have a fair value (market price) of $11 a share, or $528,000.			
Unrealized Holding Gain		No entry	
or Loss—Equity	48,000		
Securities Fair Value Adjustment			
(Available-for-Sale)	48,000		

Note that under the fair value method, Maxi reports as revenue only the cash dividends received from Mini. **The earning of net income by Mini (the investee) is not considered a proper basis for recognition of income from the investment by Maxi (the investor).** Why? Mini may permanently retain in the business any increased net assets resulting from its profitable operation. Therefore, Maxi only earns revenue when it receives dividends from Mini.

Under the equity method, Maxi reports as revenue its share of the net income reported by Mini. Maxi records the cash dividends received from Mini as a decrease in the investment carrying value. As a result, Maxi records its share of the net income of Mini in the year when it is earned. With significant influence, Maxi can ensure that Mini will pay dividends, if desired, on any net asset increases resulting from net income. To wait until receiving a dividend ignores the fact that Maxi is better off if the investee has earned income.

Using dividends as a basis for recognizing income poses an additional problem. For example, assume that the investee reports a net loss. However, the investor exerts influence to force a dividend payment from the investee. In this case, the investor reports income, even though the investee is experiencing a loss. **In other words, using dividends as a basis for recognizing income fails to report properly the economics of the situation.**

INTERNATIONAL INSIGHT

iGAAP permits companies to measure significant-influence investments using the equity, cost, or fair value methods.

For some companies, equity accounting can be a real pain to the bottom line. For example, **Amazon.com**, the pioneer of Internet retailing, at one time struggled to turn a profit. Furthermore, some of Amazon's equity investments had resulted in Amazon's earnings performance going from bad to worse. In a recent year, Amazon.com disclosed equity stakes in such companies as **Altera International, Basis Technology, Drugstore.com,** and **Eziba.com.** These equity investees reported losses that made Amazon's already bad bottom line even worse, accounting for up to 22 percent of its reported loss in one year alone.

Investee Losses Exceed Carrying Amount

Underlying Concepts

Revenue to be recognized should be earned and realized or realizable. A low level of ownership indicates that a company should defer the income from an investee until cash is received.

If an investor's share of the investee's losses exceeds the carrying amount of the investment, should the investor recognize additional losses? Ordinarily, the investor should discontinue applying the equity method and not recognize additional losses.

If the investor's potential loss is not limited to the amount of its original investment (by guarantee of the investee's obligations or other commitment to provide further financial support), or if imminent return to profitable operations by the investee appears to be assured, the investor should recognize additional losses. [7]

HOLDINGS OF MORE THAN 50%

When one corporation acquires a voting interest of more than 50 percent in another corporation, it is said to have a **controlling interest.** In such a relationship, the investor corporation is referred to as the **parent** and the investee corporation as the **subsidiary.** Companies present the investment in the common stock of the subsidiary as a long-term investment on the separate financial statements of the parent.

INTERNATIONAL INSIGHT

In contrast to U.S. firms, financial statements of non-U.S. companies often include both consolidated (group) statements and parent company financial statements.

When the parent treats the subsidiary as an investment, the parent generally prepares **consolidated financial statements.** Consolidated financial statements treat the parent and subsidiary corporations as a single economic entity. (Advanced accounting courses extensively discuss the subject of when and how to prepare consolidated financial statements.) Whether or not consolidated financial statements are prepared, the parent company generally accounts for the investment in the subsidiary **using the equity method** as explained in the previous section of this chapter.

CONSOLIDATE THIS!

What do the numbers mean?

Presently the rules for consolidation seem very straightforward: If a company owns more than 50 percent of another company, it generally should be consolidated. If it owns less than 50 percent, it is generally not consolidated. However the FASB recognizes the artificiality of the present test. Determination of who really has control often relies on factors other than stock ownership.

In fact, specific guidelines force consolidation even though stock ownership is not above 50 percent in certain limited situations. For example, Enron's failure to consolidate three special purpose entities (SPEs) that it effectively controlled led to an overstatement of income of $569 million and overstatement of equity of $1.2 billion. In each of Enron's three SPEs, the GAAP guidelines would have led to consolidation. That is, the following factors indicate that consolidation should have occurred: the majority owner of the special purpose entity (SPE) made only a modest investment; the activities of the SPE primarily benefited Enron; and the substantive risks and rewards related to the assets or debt of the SPE rested directly or indirectly with Enron.

The FASB has issued new guidelines related to SPEs, given all the reporting problems that have surfaced related to SPEs at Enron and other companies. We discuss these new rules in Appendix 17B.

FAIR VALUE OPTION

As indicated in earlier chapters, companies have the option to report most financial instruments at fair value, with all gains and losses related to changes in fair value reported in the income statement. This option is applied on an instrument-by-instrument basis. The fair value option is generally available only at the time a company first purchases the financial asset or incurs a financial liability. If a company chooses to use the fair value option, it must measure this instrument at fair value until the company no longer has ownership.

> **Objective·5**
> Describe the accounting for the fair value option.

For example, assume that **Abbott Laboratories** purchased debt securities in 2010 that it classified as held-to-maturity. Abbott does not choose to report this security using the fair value option. In 2011, Abbott buys another held-to-maturity debt security. Abbott decides to report this security using the fair value option. Once it chooses the fair value option for the security bought in 2011, the decision is irrevocable (may not be changed). In addition, Abbott does not have the option to value the held-to-maturity security purchased in 2010 at fair value in 2011 or in subsequent periods.

Many support the use of the fair value option as a step closer to total fair value reporting for financial instruments. They believe this treatment leads to an improvement in financial reporting. Others argue that the fair value option is confusing. A company can choose from period to period whether to use the fair value option for any new investment in a financial instrument. By permitting an instrument-by-instrument approach, companies are able to report some financial instruments at fair value but not others. To illustrate the accounting issues related to the fair value option, we discuss three different situations.

Available-for-Sale Securities

Available-for-sale securities are presently reported at fair value, and any unrealized gains and losses are recorded as part of other comprehensive income. Assume that Hardy Company purchases stock in Fielder Company during 2010 that it classifies as available-for-sale. At December 31, 2010, the cost of this security is $100,000; its fair value at December 31, 2010, is $125,000. If Hardy chooses the fair value option to account for the Fielder Company stock, it makes the following entry at December 31, 2010.

Investment in Fielder Stock	25,000	
Unrealized Holding Gain or Loss—Income		25,000

In this situation, Hardy uses an account titled Investment in Fielder Stock to record the change in fair value at December 31. It does not use a Securities Fair Value Adjustment account because the accounting for a fair value option is on an investment-by-investment basis rather than on a portfolio basis. Because Hardy selected the fair value option, the unrealized gain or loss is recorded as part of net income. Hardy must continue to use the fair value method to record this investment until it no longer has ownership of the security.

Equity Method of Accounting

Companies may also use the fair value option for investments that otherwise follow the equity method of accounting. To illustrate, assume that Durham Company holds a 28 percent stake in Suppan Inc. Durham purchased the investment in 2010 for $930,000. At December 31, 2010, the fair value of the investment is $900,000. Durham elects to report the investment in Suppan using the fair value option. The entry to record this investment is as follows.

Unrealized Holding Gain or Loss—Income	30,000	
Investment in Suppan Stock		30,000

In contrast to equity method accounting, if the fair value option is chosen, Durham does not have to report its pro rata share of the income or loss from Suppan. In addition, any dividend payments are credited to Dividend Revenue and therefore do not reduce the Investment in Suppan Stock account.

One major advantage of using the fair value option for this type of investment is that it addresses confusion about the equity method of accounting. In other words, what exactly does the one-line consolidation related to the equity method of accounting on the balance sheet tell investors? Many believe it does not provide information about liquidity or solvency, nor does it provide an indication of the worth of the company.

Financial Liabilities

One of the more controversial aspects of the fair value option relates to valuation of a company's own liabilities. Companies may apply the fair value option to their own debt instruments. As a result, changes in the fair value of the debt instrument are included as part of earnings in any given period.

To illustrate, Edmonds Company has issued $500,000 of 6% bonds at face value on May 1, 2010. Edmonds chooses the fair value option for these bonds. At December 31, 2010, the value of the bonds is now $480,000 because interest rates in the market have increased to 8 percent. The value of the debt securities falls because the bond is paying less than market rate for similar securities. Under the fair value option, Edmonds makes the following entry.

| Bonds Payable | 20,000 | |
| Unrealized Holding Gain or Loss—Income | | 20,000 |

As the journal entry indicates, the value of the bonds declined. This decline leads to a reduction in the bond liability and a resulting unrealized holding gain, which is reported as part of net income. The value of Edmonds' debt declined because interest rates increased. In addition, if the creditworthiness of Edmonds Company declines, the value of its debt also declines. That is, Edmonds issued debt at rates reflecting higher creditworthiness. If its creditworthiness declines, its bond investors are receiving a lower rate relative to investors with similar-risk investments. If Edmonds is using the fair value option in this case, it records an unrealized holding gain due to its worsening credit position.

Some question how Edmonds can record a gain when its creditworthiness is becoming worse. As one writer noted, "It seems counter-intuitive." However, the FASB notes that the debtholders' loss is the stockholders' gain. That is, the stockholders' claims on the assets of the company increase when the value of the debtholders declines. In addition, the worsening credit position may indicate that the assets of the company are declining in value as well. Thus, the company may be reporting losses on the asset side which will be offsetting gains on the liability side.

SECTION 3 • OTHER REPORTING ISSUES

We have identified the basic issues involved in accounting for investments in debt and equity securities. In addition, the following issues relate to both of these types of securities.

1. Impairment of value.
2. Reclassification adjustments.
3. Transfers between categories.
4. Fair value controversy.

IMPAIRMENT OF VALUE

A company should evaluate every investment, at each reporting date, to determine if it has suffered **impairment**—a loss in value that is other than temporary. For example, if an investee experiences a bankruptcy or a significant liquidity crisis, the investor may suffer a permanent loss. **If the decline is judged to be other than temporary, a company writes down the cost basis of the individual security to a new cost basis.** The company accounts for the write-down as a realized loss. Therefore, it includes the amount in net income.

> **Objective·6**
> Discuss the accounting for impairments of debt and equity investments.

For debt securities, a company uses the impairment test to determine whether "it is probable that the investor will be unable to collect all amounts due according to the contractual terms."

For equity securities, the guideline is less precise. Any time realizable value is lower than the carrying amount of the investment, a company must consider an impairment. Factors involved include the length of time and the extent to which the fair value has been less than cost; the financial condition and near-term prospects of the issuer; and the intent and ability of the investor company to retain its investment to allow for any anticipated recovery in fair value.

To illustrate an impairment, assume that Strickler Company holds available-for-sale bond securities with a par value and amortized cost of $1 million. The fair value of these securities is $800,000. Strickler has previously reported an unrealized loss on these securities of $200,000 as part of other comprehensive income. In evaluating the securities, Strickler now determines that it probably will not collect all amounts due. In this case, it reports the unrealized loss of $200,000 as a loss on impairment of $200,000. Strickler includes this amount in income, with the bonds stated at their new cost basis. It records this impairment as follows.

Loss on Impairment	200,000	
Available-for-Sale Securities		200,000

The new cost basis of the investment in debt securities is $800,000. Strickler includes subsequent increases and decreases in the fair value of impaired available-for-sale securities as other comprehensive income.[8]

Companies base impairment for debt and equity securities on a fair value test. This test differs slightly from the impairment test for loans that we discuss in Appendix 7B. The FASB rejected the discounted cash flow alternative for securities because of the availability of market price information.

An example of the criteria used by **Caterpillar** to assess impairment is provided in Illustration 17-18.

Caterpillar, Inc.
Notes to Financial Statements

Note 1. Impairment of available-for-sale securities
Available-for-sale securities are reviewed monthly to identify market values below cost of 20% or more. If a decline for a debt security is in excess of 20% for six months, the investment is evaluated to determine if the decline is due to general declines in the marketplace or if the investment has been impaired and should be written down to market value. . . . After the six-month period, debt securities with declines from cost in excess of 20% are evaluated monthly for impairment. For equity securities, if a decline from cost of 20% or more continues for a 12-month period, an other than temporary impairment is recognized without continued analysis.

ILLUSTRATION 17-18
Disclosure of Impairment Assessment Criteria

---

[8]Companies may not amortize any discount related to the debt securities after recording the impairment. The new cost basis of impaired held-to-maturity securities does not change unless additional impairment occurs.

RECLASSIFICATION ADJUSTMENTS

Objective·7

Explain why companies report reclassification adjustments.

As we indicated in Chapter 4, companies report changes in unrealized holding gains and losses related to available-for-sale securities as part of other comprehensive income. Companies may display the components of other comprehensive income in one of three ways: (1) in a combined statement of income and comprehensive income, (2) in a separate statement of comprehensive income that begins with net income, or (3) in a statement of stockholders' equity.

The reporting of changes in unrealized gains or losses in comprehensive income is straightforward unless a company sells securities during the year. In that case, double counting results when the company reports realized gains or losses as part of net income but also shows the amounts as part of other comprehensive income in the current period or in previous periods.

To ensure that gains and losses are not counted twice when a sale occurs, a **reclassification adjustment** is necessary. To illustrate, assume that Open Company has the following two available-for-sale securities in its portfolio at the end of 2009 (its first year of operations).

ILLUSTRATION 17-19
Available-for-Sale Security Portfolio (2009)

Investments	Cost	Fair Value	Unrealized Holding Gain (Loss)
Lehman Inc. common stocks	$ 80,000	$105,000	$25,000
Woods Co. common stocks	120,000	135,000	15,000
Total of portfolio	$200,000	$240,000	40,000
Previous securities fair value adjustment balance			–0–
Securities fair value adjustment—Dr.			$40,000

If Open Company reports net income in 2009 of $350,000, it presents a statement of comprehensive income as follows.

ILLUSTRATION 17-20
Statement of Comprehensive Income (2009)

OPEN COMPANY STATEMENT OF COMPREHENSIVE INCOME FOR THE YEAR ENDED DECEMBER 31, 2009	
Net income	$350,000
Other comprehensive income	
Holding gains arising during period	40,000
Comprehensive income	$390,000

During 2010, Open Company sold the Lehman Inc. common stock for $105,000 and realized a gain on the sale of $25,000 ($105,000 – $80,000). At the end of 2010, the fair value of the Woods Co. common stock increased an additional $20,000, to $155,000. Illustration 17-21 shows the computation of the change in the securities fair value adjustment account.

ILLUSTRATION 17-21
Available-for-Sale Security Portfolio (2010)

Investments	Cost	Fair Value	Unrealized Holding Gain (Loss)
Woods Co. common stocks	$120,000	$155,000	$35,000
Previous securities fair value adjustment balance—Dr.			(40,000)
Securities fair value adjustment—Cr.			$ (5,000)

Illustration 17-21 indicates that Open should report an unrealized holding loss of $5,000 in comprehensive income in 2010. In addition, Open realized a gain of $25,000 on the sale of the Lehman common stock. **Comprehensive income includes both realized and unrealized components.** Therefore, Open recognizes a total holding gain (loss) in 2010 of $20,000, computed as follows.

Unrealized holding gain (loss)	$ (5,000)
Realized holding gain	25,000
Total holding gain recognized	$20,000

ILLUSTRATION 17-22
Computation of Total Holding Gain (Loss)

Open reports net income of $720,000 in 2010, which includes the realized gain on sale of the Lehman securities. Illustration 17-23 shows a statement of comprehensive income for 2010, indicating how Open reported the components of holding gains (losses).

OPEN COMPANY
STATEMENT OF COMPREHENSIVE INCOME
FOR THE YEAR ENDED DECEMBER 31, 2010

Net income (includes $25,000 realized gain on Lehman shares)		$720,000
Other comprehensive income		
Total holding gains arising during period [$(5,000) + $25,000]	$20,000	
Less: Reclassification adjustment for gains included in net income	25,000	(5,000)
Comprehensive income		$715,000

ILLUSTRATION 17-23
Statement of Comprehensive Income (2010)

In 2009, Open included the unrealized gain on the Lehman Co. common stock in comprehensive income. In 2010, Open sold the stock. It reported the realized gain in net income, which increased comprehensive income again. To avoid double counting this gain, Open makes a reclassification adjustment to eliminate the realized gain from the computation of comprehensive income in 2010.

A company may display reclassification adjustments on the face of the financial statement in which it reports comprehensive income. Or it may disclose these reclassification adjustments in the notes to the financial statements.

Comprehensive Example

To illustrate the reporting of investment securities and related gain or loss on available-for-sale securities, assume that on January 1, 2010, Hinges Co. had cash and common stock of $50,000.[9] At that date the company had no other asset, liability, or equity balance. On January 2, Hinges purchased for cash $50,000 of equity securities classified as available-for-sale. On June 30, Hinges sold part of the available-for-sale security portfolio, realizing a gain as shown in Illustration 17-24.

Fair value of securities sold	$22,000
Less: Cost of securities sold	20,000
Realized gain	$ 2,000

ILLUSTRATION 17-24
Computation of Realized Gain

[9]We adapted this example from Dennis R. Beresford, L. Todd Johnson, and Cheri L. Reither, "Is a Second Income Statement Needed?" *Journal of Accountancy* (April 1996), p. 71.

Hinges did not purchase or sell any other securities during 2010. It received $3,000 in dividends during the year. At December 31, 2010, the remaining portfolio is as shown in Illustration 17-25.

ILLUSTRATION 17-25
Computation of
Unrealized Gain

Fair value of portfolio	$34,000
Less: Cost of portfolio	30,000
Unrealized gain	$ 4,000

Illustration 17-26 shows the company's income statement for 2010.

ILLUSTRATION 17-26
Income Statement

HINGES CO.
INCOME STATEMENT
FOR THE YEAR ENDED DECEMBER 31, 2010

Dividend revenue	$3,000
Realized gains on investment in securities	2,000
Net income	$5,000

The company reports its change in the unrealized holding gain in a statement of comprehensive income as follows.

ILLUSTRATION 17-27
Statement of
Comprehensive Income

HINGES CO.
STATEMENT OF COMPREHENSIVE INCOME
FOR THE YEAR ENDED DECEMBER 31, 2010

Net income		$5,000
Other comprehensive income:		
Holding gains arising during the period ($4,000 + $2,000)	$6,000	
Less: Reclassification adjustment for gains included in net income	2,000	4,000
Comprehensive income		$9,000

Its statement of stockholders' equity appears in Illustration 17-28.

ILLUSTRATION 17-28
Statement of Stockholders'
Equity

HINGES CO.
STATEMENT OF STOCKHOLDERS' EQUITY
FOR THE YEAR ENDED DECEMBER 31, 2010

	Common Stock	Retained Earnings	Accumulated Other Comprehensive Income	Total
Beginning balance	$50,000	$–0–	$–0–	$50,000
Add: Net income		5,000		5,000
Other comprehensive income			4,000	4,000
Ending balance	$50,000	$5,000	$4,000	$59,000

The comparative balance sheet is shown on the next page in Illustration 17-29.

ILLUSTRATION 17-29
Comparative Balance
Sheet

HINGES CO. COMPARATIVE BALANCE SHEET		
	1/1/10	12/31/10
Assets		
Cash	$50,000	$25,000
Available-for-sale securities		34,000
Total assets	$50,000	$59,000
Stockholders' equity		
Common stock	$50,000	$50,000
Retained earnings		5,000
Accumulated other comprehensive income		4,000
Total stockholders' equity	$50,000	$59,000

This example indicates how an unrealized gain or loss on available-for-sale securities affects all the financial statements. Note that a company must disclose the components that comprise accumulated other comprehensive income.

TRANSFERS BETWEEN CATEGORIES

Companies account for transfers between any of the categories at fair value. Thus, if a company transfers available-for-sale securities to held-to-maturity investments, it records the new investment (held-to-maturity) at the date of transfer at **fair value** in the new category. Similarly, if it transfers held-to-maturity investments to available-for-sale investments, it records the new investments (available-for-sale) at **fair value**. This **fair value** rule assures that a company cannot omit recognition of fair value simply by transferring securities to the held-to-maturity category. Illustration 17-30 summarizes the accounting treatment for transfers.

Objective•8
Describe the accounting for transfer of investment securities between categories.

ILLUSTRATION 17-30
Accounting for Transfers

Examples of the Entries for Recording Transfers Between Categories

Type of Transfer	Measurement Basis	Impact of Transfer on Stockholders' Equity*	Impact of Transfer on Net Income*
Transfer from trading to available-for-sale	Security transferred at fair value at the date of transfer, which is the new cost basis of the security.	The unrealized gain or loss at the date of transfer increases or decreases stockholders' equity.	The unrealized gain or loss at the date of transfer is recognized in income.
Transfer from available-for-sale to trading	Security transferred at fair value at the date of transfer, which is the new cost basis of the security.	The unrealized gain or loss at the date of transfer increases or decreases stockholders' equity.	The unrealized gain or loss at the date of transfer is recognized in income.
Transfer from held-to-maturity to available-for-sale**	Security transferred at fair value at the date of transfer.	The separate component of stockholders' equity is increased or decreased by the unrealized gain or loss at the date of transfer.	None
Transfer from available-for-sale to held-to-maturity	Security transferred at fair value at the date of transfer.	The unrealized gain or loss at the date of transfer carried as a separate component of stockholders' equity is amortized over the remaining life of the security.	None

*Assumes that adjusting entries to report changes in fair value for the current period are not yet recorded.

**According to GAAP, these types of transfers should be rare.

FAIR VALUE CONTROVERSY

The reporting of investment securities is controversial. Some believe that all securities should be reported at fair value; others believe they all should be stated at amortized cost. Others favor the present approach. In this section we look at some of the major unresolved issues.

Measurement Based on Intent

Companies classify debt securities as held-to-maturity, available-for-sale, or trading. As a result, companies can report three identical debt securities in three different ways in the financial statements. Some argue such treatment is confusing. Furthermore, the held-to-maturity category relies solely on intent, a subjective evaluation. What is not subjective is the fair value of the debt instrument. In other words, the three classifications are subjective, resulting in arbitrary classifications.

Gains Trading

Companies can classify certain debt securities as held-to-maturity and therefore report them at amortized cost. Companies can classify other debt and equity securities as available-for-sale and report them at fair value with the unrealized gain or loss reported as other comprehensive income. In either case, a company can become involved in "gains trading" (also referred to as "cherry picking," "snacking," or "sell the best and keep the rest"). In **gains trading**, companies sell their "winners," reporting the gains in income, and hold on to the losers.

Liabilities Not Fairly Valued

Many argue that if companies report investment securities at fair value, they also should report liabilities at fair value. Why? By recognizing changes in value on only one side of the balance sheet (the asset side), a high degree of volatility can occur in the income and stockholders' equity amounts. Further, financial institutions are involved in asset and liability management (not just asset management). Viewing only one side may lead managers to make uneconomic decisions as a result of the accounting.

Fair Values—Final Comment

Both the IASB and the FASB believe that fair value information for financial assets and financial liabilities provides more useful and relevant information than a cost-based system. The Boards take this position because fair value reflects the current cash equivalent of the financial instrument rather that the cost of a past transaction. As a consequence, only fair value provides an understanding of the current worth of the investment.

Companies must report fair values for some types of financial instruments. In addition, they have the option to record fair values for any of their financial instruments. How many companies will choose this fair value option? We are hopeful that many companies will select this option; we believe that the information provided by fair value reporting for financial instruments is useful and more understandable to financial statement users.

SUMMARY OF REPORTING TREATMENT OF SECURITIES

Illustration 17-31 summarizes the major debt and equity securities and their reporting treatment.

ILLUSTRATION 17-31
Summary of Treatment of
Major Debt and Equity
Securities

Category*	Balance Sheet	Income Statement
Trading (debt and equity securities)	Investments shown at fair value. Current assets.	Interest and dividends are recognized as revenue. Unrealized holding gains and losses are included in net income.
Available-for-sale (debt and equity securities)	Investments shown at fair value. Current or long-term assets. Unrealized holding gains and losses are a separate component of stockholders' equity.	Interest and dividends are recognized as revenue. Unrealized holding gains and losses are **not** included in net income but in other comprehensive income.
Held-to-maturity (debt securities)	Investments shown at amortized cost. Current or long-term assets.	Interest is recognized as revenue.
Equity method and/or consolidation (equity securities)	Investments originally are carried at cost, are periodically adjusted by the investor's share of the investee's earnings or losses, and are decreased by all dividends received from the investee. Classified as long-term.	Revenue is recognized to the extent of the investee's earnings or losses reported subsequent to the date of investment.

*Companies have the option to report financial instruments at fair value with all gains and losses related to changes in fair value reported in the income statement. If a company chooses to use the fair option for some of its financial instruments, these assets or liabilities should be reported separately from other financial instruments that used a different valuation basis. To accomplish separate reporting, a company may either (a) report separate line items for the fair value and non–fair value amounts or (b) report the total fair value and non–fair value amounts in one line and parenthetically report the fair value amount in that line also.[10]

Discussion of Special Issues Related to Investments

MORE DISCLOSURE, PLEASE

As indicated in the last two sections, the level of disclosure for investment securities is extensive. How to account for investment securities is a particularly sensitive area, given the large amounts of equity investments involved. And presently companies report investments in equity securities at cost, equity, fair value, and full consolidation, depending on the circumstances. As a recent SEC study noted, "there are so many different accounting treatments for investments that it raises the question of whether they are all needed."

Presented below is an estimate of the percentage of companies on the major exchanges that have investments in the equity of other entities.

Investments in the Equity of Other Companies

Categorized by Accounting Treatment	Percent of Companies
Presenting consolidated financial statements	91.1%
Reporting equity method investments	23.5
Reporting cost method investments*	17.4
Reporting available-for-sale investments	37.4
Reporting trading investments	6.2

*If the equity investments are not publicly traded, the company often accounts for the investment under the cost method. Changes in value are therefore not recognized unless there is impairment.

As the table indicates, many companies have equity investments of some type. These investments can be substantial. For example, based on the table above, the total amount of equity-method investments appearing on company balance sheets is approximately $403 billion, and the amount shown in the income statements in any one year for all companies is approximately $38 billion.

Source: "Report and Recommendations Pursuant to Section 401(c) of the Sarbanes-Oxley Act of 2002 on Arrangements with Off-Balance Sheet Implications, Special Purpose Entities, and Transparency of Filings by Issuers," United States Securities and Exchange Commission—Office of Chief Accountant, Office of Economic Analyses, Division of Corporation Finance (June 2005), pp. 36–39.

What do the numbers mean?

You will want to read the
CONVERGENCE CORNER on page 882

For discussion of how international convergence efforts relate to the accounting for investments.

[10]Not surprisingly, the disclosure requirements for investments and other financial assets and liabilities are extensive. We provide an expanded discussion with examples of these disclosure requirements in Appendix 17C.

CONVERGENCE CORNER

The accounting for investment securities is discussed in *IAS 27* ("Consolidated and Separate Financial Statements"), *IAS 28* ("Accounting for Investments in Associates"), and *IAS 39* ("Financial Instruments: Recognition and Measurement"). The accounting and reporting under iGAAP and U.S. GAAP are for the most part very similar, although the criteria used to determine the accounting is often different.

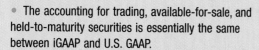 RELEVANT FACTS

• The accounting for trading, available-for-sale, and held-to-maturity securities is essentially the same between iGAAP and U.S. GAAP.

• Gains and losses related to available-for-sale securities are reported in other comprehensive income under U.S. GAAP. Under iGAAP, these gains and losses are reported directly in equity.

• Both iGAAP and U.S. GAAP use the same test to determine whether the equity method of accounting should be used—that is, significant influence with a general guide of over 20 percent ownership. iGAAP uses the term *associate investment* rather than *equity investment* to describe its investment under the equity method.

• Reclassifications of securities from one category to another generally follow the same accounting under the two GAAP systems. Reclassification in and out of trading securities is prohibited under iGAAP. It is not prohibited under U.S. GAAP, but this type of reclassification should be rare.

• Under iGAAP, both the investor and an associate

ABOUT THE NUMBERS

The following example illustrates the accounting for investment impairments under iGAAP. Belerus Company has an available-for-sale investment in the 8 percent, 10-year bonds of Wimbledon Company. The investment has a carrying value of 2,300,000 euros at December 31, 2010. Early in January 2011, Belerus learns that Wimbledon has lost a major customer. As a result, Belerus determines that this investment is impaired and now has a fair value of 1,500,000 euros. Belerus makes the following entry to record the impairment.

Loss on Impairment (€2,300,000 − €1,500,000)   800,000
    Available-for-Sale Investment   800,000

Early in 2012, Wimbledon secures several new customers, and its prospects have improved considerably. Belerus determines the fair value of its investment is now 2,000,000 euros and makes the following entry under iGAAP.

Available-for-Sale Impairment
  (€2,000,000 − €1,500,000)   500,000
    Recovery of Loss on Investment   500,000

Under U.S. GAAP, Belerus is prohibited from recording the recovery in value of the impaired investment. That is, once an investment is impaired, the impaired value becomes the new basis for the investment.

company should follow the same accounting policies. As a result, in order to prepare financial information, adjustments are made to the associate's policies to conform to the investor's books.

• The basis for consolidation under iGAAP is control. Under U.S. GAAP, a bipolar approach is used, which is a risk-and-reward model (often referred to as a *variable-entity approach*) and a voting-interest approach. However, under both systems, for consolidation to occur, the investor company must generally own 50 percent of another company.

• iGAAP and U.S. GAAP are similar in the accounting for the fair value option. That is, the selection to use the fair value method must be made at initial recognition, the selection is irrevocable, and gains and losses related to fair value changes are reported as part of income. The differences relate to disclosures and scope exceptions.

• U.S. GAAP does not permit the reversal of an impairment charge related to available-for-sale debt and equity investments. iGAAP follows the same approach for available-for-sale equity investments but permits reversal for available-for-sale debt securities and held-to-maturity securities.

ON THE HORIZON

As indicated earlier, both the FASB and IASB have indicated that they believe that all financial instruments should be reported at fair value and that changes in fair value should be reported as part of net income. It seems likely as more companies choose the fair value option for financial instruments, we will eventually arrive at fair value measurement for all financial instruments.

SUMMARY OF LEARNING OBJECTIVES

[·1] Identify the three categories of debt securities and describe the accounting and reporting treatment for each category. (1) Carry and report *held-to-maturity debt securities* at amortized cost. (2) Value *trading debt securities* for reporting purposes at fair value, with unrealized holding gains or losses included in net income. (3) Value *available-for-sale debt securities* for reporting purposes at fair value, with unrealized holding gains or losses reported as other comprehensive income and as a separate component of stockholders' equity.

[·2] Understand the procedures for discount and premium amortization on bond investments. Similar to bonds payable, companies should amortize discount or premium on bond investments using the effective-interest method. They apply the effective interest rate or yield to the beginning carrying value of the investment for each interest period in order to compute interest revenue.

[·3] Identify the categories of equity securities and describe the accounting and reporting treatment for each category. The degree to which one corporation (investor) acquires an interest in the common stock of another corporation (investee) generally determines the accounting treatment for the investment. Long-term investments by one corporation in the common stock of another can be classified according to the percentage of the voting stock of the investee held by the investor.

[·4] Explain the equity method of accounting and compare it to the fair value method for equity securities. Under the equity method the investor and the investee acknowledge a substantive economic relationship. The company originally records the investment at cost but subsequently adjusts the amount each period for changes in the net assets of the investee. That is, the investor's proportionate share of the earnings (losses) of the investee periodically increases (decreases) the investment's carrying amount. All dividends received by the investor from the investee decrease the investment's carrying amount. Under the fair value method a company reports the equity investment at fair value each reporting period irrespective of the investee's earnings or dividends paid to it. A company applies the equity method to investment holdings between 20 percent and 50 percent of ownership. It applies the fair value method to holdings below 20 percent.

[·5] Describe the accounting for the fair value option. Companies have the option to report most financial instruments at fair value, with all gains and losses related to changes in fair value reported in the income statement. This option is applied on an instrument-by-instrument basis. The fair value option is generally available only at the time a company first purchases the financial asset or incurs a financial liability. If a company chooses to use the fair value option, it must measure this instrument at fair value until the company no longer has ownership.

[·6] Discuss the accounting for impairments of debt and equity investments. Impairments of debt and equity securities are losses in value that are determined to be other than temporary, are based on a fair value test, and are charged to income.

[·7] Explain why companies report reclassification adjustments. A company needs a reclassification adjustment when it reports realized gains or losses as part of net income but also shows the amounts as part of other comprehensive income in the current or in previous periods. Companies should report unrealized holding gains or losses related to available-for-sale securities in other comprehensive income and the aggregate balance as accumulated comprehensive income on the balance sheet.

[·8] Describe the accounting for transfer of investment securities between categories. Transfers of securities between categories of investments should be accounted for at fair value, with unrealized holding gains or losses treated in accordance with the nature of the transfer.

KEY TERMS

amortized cost, *859*

available-for-sale securities, *858*

consolidated financial statements, *872*

controlling interest, *872*

debt securities, *858*

effective-interest method, *860*

equity method, *870*

equity securities, *866*

exchange for noncash consideration, *868(n)*

fair value, *859*

fair value method, *867*

gains trading, *865, 880*

held-to-maturity securities, *858*

holding gain or loss, *865*

impairment, *875*

investee, *866*

investor, *866*

parent, *872*

reclassification adjustment, *876*

Securities Fair Value Adjustment account, *863*

security, *858(n)*

significant influence, *870*

subsidiary, *872*

trading securities, *858*

| APPENDIX **17A** | **ACCOUNTING FOR DERIVATIVE INSTRUMENTS** |

Until the early 1970s, most financial managers worked in a cozy, if unthrilling, world. Since then, constant change caused by volatile markets, new technology, and deregulation has increased the risks to businesses. In response, the financial community developed products to manage these risks.

These products—called **derivative financial instruments** or simply, **derivatives**—are useful for managing risk. Companies use the fair values or cash flows of these instruments to offset the changes in fair values or cash flows of the at-risk assets. The development of powerful computing and communication technology has aided the growth in derivative use. This technology provides new ways to analyze information about markets as well as the power to process high volumes of payments.

DEFINING DERIVATIVES

In order to understand derivatives, consider the following examples.

Example 1—Forward Contract. Assume that a company like **Dell** believes that the price of **Google**'s stock will increase substantially in the next 3 months. Unfortunately, it does not have the cash resources to purchase the stock today. Dell therefore enters into a contract with a broker for delivery of 10,000 shares of Google stock in 3 months at the price of $110 per share.

Dell has entered into a **forward contract**, a type of derivative. As a result of the contract, Dell **has received the right** to receive 10,000 shares of Google stock in 3 months. Further, it **has an obligation** to pay $110 per share at that time. What is the benefit of this derivative contract? Dell can buy Google stock today and take delivery in 3 months. If the price goes up, as it expects, Dell profits. If the price goes down, Dell loses.

Example 2—Option Contract. Now suppose that Dell needs 2 weeks to decide whether to purchase Google stock. It therefore enters into a different type of contract, one that gives it the right to purchase Google stock at its current price any time within the next 2 weeks. As part of the contract, the broker charges $3,000 for holding the contract open for 2 weeks at a set price.

Dell has now entered into an **option contract**, another type of derivative. As a result of this contract, **it has received the right**, **but not the obligation** to purchase this stock. If the price of the Google stock increases in the next 2 weeks, Dell exercises its option. In this case, the cost of the stock is the price of the stock stated in the contract, plus the cost of the option contract. If the price does not increase, Dell does not exercise the contract, but still incurs the cost for the option.

The forward contract and the option contract both involve a future delivery of stock. The value of the contract relies on the underlying asset—the Google stock. Thus, these financial instruments are known as derivatives because they **derive their value from** values of other assets (e.g., stocks, bonds, or commodities). Or, put another way, their value relates to a market-determined indicator (e.g., stock price, interest rates, or the Standard and Poor's 500 stock composite index).

In this appendix, we discuss the accounting for three different types of derivatives:

1. Financial forwards or financial futures.
2. Options.
3. Swaps.

WHO USES DERIVATIVES, AND WHY?

Whether to protect for changes in interest rates, the weather, stock prices, oil prices, or foreign currencies, derivative contracts help to smooth the fluctuations caused by various types of risks. A company that wants to ensure against certain types of business risks often uses derivative contracts to achieve this objective.[11]

> **Objective•9**
> Explain who uses derivatives and why.

Producers and Consumers

To illustrate, assume that Heartland Ag is a large producer of potatoes for the consumer market. The present price for potatoes is excellent. Unfortunately, Heartland needs two months to harvest its potatoes and deliver them to the market. Because Heartland expects the price of potatoes to drop in the coming months, it signs a forward contract. It agrees to sell its potatoes today at the current market price for delivery in 2 months.

Who would buy this contract? Suppose on the other side of the contract is McDonald's Corporation. McDonald's wants to have potatoes (for French fries) in 2 months and believes that prices will increase. McDonald's is therefore agreeable to accepting delivery in 2 months at current prices. It knows that it will need potatoes in 2 months, and that it can make an acceptable profit at this price level.

In this situation, if the price of potatoes increases before delivery, Heartland loses and McDonald's wins. Conversely, if the price decreases, Heartland wins and McDonald's loses. However, the objective is not to gamble on the outcome. Regardless of which way the price moves, both Heartland and McDonald's have received a price at which they obtain an acceptable profit. In this case, although Heartland is a **producer** and McDonald's is a **consumer**, both companies are **hedgers**. They both **hedge their positions** to ensure an acceptable financial result.

Commodity prices are volatile. They depend on weather, crop production, and general economic conditions. For the producer and the consumer to plan effectively, it makes good sense to lock in specific future revenues or costs in order to run their businesses successfully.

Speculators and Arbitrageurs

In some cases, instead of McDonald's taking a position in the forward contract, a speculator may purchase the contract from Heartland. The speculator bets that the price of potatoes will rise, thereby increasing the value of the forward contract. The speculator, who may be in the market for only a few hours, will then sell the forward contract to another speculator or to a company like McDonald's.

Arbitrageurs also use derivatives. These market players attempt to exploit inefficiencies in markets. They seek to lock in profits by simultaneously entering into transactions in two or more markets. For example, an arbitrageur might trade in a futures contract. At the same time, the arbitrageur will also trade in the commodity underlying the futures contract, hoping to achieve small price gains on the difference between the two. Markets rely on speculators and arbitrageurs to keep the market liquid on a daily basis.

In these illustrations, we explained why Heartland (the producer) and McDonald's (the consumer) would become involved in a derivative contract. Consider other types of situations that companies face.

1. Airlines, like Delta, Southwest, and United, are affected by changes in the price of jet fuel.
2. Financial institutions, such as Citigroup, Bankers Trust, and M&I Bank, are involved in borrowing and lending funds that are affected by changes in interest rates.
3. Multinational corporations, like Cisco Systems, Coca-Cola, and General Electric, are subject to changes in foreign exchange rates.

[11]Derivatives are traded on many exchanges throughout the world. In addition, many derivative contracts (primarily interest rate swaps) are privately negotiated.

In fact, most corporations are involved in some form of derivatives transactions. Companies give these reasons (in their annual reports) as to why they use derivatives:

1. **ExxonMobil** uses derivatives to hedge its exposure to fluctuations in interest rates, foreign currency exchange rates, and hydrocarbon prices.
2. **Caterpillar** uses derivatives to manage foreign currency exchange rates, interest rates, and commodity price exposure.
3. **Johnson & Johnson** uses derivatives to manage the impact of interest rate and foreign exchange rate changes on earnings and cash flows.

Many corporations use derivatives extensively and successfully. However, derivatives can be dangerous. All parties involved must understand the risks and rewards associated with these contracts.[12]

BASIC PRINCIPLES IN ACCOUNTING FOR DERIVATIVES

Objective•10

Understand the basic guidelines for accounting for derivatives.

The FASB concluded that derivatives such as forwards and options are assets and liabilities. It also concluded that companies should report them in the balance sheet **at fair value.**[13] The Board believes that fair value will provide statement users the best information about derivatives. Relying on some other basis of valuation for derivatives, such as historical cost, does not make sense. Why? Because many derivatives have a historical cost of zero. Furthermore, the markets for derivatives, and the assets upon which derivatives' values rely, are well developed. As a result, the Board believes that companies can determine reliable fair value amounts for derivatives.[14]

On the income statement, a company should recognize any unrealized gain or loss in income, if it uses the derivative for speculation purposes. If using the derivative for hedging purposes, the accounting for any gain or loss depends on the type of hedge used. We discuss the accounting for hedged transactions later in the appendix.

In summary, companies follow these guidelines in accounting for derivatives.

1. Recognize derivatives in the financial statements as assets and liabilities.
2. Report derivatives at fair value.
3. Recognize gains and losses resulting from speculation in derivatives immediately in income.
4. Report gains and losses resulting from hedge transactions differently, depending on the type of hedge.

[12]There are some well-publicized examples of companies that have suffered considerable losses using derivatives. For example, companies such as **Fannie Mae** (U.S.), **Enron** (U.S.), **Showa Shell Sekiyu** (Japan), **Metallgesellschaft** (Germany), **Procter & Gamble** (U.S.), and **Air Products & Chemicals** (U.S.) incurred significant losses from investments in derivative instruments.

[13]GAAP covers accounting and reporting for all derivative instruments, whether financial or not. In this appendix we focus on derivative financial instruments because of their widespread use in practice. [8]

[14]As discussed in earlier chapters, fair value is defined as "the price that would be received to sell an asset or paid to transfer a liability in an orderly transaction between market participants at the measurement date." Fair value is therefore a market-based measure. The FASB has also developed a fair value hierarchy, which indicates the priority of valuation techniques to use to determine fair value. *Level 1* fair value measures are based on observable inputs that reflect quoted prices for identical assets or liabilities in active markets. *Level 2* measures are based on inputs other than quoted prices included in Level 1 but that can be corroborated with observable data. *Level 3* fair values are based on unobservable inputs (for example, a company's own data or assumptions). Thus, Level 1 is the most reliable because it is based on quoted prices, like a closing stock price in the *Wall Street Journal*. Level 2 is the next most reliable and would rely on evaluating similar assets or liabilities in active markets. For Level 3 (the least reliable), much judgment is needed, based on the best information available, to arrive at a relevant and reliable fair value measurement. [9]

Example of Derivative Financial Instrument—Speculation

Objective·11

Describe the accounting for derivative financial instruments.

To illustrate the measurement and reporting of a derivative for speculative purposes, we examine a derivative whose value depends on the market price of Laredo Inc. common stock. A company can realize a gain from the increase in the value of the Laredo shares with the use of a derivative, such as a call option.[15] A **call option** gives the holder the right, but not the obligation, to buy shares at a preset price. This price is often referred to as the **strike price** or the **exercise price**.

For example, assume a company enters into a call option contract with Baird Investment Co., which gives it the option to purchase Laredo stock at $100 per share.[16] If the price of Laredo stock increases above $100, the company can exercise this option and purchase the shares for $100 per share. If Laredo's stock never increases above $100 per share, the call option is worthless.

Accounting Entries. To illustrate the accounting for a call option, assume that the company purchases a call option contract on January 2, 2010, when Laredo shares are trading at $100 per share. The contract gives it the option to purchase 1,000 shares (referred to as the **notional amount**) of Laredo stock at an option price of $100 per share. The option expires on April 30, 2010. The company purchases the call option for $400 and makes the following entry.

	January 2, 2010	
Call Option	400	
Cash		400

This payment is referred to as the **option premium**. It is generally much less than the cost of purchasing the shares directly. The option premium consists of two amounts: (1) intrinsic value and (2) time value. Illustration 17A-1 shows the formula to compute the option premium.

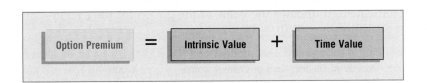

ILLUSTRATION 17A-1
Option Premium Formula

Intrinsic value is the difference between the market price and the preset strike price at any point in time. It represents the amount realized by the option holder, if exercising the option immediately. On January 2, 2010, the intrinsic value is zero because the market price equals the preset strike price.

Time value refers to the option's value over and above its intrinsic value. Time value reflects the possibility that the option has a fair value greater than zero. How? Because there is some expectation that the price of Laredo shares will increase above the strike price during the option term. As indicated, the time value for the option is $400.[17]

---

[15]Investors can use a different type of option contract—a **put option**—to realize a gain if anticipating a decline in the Laredo stock value. A put option gives the holder the option to sell shares at a preset price. Thus, a put option **increases** in value when the underlying asset **decreases** in value.

[16]Baird Investment Co. is referred to as the **counterparty**. Counterparties frequently are investment bankers or other companies that hold inventories of financial instruments.

[17]This cost is estimated using option-pricing models, such as the Black-Scholes model. The volatility of the underlying stock, the expected life of the option, the risk-free rate of interest, and expected dividends on the underlying stock during the option term affect the Black-Scholes fair value estimate.

The following additional data are available with respect to the call option.

Date	Market Price of Laredo Shares	Time Value of Call Option
March 31, 2010	$120 per share	$100
April 16, 2010	$115 per share	$60

As indicated, on March 31, 2010, the price of Laredo shares increases to $120 per share. The intrinsic value of the call option contract is now $20,000. That is, the company can exercise the call option and purchase 1,000 shares from Baird Investment for $100 per share. It can then sell the shares in the market for $120 per share. This gives the company a gain of $20,000 ($120,000 − $100,000) on the option contract.[18] It records the increase in the intrinsic value of the option as follows.

March 31, 2010

Call Option	20,000	
Unrealized Holding Gain or Loss—Income		20,000

A market appraisal indicates that the time value of the option at March 31, 2010, is $100.[19] The company records this change in value of the option as follows.

March 31, 2010

Unrealized Holding Gain or Loss—Income	300	
Call Option ($400 − $100)		300

At March 31, 2010, the company reports the call option in its balance sheet at fair value of $20,100.[20] The unrealized holding gain increases net income for the period. The loss on the time value of the option decreases net income.

On April 16, 2010, the company settles the option before it expires. To properly record the settlement, it updates the value of the option for the decrease in the intrinsic value of $5,000 ([$20 − $15]) × 1,000) as follows.

April 16, 2010

Unrealized Holding Gain or Loss—Income	5,000	
Call Option		5,000

The decrease in the time value of the option of $40 ($100 − $60) is recorded as follows.

April 16, 2010

Unrealized Holding Gain or Loss—Income	40	
Call Option		40

Thus, at the time of the settlement, the call option's carrying value is as follows.

Call Option			
January 2, 2010	400	March 31, 2010	300
March 31, 2010	20,000	April 16, 2010	5,000
		April 16, 2010	40
Balance, April 16, 2010	15,060		

[18]In practice, investors generally do not have to actually buy and sell the Laredo shares to settle the option and realize the gain. This is referred to as the net settlement feature of option contracts.

[19]The decline in value reflects both the decreased likelihood that the Laredo shares will continue to increase in value over the option period and the shorter time to maturity of the option contract.

[20]As indicated earlier, the total value of the option at any point in time equals the intrinsic value plus the time value.

The company records the settlement of the option contract with Baird as follows.

April 16, 2010

Cash	15,000	
Loss on Settlement of Call Option	60	
Call Option		15,060

Illustration 17A-2 summarizes the effects of the call option contract on net income.

Date	Transaction	Income (Loss) Effect
March 31, 2010	Net increase in value of call option ($20,000 − $300)	$19,700
April 16, 2010	Decrease in value of call option ($5,000 + $40)	(5,040)
April 16, 2010	Settle call option	(60)
	Total net income	$14,600

ILLUSTRATION 17A-2
Effect on Income—
Derivative Financial
Instrument

The accounting summarized in Illustration 17A-2 is in accord with GAAP. That is, because the call option meets the definition of an asset, the company records it in the balance sheet on March 31, 2010. Furthermore, it reports the call option at fair value, with any gains or losses reported in income.

Differences between Traditional and Derivative Financial Instruments

How does a traditional financial instrument differ from a derivative one? A derivative financial instrument has the following three basic characteristics. [10]

1. *The instrument has (1) one or more underlyings and (2) an identified payment provision.* An **underlying** is a specified interest rate, security price, commodity price, index of prices or rates, or other market-related variable. The interaction of the underlying, with the face amount or the number of units specified in the derivative contract (the notional amounts), determines payment. For example, the value of the call option increased in value when the value of the Laredo stock increased. In this case, the underlying is the stock price. To arrive at the payment provision, multiply the change in the stock price by the number of shares (notional amount).

2. *The instrument requires little or no investment at the inception of the contract.* To illustrate, the company paid a small premium to purchase the call option—an amount much less than if purchasing the Laredo shares as a direct investment.

3. *The instrument requires or permits net settlement.* As indicated in the call option example, the company could realize a profit on the call option without taking possession of the shares. This **net settlement** feature reduces the transaction costs associated with derivatives.

Illustration 17A-3 summarizes the differences between traditional and derivative financial instruments. Here, we use a trading security for the traditional financial instrument and a call option as an example of a derivative one.

Feature	Traditional Financial Instrument (Trading Security)	Derivative Financial Instrument (Call Option)
Payment provision	Stock price times the number of shares.	Change in stock price (underlying) times number of shares (notional amount).
Initial investment	Investor pays full cost.	Initial investment is much less than full cost.
Settlement	Deliver stock to receive cash.	Receive cash equivalent, based on changes in stock price times the number of shares.

ILLUSTRATION 17A-3
Features of Traditional
and Derivative Financial
Instruments

DERIVATIVES USED FOR HEDGING

Flexibility in use, and the low-cost features of derivatives relative to traditional financial instruments, explain the popularity of derivatives. An additional use for derivatives is in risk management. For example, companies such as **Coca-Cola**, **ExxonMobil**, and **General Electric** borrow and lend substantial amounts in credit markets. In doing so, they are exposed to significant **interest rate risk**. That is, they face substantial risk that the fair values or cash flows of interest-sensitive assets or liabilities will change if interest rates increase or decrease. These same companies also have significant international operations. As such, they are also exposed to **exchange rate risk**—the risk that changes in foreign currency exchange rates will negatively impact the profitability of their international businesses.

Companies can use derivatives to offset the negative impacts of changes in interest rates or foreign currency exchange rates. This use of derivatives is referred to as **hedging**.

GAAP established accounting and reporting standards for derivative financial instruments used in hedging activities. The FASB allows special accounting for two types of hedges—fair value and cash flow hedges.[21]

RISKY BUSINESS

What do the numbers mean?

As shown in the graph below, use of derivatives has grown steadily in the past several years. In fact, over *$450 trillion* (in notional amounts) in derivative contracts were in play at the end of 2007. The primary players in the market for derivatives are large companies and various financial institutions, which continue to find new uses for derivatives for speculation and risk management.

Total Swaps and Equity Derivatives
($ in trillions)

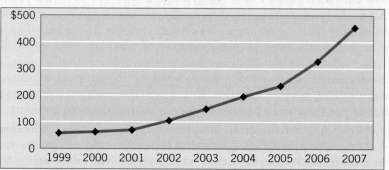

Financial engineers continue to develop new uses for derivatives, many times through the use of increasingly complex webs of transactions, spanning a number of markets. As new uses for derivatives appear, the financial system as a whole can be dramatically affected. As a result, some market-watchers are concerned about the risk that a crisis in one company or sector could bring the entire financial system to its knees.

This concern was illustrated recently when both **Fannie Mae** and **Freddie Mac** (two federally-chartered mortgage companies) indicated problems with their derivative accounting, and both of these companies had to restate their financial results for prior periods. This has led Congress to study whether the concentration of mortgages in these institutions is too high. With so many home buyers dependent on Fannie and Freddie, there is concern that these companies may be too loaded down with debt, which could negatively affect the home mortgage market.

Source: Data from International Swaps and Derivatives Association Market Survey (2007).

---

[21]GAAP also addresses the accounting for certain foreign currency hedging transactions. In general, these transactions are special cases of the two hedges we discuss here. [11] Understanding of foreign currency hedging transactions requires knowledge related to consolidation of multinational entities, which is beyond the scope of this textbook.

Fair Value Hedge

In a **fair value hedge**, a company uses a derivative to hedge (offset) the exposure to changes in the fair value of a recognized asset or liability or of an unrecognized commitment. In a perfectly hedged position, the gain or loss on the fair value of the derivative equals and offsets that of the hedged asset or liability.

Companies commonly use several types of fair value hedges. For example, companies use interest rate swaps to hedge the risk that changes in interest rates will impact the fair value of debt obligations. Or, they use put options to hedge the risk that an equity investment will decline in value.

To illustrate a fair value hedge, assume that on April 1, 2010, Hayward Co. purchases 100 shares of Sonoma stock at a market price of $100 per share. Hayward does not intend to actively trade this investment. It consequently classifies the Sonoma investment as available-for-sale. Hayward records this available-for-sale investment as follows.

April 1, 2010

Available-for-Sale Securities	10,000	
Cash		10,000

Hayward records available-for-sale securities at fair value on the balance sheet. It reports unrealized gains and losses in equity as part of other comprehensive income.[22] Fortunately for Hayward, the value of the Sonoma shares increases to $125 per share during 2010. Hayward records the gain on this investment as follows.

December 31, 2010

Security Fair Value Adjustment (Available-for-Sale)	2,500	
Unrealized Holding Gain or Loss—Equity		2,500

Illustration 17A-4 indicates how Hayward reports the Sonoma investment in its balance sheet.

HAYWARD CO.
BALANCE SHEET (PARTIAL)
DECEMBER 31, 2010

Assets	
Available-for-sale securities (at fair value)	$12,500
Stockholders' Equity	
Accumulated other comprehensive income	
Unrealized holding gain	$2,500

ILLUSTRATION 17A-4
Balance Sheet Presentation of Available-for-Sale Securities

While Hayward benefits from an increase in the price of Sonoma shares, it is exposed to the risk that the price of the Sonoma stock will decline. To hedge this risk, Hayward locks in its gain on the Sonoma investment by purchasing a put option on 100 shares of Sonoma stock.

Hayward enters into the put option contract on January 2, 2011, and designates the option as a fair value hedge of the Sonoma investment. This put option (which expires in two years) gives Hayward the option to sell Sonoma shares at a price of $125. Since the exercise price equals the current market price, no entry is necessary at inception of the put option.[23]

January 2, 2011

No entry required. A memorandum indicates the signing of the put option contract and its designation as a fair value hedge for the Sonoma investment.

---

[22]We discussed the distinction between trading and available-for-sale investments in the chapter.

[23]To simplify the example, we assume no premium is paid for the option.

At December 31, 2011, the price of the Sonoma shares has declined to $120 per share. Hayward records the following entry for the Sonoma investment.

December 31, 2011

Unrealized Holding Gain or Loss—Income	500	
Security Fair Value Adjustment (Available-for-Sale)		500

Note that upon designation of the hedge, the accounting for the available-for-sale security changes from regular GAAP. That is, Hayward records the unrealized holding loss in income, not in equity. If Hayward had not followed this accounting, a mismatch of gains and losses in the income statement would result. Thus, special accounting for the hedged item (in this case, an available-for-sale security) is necessary in a fair value hedge.

The following journal entry records the increase in value of the put option on Sonoma shares.

December 31, 2011

Put Option	500	
Unrealized Holding Gain or Loss—Income		500

The decline in the price of Sonoma shares results in an increase in the fair value of the put option. That is, Hayward could realize a gain on the put option by purchasing 100 shares in the open market for $120 and then exercise the put option, selling the shares for $125. This results in a gain to Hayward of $500 (100 shares $\times$ [$125 − $120]).[24]

Illustration 17A-5 indicates how Hayward reports the amounts related to the Sonoma investment and the put option.

ILLUSTRATION 17A-5
Balance Sheet Presentation of Fair Value Hedge

HAYWARD CO. BALANCE SHEET (PARTIAL) DECEMBER 31, 2011	
Assets	
Available-for-sale securities (at fair value)	$12,000
Put option	500

The increase in fair value on the option offsets or hedges the decline in value on Hayward's available-for-sale security. By using fair value accounting for both financial instruments, the financial statements reflect the underlying substance of Hayward's net exposure to the risks of holding Sonoma stock. By using fair value accounting for both these financial instruments, the balance sheet reports the amount that Hayward would receive on the investment and the put option contract if Hayward sold and settled them, respectively.

Illustration 17A-6 illustrates the reporting of the effects of the hedging transaction on income for the year ended December 31, 2011.

ILLUSTRATION 17A-6
Income Statement Presentation of Fair Value Hedge

HAYWARD CO. INCOME STATEMENT (PARTIAL) FOR THE YEAR ENDED DECEMBER 31, 2011	
Other Income	
Unrealized holding gain—put option	$ 500
Unrealized holding loss—available-for-sale securities	(500)

[24]In practice, Hayward generally does not have to actually buy and sell the Sonoma shares to realize this gain. Rather, unless the counterparty wants to hold Hayward shares, Hayward can "close out" the contract by having the counterparty pay it $500 in cash. This is an example of the net settlement feature of derivatives.

The income statement indicates that the gain on the put option offsets the loss on the available-for-sale securities.[25] The reporting for these financial instruments, even when they reflect a hedging relationship, illustrates why the FASB argued that fair value accounting provides the most relevant information about financial instruments, including derivatives.

Cash Flow Hedge

Companies use **cash flow hedges** to hedge exposures to **cash flow risk**, which results from the variability in cash flows. The FASB allows special accounting for cash flow hedges. Generally, companies measure and report derivatives at fair value on the balance sheet. They report gains and losses directly in net income. However, companies account for derivatives used in cash flow hedges at fair value on the balance sheet, but they **record gains or losses in equity, as part of other comprehensive income**.

> **Objective•13**
> Explain how to account for a cash flow hedge.

To illustrate, assume that in September 2010 Allied Can Co. anticipates purchasing 1,000 metric tons of aluminum in January 2011. Concerned that prices for aluminum will increase in the next few months, Allied wants to hedge the risk that it might pay higher prices for inventory in January 2011. As a result, Allied enters into an aluminum futures contract.

> **INTERNATIONAL INSIGHT**
> Under iGAAP, companies record unrealized holding gains or losses on cash flow hedges as adjustments to the value of the hedged item, not as "Other comprehensive income."

A **futures contract** gives the holder the right and the obligation to purchase an asset at a preset price for a specified period of time.[26] In this case, the aluminum futures contract gives Allied the right and the obligation to purchase 1,000 metric tons of aluminum for $1,550 per ton. This contract price is good until the contract expires in January 2011. The underlying for this derivative is the price of aluminum. If the price of aluminum rises above $1,550, the value of the futures contract to Allied increases. Why? Because Allied will be able to purchase the aluminum at the lower price of $1,550 per ton.[27]

Allied enters into the futures contract on September 1, 2010. Assume that the price to be paid today for inventory to be delivered in January—the **spot price**—equals the contract price. With the two prices equal, the futures contract has no value. Therefore no entry is necessary.

September 2010

No entry required. A memorandum indicates
the signing of the futures contract.

At December 31, 2010, the price for January delivery of aluminum increases to $1,575 per metric ton. Allied makes the following entry to record the increase in the value of the futures contract.

December 31, 2010

Futures Contract	25,000	
Unrealized Holding Gain or Loss—Equity		25,000
([$1,575 − $1,550] × 1,000 tons)		

Allied reports the futures contract in the balance sheet as a current asset. It reports the gain on the futures contract as part of other comprehensive income.

Since Allied has not yet purchased and sold the inventory, this gain arises from an **anticipated transaction**. In this type of transaction, a company accumulates in equity gains or losses on the futures contract as part of other comprehensive income until the period in which it sells the inventory, thereby affecting earnings.

---

[25]Note that the fair value changes in the option contract will not offset **increases** in the value of the Hayward investment. Should the price of Sonoma stock increase above $125 per share, Hayward would have no incentive to exercise the put option.

[26]A **futures contract** is a firm contractual agreement between a buyer and seller for a specified asset on a fixed date in the future. The contract also has a standard specification so both parties know exactly what is being traded. A **forward** is similar but is not traded on an exchange and does not have standardized conditions.

[27]As with the earlier call option example, the actual aluminum does not have to be exchanged. Rather, the parties to the futures contract settle by paying the cash difference between the futures price and the price of aluminum on each settlement date.

In January 2011, Allied purchases 1,000 metric tons of aluminum for $1,575 and makes the following entry.[28]

January 2011

Aluminum Inventory	1,575,000	
Cash ($1,575 × 1,000 tons)		1,575,000

At the same time, Allied makes final settlement on the futures contract. It records the following entry.

January 2011

Cash	25,000	
Futures Contract ($1,575,000 − $1,550,000)		25,000

Through use of the futures contract derivative, Allied fixes the cost of its inventory. The $25,000 futures contract settlement offsets the amount paid to purchase the inventory at the prevailing market price of $1,575,000. The result: net cash outflow of $1,550 per metric ton, as desired. As Illustration 17A-7 shows, Allied has therefore effectively hedged the cash flow for the purchase of inventory.

ILLUSTRATION 17A-7
Effect of Hedge on Cash Flows

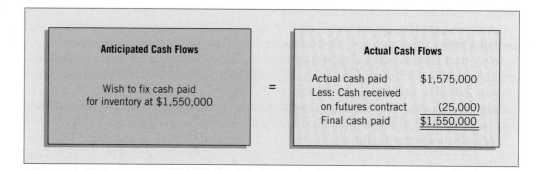

There are no income effects at this point. Allied accumulates in equity the gain on the futures contract as part of other comprehensive income until the period when it sells the inventory, affecting earnings through cost of goods sold.

For example, assume that Allied processes the aluminum into finished goods (cans). The total cost of the cans (including the aluminum purchases in January 2011) is $1,700,000. Allied sells the cans in July 2011 for $2,000,000, and records this sale as follows.

July 2011

Cash	2,000,000	
Sales Revenue		2,000,000
Cost of Goods Sold	1,700,000	
Inventory (Cans)		1,700,000

Since the effect of the anticipated transaction has now affected earnings, Allied makes the following entry related to the hedging transaction.

July 2011

Unrealized Holding Gain or Loss—Equity	25,000	
Cost of Goods Sold		25,000

The gain on the futures contract, which Allied reported as part of other comprehensive income, now reduces cost of goods sold. As a result, the cost of aluminum included in the overall cost of goods sold is $1,550,000. The futures contract has worked as planned. Allied has managed the cash paid for aluminum inventory and the amount of cost of goods sold.

---

[28]In practice, futures contracts are settled on a daily basis. For our purposes, we show only one settlement for the entire amount.

OTHER REPORTING ISSUES

The preceding examples illustrate the basic reporting issues related to the accounting for derivatives. Next, we discuss the following additional issues:

> **Objective·14**
> Identify special reporting issues related to derivative financial instruments that cause unique accounting problems.

1. The accounting for embedded derivatives.
2. Qualifying hedge criteria.

Embedded Derivatives

As we indicated at the beginning of this appendix, rapid innovation in the development of complex financial instruments drove efforts toward unifying and improving the accounting standards for derivatives. In recent years, this innovation has led to the development of **hybrid securities**. These securities have characteristics of both debt and equity. They often combine traditional and derivative financial instruments.

For example, a convertible bond (discussed in Chapter 16) is a hybrid instrument. It consists of two parts: (1) a debt security, referred to as the **host security**, combined with (2) an option to convert the bond to shares of common stock, the **embedded derivative**.

To provide consistency in accounting for similar derivatives, a company must account for embedded derivatives similarly to other derivatives. Therefore, to account for an embedded derivative, a company **should separate it from the host security** and then account for it using the accounting for derivatives. This separation process is referred to as **bifurcation**.[29] Thus, a company investing in a convertible bond must separate the stock option component of the instrument. It then accounts for the derivative (the stock option) at fair value and the host instrument (the debt) according to GAAP, as if there were no embedded derivative.[30]

Qualifying Hedge Criteria

> **INTERNATIONAL INSIGHT**
> iGAAP qualifying hedge criteria are similar to those used in U.S. GAAP.

The FASB identified certain criteria that hedging transactions must meet before requiring the special accounting for hedges. The FASB designed these criteria to ensure the use of hedge accounting in a consistent manner across different hedge transactions. The general criteria relate to the following areas.

1. *Documentation, risk management, and designation.* At inception of the hedge, there must be formal **documentation** of the hedging relationship, the company's **risk management** objective, and the strategy for undertaking the hedge. **Designation** refers to identifying the hedging instrument, the hedged item or transaction, the nature of the risk being hedged, and how the hedging instrument will offset changes in the fair value or cash flows attributable to the hedged risk.

   The FASB decided that documentation and designation are critical to the implementation of the special accounting for hedges. Without these requirements, companies might try to apply the hedge accounting provisions retroactively, only in response to negative changes in market conditions, to offset the negative impact of a transaction on the financial statements. Allowing special hedge accounting in such a setting could mask the speculative nature of the original transaction.

2. *Effectiveness of the hedging relationship.* At inception and on an ongoing basis, the hedging relationship should be **highly effective** in achieving offsetting changes in fair value or cash flows. Companies must assess effectiveness whenever preparing financial statements.

[29]A company can also designate such a derivative as a hedging instrument. The company would apply the hedge accounting provisions outlined earlier in the chapter.

[30]The **issuer** of the convertible bonds would not bifurcate the option component of the convertible bonds payable. GAAP explicitly precludes embedded derivative accounting for an embedded derivative that is indexed to a company's own common stock. If the conversion feature was tied to **another company's** stock, then the derivative would be bifurcated.

The general guideline for effectiveness is that the fair values or cash flows of the hedging instrument (the derivative) and the hedged item exhibit a high degree of correlation. In practice, high effectiveness is assumed when the correlation is close to one (e.g., within plus or minus .10). In our earlier hedging examples (put option and the futures contract on aluminum inventory), the fair values and cash flows are perfectly correlated. That is, when the cash payment for the inventory purchase increased, it offset, dollar for dollar, the cash received on the futures contract.

If the effectiveness criterion is not met, either at inception or because of changes following inception of the hedging relationship, the FASB no longer allows special hedge accounting. The company should then account for the derivative as a free-standing derivative.[31]

3. **Effect on reported earnings of changes in fair values or cash flows.** A change in the fair value of a hedged item or variation in the cash flow of a hedged forecasted transaction must have the potential to change the amount recognized in reported earnings.[32] There is no need for special hedge accounting if a company accounts for both the hedging instrument and the hedged item at fair value under existing GAAP. In this case, earnings will properly reflect the offsetting gains and losses.

For example, special accounting is not needed for a fair value hedge of a trading security, because a company accounts for both the investment and the derivative at fair value on the balance sheet with gains or losses reported in earnings. Thus, "special" hedge accounting is necessary only when there is a mismatch of the accounting effects for the hedging instrument and the hedged item under GAAP.[33]

Summary of Derivatives Accounting

Illustration 17A-8 summarizes the accounting provisions for derivatives and hedging transactions.

ILLUSTRATION 17A-8
Summary of Derivative
Accounting under GAAP

Derivative Use	Accounting for Derivative	Accounting for Hedged Item	Common Example
Speculation	At fair value with unrealized holding gains and losses recorded in income.	Not applicable	Call or put option on an equity security.
Hedging Fair value	At fair value with holding gains and losses recorded in income.	At fair value with gains and losses recorded in income.	Put option to hedge an equity investment.
Cash flow	At fair value with unrealized holding gains and losses from the hedge recorded in other comprehensive income, and reclassified in income when the hedged transaction's cash flows affect earnings.	Use other generally accepted accounting principles for the hedged item.	Use of a futures contract to hedge a forecasted purchase of inventory.

---

[31]The accounting for the part of a derivative that is not effective in a hedge is at fair value, with gains and losses recorded in income.

[32]GAAP gives companies the option to measure most types of financial instruments—from equity investments to debt issued by the company—at fair value. Changes in fair value are recognized in net income each reporting period. Thus, GAAP provides companies with the opportunity to hedge their financial instruments without the complexity inherent in applying hedge accounting provisions. For example, if the fair value option is used, bifurcation of an embedded derivative is not required. [12]

[33]An important criterion specific to cash flow hedges is that the forecasted transaction in a cash flow hedge "is likely to occur." A company should support this probability (defined as significantly greater than the term "more likely than not") by observable facts such as frequency of similar past transactions and its financial and operational ability to carry out the transaction.

As indicated, the general accounting for derivatives relies on fair values. GAAP also establishes special accounting guidance when companies use derivatives **for hedging purposes**. For example, when a company uses a put option to hedge price changes in an available-for-sale stock investment in a fair value hedge (see the Hayward example earlier), it records unrealized gains on the investment in earnings, which is not GAAP for available-for-sale securities without such a hedge. This special accounting is justified in order to accurately report the nature of the hedging relationship in the balance sheet (recording both the put option and the investment at fair value) and in the income statement (reporting offsetting gains and losses in the same period).

Special accounting also is used for cash flow hedges. Companies account for derivatives used in qualifying cash flow hedges at fair value on the balance sheet, but record unrealized holding gains or losses in other comprehensive income until selling or settling the hedged item. In a cash flow hedge, a company continues to record the hedged item at its historical cost.

Disclosure requirements for derivatives are complex. Recent pronouncements on fair value information and financial instruments provide a helpful disclosure framework for reporting derivative instruments. Appendix 17C illustrates many of these disclosures, except for discussion of hedging issues. In general, companies that have derivatives are required to disclose the objectives for holding or issuing those instruments (speculation or hedging), the hedging context (fair value or cash flow), and the strategies for achieving risk-management objectives.

COMPREHENSIVE HEDGE ACCOUNTING EXAMPLE

To provide a comprehensive example of hedge accounting, we examine the use of an interest rate swap. First, let's consider how swaps work and why companies use them.

Options and futures trade on organized securities exchanges. Because of this, options and futures have standardized terms. Although that standardization makes the trading easier, it limits the flexibility needed to tailor contracts to specific circumstances. In addition, most types of derivatives have relatively short time horizons, thereby excluding their use for reducing long-term risk exposure.

As a result, many corporations instead turn to the swap, a very popular type of derivative. A **swap** is a transaction between two parties in which the first party promises to make a payment to the second party. Similarly, the second party promises to make a simultaneous payment to the first party.

The most common type of swap is the **interest rate swap**. In this type, one party makes payments based on a fixed or floating rate, and the second party does just the opposite. In most cases, large money-center banks bring together the two parties. These banks handle the flow of payments between the parties, as shown in Illustration 17A-9.

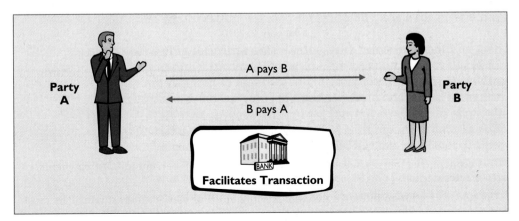

ILLUSTRATION 17A-9
Swap Transaction

Fair Value Hedge

To illustrate the use of a swap in a fair value hedge, assume that Jones Company issues $1,000,000 of five-year, 8 percent bonds on January 2, 2010. Jones records this transaction as follows.

January 2, 2010

Cash	1,000,000	
Bonds Payable		1,000,000

Jones offered a fixed interest rate to appeal to investors. But Jones is concerned that if market interest rates decline, the fair value of the liability will increase. The company will then suffer an economic loss.[34] To protect against the risk of loss, Jones hedges the risk of a decline in interest rates by entering into a five-year interest rate swap contract. Jones agrees to the following terms:

1. Jones will receive fixed payments at 8 percent (based on the $1,000,000 amount).
2. Jones will pay variable rates, based on the market rate in effect for the life of the swap contract. The variable rate at the inception of the contract is 6.8 percent.

As Illustration 17A-10 shows, this swap allows Jones to change the interest on the bonds payable from a fixed rate to a variable rate.

ILLUSTRATION 17A-10
Interest Rate Swap

The settlement dates for the swap correspond to the interest payment dates on the debt (December 31). On each interest payment (settlement) date, Jones and the counterparty compute the difference between current market interest rates and the fixed rate of 8 percent, and determine the value of the swap.[35] If interest rates decline, the value of the swap contract to Jones increases (Jones has a gain), while at the same time Jones's fixed-rate debt obligation increases (Jones has an economic loss).

The swap is an effective risk-management tool in this setting. Its value relates to the same underlying (interest rates) that will affect the value of the fixed-rate bond payable. Thus, if the value of the swap goes up, it offsets the loss related to the debt obligation.

Assuming that Jones enters into the swap on January 2, 2010 (the same date as the issuance of the debt), the swap at this time has no value. Therefore no entry is necessary.

January 2, 2010

No entry required. A memorandum indicates the signing of the swap contract.

At the end of 2010, Jones makes the interest payment on the bonds. It records this transaction as follows.

December 31, 2010

Interest Expense	80,000	
Cash (8% × $1,000,000)		80,000

[34]This economic loss arises because Jones is locked into the 8 percent interest payments even if rates decline.

[35]The underlying for an interest rate swap is some index of market interest rates. The most commonly used index is the London Interbank Offer Rate, or LIBOR. In this example, we assume the LIBOR is 6.8 percent.

At the end of 2010, market interest rates have declined substantially. Therefore the value of the swap contract increases. Recall (see Illustration 17A-9) that in the swap, Jones receives a fixed rate of 8 percent, or $80,000 ($1,000,000 × 8%), and pays a variable rate (6.8%), or $68,000. Jones therefore receives $12,000 ($80,000 – $68,000) as a settlement payment on the swap contract on the first interest payment date. Jones records this transaction as follows.

December 31, 2010

Cash	12,000	
Interest Expense		12,000

In addition, a market appraisal indicates that the value of the interest rate swap has increased $40,000. Jones records this increase in value as follows.[36]

December 31, 2010

Swap Contract	40,000	
Unrealized Holding Gain or Loss—Income		40,000

Jones reports this swap contract in the balance sheet. It reports the gain on the hedging transaction in the income statement. Because interest rates have declined, the company records a loss and a related increase in its liability as follows.

December 31, 2010

Unrealized Holding Gain or Loss—Income	40,000	
Bonds Payable		40,000

Jones reports the loss on the hedging activity in net income. It adjusts bonds payable in the balance sheet to fair value.

Financial Statement Presentation of an Interest Rate Swap

Illustration 17A-11 indicates how Jones reports the asset and liability related to this hedging transaction on the balance sheet.

ILLUSTRATION 17A-11
Balance Sheet Presentation
of Fair Value Hedge

JONES COMPANY BALANCE SHEET (PARTIAL) DECEMBER 31, 2010	
Current assets	
Swap contract	$40,000
Long-term liabilities	
Bonds payable	$1,040,000

The effect on Jones's balance sheet is the addition of the swap asset and an increase in the carrying value of the bonds payable. Illustration 17A-12 indicates how Jones reports the effects of this swap transaction in the income statement.

ILLUSTRATION 17A-12
Income Statement
Presentation of Fair
Value Hedge

JONES COMPANY INCOME STATEMENT (PARTIAL) FOR THE YEAR ENDED DECEMBER 31, 2010		
Interest expense ($80,000 – $12,000)		$68,000
Other income		
Unrealized holding gain—swap contract	$40,000	
Unrealized holding loss—bonds payable	(40,000)	
Net gain (loss)		$–0–

[36]Theoretically, this fair value change reflects the present value of expected future differences in variable and fixed interest rates.

On the income statement, Jones reports interest expense of $68,000. Jones has effectively changed the debt's interest rate from fixed to variable. That is, by receiving a fixed rate and paying a variable rate on the swap, the company converts the fixed rate on the bond payable to variable. This results in an effective interest rate of 6.8 percent in 2010.[37] Also, the gain on the swap offsets the loss related to the debt obligation. Therefore the net gain or loss on the hedging activity is zero.

Illustration 17A-13 shows the overall impact of the swap transaction on the financial statements.

ILLUSTRATION 17A-13
Impact on Financial Statements of Fair Value Hedge

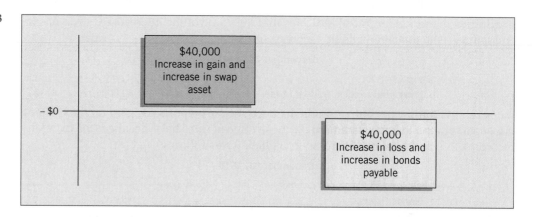

In summary, to account for fair value hedges (as illustrated in the Jones example) **record the derivative at its fair value in the balance sheet, and record any gains and losses in income**. Thus, the gain on the swap offsets or hedges the loss on the bond payable, due to the decline in interest rates.

By adjusting the hedged item (the bond payable in the Jones case) to fair value, with the gain or loss recorded in earnings, the accounting for the Jones bond payable deviates from amortized cost. This special accounting is justified in order to report accurately the nature of the hedging relationship between the swap and the bond payable in the balance sheet (both the swap and the debt obligation are recorded at fair value) and in the income statement (offsetting gains and losses are reported in the same period).[38]

CONTROVERSY AND CONCLUDING REMARKS

Companies need rules to properly measure and report derivatives in financial statements. However, some argue that reporting derivatives at fair value results in unrealized gains and losses that are difficult to interpret. Still, others raise concerns about the complexity and cost of implementing GAAP in this area.

However, we believe that the long-term benefits of using fair value and reporting derivatives at fair value will far outweigh any short-term implementation costs. As the volume and complexity of derivatives and hedging transactions continue to grow, so does the risk that investors and creditors will be exposed to unexpected losses arising

---

[37]Jones will apply similar accounting and measurement at future interest payment dates. Thus, if interest rates increase, Jones will continue to receive 8 percent on the swap (records a loss) but will also be locked into the fixed payments to the bondholders at an 8 percent rate (records a gain).

[38]An interest rate swap can also be used in a cash flow hedge. A common setting is the cash flow risk inherent in having variable rate debt as part of a company's debt structure. In this situation, the variable debt issuer can hedge the cash flow risk by entering into a swap contract to receive variable rate cash flows but pay fixed rate. The cash received on the swap contract will offset the variable cash flows to be paid on the debt obligation.

from derivative transactions. Statement readers must have comprehensive information concerning many derivative financial instruments and the effects of hedging transactions using derivatives.

SUMMARY OF LEARNING OBJECTIVES FOR APPENDIX 17A

•9 **Explain who uses derivatives and why.** Any company or individual that wants to ensure against different types of business risks may use derivative contracts to achieve this objective. In general, these transactions involve some type of hedge. Speculators also use derivatives, attempting to find an enhanced return. Speculators are very important to the derivatives market because they keep it liquid on a daily basis. Arbitrageurs attempt to exploit inefficiencies in various derivative contracts. A company primarily uses derivatives for purposes of hedging its exposure to fluctuations in interest rates, foreign currency exchange rates, and commodity prices.

•10 **Understand the basic guidelines for accounting for derivatives.** Companies should recognize derivatives in the financial statements as assets and liabilities, and report them at fair value. Companies should recognize gains and losses resulting from speculation immediately in income. They report gains and losses resulting from hedge transactions in different ways, depending on the type of hedge.

•11 **Describe the accounting for derivative financial instruments.** Companies report derivative financial instruments in the balance sheet, and record them at fair value. Except for derivatives used in hedging, companies record realized and unrealized gains and losses on derivative financial instruments in income.

•12 **Explain how to account for a fair value hedge.** A company records the derivative used in a qualifying fair value hedge at its fair value in the balance sheet, recording any gains and losses in income. In addition, the company also accounts for the item being hedged with the derivative at fair value. By adjusting the hedged item to fair value, with the gain or loss recorded in earnings, the accounting for the hedged item may deviate from GAAP in the absence of a hedge relationship. This special accounting is justified in order to report accurately the nature of the hedging relationship between the derivative hedging instruments and the hedged item. A company reports both in the balance sheet, reporting offsetting gains and losses in income in the same period.

•13 **Explain how to account for a cash flow hedge.** Companies account for derivatives used in qualifying cash flow hedges at fair value on the balance sheet, but record gains or losses in equity as part of other comprehensive income. Companies accumulate these gains or losses, and reclassify them in income when the hedged transaction's cash flows affect earnings. Accounting is according to GAAP for the hedged item.

•14 **Identify special reporting issues related to derivative financial instruments that cause unique accounting problems.** A company should separate a derivative that is embedded in a hybrid security from the host security, and account for it using the accounting for derivatives. This separation process is referred to as bifurcation. Special hedge accounting is allowed only for hedging relationships that meet certain criteria. The main criteria are: (1) There is formal documentation of the hedging relationship, the company's risk management objective, and the strategy for undertaking the hedge, and the company designates the derivative as either a cash flow or fair value hedge. (2) The company expects the hedging relationship to be highly effective in achieving offsetting

KEY TERMS

anticipated transaction, *893*

arbitrageurs, *885*

bifurcation, *895*

call option, *887*

cash flow hedge, *893*

counterparty, *887(n)*

derivative financial instrument, derivative, *884*

designation, *895*

documentation, *895*

embedded derivative, *895*

fair value hedge, *891*

forward contract, *884*

futures contract, *893*

hedging, *890*

highly effective, *895*

host security, *895*

hybrid security, *895*

interest rate swap, *897*

intrinsic value, *887*

net settlement, *888(n)*

notional amount, *887*

option contract, *884*

option premium, *887*

put option, *887(n)*

risk management, *895*

speculators, *885*

spot price, *893*

strike (exercise) price, *887*

swap, *897*

time value, *887*

underlying, *889*

changes in fair value or cash flows. (3) "Special" hedge accounting is necessary only when there is a mismatch of the accounting effects for the hedging instrument and the hedged item under GAAP.

APPENDIX 17B   VARIABLE-INTEREST ENTITIES

Objective·15

Describe the accounting for the variable-interest entitles.

The FASB has issued an interpretation to address the concern that some companies are not reporting the risks and rewards of certain investments and other financial arrangements in their consolidated financial statements. [13] As one analyst noted, **Enron** showed the world the power of the idea that "if investors can't see it, they can't ask you about it—the 'it' being assets and liabilities."

What exactly did Enron do? First, it created a number of entities whose purpose was to hide debt, avoid taxes, and enrich certain management personnel to the detriment of the company and its stockholders. In effect, these entities, called **special purpose entities (SPEs)**, appeared to be separate entities for which Enron had a limited economic interest. For many of these arrangements, Enron actually had a substantial economic interest; the risks and rewards of ownership were not shifted to the entities but remained with Enron. In short, Enron was obligated to repay investors in these SPEs when they were unsuccessful. Once Enron's problems were discovered, it soon became apparent that many other companies had similar problems.

WHAT ABOUT GAAP?

A reasonable question to ask with regard to SPEs is, "Why didn't GAAP prevent companies from hiding SPE debt and other risks, by forcing companies to include these obligations in their consolidated financial statements?" To understand why, we have to look at the basic rules of consolidation.

The GAAP rules indicate that consolidated financial statements are "usually necessary for a fair presentation when one of the companies in the group directly or indirectly has a controlling financial interest in other companies." They further note that "the usual condition for a controlling financial interest is ownership of a majority voting interest."[39] In other words, if a company, like **Intel**, owns more than 50 percent of the voting stock of another company, Intel consolidates that company. GAAP also indicates that controlling financial interest may be achieved through arrangements that do not involve voting interests. However, applying these guidelines in practice is difficult.

Whenever GAAP uses a clear line, like "greater than 50 percent," companies sometimes exploit the criterion. For example, some companies set up joint ventures in which each party owns exactly 50 percent. In that case, neither party consolidates. Or like **Coca-Cola** in the opening story, a company may own less than 50 percent of the voting stock, but maintain effective control through board of director relationships, supply relationships, or through some other type of financial arrangement.

So the FASB realized that changes had to be made to GAAP for consolidations, and it issued new guidelines. These guidelines define when a company should use factors other than voting interest to determine controlling financial interest. In this pronouncement, the FASB created a new risk-and-reward model to be used in situations where voting interests were unclear. The risk-and-reward model answers the basic questions of who stands to gain or lose the most from ownership in an SPE when ownership is uncertain.

[39]"Consolidation of Certain Special Purpose Entities," Proposed Interpretation (Norwalk, Conn.: FASB, June 28, 2002).

In other words, we now have two models for consolidation:

1. **Voting-interest model**—If a company owns more than 50 percent of another company, then consolidate in most cases.
2. **Risk-and-reward model**—If a company is involved substantially in the economics of another company, then consolidate.

Operationally, the voting-interest model is easy to apply: It sets a "bright line" ownership standard of more than 50 percent of the voting stock. However, if companies cannot determine control based on voting interest, they may use the risk-and-reward model.

CONSOLIDATION OF VARIABLE-INTEREST ENTITIES

To answer the question of who gains or loses when voting rights do not determine consolidation, the FASB developed the risk-and-reward model. In this model, the FASB introduced the notion of a variable-interest entity. A **variable-interest entity (VIE)** is an entity that has one of the following characteristics:

1. *Insufficient equity investment at risk.* Stockholders are assumed to have sufficient capital investment to support the entity's operations. If thinly capitalized, the entity is considered a VIE and is subject to the risk-and-reward model.
2. *Stockholders lack decision-making rights.* In some cases, stockholders do not have the influence to control the company's destiny.
3. *Stockholders do not absorb the losses or receive the benefits of a normal stockholder.* In some entities, stockholders are shielded from losses related to their primary risks, or their returns are capped or must be shared with other parties.

Once the company determines that an entity is a variable-interest entity, it no longer can use the voting-interest model. The question that must then be asked is, "What party is exposed to the majority of the risks and rewards associated with the VIE?" This party is called the primary beneficiary and must consolidate the VIE. Illustration 17B-1 shows the decision model for the VIE consolidation model.

ILLUSTRATION 17B-1
VIE Consolidation Model

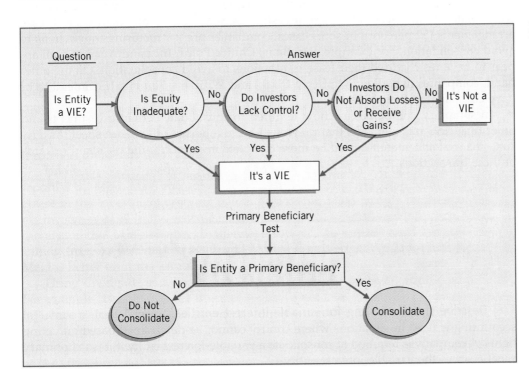

Some Examples

Let's look at a couple of examples to illustrate how this process works.

Example 1

Assume that Citigroup sells notes receivable to another entity called RAKO. RAKO's assets are financed in two ways: Lenders provide 90 percent, and investors provide the remaining 10 percent as an equity investment. If Citigroup does not guarantee the debt, Citigroup has low or nonexistent risk. Therefore, Citigroup would not consolidate the assets and liabilities of RAKO. On the other hand, if Citigroup guarantees RAKO's debt, then RAKO is a VIE, and Citigroup is the primary beneficiary. In that case, Citigroup must consolidate.

Example 2

San Diego Gas and Electric (SDGE) is required by law to buy power from small, local producers. In some cases, SDGE has contracts requiring it to purchase substantially all the power generated by these local companies over their lifetime. Because SDGE controls the outputs of the producers, they are VIEs. In this case, the risks and rewards related to ownership apply to SDGE. In other words, it is the primary beneficiary, and SDGE should include these producers in the consolidated financial statements.

Note that the primary beneficiary may have the risks and rewards of ownership through use of a variety of instruments and financial arrangements, such as equity investments, loans to the VIE, leases, derivatives, and guarantees. Potential VIEs include the following: corporations, partnerships, limited liability companies, and majority-owned subsidiaries.

ILLUSTRATION 17B-2
Impact of Rule Involving Risk-and-Reward Model

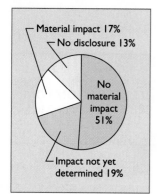

Material impact 17%
No disclosure 13%
No material impact 51%
Impact not yet determined 19%

Source: Company Reports, *Glass, Lewis, & Co. Research Report* (November 6, 2003).

What Is Happening in Practice?

For most companies, the new reporting related to VIEs will not materially affect their financial statements. As shown in Illustration 17B-2, one study of 509 companies with total market values over $500 million found that just 17 percent of the companies reviewed have a material impact.

Of the material VIEs disclosed in the study, the most common types (42 percent) were related to joint-venture equity investments, followed by off-balance-sheet lease arrangements (22 percent). In some cases, companies are restructuring transactions to avoid consolidation. For example, Pep Boys, Choice Point, Inc., and Anadarko all appear to have restructured their lease transactions to avoid consolidation. On the other hand, companies like eBay, Kimberly-Clark, and Williams-Sonoma Inc. intend to or have consolidated their VIEs.

In summary, companies are now required to consolidate certain investments and other financing arrangements that previously were reported off-balance-sheet. As a result, financial statements should be more complete in reporting the risks and rewards of these transactions.

KEY TERMS

risk-and-reward model, *903*

special purpose entity (SPE), *902*

variable-interest entity (VIE), *903*

voting-interest model, *903*

SUMMARY OF LEARNING OBJECTIVE FOR APPENDIX 17B

•15 **Describe the accounting for variable-interest entities.** Special variable-interest accounting is used in situations where control cannot be determined based on voting rights. A company is required to consolidate a variable-interest entity if it is the primary beneficiary of the variable-interest entity.

| APPENDIX **17C** | FAIR VALUE MEASUREMENTS AND DISCLOSURES |

As indicated in the chapter, the FASB believes that fair value information is relevant for making effective business decisions. However, others express concern about fair value measurements for two reasons: (1) the lack of reliability related to the fair value measurement in certain cases, and (2) the ability to manipulate fair value measurements to achieve financial results inconsistent with the underlying economics of the situation.

The Board recognizes these concerns and has attempted to develop a sound conceptual basis for measuring and reporting fair value information. In addition, it has placed emphasis on developing guidelines for reporting fair value information for financial instruments, because many of these instruments have relatively active markets for which valuations can be reliably determined. The purpose of this appendix is to explain the disclosure requirements for financial instruments related to fair value information.

DISCLOSURE OF FAIR VALUE INFORMATION: FINANCIAL INSTRUMENTS—NO FAIR VALUE OPTION

One requirement related to fair value disclosure is that both the cost and the fair value of all financial instruments be reported in the notes to the financial statements. [14] This enables readers of the financial statements to understand the fair value of the company's financial instruments and the potential gains and losses that might occur in the future as a result of these instruments.

The Board also decided that companies should disclose information that enables users to determine the extent of usage of fair value and the inputs used to implement fair value measurement. Two reasons for additional disclosure beyond the simple itemization of fair values are:

1. Differing levels of reliability exist in the measurement of fair value information; it therefore is important to understand the varying risks involved in measurement. It is difficult to incorporate these levels of uncertainty into the financial statements. Disclosure provides a framework for addressing the qualitative aspects related to risk and measurement.

2. Changes in the fair value of financial instruments are reported differently in the financial statements, depending upon the type of financial instrument involved and whether the fair value option is employed. Note disclosure provides an opportunity to explain more precisely the impact that changes in the value of financial instruments have on financial results. In assessing the inputs, the Board recognizes that the reliability of the fair value measurement is of extreme importance. Many financial instruments are traded in active markets, and their valuation is not difficult. Other instruments are complex/illiquid, and their valuation is difficult.

To highlight these levels of reliability in valuation, the FASB established a fair value hierarchy. As discussed in Chapter 2 (page 43), this hierarchy identifies three broad levels—1, 2, and 3—related to the measurement of fair values. Level 1 is the most reliable measurement because fair value is based on quoted prices in active markets *for identical assets or liabilities*. Level 2 is less reliable; it is not based on quoted market prices for identical assets and liabilities but instead may be based on *similar assets or liabilities*. Level 3 is least reliable; it uses unobservable inputs that reflect the company's assumption as to the value of the financial instrument.

Illustration 17C-1 is an example of a fair value note disclosure for Sabathia Company. It includes both the fair value amounts and the reliability level. (A similar disclosure would be presented for liabilities.)

ILLUSTRATION 17C-1
Example of Fair Value
Hierarchy

		SABATHIA COMPANY		
		NOTES TO THE FINANCIAL STATEMENTS		
($ in 000s)		Fair Value Measurements at Reporting Data Using		
Description	Fair Value 12/31/10	Quoted Prices in Active Markets for Identical Assets (Level 1)	Significant Other Observable Inputs (Level 2)	Significant Unobservable Inputs (Level 3)
Trading securities	$115	$105	$10	
Available-for-sale securities	75	75		
Derivatives	60	25	15	$20
Venture capital investments	10			10
Total	$260	$205	$25	$30

For assets and liabilities measured at fair value and classified as Level 3, a reconciliation of Level 3 changes for the period is required. In addition, companies should report an analysis of how Level 3 changes in fair value affect total gains and losses and their impact on net income. Illustration 17C-2 is an example of this disclosure.

ILLUSTRATION 17C-2
Reconciliation of Level 3
Inputs

	SABATHIA COMPANY		
	NOTES TO THE FINANCIAL STATEMENTS		
($ in 000s)	Fair Value Measurements Using Significant Unobservable Inputs (Level 3)		
	Derivatives	Venture Capital Investments	Total
Beginning balance	$14	$11	$25
Total gains or losses (realized/unrealized)			
Included in earnings (or changes in net assets)	11	(3)	8
Included in other comprehensive income	4		4
Purchases, issuances, and settlements	(7)	2	(5)
Transfers in and/or out of Level 3	(2)		(2)
Ending balance	$20	$10	$30
The amount of total gains or losses for the period included in earnings (or changes in net assets) attributable to the change in unrealized gains or losses relating to assets still held at the reporting date	$7	$2	$9

Gains and losses (realized and unrealized) included in earnings (or changes in net assets) for the period (above) are reported in trading revenues and in other revenues as follows.

	Trading Revenues	Other Revenues
Total gains or losses included in earnings (or changes in net assets) for the period (as shown in the table above)	$11	$(3)
Change in unrealized gains or losses relating to assets still held at reporting date	$7	$2

Sabathia Company's disclosure provides to the user of the financial statements an understanding of the following:

1. The carrying amount and the fair value of the company's financial instruments segregated by level of reliability. Thus the reader of the financial statements has a basis for judging what credence should be given to the fair value amounts.

2. For Level 3 financial instruments, a reconciliation of the balance from the beginning to the end of the period. This reconciliation enables the reader to understand the composition of the change. It is important because these calculations are most affected by subjective estimates and could be subject to manipulation.

3. The impact of changes in fair value on the net assets of the company from one period to the next.

DISCLOSURE OF FAIR VALUE INFORMATION: FINANCIAL INSTRUMENTS—FAIR VALUE OPTION

Some companies may choose to use the fair value option for some or all of their financial instruments. [15] In that case, companies have the option of incorporating the entire guidelines related to fair value measurement into one master schedule, or they can provide in a separate schedule information related solely to the fair value option. Illustration 17C-3 for Sheets Company includes only information related to the fair value option. It integrates the disclosure of the carrying amount in addition to the fair value disclosure.

ILLUSTRATION 17C-3
Disclosure of Fair Value Option

SHEETS COMPANY NOTES TO THE FINANCIAL STATEMENTS								
($ in 000s)		Fair Value Measurements at December 31, 2010 Using			Changes in Fair Values for the 12-Month Period Ended December 31, 2010, for Items Measured at Fair Value Pursuant to Election of the Fair Value Option			
Description	Fair Value Measurements 12/31/10	Quoted Prices in Active Markets for Identical Assets (Level 1)	Significant Other Observable Inputs (Level 2)	Significant Unobservable Inputs (Level 3)	Other Gains and Losses	Interest Income on Loans	Interest Expense on Long-Term Debt	Total Changes in Fair Values Included in Current-Period Earnings
Trading securities	$115	$105	$ 10					
Available-for-sale securities	75	75						
Loans	150	0	100	$ 50	$ (3)	$10		$ 7
Derivatives	60	25	15	20				
Private equity investments*	75	0	25	50	(18)			(18)
Long-term debt	(60)	(30)	(10)	(20)	13		$(4)	9

*Represents investments that would otherwise be accounted for under the equity method of accounting.

Loans are included in loans and lease receivables in the statement of financial position. As of December 31, 2010, approximately $160,000 of lease receivables are included in loans and lease receivables in the statement of financial position and are not eligible for the fair value option.

Source: Adapted from *FASB ASC 825-10-25* (Norwalk, Conn.: FASB, February 2007), Table 2, p. 47.

DISCLOSURE OF FAIR VALUES: IMPAIRED ASSETS OR LIABILITIES

In addition to financial instruments, companies often have assets or liabilities that are remeasured on a nonrecurring basis due to impairment. In this case the fair value hierarchy can highlight the reliability of the measurement, coupled with the related gain or loss for the period. Illustration 17C-4 highlights this disclosure for McClung Company.

ILLUSTRATION 17C-4
Disclosure of Fair Value, with Impairment

($ in millions)		Fair Value Measurements Using		
Description	Year Ended 12/31/10	Quoted Prices in Active Markets for Identical Assets (Level 1)	Significant Other Observable Inputs (Level 2)	Significant Unobservable Inputs (Level 3)
Long-lived assets held and used	$75		$75	
Goodwill	30			$30
Long-lived assets held for sale	26		26	

McCLUNG COMPANY
NOTES TO THE FINANCIAL STATEMENTS

Long-lived assets held and used with a carrying amount of $100 million were written down to their fair value of $75 million, resulting in an impairment charge of $25 million, which was included in earnings for the period.

Goodwill with a carrying amount of $65 million was written down to its implied fair value of $30 million, resulting in an impairment charge of $35 million, which was included in earnings for the period.

In accordance with the provisions of the Impairment or Disposal of Long-Lived Assets Subsections of FASB Codification Subtopic 360-10, long-lived assets held for sale with a carrying amount of $35 million were written down to their fair value of $26 million, less cost to sell of $6 million (or $20 million), resulting in a loss of $15 million, which was included in earnings for the period.

FASB CODIFICATION

FASB Codification References

[1] FASB ASC 810-10-25. [Predecessor literature: "Consolidation of Variable Interest Entities (revised)—An Interpretation of *ARB No. 51*," *Financial Accounting Standards Interpretation No. 46(R)* (Norwalk, Conn.: FASB, December 2003.]

[2] FASB ASC Glossary. [Predecessor literature: "Accounting for Certain Investments in Debt and Equity Securities," *Statement of Financial Accounting Standards No. 115* (Norwalk, Conn.: FASB 1993), par. 137.]

[3] FASB ASC 820-10-20. [Predecessor literature: "Fair Value Measurement," *Statement of Financial Accounting Standards No. 157* (Norwalk, Conn.: FASB, September 2006).]

[4] FASB ASC 220. [Predecessor literature: "Reporting Comprehensive Income," *Statement of Financial Accounting Standards No. 130* (Norwalk, Conn.: FASB, 1997).]

[5] FASB ASC 323-10-15. [Predecessor literature: "The Equity Method of Accounting for Investments in Common Stock," *Opinions of the Accounting Principles Board No. 18* (New York: AICPA, 1971), par. 17.]

[6] FASB ASC 323-10-15-10. [Predecessor literature: "Criteria for Applying the Equity Method of Accounting for Investments in Common Stock," *Interpretations of the Financial Accounting Standards Board No. 35* (Stamford, Conn.: FASB, 1981).]

[7] FASB ASC 323-10-35. [Predecessor literature: "The Equity Method of Accounting for Investments in Common Stock," *Opinions of the Accounting Principles Board No. 18* (New York: AICPA, 1971), par. 19(i).]

[8] FASB ASC 815-10-05. [Predecessor literature: "Accounting for Derivative Instruments and Hedging Activities," *Statement of Financial Accounting Standards No. 133* (Stamford, Conn.: FASB, 1998).]

[9] FASB ASC 820-10. [Predecessor literature: "Fair Value Measurement," *Statement of Financial Accounting Standards No. 157* (Norwalk, Conn.: FASB, September 2006).]

[10] FASB ASC 815-10-05-4. [Predecessor literature: "Accounting for Derivative Instruments and Hedging Activities," *Statement of Financial Accounting Standards No. 133* (Stamford, Conn.: FASB, 1998), par. 249.]

[11] FASB ASC 815-10-05-4. [Predecessor literature: "Accounting for Derivative Instruments and Hedging Activities," *Statement of Financial Accounting Standards No. 133* (Stamford, Conn.: FASB, 1998).]

[12] FASB ASC 825-10-25-1. [Predecessor literature: "The Fair Value Option for Financial Assets and Liabilities, Including an Amendment of FASB Statement No. 115," *Statement of Financial Accounting Standards No. 159* (Norwalk, Conn.: FASB, February 2007).]

[13] FASB ASC 810-10-05. [Predecessor literature: "Consolidation of Variable Interest Entities (revised)—An Interpretation of *ARB No. 51*," *Financial Accounting Standards Interpretation No. 46(R)* (FASB, Norwalk, Conn.: December 2003).]

[14] FASB ASC 820-10. [Predecessor literature: "Fair Value Measurement," *Statement of Financial Accounting Standards No. 157* (Norwalk, Conn.: FASB, September 2006).]

[15] FASB ASC 825-10-25-1. (Predecessor literature: "The Fair Value Option for Financial Assets and Liabilities, Including an Amendment of FASB Statement No. 115," *Statement of Financial Accounting Standards No. 159* (Norwalk, Conn.: FASB, February 2007).]

Exercises

Access the FASB Codification at *http://asc.fasb.org/home* to prepare responses to the following exercises. Provide Codification references for your responses.

CE17-1 Access the glossary ("Master Glossary") to answer the following.

  (a) What are trading securities?
  (b) What is the definition of "holding gain or loss"?
  (c) What is a cash flow hedge?
  (d) What is a fair value hedge?

CE17-2 What guidance does the SEC give for disclosures regarding accounting policies used for derivatives?

CE17-3 When would an investor discontinue applying the equity method in an investment? Are there any exceptions to this rule?

CE17-4 For balance sheet purposes, can the fair value of a derivative in a loss position be netted against the fair value of a derivative in a gain position?

An additional Codification case can be found in the Using Your Judgment section, on page 928.

Be sure to check the companion website for a Review and Analysis Exercise, with solution.

Note: All asterisked Questions, Exercises, and Problems relate to material in the appendices to the chapter.

QUESTIONS

1. Distinguish between a debt security and an equity security.

2. What purpose does the variety in bond features (types and characteristics) serve?

3. What is the cost of a long-term investment in bonds?

4. Identify and explain the three types of classifications for investments in debt securities.

5. When should a debt security be classified as held-to-maturity?

6. Explain how trading securities are accounted for and reported.

7. At what amount should trading, available-for-sale, and held-to-maturity securities be reported on the balance sheet?

8. On July 1, 2010, Wheeler Company purchased $4,000,000 of Duggen Company's 8% bonds, due on July 1, 2017. The bonds, which pay interest semiannually on January 1 and July 1, were purchased for $3,500,000 to yield 10%. Determine the amount of interest revenue Wheeler should report on its income statement for year ended December 31, 2010.

9. If the bonds in question 8 are classified as available-for-sale and they have a fair value at December 31, 2010, of

$3,604,000, prepare the journal entry (if any) at December 31, 2010, to record this transaction.

10. Indicate how unrealized holding gains and losses should be reported for investment securities classified as trading, available-for-sale, and held-to-maturity.

11. (a) Assuming no Securities Fair Value Adjustment (Available-for-Sale) account balance at the beginning of the year, prepare the adjusting entry at the end of the year if Laura Company's available-for-sale securities have a market value $60,000 below cost. (b) Assume the same information as part (a), except that Laura Company has a debit balance in its Securities Fair Value Adjustment (Available-for-Sale) account of $10,000 at the beginning of the year. Prepare the adjusting entry at year-end.

12. Identify and explain the different types of classifications for investment in equity securities.

13. Why are held-to-maturity investments applicable only to debt securities?

14. Hayes Company sold 10,000 shares of Kenyon Co. common stock for $27.50 per share, incurring $1,770 in brokerage commissions. These securities were classified as trading and originally cost $260,000. Prepare the entry to record the sale of these securities.

15. Distinguish between the accounting treatment for available-for-sale equity securities and trading equity securities.

16. What constitutes "significant influence" when an investor's financial interest is below the 50% level?

17. Explain how the investment account is affected by investee activities under the equity method.

18. When the equity method is applied, what disclosures should be made in the investor's financial statements?

19. Hiram Co. uses the equity method to account for investments in common stock. What accounting should be made for dividends received from these investments subsequent to the date of investment?

20. Raleigh Corp. has an investment with a carrying value (equity method) on its books of $170,000 representing a 30% interest in Borg Company, which suffered a $620,000 loss this year. How should Raleigh Corp. handle its proportionate share of Borg's loss?

21. Where on the asset side of the balance sheet are trading securities, available-for-sale securities, and held-to-maturity securities reported? Explain.

22. Explain why reclassification adjustments are necessary.

23. Briefly discuss how a transfer of securities from the available-for-sale category to the trading category affects stockholders' equity and income.

24. When is a debt security considered impaired? Explain how to account for the impairment of an available-for-sale debt security.

25. What is the GAAP definition of fair value?

26. What is the fair value option?

27. Franklin Corp. has an investment that it has held for several years. When it purchased the investment, Franklin classified and accounted for it as available-for-sale. Can Franklin use the fair value option for this investment? Explain.

28. Where can authoritative iGAAP be found related to investments?

29. Briefly describe some of the similarities and differences between U.S. GAAP and iGAAP with respect to the accounting for investments.

30. Ramirez Company has an available-for-sale investment in the 6%, 20-year bonds of Soto Company. The investment was originally purchased for $1,200,000 in 2009. Early in 2010, Ramirez recorded an impairment of $300,000 on the Soto investment, due to Soto's financial distress. In 2011, Soto returned to profitability and the Soto investment was no longer impaired. What entry does Ramirez make in 2011 under (a) U.S. GAAP and (b) iGAAP?

*31. What is meant by the term underlying as it relates to derivative financial instruments?

*32. What are the main distinctions between a traditional financial instrument and a derivative financial instrument?

*33. What is the purpose of a fair value hedge?

*34. In what situation will the unrealized holding gain or loss on an available-for-sale security be reported in income?

*35. Why might a company become involved in an interest rate swap contract to receive fixed interest payments and pay variable?

*36. What is the purpose of a cash flow hedge?

*37. Where are gains and losses related to cash flow hedges involving anticipated transactions reported?

*38. What are hybrid securities? Give an example of a hybrid security.

*39. Explain the difference between the voting-interest model and the risk-and-reward model used for consolidation.

*40. What is a variable-interest entity?

BRIEF EXERCISES

BE17-1 Garfield Company purchased, as a held-to-maturity investment, $80,000 of the 9%, 5-year bonds of Chester Corporation for $74,086, which provides an 11% return. Prepare Garfield's journal entries for (a) the purchase of the investment, and (b) the receipt of annual interest and discount amortization. Assume effective-interest amortization is used.

•2 **BE17-2** Use the information from BE17-1, but assume the bonds are purchased as an available-for-sale security. Prepare Garfield's journal entries for (a) the purchase of the investment, (b) the receipt of annual interest and discount amortization, and (c) the year-end fair value adjustment. The bonds have a year-end fair value of $75,500.

•2 **BE17-3** Carow Corporation purchased, as a held-to-maturity investment, $60,000 of the 8%, 5-year bonds of Harrison, Inc. for $65,118, which provides a 6% return. The bonds pay interest semiannually. Prepare Carow's journal entries for (a) the purchase of the investment, and (b) the receipt of semiannual interest and premium amortization. Assume effective-interest amortization is used.

•2 **BE17-4** Hendricks Corporation purchased trading investment bonds for $50,000 at par. At December 31, Hendricks received annual interest of $2,000, and the fair value of the bonds was $47,400. Prepare Hendricks' journal entries for (a) the purchase of the investment, (b) the interest received, and (c) the fair value adjustment.

•3 **BE17-5** Fairbanks Corporation purchased 400 shares of Sherman Inc. common stock as an available-for-sale investment for $13,200. During the year, Sherman paid a cash dividend of $3.25 per share. At year-end, Sherman stock was selling for $34.50 per share. Prepare Fairbanks's journal entries to record (a) the purchase of the investment, (b) the dividends received, and (c) the fair value adjustment.

•3 **BE17-6** Use the information from BE17-5 but assume the stock was purchased as a trading security. Prepare Fairbanks's journal entries to record (a) the purchase of the investment, (b) the dividends received, and (c) the fair value adjustment.

•4 **BE17-7** Zoop Corporation purchased for $300,000 a 30% interest in Murphy, Inc. This investment enables Zoop to exert significant influence over Murphy. During the year Murphy earned net income of $180,000 and paid dividends of $60,000. Prepare Zoop's journal entries related to this investment.

•3 **BE17-8** Cleveland Company has a stock portfolio valued at $4,000. Its cost was $3,300. If the Securities Fair Value Adjustment (Available-for-Sale) account has a debit balance of $200, prepare the journal entry at year-end.

•7 **BE17-9** The following information relates to Starbucks for 2007: net income $672.638 million; unrealized holding loss of $20.380 million related to available-for-sale securities during the year; accumulated other comprehensive income of $37.273 million on October 1, 2006. Assuming no other changes in accumulated other comprehensive income, determine (a) other comprehensive income for 2007, (b) comprehensive income for 2007, and (c) accumulated other comprehensive income at September 30, 2007.

•6 **BE17-10** Hillsborough Co. has an available-for-sale investment in the bonds of Schuyler Corp. with a carrying (and fair) value of $70,000. Hillsborough determined that due to poor economic prospects for Schuyler, the bonds have decreased in value to $60,000. It is determined that this loss in value is other-than-temporary. Prepare the journal entry, if any, to record the reduction in value.

EXERCISES

•1 •3 **E17-1** **(Investment Classifications)** For the following investments identify whether they are:

1. Trading Securities
2. Available-for-Sale Securities
3. Held-to-Maturity Securities

Each case is independent of the other.

(a) A bond that will mature in 4 years was bought 1 month ago when the price dropped. As soon as the value increases, which is expected next month, it will be sold.

(b) 10% of the outstanding stock of Farm-Co was purchased. The company is planning on eventually getting a total of 30% of its outstanding stock.

(c) 10-year bonds were purchased this year. The bonds mature at the first of next year.

(d) Bonds that will mature in 5 years are purchased. The company would like to hold them until they mature, but money has been tight recently and they may need to be sold.

(e) A bond that matures in 10 years was purchased. The company is investing money set aside for an expansion project planned 10 years from now.

(f) Preferred stock was purchased for its constant dividend. The company is planning to hold the preferred stock for a long time.

E17-2 (Entries for Held-to-Maturity Securities) On January 1, 2010, Jennings Company purchased at par 10% bonds having a maturity value of $300,000. They are dated January 1, 2010, and mature January 1, 2015, with interest receivable December 31 of each year. The bonds are classified in the held-to-maturity category.

Instructions

(a) Prepare the journal entry at the date of the bond purchase.
(b) Prepare the journal entry to record the interest received for 2010.
(c) Prepare the journal entry to record the interest received for 2011.

E17-3 (Entries for Held-to-Maturity Securities) On January 1, 2009, Roosevelt Company purchased 12% bonds, having a maturity value of $500,000, for $537,907.40. The bonds provide the bondholders with a 10% yield. They are dated January 1, 2009, and mature January 1, 2014, with interest receivable December 31 of each year. Roosevelt Company uses the effective-interest method to allocate unamortized discount or premium. The bonds are classified in the held-to-maturity category.

Instructions

(a) Prepare the journal entry at the date of the bond purchase.
(b) Prepare a bond amortization schedule.
(c) Prepare the journal entry to record the interest received and the amortization for 2009.
(d) Prepare the journal entry to record the interest received and the amortization for 2010.

E17-4 (Entries for Available-for-Sale Securities) Assume the same information as in E17-3 except that the securities are classified as available-for-sale. The fair value of the bonds at December 31 of each year-end is as follows.

2009	$534,200	2012	$517,000
2010	$515,000	2013	$500,000
2011	$513,000		

Instructions

(a) Prepare the journal entry at the date of the bond purchase.
(b) Prepare the journal entries to record the interest received and recognition of fair value for 2009.
(c) Prepare the journal entry to record the recognition of fair value for 2010.

E17-5 (Effective-Interest versus Straight-Line Bond Amortization) On January 1, 2010, Morgan Company acquires $300,000 of Nicklaus, Inc., 9% bonds at a price of $278,384. The interest is payable each December 31, and the bonds mature December 31, 2012. The investment will provide Morgan Company a 12% yield. The bonds are classified as held-to-maturity.

Instructions

(a) Prepare a 3-year schedule of interest revenue and bond discount amortization, applying the straight-line method. (Round to nearest dollar.)
(b) Prepare a 3-year schedule of interest revenue and bond discount amortization, applying the effective-interest method. (Round to nearest cent.)
(c) Prepare the journal entry for the interest receipt of December 31, 2011, and the discount amortization under the straight-line method.
(d) Prepare the journal entry for the interest receipt of December 31, 2011, and the discount amortization under the effective-interest method.

E17-6 (Entries for Available-for-Sale and Trading Securities) The following information is available for Kinney Company at December 31, 2010, regarding its investments.

Securities	Cost	Fair Value
3,000 shares of Petty Corporation Common Stock	$40,000	$46,000
1,000 shares of Dowe Incorporated Preferred Stock	25,000	22,000
	$65,000	$68,000

Instructions

(a) Prepare the adjusting entry (if any) for 2010, assuming the securities are classified as trading.
(b) Prepare the adjusting entry (if any) for 2010, assuming the securities are classified as available-for-sale.
(c) Discuss how the amounts reported in the financial statements are affected by the entries in (a) and (b).

•3 E17-7 (Trading Securities Entries) On December 21, 2010, Zurich Company provided you with the following information regarding its trading securities.

December 31, 2010

Investments (Trading)	Cost	Fair Value	Unrealized Gain (Loss)
Stargate Corp. stock	$20,000	$19,000	$(1,000)
Carolina Co. stock	10,000	9,000	(1,000)
Vectorman Co. stock	20,000	20,600	600
Total of portfolio	$50,000	$48,600	(1,400)
Previous securities fair value adjustment balance			–0–
Securities fair value adjustment—Cr.			$(1,400)

During 2011, Carolina Company stock was sold for $9,500. The fair value of the stock on December 31, 2011, was: Stargate Corp. stock—$19,300; Vectorman Co. stock—$20,500.

Instructions
(a) Prepare the adjusting journal entry needed on December 31, 2010.
(b) Prepare the journal entry to record the sale of the Carolina Company stock during 2011.
(c) Prepare the adjusting journal entry needed on December 31, 2011.

•3 E17-8 (Available-for-Sale Securities Entries and Reporting) Player Corporation purchases equity securities costing $73,000 and classifies them as available-for-sale securities. At December 31, the fair value of the portfolio is $67,000.

Instructions
Prepare the adjusting entry to report the securities properly. Indicate the statement presentation of the accounts in your entry.

•3 E17-9 (Available-for-Sale Securities Entries and Financial Statement Presentation) At December 31, 2010, the available-for-sale equity portfolio for Wenger, Inc. is as follows.

Security	Cost	Fair Value	Unrealized Gain (Loss)
A	$17,500	$15,000	($2,500)
B	12,500	14,000	1,500
C	23,000	25,500	2,500
Total	$53,000	$54,500	1,500
Previous securities fair value adjustment balance—Dr.			200
Securities fair value adjustment—Dr.			$1,300

On January 20, 2011, Wenger, Inc. sold security A for $15,300. The sale proceeds are net of brokerage fees.

Instructions
(a) Prepare the adjusting entry at December 31, 2010, to report the portfolio at fair value.
(b) Show the balance sheet presentation of the investment related accounts at December 31, 2010. (Ignore notes presentation.)
(c) Prepare the journal entry for the 2011 sale of security A.

•7 E17-10 (Comprehensive Income Disclosure) Assume the same information as E17-9 and that Wenger, Inc. reports net income in 2010 of $120,000 and in 2011 of $140,000. Total holding gains (including any realized holding gain or loss) arising during 2011 total $30,000.

Instructions
(a) Prepare a statement of comprehensive income for 2010 starting with net income.
(b) Prepare a statement of comprehensive income for 2011 starting with net income.

•3 E17-11 (Equity Securities Entries) Capriati Corporation made the following cash purchases of securities during 2010, which is the first year in which Capriati invested in securities.

1. On January 15, purchased 9,000 shares of Gonzalez Company's common stock at $33.50 per share plus commission $1,980.
2. On April 1, purchased 5,000 shares of Belmont Co.'s common stock at $52.00 per share plus commission $3,370.
3. On September 10, purchased 7,000 shares of Thep Co.'s preferred stock at $26.50 per share plus commission $4,910.

On May 20, 2010, Capriati sold 3,000 shares of Gonzalez Company's common stock at a market price of $35 per share less brokerage commissions, taxes, and fees of $2,850. The year-end fair values per share were: Gonzalez $30, Belmont $55, and Thep $28. In addition, the chief accountant of Capriati told you that Capriati Corporation plans to hold these securities for the long term but may sell them in order to earn profits from appreciation in prices.

Instructions

(a) Prepare the journal entries to record the above three security purchases.
(b) Prepare the journal entry for the security sale on May 20.
(c) Compute the unrealized gains or losses and prepare the adjusting entries for Capriati on December 31, 2010.

•3 •4 E17-12 (Journal Entries for Fair Value and Equity Methods) Presented below are two independent situations.

Situation 1

Hatcher Cosmetics acquired 10% of the 200,000 shares of common stock of Ramirez Fashion at a total cost of $14 per share on March 18, 2010. On June 30, Ramirez declared and paid a $75,000 cash dividend. On December 31, Ramirez reported net income of $122,000 for the year. At December 31, the market price of Ramirez Fashion was $15 per share. The securities are classified as available-for-sale.

Situation 2

Holmes, Inc. obtained significant influence over Nadal Corporation by buying 25% of Nadal's 30,000 outstanding shares of common stock at a total cost of $9 per share on January 1, 2010. On June 15, Nadal declared and paid a cash dividend of $36,000. On December 31, Nadal reported a net income of $85,000 for the year.

Instructions

Prepare all necessary journal entries in 2010 for both situations.

•4 E17-13 (Equity Method) Gator Co. invested $1,000,000 in Demo Co. for 25% of its outstanding stock. Demo Co. pays out 40% of net income in dividends each year.

Instructions

Use the information in the following T-account for the investment in Demo to answer the following questions.

Investment in Demo Co.

1,000,000	
130,000	
	52,000

(a) How much was Gator Co.'s share of Demo Co.'s net income for the year?
(b) How much was Gator Co.'s share of Demo Co.'s dividends for the year?
(c) What was Demo Co.'s total net income for the year?
(d) What was Demo Co.'s total dividends for the year?

•3 E17-14 (Equity Investment—Trading) Feiner Co. had purchased 300 shares of Guttman Co. for $40 each this year and classified the investment as a trading security. Feiner Co. sold 100 shares of the stock for $43 each. At year end the price per share of the Guttman Co. stock had dropped to $35.

Instructions

Prepare the journal entries for these transactions and any year-end adjustments.

•3 E17-15 (Equity Investments—Trading) Swanson Company has the following securities in its trading portfolio of securities on December 31, 2010.

Investments (Trading)	Cost	Fair Value
1,500 shares of Parker, Inc., Common	$ 71,500	$ 69,000
5,000 shares of Beilman Corp., Common	180,000	175,000
400 shares of Duncan, Inc., Preferred	60,000	61,600
	$311,500	$305,600

All of the securities were purchased in 2010.
In 2011, Swanson completed the following securities transactions.

March 1 Sold the 1,500 shares of Parker, Inc., Common, @ $45 less fees of $1,200.
April 1 Bought 700 shares of McDowell Corp., Common, @ $75 plus fees of $1,300.

Swanson Company's portfolio of trading securities appeared as follows on December 31, 2011.

Investments (Trading)	Cost	Fair Value
5,000 shares of Beilman Corp., Common	$180,000	$175,000
700 shares of McDowell Corp., Common	53,800	50,400
400 shares of Duncan, Inc., Preferred	60,000	58,000
	$293,800	$283,400

Instructions
Prepare the general journal entries for Swanson Company for:

(a) The 2010 adjusting entry.
(b) The sale of the Parker stock.
(c) The purchase of the McDowell stock.
(d) The 2011 adjusting entry for the trading portfolio.

•3 •4 E17-16 (Fair Value and Equity Method Compared) Gregory Inc. acquired 20% of the outstanding common stock of Handerson Inc. on December 31, 2010. The purchase price was $1,250,000 for 50,000 shares. Handerson Inc. declared and paid an $0.80 per share cash dividend on June 30 and on December 31, 2011. Handerson reported net income of $730,000 for 2011. The fair value of Handerson's stock was $27 per share at December 31, 2011.

Instructions

(a) Prepare the journal entries for Gregory Inc. for 2010 and 2011, assuming that Gregory cannot exercise significant influence over Handerson. The securities should be classified as available-for-sale.
(b) Prepare the journal entries for Gregory Inc. for 2010 and 2011, assuming that Gregory can exercise significant influence over Handerson.
(c) At what amount is the investment in securities reported on the balance sheet under each of these methods at December 31, 2011? What is the total net income reported in 2011 under each of these methods?

•4 E17-17 (Equity Method) On January 1, 2010, Meredith Corporation purchased 25% of the common shares of Pirates Company for $200,000. During the year, Pirates earned net income of $80,000 and paid dividends of $20,000.

Instructions
Prepare the entries for Meredith to record the purchase and any additional entries related to this investment in Pirates Company in 2010.

•6 E17-18 (Impairment of Debt Securities) Cairo Corporation has municipal bonds classified as available-for-sale at December 31, 2010. These bonds have a par value of $800,000, an amortized cost of $800,000, and a fair value of $740,000. The unrealized loss of $60,000 previously recognized as other comprehensive income and as a separate component of stockholders' equity is now determined to be other than temporary. That is, the company believes that impairment accounting is now appropriate for these bonds.

Instructions

(a) Prepare the journal entry to recognize the impairment.
(b) What is the new cost basis of the municipal bonds? Given that the maturity value of the bonds is $800,000, should Cairo Corporation amortize the difference between the carrying amount and the maturity value over the life of the bonds?
(c) At December 31, 2011, the fair value of the municipal bonds is $760,000. Prepare the entry (if any) to record this information.

•3 •5 E17-19 (Fair Value Measurement) Presented below is information related to the purchases of common stock by Lilly Company during 2010.

	Cost (at purchase date)	Fair Value (at December 31)
Investment in Arroyo Company stock	$100,000	$ 80,000
Investment in Lee Corporation stock	250,000	300,000
Investment in Woods Inc. stock	180,000	190,000
Total	$530,000	$570,000

Instructions

(a) What entry would Lilly make at December 31, 2010, to record the investment in Arroyo Company stock if it chooses to report this security using the fair value option?

(b) What entry would Lilly make at December 31, 2010, to record the investment in Lee Corporation, assuming that Lilly wants to classify this security as available-for-sale? This security is the only available-for-sale security that Lilly presently owns.

(c) What entry would Lilly make at December 31, 2010, to record the investment in Woods Inc., assuming that Lilly wants to classify this investment as a trading security?

·3·5 E17-20 (Fair Value Measurement Issues) Assume the same information as in E17-19 for Lilly Company. In addition, assume that the investment in the Woods Inc. stock was sold during 2011 for $195,000. At December 31, 2011, the following information relates to its two remaining investments of common stock.

	Cost (at purchase date)	Fair Value (at December 31)
Investment in Arroyo Company stock	$100,000	$140,000
Investment in Lee Corporation stock	250,000	310,000
Total	$350,000	$450,000

Net income before any security gains and losses for 2011 was $905,000.

Instructions

(a) Compute the amount of net income or net loss that Lilly should report for 2011, taking into consideration Lilly's security transactions for 2011.

(b) Prepare the journal entry to record unrealized gain or loss related to the investment in Arroyo Company stock at December 31, 2011.

·2·3·5 E17-21 (Fair Value Option) Presented below is selected information related to the financial instruments of Dawson Company at December 31, 2010. This is Dawson Company's first year of operations.

	Carrying Amount	Fair Value (at December 31)
Investment in debt securities (intent is to hold to maturity)	$ 40,000	$ 41,000
Investment in Chen Company stock	800,000	910,000
Bonds payable	220,000	195,000

Instructions

(a) Dawson elects to use the fair value option whenever possible. Assuming that Dawson's net income is $100,000 in 2010 before reporting any securities gains or losses, determine Dawson's net income for 2010.

(b) Record the journal entry, if any, necessary at December 31, 2010, to record the fair value option for the bonds payable.

·11 *E17-22 (Derivative Transaction) On January 2, 2010, Jones Company purchases a call option for $300 on Merchant common stock. The call option gives Jones the option to buy 1,000 shares of Merchant at a strike price of $50 per share. The market price of a Merchant share is $50 on January 2, 2010 (the intrinsic value is therefore $0). On March 31, 2010, the market price for Merchant stock is $53 per share, and the time value of the option is $200.

Instructions

(a) Prepare the journal entry to record the purchase of the call option on January 2, 2010.

(b) Prepare the journal entry(ies) to recognize the change in the fair value of the call option as of March 31, 2010.

(c) What was the effect on net income of entering into the derivative transaction for the period January 2 to March 31, 2010? (Ignore tax effects.)

·12 *E17-23 (Fair Value Hedge) On January 2, 2010, MacCloud Co. issued a 4-year, $100,000 note at 6% fixed interest, interest payable semiannually. MacCloud now wants to change the note to a variable-rate note.

As a result, on January 2, 2010, MacCloud Co. enters into an interest rate swap where it agrees to receive 6% fixed and pay LIBOR of 5.7% for the first 6 months on $100,000. At each 6-month period, the variable rate will be reset. The variable rate is reset to 6.7% on June 30, 2010.

Instructions

(a) Compute the net interest expense to be reported for this note and related swap transaction as of June 30, 2010.

(b) Compute the net interest expense to be reported for this note and related swap transaction as of December 31, 2010.

·13 *E17-24 (Cash Flow Hedge)** On January 2, 2010, Parton Company issues a 5-year, $10,000,000 note at LIBOR, with interest paid annually. The variable rate is reset at the end of each year. The LIBOR rate for the first year is 5.8%.

Parton Company decides it prefers fixed-rate financing and wants to lock in a rate of 6%. As a result, Parton enters into an interest rate swap to pay 6% fixed and receive LIBOR based on $10 million. The variable rate is reset to 6.6% on January 2, 2011.

Instructions
(a) Compute the net interest expense to be reported for this note and related swap transactions as of December 31, 2010.
(b) Compute the net interest expense to be reported for this note and related swap transactions as of December 31, 2011.

·12 *E17-25 (Fair Value Hedge)** Sarazan Company issues a 4-year, 7.5% fixed-rate interest only, nonprepayable $1,000,000 note payable on December 31, 2010. It decides to change the interest rate from a fixed rate to variable rate and enters into a swap agreement with M&S Corp. The swap agreement specifies that Sarazan will receive a fixed rate at 7.5% and pay variable with settlement dates that match the interest payments on the debt. Assume that interest rates have declined during 2011 and that Sarazan received $13,000 as an adjustment to interest expense for the settlement at December 31, 2011. The loss related to the debt (due to interest rate changes) was $48,000. The value of the swap contract increased $48,000.

Instructions
(a) Prepare the journal entry to record the payment of interest expense on December 31, 2011.
(b) Prepare the journal entry to record the receipt of the swap settlement on December 31, 2011.
(c) Prepare the journal entry to record the change in the fair value of the swap contract on December 31, 2011.
(d) Prepare the journal entry to record the change in the fair value of the debt on December 31, 2011.

·11 *E17-26 (Call Option)** On August 15, 2010. Outkast Co. invested idle cash by purchasing a call option on Counting Crows Inc. common shares for $360. The notional value of the call option is 400 shares, and the option price is $40. (Market price of an Outkast share is $40.) The option expires on January 31, 2011. The following data are available with respect to the call option.

Date	Market Price of Counting Crows Shares	Time Value of Call Option
September 30, 2010	$48 per share	$180
December 31, 2010	$46 per share	65
January 15, 2011	$47 per share	30

Instructions
Prepare the journal entries for Outkast for the following dates.

(a) Investment in call option on Counting Crows shares on August 15, 2010.
(b) September 30, 2010—Outkast prepares financial statements.
(c) December 31, 2010—Outkast prepares financial statements.
(d) January 15, 2011—Outkast settles the call option on the Counting Crows shares.

·13 *E17-27 (Cash Flow Hedge)** Hart Golf Co. uses titanium in the production of its specialty drivers. Hart anticipates that it will need to purchase 200 ounces of titanium in October 2010, for clubs that will be shipped in the holiday shopping season. However, if the price of titanium increases, this will increase the cost to produce the clubs, which will result in lower profit margins.

To hedge the risk of increased titanium prices, on May 1, 2010, Hart enters into a titanium futures contract and designates this futures contract as cash flow hedge of the anticipated titanium purchase. The notional amount of the contract is 200 ounces, and the terms of the contract give Hart the right and the obligation to purchase titanium at a price of $500 per ounce. The price will be good until the contract expires on November 30, 2010.

Assume the following data with respect to the price of the call options and the titanium inventory purchase.

Date	Spot Price for November Delivery
May 1, 2010	$500 per ounce
June 30, 2010	520 per ounce
September 30, 2011	525 per ounce

Instructions

Present the journal entries for the following dates/transactions.

(a) May 1, 2010—Inception of futures contract, no premium paid.

(b) June 30, 2010—Hart prepares financial statements.

(c) September 30, 2010—Hart prepares financial statements.

(d) October 5, 2010—Hart purchases 200 ounces of titanium at $525 per ounce and settles the futures contract.

(e) December 15, 2010—Hart sells clubs containing titanium purchased in October 2010 for $250,000. The cost of the finished goods inventory is $140,000.

(f) Indicate the amount(s) reported in the income statement related to the futures contract and the inventory transactions on December 31, 2010.

See the book's companion website, www.wiley.com/college/kieso, for a set of B Exercises.

PROBLEMS

•2 **P17-1** **(Debt Securities)** Presented below is an amortization schedule related to Spangler Company's 5-year, $100,000 bond with a 7% interest rate and a 5% yield, purchased on December 31, 2008, for $108,660.

Date	Cash Received	Interest Revenue	Bond Premium Amortization	Carrying Amount of Bonds
12/31/08				$108,660
12/31/09	$7,000	$5,433	$1,567	107,093
12/31/10	7,000	5,354	1,646	105,447
12/31/11	7,000	5,272	1,728	103,719
12/31/12	7,000	5,186	1,814	101,905
12/31/13	7,000	5,095	1,905	100,000

The following schedule presents a comparison of the amortized cost and fair value of the bonds at year-end.

	12/31/09	12/31/10	12/31/11	12/31/12	12/31/13
Amortized cost	$107,093	$105,447	$103,719	$101,905	$100,000
Fair value	$106,500	$107,500	$105,650	$103,000	$100,000

Instructions

(a) Prepare the journal entry to record the purchase of these bonds on December 31, 2008, assuming the bonds are classified as held-to-maturity securities.

(b) Prepare the journal entry(ies) related to the held-to-maturity bonds for 2009.

(c) Prepare the journal entry(ies) related to the held-to-maturity bonds for 2011.

(d) Prepare the journal entry(ies) to record the purchase of these bonds, assuming they are classified as available-for-sale.

(e) Prepare the journal entry(ies) related to the available-for-sale bonds for 2009.

(f) Prepare the journal entry(ies) related to the available-for-sale bonds for 2011.

•2 **P17-2** **(Available-for-Sale Debt Securities)** On January 1, 2010, Novotna Company purchased $400,000, 8% bonds of Aguirre Co. for $369,114. The bonds were purchased to yield 10% interest. Interest is payable semiannually on July 1 and January 1. The bonds mature on January 1, 2015. Novotna Company uses the effective-interest method to amortize discount or premium. On January 1, 2012, Novotna Company sold the bonds for $370,726 after receiving interest to meet its liquidity needs.

Instructions

(a) Prepare the journal entry to record the purchase of bonds on January 1. Assume that the bonds are classified as available-for-sale.

(b) Prepare the amortization schedule for the bonds.

(c) Prepare the journal entries to record the semiannual interest on July 1, 2010, and December 31, 2010.

(d) If the fair value of Aguirre bonds is $372,726 on December 31, 2011, prepare the necessary adjusting entry. (Assume the securities fair value adjustment balance on January 1, 2011, is a debit of $3,375.)

(e) Prepare the journal entry to record the sale of the bonds on January 1, 2012.

•2 •3 P17-3 (Available-for-Sale Investments) Cardinal Paz Corp. carries an account in its general ledger called Investments, which contained debits for investment purchases, and no credits, with the following descriptions.

Feb. 1, 2010	Sharapova Company common stock, $100 par, 200 shares	$ 37,400
April 1	U.S. government bonds, 11%, due April 1, 2020, interest payable April 1 and October 1, 110 bonds of $1,000 par each	110,000
July 1	McGrath Company 12% bonds, par $50,000, dated March 1, 2010 purchased at 104 plus accrued interest, interest payable annually on March 1, due March 1, 2030	54,000

Instructions
(Round all computations to the nearest dollar.)

(a) Prepare entries necessary to classify the amounts into proper accounts, assuming that all the securities are classified as available-for-sale.

(b) Prepare the entry to record the accrued interest and the amortization of premium on December 31, 2010 using the straight-line method.

(c) The fair values of the securities on December 31, 2010, were:

Sharapova Company common stock	$ 31,800
U.S. government bonds	124,700
McGrath Company bonds	58,600

What entry or entries, if any, would you recommend be made?

(d) The U.S. government bonds were sold on July 1, 2011, for $119,200 plus accrued interest. Give the proper entry.

•2 P17-4 (Available-for-Sale Debt Securities) Presented below is information taken from a bond investment amortization schedule with related fair values provided. These bonds are classified as available-for-sale.

	12/31/10	12/31/11	12/31/12
Amortized cost	$491,150	$519,442	$550,000
Fair value	$497,000	$509,000	$550,000

Instructions

(a) Indicate whether the bonds were purchased at a discount or at a premium.

(b) Prepare the adjusting entry to record the bonds at fair value at December 31, 2010. The Securities Fair Value Adjustment account has a debit balance of $1,000 prior to adjustment.

(c) Prepare the adjusting entry to record the bonds at fair value at December 31, 2011.

 •3 P17-5 (Equity Securities Entries and Disclosures) Parnevik Company has the following securities in its investment portfolio on December 31, 2010 (all securities were purchased in 2010): (1) 3,000 shares of Anderson Co. common stock which cost $58,500, (2) 10,000 shares of Munter Ltd. common stock which cost $580,000, and (3) 6,000 shares of King Company preferred stock which cost $255,000. The Securities Fair Value Adjustment account shows a credit of $10,100 at the end of 2010.

In 2011, Parnevik completed the following securities transactions.

1. On January 15, sold 3,000 shares of Anderson's common stock at $22 per share less fees of $2,150.
2. On April 17, purchased 1,000 shares of Castle's common stock at $33.50 per share plus fees of $1,980.

On December 31, 2011, the market values per share of these securities were: Munter $61, King $40, and Castle $29. In addition, the accounting supervisor of Parnevik told you that, even though all these securities have readily determinable fair values, Parnevik will not actively trade these securities because the top management intends to hold them for more than one year.

Instructions

(a) Prepare the entry for the security sale on January 15, 2011.

(b) Prepare the journal entry to record the security purchase on April 17, 2011.

(c) Compute the unrealized gains or losses and prepare the adjusting entry for Parnevik on December 31, 2011.

(d) How should the unrealized gains or losses be reported on Parnevik's balance sheet?

•3 P17-6 (Trading and Available-for-Sale Securities Entries) McElroy Company has the following portfolio of investment securities at September 30, 2010, its last reporting date.

Trading Securities	Cost	Fair Value
Horton, Inc. common (5,000 shares)	$215,000	$200,000
Monty, Inc. preferred (3,500 shares)	133,000	140,000
Oakwood Corp. common (1,000 shares)	180,000	179,000

On October 10, 2010, the Horton shares were sold at a price of $54 per share. In addition, 3,000 shares of Patriot common stock were acquired at $54.50 per share on November 2, 2010. The December 31, 2010, fair values were: Monty $106,000, Patriot $132,000, and the Oakwood common $193,000. All the securities are classified as trading.

Instructions

(a) Prepare the journal entries to record the sale, purchase, and adjusting entries related to the trading securities in the last quarter of 2010.

(b) How would the entries in part (a) change if the securities were classified as available-for-sale?

·2 P17-7 (Available-for-Sale and Held-to-Maturity Debt Securities Entries) The following information relates to the debt securities investments of Wildcat Company.

1. On February 1, the company purchased 10% bonds of Gibbons Co. having a par value of $300,000 at 100 plus accrued interest. Interest is payable April 1 and October 1.
2. On April 1, semiannual interest is received.
3. On July 1, 9% bonds of Sampson, Inc. were purchased. These bonds with a par value of $200,000 were purchased at 100 plus accrued interest. Interest dates are June 1 and December 1.
4. On September 1, bonds with a par value of $60,000, purchased on February 1, are sold at 99 plus accrued interest.
5. On October 1, semiannual interest is received.
6. On December 1, semiannual interest is received.
7. On December 31, the fair value of the bonds purchased February 1 and July 1 are 95 and 93, respectively.

Instructions

(a) Prepare any journal entries you consider necessary, including year-end entries (December 31), assuming these are available-for-sale securities.

(b) If Wildcat classified these as held-to-maturity securities, explain how the journal entries would differ from those in part (a).

·3 ·4 ·5 P17-8 (Fair Value and Equity Methods) Brooks Corp. is a medium-sized corporation specializing in quarrying stone for building construction. The company has long dominated the market, at one time achieving a 70% market penetration. During prosperous years, the company's profits, coupled with a conservative dividend policy, resulted in funds available for outside investment. Over the years, Brooks has had a policy of investing idle cash in equity securities. In particular, Brooks has made periodic investments in the company's principal supplier, Norton Industries. Although the firm currently owns 12% of the outstanding common stock of Norton Industries, Brooks does not have significant influence over the operations of Norton Industries.

Cheryl Thomas has recently joined Brooks as assistant controller, and her first assignment is to prepare the 2010 year-end adjusting entries for the accounts that are valued by the "fair value" rule for financial reporting purposes. Thomas has gathered the following information about Brooks's pertinent accounts.

1. Brooks has trading securities related to Delaney Motors and Patrick Electric. During this fiscal year, Brooks purchased 100,000 shares of Delaney Motors for $1,400,000; these shares currently have a market value of $1,600,000. Brooks' investment in Patrick Electric has not been profitable; the company acquired 50,000 shares of Patrick in April 2010 at $20 per share, a purchase that currently has a value of $720,000.
2. Prior to 2010, Brooks invested $22,500,000 in Norton Industries and has not changed its holdings this year. This investment in Norton Industries was valued at $21,500,000 on December 31, 2009. Brooks' 12% ownership of Norton Industries has a current market value of $22,225,000.

Instructions

(a) Prepare the appropriate adjusting entries for Brooks as of December 31, 2010, to reflect the application of the "fair value" rule for both classes of securities described above.

(b) For both classes of securities presented above, describe how the results of the valuation adjustments made in (a) would be reflected in the body of and notes to Brooks' 2010 financial statements.

(c) Prepare the entries for the Norton investment, assuming that Brooks owns 25% of Norton's shares. Norton reported income of $500,000 in 2010 and paid cash dividends of $100,000.

·3 ·5 P17-9 (Financial Statement Presentation of Available-for-Sale Investments) Kennedy Company has the following portfolio of available-for-sale securities at December 31, 2010.

Security	Quantity	Percent Interest	Per Share Cost	Per Share Market
Frank, Inc.	2,000 shares	8%	$11	$16
Ellis Corp.	5,000 shares	14%	23	19
Mendota Company	4,000 shares	2%	31	24

Instructions

(a) What should be reported on Kennedy's December 31, 2010, balance sheet relative to these long-term available-for-sale securities?

On December 31, 2011, Kennedy's portfolio of available-for-sale securities consisted of the following common stocks.

Security	Quantity	Percent Interest	Per Share Cost	Per Share Market
Ellis Corp.	5,000 shares	14%	$23	$28
Mendota Company	4,000 shares	2%	31	23
Mendota Company	2,000 shares	1%	25	23

At the end of year 2011, Kennedy Company changed its intent relative to its investment in Frank, Inc. and reclassified the shares to trading securities status when the shares were selling for $8 per share.

(b) What should be reported on the face of Kennedy's December 31, 2011, balance sheet relative to available-for-sale securities investments? What should be reported to reflect the transactions above in Kennedy's 2011 income statement?

(c) Assuming that comparative financial statements for 2010 and 2011 are presented, draft the footnote necessary for full disclosure of Kennedy's transactions and position in equity securities.

•3 •5 **P17-10** **(Gain on Sale of Securities and Comprehensive Income)** On January 1, 2010, Acker Inc. had the following balance sheet.

ACKER INC.			
BALANCE SHEET			
AS OF JANUARY 1, 2010			
Assets		Equity	
Cash	$ 50,000	Common stock	$260,000
Available-for-sale securities	240,000	Accumulated other comprehensive income	30,000
Total	$290,000	Total	$290,000

The accumulated other comprehensive income related to unrealized holding gains on available-for-sale securities. The fair value of Acker Inc.'s available-for-sale securities at December 31, 2010, was $190,000; its cost was $140,000. No securities were purchased during the year. Acker Inc.'s income statement for 2010 was as follows. (Ignore income taxes.)

ACKER INC.	
INCOME STATEMENT	
FOR THE YEAR ENDED DECEMBER 31, 2010	
Dividend revenue	$ 5,000
Gain on sale of available-for-sale securities	30,000
Net income	$35,000

Instructions

(Assume all transactions during the year were for cash.)

(a) Prepare the journal entry to record the sale of the available-for-sale securities in 2010.

(b) Prepare a statement of comprehensive income for 2010.

(c) Prepare a balance sheet as of December 31, 2010.

•3 **P17-11** **(Equity Investments—Available-for-Sale)** Castleman Holdings, Inc. had the following available-for-sale investment portfolio at January 1, 2010.

Evers Company	1,000 shares @ $15 each	$15,000
Rogers Company	900 shares @ $20 each	18,000
Chance Company	500 shares @ $9 each	4,500
Available-for-sale securities @ cost		37,500
Securities fair value adjustment—Available-for-sale		(7,500)
Available-for-sale securities @ fair value		$30,000

During 2010, the following transactions took place.

1. On March 1, Rogers Company paid a $2 per share dividend.
2. On April 30, Castleman Holdings, Inc. sold 300 shares of Chance Company for $11 per share.
3. On May 15, Castleman Holdings, Inc. purchased 100 more shares of Evers Co. stock at $16 per share.
4. At December 31, 2010, the stocks had the following price per share values: Evers $17, Rogers $19, and Chance $8.

During 2011, the following transactions took place.

5. On February 1, Castleman Holdings, Inc. sold the remaining Chance shares for $8 per share.
6. On March 1, Rogers Company paid a $2 per share dividend.
7. On December 21, Evers Company declared a cash dividend of $3 per share to be paid in the next month.
8. At December 31, 2011, the stocks had the following price per shares values: Evers $19 and Rogers $21.

Instructions

(a) Prepare journal entries for each of the above transactions.
(b) Prepare a partial balance sheet showing the Investments account at December 31, 2010 and 2011.

•3 •5 P17-12 (Available-for-Sale Securities—Statement Presentation) Fernandez Corp. invested its excess cash in available-for-sale securities during 2010. As of December 31, 2010, the portfolio of available-for-sale securities consisted of the following common stocks.

Security	Quantity		Cost	Fair Value
Lindsay Jones, Inc.	1,000 shares		$ 15,000	$ 21,000
Poley Corp.	2,000 shares		40,000	42,000
Arnold Aircraft	2,000 shares		72,000	60,000
		Totals	$127,000	$123,000

Instructions

(a) What should be reported on Fernandez's December 31, 2010, balance sheet relative to these securities? What should be reported on Fernandez's 2010 income statement?

On December 31, 2011, Fernandez's portfolio of available-for-sale securities consisted of the following common stocks.

Security	Quantity		Cost	Fair Value
Lindsay Jones, Inc.	1,000 shares		$ 15,000	$20,000
Lindsay Jones, Inc.	2,000 shares		33,000	40,000
Duff Company	1,000 shares		16,000	12,000
Arnold Aircraft	2,000 shares		72,000	22,000
		Totals	$136,000	$94,000

During the year 2011, Fernandez Corp. sold 2,000 shares of Poley Corp. for $38,200 and purchased 2,000 more shares of Lindsay Jones, Inc. and 1,000 shares of Duff Company.

(b) What should be reported on Fernandez's December 31, 2011, balance sheet? What should be reported on Fernandez's 2011 income statement?

On December 31, 2012, Fernandez's portfolio of available-for-sale securities consisted of the following common stocks.

Security	Quantity		Cost	Fair Value
Arnold Aircraft	2,000 shares		$72,000	$82,000
Duff Company	500 shares		8,000	6,000
		Totals	$80,000	$88,000

During the year 2012, Fernandez Corp. sold 3,000 shares of Lindsay Jones, Inc. for $39,900 and 500 shares of Duff Company at a loss of $2,700.

(c) What should be reported on the face of Fernandez's December 31, 2012, balance sheet? What should be reported on Fernandez's 2012 income statement?
(d) What would be reported in a statement of comprehensive income at (1) December 31, 2010, and (2) December 31, 2011?

•11 *P17-13 (Derivative Financial Instrument) The treasurer of Miller Co. has read on the Internet that the stock price of Wade Inc. is about to take off. In order to profit from this potential development, Miller Co. purchased a call option on Wade common shares on July 7, 2010, for $240. The call option is for 200 shares (notional value), and the strike price is $70. (The market price of a share of Wade stock on that date is $70.) The option expires on January 31, 2011. The following data are available with respect to the call option.

Date	Market Price of Wade Shares	Time Value of Call Option
September 30, 2010	$77 per share	$180
December 31, 2010	75 per share	65
January 4, 2011	76 per share	30

Instructions

Prepare the journal entries for Miller Co. for the following dates.

(a) July 7, 2010—Investment in call option on Wade shares.
(b) September 30, 2010—Miller prepares financial statements.
(c) December 31, 2010—Miller prepares financial statements.
(d) January 4, 2011—Miller settles the call option on the Wade shares.

•11 ***P17-14 (Derivative Financial Instrument)** Johnstone Co. purchased a put option on Ewing common shares on July 7, 2010, for $240. The put option is for 200 shares, and the strike price is $70. (The market price of a share of Ewing stock on that date is $70.) The option expires on January 31, 2011. The following data are available with respect to the put option.

Date	Market Price of Ewing Shares	Time Value of Put Option
September 30, 2010	$77 per share	$125
December 31, 2010	75 per share	50
January 31, 2011	78 per share	0

Instructions

Prepare the journal entries for Johnstone Co. for the following dates.

(a) July 7, 2010—Investment in put option on Ewing shares.
(b) September 30, 2010—Johnstone prepares financial statements.
(c) December 31, 2010—Johnstone prepares financial statements.
(d) January 31, 2011—Put option expires.

•11 ***P17-15 (Free-Standing Derivative)** Warren Co. purchased a put option on Echo common shares on January 7, 2010, for $360. The put option is for 400 shares, and the strike price is $85 (which equals the price of an Echo share on the purchase date). The option expires on July 31, 2010. The following data are available with respect to the put option.

Date	Market Price of Echo Shares	Time Value of Put Option
March 31, 2010	$80 per share	$200
June 30, 2010	82 per share	90
July 6, 2010	77 per share	25

Instructions

Prepare the journal entries for Warren Co. for the following dates.

(a) January 7, 2010—Investment in put option on Echo shares.
(b) March 31, 2010—Warren prepares financial statements.
(c) June 30, 2010—Warren prepares financial statements.
(d) July 6, 2010—Warren settles the put option on the Echo shares.

•12 ***P17-16 (Fair Value Hedge Interest Rate Swap)** On December 31, 2010, Mercantile Corp. had a $10,000,000, 8% fixed-rate note outstanding, payable in 2 years. It decides to enter into a 2-year swap with Chicago First Bank to convert the fixed-rate debt to variable-rate debt. The terms of the swap indicate that Mercantile will receive interest at a fixed rate of 8.0% and will pay a variable rate equal to the 6-month LIBOR rate, based on the $10,000,000 amount. The LIBOR rate on December 31, 2010, is 7%. The LIBOR rate will be reset every 6 months and will be used to determine the variable rate to be paid for the following 6-month period.

Mercantile Corp. designates the swap as a fair value hedge. Assume that the hedging relationship meets all the conditions necessary for hedge accounting. The 6-month LIBOR rate and the swap and debt fair values are as follows.

Date	6-Month LIBOR Rate	Swap Fair Value	Debt Fair Value
December 31, 2010	7.0%	—	$10,000,000
June 30, 2011	7.5%	(200,000)	9,800,000
December 31, 2011	6.0%	60,000	10,060,000

Instructions

(a) Present the journal entries to record the following transactions.
 (1) The entry, if any, to record the swap on December 31, 2010.
 (2) The entry to record the semiannual debt interest payment on June 30, 2011.

(3) The entry to record the settlement of the semiannual swap amount receivables at 8%, less amount payable at LIBOR, 7%.

(4) The entry to record the change in the fair value of the debt on June 30, 2011.

(5) The entry to record the change in the fair value of the swap at June 30, 2011.

(b) Indicate the amount(s) reported on the balance sheet and income statement related to the debt and swap on December 31, 2010.

(c) Indicate the amount(s) reported on the balance sheet and income statement related to the debt and swap on June 30, 2011.

(d) Indicate the amount(s) reported on the balance sheet and income statement related to the debt and swap on December 31, 2011.

•13 *P17-17 **(Cash Flow Hedge)** LEW Jewelry Co. uses gold in the manufacture of its products. LEW anticipates that it will need to purchase 500 ounces of gold in October 2010, for jewelry that will be shipped for the holiday shopping season. However, if the price of gold increases, LEW's cost to produce its jewelry will increase, which would reduce its profit margins.

To hedge the risk of increased gold prices, on April 1, 2010, LEW enters into a gold futures contract and designates this futures contract as a cash flow hedge of the anticipated gold purchase. The notional amount of the contract is 500 ounces, and the terms of the contract give LEW the right and the obligation to purchase gold at a price of $300 per ounce. The price will be good until the contract expires on October 31, 2010.

Assume the following data with respect to the price of the call options and the gold inventory purchase.

Date	Spot Price for October Delivery
April 1, 2010	$300 per ounce
June 30, 2010	310 per ounce
September 30, 2010	315 per ounce

Instructions

Prepare the journal entries for the following transactions.

(a) April 1, 2010—Inception of the futures contract, no premium paid.

(b) June 30, 2010—LEW Co. prepares financial statements.

(c) September 30, 2010—LEW Co. prepares financial statements.

(d) October 10, 2010—LEW Co. purchases 500 ounces of gold at $315 per ounce and settles the futures contract.

(e) December 20, 2010—LEW sells jewelry containing gold purchased in October 2010 for $350,000. The cost of the finished goods inventory is $200,000.

(f) Indicate the amount(s) reported on the balance sheet and income statement related to the futures contract on June 30, 2010.

(g) Indicate the amount(s) reported in the income statement related to the futures contract and the inventory transactions on December 31, 2010.

•12 *P17-18 **(Fair Value Hedge)** On November 3, 2010, Sprinkle Co. invested $200,000 in 4,000 shares of the common stock of Pratt Co. Sprinkle classified this investment as available-for-sale. Sprinkle Co. is considering making a more significant investment in Pratt Co. at some point in the future but has decided to wait and see how the stock does over the next several quarters.

To hedge against potential declines in the value of Pratt stock during this period, Sprinkle also purchased a put option on the Pratt stock. Sprinkle paid an option premium of $600 for the put option, which gives Sprinkle the option to sell 4,000 Pratt shares at a strike price of $50 per share. The option expires on July 31, 2011. The following data are available with respect to the values of the Pratt stock and the put option.

Date	Market Price of Pratt Shares	Time Value of Put Option
December 31, 2010	$50 per share	$375
March 31, 2011	45 per share	175
June 30, 2011	43 per share	40

Instructions

(a) Prepare the journal entries for Sprinkle Co. for the following dates.

(1) November 3, 2010—Investment in Pratt stock and the put option on Pratt shares.

(2) December 31, 2011—Sprinkle Co. prepares financial statements.

(3) March 31, 2011—Sprinkle prepares financial statements.

(4) June 30, 2011—Sprinkle prepares financial statements.

(5) July 1, 2011—Sprinkle settles the put option and sells the Pratt shares for $43 per share.

(b) Indicate the amount(s) reported on the balance sheet and income statement related to the Pratt investment and the put option on December 31, 2010.

(c) Indicate the amount(s) reported on the balance sheet and income statement related to the Pratt investment and the put option on June 30, 2011.

CA17-1 (Issues Raised about Investment Securities) You have just started work for Warren Co. as part of the controller's group involved in current financial reporting problems. Jane Henshaw, controller for Warren, is interested in your accounting background because the company has experienced a series of financial reporting surprises over the last few years. Recently, the controller has learned from the company's auditors that there is authoritative literature that may apply to its investment in securities. She assumes that you are familiar with this pronouncement and asks how the following situations should be reported in the financial statements.

Situation 1
Trading securities in the current assets section have a fair value that is $4,200 lower than cost.

Situation 2
A trading security whose fair value is currently less than cost is transferred to the available-for-sale category.

Situation 3
An available-for-sale security whose fair value is currently less than cost is classified as noncurrent but is to be reclassified as current.

Situation 4
A company's portfolio of available-for-sale securities consists of the common stock of one company. At the end of the prior year the fair value of the security was 50% of original cost, and this reduction in market value was reported as an other than temporary impairment. However, at the end of the current year the fair value of the security had appreciated to twice the original cost.

Situation 5
The company has purchased some convertible debentures that it plans to hold for less than a year. The fair value of the convertible debentures is $7,700 below its cost.

Instructions
What is the effect upon carrying value and earnings for each of the situations above? Assume that these situations are unrelated.

CA17-2 (Equity Securities) Lexington Co. has the following available-for-sale securities outstanding on December 31, 2010 (its first year of operations).

	Cost	Fair Value
Greenspan Corp. Stock	$20,000	$19,000
Summerset Company Stock	9,500	8,800
Tinkers Company Stock	20,000	20,600
	$49,500	$48,400

During 2011 Summerset Company stock was sold for $9,200, the difference between the $9,200 and the "fair value" of $8,800 being recorded as a "Gain on Sale of Securities." The market price of the stock on December 31, 2011, was: Greenspan Corp. stock $19,900; Tinkers Company stock $20,500.

Instructions
(a) What justification is there for valuing available-for-sale securities at fair value and reporting the unrealized gain or loss as part of stockholders' equity?
(b) How should Lexington Company apply this rule on December 31, 2010? Explain.
(c) Did Lexington Company properly account for the sale of the Summerset Company stock? Explain.
(d) Are there any additional entries necessary for Lexington Company at December 31, 2011, to reflect the facts on the financial statements in accordance with generally accepted accounting principles? Explain.

(AICPA adapted)

CA17-3 (Financial Statement Effect of Equity Securities) Presented below are three unrelated situations involving equity securities.

Situation 1
An equity security, whose market value is currently less than cost, is classified as available-for-sale but is to be reclassified as trading.

Situation 2
A noncurrent portfolio with an aggregate market value in excess of cost includes one particular security whose market value has declined to less than one-half of the original cost. The decline in value is considered to be other than temporary.

Situation 3

The portfolio of trading securities has a cost in excess of fair value of $13,500. The available-for-sale portfolio has a fair value in excess of cost of $28,600.

Instructions

What is the effect upon carrying value and earnings for each of the situations above?

CA17-4   (Equity Securities)   The Financial Accounting Standards Board issued accounting guidance to clarify accounting methods and procedures with respect to certain debt and all equity securities. An important part of the statement concerns the distinction between held-to-maturity, available-for-sale, and trading securities.

Instructions

  (a) Why does a company maintain an investment portfolio of held-to-maturity, available-for-sale, and trading securities?
• (b) What factors should be considered in determining whether investments in securities should be classified as held-to-maturity, available-for-sale, and trading? How do these factors affect the accounting treatment for unrealized losses?

CA17-5   (Investment Accounted for under the Equity Method)   On July 1, 2011, Fontaine Company purchased for cash 40% of the outstanding capital stock of Knoblett Company. Both Fontaine Company and Knoblett Company have a December 31 year-end. Knoblett Company, whose common stock is actively traded in the over-the-counter market, reported its total net income for the year to Fontaine Company and also paid cash dividends on November 15, 2011, to Fontaine Company and its other stockholders.

Instructions

How should Fontaine Company report the above facts in its December 31, 2011, balance sheet and its income statement for the year then ended? Discuss the rationale for your answer.

(AICPA adapted)

CA17-6   (Equity Investment)   On July 1, 2010, Selig Company purchased for cash 40% of the outstanding capital stock of Spoor Corporation. Both Selig and Spoor have a December 31 year-end. Spoor Corporation, whose common stock is actively traded on the American Stock Exchange, paid a cash dividend on November 15, 2010, to Selig Company and its other stockholders. It also reported its total net income for the year of $920,000 to Selig Company.

Instructions

Prepare a one-page memorandum of instructions on how Selig Company should report the above facts in its December 31, 2010, balance sheet and its 2010 income statement. In your memo, identify and describe the method of valuation you recommend. Provide rationale where you can. Address your memo to the chief accountant at Selig Company.

CA17-7   (Fair Value)   Addison Manufacturing holds a large portfolio of debt and equity securities as an investment. The fair value of the portfolio is greater than its original cost, even though some securities have decreased in value. Sam Beresford, the financial vice president, and Angie Nielson, the controller, are near year-end in the process of classifying for the first time this securities portfolio in accordance with GAAP. Beresford wants to classify those securities that have increased in value during the period as trading securities in order to increase net income this year. He wants to classify all the securities that have decreased in value as available-for-sale (the equity securities) and as held-to-maturity (the debt securities).

Nielson disagrees. She wants to classify those securities that have decreased in value as trading securities and those that have increased in value as available-for-sale (equity) and held-to-maturity (debt). She contends that the company is having a good earnings year and that recognizing the losses will help to smooth the income this year. As a result, the company will have built-in gains for future periods when the company may not be as profitable.

Instructions

Answer the following questions.

  (a) Will classifying the portfolio as each proposes actually have the effect on earnings that each says it will?
  (b) Is there anything unethical in what each of them proposes? Who are the stakeholders affected by their proposals?
  (c) Assume that Beresford and Nielson properly classify the entire portfolio into trading, available-for-sale, and held-to-maturity categories. But then each proposes to sell just before year-end the securities with gains or with losses, as the case may be, to accomplish their effect on earnings. Is this unethical?

USING YOUR JUDGMENT

FINANCIAL REPORTING

Financial Reporting Problem

P&G The Procter & Gamble Company (P&G)

The financial statements of **P&G** are presented in Appendix 5B or can be accessed at the book's companion website, **www.wiley.com/college/kieso.**

Instructions

Refer to P&G's financial statements and the accompanying notes to answer the following questions.

(a) What investments does P&G report in 2007, and where are these investments reported in its financial statements?

(b) How are P&G's investments valued? How does P&G determine fair value?

(c) How does P&G use derivative financial instruments?

Comparative Analysis Case

The Coca-Cola Company and PepsiCo, Inc.

The Coca-Cola Company

 PEPSICO

Instructions

Go to the book's companion website and use information found there to answer the following questions related to **The Coca-Cola Company** and **PepsiCo, Inc.**

(a) Based on the information contained in these financial statements, determine each of the following for each company.

(1) Cash used in (for) investing activities during 2007 (from the statement of cash flows).

(2) Cash used for acquisitions and investments in unconsolidated affiliates (or principally bottling companies) during 2007.

(3) Total investment in unconsolidated affiliates (or investments and other assets) at the end of 2007.

(4) What conclusions concerning the management of investments can be drawn from these data?

(b) (1) Briefly identify from Coca-Cola's December 31, 2007, balance sheet the investments it reported as being accounted for under the equity method. (2) What is the amount of investments that Coca-Cola reported in its 2007 balance sheet as "cost method investments," and what is the nature of these investments?

(c) In its Note number 9 on Financial Instruments, what total amounts did Coca-Cola report at December 31, 2007, as: (1) trading securities, (2) available-for-sale securities, and (3) held-to-maturity securities?

Financial Statement Analysis Case

Union Planters

Union Planters is a Tennessee bank holding company (that is, a corporation that owns banks). (Union Planters is now part of **Regions Bank**.) Union Planters manages $32 billion in assets, the largest of which is its loan portfolio of $19 billion. In addition to its loan portfolio, however, like other banks it has significant debt investments. The nature of these investments varies from short-term in nature to long-term in nature. As a consequence, consistent with the requirements of accounting rules, Union Planters reports its investments in two different categories—trading and available-for-sale. The following facts were found in a recent Union Planters' annual report.

(all dollars in millions)	Amortized Cost	Gross Unrealized Gains	Gross Unrealized Losses	Fair Value
Trading account assets	$ 275	—	—	$ 275
Securities available for sale	8,209	$108	$15	8,302
Net income				224
Net securities gains (losses)				(9)

Instructions

(a) Why do you suppose Union Planters purchases investments, rather than simply making loans? Why does it purchase investments that vary in nature both in terms of their maturities and in type (debt versus stock)?

(b) How must Union Planters account for its investments in each of the two categories?

(c) In what ways does classifying investments into two different categories assist investors in evaluating the profitability of a company like Union Planters?

(d) Suppose that the management of Union Planters was not happy with its net income for the year. What step could it have taken with its investment portfolio that would have definitely increased reported profit? How much could it have increased reported profit? Why do you suppose it chose not to do this?

BRIDGE TO THE PROFESSION

Professional Research: FASB Codification

Your client, Cascade Company, is planning to invest some of its excess cash in 5-year revenue bonds issued by the county and in the stock of one of its suppliers, Teton Co. Teton's shares trade on the over-the-counter market. Cascade plans to classify these investments as available-for-sale. They would like you to conduct some research on the accounting for these investments.

Instructions

Access the FASB Codification at *http://asc.fasb.org/home* to conduct research using the Codification Research System to prepare responses to the following items. Provide Codification references for your responses.

(a) Since the Teton shares do not trade on one of the large stock markets, Cascade argues that the fair value of this investment is not readily available. According to the authoritative literature, when is the fair value of a security "readily determinable"?

(b) How is an impairment of a security accounted for?

(c) To avoid volatility in their financial statements due to fair value adjustments, Cascade debated whether the bond investment could be classified as held-to-maturity; Cascade is pretty sure it will hold the bonds for 5 years. How close to maturity could Cascade sell an investment and still classify it as held-to-maturity?

(d) What disclosures must be made for any sale or transfer from securities classified as held-to-maturity?

Professional Simulation

Go to the book's companion website, at **www.wiley.com.college/kieso**, to find an interactive problem that simulates the computerized CPA exam. The professional simulation for this chapter asks you to address questions related to the accounting for investments.

Remember to check the book's companion website to find additional resources for this chapter.

CHAPTER 18

REVENUE RECOGNITION

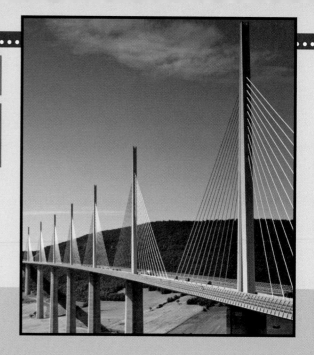

LEARNING OBJECTIVES

After studying this chapter, you should be able to:

- **•1** Apply the revenue recognition principle.
- **•2** Describe accounting issues for revenue recognition at point of sale.
- **•3** Apply the percentage-of-completion method for long-term contracts.
- **•4** Apply the completed-contract method for long-term contracts.
- **•5** Identify the proper accounting for losses on long-term contracts.
- **•6** Describe the installment-sales method of accounting.
- **•7** Explain the cost-recovery method of accounting.

| IT'S BACK |

Several years after passage, the accounting world continues to be preoccupied with the Sarbanes-Oxley Act of 2002 (SOX). Unfortunately, SOX did not solve one of the classic accounting issues—how to properly account for revenue. In fact, revenue recognition practices are the most prevalent reasons for accounting restatements. A number of the revenue recognition issues relate to possible fraudulent behavior by company executives and employees. Consider some of the recent SEC actions:

- The SEC charged the former co-chairman and CEO of **Qwest Communications International Inc.** and eight other former Qwest officers and employees with fraud and other violations of the federal securities laws. Three of these people fraudulently characterized nonrecurring revenue from one-time sales as revenue from recurring data and Internet services. The SEC release notes that internal correspondence likened Qwest's dependence on these transactions to fill the gap between actual and projected revenue to an addiction.

- The SEC filed a complaint against three former senior officers of **iGo Corp.**, alleging that the defendants collectively caused iGo to improperly recognize revenue on consignment sales and products that were not shipped or that were shipped after the end of a fiscal quarter.

- The SEC filed a complaint against the former CEO and chairman of **Homestore Inc.** and its former executive vice president of business development, alleging that they engaged in a fraudulent scheme to overstate advertising and subscription revenues. The scheme involved a complex structure of "round-trip" transactions using various third-party companies that, in essence, allowed Homestore to recognize its own cash as revenue.

- The SEC claims that **Lantronix** deliberately sent excessive product to distributors and granted them generous return rights and extended payment terms. In addition, as part of its alleged channel stuffing and to prevent product returns, Lantronix loaned funds to a third party to purchase Lantronix products from one of its distributors. The third party later returned the product. The SEC also asserted that Lantronix engaged in other improper revenue recognition practices, including shipping without a purchase order and recognizing revenue on a contingent sale.

Though the cases cited involved fraud and irregularity, not all revenue recognition errors are intentional. For example, in April 2005 **American Home Mortgage Investment Corp.** announced that it would reverse revenue recognized from its fourth-quarter 2004 loan securitization, and would recognize it in the first quarter of 2005 instead. As a result, American Home restated its financial results for 2004.

So, how does a company ensure that revenue transactions are recorded properly? Some answers will become apparent after you study this chapter.

Sources: Cheryl de Mesa Graziano, "Revenue Recognition: A Perennial Problem," *Financial Executive* (July 14, 2005), *www.fei.org/mag/articles/7-2005_revenue.cfm*; and S. Taub, "SEC Accuses Ex-CFO of Channel Stuffing," *CFO.com* (September 30, 2006).

PREVIEW OF CHAPTER 18

As indicated in the opening story, the issue of when revenue should be recognized is complex. The many methods of marketing products and services make it difficult to develop guidelines that will apply to all situations. This chapter provides you with general guidelines used in most business transactions. The content and organization of the chapter are as follows.

REVENUE RECOGNITION

CURRENT ENVIRONMENT	REVENUE RECOGNITION AT POINT OF SALE	REVENUE RECOGNITION BEFORE DELIVERY	REVENUE RECOGNITION AFTER DELIVERY
• Guidelines for revenue recognition • Departures from sale basis	• Sales with buyback agreements • Sales when right of return exists • Trade loading and channel stuffing	• Percentage-of-completion method • Completed-contract method • Long-term contract losses • Disclosures • Completion-of-production basis	• Installment-sales method • Cost-recovery method • Deposit method • Summary of bases • Concluding remarks

THE CURRENT ENVIRONMENT

According to one study, revenue recognition has been the largest single source of public-company restatements over the past decade. The study noted the following:

1. Restatements for improper revenue recognition result in larger drops in market capitalization than any other type of restatement.
2. Revenue problems caused eight of the top ten market value losses in a recent year.
3. Of the ten companies, the leading three lost $20 billion in market value in just three days following disclosure of revenue recognition problems.[1]

INTERNATIONAL INSIGHT

iGAAP has less-detailed revenue recognition rules compared to U.S. GAAP.

As a result of such revenue recognition problems, the SEC has increased its enforcement actions in this area (as evidenced in the opening story). In some of these cases, companies made significant adjustments to previously issued financial statements. As Lynn Turner, a former chief accountant of the SEC, indicated, "When people cross over the boundaries of legitimate reporting, the Commission will take appropriate action to ensure the fairness and integrity that investors need and depend on every day."[2]

Inappropriate recognition of revenue can occur in any industry. Products that are sold to distributors for resale pose different risks than products or services that are sold directly to customers. Sales in high-technology industries, where rapid product obsolescence is a significant issue, pose different risks than sale of inventory with a longer life, such as farm or construction equipment, automobiles, trucks, and appliances.[3]

As indicated in Chapter 10, telecom companies such as **Global Crossing** and **Qwest Communications** swapped fiber-optic capacity to increase revenue. The SEC has expressed concern that dot-coms also are increasing their revenue by including product sales in their revenue even though they are acting only as the distributor (intermediary) on behalf of other companies. Instead, dot-coms should be reporting only a distribution (brokerage) fee for selling another company's products.[4]

What do the numbers mean?

GROSSED OUT

Consider **Priceline.com**, the company made famous by William Shatner's ads about "naming your own price" for airline tickets and hotel rooms. In one of its quarterly SEC filings, Priceline reported that it earned $152 million in revenues. But that included the full amount customers paid for tickets, hotel rooms, and rental cars. Traditional travel agencies call that amount "gross bookings," not revenues. And much like regular travel agencies, Priceline keeps only a small portion of gross bookings—namely, the spread between the customers' accepted bids and the price it paid for the merchandise. The rest, which Priceline calls "product costs," it pays to the airlines and hotels that supply the tickets and rooms.

[1]PricewaterhouseCoopers, "Current Developments for Audit Committees 2002" (Florham Park, N.J.: PricewaterhouseCoopers, 2002), p. 65.

[2]The Sarbanes-Oxley Act of 2002 also makes it clear that Congress will not tolerate abuses of the financial reporting process and that those who fail to adhere to "certain standards" will be prosecuted.

[3]Adapted from American Institute of Certified Public Accountants, Inc., *Audit Issues in Revenue Recognition* (New York: AICPA, 1999).

[4]"Revenue Recognition in Financial Statements," *SEC Staff Accounting Bulletin No. 101*, December 3, 1999).

However, Priceline's product costs came to $134 million, leaving Priceline just $18 million of what it calls "gross profit" and what most other companies would call revenues. And that's before all of Priceline's other costs—like advertising and salaries—which netted out to a loss of $102 million. The difference isn't academic: Priceline stock traded at about 23 times its reported revenues but at a mind-boggling 214 times its "gross profit." This and other aggressive recognition practices led the SEC to issue stricter revenue recogniton guidance indicating that if a company performs as an agent or broker without assuming the risks and rewards of ownership of the goods, the company should report sales on a net (fee) basis. [1]

What do the numbers mean?

(continued)

Source: Jeremy Kahn, "Presto Chango! Sales Are Huge," *Fortune* (March 20, 2000), p. 44.

Guidelines for Revenue Recognition

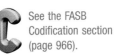

See the FASB Codification section (page 966).

In general, the guidelines for revenue recognition are quite broad. On top of the broad guidelines, certain industries have specific additional guidelines that provide further insight into when revenue should be recognized. The **revenue recognition principle** provides that companies should recognize revenue[5] (1) when it is realized or realizable and (2) when it is earned.[6] Therefore, proper revenue recognition revolves around three terms:

> **Objective·1**
> Apply the revenue recognition principle.

> Revenues are **realized** when a company exchanges goods and services for cash or claims to cash (receivables).
>
> Revenues are **realizable** when assets a company receives in exchange are readily convertible to known amounts of cash or claims to cash.
>
> Revenues are **earned** when a company has substantially accomplished what it must do to be entitled to the benefits represented by the revenues—that is, when the earnings process is complete or virtually complete.[7]

Four revenue transactions are recognized in accordance with this principle:

1. Companies recognize revenue from selling products at the date of sale. This date is usually interpreted to mean the date of delivery to customers.
2. Companies recognize revenue from services provided, when services have been performed and are billable.
3. Companies recognize revenue from permitting others to use enterprise assets, such as interest, rent, and royalties, as time passes or as the assets are used.
4. Companies recognize revenue from disposing of assets other than products at the date of sale.

Underlying Concepts

Revenues are inflows of assets and/or settlements of liabilities from delivering or producing goods, providing services, or other earning activities that constitute a company's ongoing major or central operations during a period.

---

[5]Recognition is "the process of formally recording or incorporating an item in the accounts and financial statements of an entity" (*SFAC No. 3*, par. 83). "Recognition includes depiction of an item in both words and numbers, with the amount included in the totals of the financial statements" (*SFAC No. 5*, par. 6). For an asset or liability, recognition involves recording not only acquisition or incurrence of the item but also later changes in it, including removal from the financial statements previously recognized.

Recognition is not the same as realization, although the two are sometimes used interchangeably in accounting literature and practice. *Realization* is "the process of converting noncash resources and rights into money and is most precisely used in accounting and financial reporting to refer to sales of assets for cash or claims to cash" (*SFAC No. 3*, par. 83).

[6]"Recognition and Measurement in Financial Statements of Business Enterprises," *Statement of Financial Accounting Concepts No. 5* (Stamford, Conn.: FASB, 1984), par. 83.

[7]Gains (as contrasted to revenues) commonly result from transactions and other events that do not involve an "earning process." For gain recognition, being earned is generally less significant than being realized or realizable. Companies commonly recognize gains at the time of an asset's sale, disposition of a liability, or when prices of certain assets change.

These revenue transactions are diagrammed in Illustration 18-1.

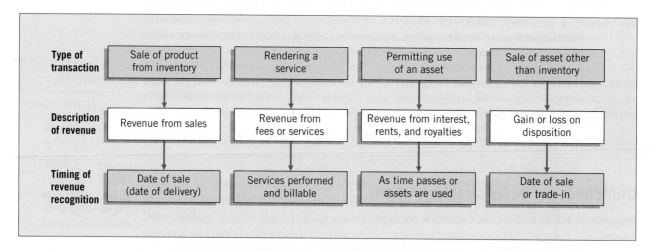

ILLUSTRATION 18-1
Revenue Recognition
Classified by Nature of
Transaction

The preceding statements are the basis of accounting for revenue transactions. Yet, in practice there are departures from the revenue recognition principle. Companies sometimes recognize revenue at other points in the earning process, owing in great measure to the considerable variety of revenue transactions.[8]

Departures from the Sale Basis

An FASB study found some common **reasons for departures from the sale basis**.[9] One reason is a desire to **recognize earlier** than the time of sale the effect of earning activities. Earlier recognition is appropriate if there is a high degree of certainty about the amount of revenue earned. A second reason is a desire to **delay recognition** of revenue beyond the time of sale. Delayed recognition is appropriate if the degree of uncertainty concerning the amount of either revenue or costs is sufficiently high or if the sale does not represent substantial completion of the earnings process.

This chapter focuses on two of the four general types of revenue transactions described earlier: (1) selling products and (2) providing services. Both of these are **sales transactions**. (In several other sections of the textbook, we discuss the other two types of revenue transactions—revenue from permitting others to use enterprise assets, and revenue from disposing of assets other than products.) Our discussion of product sales transactions in this chapter is organized around the following topics:

1. Revenue recognition at point of sale (delivery).
2. Revenue recognition before delivery.
3. Revenue recognition after delivery.
4. Revenue recognition for special sales transactions—franchises and consignments.

Examples of Revenue Recognition Policies

---

[8]The FASB and IASB are now involved in a joint project on revenue recognition. The purpose of this project is to develop comprehensive conceptual guidance on when to recognize revenue. Presently, the Boards are evaluating a customer-consideration model. In this model, a company accounts for the contract asset or liability that arises from the rights and performance obligations in an enforceable contract with the customer. At contract inception, the rights in the contract are measured at the amount of the promised customer payment (that is, the customer consideration). That amount is then allocated to the individual performance obligations identified within the contract in proportion to the standalone selling price of each good or service underlying the performance obligation. It is hoped that this approach (rather than using the earned and realized or realized criteria) will lead to a better basis for revenue recognition. (See *www.fasb.org/project/revenue_recognition.shtml*.)

[9]Henry R. Jaenicke, Survey of Present Practices in Recognizing Revenues, Expenses, Gains, and Losses, A Research Report (Stamford, Conn.: FASB, 1981), p. 11.

Illustration 18-2 depicts this organization of revenue recognition topics.

ILLUSTRATION 18-2
Revenue Recognition
Alternatives

At point of sale (delivery)	Before delivery			After delivery		Special sales	
"The General Rule"	Before production	During production	At completion of production	As cash is collected	After costs are recovered	Franchises	Consignments

REVENUE RECOGNITION AT POINT OF SALE (DELIVERY)

According to the FASB's *Concepts Statement No. 5*, companies usually meet the two conditions for recognizing revenue (being realized or realizable and being earned) by the time they deliver products or render services to customers.[10] Therefore, companies commonly recognize revenues from manufacturing and selling activities at **point of sale** (usually meaning delivery).[11] Implementation problems, however, can arise. We discuss three such problematic situations on the following pages.

> **Objective·2**
> Describe accounting issues for revenue recognition at point of sale.

Sales with Buyback Agreements

If a company sells a product in one period and agrees to buy it back in the next accounting period, has the company sold the product? As indicated in Chapter 8, legal title has transferred in this situation. However, the economic substance of the transaction is that the seller retains the risks of ownership. The FASB has curtailed recognition of revenue using this practice. When a repurchase agreement exists at a set price and this price covers all cost of the inventory plus related holding costs, the inventory and related liability remain on the seller's books. [3] In other words, no sale.

Sales When Right of Return Exists

Whether cash or credit sales are involved, a special problem arises with claims for returns and allowances. In Chapter 7, we presented the accounting treatment for normal returns and allowances. However, certain companies experience such a **high rate of returns**—a high ratio of returned merchandise to sales—that they find it necessary to postpone reporting sales until the return privilege has substantially expired.

For example, in the publishing industry, the rate of return approaches 25 percent for hardcover books and 65 percent for some magazines. Other types of companies that experience high return rates are perishable food dealers, distributors who sell to retail outlets, recording-industry companies, and some toy and sporting goods manufacturers. Returns in these industries are frequently made either through a right of contract or as a matter of practice involving "guaranteed sales" agreements or consignments.

> **Underlying Concepts**
> This is an example of *realized but unearned revenue*. When high rates of return exist and cannot be reasonably estimated, a question arises as to whether the earnings process has been substantially completed.

---

[10]The SEC believes that revenue is realized or realizable and earned when **all** of the following criteria are met: (1) Persuasive evidence of an arrangement exists; (2) delivery has occurred or services have been provided; (3) the seller's price to the buyer is fixed or determinable; and (4) collectibility is reasonably assured. [2] The SEC provided more specific guidance because the general criteria were difficult to interpret.

[11]*Statement of Financial Accounting Concepts No. 5*, op. cit., par. 84.

Three alternative revenue recognition methods are available when the right of return exposes the seller to continued risks of ownership. These are: (1) not recording a sale until all return privileges have expired; (2) recording the sale, but reducing sales by an estimate of future returns; and (3) recording the sale and accounting for the returns as they occur. The FASB concluded that if a company sells its product but gives the buyer the right to return it, the company should **recognize revenue** from the sales transactions at the time of sale **only if all of the following six conditions** have been met. [4]

1. The seller's price to the buyer is substantially fixed or determinable at the date of sale.
2. The buyer has paid the seller, or the buyer is obligated to pay the seller, and the obligation is not contingent on resale of the product.
3. The buyer's obligation to the seller would not be changed in the event of theft or physical destruction or damage of the product.
4. The buyer acquiring the product for resale has economic substance apart from that provided by the seller.
5. The seller does not have significant obligations for future performance to directly bring about resale of the product by the buyer.
6. The seller can reasonably estimate the amount of future returns.

What if the six conditions are not met? In that case, the company must recognize sales revenue and cost of sales either when the return privilege has substantially expired or when those six conditions subsequently are met, **whichever occurs first**. In the income statement, the company must reduce sales revenue and cost of sales by the amount of the estimated returns.

Trade Loading and Channel Stuffing

Some companies record revenues at date of delivery with neither buyback nor unlimited return provisions. Although they appear to be following acceptable point-of-sale revenue recognition practices, they are recognizing revenues and earnings prematurely.

For example, the domestic cigarette industry at one time engaged in a distribution practice known as **trade loading**. As one commentator described this practice, "Trade loading is a crazy, uneconomic, insidious practice through which manufacturers—trying to show sales, profits, and market share they don't actually have—induce their wholesale customers, known as the trade, to buy more product than they can promptly resell."[12] In total, the cigarette industry appears to have exaggerated a couple years' operating profits by as much as $600 million by taking the profits from future years.

In the computer software industry, a similar practice is referred to as **channel stuffing**. When a software maker needed to make its financial results look good, it offered deep discounts to its distributors to overbuy, and then recorded revenue when the software left the loading dock.[13] Of course, the distributors' inventories become bloated and the marketing channel gets too filled with product, but the software maker's current-period financials are improved. However, financial results in future periods will suffer, unless the company repeats the process.

Trade loading and channel stuffing distort operating results and "window dress" financial statements. If used without an appropriate allowance for sales returns, channel stuffing is a classic example of booking tomorrow's revenue today. Business managers need to be aware of the ethical dangers of misleading the financial community by engaging in such practices to improve their financial statements.

---

[12]"The $600 Million Cigarette Scam," *Fortune* (December 4, 1989), p. 89.
[13]"Software's Dirty Little Secret," *Forbes* (May 15, 1989), p. 128.

NO TAKE-BACKS

What do the numbers mean?

Investors in **Lucent Technologies** were negatively affected when Lucent violated one of the fundamental criteria for revenue recognition—the "no take-back" rule. This rule holds that revenue should not be booked on inventory that is shipped if the customer can return it at some point in the future. In this particular case, Lucent agreed to take back shipped inventory from its distributors, if the distributors were unable to sell the items to their customers.

In essence, Lucent was "stuffing the channel." By booking sales when goods were shipped, even though they most likely would get them back, Lucent was able to report continued sales growth. However, Lucent investors got a nasty surprise when distributors returned those goods and Lucent had to restate its financial results. The restatement erased $679 million in revenues, turning an operating profit into a loss. In response to this bad news, Lucent's stock price declined $1.31 per share, or 8.5 percent. Lucent is not alone in this practice. **Sunbeam** got caught stuffing the sales channel with barbeque grills and other outdoor items, which contributed to its troubles when it was forced to restate its earnings.

Investors can be tipped off to potential channel stuffing by carefully reviewing a company's revenue recognition policy for generous return policies and by watching inventory and receivable levels. When sales increase along with receivables, that's one sign that customers are not paying for goods shipped on credit. And growing inventory levels are an indicator that customers have all the goods they need. Both scenarios suggest a higher likelihood of goods being returned and revenues and income being restated. So remember, no take-backs!

Source: Adapted from S. Young, "Lucent Slashes First Quarter Outlook, Erases Revenue from Latest Quarter," *Wall Street Journal Online* (December 22, 2000); and Tracey Byrnes, "Too Many Thin Mints: Spotting the Practice of Channel Stuffing," *Wall Street Journal Online* (February 7, 2002).

REVENUE RECOGNITION BEFORE DELIVERY

For the most part, companies recognize revenue at the point of sale (delivery) because at point of sale most of the uncertainties in the earning process are removed and the exchange price is known. Under certain circumstances, however, companies recognize revenue prior to completion and delivery. The most notable example is long-term construction contract accounting, which uses the percentage-of-completion method.

Additional Disclosures of Revenue Recognition Policies

Long-term contracts frequently provide that the seller (builder) may bill the purchaser at intervals, as it reaches various points in the project. Examples of long-term contracts are construction-type contracts, development of military and commercial aircraft, weapons-delivery systems, and space exploration hardware. When the project consists of separable units, such as a group of buildings or miles of roadway, contract provisions may provide for delivery in installments. In that case, the seller would bill the buyer and transfer title at stated stages of completion, such as the completion of each building unit or every 10 miles of road. The accounting records should record sales when installments are "delivered."[14]

Two distinctly different methods of accounting for long-term construction contracts are recognized.[15] They are:

- **Percentage-of-Completion Method.** Companies recognize revenues and gross profits each period based upon the progress of the construction—that is, the percentage of completion. The company accumulates construction costs **plus gross profit earned to date** in an inventory account (Construction in Process), and it accumulates progress billings in a contra inventory account (Billings on Construction in Progress).

---

[14]*Statement of Financial Accounting Concepts No. 5,* **par. 84,** item c.

[15]*Accounting Trends and Techniques—2007* reports that of the 90 of its 600 sample companies that referred to long-term construction contracts, 81 used the percentage-of-completion method and 9 used the completed-contract method.

- **Completed-Contract Method.** Companies recognize revenues and gross profit **only** when the contract is completed. The company accumulates construction costs in an inventory account (Construction in Process), and it accumulates progress billings in a contra inventory account (Billings on Construction in Process).

The rationale for using percentage-of-completion accounting is that under most of these contracts the buyer and seller have enforceable rights. The buyer has the legal right to require specific performance on the contract. The seller has the right to require progress payments that provide evidence of the buyer's ownership interest. As a result, a continuous sale occurs as the work progresses. Companies should recognize revenue according to that progression.

Underlying Concepts

The percentage-of-completion method recognizes revenue from long-term contracts in the periods in which the revenue is earned. The firm contract fixes the selling price. And, if costs are estimable and collection reasonably assured, the revenue recognition concept is not violated.

Companies *must* use the percentage-of-completion method when estimates of progress toward completion, revenues, and costs are reasonably dependable and **all of the following conditions** exist. [5]

1. The contract clearly specifies the enforceable rights regarding goods or services to be provided and received by the parties, the consideration to be exchanged, and the manner and terms of settlement.
2. The buyer can be expected to satisfy all obligations under the contract.
3. The contractor can be expected to perform the contractual obligations.

Companies should use the completed-contract method when one of the following conditions applies:

- when a company has primarily short-term contracts, *or*
- when a company cannot meet the conditions for using the percentage-of-completion method, *or*
- when there are inherent hazards in the contract beyond the normal, recurring business risks.

The presumption is that percentage-of-completion is the better method. Therefore, companies should use the completed-contract method only when the percentage-of-completion method is inappropriate. We discuss the two methods in more detail in the following sections.

Percentage-of-Completion Method

Objective·3

Apply the percentage-of-completion method for long-term contracts.

The **percentage-of-completion method** recognizes revenues, costs, and gross profit as a company makes progress toward completion on a long-term contract. To defer recognition of these items until completion of the entire contract is to misrepresent the efforts (costs) and accomplishments (revenues) of the accounting periods during the contract. In order to apply the percentage-of-completion method, a company must have some basis or standard for measuring the progress toward completion at particular interim dates.

Measuring the Progress toward Completion

As one practicing accountant wrote, "The big problem in applying the percentage-of-completion method . . . has to do with the ability to make reasonably accurate estimates of completion and the final gross profit."[16] Companies use various methods to determine the **extent of progress toward completion**. The most common are the *cost-to-cost* and *units-of-delivery* methods.[17]

---

[16]Richard S. Hickok, "New Guidance for Construction Contractors: 'A Credit Plus,'" *The Journal of Accountancy* (March 1982), p. 46.

[17]R. K. Larson and K. L. Brown, "Where Are We with Long-Term Contract Accounting?" *Accounting Horizons* (September 2004), pp. 207–219.

The objective of all these methods is to measure the extent of progress in terms of costs, units, or value added. Companies identify the various measures (costs incurred, labor hours worked, tons produced, floors completed, etc.) and classify them as input or output measures. **Input measures** (costs incurred, labor hours worked) are efforts devoted to a contract. **Output measures** (with units of delivery measured as tons produced, floors of a building completed, miles of a highway completed) track results. Neither are universally applicable to all long-term projects. Their use requires the exercise of judgment and careful tailoring to the circumstances.

Both input and output measures have certain disadvantages. The input measure is based on an established relationship between a unit of input and productivity. If inefficiencies cause the productivity relationship to change, inaccurate measurements result. Another potential problem is front-end loading, in which significant up-front costs result in higher estimates of completion. To avoid this problem, companies should disregard some early-stage construction costs—for example, costs of uninstalled materials or costs of subcontracts not yet performed—if they do not relate to contract performance.

Similarly, output measures can produce inaccurate results if the units used are not comparable in time, effort, or cost to complete. For example, using floors (stories) completed can be deceiving. Completing the first floor of an eight-story building may require more than one-eighth the total cost because of the substructure and foundation construction.

The most popular input measure used to determine the progress toward completion is the **cost-to-cost basis**. Under this basis, a company like **EDS** measures the percentage of completion by comparing costs incurred to date with the most recent estimate of the total costs required to complete the contract. Illustration 18-3 shows the formula for the cost-to-cost basis.

$$\frac{\text{Costs incurred to date}}{\text{Most recent estimate of total costs}} = \text{Percent complete}$$

ILLUSTRATION 18-3
Formula for Percentage-of-Completion, Cost-to-Cost Basis

Once EDS knows the percentage that costs incurred bear to total estimated costs, it applies that percentage to the total revenue or the estimated total gross profit on the contract. The resulting amount is the revenue or the gross profit to be recognized to date. Illustration 18-4 shows this computation.

$$\begin{array}{c}\text{Percent} \\ \text{complete}\end{array} \times \begin{array}{c}\text{Estimated} \\ \text{total revenue} \\ \text{(or gross profit)}\end{array} = \begin{array}{c}\text{Revenue (or gross} \\ \text{profit) to be} \\ \text{recognized to date}\end{array}$$

ILLUSTRATION 18-4
Formula for Total Revenue to Be Recognized to Date

To find the amounts of revenue and gross profit recognized each period, EDS subtracts total revenue or gross profit recognized in prior periods, as shown in Illustration 18-5.

$$\begin{array}{c}\text{Revenue (or gross} \\ \text{profit) to be} \\ \text{recognized to date}\end{array} - \begin{array}{c}\text{Revenue (or gross} \\ \text{profit) recognized} \\ \text{in prior periods}\end{array} = \begin{array}{c}\text{Current-period} \\ \text{revenue} \\ \text{(or gross profit)}\end{array}$$

ILLUSTRATION 18-5
Formula for Amount of Current-Period Revenue, Cost-to-Cost Basis

Because **the cost-to-cost method is widely used** (without excluding other bases for measuring progress toward completion), we have adopted it for use in our examples. [6]

Example of Percentage-of-Completion Method—Cost-to-Cost Basis

To illustrate the percentage-of-completion method, assume that Hardhat Construction Company has a contract to construct a $4,500,000 bridge at an estimated cost of $4,000,000. The contract is to start in July 2010, and the bridge is to be completed in October 2012. The following data pertain to the construction period. (Note that by the end of 2011 Hardhat has revised the estimated total cost from $4,000,000 to $4,050,000.)

	2010	2011	2012
Costs to date	$1,000,000	$2,916,000	$4,050,000
Estimated costs to complete	3,000,000	1,134,000	—
Progress billings during the year	900,000	2,400,000	1,200,000
Cash collected during the year	750,000	1,750,000	2,000,000

Hardhat would compute the percentage complete as shown in Illustration 18-6.

ILLUSTRATION 18-6
Application of Percentage-of-Completion Method, Cost-to-Cost Basis

	2010	2011	2012
Contract price	$4,500,000	$4,500,000	$4,500,000
Less estimated cost:			
Costs to date	1,000,000	2,916,000	4,050,000
Estimated costs to complete	3,000,000	1,134,000	—
Estimated total costs	4,000,000	4,050,000	4,050,000
Estimated total gross profit	$ 500,000	$ 450,000	$ 450,000
Percent complete	25%	72%	100%
	$\left(\dfrac{\$1,000,000}{\$4,000,000}\right)$	$\left(\dfrac{\$2,916,000}{\$4,050,000}\right)$	$\left(\dfrac{\$4,050,000}{\$4,050,000}\right)$

On the basis of the data above, Hardhat would make the following entries to record (1) the costs of construction, (2) progress billings, and (3) collections. These entries appear as summaries of the many transactions that would be entered individually as they occur during the year.

ILLUSTRATION 18-7
Journal Entries—Percentage-of-Completion Method, Cost-to-Cost Basis

	2010		2011		2012	
To record cost of construction:						
Construction in Process	1,000,000		1,916,000		1,134,000	
Materials, Cash, Payables, etc.		1,000,000		1,916,000		1,134,000
To record progress billings:						
Accounts Receivable	900,000		2,400,000		1,200,000	
Billings on Construction in Process		900,000		2,400,000		1,200,000
To record collections:						
Cash	750,000		1,750,000		2,000,000	
Accounts Receivable		750,000		1,750,000		2,000,000

In this example, the costs incurred to date are a measure of the extent of progress toward completion. To determine this, Hardhat evaluates the costs incurred to date as a proportion of the estimated total costs to be incurred on the project. The estimated revenue and gross profit that Hardhat will recognize for each year are calculated as shown in Illustration 18-8 (on page 941).

ILLUSTRATION 18-8
Percentage-of-Completion,
Revenue and Gross Profit,
by Year

	2010	2011	2012
Revenue recognized in:			
2010 $4,500,000 × 25%	$1,125,000		
2011 $4,500,000 × 72%		$3,240,000	
Less: Revenue recognized in 2010		1,125,000	
Revenue in 2011		$2,115,000	
2012 $4,500,000 × 100%			$4,500,000
Less: Revenue recognized in 2010 and 2011			3,240,000
Revenue in 2012			$1,260,000
Gross profit recognized in:			
2010 $500,000 × 25%	$ 125,000		
2011 $450,000 × 72%		$ 324,000	
Less: Gross profit recognized in 2010		125,000	
Gross profit in 2011		$ 199,000	
2012 $450,000 × 100%			$ 450,000
Less: Gross profit recognized in 2010 and 2011			324,000
Gross profit in 2012			$ 126,000

Illustration 18-9 shows Hardhat's entries to recognize revenue and gross profit each year and to record completion and final approval of the contract.

ILLUSTRATION 18-9
Journal Entries to
Recognize Revenue and
Gross Profit and to Record
Contract Completion—
Percentage-of-Completion
Method, Cost-to-Cost
Basis

	2010	2011	2012
To recognize revenue and gross profit:			
Construction in Process (gross profit)	125,000	199,000	126,000
Construction Expenses	1,000,000	1,916,000	1,134,000
Revenue from Long-Term Contracts	1,125,000	2,115,000	1,260,000
To record completion of the contract:			
Billings on Construction in Process			4,500,000
Construction in Process			4,500,000

Note that Hardhat debits gross profit (as computed in Illustration 18-8) to Construction in Process. Similarly, it credits Revenue from Long-Term Contracts for the amounts computed in Illustration 18-8. Hardhat then debits the difference between the amounts recognized each year for revenue and gross profit to a nominal account, Construction Expenses (similar to Cost of Goods Sold in a manufacturing company). It reports that amount in the income statement as the actual cost of construction incurred in that period. For example, Hardhat uses the actual costs of $1,000,000 to compute both the gross profit of $125,000 and the percent complete (25 percent).

Hardhat continues to accumulate costs in the Construction in Process account, in order to maintain a record of total costs incurred (plus recognized profit) to date. Although theoretically a series of "sales" takes place using the percentage-of-completion method, the selling company cannot remove the inventory cost until the construction is completed and transferred to the new owner. Hardhat's Construction in Process account for the bridge would include the following summarized entries over the term of the construction project.

ILLUSTRATION 18-10
Content of Construction
in Process Account—
Percentage-of-Completion
Method

Construction in Process				
2010 construction costs	$1,000,000	12/31/12	to close	
2010 recognized gross profit	125,000		completed	
2011 construction costs	1,916,000		project	$4,500,000
2011 recognized gross profit	199,000			
2012 construction costs	1,134,000			
2012 recognized gross profit	126,000			
Total	$4,500,000	Total		$4,500,000

Recall that the Hardhat Construction Company example contained a **change in estimate**: In the second year, 2011, it increased the estimated total costs from $4,000,000 to $4,050,000. The change in estimate is accounted for in a **cumulative catch-up manner**. This is done by, first, adjusting the percent completed to the new estimate of total costs. Next, Hardhat deducts the amount of revenues and gross profit recognized in prior periods from revenues and gross profit computed for progress to date. That is, it accounts for the change in estimate in the period of change. That way, the balance sheet at the end of the period of change and the accounting in subsequent periods are as they would have been if the revised estimate had been the original estimate.

Financial Statement Presentation—Percentage-of-Completion

Generally, when a company records a receivable from a sale, it reduces the Inventory account. Under the percentage-of-completion method, however, the company continues to carry both the receivable and the inventory. Subtracting the balance in the **Billings account** from Construction in Process avoids double-counting the inventory. During the life of the contract, Hardhat reports in the balance sheet the difference between the Construction in Process and the Billings on Construction in Process accounts. If that amount is a debit, Hardhat reports it **as a current asset**; if it is a credit, it reports it **as a current liability**.

At times, the costs incurred plus the gross profit recognized to date (the balance in Construction in Process) exceed the billings. In that case, Hardhat reports this excess as a current asset entitled "Cost and recognized profit in excess of billings." Hardhat can at any time calculate the unbilled portion of revenue recognized to date by subtracting the billings to date from the revenue recognized to date, as illustrated for 2010 for Hardhat Construction in Illustration 18-11.

ILLUSTRATION 18-11
Computation of Unbilled
Contract Price at
12/31/10

Contract revenue recognized to date: $4,500,000 × $\dfrac{\$1,000,000}{\$4,000,000}$		$1,125,000
Billings to date		900,000
Unbilled revenue		$ 225,000

At other times, the billings exceed costs incurred and gross profit to date. In that case, Hardhat reports this excess as a current liability entitled "Billings in excess of costs and recognized profit."

It probably has occurred to you that companies often have more than one project going at a time. When a company has a number of projects, costs exceed billings on some contracts and billings exceed costs on others. In such a case, the company segregates the contracts. The asset side includes only those contracts on which costs and recognized profit exceed billings. The liability side includes only those on which billings exceed costs and recognized profit. Separate disclosures of the dollar volume of billings and costs are preferable to a summary presentation of the net difference.

Using data from the bridge example, Hardhat Construction Company would report the status and results of its long-term construction activities under the perentage-of-completion method as shown in Illustration 18-12 (on page 943).

ILLUSTRATION 18-12
Financial Statement
Presentation—Percentage-
of-Completion Method

HARDHAT CONSTRUCTION COMPANY

	2010	2011	2012
Income Statement			
Revenue from long-term contracts	$1,125,000	$2,115,000	$1,260,000
Costs of construction	1,000,000	1,916,000	1,134,000
Gross profit	$ 125,000	$ 199,000	$ 126,000

Balance Sheet (12/31)

Current assets			
Accounts receivable		$ 150,000	$ 800,000
Inventories			
Construction in process	$1,125,000		
Less: Billings	900,000		
Costs and recognized profit in excess of billings		225,000	
Current liabilities			
Billings ($3,300,000) in excess of costs and recognized profit ($3,240,000)			$ 60,000

Note 1. Summary of significant accounting policies.
Long-Term Construction Contracts. The company recognizes revenues and reports profits from long-term construction contracts, its principal business, under the percentage-of-completion method of accounting. These contracts generally extend for periods in excess of one year. The amounts of revenues and profits recognized each year are based on the ratio of costs incurred to the total estimated costs. Costs included in construction in process include direct materials, direct labor, and project-related overhead. Corporate general and administrative expenses are charged to the periods as incurred and are not allocated to construction contracts.

Completed-Contract Method

Under the **completed-contract method**, companies recognize revenue and gross profit only at point of sale—that is, when the contract is completed. Under this method, companies accumulate costs of long-term contracts in process, but they make no interim charges or credits to income statement accounts for revenues, costs, or gross profit.

The principal advantage of the completed-contract method is that reported revenue reflects final results rather than *estimates* of unperformed work. Its major disadvantage is that it does not reflect current performance when the period of a contract extends into more than one accounting period. Although operations may be fairly uniform during the period of the contract, the company will not report revenue until the year of completion, creating a distortion of earnings.

Under the completed-contract method, the company would make the same **annual entries** to record costs of construction, progress billings, and collections from customers as those illustrated under the percentage-of-completion method. The significant difference is that the company **would not make entries to recognize revenue and gross profit**.

For example, under the completed-contract method for the bridge project illustrated on the preceding pages, Hardhat Construction Company would make the following entries in 2012 to recognize revenue and costs and to close out the inventory and billing accounts.

Billings on Construction in Process	4,500,000	
Revenue from Long-Term Contracts		4,500,000
Costs of Construction	4,050,000	
Construction in Process		4,050,000

Objective·4
Apply the completed-contract method for long-term contracts.

INTERNATIONAL INSIGHT

iGAAP prohibits the use of the completed-contract method of accounting for long-term construction contracts. Companies must use the percentage-of-completion method. If revenues and costs are difficult to estimate, then companies recognize revenue only to the extent of the cost incurred—a zero-profit approach.

Illustration 18-13 compares the amount of gross profit that Hardhat Construction Company would recognize for the bridge project under the two revenue-recognition methods.

ILLUSTRATION 18-13
Comparison of Gross
Profit Recognized under
Different Methods

	Percentage-of-Completion	Completed-Contract
2010	$125,000	$ 0
2011	199,000	0
2012	126,000	450,000

Under the completed-contract method, Hardhat Construction would report its long-term construction activities as follows.

ILLUSTRATION 18-14
Financial Statement
Presentation—
Completed-Contract
Method

HARDHAT CONSTRUCTION COMPANY

	2010	2011	2012
Income Statement			
Revenue from long-term contracts	—	—	$4,500,000
Costs of construction	—	—	4,050,000
Gross profit	—	—	$ 450,000

Balance Sheet (12/31)			
Current assets			
Accounts receivable		$150,000	$800,000
Inventories			
Construction in process	$1,000,000		
Less: Billings	900,000		
Unbilled contract costs		100,000	
Current liabilities			
Billings ($3,300,000) in excess of contract			
costs ($2,916,000)			$384,000

Note 1. Summary of significant accounting policies.
Long-Term Construction Contracts. The company recognizes revenues and reports profits from long-term construction contracts, its principal business, under the completed-contract method. These contracts generally extend for periods in excess of one year. Contract costs and billings are accumulated during the periods of construction, but no revenues or profits are recognized until completion of the contract. Costs included in construction in process include direct material, direct labor, and project-related overhead. Corporate general and administrative expenses are charged to the periods as incurred.

Long-Term Contract Losses

Two types of losses can become evident under long-term contracts:[18]

Objective•5
Identify the proper accounting for
losses on long-term contracts.

1. *Loss in the Current Period on a Profitable Contract.* This condition arises when, during construction, there is a significant increase in the estimated total contract costs but the increase does not eliminate all profit on the contract. Under the percentage-of-completion method only, the estimated cost increase requires a current-period adjustment of excess gross profit recognized on the project in prior periods. The company records this adjustment as a loss in the current period because it is a **change in accounting estimate** (discussed in Chapter 22).

[18]Sak Bhamornsiri, "Losses from Construction Contracts," *The Journal of Accountancy* (April 1982), p. 26.

2. *Loss on an Unprofitable Contract.* Cost estimates at the end of the current period may indicate that a loss will result on completion of the *entire* contract. Under both the percentage-of-completion and the completed-contract methods, the company must recognize in the current period the entire expected contract loss.

Underlying Concepts

Conservatism justifies recognizing the losses immediately. Loss recognition does not require *realization;* it only requires evidence that an impairment of asset value has occurred.

The treatment described for unprofitable contracts is consistent with the accounting custom of anticipating foreseeable losses to avoid overstatement of current and future income (conservatism).

Loss in Current Period

To illustrate a loss in the current period on a contract expected to be profitable upon completion, we'll continue with the Hardhat Construction Company bridge project. Assume that on December 31, 2011, Hardhat estimates the costs to complete the bridge contract at $1,468,962 instead of $1,134,000 (refer to page 940). Assuming all other data are the same as before, Hardhat would compute the percentage complete and recognize the loss as shown in Illustration 18-15. Compare these computations with those for 2011 in Illustration 18-6 (page 940). The "percent complete" has dropped, from 72 percent to 66½ percent, due to the increase in estimated future costs to complete the contract.

Cost to date (12/31/11)	$2,916,000
Estimated costs to complete (revised)	1,468,962
Estimated total costs	$4,384,962
Percent complete ($2,916,000 ÷ $4,384,962)	66½%
Revenue recognized in 2011	
($4,500,000 × 66½%) − $1,125,000	$1,867,500
Costs incurred in 2011	1,916,000
Loss recognized in 2011	$ 48,500

ILLUSTRATION 18-15
Computation of Recognizable Loss, 2011—Loss in Current Period

The 2011 loss of $48,500 is a cumulative adjustment of the "excessive" gross profit recognized on the contract in 2010. Instead of restating the prior period, the company absorbs the prior period misstatement entirely in the current period. In this illustration, the adjustment was large enough to result in recognition of a loss.

Hardhat Construction would record the loss in 2011 as follows.

Construction Expenses	1,916,000	
Construction in Process (loss)		48,500
Revenue from Long-Term Contracts		1,867,500

Hardhat will report the loss of $48,500 on the 2011 income statement as the difference between the reported revenues of $1,867,500 and the costs of $1,916,000.[19] **Under the completed-contract method, the company does not recognize a loss in 2011.** Why not? Because the company still expects the contract **to result in a profit**, to be recognized in the year of completion.

Loss on an Unprofitable Contract

To illustrate the accounting for an **overall loss on a long-term contract**, assume that at December 31, 2011, Hardhat Construction Company estimates the costs to complete the

---

[19]In 2012 Hardhat Construction will recognize the remaining 33½ percent of the revenue ($1,507,500), with costs of $1,468,962 as expected, and will report a gross profit of $38,538. The total gross profit over the three years of the contract would be $115,038 [$125,000 (2010) − $48,500 (2011) + $38,538 (2012)]. This amount is the difference between the total contract revenue of $4,500,000 and the total contract costs of $4,384,962.

bridge contract at $1,640,250 instead of $1,134,000. Revised estimates for the bridge contract are as follows.

	2010 Original Estimates	2011 Revised Estimates
Contract price	$4,500,000	$4,500,000
Estimated total cost	4,000,000	4,556,250*
Estimated gross profit	$ 500,000	
Estimated loss		$ (56,250)

*($2,916,000 + $1,640,250)

Under the percentage-of-completion method, Hardhat recognized $125,000 of gross profit in 2010 (see Illustration 18-8 on page 941). This amount must be offset in 2011 because it is no longer expected to be realized. In addition, since losses must be recognized as soon as estimable, the company must recognize the total estimated loss of $56,250 in 2011. Therefore, Hardhat must recognize a total loss of $181,250 ($125,000 + $56,250) in 2011.

Illustration 18-16 shows Hardhat's computation of the revenue to be recognized in 2011.

ILLUSTRATION 18-16
Computation of Revenue Recognizable, 2011—Unprofitable Contract

Revenue recognized in 2011:		
Contract price		$4,500,000
Percent complete		× 64%*
Revenue recognizable to date		2,880,000
Less: Revenue recognized prior to 2011		1,125,000
Revenue recognized in 2011		$1,755,000
*Cost to date (12/31/11)	$2,916,000	
Estimated cost to complete	1,640,250	
Estimated total costs	$4,556,250	
Percent complete: $2,916,000 ÷ $4,556,250 = 64%		

To compute the construction costs to be expensed in 2011, Hardhat adds the total loss to be recognized in 2011 ($125,000 + $56,250) to the revenue to be recognized in 2011. Illustration 18-17 shows this computation.

ILLUSTRATION 18-17
Computation of Construction Expense, 2011—Unprofitable Contract

Revenue recognized in 2011 (computed above)		$1,755,000
Total loss recognized in 2011:		
Reversal of 2010 gross profit	$125,000	
Total estimated loss on the contract	56,250	181,250
Construction cost expensed in 2011		$1,936,250

Hardhat Construction would record the long-term contract revenues, expenses, and loss in 2011 as follows.

Construction Expenses	1,936,250	
Construction in Process (Loss)		181,250
Revenue from Long-Term Contracts		1,755,000

At the end of 2011, Construction in Process has a balance of $2,859,750 as shown below.[20]

Construction in Process			
2010 Construction costs	1,000,000		
2010 Recognized gross profit	125,000		
2011 Construction costs	1,916,000	2011 Recognized loss	181,250
Balance	**2,859,750**		

ILLUSTRATION 18-18
Content of Construction
in Process Account at End
of 2011—Unprofitable
Contract

Under the completed-contract method, Hardhat also would recognize the contract loss of $56,250, through the following entry in 2011 (the year in which the loss first became evident).

Loss from Long-Term Contracts	56,250	
Construction in Process (Loss)		56,250

Just as the Billings account balance cannot exceed the contract price, neither can the balance in Construction in Process exceed the contract price. In circumstances where the Construction in Process balance exceeds the billings, the company can deduct the recognized loss from such accumulated costs on the balance sheet. That is, under both the percentage-of-completion and the completed-contract methods, the provision for the loss (the credit) may be combined with Construction in Process, thereby reducing the inventory balance. In those circumstances, however (as in the 2011 example above), where the billings exceed the accumulated costs, Hardhat must report separately on the balance sheet, as a current liability, the amount of the estimated loss. That is, under both the percentage-of-completion and the completed-contract methods, Hardhat would take the $56,250 loss, as estimated in 2011, from the Construction in Process account and report it separately as a current liability titled "Estimated liability from long-term contracts." [7]

Disclosures in Financial Statements

Construction contractors usually make some unique financial statement disclosures in addition to those required of all businesses. Generally these additional disclosures are made in the notes to the financial statements. For example, a construction contractor should disclose the following: the method of recognizing revenue, [8] the basis used to classify assets and liabilities as current (the nature and length of the operating cycle), the basis for recording inventory, the effects of any revision of estimates, the amount of backlog on uncompleted contracts, and the details about receivables (billed and unbilled, maturity, interest rates, retainage provisions, and significant individual or group concentrations of credit risk).

[20]If the costs in 2012 are $1,640,250 as projected, at the end of 2012 the Construction in Process account will have a balance of $1,640,250 + $2,859,750, or $4,500,000, equal to the contract price. When the company matches the revenue remaining to be recognized in 2012 of $1,620,000 [$4,500,000 (total contract price) − $1,125,000 (2010) − $1,755,000 (2011)] with the construction expense to be recognized in 2012 of $1,620,000 [total costs of $4,556,250 less the total costs recognized in prior years of $2,936,250 (2010, $1,000,000; 2011, $1,936,250)], a zero profit results. Thus the total loss has been recognized in 2011, the year in which it first became evident.

**What do the
numbers mean?**

Halliburton provides engineering- and construction-related services, in jobs around the world. Much of the company's work is completed under contract over long periods of time. The company uses percentage-of-completion accounting. The SEC started enforcement proceedings against the company related to its accounting for contract claims and disagreements with customers, including those arising from change orders and disputes about billable amounts and costs associated with a construction delay.

Prior to 1998, Halliburton took a very conservative approach to its accounting for disputed claims. As stated in the company's 1997 annual report, "Claims for additional compensation are recognized during the period such claims are resolved." That is, the company waited until all disputes were resolved before recognizing associated revenues. In contrast, in 1998 the company recognized revenue for disputed claims before their resolution, using estimates of amounts expected to be recovered. Such revenue and its related profit are more tentative and are subject to possible later adjustment than revenue and profit recognized when all claims have been resolved. As a case in point, the company noted that it incurred losses of $99 million in 1998 related to customer claims.

The accounting method put in place in 1998 is more aggressive than the company's former policy, but it is still within the boundaries of generally accepted accounting principles. However, the SEC noted that over six quarters, Halliburton failed to disclose its change in accounting practice. In the absence of any disclosure the SEC believed the investing public was misled about the precise nature of Halliburton's income in comparison to prior periods. The Halliburton situation illustrates the difficulty of using estimates in percentage-of-completion accounting and the impact of those estimates on the financial statements.

Source: "Failure to Disclose a 1998 Change in Accounting Practice," SEC (August 3, 2004), *www.sec.gov/news/press/ 2004-104.htm*. See also "Accounting Ace Charles Mulford Answers Accounting Questions," *Wall Street Journal Online* (June 7, 2002).

Completion-of-Production Basis

Underlying Concepts

This is not an exception to the revenue recognition principle. At the completion of production, realization is virtually assured and the earning process is substantially completed.

In certain cases companies recognize revenue at the completion of **production** even though no sale has been made. Examples of such situations involve precious metals or agricultural products with assured prices. Under the **completion-of-production basis**, companies recognize revenue when these metals are mined or agricultural crops harvested because the sales price is reasonably assured, the units are interchangeable, and no significant costs are involved in distributing the product.[21] (See discussion in Chapter 9, page 445, "Valuation at Net Realizable Value.")

Likewise, when sale or cash receipt precedes production and delivery, as in the case of magazine subscriptions, companies recognize revenues as earned by production and delivery.[22]

REVENUE RECOGNITION AFTER DELIVERY

In some cases, the collection of the sales price is not reasonably assured and revenue recognition is deferred. One of two methods is generally employed to defer revenue recognition until the company receives cash: the **installment-sales method** or the **cost-recovery method**. A third method, the **deposit method**, applies in situations in which a company receives cash prior to delivery or transfer of the property; the company records that receipt as a deposit because the sale transaction is incomplete. This section examines these three methods.

---

[21]Such revenue satisfies the criteria of *Concepts Statement No. 5* since the assets are readily realizable and the earning process is virtually complete (see par. 84, item c).

[22]*Statement of Financial Accounting Concepts No. 5*, par. 84, item b.

Installment-Sales Method

The **installment-sales method** recognizes income in the periods of collection rather than in the period of sale. The logic underlying this method is that when there is no reasonable approach for estimating the degree of collectibility, companies should not recognize revenue until cash is collected.

The expression "installment sales" generally describes any type of sale for which payment is required in periodic installments over an extended period of time. All types of farm and home equipment as well as home furnishings are sold on an installment basis. The heavy equipment industry also sometimes uses the method for machine installations paid for over a long period. Another application of the method is in land-development sales.

Because payment is spread over a relatively long period, the risk of loss resulting from uncollectible accounts is greater in installment-sales transactions than in ordinary sales. Consequently, selling companies use various devices to protect themselves. Two common devices are: (1) the use of a *conditional sales contract*, which specifies that title to the item sold does not pass to the purchaser until all payments are made, and (2) use of notes secured by a *chattel* (personal property) *mortgage* on the article sold. Either of these permits the seller to "repossess" the goods sold if the purchaser defaults on one or more payments. The seller can then resell the repossessed merchandise at whatever price it will bring to compensate for the uncollected installments and the expense of repossession.

Under the installment-sales method of accounting, companies defer income recognition until the period of cash collection. They recognize both revenues and costs of sales in the period of sale, but defer the related gross profit to those periods in which they collect the cash. Thus, **instead of deferring the sale**, **along with related costs and expenses, to the future periods of anticipated collection, the company defers only the proportional gross profit**. This approach is equivalent to deferring both sales and cost of sales. Other expenses—that is, selling expense, administrative expense, and so on—are not deferred.

Thus, the installment-sales method matches cost and expenses against sales through the gross profit figure, but no further. Companies using the installment-sales method generally record operating expenses without regard to the fact that they will defer some portion of the year's gross profit. This practice is often justified on the basis that (1) these expenses do not follow sales as closely as does the cost of goods sold, and (2) accurate apportionment among periods would be so difficult that it could not be justified by the benefits gained.[23]

Acceptability of the Installment-Sales Method

The use of the installment-sales method for revenue recognition has fluctuated widely. At one time it was widely accepted for installment-sales transactions. Somewhat paradoxically, as installment-sales transactions increased in popularity, acceptance and use of the installment-sales method decreased. Finally, the profession concluded that except in special circumstances, "the installment method of recognizing revenue is not acceptable." [9] The rationale for this position is simple: Because the installment method recognizes no income until cash is collected, it is not in accordance with the accrual accounting concept.

Use of the installment-sales method was often justified on the grounds that the risk of not collecting an account receivable may be so great that the sale itself is not sufficient evidence that recognition should occur. In some cases, this reasoning is valid, but not in a majority of cases. The general approach is that a company should recognize a completed sale. If the company expects bad debts, it should record this possibility as separate estimates of uncollectibles. Although collection expenses, repossession

---

[23]In addition, other theoretical deficiencies of the installment-sales method could be cited. For example, see Richard A. Scott and Rita K. Scott, "Installment Accounting: Is It Inconsistent?" *The Journal of Accountancy* (November 1979).

expenses, and bad debts are an unavoidable part of installment-sales activities, the incurrence of these costs and the collectibility of the receivables are reasonably predictable.

We study this topic in intermediate accounting because the method is acceptable in cases where a company believes there to be no reasonable basis of estimating the degree of collectibility. In addition, the sales method of revenue recognition has certain weaknesses when used for franchise and land-development operations. Application of the sales method to **franchise and license operations** has resulted in the abuse described earlier as "front-end loading." In some cases, franchisors recognized revenue prematurely, when they granted a franchise or issued a license, rather than when revenue was earned or the cash is received. Many **land-development** ventures were susceptible to the same abuses. As a result, the FASB prescribes application of the installment-sales method of accounting for sales of real estate under certain circumstances. **[10]**[24]

Procedure for Deferring Revenue and Cost of Sales of Merchandise

One could work out a procedure that deferred both the uncollected portion of the sales price and the proportionate part of the cost of the goods sold. Instead of apportioning both sales price and cost over the period of collection, however, the installment-sales method defers **only the gross profit**. This procedure has exactly the same effect as deferring both sales and cost of sales, but it requires only one deferred account rather than two.

For the **sales in any one year**, the steps companies use to defer gross profit are as follows.

1. During the year, record both sales and cost of sales in the regular way, using the special accounts described later, and compute the rate of gross profit on installment-sales transactions.
2. At the end of the year, apply the rate of gross profit to the cash collections of the current year's installment sales, to arrive at the realized gross profit.
3. Defer to future years the gross profit not realized.

For **sales made in prior years**, companies apply the gross profit rate of each year's sales against cash collections of accounts receivable resulting from that year's sales, to arrive at the realized gross profit.

Special accounts must be used in the installment-sales method. These accounts provide certain special information required to determine the realized and unrealized gross profit in each year of operations. In computing net income under the installment-sales method as generally applied, the only peculiarity is the **deferral of gross profit until realized by accounts receivable collection**. We will use the following data to illustrate the installment-sales method in accounting for the sales of merchandise.

	2010	2011	2012
Installment sales	$200,000	$250,000	$240,000
Cost of installment sales	150,000	190,000	168,000
Gross profit	$ 50,000	$ 60,000	$ 72,000
Rate of gross profit on sales	25%[a]	24%[b]	30%[c]
Cash receipts			
2010 sales	$ 60,000	$100,000	$ 40,000
2011 sales		100,000	125,000
2012 sales			80,000
	[a] $50,000	[b] $60,000	[c] $72,000
	$200,000	$250,000	$240,000

[24]The installment-sales method of accounting must be applied to a retail land sale that meets **all** of the following criteria: (1) the period of cancellation of the sale with refund of the down payment and any subsequent payments has expired; (2) cumulative cash payments equal or exceed 10 percent of the sales value; and (3) the seller is financially capable of providing all promised contract representations (e.g., land improvements, off-site facilities).

To simplify this example, we have excluded interest charges. Summary entries in general journal form for the year 2010 are as follows.

2010

Installment Accounts Receivable, 2010	200,000	
Installment Sales		200,000
(To record sales made on installment in 2010)		
Cash	60,000	
Installment Accounts Receivable, 2010		60,000
(To record cash collected on installment receivables)		
Cost of Installment Sales	150,000	
Inventory (or Purchases)		150,000
(To record cost of goods sold on installment in 2010 on either a perpetual or a periodic inventory basis)		
Installment Sales	200,000	
Cost of Installment Sales		150,000
Deferred Gross Profit, 2010		50,000
(To close installment sales and cost of installment sales for the year)		
Deferred Gross Profit, 2010	15,000	
Realized Gross Profit on Installment Sales		15,000
(To remove from deferred gross profit the profit realized through cash collections; $60,000 × 25%)		
Realized Gross Profit on Installment Sales	15,000	
Income Summary		15,000
(To close profits realized by collections)		

Illustration 18-19 shows computation of the realized and deferred gross profit for the year 2010.

2010	
Rate of gross profit current year	25%
Cash collected on current year's sales	$60,000
Realized gross profit (25% of $60,000)	15,000
Gross profit to be deferred ($50,000 − $15,000)	35,000

ILLUSTRATION 18-19
Computation of Realized and Deferred Gross Profit, 2010

Summary entries in journal form for year 2 (2011) are as follows.

2011

Installment Accounts Receivable, 2011	250,000	
Installment Sales		250,000
(To record sales made on installment in 2011)		
Cash	200,000	
Installment Accounts Receivable, 2010		100,000
Installment Accounts Receivable, 2011		100,000
(To record cash collected on installment receivables)		
Cost of Installment Sales	190,000	
Inventory (or Purchases)		190,000
(To record cost of goods sold on installment in 2011)		
Installment Sales	250,000	
Cost of Installment Sales		190,000
Deferred Gross Profit, 2011		60,000
(To close installment sales and cost of installment sales for the year)		
Deferred Gross Profit, 2010 ($100,000 × 25%)	25,000	
Deferred Gross Profit, 2011 ($100,000 × 24%)	24,000	
Realized Gross Profit on Installment Sales		49,000
(To remove from deferred gross profit the profit realized through cash collections)		
Realized Gross Profit on Installment Sales	49,000	
Income Summary		49,000
(To close profits realized by collections)		

Illustration 18-20 shows computation of the realized and deferred gross profit for the year 2011.

ILLUSTRATION 18-20
Computation of Realized and Deferred Gross Profit, 2011

2011	
Current year's sales	
Rate of gross profit	24%
Cash collected on current year's sales	$100,000
Realized gross profit (24% of $100,000)	24,000
Gross profit to be deferred ($60,000 − $24,000)	36,000
Prior year's sales	
Rate of gross profit—2010	25%
Cash collected on 2010 sales	$100,000
Gross profit realized in 2011 on 2010 sales (25% of $100,000)	25,000
Total gross profit realized in 2011	
Realized on collections of 2010 sales	$ 25,000
Realized on collections of 2011 sales	24,000
Total	$ 49,000

The entries in 2012 would be similar to those of 2011, and the total gross profit taken up or realized would be $64,000, as shown by the computations in Illustration 18-21.

ILLUSTRATION 18-21
Computation of Realized and Deferred Gross Profit, 2012

2012	
Current year's sales	
Rate of gross profit	30%
Cash collected on current year's sales	$ 80,000
Gross profit realized on 2012 sales (30% of $80,000)	24,000
Gross profit to be deferred ($72,000 − $24,000)	48,000
Prior years' sales	
2010 sales	
Rate of gross profit	25%
Cash collected	$ 40,000
Gross profit realized in 2012 on 2010 sales (25% of $40,000)	10,000
2011 sales	
Rate of gross profit	24%
Cash collected	$125,000
Gross profit realized in 2012 on 2011 sales (24% of $125,000)	30,000
Total gross profit realized in 2012	
Realized on collections of 2010 sales	$ 10,000
Realized on collections of 2011 sales	30,000
Realized on collections of 2012 sales	24,000
Total	$ 64,000

In summary, here are the basic concepts you should understand about accounting for installment sales:

1. How to compute a proper gross profit percentage.
2. How to record installment sales, cost of installment sales, and deferred gross profit.
3. How to compute realized gross profit on installment receivables.
4. How the deferred gross profit balance at the end of the year results from applying the gross profit rate to the installment accounts receivable.

Additional Problems of Installment-Sales Accounting

In addition to computing realized and deferred gross profit currently, other problems are involved in accounting for installment-sales transactions. These problems are related to:

1. Interest on installment contracts.

2. Uncollectible accounts.

3. Defaults and repossessions.

Interest on Installment Contracts. Because the collection of installment receivables is spread over a long period, it is customary to charge the buyer interest on the unpaid balance. The seller and buyer set up a schedule of equal payments consisting of interest and principal. Each successive payment is attributable to a smaller amount of interest and a correspondingly larger amount of principal, as shown in Illustration 18-22. This illustration assumes that a company sells for $3,000 an asset costing $2,400 (rate of gross profit = 20%), with interest of 8 percent included in the three installments of $1,164.10.

ILLUSTRATION 18-22
Installment Payment Schedule

Date	Cash (Debit)	Interest Earned (Credit)	Installment Receivables (Credit)	Installment Unpaid Balance	Realized Gross Profit (20%)
1/2/10	—	—	—	$3,000.00	—
1/2/11	$1,164.10[a]	$240.00[b]	$ 924.10[c]	2,075.90[d]	$184.82[e]
1/2/12	1,164.10	166.07	998.03	1,077.87	199.61
1/2/13	1,164.10	86.23	1,077.87	–0–	215.57
					$600.00

[a]Periodic payment = Original unpaid balance ÷ PV of an annuity of $1.00 for three periods at 8%; $1,164.10 = $3,000 ÷ 2.57710.
[b]$3,000.00 × .08 = $240.
[c]$1,164.10 − $240.00 = $924.10.
[d]$3,000.00 − $924.10 = $2,075.90.
[e]$924.10 × .20 = $184.82.

The company accounts for interest separate from the gross profit recognized on the installment-sales collections during the period, by recognizing interest revenue at the time of its cash receipt.

Uncollectible Accounts. The problem of bad debts or uncollectible accounts receivable is somewhat different for concerns selling on an installment basis because of a repossession feature commonly incorporated in the sales agreement. This feature gives the selling company an opportunity to recoup an uncollectible account through repossession and resale of repossessed merchandise. If the experience of the company indicates that repossessions do not, as a rule, compensate for uncollectible balances, it may be advisable to provide for such losses through charges to a special bad debt expense account, just as is done for other credit sales.

Defaults and Repossessions. Depending on the terms of the sales contract and the policy of the credit department, the seller can repossess merchandise sold under an installment arrangement if the purchaser fails to meet payment requirements. The seller may then recondition repossessed merchandise before offering it for re-sale, for cash or installment payments.

The accounting for **repossessions** recognizes that the company is not likely to collect the related installment receivable and should write it off. Along with the installment account receivable, the company must remove the applicable deferred gross profit using the following entry:

Repossessed Merchandise (an inventory account)	xxx
Deferred Gross Profit	xxx
Installment Accounts Receivable	xxx

This entry assumes that the company will record the repossessed merchandise at exactly the amount of the uncollected account less the deferred gross profit applicable. This assumption may or may not be proper. To determine the correct amount, the company should consider the condition of the repossessed merchandise, the cost of reconditioning, and the market for second-hand merchandise of that particular type. The objective should be to put any asset acquired on the books at its fair value, or at the best possible approximation of fair value when fair value is not determinable. A loss can occur if the fair value of the repossessed merchandise is less than the uncollected balance less the deferred gross profit. In that case, the company should record a "loss on repossession" at the date of repossession.[25]

To illustrate the required entry, assume that Klein Brothers sells a refrigerator to Marilyn Hunt for $1,500 on September 1, 2010. Terms require a down payment of $600 and $60 on the first of every month for 15 months, starting October 1, 2010. It is further assumed that the refrigerator cost $900, and that Klein Brothers priced it to provide a 40 percent rate of gross profit on selling price. At the year-end, December 31, 2010, Klein Brothers should have collected a total of $180 in addition to the original down payment.

If Hunt makes her January and February payments in 2011 and then defaults, the account balances applicable to Hunt at time of default are as shown in Illustration 18-23.

ILLUSTRATION 18-23
Computation of Installment Receivable Balances

Installment accounts receivable (September 1, 2010)		$1,500
Less: Down payment:	$600	
Payments to date ($60 × 5)	300	900
Installment accounts receivable (March 1, 2011)		$ 600
Installment accounts receivable (March 1, 2011)		$600
Gross profit rate		× 40%
Deferred gross profit		$240

As indicated, Klein Brothers compute the balance of deferred gross profit applicable to Hunt's account by applying the gross profit rate for the year of sale to the balance of Hunt's account receivable: 40 percent of $600, or $240. The account balances are therefore:

Installment Account Receivable, 2010	600 (dr.)
Deferred Gross Profit, 2010	240 (cr.)

Klein repossesses the refrigerator following Hunt's default. If Klein sets the estimated fair value of the repossessed article at $150, it would make the following entry to record the repossession.

Deferred Gross Profit, 2010	240	
Repossessed Merchandise	150	
Loss on Repossession	210	
Installment Accounts Receivable, 2010		600

[25]Some contend that a company should record repossessed merchandise at a valuation that will permit the company to make its regular rate of gross profit on resale. If the company enters the value at its approximated cost to purchase, the regular rate of gross profit could be provided for upon its ultimate sale, but that is completely a secondary consideration. It is more important that the company record the repossessed asset at fair value. This accounting would be in accordance with the general practice of carrying assets at acquisition price, as represented by the fair value at the date of acquisition.

Klein determines the amount of the loss in two steps: (1) It subtracts the deferred gross profit from the amount of the account receivable, to determine the unrecovered cost (or book value) of the merchandise repossessed. (2) It then subtracts the estimated fair value of the merchandise repossessed from the unrecovered cost, to get the amount of the loss on repossession. Klein Brothers computes the loss on the refrigerator as shown in Illustration 18-24.

Balance of account receivable (representing uncollected selling price)	$600
Less: Deferred gross profit	240
Unrecovered cost	360
Less: Estimated fair value of merchandise repossessed	150
Loss (Gain) on repossession	$210

ILLUSTRATION 18-24
Computation of Loss on Repossession

As pointed out earlier, the loss on repossession may be charged to Allowance for Doubtful Accounts if a company carries such an account.

Financial Statement Presentation of Installment-Sales Transactions

If installment-sales transactions represent a significant part of total sales, it is desirable to make full disclosure of installment sales, the cost of installment sales, and any expenses allocable to installment sales. However, if installment-sales transactions constitute an insignificant part of total sales, it may be satisfactory to include only the realized gross profit in the income statement as a special item following the gross profit on sales. Illustration 18-25 shows this simpler presentation.

HEALTH MACHINE COMPANY
INCOME STATEMENT
FOR THE YEAR ENDED DECEMBER 31, 2011

Sales	$620,000
Cost of goods sold	490,000
Gross profit	130,000
Gross profit realized on installment sales	51,000
Total gross profit	$181,000

ILLUSTRATION 18-25
Disclosure of Installment-Sales Transactions—Insignificant Amount

If a company wants more complete disclosure of installment-sales transactions, it would use a presentation similar to that shown in Illustration 18-26.

ILLUSTRATION 18-26
Disclosure of Installment-Sales Transactions—Significant Amount

HEALTH MACHINE COMPANY
INCOME STATEMENT
FOR THE YEAR ENDED DECEMBER 31, 2011

	Installment Sales	Other Sales	Total
Sales	$248,000	$620,000	$868,000
Cost of goods sold	182,000	490,000	672,000
Gross profit	66,000	130,000	196,000
Less: Deferred gross profit on installment sales of this year	47,000		47,000
Realized gross profit on this year's sales	19,000	130,000	149,000
Add: Gross profit realized on installment sales of prior years	32,000		32,000
Gross profit realized this year	$ 51,000	$130,000	$181,000

The presentation in Illustration 18-26 is awkward. Yet the awkwardness of this method is difficult to avoid if a company wants to provide full disclosure of installment-sales transactions in the income statement. One solution, of course, is to prepare a separate schedule showing installment-sales transactions, with only the final figure carried into the income statement.

In the balance sheet it is generally considered desirable to classify installment accounts receivable by year of collectibility. There is some question as to whether companies should include in current assets installment accounts that are not collectible for two or more years. Yet if installment sales are **part of normal operations**, companies may consider them as current assets because they are collectible within the operating cycle of the business. Little confusion should result from this practice if the company fully discloses maturity dates, as illustrated in the following example.

ILLUSTRATION 18-27
Disclosure of Installment
Accounts Receivable,
by Year

Current assets		
Notes and accounts receivable		
Trade customers	$78,800	
Less: Allowance for doubtful accounts	3,700	
	75,100	
Installment accounts collectible in 2011	22,600	
Installment accounts collectible in 2012	47,200	$144,900

On the other hand, a company may have receivables from an installment contract, resulting from a transaction not related to normal operations. In that case, the company should report such receivable in the "Other assets" section if due beyond one year.

Repossessed merchandise is a part of inventory, and companies should report it as such in the "Current assets" section of the balance sheet. They should include any gain or loss on repossession in the income statement in the "Other revenues and gains" or "Other expenses and losses" section.

If a company has **deferred gross profit on installment sales**, it generally treats it as unearned revenue and classifies it as a current liability. Theoretically, deferred gross profit consists of three elements: (1) income tax liability to be paid when the sales are reported as realized revenue (current liability); (2) allowance for collection expense, bad debts, and repossession losses (deduction from installment accounts receivable); and (3) net income (retained earnings, restricted as to dividend availability). Because of the difficulty in allocating deferred gross profit among these three elements, however, companies frequently report the whole amount as unearned revenue.

In contrast, the FASB in *SFAC No. 6* states that "no matter how it is displayed in financial statements, deferred gross profit on installment sales is conceptually an asset valuation—that is, a reduction of an asset."[26] We support the FASB position, but we recognize that until an official standard on this topic is issued, financial statements will probably continue to report such deferred gross profit as a current liability.

Cost-Recovery Method

Objective·7
Explain the cost-recovery method of accounting.

Under the **cost-recovery method**, a company recognizes no profit until cash payments by the buyer exceed the cost of the merchandise sold. After the seller has recovered all costs, it includes in income any additional cash collections. The seller's income statement for the period reports sales revenue, the cost of goods

---

[26]See *Statement of Financial Accounting Concepts No. 6*, pars. 232–234.

sold, and the gross profit—both the amount (if any) that is recognized during the period and the amount that is deferred. The deferred gross profit is offset against the related receivable—reduced by collections—on the balance sheet. Subsequent income statements report the gross profit as a separate item of revenue when the company recognizes it as earned.

A seller is permitted to use the cost-recovery method to account for sales in which "there is no reasonable basis for estimating collectibility." In addition, use of this method is required where a high degree of uncertainty exists related to the collection of receivables. [11], [12], [13]

To illustrate the cost-recovery method, assume that early in 2010, Fesmire Manufacturing sells inventory with a cost of $25,000 to Higley Company for $36,000. Higley will make payments of $18,000 in 2010, $12,000 in 2011, and $6,000 in 2012. If the cost-recovery method applies to this transaction and Higley makes the payments as scheduled, Fesmire recognizes cash collections, revenue, cost, and gross profit as follows.[27]

ILLUSTRATION 18-28
Computation of Gross
Profit—Cost-Recovery
Method

	2010	2011	2012
Cash collected	$18,000	$12,000	$6,000
Revenue	$36,000	-0-	-0-
Cost of goods sold	25,000	-0-	-0-
Deferred gross profit	11,000	$11,000	$6,000
Recognized gross profit	-0-	5,000*	6,000
Deferred gross profit balance (end of period)	$11,000	$ 6,000	$ -0-

*$25,000 − $18,000 = $7,000 of unrecovered cost at the end of 2010; $12,000 − $7,000 = $5,000, the excess of cash received in 2011 over unrecovered cost.

Under the cost-recovery method, Fesmire reports total revenue and cost of goods sold in the period of sale, similar to the installment-sales method. However, unlike the installment-sales method, which recognizes income as cash is collected, Fesmire recognizes profit under the cost-recovery method **only when cash collections exceed the total cost of the goods sold**.

Therefore, Fesmire's journal entry to record the deferred gross profit on the Higley sale transaction (after recording the sale and the cost of sale in the normal manner) at the end of 2010 is as follows.

2010

Sales	36,000	
Cost of Sales		25,000
Deferred Gross Profit		11,000
(To close sales and cost of sales and to record deferred gross profit on sales accounted for under the cost-recovery method)		

[27]An alternative format for computing the amount of gross profit recognized annually is shown below.

Year	Cash Received	Original Cost Recovered	Balance of Unrecovered Cost	Gross Profit Realized
Beginning balance	—	—	$25,000	—
12/31/10	$18,000	$18,000	7,000	$ -0-
12/31/11	12,000	7,000	-0-	5,000
12/31/12	6,000	-0-	-0-	6,000

In 2011 and 2012, the deferred gross profit becomes realized gross profit as the cumulative cash collections exceed the total costs, by recording the following entries.

2011

Deferred Gross Profit	5,000	
Realized Gross Profit		5,000
(To recognize gross profit to the extent that		
cash collections in 2011 exceed costs)		

2012

Deferred Gross Profit	6,000	
Realized Gross Profit		6,000
(To recognize gross profit to the extent that		
cash collections in 2012 exceed costs)		

What do the numbers mean?

LIABILITY OR REVENUE?

Suppose you purchased a gift card for spa services at Sundara Spa for $300. The gift card expires at the end of six months. When should Sundara record the revenue? Here are two choices:

1. At the time Sundara receives the cash for the gift card.
2. At the time Sundara provides the service to the gift-card holder.

If you answered number 2, you would be right. Companies should recognize revenue when the obligation is satisfied—which is when Sundara performs the service.

Now let's add a few more facts. Suppose that the gift-card holder fails to use the card in the six-month period. Statistics show that between 2 and 15 percent of gift-card holders never redeem their cards. So, do you still believe that Sundara should record the revenue at the expiration date?

If you say you are not sure, you are probably right. Here is why: Certain states (such as California) do not recognize expiration dates, and therefore the customer has the right to redeem an otherwise expired gift card at any time. Let's for the moment say we are in California. Because the card holder may never redeem, when can Sundara recognize the revenue? In that case Sundara would have to show statistically that after a certain period of time, the likelihood of redemption is remote. If it can make that case, it can recognize the revenue. Otherwise it may have to wait a long time.

Unfortunately Sundara may still have a problem. It may be required to turn over the value of the spa service to the state. The treatment for unclaimed gift cards may fall under the state abandoned-and-unclaimed-property laws. Most common unclaimed items are required to be remitted to the states after a five-year period. Failure to report and remit the property can result in additional fines and penalties. So if Sundara is in a state where unclaimed property must be sent to the state, Sundara should report a liability on its balance sheet.

Source: PricewaterhouseCoopers, "Issues Surrounding the Recognition of Gift Card Sales and Escheat Liabilities," *Quick Brief* (December 2004).

Deposit Method

In some cases, a company receives cash from the buyer before it transfers the goods or property. In such cases the seller has not performed under the contract and has no claim against the purchaser. There is not sufficient transfer of the risks and rewards of ownership for a sale to be recorded. The method of accounting for these incomplete transactions is the **deposit method**.

Under the **deposit method** the seller reports the cash received from the buyer as a deposit on the contract and classifies it on the balance sheet as a liability (refundable deposit or customer advance). The seller continues to report the property as an asset on its balance sheet, along with any related existing debt. Also, the seller continues to charge depreciation expense as a period cost for the property. **The seller does not recognize revenue or income until the sale is complete.** [14] At that time, it closes the deposit account and applies one of the revenue recognition methods discussed in this chapter to the sale.

The **major difference between the installment-sales and cost-recovery methods and the deposit method** relates to contract performance. In the installment-sales and cost-recovery methods it is assumed that the seller has performed on the contract, but cash collection is highly uncertain. In the deposit method, the seller has *not* performed and no legitimate claim exists. The deposit method postpones recognizing a sale until the company determines that a sale has occurred for accounting purposes. If there has not been sufficient transfer of risks and rewards of ownership, even if the selling company has received a deposit, the company postpones recognition of the sale until sufficient transfer has occurred. In that sense, the deposit method is not a revenue recognition method as are the installment-sales and cost-recovery methods.

Summary of Product Revenue Recognition Bases

Illustration 18-29 summarizes the revenue-recognition bases or methods, the criteria for their use, and the reasons for departing from the sale basis.[28]

ILLUSTRATION 18-29
Revenue Recognition
Bases Other Than the Sale
Basis for Products

Recognition Basis (or Method of Applying a Basis)	Criteria for Use	Reason(s) for Departing from Sale Basis
Percentage-of-completion method	Long-term construction of property; dependable estimates of extent of progress and cost to complete; reasonable assurance of collectibility of contract price; expectation that both contractor and buyer can meet obligations; and absence of inherent hazards that make estimates doubtful.	Availability of evidence of ultimate proceeds; better measure of periodic income; avoidance of fluctuations in revenues, expenses, and income; performance is a "continuous sale" and therefore not a departure from the sale basis.
Completed-contract method	Use on short-term contracts, and whenever percentage-of-completion cannot be used on long-term contracts.	Existence of inherent hazards in the contract beyond the normal, recurring business risks; conditions for using the percentage-of-completion method are absent.
Completion-of-production basis	Immediate marketability at quoted prices; unit interchangeability; and no significant distribution costs.	Known or determinable revenues; inability to determine costs and thereby defer expense recognition until sale.
Installment-sales method and cost-recovery method	Absence of reasonable basis for estimating degree of collectibility and costs of collection.	Collectibility of the receivable is so uncertain that gross profit (or income) is not recognized until cash is actually received.
Deposit method	Cash received before the sales transaction is completed.	No recognition of revenue and income because there is not sufficient transfer of the risks and rewards of ownership.

CONCLUDING REMARKS

As indicated, revenue recognition principles are sometimes difficult to apply and often vary by industry. Recently, the SEC has attempted to provide more guidance in this area because of concern that the revenue recognition principle is sometimes being incorrectly applied. Many cases of intentional misstatement of revenue to achieve better financial results have recently come to light. Such practices are fraudulent, and the SEC is vigorously prosecuting these situations.

For our capital markets to be efficient, investors must have confidence that the financial information provided is both relevant and reliable. As a result, it is imperative that the accounting profession, regulators, and companies eliminate aggressive revenue recognition practices. It is our hope that recent efforts by the SEC and the accounting profession will lead to higher-quality reporting in this area.

INTERNATIONAL INSIGHT

There is no international enforcement body comparable to the U.S. SEC.

You will want to read the **CONVERGENCE CORNER** on page 960

For discussion of how international convergence efforts relate to revenue recognition.

[28]Adapted from *Survey of Present Practices in Recognizing Revenues, Expenses, Gains, and Losses,* op. cit., pp. 12–13.

CONVERGENCE CORNER

REVENUE RECOGNITION

The general concepts and principles used for revenue recognition are similar between U.S. GAAP and international GAAP (iGAAP). Where they differ is in the detail. As indicated in the chapter, U.S. GAAP provides specific guidance related to revenue recognition for many different industries. That is not the case for iGAAP. Also the SEC has issued broad and specific guidance for public companies in the United States related to revenue recognition. Again, the IASB does not have a regulatory body that provides additional guidance.

✳ RELEVANT FACTS

• The IASB defines revenue to include both revenues and gains. U.S. GAAP provides separate definitions for revenues and gains.

• Revenue recognition fraud is a major issue in U.S. financial reporting. The same situation occurs overseas as evidenced by revenue recognition breakdowns at Dutch software company **Baan NV**, Japanese electronics giant **NEC**, and Dutch grocer **AHold NV**.

• A specific standard exists for revenue recognition under iGAAP *(IAS 18)*. In general, the standard is based on the probability that the economic benefits associated with the transaction will flow to the company selling the goods, rendering the service, or receiving investment income. In addition, the revenues and costs must be capable of being measured reliably. U.S. GAAP uses concepts such as realized, realizable, and earned as a basis for revenue recognition.

• iGAAP prohibits the use of the completed-contract method of accounting for long-term construction contracts *(IAS 13)*. Companies must use the percentage-of-completion method. If revenues and costs are difficult to estimate, then companies recognize revenue only to the extent of the cost incurred—a zero-profit approach.

• In long-term construction contracts, iGAAP requires recognition of a loss immediately if the overall contract is going to be unprofitable. In other words, U.S. GAAP and iGAAP are the same regarding this issue.

✳ ABOUT THE NUMBERS

As mentioned, iGAAP does not permit the completed-contract method of accounting for long-term construction contracts. If costs or revenues cannot be reliably determined, then how does a company report revenues related to its construction contracts using iGAAP? To illustrate, assume the following facts for England Construction Co. for a contract to build a dam at Windswept Canyon.

• The contract price to construct the dam is $400 million.

• Estimated incurred costs are $54 million in 2010, $180 million in 2011, and $126 million in 2012.

• England uses iGAAP but is uncertain as regards these cost numbers.

In this situation, England recognizes revenue up to the cost incurred until the cost numbers can be more reliably determined. For example, assume that England incurred $55 million in costs in 2010. The presentation on its income statement would be as follows.

England Construction Co. Income Statement (partial) for 2010	
Revenue from long-term contracts	$55,000,000
Costs of construction	55,000,000
Gross profit	$ –0–

Under iGAAP, zero profit is recognized. Once costs can be reliably determined, the percentage-of-completion method is used in future periods.

✳ ON THE HORIZON

The FASB and IASB are now involved in a joint project on revenue recognition. The objective of the project is to develop coherent conceptual guidance for revenue recognition and a comprehensive statement on revenue recognition based on those concepts. In particular, the project is intended to improve financial reporting by (1) converging U.S. and international standards on revenue recognition, (2) eliminating inconsistencies in the existing conceptual guidance on revenue recognition, (3) providing conceptual guidance that would be useful in addressing future revenue recognition issues, (4) eliminating inconsistencies in existing standards-level authoritative literature and accepted practices, (5) filling voids in revenue recognition guidance that have developed over time, and (6) establishing a single, comprehensive standard on revenue recognition. Presently, the Boards are evaluating a "customer-consideration" model. It is hoped that this approach (rather than using the earned and realized or realized criteria) will lead to a better basis for revenue recognition. For more on this topic, see *http://www.fasb.org/project/revenue_recognition.shtml.*

SUMMARY OF LEARNING OBJECTIVES

·1 Apply the revenue recognition principle. The revenue recognition principle provides that a company should recognize revenue (1) when revenue is realized or realizable and (2) when it is earned. Revenues are realized when goods or services are exchanged for cash or claims to cash. Revenues are realizable when assets received in exchanges are readily convertible to known amounts of cash or claims to cash. Revenues are earned when a company has substantially accomplished what it must do to be entitled to the benefits represented by the revenues—that is, when the earnings process is complete or virtually complete.

·2 Describe accounting issues for revenue recognition at point of sale. The two conditions for recognizing revenue are usually met by the time a company delivers products or merchandise or provides services to customers. Companies commonly recognize revenue from manufacturing and selling activities at time of sale. Problems of implementation can arise because of (1) sales with buyback agreements, (2) revenue recognition when right of return exists, and (3) trade loading and channel stuffing.

·3 Apply the percentage-of-completion method for long-term contracts. To apply the percentage-of-completion method to long-term contracts, a company must have some basis for measuring the progress toward completion at particular interim dates. One of the most popular input measures used to determine the progress toward completion is the cost-to-cost basis. Using this basis, a company measures the percentage of completion by comparing costs incurred to date with the most recent estimate of the total costs to complete the contract. The company applies that percentage to the total revenue or the estimated total gross profit on the contract, to arrive at the amount of revenue or gross profit to be recognized to date.

·4 Apply the completed-contract method for long-term contracts. Under this method, companies recognize revenue and gross profit only at point of sale—that is, when the company completes the contract. The company accumulates costs of long-term contracts in process and current billings. It makes no interim charges or credits to income statement accounts for revenues, costs, and gross profit. The annual entries to record costs of construction, progress billings, and collections from customers would be identical to those for the percentage-of-completion method—with the significant exclusion of the recognition of revenue and gross profit.

·5 Identify the proper accounting for losses on long-term contracts. Two types of losses can become evident under long-term contracts: (1) *Loss in current period on a profitable contract*: Under the percentage-of-completion method only, the estimated cost increase requires a current-period adjustment of excess gross profit recognized on the project in prior periods. The company records this adjustment as a loss in the current period because it is a change in accounting estimate. (2) *Loss on an unprofitable contract*: Under both the percentage-of-completion and the completed-contract methods, the company must recognize the entire expected contract loss in the current period.

·6 Describe the installment-sales method of accounting. The installment-sales method recognizes income in the periods of collection rather than in the period of sale. The installment-sales method of accounting is justified on the basis that when there is no reasonable approach for estimating the degree of collectibility, a company should not recognize revenue until it has collected cash.

·7 Explain the cost-recovery method of accounting. Under the cost-recovery method, companies do not recognize profit until cash payments by the buyer exceed the seller's cost of the merchandise sold. After the seller has recovered all costs, it includes in income any additional cash collections. The income statement for the period of sale reports sales revenue, the cost of goods sold, and the gross profit—both the amount recognized during the period and the amount deferred. The deferred gross profit is offset against the related receivable on the balance sheet. Subsequent income statements report the gross profit as a separate item of revenue when revenue is recognized as earned.

APPENDIX **18A**   **REVENUE RECOGNITION FOR SPECIAL SALES TRANSACTIONS**

To supplement our presentation of revenue recognition, in this appendix we cover two common yet unique types of business transactions—**franchises** and **consignments**.

FRANCHISES

Objective·8
Explain revenue recognition for franchises and consignment sales.

As indicated throughout this chapter, companies recognize revenue on the basis of two criteria: (1) when it is realized or realizable (occurrence of an exchange for cash or claims to cash), and (2) when it is earned (completion or virtual completion of the earnings process). These criteria are appropriate for most business activities. For some sales transactions, though, they do not adequately define when a company should recognize revenue. The fast-growing franchise industry is of special concern and challenge.

In accounting for franchise sales, a company must analyze the transaction and, considering all the circumstances, use judgment in selecting one or more of the revenue recognition bases, and then possibly must monitor the situation over a long period of time.

Four types of franchising arrangements have evolved: (1) manufacturer-retailer, (2) manufacturer-wholesaler, (3) service sponsor-retailer, and (4) wholesaler-retailer. The fastest-growing category of franchising, and the one that caused a reexamination of appropriate accounting, has been the third category, **service sponsor-retailer**. Included in this category are such industries and businesses as:

Soft ice cream/frozen yogurt stores (**Tastee Freeze, TCBY, Dairy Queen**)
Food drive-ins (**McDonald's, KFC, Burger King**)
Restaurants (**TGI Friday's, Pizza Hut, Denny's**)
Motels (**Holiday Inn, Marriott, Best Western**)
Auto rentals (**Avis, Hertz, National**)
Others (**H & R Block, Meineke Mufflers, 7-Eleven Stores, Kelly Services**)

Franchise companies derive their revenue from one or both of two sources: (1) from the sale of initial franchises and related assets or services, and (2) from continuing fees based on the operations of franchises. The **franchisor** (the party who grants business rights under the franchise) normally provides the **franchisee** (the party who operates the franchised business) with the following services.

1. Assistance in site selection: (a) analyzing location and (b) negotiating lease.
2. Evaluation of potential income.
3. Supervision of construction activity: (a) obtaining financing, (b) designing building, and (c) supervising contractor while building.
4. Assistance in the acquisition of signs, fixtures, and equipment.
5. Bookkeeping and advisory services: (a) setting up franchisee's records; (b) advising on income, real estate, and other taxes; and (c) advising on local regulations of the franchisee's business.

6. Employee and management training.

7. Quality control.

8. Advertising and promotion.[29]

In the past, it was standard practice for franchisors to recognize the entire franchise fee at the date of sale, whether the fee was received then or was collectible over a long period of time. Frequently, franchisors recorded the entire amount as revenue in the year of sale, even though many of the services were yet to be performed and uncertainty existed regarding the collection of the entire fee.[30] (In effect, the franchisors were counting their fried chickens before they were hatched.) However, a **franchise agreement** may provide for refunds to the franchisee if certain conditions are not met, and franchise fee profit can be reduced sharply by future costs of obligations and services to be rendered by the franchisor. To curb the abuses in revenue recognition that existed and to standardize the accounting and reporting practices in the franchise industry, the FASB issued rules which form the basis for the accounting discussed below.

Initial Franchise Fees

The **initial franchise fee** is payment for establishing the franchise relationship and providing some initial services. Franchisors record initial franchise fees as revenue only when and as they make "substantial performance" of the services they are obligated to perform and when collection of the fee is reasonably assured. **Substantial performance** occurs when the franchisor has no remaining obligation to refund any cash received or excuse any nonpayment of a note and has performed all the initial services required under the contract. Commencement of operations by the franchisee shall be presumed to be the earliest point at which substantial performance has occurred, unless it can be demonstrated that substantial performance of all obligations, including services rendered voluntarily, has occurred before that time. **[15]**

Example of Entries for Initial Franchise Fee

To illustrate, assume that Tum's Pizza Inc. charges an initial franchise fee of $50,000 for the right to operate as a franchisee of Tum's Pizza. Of this amount, $10,000 is payable when the franchisee signs the agreement, and the balance is payable in five annual payments of $8,000 each. In return for the initial franchise fee, Tum's will help locate the site, negotiate the lease or purchase of the site, supervise the construction activity, and provide the bookkeeping services. The credit rating of the franchisee indicates that money can be borrowed at 8 percent. The present value of an ordinary annuity of five annual receipts of $8,000 each discounted at 8 percent is $31,941.68. The discount of $8,058.32 represents the interest revenue to be accrued by the franchisor over the payment period. The following examples show the entries that Tum's Pizza Inc. would make under various conditions.

1. If there is reasonable expectation that Tum's Pizza Inc. may refund the down payment and if substantial future services remain to be performed by Tum's Pizza Inc., the entry should be:

Cash	10,000.00	
Notes Receivable	40,000.00	
Discount on Notes Receivable		8,058.32
Unearned Franchise Fees		41,941.68

[29]Archibald E. MacKay, "Accounting for Initial Franchise Fee Revenue," *The Journal of Accountancy* (January 1970), pp. 66–67.

[30]In 1987 and 1988 the SEC ordered a half-dozen fast-growing startup franchisors, including Jiffy Lube International, Moto Photo, Inc., Swensen's, Inc., and LePeep Restaurants, Inc., to defer their initial franchise fee recognition until earned. See "Claiming Tomorrow's Profits Today," *Forbes* (October 17, 1988), p. 78.

2. If the probability of refunding the initial franchise fee is extremely low, the amount of future services to be provided to the franchisee is minimal, collectibility of the note is reasonably assured, and substantial performance has occurred, the entry should be:

Cash	10,000.00	
Notes Receivable	40,000.00	
Discount on Notes Receivable		8,058.32
Revenue from Franchise Fees		41,941.68

3. If the initial down payment is not refundable, represents a fair measure of the services already provided, with a significant amount of services still to be performed by Tum's Pizza in future periods, and collectibility of the note is reasonably assured, the entry should be:

Cash	10,000.00	
Notes Receivable	40,000.00	
Discount on Notes Receivable		8,058.32
Revenue from Franchise Fees		10,000.00
Unearned Franchise Fees		31,941.68

4. If the initial down payment is not refundable and no future services are required by the franchisor, but collection of the note is so uncertain that recognition of the note as an asset is unwarranted, the entry should be:

Cash	10,000.00	
Revenue from Franchise Fees		10,000.00

5. Under the same conditions as those listed in case 4 above, except that the down payment is refundable or substantial services are yet to be performed, the entry should be:

Cash	10,000.00	
Unearned Franchise Fees		10,000.00

In cases 4 and 5—where collection of the note is extremely uncertain—franchisors may recognize cash collections using the installment-sales method or the cost-recovery method.[31]

Continuing Franchise Fees

Continuing franchise fees are received in return for the continuing rights granted by the franchise agreement and for providing such services as management training, advertising and promotion, legal assistance, and other support. Franchisors report continuing fees as revenue when they are earned and receivable from the franchisee, unless a portion of them has been designated for a particular purpose, such as providing a specified amount for building maintenance or local advertising. In that case, the portion deferred shall be an amount sufficient to cover the estimated cost in excess of continuing franchise fees and provide a reasonable profit on the continuing services.

Bargain Purchases

In addition to paying continuing franchise fees, franchisees frequently purchase some or all of their equipment and supplies from the franchisor. The franchisor would account for these sales as it would for any other product sales.

Sometimes, however, the franchise agreement grants the franchisee the right to make **bargain purchases** of equipment or supplies after the franchisee has paid the initial franchise fee. If the bargain price is lower than the normal selling price of the same product, or if it does not provide the franchisor a reasonable profit, then the franchisor should defer a portion of the initial franchise fee. The franchisor would account for the deferred portion as an adjustment of the selling price when the franchisee subsequently purchases the equipment or supplies.

[31]A study that compared four revenue recognition procedures—installment-sales basis, spreading recognition over the contract life, percentage-of-completion basis, and substantial performance—for franchise sales concluded that the percentage-of-completion method is the most acceptable revenue recognition method; the substantial-performance method was found sometimes to yield ultra-conservative results. See Charles H. Calhoun III, "Accounting for Initial Franchise Fees: Is It a Dead Issue?" *The Journal of Accountancy* (February 1975), pp. 60–67.

Options to Purchase

A franchise agreement may give the franchisor an **option to purchase** the franchisee's business. As a matter of management policy, the franchisor may reserve the right to purchase a profitable franchise outlet, or to purchase one that is in financial difficulty.

If it is **probable** at the time the option is given that the franchisor will ultimately purchase the outlet, then the franchisor should not recognize the initial franchise fee as revenue but should instead record it as a liability. When the franchisor exercises the option, the liability would reduce the franchisor's investment in the outlet.

Franchisor's Cost

Franchise accounting also involves proper accounting for the **franchisor's cost**. The objective is to match related costs and revenues by reporting them as components of income in the same accounting period. Franchisors should ordinarily defer **direct costs** (usually incremental costs) relating to specific franchise sales for which revenue has not yet been recognized. They should not, however, defer costs without reference to anticipated revenue and its realizability. **[16]** **Indirect costs** of a regular and recurring nature, such as selling and administrative expenses that are incurred irrespective of the level of franchise sales, should be expensed as incurred.

Disclosures of Franchisors

Franchisors must disclose all significant commitments and obligations resulting from franchise agreements, including a description of services that have not yet been substantially performed. They also should disclose any resolution of uncertainties regarding the collectibility of franchise fees. Franchisors segregate initial franchise fees from other franchise fee revenue if they are significant. Where possible, revenues and costs related to franchisor-owned outlets should be distinguished from those related to franchised outlets.

CONSIGNMENTS

In some cases, manufacturers (or wholesalers) deliver goods but retain title to the goods until they are sold. This specialized method of marketing certain types of products makes use of a device known as a **consignment**. Under this arrangement, the **consignor** (manufacturer or wholesaler) ships merchandise to the **consignee** (dealer), who is to act as an agent for the consignor in selling the merchandise. Both consignor and consignee are interested in selling—the former to make a profit or develop a market, the latter to make a commission on the sale.

The consignee accepts the merchandise and agrees to exercise due diligence in caring for and selling it. The consignee remits to the consignor cash received from customers, after deducting a sales commission and any chargeable expenses.

In consignment sales, the consignor uses a modified version of the sale basis of revenue recognition. That is, the consignor recognizes revenue only after receiving notification of sale and the cash remittance from the consignee. The consignor carries the merchandise as inventory throughout the consignment, separately classified as Merchandise on Consignment. **The consignee does not record the merchandise as an asset on its books.** Upon sale of the merchandise, the consignee has **a liability for the net amount due the consignor**. The consignor periodically receives from the consignee a report called **account sales** that shows the merchandise received, merchandise sold, expenses chargeable to the consignment, and the cash remitted. Revenue is then recognized by the consignor.

To illustrate consignment accounting entries, assume that Nelba Manufacturing Co. ships merchandise costing $36,000 on consignment to Best Value Stores. Nelba pays $3,750 of freight costs, and Best Value pays $2,250 for local advertising costs that are reimbursable from Nelba. By the end of the period, Best Value has sold two-thirds of the consigned merchandise for $40,000 cash. Best Value notifies Nelba of the sales, retains a 10 percent commission, and remits the cash due Nelba. Illustration 18A-1 (on page 966) shows the journal entries of the consignor (Nelba) and the consignee (Best Value).

ILLUSTRATION 18A-1
Entries for Consignment
Sales

NELBA MFG. CO. (CONSIGNOR)			BEST VALUE STORES (CONSIGNEE)		
Shipment of consigned merchandise					
Inventory on Consignment	36,000		No entry (record memo of merchandise		
Finished Goods Inventory		36,000	received).		
Payment of freight costs by consignor					
Inventory on Consignment	3,750		No entry.		
Cash		3,750			
Payment of advertising by consignee					
No entry until notified.			Receivable from Consignor	2,250	
			Cash		2,250
Sales of consigned merchandise					
No entry until notified.			Cash	40,000	
			Payable to Consignor		40,000
Notification of sales and expenses and remittance of amount due					
Cash	33,750		Payable to Consignor	40,000	
Advertising Expense	2,250		Receivable from		
Commission Expense	4,000		Consignor		2,250
Revenue from			Commission Revenue		4,000
Consignment Sales		40,000	Cash		33,750
Adjustment of inventory on consignment for cost of sales					
Cost of Goods Sold	26,500		No entry.		
Inventory on Consignment		26,500			
[2/3 ($36,000 + $3,750) = $26,500]					

Under the consignment arrangement, the consignor accepts the risk that the merchandise might not sell and relieves the consignee of the need to commit part of its working capital to inventory. Companies use a variety of different systems and account titles to record consignments, but they all share the common goal of postponing the recognition of revenue until it is known that a sale to a third party has occurred.

KEY TERMS

account sales, *965*

consignee, *965*

consignment, *965*

consignor, *965*

continuing franchise
  fees, *964*

franchisee, *962*

franchisor, *962*

initial franchise fee, *963*

substantial performance,
  963

SUMMARY OF LEARNING OBJECTIVE FOR APPENDIX 18A

[•8] Explain revenue recognition for franchises and consignment sales. In a franchise arrangement, the franchisor records as revenue the initial franchise fee as it makes substantial performance of the services it is obligated to perform and collection of the fee is reasonably assured. Franchisors recognize continuing franchise fees as revenue when they are earned and receivable from the franchisee. In a consignment sale, the consignor recognizes revenue when it receives cash and notification of the sale from the consignee.

FASB CODIFICATION

FASB Codification References

[1] FASB ASC 605-10-S99-1. [Predecessor literature: "Revenue Recognition in Financial Statements," *SEC Staff Accounting Bulletin No. 101* (December 3, 1999), and "Revenue Recognition," *SEC Staff Accounting Bulletin No. 104* (December 17, 2003).]

[2] FASB ASC 605-10-S99-1. [Predecessor literature: "Revenue Recognition in Financial Statements," *SEC Staff Accounting Bulletin No. 101* December 3, 1999), and "Revenue Recognition," *SEC Staff Accounting Bulletin No. 104* (December 17, 2003).]

[3] FASB ASC 470-40-25. [Predecessor literature: "Accounting for Product Financing Arrangements," *Statement of Financial Accounting Standards No. 49* (Stamford, Conn.: FASB, 1981).]

[4] FASB ASC 605-15-25-1. [Predecessor literature: "Revenue Recognition When Right of Return Exists," *Statement of Financial Accounting Standards No. 48* (Stamford, Conn.: FASB, 1981), par. 6.]

[5] FASB ASC 605-35-25-57. [Predecessor literature: "Accounting for Performance of Construction-Type and Certain Production-Type Contracts," *Statement of Position 81-1* (New York: AICPA, 1981), par. 23.]

[6] FASB ASC 605-35-05-7. [Predecessor literature: Committee on Accounting Procedure, "Long-Term Construction-Type Contracts," *Accounting Research Bulletin No. 45* (New York: AICPA, 1955), p. 7.]

[7] FASB ASC 910-405. [Predecessor literature: *Construction Contractors*, Audit and Accounting Guide (New York: AICPA, 1981), pp. 148–149.]

[8] FASB ASC 910-605-50-1. [Predecessor literature: *Construction Contractors*, Audit and Accounting Guide (New York: AICPA, 1981), p. 30.]

[9] FASB ASC 605-10-25-3. [Predecessor literature: "Omnibus Opinion," *Opinions of the Accounting Principles Board No. 10* (New York: AICPA, 1966), par. 12.]

[10] FASB ASC 976-605-25. [Predecessor literature: "Accounting for Sales of Real Estate," *Statement of Financial Accounting Standards No. 66* (Norwalk, Conn.: FASB, 1982), pars. 45–47.]

[11] FASB ASC 605-10-25-4. [Predecessor literature: "Omnibus Opinion," *Opinions of the Accounting Principles Board No. 10* (New York: AICPA, 1966), footnote 8, p. 149.]

[12] FASB ASC 952-605-25-7. [Predecessor literature: "Accounting for Franchise Fee Revenue," *Statement of Financial Accounting Standards No. 45* (Stamford, Conn.: FASB, 1981), par. 6.]

[13] FASB ASC 360-20-55-13. [Predecessor literature: "Accounting for Sales of Real Estate," *Statement of Financial Accounting Standards No. 66*, pars. 62 and 63.]

[14] FASB ASC 360-20-55-17. [Predecessor literature: "Accounting for Sales of Real Estate," *Statement of Financial Accounting Standards No. 66*, pars. 65.]

[15] FASB ASC 952-605-25-3. [Predecessor literature: "Accounting for Franchise Fee Revenue," *Statement of Financial Accounting Standards No. 45* (Stamford, Conn.: FASB, 1981), par. 5.]

[16] FASB ASC 952-340-25. [Predecessor literature: "Accounting for Franchise Fee Revenue," *Statement of Financial Accounting Standards No. 45* (Stamford, Conn.: FASB, 1981), p. 17.]

Exercises

Access the FASB Codification at *http://asc.fasb.org/home* to prepare responses to the following exercises. Provide Codification references for your responses.

CE18-1   Access the glossary ("Master Glossary") to answer the following.

(a) What is the cost-recovery method?
(b) What is the percentage-of-completion method?
(c) What is the deposit method?
(d) What is the installment method?

CE18-2   Is the installment method of recognizing revenue generally acceptable? Why or why not?

CE18-3   When would a construction company be allowed to use the completed-contract method?

CE18-4   When is it appropriate to use the cost-recovery method?

An additional Codification case can be found in the Using Your Judgment section, on page 988.

Be sure to check the companion website for a Review and Analysis Exercise, with solution.

Note: All asterisked Questions, Exercises, and Problems relate to material in the appendix to the chapter.

QUESTIONS

1. Explain the current environment regarding revenue recognition.

2. When is revenue conventionally recognized? What conditions should exist for the recognition at date of sale of all or part of the revenue of any sale transaction?

3. When is revenue recognized in the following situations: (a) Revenue from selling products? (b) Revenue from services rendered? (c) Revenue from permitting others to use enterprise assets? (d) Revenue from disposing of assets other than products?

4. Identify several types of sales transactions and indicate the types of business for which that type of transaction is common.

5. What are the three alternative accounting methods available to a seller that is exposed to continued risks of ownership through return of the product?

6. Under what conditions may a seller who is exposed to continued risks of a high rate of return of the product sold recognize sales transactions as current revenue?

7. What are the two basic methods of accounting for long-term construction contracts? Indicate the circumstances that determine when one or the other of these methods should be used.

8. Hawkins Construction Co. has a $60 million contract to construct a highway overpass and cloverleaf. The total estimated cost for the project is $50 million. Costs incurred in the first year of the project are $8 million. Hawkins Construction Co. appropriately uses the percentage-of-completion method. How much revenue and gross profit should Hawkins recognize in the first year of the project?

9. For what reasons should the percentage-of-completion method be used over the completed-contract method whenever possible?

10. What methods are used in practice to determine the extent of progress toward completion? Identify some "input measures" and some "output measures" that might be used to determine the extent of progress.

11. What are the two types of losses that can become evident in accounting for long-term contracts? What is the nature of each type of loss? How is each type accounted for?

12. Under the percentage-of-completion method, how are the Construction in Process and the Billings on Construction in Process accounts reported in the balance sheet?

13. Explain the differences between the installment-sales method and the cost-recovery method.

14. Identify and briefly describe the two methods generally employed to account for the cash received in situations where the collection of the sales price is not reasonably assured.

15. What is the deposit method and when might it be applied?

16. What is the nature of an installment sale? How do installment sales differ from ordinary credit sales?

17. Describe the installment-sales method of accounting.

18. How are operating expenses (not included in cost of goods sold) handled under the installment-sales method of accounting? What is the justification for such treatment?

19. Mojave sold her condominium for $500,000 on September 14, 2010; she had paid $330,000 for it in 2002. Mojave collected the selling price as follows: 2010, $80,000; 2011, $320,000; and 2012, $100,000. Mojave appropriately uses the installment-sales method. Prepare a schedule to determine the gross profit for 2010, 2011, and 2012 from the installment sale.

20. When interest is involved in installment-sales transactions, how should it be treated for accounting purposes?

21. How should the results of installment sales be reported on the income statement?

22. At what time is it proper to recognize income in the following cases: (a) Installment sales with no reasonable basis for estimating the degree of collectibility? (b) Sales for future delivery? (c) Merchandise shipped on consignment? (d) Profit on incomplete construction contracts? (e) Subscriptions to publications?

23. When is revenue recognized under the cost-recovery method?

24. When is revenue recognized under the deposit method? How does the deposit method differ from the installment-sales and cost-recovery methods?

25. What is a major difference between iGAAP and U.S. GAAP as regards revenue recognition practices?

26. iGAAP prohibits the use of the completed-contract method in accounting for long-term contracts. If revenues and costs are difficult to estimate, how must companies account for long-term contracts?

27. Livesey Company has signed a long-term contract to build a new basketball arena. The total revenue related to the contract is $120 million. Estimated costs for building the arena are $40 million in the first year and $30 million in both the second and third year. The costs cannot be reliably estimated. How much revenue should Livesey Company report in the first year under iGAAP?

*28. Why in franchise arrangements may it not be proper to recognize the entire franchise fee as revenue at the date of sale?

*29. How does the concept of "substantial performance" apply to accounting for franchise sales?

*30. How should a franchisor account for continuing franchise fees and routine sales of equipment and supplies to franchisees?

*31 What changes are made in the franchisor's recording of the initial franchise fee when the franchise agreement:

    (a) Contains an option allowing the franchisor to purchase the franchised outlet, and it is likely that the option will be exercised?

    (b) Allows the franchisee to purchase equipment and supplies from the franchisor at bargain prices?

*32 What is the nature of a sale on consignment? When is revenue recognized from a consignment sale?

BRIEF EXERCISES

·1 ·2 BE18-1 Aamodt Music sold CDs to retailers and recorded sales revenue of $700,000. During 2010, retailers returned CDs to Aamodt and were granted credit of $78,000. Past experience indicates that the normal return rate is 15%. Prepare Aamodt's entries to record (a) the $78,000 of returns and (b) estimated returns at December 31, 2010.

·3 BE18-2 Turner, Inc. began work on a $7,000,000 contract in 2010 to construct an office building. During 2010, Turner, Inc. incurred costs of $1,700,000, billed their customers for $1,200,000, and collected $960,000. At December 31, 2010, the estimated future costs to complete the project total $3,300,000. Prepare Turner's 2010 journal entries using the percentage-of-completion method.

·3 BE18-3 O'Neil, Inc. began work on a $7,000,000 contract in 2010 to construct an office building. O'Neil uses the percentage-of-completion method. At December 31, 2010, the balances in certain accounts were: construction in process $2,450,000; accounts receivable $240,000; and billings on construction in process $1,400,000. Indicate how these accounts would be reported in O'Neil's December 31, 2010 balance sheet.

·4 BE18-4 Use the information from BE18-2, but assume Turner uses the completed-contract method. Prepare the company's 2010 journal entries.

·4 BE18-5 Guillen, Inc. began work on a $7,000,000 contract in 2010 to construct an office building. Guillen uses the completed-contract method. At December 31, 2010, the balances in certain accounts were construction in process $1,715,000; accounts receivable $240,000; and billings on construction in process $1,000,000. Indicate how these accounts would be reported in Guillen's December 31, 2010, balance sheet.

·5 BE18-6 Archer Construction Company began work on a $420,000 construction contract in 2010. During 2010, Archer incurred costs of $278,000, billed its customer for $215,000, and collected $175,000. At December 31, 2010, the estimated future costs to complete the project total $162,000. Prepare Archer's journal entry to record profit or loss using (a) the percentage-of-completion method and (b) the completed-contract method, if any.

·6 BE18-7 Gordeeva Corporation began selling goods on the installment basis on January 1, 2010. During 2010, Gordeeva had installment sales of $150,000; cash collections of $54,000; cost of installment sales of $102,000. Prepare the company's entries to record installment sales, cash collected, cost of installment sales, deferral of gross profit, and gross profit recognized, using the installment-sales method.

·6 BE18-8 Lazaro Inc. sells goods on the installment basis and uses the installment-sales method. Due to a customer default, Lazaro repossessed merchandise that was originally sold for $800, resulting in a gross profit rate of 40%. At the time of repossession, the uncollected balance is $520, and the fair value of the repossessed merchandise is $275. Prepare Lazaro's entry to record the repossession.

·6 BE18-9 At December 31, 2010, Grinkov Corporation had the following account balances.

Installment Accounts Receivable, 2009	$ 65,000
Installment Accounts Receivable, 2010	110,000
Deferred Gross Profit, 2009	23,400
Deferred Gross Profit, 2010	41,800

Most of Grinkov's sales are made on a 2-year installment basis. Indicate how these accounts would be reported in Grinkov's December 31, 2010, balance sheet. The 2009 accounts are collectible in 2011, and the 2010 accounts are collectible in 2012.

·7 **BE18-10** Schuss Corporation sold equipment to Potsdam Company for $20,000. The equipment is on Schuss's books at a net amount of $13,000. Schuss collected $10,000 in 2010, $5,000 in 2011, and $5,000 in 2012. If Schuss uses the cost-recovery method, what amount of gross profit will be recognized in each year?

·8 ***BE18-11** Frozen Delight, Inc. charges an initial franchise fee of $75,000 for the right to operate as a franchisee of Frozen Delight. Of this amount, $25,000 is collected immediately. The remainder is collected in 4 equal annual installments of $12,500 each. These installments have a present value of $41,402. There is reasonable expectation that the down payment may be refunded and substantial future services be performed by Frozen Delight, Inc. Prepare the journal entry required by Frozen Delight to record the franchise fee.

·8 ***BE18-12** Jansen Corporation shipped $20,000 of merchandise on consignment to Gooch Company. Jansen paid freight costs of $2,000. Gooch Company paid $500 for local advertising which is reimbursable from Jansen. By year-end, 60% of the merchandise had been sold for $21,500. Gooch notified Jansen, retained a 10% commission, and remitted the cash due to Jansen. Prepare Jansen's entry when the cash is received.

· **EXERCISES** · · · · · · · · · · · · · · ·

·1 ·2 **E18-1** **(Revenue Recognition on Book Sales with High Returns)** Uddin Publishing Co. publishes college textbooks that are sold to bookstores on the following terms. Each title has a fixed wholesale price, terms f.o.b. shipping point, and payment is due 60 days after shipment. The retailer may return a maximum of 30% of an order at the retailer's expense. Sales are made only to retailers who have good credit ratings. Past experience indicates that the normal return rate is 12%, and the average collection period is 72 days.

Instructions
(a) Identify alternative revenue recognition criteria that Uddin could employ concerning textbook sales.
(b) Briefly discuss the reasoning for your answers in (a) above.
(c) In late July, Uddin shipped books invoiced at $15,000,000. Prepare the journal entry to record this event that best conforms to generally accepted accounting principles and your answer to part (b).
(d) In October, $2 million of the invoiced July sales were returned according to the return policy, and the remaining $13 million was paid. Prepare the entries recording the return and payment.

·1 ·2 **E18-2** **(Sales Recorded Both Gross and Net)** On June 3, Hunt Company sold to Ann Mount merchandise having a sale price of $8,000 with terms of 2/10, n/60, f.o.b. shipping point. An invoice totaling $120, terms n/30, was received by Mount on June 8 from the Olympic Transport Service for the freight cost. Upon receipt of the goods, June 5, Mount notified Hunt Company that merchandise costing $600 contained flaws that rendered it worthless. The same day Hunt Company issued a credit memo covering the worthless merchandise and asked that it be returned at company expense. The freight on the returned merchandise was $24, paid by Hunt Company on June 7. On June 12, the company received a check for the balance due from Mount.

Instructions
(a) Prepare journal entries on Hunt Company books to record all the events noted above under each of the following bases.
   (1) Sales and receivables are entered at gross selling price.
   (2) Sales and receivables are entered net of cash discounts.
(b) Prepare the journal entry under basis 2, assuming that Ann Mount did not remit payment until August 5.

·1 ·2 **E18-3** **(Revenue Recognition on Marina Sales with Discounts)** Taylor Marina has 300 available slips that rent for $800 per season. Payments must be made in full at the start of the boating season, April 1, 2011. Slips for the next season may be reserved if paid for by December 31, 2010. Under a new policy, if payment is made by December 31, 2010 a 5% discount is allowed. The boating season ends October 31, and the marina has a December 31 year-end. To provide cash flow for major dock repairs, the marina operator is also offering a 20% discount to slip renters who pay for the 2012 season.

For the fiscal year ended December 31, 2010, all 300 slips were rented at full price. Two hundred slips were reserved and paid for for the 2011 boating season, and 60 slips were reserved and paid for for the 2012 boating season.

Instructions
(a) Prepare the appropriate journal entries for fiscal 2010.
(b) Assume the marina operator is unsophisticated in business. Explain the managerial significance of the accounting above to this person.

·3 ·4 **E18-4** **(Recognition of Profit on Long-Term Contracts)** During 2010 Nilsen Company started a construction job with a contract price of $1,600,000. The job was completed in 2012. The following information is available.

	2010	2011	2012
Costs incurred to date	$400,000	$825,000	$1,070,000
Estimated costs to complete	600,000	275,000	–0–
Billings to date	300,000	900,000	1,600,000
Collections to date	270,000	810,000	1,425,000

Instructions
(a) Compute the amount of gross profit to be recognized each year assuming the percentage-of-completion method is used.
(b) Prepare all necessary journal entries for 2011.
(c) Compute the amount of gross profit to be recognized each year assuming the completed-contract method is used.

·3 **E18-5** **(Analysis of Percentage-of-Completion Financial Statements)** In 2010, Steinrotter Construction Corp. began construction work under a 3-year contract. The contract price was $1,000,000. Steinrotter uses the percentage-of-completion method for financial accounting purposes. The income to be recognized each year is based on the proportion of cost incurred to total estimated costs for completing the contract. The financial statement presentations relating to this contract at December 31, 2010, follow.

Balance Sheet

Accounts receivable—construction contract billings		$18,000
Construction in progress	$65,000	
Less: Contract billings	61,500	
Cost of uncompleted contract in excess of billings		3,500

Income Statement

Income (before tax) on the contract recognized in 2010	$19,500

Instructions
(a) How much cash was collected in 2010 on this contract?
(b) What was the initial estimated total income before tax on this contract?

(AICPA adapted)

·3 **E18-6** **(Gross Profit on Uncompleted Contract)** On April 1, 2010, Dougherty Inc. entered into a cost-plus-fixed-fee contract to construct an electric generator for Altom Corporation. At the contract date, Dougherty estimated that it would take 2 years to complete the project at a cost of $2,000,000. The fixed fee stipulated in the contract is $450,000. Dougherty appropriately accounts for this contract under the percentage-of-completion method. During 2010 Dougherty incurred costs of $800,000 related to the project. The estimated cost at December 31, 2010, to complete the contract is $1,200,000. Altom was billed $600,000 under the contract.

Instructions
Prepare a schedule to compute the amount of gross profit to be recognized by Dougherty under the contract for the year ended December 31, 2010. Show supporting computations in good form.

(AICPA adapted)

·3 **E18-7** **(Recognition of Profit, Percentage-of-Completion)** In 2010 Gurney Construction Company agreed to construct an apartment building at a price of $1,200,000. The information relating to the costs and billings for this contract is shown below.

	2010	2011	2012
Costs incurred to date	$280,000	$600,000	$ 785,000
Estimated costs yet to be incurred	520,000	200,000	–0–
Customer billings to date	150,000	500,000	1,200,000
Collection of billings to date	120,000	320,000	940,000

Instructions
(a) Assuming that the percentage-of-completion method is used, (1) compute the amount of gross profit to be recognized in 2010 and 2011, and (2) prepare journal entries for 2011.
(b) For 2011, show how the details related to this construction contract would be disclosed on the balance sheet and on the income statement.

·3 ·4 E18-8 (Recognition of Revenue on Long-Term Contract and Entries) Hamilton Construction Company uses the percentage-of-completion method of accounting. In 2010, Hamilton began work under contract #E2-D2, which provided for a contract price of $2,200,000. Other details follow:

	2010	2011
Costs incurred during the year	$640,000	$1,425,000
Estimated costs to complete, as of December 31	960,000	–0–
Billings during the year	420,000	1,680,000
Collections during the year	350,000	1,500,000

Instructions

(a) What portion of the total contract price would be recognized as revenue in 2010? In 2011?

(b) Assuming the same facts as those above except that Hamilton uses the completed-contract method of accounting, what portion of the total contract price would be recognized as revenue in 2011?

(c) Prepare a complete set of journal entries for 2010 (using the percentage-of-completion method).

·3 ·4 E18-9 (Recognition of Profit and Balance Sheet Amounts for Long-Term Contracts) Yanmei Construction Company began operations January 1, 2010. During the year, Yanmei Construction entered into a contract with Lundquist Corp. to construct a manufacturing facility. At that time, Yanmei estimated that it would take 5 years to complete the facility at a total cost of $4,500,000. The total contract price for construction of the facility is $6,000,000. During the year, Yanmei incurred $1,185,800 in construction costs related to the construction project. The estimated cost to complete the contract is $4,204,200. Lundquist Corp. was billed and paid 25% of the contract price.

Instructions

Prepare schedules to compute the amount of gross profit to be recognized for the year ended December 31, 2010, and the amount to be shown as "costs and recognized profit on uncompleted contract in excess of related billings" or "billings on uncompleted contract in excess of related costs and recognized profit" at December 31, 2010, under each of the following methods.

(a) Completed-contract method.

(b) Percentage-of-completion method.

Show supporting computations in good form.

(AICPA adapted)

·4 ·5 E18-10 (Long-Term Contract Reporting) Berstler Construction Company began operations in 2010. Construction activity for the first year is shown below. All contracts are with different customers, and any work remaining at December 31, 2010, is expected to be completed in 2011.

Project	Total Contract Price	Billings through 12/31/10	Cash Collections through 12/31/10	Contract Costs Incurred through 12/31/10	Estimated Additional Costs to Complete
1	$ 560,000	$ 360,000	$340,000	$450,000	$130,000
2	670,000	220,000	210,000	126,000	504,000
3	520,000	500,000	440,000	330,000	–0–
	$1,750,000	$1,080,000	$990,000	$906,000	$634,000

Instructions

Prepare a partial income statement and balance sheet to indicate how the above information would be reported for financial statement purposes. Berstler Construction Company uses the completed-contract method.

·6 E18-11 (Installment-Sales Method Calculations, Entries) Coffin Corporation appropriately uses the installment-sales method of accounting to recognize income in its financial statements. The following information is available for 2010 and 2011.

	2010	2011
Installment sales	$900,000	$1,000,000
Cost of installment sales	594,000	680,000
Cash collections on 2010 sales	370,000	350,000
Cash collections on 2011 sales	–0–	450,000

Instructions

(a) Compute the amount of realized gross profit recognized in each year.

(b) Prepare all journal entries required in 2011.

•6 **E18-12** **(Analysis of Installment-Sales Accounts)** Samuels Co. appropriately uses the installment-sales method of accounting. On December 31, 2012, the books show balances as follows.

Installment Receivables		Deferred Gross Profit		Gross Profit on Sales	
2010	$12,000	2010	$ 7,000	2010	35%
2011	40,000	2011	26,000	2011	33%
2012	80,000	2012	95,000	2012	32%

Instructions

(a) Prepare the adjusting entry or entries required on December 31, 2012 to recognize 2012 realized gross profit. (Installment receivables have already been credited for cash receipts during 2012.)

(b) Compute the amount of cash collected in 2012 on accounts receivable each year.

•6 **E18-13** **(Gross Profit Calculations and Repossessed Merchandise)** Basler Corporation, which began business on January 1, 2010, appropriately uses the installment-sales method of accounting. The following data were obtained for the years 2010 and 2011.

	2010	2011
Installment sales	$750,000	$840,000
Cost of installment sales	510,000	588,000
General & administrative expenses	70,000	84,000
Cash collections on sales of 2010	310,000	300,000
Cash collections on sales of 2011	–0–	400,000

Instructions

(a) Compute the balance in the deferred gross profit accounts on December 31, 2010, and on December 31, 2011.

(b) A 2010 sale resulted in default in 2012. At the date of default, the balance on the installment receivable was $12,000, and the repossessed merchandise had a fair value of $8,000. Prepare the entry to record the repossession.

(AICPA adapted)

•6 **E18-14** **(Interest Revenue from Installment Sale)** Becker Corporation sells farm machinery on the installment plan. On July 1, 2010, Becker entered into an installment-sale contract with Valente Inc. for a 8-year period. Equal annual payments under the installment sale are $100,000 and are due on July 1. The first payment was made on July 1, 2010.

Additional information

1. The amount that would be realized on an outright sale of similar farm machinery is $586,842.
2. The cost of the farm machinery sold to Valente Inc. is $425,000.
3. The finance charges relating to the installment period are based on a stated interest rate of 10%, which is appropriate.
4. Circumstances are such that the collection of the installments due under the contract is reasonably assured.

Instructions

What income or loss before income taxes should Becker record for the year ended December 31, 2010, as a result of the transaction above?

(AICPA adapted)

•6 •7 **E18-15** **(Installment-Sales Method and Cost-Recovery Method)** Swift Corp., a capital goods manufacturing business that started on January 4, 2010, and operates on a calendar-year basis, uses the installment-sales method of profit recognition in accounting for all its sales. The following data were taken from the 2010 and 2011 records.

	2010	2011
Installment sales	$480,000	$620,000
Gross profit as a percent of costs	25%	28%
Cash collections on sales of 2010	$130,000	$240,000
Cash collections on sales of 2011	–0–	$160,000

The amounts given for cash collections exclude amounts collected for interest charges.

Instructions

(a) Compute the amount of realized gross profit to be recognized on the 2011 income statement, prepared using the installment-sales method.

(b) State where the balance of Deferred Gross Profit would be reported on the financial statements for 2011.

(c) Compute the amount of realized gross profit to be recognized on the income statement, prepared using the cost-recovery method.

(CIA adapted)

·6 ·7 E18-16 (Installment-Sales Method and Cost-Recovery Method) On January 1, 2010, Wetzel Company sold property for $250,000. The note will be collected as follows: $120,000 in 2010, $90,000 in 2011, and $40,000 in 2012. The property had cost Wetzel $150,000 when it was purchased in 2008.

Instructions

(a) Compute the amount of gross profit realized each year, assuming Wetzel uses the cost-recovery method.

(b) Compute the amount of gross profit realized each year, assuming Wetzel uses the installment-sales method.

·6 E18-17 (Installment Sales—Default and Repossession) Crawford Imports Inc. was involved in two default and repossession cases during the year:

1. A refrigerator was sold to Cindy McClary for $1,800, including a 30% markup on selling price. McClary made a down payment of 20%, four of the remaining 16 equal payments, and then defaulted on further payments. The refrigerator was repossessed, at which time the fair value was determined to be $800.

2. An oven that cost $1,200 was sold to Travis Longman for $1,500 on the installment basis. Longman made a down payment of $240 and paid $80 a month for six months, after which he defaulted. The oven was repossessed and the estimated fair value at time of repossession was determined to be $750.

Instructions

Prepare journal entries to record each of these repossessions using a fair value approach. (Ignore interest charges.)

·6 E18-18 (Installment Sales—Default and Repossession) Seaver Company uses the installment-sales method in accounting for its installment sales. On January 1, 2010, Seaver Company had an installment account receivable from Jan Noble with a balance of $1,800. During 2010, $500 was collected from Noble. When no further collection could be made, the merchandise sold to Noble was repossessed. The merchandise had a fair value of $650 after the company spent $60 for reconditioning of the merchandise. The merchandise was originally sold with a gross profit rate of 30%.

Instructions

Prepare the entries on the books of Seaver Company to record all transactions related to Noble during 2010. (Ignore interest charges.)

·8 *E18-19 (Franchise Entries) Pacific Crossburgers Inc. charges an initial franchise fee of $70,000. Upon the signing of the agreement, a payment of $28,000 is due. Thereafter, three annual payments of $14,000 are required. The credit rating of the franchisee is such that it would have to pay interest at 10% to borrow money.

Instructions

Prepare the entries to record the initial franchise fee on the books of the franchisor under the following assumptions.

(a) The down payment is not refundable, no future services are required by the franchisor, and collection of the note is reasonably assured.

(b) The franchisor has substantial services to perform, the down payment is refundable, and the collection of the note is very uncertain.

(c) The down payment is not refundable, collection of the note is reasonably certain, the franchisor has yet to perform a substantial amount of services, and the down payment represents a fair measure of the services already performed.

·8 *E18-20 (Franchise Fee, Initial Down Payment) On January 1, 2010, Lesley Benjamin signed an agreement to operate as a franchisee of Campbell Inc. for an initial franchise fee of $50,000. The amount of $10,000 was paid when the agreement was signed, and the balance is payable in five annual payments of $8,000 each, beginning January 1, 2011. The agreement provides that the down payment is not refundable and that no future services are required of the franchisor. Lesley Benjamin's credit rating indicates that she can borrow money at 11% for a loan of this type.

Instructions

(a) How much should Campbell record as revenue from franchise fees on January 1, 2010? At what amount should Benjamin record the acquisition cost of the franchise on January 1, 2010?

(b) What entry would be made by Campbell on January 1, 2010, if the down payment is refundable and substantial future services remain to be performed by Campbell?

(c) How much revenue from franchise fees would be recorded by Campbell on January 1, 2010, if:

   (1) The initial down payment is not refundable, it represents a fair measure of the services already provided, a significant amount of services is still to be performed by Campbell in future periods, and collectibility of the note is reasonably assured?

   (2) The initial down payment is not refundable and no future services are required by the franchisor, but collection of the note is so uncertain that recognition of the note as an asset is unwarranted?

   (3) The initial down payment has not been earned and collection of the note is so uncertain that recognition of the note as an asset is unwarranted?

·8 *E18-21 (Consignment Computations) On May 3, 2010, Eisler Company consigned 80 freezers, costing $500 each, to Remmers Company. The cost of shipping the freezers amounted to $840 and was paid by Eisler Company. On December 30, 2010, a report was received from the consignee, indicating that 40 freezers had been sold for $750 each. Remittance was made by the consignee for the amount due, after deducting a commission of 6%, advertising of $200, and total installation costs of $320 on the freezers sold.

Instructions

(a) Compute the inventory value of the units unsold in the hands of the consignee.

(b) Compute the profit for the consignor for the units sold.

(c) Compute the amount of cash that will be remitted by the consignee.

> **See the book's companion website, www.wiley.com/college/kieso, for a set of B Exercises.**

PROBLEMS

·2 ·3 ·4 ·6 P18-1 (Comprehensive Three-Part Revenue Recognition) Van Hatten Industries has three operating divisions—Depp Construction Division, DeMent Publishing Division, and Ankiel Securities Division. Each division maintains its own accounting system and method of revenue recognition.

Depp Construction Division

During the fiscal year ended November 30, 2010, Depp Construction Division had one construction project in process. A $30,000,000 contract for construction of a civic center was granted on June 19, 2010, and construction began on August 1, 2010. Estimated costs of completion at the contract date were $25,000,000 over a 2-year time period from the date of the contract. On November 30, 2010, construction costs of $7,200,000 had been incurred and progress billings of $9,500,000 had been made. The construction costs to complete the remainder of the project were reviewed on November 30, 2010, and were estimated to amount to only $16,800,000 because of an expected decline in raw materials costs. Revenue recognition is based upon a percentage-of-completion method.

DeMent Publishing Division

The DeMent Publishing Division sells large volumes of novels to a few book distributors, which in turn sell to several national chains of bookstores. DeMent allows distributors to return up to 30% of sales, and distributors give the same terms to bookstores. While returns from individual titles fluctuate greatly, the returns from distributors have averaged 20% in each of the past 5 years. A total of $7,000,000 of paperback novel sales were made to distributors during fiscal 2010. On November 30, 2010 (the end of the fiscal year) $1,500,000 of fiscal 2010 sales were still subject to return privileges over the next 6 months. The remaining $5,500,000 of fiscal 2010 sales had actual returns of 21%. Sales from fiscal 2009 totaling $2,000,000 were collected in fiscal 2010 less 18% returns. This division records revenue according to the method referred to as revenue recognition when the right of return exists.

Ankiel Securities Division

Ankiel Securities Division works through manufacturers' agents in various cities. Orders for alarm systems and down payments are forwarded from agents, and the Division ships the goods f.o.b. factory directly to customers (usually police departments and security guard companies). Customers are billed directly for the balance due plus actual shipping costs. The company received orders for $6,000,000 of goods during the fiscal year ended November 30, 2010. Down payments of $600,000 were received, and $5,200,000 of goods were billed and shipped. Actual freight costs of $100,000 were also billed. Commissions of 10% on product price are paid to manufacturing agents after goods are shipped to customers. Such goods are warranted for 90 days after shipment, and warranty returns have been about 1% of sales. Revenue is recognized at the point of sale by this division.

Instructions

(a) There are a variety of methods of revenue recognition. Define and describe each of the following methods of revenue recognition, and indicate whether each is in accordance with generally accepted accounting principles.
  (1) Point of sale.
  (2) Completion-of-production.
  (3) Percentage-of-completion.
  (4) Installment-sales.

(b) Compute the revenue to be recognized in fiscal year 2010 for each of the three operating divisions of Van Hatten Industries in accordance with generally accepted accounting principles.

 P18-2 (Recognition of Profit on Long-Term Contract) Shanahan Construction Company has entered into a contract beginning January 1, 2010, to build a parking complex. It has been estimated that the complex will cost $600,000 and will take 3 years to construct. The complex will be billed to the purchasing company at $900,000. The following data pertain to the construction period.

	2010	2011	2012
Costs to date	$270,000	$450,000	$610,000
Estimated costs to complete	330,000	150,000	–0–
Progress billings to date	270,000	550,000	900,000
Cash collected to date	240,000	500,000	900,000

Instructions

(a) Using the percentage-of-completion method, compute the estimated gross profit that would be recognized during each year of the construction period.

(b) Using the completed-contract method, compute the estimated gross profit that would be recognized during each year of the construction period.

 P18-3 (Recognition of Profit and Entries on Long-Term Contract) On March 1, 2010, Chance Company entered into a contract to build an apartment building. It is estimated that the building will cost $2,000,000 and will take 3 years to complete. The contract price was $3,000,000. The following information pertains to the construction period.

	2010	2011	2012
Costs to date	$ 600,000	$1,560,000	$2,100,000
Estimated costs to complete	1,400,000	520,000	–0–
Progress billings to date	1,050,000	2,000,000	3,000,000
Cash collected to date	950,000	1,950,000	2,850,000

Instructions

(a) Compute the amount of gross profit to be recognized each year assuming the percentage-of-completion method is used.

(b) Prepare all necessary journal entries for 2012.

(c) Prepare a partial balance sheet for December 31, 2011, showing the balances in the receivables and inventory accounts.

 P18-4 (Recognition of Profit and Balance Sheet Presentation, Percentage-of-Completion) On February 1, 2010, Hewitt Construction Company obtained a contract to build an athletic stadium. The stadium was to be built at a total cost of $5,400,000 and was scheduled for completion by September 1, 2012. One clause of the contract stated that Hewitt was to deduct $15,000 from the $6,600,000 billing price for each week that completion was delayed. Completion was delayed 6 weeks, which resulted in a $90,000 penalty. Below are the data pertaining to the construction period.

	2010	2011	2012
Costs to date	$1,620,000	$3,850,000	$5,500,000
Estimated costs to complete	3,780,000	1,650,000	–0–
Progress billings to date	1,200,000	3,300,000	6,510,000
Cash collected to date	1,000,000	2,800,000	6,510,000

Instructions

(a) Using the percentage-of-completion method, compute the estimated gross profit recognized in the years 2010–2012.

(b) Prepare a partial balance sheet for December 31, 2011, showing the balances in the receivable and inventory accounts.

·3 ·4 ·5 P18-5 (Completed Contract and Percentage of Completion with Interim Loss) Reynolds Custom Builders (RCB) was established in 1985 by Avery Conway and initially built high-quality customized homes under contract with specific buyers. In the 1990s, Conway's two sons joined the company and expanded RCB's activities into the high-rise apartment and industrial plant markets. Upon the retirement of RCB's long-time financial manager, Conway's sons recently hired Ed Borke as controller for RCB. Borke, a former college friend of Conway's sons, has been associated with a public accounting firm for the last 6 years.

Upon reviewing RCB's accounting practices, Borke observed that RCB followed the completed-contract method of revenue recognition, a carryover from the years when individual home building was the majority of RCB's operations. Several years ago, the predominant portion of RCB's activities shifted to the high-rise and industrial building areas. From land acquisition to the completion of construction, most building contracts cover several years. Under the circumstances, Borke believes that RCB should follow the percentage-of-completion method of accounting. From a typical building contract, Borke developed the following data.

BLUESTEM TRACTOR PLANT

Contract price: $8,000,000

	2010	2011	2012
Estimated costs	$1,600,000	$2,880,000	$1,920,000
Progress billings	1,000,000	2,500,000	4,500,000
Cash collections	800,000	2,300,000	4,900,000

Instructions

(a) Explain the difference between completed-contract revenue recognition and percentage-of-completion revenue recognition.

(b) Using the data provided for the Bluestem Tractor Plant and assuming the percentage-of-completion method of revenue recognition is used, calculate RCB's revenue and gross profit for 2010, 2011, and 2012, under **each** of the following circumstances.

  (1) Assume that all costs are incurred, all billings to customers are made, and all collections from customers are received within 30 days of billing, as planned.

  (2) Further assume that, as a result of unforeseen local ordinances and the fact that the building site was in a wetlands area, RCB experienced cost overruns of $800,000 in 2010 to bring the site into compliance with the ordinances and to overcome wetlands barriers to construction.

  (3) Further assume that, in addition to the cost overruns of $800,000 for this contract incurred under part (b)2, inflationary factors over and above those anticipated in the development of the original contract cost have caused an additional cost overrun of $850,000 in 2011. It is not anticipated that any cost overruns will occur in 2012.

(CMA adapted)

·3 ·4 ·5 P18-6 (Long-Term Contract with Interim Loss) On March 1, 2010, Pechstein Construction Company contracted to construct a factory building for Fabrik Manufacturing Inc. for a total contract price of $8,400,000. The building was completed by October 31, 2012. The annual contract costs incurred, estimated costs to complete the contract, and accumulated billings to Fabrik for 2010, 2011, and 2012 are given below.

	2010	2011	2012
Contract costs incurred during the year	$2,880,000	$2,230,000	$2,190,000
Estimated costs to complete the contract at 12/31	3,520,000	2,190,000	–0–
Billings to Fabrik during the year	3,200,000	3,500,000	1,700,000

Instructions

(a) Using the percentage-of-completion method, prepare schedules to compute the profit or loss to be recognized as a result of this contract for the years ended December 31, 2010, 2011, and 2012. (Ignore income taxes.)

(b) Using the completed-contract method, prepare schedules to compute the profit or loss to be recognized as a result of this contract for the years ended December 31, 2010, 2011, and 2012. (Ignore incomes taxes.)

•3 •4 •5 P18-7 (Long-Term Contract with an Overall Loss) On July 1, 2010, Torvill Construction Company Inc. contracted to build an office building for Gumbel Corp. for a total contract price of $1,900,000. On July 1, Torvill estimated that it would take between 2 and 3 years to complete the building. On December 31, 2012, the building was deemed substantially completed. Following are accumulated contract costs incurred, estimated costs to complete the contract, and accumulated billings to Gumbel for 2010, 2011, and 2012.

	At 12/31/10	At 12/31/11	At 12/31/12
Contract costs incurred to date	$ 300,000	$1,200,000	$2,100,000
Estimated costs to complete the contract	1,200,000	800,000	–0–
Billings to Gumbel	300,000	1,100,000	1,850,000

Instructions

(a) Using the percentage-of-completion method, prepare schedules to compute the profit or loss to be recognized as a result of this contract for the years ended December 31, 2010, 2011, and 2012. (Ignore income taxes.)

(b) Using the completed-contract method, prepare schedules to compute the profit or loss to be recognized as a result of this contract for the years ended December 31, 2010, 2011, and 2012. (Ignore income taxes.)

•6 P18-8 (Installment-Sales Computations and Entries) Presented below is summarized information for Johnston Co., which sells merchandise on the installment basis.

	2010	2011	2012
Sales (on installment plan)	$250,000	$260,000	$280,000
Cost of sales	155,000	163,800	182,000
Gross profit	$ 95,000	$ 96,200	$ 98,000
Collections from customers on:			
2010 installment sales	$ 75,000	$100,000	$ 50,000
2011 installment sales		100,000	120,000
2012 installment sales			100,000

Instructions

(a) Compute the realized gross profit for each of the years 2010, 2011, and 2012.

(b) Prepare in journal form all entries required in 2012, applying the installment-sales method of accounting. (Ignore interest charges.)

•6 P18-9 (Installment-Sales Income Statements) Chantal Stores sells merchandise on open account as well as on installment terms.

	2010	2011	2012
Sales on account	$385,000	$426,000	$525,000
Installment sales	320,000	275,000	380,000
Collections on installment sales			
Made in 2010	100,000	90,000	40,000
Made in 2011		110,000	140,000
Made in 2012			125,000
Cost of sales			
Sold on account	270,000	277,000	341,000
Sold on installment	214,400	176,000	228,000
Selling expenses	77,000	87,000	92,000
Administrative expenses	50,000	51,000	52,000

Instructions

From the data above, which cover the 3 years since Chantal Stores commenced operations, determine the net income for each year, applying the installment-sales method of accounting. (Ignore interest charges.)

·6 **P18-10** **(Installment-Sales Computations and Entries)** Paul Dobson Stores sell appliances for cash and also on the installment plan. Entries to record cost of sales are made monthly.

PAUL DOBSON STORES
TRIAL BALANCE
DECEMBER 31, 2011

	Dr.	Cr.
Cash	$153,000	
Installment Accounts Receivable, 2010	56,000	
Installment Accounts Receivable, 2011	91,000	
Inventory—New Merchandise	123,200	
Inventory—Repossessed Merchandise	24,000	
Accounts Payable		$ 98,500
Deferred Gross Profit, 2010		45,600
Capital Stock		170,000
Retained Earnings		93,900
Sales		343,000
Installment Sales		200,000
Cost of Sales	255,000	
Cost of Installment Sales	120,000	
Loss on Repossession	800	
Selling and Administrative Expenses	128,000	
	$951,000	$951,000

The accounting department has prepared the following analysis of cash receipts for the year.

Cash sales (including repossessed merchandise)	$424,000
Installment accounts receivable, 2010	96,000
Installment accounts receivable, 2011	109,000
Other	36,000
Total	$665,000

Repossessions recorded during the year are summarized as follows.

	2010
Uncollected balance	$8,000
Loss on repossession	800
Repossessed merchandise	4,800

Instructions
From the trial balance and accompanying information:

(a) Compute the rate of gross profit on installment sales for 2010 and 2011.
(b) Prepare closing entries as of December 31, 2011, under the installment-sales method of accounting.
(c) Prepare an income statement for the year ended December 31, 2011. Include only the realized gross profit in the income statement.

·6 **P18-11** **(Installment-Sales Entries)** The following summarized information relates to the installment-sales activity of Phillips Stores, Inc. for the year 2010.

Installment sales during 2010	$500,000
Cost of goods sold on installment basis	350,000
Collections from customers	180,000
Unpaid balances on merchandise repossessed	24,000
Estimated value of merchandise repossessed	11,200

Instructions
(a) Prepare journal entries at the end of 2010 to record on the books of Phillips Stores, Inc. the summarized data above.
(b) Prepare the entry to record the gross profit realized during 2010.

·6 **P18-12** **(Installment-Sales Computation and Entries—Periodic Inventory)** Mantle Inc. sells merchandise for cash and also on the installment plan. Entries to record cost of goods sold are made at the end of each year.

Repossessions of merchandise (sold in 2010) were made in 2011 and were recorded correctly as follows.

Deferred Gross Profit, 2010	7,200	
Repossessed Merchandise	8,000	
Loss on Repossession	2,800	
Installment Accounts Receivable, 2010		18,000

Part of this repossessed merchandise was sold for cash during 2011, and the sale was recorded by a debit to Cash and a credit to Sales.

The inventory of repossessed merchandise on hand December 31, 2011, is $4,000; of new merchandise, $127,400. There was no repossessed merchandise on hand January 1, 2011.

Collections on accounts receivable during 2011 were:

Installment Accounts Receivable, 2010	$80,000
Installment Accounts Receivable, 2011	50,000

The cost of the merchandise sold under the installment plan during 2011 was $111,600.

The rate of gross profit on 2010 and on 2011 installment sales can be computed from the information given.

MANTLE INC.
TRIAL BALANCE
DECEMBER 31, 2011

	Dr.	Cr.
Cash	$118,400	
Installment Accounts Receivable, 2010	80,000	
Installment Accounts Receivable, 2011	130,000	
Inventory, Jan. 1, 2011	120,000	
Repossessed Merchandise	8,000	
Accounts Payable		$ 47,200
Deferred Gross Profit, 2010		64,000
Capital Stock, Common		200,000
Retained Earnings		40,000
Sales		400,000
Installment Sales		180,000
Purchases	360,000	
Loss on Repossession	2,800	
Operating Expenses	112,000	
	$931,200	$931,200

Instructions

(a) From the trial balance and other information given above, prepare adjusting and closing entries as of December 31, 2011.

(b) Prepare an income statement for the year ended December 31, 2011. Include only the realized gross profit in the income statement.

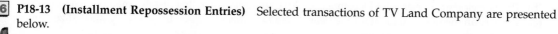 **P18-13** **(Installment Repossession Entries)** Selected transactions of TV Land Company are presented below.

1. A television set costing $540 is sold to Jack Matre on November 1, 2010, for $900. Matre makes a down payment of $300 and agrees to pay $30 on the first of each month for 20 months thereafter.
2. Matre pays the $30 installment due December 1, 2010.
3. On December 31, 2010, the appropriate entries are made to record profit realized on the installment sales.
4. The first seven 2011 installments of $30 each are paid by Matre. (Make one entry.)
5. In August 2011 the set is repossessed, after Matre fails to pay the August 1 installment and indicates that he will be unable to continue the payments. The estimated fair value of the repossessed set is $100.

Instructions

Prepare journal entries to record the transactions above on the books of TV Land Company. Closing entries should not be made.

P18-14 **(Installment-Sales Computations and Schedules)** Saprano Company, on January 2, 2010, entered into a contract with a manufacturing company to purchase room-size air conditioners and to sell the units on an installment plan with collections over approximately 30 months with no carrying charge.

For income tax purposes Saprano Company elected to report income from its sales of air conditioners according to the installment-sales method.

Purchases and sales of new units were as follows.

	Units Purchased		Units Sold	
Year	Quantity	Price Each	Quantity	Price Each
2010	1,400	$130	1,100	$200
2011	1,200	112	1,500	170
2012	900	136	800	205

Collections on installment sales were as follows.

	Collections Received		
	2010	2011	2012
2010 sales	$42,000	$88,000	$ 80,000
2011 sales		51,000	110,000
2012 sales			34,600

In 2012, 50 units from the 2011 sales were repossessed and sold for $120 each on the installment plan. At the time of repossession, $2,000 had been collected from the original purchasers, and the units had a fair value of $3,000.

General and administrative expenses for 2012 were $60,000. No charge has been made against current income for the applicable insurance expense from a 3-year policy expiring June 30, 2013, costing $7,200, and for an advance payment of $12,000 on a new contract to purchase air conditioners beginning January 2, 2013.

Instructions

Assuming that the weighted-average method is used for determining the inventory cost, including repossessed merchandise, prepare schedules computing for 2010, 2011, and 2012:

(a) (1) The cost of goods sold on installments.
   (2) The average unit cost of goods sold on installments for each year.
(b) The gross profit percentages for 2010, 2011, and 2012.
(c) The gain or loss on repossessions in 2012.
(d) The net income from installment sales for 2012. (Ignore income taxes.)

(AICPA adapted)

·4·5 P18-15 (Completed-Contract Method) Monat Construction Company, Inc., entered into a firm fixed-price contract with Hyatt Clinic on July 1, 2010, to construct a four-story office building. At that time, Monat estimated that it would take between 2 and 3 years to complete the project. The total contract price for construction of the building is $4,400,000. Monat appropriately accounts for this contract under the completed-contract method in its financial statements and for income tax reporting. The building was deemed substantially completed on December 31, 2012. Estimated percentage of completion, accumulated contract costs incurred, estimated costs to complete the contract, and accumulated billings to the Hyatt Clinic under the contract are shown below.

	At December 31, 2010	At December 31, 2011	At December 31, 2012
Percentage of completion	30%	70%	100%
Contract costs incurred	$1,140,000	$3,290,000	$4,800,000
Estimated costs to complete the contract	$2,660,000	$1,410,000	–0–
Billings to Hyatt Clinic	$1,400,000	$2,500,000	$4,300,000

Instructions

(a) Prepare schedules to compute the amount to be shown as "Cost of uncompleted contract in excess of related billings" or "Billings on uncompleted contract in excess of related costs" at December 31, 2010, 2011, and 2012. Ignore income taxes. Show supporting computations in good form.
(b) Prepare schedules to compute the profit or loss to be recognized as a result of this contract for the years ended December 31, 2010, 2011, and 2012. Ignore income taxes. Show supporting computations in good form.

(AICPA adapted)

·3·4 P18-16 (Revenue Recognition Methods—Comparison) Sue's Construction is in its fourth year of business. Sue performs long-term construction projects and accounts for them using the completed-contract method. Sue built an apartment building at a price of $1,100,000. The costs and billings for this contract for the first three years are as follows.

	2010	2011	2012
Costs incurred to date	$240,000	$600,000	$ 790,000
Estimated costs yet to be incurred	560,000	200,000	–0–
Customer billings to date	150,000	410,000	1,100,000
Collection of billings to date	120,000	340,000	950,000

Sue has contacted you, a certified public accountant, about the following concern. She would like to attract some investors, but she believes that in order to recognize revenue she must first "deliver" the product. Therefore, on her balance sheet, she did not recognize any gross profits from the above contract until 2012, when she recognized the entire $310,000. That looked good for 2012, but the preceding years looked grim by comparison. She wants to know about an alternative to this completed-contract revenue recognition.

Instructions

Draft a letter to Sue, telling her about the percentage-of-completion method of recognizing revenue. Compare it to the completed-contract method. Explain the idea behind the percentage-of-completion method. In addition, illustrate how much revenue she could have recognized in 2010, 2011, and 2012 if she had used this method.

P18-17 (Comprehensive Problem—Long-Term Contracts) You have been engaged by Buhl Construction Company to advise it concerning the proper accounting for a series of long-term contracts. Buhl commenced doing business on January 1, 2010. Construction activities for the first year of operations are shown below. All contract costs are with different customers, and any work remaining at December 31, 2010, is expected to be completed in 2011.

Project	Total Contract Price	Billings Through 12/31/10	Cash Collections Through 12/31/10	Contract Costs Incurred Through 12/31/10	Estimated Additional Costs to Complete
A	$ 300,000	$200,000	$180,000	$248,000	$ 72,000
B	350,000	110,000	105,000	67,800	271,200
C	280,000	280,000	255,000	186,000	–0–
D	200,000	35,000	25,000	118,000	87,000
E	240,000	205,000	200,000	190,000	10,000
	$1,370,000	$830,000	$765,000	$809,800	$440,200

Instructions

(a) Prepare a schedule to compute gross profit (loss) to be reported, unbilled contract costs and recognized profit, and billings in excess of costs and recognized profit using the percentage-of-completion method.

(b) Prepare a partial income statement and balance sheet to indicate how the information would be reported for financial statement purposes.

(c) Repeat the requirements for part (a) assuming Buhl uses the completed-contract method.

(d) Using the responses above for illustrative purposes, prepare a brief report comparing the conceptual merits (both positive and negative) of the two revenue recognition approaches.

CONCEPTS FOR ANALYSIS

CA18-1 (Revenue Recognition—Alternative Methods) Peterson Industries has three operating divisions—Farber Mining, Glesen Paperbacks, and Enyart Protection Devices. Each division maintains its own accounting system and method of revenue recognition.

Farber Mining

Farber Mining specializes in the extraction of precious metals such as silver, gold, and platinum. During the fiscal year ended November 30, 2010, Farber entered into contracts worth $2,250,000 and shipped metals worth $2,000,000. A quarter of the shipments were made from inventories on hand at the beginning of the fiscal year, and the remainder were made from metals that were mined during the year. Mining totals for the year, valued at market prices, were: silver at $750,000, gold at $1,400,000, and platinum at $490,000. Farber uses the completion-of-production method to recognize revenue, because its operations meet the specified criteria—i.e., reasonably assured sales prices, interchangeable units, and insignificant distribution costs.

Enyart Paperbacks

Enyart Paperbacks sells large quantities of novels to a few book distributors that in turn sell to several national chains of bookstores. Enyart allows distributors to return up to 30% of sales, and distributors give the same terms to bookstores. While returns from individual titles fluctuate greatly, the returns from distributors have averaged 20% in each of the past 5 years. A total of $7,000,000 of paperback novel sales were made to distributors during the fiscal year. On November 30, 2010, $2,200,000 of fiscal 2010 sales were still subject to return privileges over the next 6 months. The remaining $4,800,000 of fiscal 2010 sales had actual returns of 21%. Sales from fiscal 2009 totaling $2,500,000 were collected in fiscal 2010, with less than 18% of sales returned. Enyart records revenue according to the method referred to as revenue recognition when the right of return exits, because all applicable criteria for use of this method are met by Enyart's operations.

Glesen Protection Devices

Glesen Protection Devices works through manufacturers' agents in various cities. Orders for alarm systems and down payments are forwarded from agents, and Glesen ships the goods f.o.b. shipping point. Customers are billed for the balance due plus actual shipping costs. The firm received orders for $6,000,000 of goods during the fiscal year ended November 30, 2010. Down payments of $600,000 were received, and $5,000,000 of goods were billed and shipped. Actual freight costs of $100,000 were also billed. Commissions of 10% on product price were paid to manufacturers' agents after the goods were shipped to customers. Such goods are warranted for 90 days after shipment, and warranty returns have been about 1% of sales. Revenue is recognized at the point of sale by Glesen.

Instructions

(a) There are a variety of methods for revenue recognition. Define and describe each of the following methods of revenue recognition, and indicate whether each is in accordance with generally accepted accounting principles.

(1) Completion-of-production method.

(2) Percentage-of-completion method.

(3) Installment-sales method.

(b) Compute the revenue to be recognized in the fiscal year ended November 30, 2010, for

(1) Farber Mining.

(2) Enyart Paperbacks.

(3) Glesen Protection Devices.

(CMA adapted)

CA18-2 (Recognition of Revenue—Theory) Revenue is usually recognized at the point of sale. Under special circumstances, however, bases other than the point of sale are used for the timing of revenue recognition.

Instructions

(a) Why is the point of sale usually used as the basis for the timing of revenue recognition?

(b) Disregarding the special circumstances when bases other than the point of sale are used, discuss the merits of each of the following objections to the sales basis of revenue recognition:

(1) It is too conservative because revenue is earned throughout the entire process of production.

(2) It is not conservative enough because accounts receivable do not represent disposable funds, sales returns and allowances may be made, and collection and bad debt expenses may be incurred in a later period.

(c) Revenue may also be recognized (1) during production and (2) when cash is received. For each of these two bases of timing revenue recognition, give an example of the circumstances in which it is properly used and discuss the accounting merits of its use in lieu of the sales basis.

(AICPA adapted)

CA18-3 (Recognition of Revenue—Theory) The earning of revenue by a business enterprise is recognized for accounting purposes when the transaction is recorded. In some situations, revenue is recognized approximately as it is earned in the economic sense. In other situations, however, accountants have developed guidelines for recognizing revenue by other criteria, such as at the point of sale.

Instructions

(Ignore income taxes.)

(a) Explain and justify why revenue is often recognized as earned at time of sale.

(b) Explain in what situations it would be appropriate to recognize revenue as the productive activity takes place.

(c) At what times, other than those included in (a) and (b) above, may it be appropriate to recognize revenue? Explain.

CA18-4 **(Recognition of Revenue—Bonus Dollars)** Griseta & Dubel Inc. was formed early this year to sell merchandise credits to merchants who distribute the credits free to their customers. For example, customers can earn additional credits based on the dollars they spend with a merchant (e.g., airlines and hotels). Accounts for accumulating the credits and catalogs illustrating the merchandise for which the credits may be exchanged are maintained online. Centers with inventories of merchandise premiums have been established for redemption of the credits. Merchants may not return unused credits to Griseta & Dubel.

The following schedule expresses Griseta & Dubel's expectations as to percentages of a normal month's activity that will be attained. For this purpose, a "normal month's activity" is defined as the level of operations expected when expansion of activities ceases or tapers off to a stable rate. The company expects that this level will be attained in the third year and that sales of credits will average $6,000,000 per month throughout the third year.

Month	Actual Credit Sales Percent	Merchandise Premium Purchases Percent	Credit Redemptions Percent
6th	30%	40%	10%
12th	60	60	45
18th	80	80	70
24th	90	90	80
30th	100	100	95

Griseta & Dubel plans to adopt an annual closing date at the end of each 12 months of operation.

Instructions

(a) Discuss the factors to be considered in determining when revenue should be recognized in measuring the income of a business enterprise.

(b) Discuss the accounting alternatives that should be considered by Griseta & Dubel Inc. for the recognition of its revenues and related expenses.

(c) For each accounting alternative discussed in (b), give balance sheet accounts that should be used and indicate how each should be classified.

(AICPA adapted)

CA18-5 **(Recognition of Revenue from Subscriptions)** *Cutting Edge* is a monthly magazine that has been on the market for 18 months. It currently has a circulation of 1.4 million copies. Negotiations are underway to obtain a bank loan in order to update the magazine's facilities. They are producing close to capacity and expect to grow at an average of 20% per year over the next 3 years.

After reviewing the financial statements of *Cutting Edge*, Andy Rich, the bank loan officer, had indicated that a loan could be offered to *Cutting Edge* only if it could increase its current ratio and decrease its debt to equity ratio to a specified level.

Jonathan Embry, the marketing manager of *Cutting Edge*, has devised a plan to meet these requirements. Embry indicates that an advertising campaign can be initiated to immediately increase circulation. The potential customers would be contacted after the purchase of another magazine's mailing list. The campaign would include:

1. An offer to subscribe to *Cutting Edge* at 3/4 the normal price.
2. A special offer to all new subscribers to receive the most current world atlas whenever requested at a guaranteed price of $2.
3. An unconditional guarantee that any subscriber will receive a full refund if dissatisfied with the magazine.

Although the offer of a full refund is risky, Embry claims that few people will ask for a refund after receiving half of their subscription issues. Embry notes that other magazine companies have tried this sales promotion technique and experienced great success. Their average cancellation rate was 25%. On average, each company increased its initial circulation threefold and in the long run increased circulation to twice that which existed before the promotion. In addition, 60% of the new subscribers are expected to take advantage of the atlas premium. Embry feels confident that the increased subscriptions from the advertising campaign will increase the current ratio and decrease the debt to equity ratio.

You are the controller of *Cutting Edge* and must give your opinion of the proposed plan.

Instructions

(a) When should revenue from the new subscriptions be recognized?

(b) How would you classify the estimated sales returns stemming from the unconditional guarantee?

(c) How should the atlas premium be recorded? Is the estimated premium claims a liability? Explain.

(d) Does the proposed plan achieve the goals of increasing the current ratio and decreasing the debt to equity ratio?

CA18-6 (Long-Term Contract—Percentage-of-Completion) Widjaja Company is accounting for a long-term construction contract using the percentage-of-completion method. It is a 4-year contract that is currently in its second year. The latest estimates of total contract costs indicate that the contract will be completed at a profit to Widjaja Company.

Instructions
- **(a)** What theoretical justification is there for Widjaja Company's use of the percentage-of-completion method?
- **(b)** How would progress billings be accounted for? Include in your discussion the classification of progress billings in Widjaja Company financial statements.
- **(c)** How would the income recognized in the second year of the 4-year contract be determined using the cost-to-cost method of determining percentage of completion?
- **(d)** What would be the effect on earnings per share in the second year of the 4-year contract of using the percentage-of-completion method instead of the completed-contract method? Discuss.

(AICPA adapted)

CA18-7 (Revenue Recognition—Real Estate Development) Lillehammer Lakes is a new recreational real estate development which consists of 500 lake-front and lake-view lots. As a special incentive to the first 100 buyers of lake-view lots, the developer is offering 3 years of free financing on 10-year, 12% notes, no down payment, and one week at a nearby established resort—"a $1,200 value." The normal price per lot is $15,000. The cost per lake-view lot to the developer is an estimated average of $3,000. The development costs continue to be incurred; the actual average cost per lot is not known at this time. The resort promotion cost is $700 per lot. The notes are held by Harper Corp., a wholly owned subsidiary.

Instructions
- **(a)** Discuss the revenue recognition and gross profit measurement issues raised by this situation.
- **(b)** How would the developer's past financial and business experience influence your decision concerning the recording of these transactions?
- **(c)** Assume 50 persons have accepted the offer, signed 10-year notes, and have stayed at the local resort. Prepare the journal entries that you believe are proper.
- **(d)** What should be disclosed in the notes to the financial statements?

CA18-8 (Revenue Recognition) Nimble Health and Racquet Club (NHRC), which operates eight clubs in the Chicago metropolitan area, offers one-year memberships. The members may use any of the eight facilities but must reserve racquetball court time and pay a separate fee before using the court. As an incentive to new customers, NHRC advertised that any customers not satisfied for any reason could receive a refund of the remaining portion of unused membership fees. Membership fees are due at the beginning of the individual membership period. However, customers are given the option of financing the membership fee over the membership period at a 9% interest rate.

Some customers have expressed a desire to take only the regularly scheduled aerobic classes without paying for a full membership. During the current fiscal year, NHRC began selling coupon books for aerobic classes to accommodate these customers. Each book is dated and contains 50 coupons that may be redeemed for any regularly scheduled aerobics class over a one-year period. After the one-year period, unused coupons are no longer valid.

During 2008, NHRC expanded into the health equipment market by purchasing a local company that manufactures rowing machines and cross-country ski machines. These machines are used in NHRC's facilities and are sold through the clubs and mail order catalogs. Customers must make a 20% down payment when placing an equipment order; delivery is 60–90 days after order placement. The machines are sold with a 2-year unconditional guarantee. Based on past experience, NHRC expects the costs to repair machines under guarantee to be 4% of sales.

NHRC is in the process of preparing financial statements as of May 31, 2011, the end of its fiscal year. Marvin Bush, corporate controller, expressed concern over the company's performance for the year and decided to review the preliminary financial statements prepared by Joyce Kiley, NHRC's assistant controller. After reviewing the statements, Bush proposed that the following changes be reflected in the May 31, 2011, published financial statements.

1. Membership revenue should be recognized when the membership fee is collected.
2. Revenue from the coupon books should be recognized when the books are sold.
3. Down payments on equipment purchases and expenses associated with the guarantee on the rowing and cross-country machines should be recognized when paid.

Kiley indicated to Bush that the proposed changes are not in accordance with generally accepted accounting principles, but Bush insisted that the changes be made. Kiley believes that Bush wants to manage income to forestall any potential financial problems and increase his year-end bonus. At this point, Kiley is unsure what action to take.

Instructions

(a) (1) Describe when Nimble Health and Racquet Club (NHRC) should recognize revenue from membership fees, court rentals, and coupon book sales.

   (2) Describe how NHRC should account for the down payments on equipment sales, explaining when this revenue should be recognized.

   (3) Indicate when NHRC should recognize the expense associated with the guarantee of the rowing and cross-country machines.

(b) Discuss why Marvin Bush's proposed changes and his insistence that the financial statement changes be made is unethical. Structure your answer around or to include the following aspects of ethical conduct: competence, confidentiality, integrity, and/or objectivity.

(c) Identify some specific actions Joyce Kiley could take to resolve this situation.

(CMA adapted)

CA18-9 (Revenue Recognition—Membership Fees) Midwest Health Club offers one-year memberships. Membership fees are due in full at the beginning of the individual membership period. As an incentive to new customers, MHC advertised that any customers not satisfied for any reason could receive a refund of the remaining portion of unused membership fees. As a result of this policy, Richard Nies, corporate controller, recognized revenue ratably over the life of the membership.

MHC is in the process of preparing its year-end financial statements. Rachel Avery, MHC's treasurer, is concerned about the company's lackluster performance this year. She reviews the financial statements Nies prepared and tells Nies to recognize membership revenue when the fees are received.

Instructions

Answer the following questions.

(a) What are the ethical issues involved?

(b) What should Nies do?

*CA18-10 (Franchise Revenue) Amigos Burrito Inc. sells franchises to independent operators throughout the northwestern part of the United States. The contract with the franchisee includes the following provisions.

1. The franchisee is charged an initial fee of $120,000. Of this amount, $20,000 is payable when the agreement is signed, and a $20,000 non-interest-bearing note is payable at the end of each of the 5 subsequent years.

2. All of the initial franchise fee collected by Amigos is to be refunded and the remaining obligation canceled if, for any reason, the franchisee fails to open his or her franchise.

3. In return for the initial franchise fee, Amigos agrees to (a) assist the franchisee in selecting the location for the business, (b) negotiate the lease for the land, (c) obtain financing and assist with building design, (d) supervise construction, (e) establish accounting and tax records, and (f) provide expert advice over a 5-year period relating to such matters as employee and management training, quality control, and promotion.

4. In addition to the initial franchise fee, the franchisee is required to pay to Amigos a monthly fee of 2% of sales for menu planning, receipt innovations, and the privilege of purchasing ingredients from Amigos at or below prevailing market prices.

Management of Amigos Burrito estimates that the value of the services rendered to the franchisee at the time the contract is signed amounts to at least $20,000. All franchisees to date have opened their locations at the scheduled time, and none have defaulted on any of the notes receivable.

The credit ratings of all franchisees would entitle them to borrow at the current interest rate of 10%. The present value of an ordinary annuity of five annual receipts of $20,000 each discounted at 10% is $75,816.

Instructions

(a) Discuss the alternatives that Amigos Burrito Inc. might use to account for the initial franchise fees, evaluate each by applying generally accepted accounting principles, and give illustrative entries for each alternative.

(b) Given the nature of Amigos Burrito's agreement with its franchisees, when should revenue be recognized? Discuss the question of revenue recognition for both the initial franchise fee and the additional monthly fee of 2% of sales, and give illustrative entries for both types of revenue.

(c) Assume that Amigos Burrito sells some franchises for $100,000, which includes a charge of $20,000 for the rental of equipment for its useful life of 10 years; that $50,000 of the fee is payable immediately and the balance on non-interest-bearing notes at $10,000 per year; that no portion of the $20,000 rental payment is refundable in case the franchisee goes out of business; and that title to the equipment remains with the franchisor. Under those assumptions, what would be the preferable method of accounting for the rental portion of the initial franchise fee? Explain.

(AICPA adapted)

USING YOUR JUDGMENT

FINANCIAL REPORTING

Financial Reporting Problem

 The Procter & Gamble Company (P&G)

The financial statements of **P&G** are presented in Appendix 5B or can be accessed at the book's companion website, **www.wiley.com/college/kieso**.

Instructions

Refer to P&G's financial statements and the accompanying notes to answer the following questions.

(a) What were P&G's sales for 2007?

(b) What was the percentage of increase or decrease in P&G's sales from 2006 to 2007? From 2005 to 2006? From 2002 to 2007?

(c) In its notes to the financial statements, what criteria does P&G use to recognize revenue?

(d) How does P&G account for trade promotions? Does the accounting conform to accrual accounting concepts? Explain.

Comparative Analysis Case

The Coca-Cola Company

The Coca-Cola Company and PepsiCo, Inc.

 PEPSICO

Instructions

Go to book's companion website and use information found there to answer the following questions related to **The Coca-Cola Company** and **PepsiCo, Inc.**

(a) What were Coca-Cola's and PepsiCo's net revenues (sales) for the year 2007? Which company increased its revenues more (dollars and percentage) from 2006 to 2007?

(b) Are the revenue recognition policies of Coca-Cola and PepsiCo similar? Explain.

(c) In which foreign countries (geographic areas) did Coca-Cola (see Note 21) and PepsiCo experience significant revenues in 2007? Compare the amounts of foreign revenues to U.S. revenues for both Coca-Cola and PepsiCo.

Financial Statement Analysis Case

Westinghouse Electric Corporation

The following note appears in the "Summary of Significant Accounting Policies" section of the Annual Report of Westinghouse Electric Corporation.

> **Note 1 (in part): Revenue Recognition.** Sales are primarily recorded as products are shipped and services are rendered. The percentage-of-completion method of accounting is used for nuclear steam supply system orders with delivery schedules generally in excess of five years and for certain construction projects where this method of accounting is consistent with industry practice.
>
> WFSI revenues are generally recognized on the accrual method. When accounts become delinquent for more than two payment periods, usually 60 days, income is recognized only as payments are received. Such delinquent accounts for which no payments are received in the current month, and other accounts on which income is not being recognized because the receipt of either principal or interest is questionable, are classified as nonearning receivables.

Instructions

(a) Identify the revenue recognition methods used by Westinghouse Electric as discussed in its note on significant accounting policies.

(b) Under what conditions are the revenue recognition methods identified in the first paragraph of Westinghouse's note above acceptable?

(c) From the information provided in the second paragraph of Westinghouse's note, identify the type of operation being described and defend the acceptability of the revenue recognition method.

BRIDGE TO THE PROFESSION

Professional Research: FASB Codification

Employees at your company disagree about the accounting for sales returns. The sales manager believes that granting more generous return provisions can give the company a competitive edge and increase sales revenue. The controller cautions that, depending on the terms granted, loose return provisions might lead to non-GAAP revenue recognition. The company CFO would like you to research the issue to provide an authoritative answer.

Instructions

Access the FASB Codification at *http://asc.fasb.org/home* to conduct research using the Codification Research System to prepare responses to the following items. Provide Codification references for your responses.

(a) What is the authoritative literature addressing revenue recognition when right of return exists?

(b) What is meant by "right of return"?

(c) When there is a right of return, what conditions must the company meet to recognize the revenue at the time of sale?

(d) What factors may impair the ability to make a reasonable estimate of future returns?

Professional Simulation

Go to the book's companion website, at **www.wiley.com/college/kieso**, to find an interactive problem that simulates the computerized CPA exam. The professional simulation for this chapter asks you to address questions related to the accounting for revenue recognition.

Remember to check the book's companion website to find additional resources for this chapter.

CHAPTER 19

ACCOUNTING FOR INCOME TAXES

LEARNING OBJECTIVES

After studying this chapter, you should be able to:

- **•1** Identify differences between pretax financial income and taxable income.
- **•2** Describe a temporary difference that results in future taxable amounts.
- **•3** Describe a temporary difference that results in future deductible amounts.
- **•4** Explain the purpose of a deferred tax asset valuation allowance.
- **•5** Describe the presentation of income tax expense in the income statement.
- **•6** Describe various temporary and permanent differences.
- **•7** Explain the effect of various tax rates and tax rate changes on deferred income taxes.
- **•8** Apply accounting procedures for a loss carryback and a loss carryforward.
- **•9** Describe the presentation of deferred income taxes in financial statements.
- **•10** Indicate the basic principles of the asset-liability method.

TAX UNCERTAINTY

One set of costs that companies manage are those related to taxes. In fact, in today's competitive markets, managers are expected to look for places in the tax code that a company can exploit to pay less tax to state and federal governments. By paying less in taxes, companies have more cash available to fund operations, finance expansion, and create new jobs. What happens, though, when companies push the tax-saving envelope? Well, they may face a tax audit, the results of which could hurt their financial statements.

A notable example of corporate maneuvering to reduce taxable income involved **Limited Brands Inc.** It managed state-tax costs downward by locating part of its business in low-tax-rate states while operating retail outlets elsewhere. For example, by basing a subsidiary (which does nothing more than hold the trademarks for Bath and Body Works and Victoria's Secret) in Delaware, it is able to transfer hundreds of millions of dollars from Limited's retail outlets in high-tax states into Delaware, which has a state tax rate of zero.

However, the IRS and some states have been increasing their scrutiny of transactions that seem done only to avoid taxes and that do not serve a legitimate business purpose. In one case, an attorney for North Carolina alleged that Limited Brands Inc. ". . . engaged in hocus pocus bookkeeping and deceptive accounting," the sole purpose of which was to reduce its state-tax bill. The court agreed, and Limited Inc. had to pay millions of dollars in taxes dating back to 1994.

Limited Brands shareholders likely got an unpleasant surprise when they learned the company also had a big tax obligation from its "uncertain tax position" related to off-shore locations. The same can be said for many other companies that take tax deductions that may not hold up under the scrutiny of the tax court or an IRS audit. Unfortunately, at the time, accounting rules were not very specific on when companies had to record an obligation for taxes owed on uncertain tax positions. Recently the FASB has clarified the rules for accounting for uncertain tax positions. Under these new guidelines, some companies will be winners, and some companies will be losers. Companies that have used stricter guidelines in accounting for these situations may have their tax liabilities decrease or their tax assets increase. Others that followed less-conservative guidelines may have to increase their liabilities or reduce their assets, with a resulting negative effect on net income.

Source: See Glenn Simpson, "A Tax Maneuver in Delaware Puts Squeeze on States," *Wall Street Journal* (August 9, 2002), p. A1.

PREVIEW OF CHAPTER 19

As our opening story indicates, companies spend a considerable amount of time and effort to minimize their income tax payments. And with good reason, as income taxes are a major cost of doing business for most corporations. Yet, at the same time, companies must present financial information to the investment community that provides a clear picture of present and potential tax obligations and tax benefits. In this chapter, we discuss the basic guidelines that companies must follow in reporting income taxes. The content and organization of the chapter are as follows.

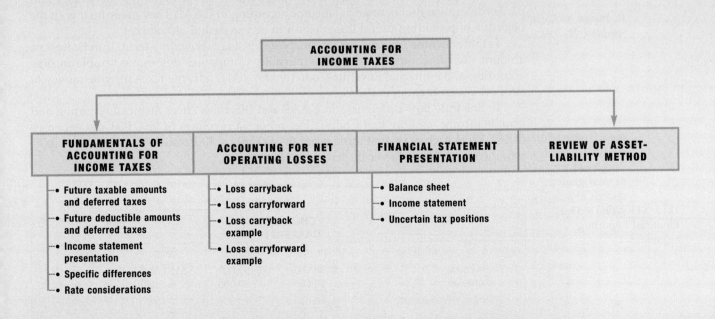

FUNDAMENTALS OF ACCOUNTING FOR INCOME TAXES

Objective·1

Identify differences between pretax financial income and taxable income.

Up to this point, you have learned the basic guidelines that corporations use to report information to investors and creditors. Corporations also must file income tax returns following the guidelines developed by the Internal Revenue Service (IRS). Because GAAP and tax regulations differ in a number of ways, so frequently do pretax financial income and taxable income. Consequently, the amount that a company reports as tax expense will differ from the amount of taxes payable to the IRS. Illustration 19-1 highlights these differences.

ILLUSTRATION 19-1
Fundamental Differences between Financial and Tax Reporting

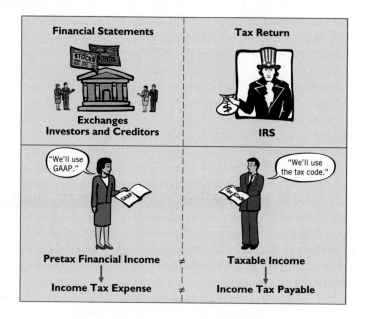

Pretax financial income is a *financial reporting* term. It also is often referred to as *income before taxes, income for financial reporting purposes,* or *income for book purposes.* Companies determine pretax financial income according to GAAP. They measure it with the objective of providing useful information to investors and creditors.

Taxable income (income for tax purposes) is a *tax accounting* term. It indicates the amount used to compute income tax payable. Companies determine taxable income according to the Internal Revenue Code (the tax code). Income taxes provide money to support government operations.

To illustrate how differences in GAAP and IRS rules affect financial reporting and taxable income, assume that Chelsea Inc. reported revenues of $130,000 and expenses of $60,000 in each of its first three years of operations. Illustration 19-2 shows the (partial) income statement over these three years.

ILLUSTRATION 19-2
Financial Reporting Income

CHELSEA INC. GAAP REPORTING				
	2010	2011	2012	Total
Revenues	$130,000	$130,000	$130,000	
Expenses	60,000	60,000	60,000	
Pretax financial income	$ 70,000	$ 70,000	$ 70,000	$ 210,000
Income tax expense (40%)	$ 28,000	$ 28,000	$ 28,000	$ 84,000

For tax purposes (following the tax code), Chelsea reported the same expenses to the IRS in each of the years. But, as Illustration 19-3 shows, Chelsea reported taxable revenues of $100,000 in 2010, $150,000 in 2011, and $140,000 in 2012.

CHELSEA INC. TAX REPORTING				
	2010	2011	2012	Total
Revenues	$100,000	$150,000	$140,000	
Expenses	60,000	60,000	60,000	
Taxable income	$ 40,000	$ 90,000	$ 80,000	$ 210,000
Income tax payable (40%)	$ 16,000	$ 36,000	$ 32,000	$ 84,000

ILLUSTRATION 19-3
Tax Reporting Income

Income tax expense and income tax payable differed over the three years, but were equal **in total**, as Illustration 19-4 shows.

CHELSEA INC. INCOME TAX EXPENSE AND INCOME TAX PAYABLE				
	2010	2011	2012	Total
Income tax expense	$28,000	$28,000	$28,000	$84,000
Income tax payable	16,000	36,000	32,000	84,000
Difference	$12,000	$ (8,000)	$ (4,000)	$ 0

ILLUSTRATION 19-4
Comparison of Income Tax Expense to Income Tax Payable

The differences between income tax expense and income tax payable in this example arise for a simple reason. For financial reporting, companies use the full accrual method to report revenues. For tax purposes, they use a modified cash basis. As a result, Chelsea reports pretax financial income of $70,000 and income tax expense of $28,000 for each of the three years. However, taxable income fluctuates. For example, in 2010 taxable income is only $40,000, so Chelsea owes just $16,000 to the IRS that year. Chelsea classifies the income tax payable as a current liability on the balance sheet.

As Illustration 19-4 indicates, for Chelsea the $12,000 ($28,000 − $16,000) difference between income tax expense and income tax payable in 2010 reflects taxes that it will pay in future periods. This $12,000 difference is often referred to as a **deferred tax amount**. In this case it is a **deferred tax liability**. In cases where taxes will be lower in the future, Chelsea records a **deferred tax asset**. We explain the measurement and accounting for deferred tax liabilities and assets in the following two sections.[1]

> **INTERNATIONAL INSIGHT**
>
> In some countries, taxable income equals pretax financial income. As a consequence, accounting for differences between tax and book income is insignificant.

Future Taxable Amounts and Deferred Taxes

The example summarized in Illustration 19-4 shows how income tax payable can differ from income tax expense. This can happen when there are temporary differences between the amounts reported for tax purposes and those reported for book purposes. A **temporary difference** is the difference between the tax basis of an asset or liability and its reported (carrying or book) amount in the financial statements, which will result in taxable amounts or deductible amounts in future

> **Objective·2**
> Describe a temporary difference that results in future taxable amounts.

[1]Determining the amount of tax to pay the IRS is a costly exercise for both individuals and companies. For example, a recent study documented that the average person spends about $200 annually collecting, calculating, and compiling tax data. U.S. corporations had a total cost of compliance of $170 billion. This is not surprising, when you consider that General Electric filed a return equivalent to 24,000 printed pages. J. Abrams, "Americans Spend 27 Hours, $200," *Naples (FL) Daily News* (April 15, 2008), p. 3a.

years. **Taxable amounts** increase taxable income in future years. **Deductible amounts** decrease taxable income in future years.

In Chelsea's situation, the only difference between the book basis and tax basis of the assets and liabilities relates to accounts receivable that arose from revenue recognized for book purposes. Illustration 19-5 indicates that Chelsea reports accounts receivable at $30,000 in the December 31, 2010, GAAP-basis balance sheet. However, the receivables have a zero tax basis.

ILLUSTRATION 19-5
Temporary Difference,
Sales Revenue

	Per Books	12/31/10	Per Tax Return	12/31/10
	Accounts receivable	$30,000	Accounts receivable	$–0–

What will happen to the $30,000 temporary difference that originated in 2010 for Chelsea? Assuming that Chelsea expects to collect $20,000 of the receivables in 2011 and $10,000 in 2012, this collection results in future taxable amounts of $20,000 in 2011 and $10,000 in 2012. These future taxable amounts will cause taxable income to exceed pretax financial income in both 2011 and 2012.

An assumption inherent in a company's GAAP balance sheet is that companies recover and settle the assets and liabilities at their reported amounts (carrying amounts). This assumption creates a requirement under accrual accounting to recognize *currently* the deferred tax consequences of temporary differences. That is, companies recognize the amount of income taxes that are payable (or refundable) when they recover and settle the reported amounts of the assets and liabilities, respectively. Illustration 19-6 shows the reversal of the temporary difference described in Illustration 19-5 and the resulting taxable amounts in future periods.

ILLUSTRATION 19-6
Reversal of Temporary
Difference, Chelsea Inc.

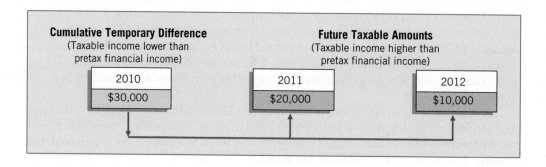

Chelsea assumes that it will collect the accounts receivable and report the $30,000 collection as taxable revenues in future tax returns. A payment of income tax in both 2011 and 2012 will occur. Chelsea should therefore record in its books in 2010 the deferred tax consequences of the revenue and related receivables reflected in the 2010 financial statements. Chelsea does this by recording a deferred tax liability.

Deferred Tax Liability

A **deferred tax liability** is the deferred tax consequences attributable to taxable temporary differences. In other words, **a deferred tax liability represents the increase in taxes payable in future years as a result of taxable temporary differences existing at the end of the current year**.

Recall from the Chelsea example that income tax payable is $16,000 ($40,000 × 40%) in 2010 (Illustration 19-4 on page 993). In addition, a temporary difference exists at year-end because Chelsea reports the revenue and related accounts receivable differently for book and tax purposes. The book basis of accounts receivable is $30,000, and the tax basis is zero. Thus, the total deferred tax liability at the end of 2010 is $12,000, computed as shown in Illustration 19-7 (on page 995).

Book basis of accounts receivable	$30,000	
Tax basis of accounts receivable	–0–	
Cumulative temporary difference at the end of 2010	30,000	
Tax rate	40%	
Deferred tax liability at the end of 2010	$12,000	

ILLUSTRATION 19-7
Computation of Deferred
Tax Liability, End of 2010

Companies may also compute the deferred tax liability by preparing a schedule that indicates the future taxable amounts due to existing temporary differences. Such a schedule, as shown in Illustration 19-8, is particularly useful when the computations become more complex.

	Future Years		
	2011	2012	Total
Future taxable amounts	$20,000	$10,000	$30,000
Tax rate	40%	40%	
Deferred tax liability at the end of 2010	$ 8,000	$ 4,000	$12,000

ILLUSTRATION 19-8
Schedule of Future
Taxable Amounts

Because it is the first year of operations for Chelsea, there is no deferred tax liability at the beginning of the year. Chelsea computes the income tax expense for 2010 as shown in Illustration 19-9.

Deferred tax liability at end of 2010	$12,000
Deferred tax liability at beginning of 2010	–0–
Deferred tax expense for 2010	12,000
Current tax expense for 2010 (Income tax payable)	16,000
Income tax expense (total) for 2010	$28,000

ILLUSTRATION 19-9
Computation of Income
Tax Expense, 2010

This computation indicates that income tax expense has two components—**current tax expense** (the amount of income tax payable for the period) and deferred tax expense. **Deferred tax expense** is the increase in the deferred tax liability balance from the beginning to the end of the accounting period.

Companies credit taxes due and payable to Income Tax Payable, and credit the increase in deferred taxes to Deferred Tax Liability. They then debit the sum of those two items to Income Tax Expense. For Chelsea, it makes the following entry at the end of 2010.

Income Tax Expense	28,000	
Income Tax Payable		16,000
Deferred Tax Liability		12,000

At the end of 2011 (the second year), the difference between the book basis and the tax basis of the accounts receivable is $10,000. Chelsea multiplies this difference by the applicable tax rate to arrive at the deferred tax liability of $4,000 ($10,000 × 40%), which it reports at the end of 2011. Income tax payable for 2011 is $36,000 (Illustration 19-3 on page 993), and the income tax expense for 2011 is as shown in Illustration 19-10.

Deferred tax liability at end of 2011	$ 4,000
Deferred tax liability at beginning of 2011	12,000
Deferred tax expense (benefit) for 2011	(8,000)
Current tax expense for 2011 (Income tax payable)	36,000
Income tax expense (total) for 2011	$28,000

ILLUSTRATION 19-10
Computation of Income
Tax Expense, 2011

Chelsea records income tax expense, the change in the deferred tax liability, and income tax payable for 2011 as follows.

Income Tax Expense	28,000	
Deferred Tax Liability	8,000	
Income Tax Payable		36,000

The entry to record income taxes at the end of 2012 reduces the Deferred Tax Liability by $4,000. The Deferred Tax Liability account appears as follows at the end of 2012.

ILLUSTRATION 19-11
Deferred Tax Liability Account after Reversals

Deferred Tax Liability			
2011	8,000	2010	12,000
2012	4,000		

The Deferred Tax Liability account has a zero balance at the end of 2012.

"REAL LIABILITIES"

What do the numbers mean?

Some analysts dismiss deferred tax liabilities when assessing the financial strength of a company. But the FASB indicates that the deferred tax liability meets the definition of a liability established in *Statement of Financial Accounting Concepts No. 6*, "Elements of Financial Statements" because:

1. *It results from a past transaction.* In the Chelsea example, the company performed services for customers and recognized revenue in 2010 for financial reporting purposes but deferred it for tax purposes.

2. *It is a present obligation.* Taxable income in future periods will exceed pretax financial income as a result of this temporary difference. Thus, a present obligation exists.

3. *It represents a future sacrifice.* Taxable income and taxes due in future periods will result from past events. The payment of these taxes when they come due is the future sacrifice.

A study by B. Ayers indicates that the market views deferred tax assets and liabilities similarly to other assets and liabilities. Further, the study concludes that the FASB rules in this area increased the usefulness of deferred tax amounts in financial statements.

Source: B. Ayers, "Deferred Tax Accounting Under *SFAS No. 109*: An Empirical Investigation of Its Incremental Value-Relevance Relative to *APB No. 11*," *The Accounting Review* (April 1998).

Summary of Income Tax Accounting Objectives

One objective of accounting for income taxes is to recognize the amount of taxes payable or refundable for the current year. In Chelsea's case, income tax payable is $16,000 for 2010.

A **second objective** is to recognize deferred tax liabilities and assets for the future tax consequences of events already recognized in the financial statements or tax returns. For example, Chelsea sold services to customers that resulted in accounts receivable of $30,000 in 2010. It reported that amount on the 2010 income statement, but not on the tax return as income. That amount will appear on future tax returns as income for the period **when collected**. As a result, a $30,000 temporary difference exists at the end of 2010, which will cause future taxable amounts. Chelsea reports a deferred tax liability of $12,000 on the balance sheet at the end of 2010, which represents the increase in taxes payable in future years ($8,000 in 2011 and $4,000 in 2012) as a result of a temporary difference existing at the end of the current year. The related deferred tax liability is reduced by $8,000 at the end of 2011 and by another $4,000 at the end of 2012.

In addition to affecting the balance sheet, deferred taxes impact income tax expense in each of the three years affected. In 2010, taxable income ($40,000) is less than pretax financial income ($70,000). Income tax payable for 2010 is therefore $16,000 (based on taxable income). Deferred tax expense of $12,000 results from the increase in the Deferred Tax Liability account on the balance sheet. Income tax expense is then $28,000 for 2010.

In 2011 and 2012, however, taxable income will exceed pretax financial income, due to the reversal of the temporary difference ($20,000 in 2011 and $10,000 in 2012). Income tax payable will therefore exceed income tax expense in 2011 and 2012. Chelsea will debit the Deferred Tax Liability account for $8,000 in 2011 and $4,000 in 2012. It records credits for these amounts in Income Tax Expense. These credits are often referred to as a **deferred tax benefit** (which we discuss again later on).

Future Deductible Amounts and Deferred Taxes

Assume that during 2010, Cunningham Inc. estimated its warranty costs related to the sale of microwave ovens to be $500,000, paid evenly over the next two years. For book purposes, in 2010 Cunningham reported warranty expense and a related estimated liability for warranties of $500,000 in its financial statements. For tax purposes, **the warranty tax deduction is not allowed until paid**. Therefore, Cunningham recognizes no warranty liability on a tax-basis balance sheet. Illustration 19-12 shows the balance sheet difference at the end of 2010.

> **Objective·3**
> Describe a temporary difference that results in future deductible amounts.

Per Books	12/31/10	Per Tax Return	12/31/10
Estimated liability for warranties	$500,000	Estimated liability for warranties	$–0–

ILLUSTRATION 19-12
Temporary Difference, Warranty Liability

When Cunningham pays the warranty liability, it reports an expense (deductible amount) for tax purposes. Because of this temporary difference, Cunningham should recognize in 2010 the tax benefits (positive tax consequences) for the tax deductions that will result from the future settlement of the liability. Cunningham reports this future tax benefit in the December 31, 2010, balance sheet as a **deferred tax asset**.

We can think about this situation another way. Deductible amounts occur in future tax returns. These **future deductible amounts** cause taxable income to be less than pretax financial income in the future as a result of an existing temporary difference. Cunningham's temporary difference originates (arises) in one period (2010) and reverses over two periods (2011 and 2012). Illustration 19-13 diagrams this situation.

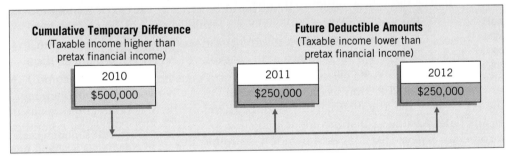

ILLUSTRATION 19-13
Reversal of Temporary Difference, Cunningham Inc.

Deferred Tax Asset

A **deferred tax asset** is the deferred tax consequence attributable to deductible temporary differences. In other words, a **deferred tax asset represents the increase in taxes refundable (or saved) in future years as a result of deductible temporary differences existing at the end of the current year**.

To illustrate, assume that Hunt Co. accrues a loss and a related liability of $50,000 in 2010 for financial reporting purposes because of pending litigation. Hunt cannot deduct this amount for tax purposes until the period it pays the liability, expected in 2011. As a result, a deductible amount will occur in 2011 when Hunt settles the liability (Estimated Litigation Liability), causing taxable income to be lower than pretax financial income. Illustration 19-14 (on page 998) shows the computation of the deferred tax asset at the end of 2010 (assuming a 40 percent tax rate).

ILLUSTRATION 19-14
Computation of Deferred
Tax Asset, End of 2010

Book basis of litigation liability	$50,000
Tax basis of litigation liability	–0–
Cumulative temporary difference at the end of 2010	50,000
Tax rate	40%
Deferred tax asset at the end of 2010	$20,000

Hunt can also compute the deferred tax asset by preparing a schedule that indicates the future deductible amounts due to deductible temporary differences. Illustration 19-15 shows this schedule.

ILLUSTRATION 19-15
Schedule of Future
Deductible Amounts

	Future Years
Future deductible amounts	$50,000
Tax rate	40%
Deferred tax asset at the end of 2010	$20,000

Assuming that 2010 is Hunt's first year of operations, and income tax payable is $100,000, Hunt computes its income tax expense as follows.

ILLUSTRATION 19-16
Computation of Income
Tax Expense, 2010

Deferred tax asset at end of 2010	$ 20,000
Deferred tax asset at beginning of 2010	–0–
Deferred tax expense (benefit) for 2010	(20,000)
Current tax expense for 2010 (Income tax payable)	100,000
Income tax expense (total) for 2010	$ 80,000

The **deferred tax benefit** results from the increase in the deferred tax asset from the beginning to the end of the accounting period (similar to the Chelsea example earlier). The deferred tax benefit is a negative component of income tax expense. The total income tax expense of $80,000 on the income statement for 2010 thus consists of two elements—current tax expense of $100,000 and a deferred tax benefit of $20,000. For Hunt, it makes the following journal entry at the end of 2010 to record income tax expense, deferred income taxes, and income tax payable.

Income Tax Expense	80,000	
Deferred Tax Asset	20,000	
Income Tax Payable		100,000

At the end of 2011 (the second year), the difference between the book value and the tax basis of the litigation liability is zero. Therefore, there is no deferred tax asset at this date. Assuming that income tax payable for 2011 is $140,000, Hunt computes income tax expense for 2011 as shown in Illustration 19-17.

ILLUSTRATION 19-17
Computation of Income
Tax Expense, 2011

Deferred tax asset at the end of 2011	$ –0–
Deferred tax asset at the beginning of 2011	20,000
Deferred tax expense (benefit) for 2011	20,000
Current tax expense for 2011 (Income tax payable)	140,000
Income tax expense (total) for 2011	$160,000

The company records income taxes for 2011 as follows.

Income Tax Expense	160,000	
Deferred Tax Asset		20,000
Income Tax Payable		140,000

The total income tax expense of $160,000 on the income statement for 2011 thus consists of two elements—current tax expense of $140,000 and deferred tax expense of $20,000. Illustration 19-18 shows the Deferred Tax Asset account at the end of 2011.

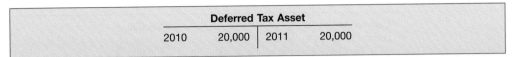

Deferred Tax Asset

| 2010 | 20,000 | 2011 | 20,000 |

ILLUSTRATION 19-18
Deferred Tax Asset
Account after Reversals

"REAL ASSETS"

A key issue in accounting for income taxes is whether a company should recognize a deferred tax asset in the financial records. Based on the conceptual definition of an asset, a deferred tax asset meets the three main conditions for an item to be recognized as an asset:

What do the numbers mean?

1. **It results from a past transaction.** In the Hunt example, the accrual of the loss contingency is the past event that gives rise to a future deductible temporary difference.
2. **It gives rise to a probable benefit in the future.** Taxable income exceeds pretax financial income in the current year (2010). However, in the next year the exact opposite occurs. That is, taxable income is lower than pretax financial income. Because this deductible temporary difference reduces taxes payable in the future, a probable future benefit exists at the end of the current period.
3. **The entity controls access to the benefits.** Hunt can obtain the benefit of existing deductible temporary differences by reducing its taxes payable in the future. Hunt has the exclusive right to that benefit and can control others' access to it.

Market analysts' reactions to the **write-off** of deferred tax assets also supports their treatment as assets. When **Bethlehem Steel** reported a $1 billion charge in a recent year to write off a deferred tax asset, analysts believed that Bethlehem was signaling that it would not realize the future benefits of the tax deductions. Thus, Bethlehem should write down the asset like other assets.

Source: J. Weil and S. Liesman, "Stock Gurus Disregard Most Big Write-Offs But They Often Hold Vital Clues to Outlook," *Wall Street Journal Online* (December 31, 2001).

Deferred Tax Asset—Valuation Allowance

Companies recognize a deferred tax asset for all deductible temporary differences. However, based on available evidence, a company should reduce a deferred tax asset by a **valuation allowance** if **it is more likely than not** that it **will not realize** some portion or all of the deferred tax asset. **"More likely than not"** means a level of likelihood of at least slightly more than 50 percent.

Objective·4
Explain the purpose of a deferred tax asset valuation allowance.

Assume that Jensen Co. has a deductible temporary difference of $1,000,000 at the end of its first year of operations. Its tax rate is 40 percent, which means it records a deferred tax asset of $400,000 ($1,000,000 × 40%). Assuming $900,000 of income taxes payable, Jensen records income tax expense, the deferred tax asset, and income tax payable as follows.

Income Tax Expense	500,000	
Deferred Tax Asset	400,000	
Income Tax Payable		900,000

After careful review of all available evidence, Jensen determines that it is more likely than not that it will not realize $100,000 of this deferred tax asset. Jensen records this reduction in asset value as follows.

Income Tax Expense	100,000	
Allowance to Reduce Deferred Tax Asset		
to Expected Realizable Value		100,000

This journal entry increases income tax expense in the current period because Jensen does not expect to realize a favorable tax benefit for a portion of the deductible temporary difference. Jensen **simultaneously establishes a valuation allowance to recognize the reduction in the carrying amount of the deferred tax asset**. This valuation account is a contra account. Jensen reports it on the financial statements in the following manner.

ILLUSTRATION 19-19
Balance Sheet Presentation
of Valuation Allowance
Account

Deferred tax asset	$400,000
Less: Allowance to reduce deferred tax	
asset to expected realizable value	100,000
Deferred tax asset (net)	$300,000

Jensen then evaluates this allowance account at the end of each accounting period. If, at the end of the next period, the deferred tax asset is still $400,000, but now it expects to realize $350,000 of this asset, Jensen makes the following entry to adjust the valuation account.

Allowance to Reduce Deferred Tax Asset to Expected Realizable Value	50,000	
Income Tax Expense		50,000

Jensen should consider all available evidence, both positive and negative, to determine whether, based on the weight of available evidence, it needs a valuation allowance. For example, if Jensen has been experiencing a series of loss years, it reasonably assumes that these losses will continue. Therefore, Jensen will lose the benefit of the future deductible amounts. We discuss the use of a valuation account under other conditions later in the chapter.

Income Statement Presentation

Objective·5
Describe the presentation of income tax expense in the income statement.

Circumstances dictate whether a company should add or subtract the change in deferred income taxes to or from income tax payable in computing income tax expense. For example, a company adds an increase in a deferred tax liability to income tax payable. On the other hand, it subtracts an increase in a deferred tax asset from income tax payable. The formula in Illustration 19-20 is used to compute income tax expense (benefit).

ILLUSTRATION 19-20
Formula to Compute
Income Tax Expense

Income Tax Payable or Refundable	±	**Change in Deferred Income Taxes**	=	**Total Income Tax Expense or Benefit**

In the income statement or in the notes to the financial statements, a company should disclose the significant components of income tax expense attributable to continuing operations. Given the information related to Chelsea on page 993, Chelsea reports its income statement as follows.

ILLUSTRATION 19-21
Income Statement
Presentation of Income
Tax Expense

CHELSEA INC.
INCOME STATEMENT
FOR THE YEAR ENDING DECEMBER 31, 2010

Revenues		$130,000
Expenses		60,000
Income before income taxes		70,000
Income tax expense		
Current	$16,000	
Deferred	12,000	28,000
Net income		$ 42,000

As illustrated, Chelsea reports both the current portion (amount of income tax payable for the period) and the deferred portion of income tax expense. Another option is to simply report the total income tax expense on the income statement, and then indicate in the notes to the financial statements the current and deferred portions. Income tax expense is often referred to as "Provision for income taxes." Using this terminology, the current provision is $16,000, and the provision for deferred taxes is $12,000.

Specific Differences

Numerous items create differences between pretax financial income and taxable income. For purposes of accounting recognition, these differences are of two types: (1) temporary, and (2) permanent.

> **Objective·6**
> Describe various temporary and permanent differences.

Temporary Differences

Taxable temporary differences are temporary differences that will result in taxable amounts in future years when the related assets are recovered. **Deductible temporary differences** are temporary differences that will result in deductible amounts in future years, when the related book liabilities are settled. Taxable temporary differences give rise to recording deferred tax liabilities. Deductible temporary differences give rise to recording deferred tax assets. Illustration 19-22 provides examples of temporary differences.

ILLUSTRATION 19-22
Examples of Temporary Differences

A. **Revenues or gains are taxable after they are recognized in financial income.**
   An asset (e.g., accounts receivable or investment) may be recognized for revenues or gains that will result in **taxable amounts in future years** when the asset is recovered. Examples:
   1. Sales accounted for on the accrual basis for financial reporting purposes and on the installment (cash) basis for tax purposes.
   2. Contracts accounted for under the percentage-of-completion method for financial reporting purposes and a portion of related gross profit deferred for tax purposes.
   3. Investments accounted for under the equity method for financial reporting purposes and under the cost method for tax purposes.
   4. Gain on involuntary conversion of nonmonetary asset which is recognized for financial reporting purposes but deferred for tax purposes.
   5. Unrealized holding gains for financial reporting purposes (including use of the fair value option), but deferred for tax purposes.

B. **Expenses or losses are deductible after they are recognized in financial income.**
   A liability (or contra asset) may be recognized for expenses or losses that will result in **deductible amounts in future years** when the liability is settled. Examples:
   1. Product warranty liabilities.
   2. Estimated liabilities related to discontinued operations or restructurings.
   3. Litigation accruals.
   4. Bad debt expense recognized using the allowance method for financial reporting purposes; direct write-off method used for tax purposes.
   5. Stock-based compensation expense.
   6. Unrealized holding losses for financial reporting purposes (including use of the fair value option), but deferred for tax purposes.

C. **Revenues or gains are taxable before they are recognized in financial income.**
   A liability may be recognized for an advance payment for goods or services to be provided in future years. For tax purposes, the advance payment is included in taxable income upon the receipt of cash. Future sacrifices to provide goods or services (or future refunds to those who cancel their orders) that settle the liability will result in **deductible amounts in future years**. Examples:
   1. Subscriptions received in advance.
   2. Advance rental receipts.
   3. Sales and leasebacks for financial reporting purposes (income deferral) but reported as sales for tax purposes.
   4. Prepaid contracts and royalties received in advance.

D. **Expenses or losses are deductible before they are recognized in financial income.**
   The cost of an asset may have been deducted for tax purposes faster than it was expensed for financial reporting purposes. Amounts received upon future recovery of the amount of the asset for financial reporting (through use or sale) will exceed the remaining tax basis of the asset and thereby result in **taxable amounts in future years**. Examples:
   1. Depreciable property, depletable resources, and intangibles.
   2. Deductible pension funding exceeding expense.
   3. Prepaid expenses that are deducted on the tax return in the period paid.

Determining a company's temporary differences may prove difficult. A company should prepare a balance sheet for tax purposes that it can compare with its GAAP balance sheet. Many of the differences between the two balance sheets are temporary differences.

Originating and Reversing Aspects of Temporary Differences. An **originating temporary difference** is the initial difference between the book basis and the tax basis of an asset or liability, regardless of whether the tax basis of the asset or liability exceeds or is exceeded by the book basis of the asset or liability. A **reversing difference**, on the other hand, occurs when eliminating a temporary difference that originated in prior periods and then removing the related tax effect from the deferred tax account.

For example, assume that Sharp Co. has tax depreciation in excess of book depreciation of $2,000 in 2008, 2009, and 2010. Further, it has an excess of book depreciation over tax depreciation of $3,000 in 2011 and 2012 for the same asset. Assuming a tax rate of 30 percent for all years involved, the Deferred Tax Liability account reflects the following.

ILLUSTRATION 19-23
Tax Effects of Originating and Reversing Differences

	Deferred Tax Liability						
Tax Effects of Reversing Differences	2011	900	2008	600	Tax Effects of Originating Differences		
	2012	900	2009	600			
			2010	600			

The originating differences for Sharp in each of the first three years are $2,000. The related tax effect of each originating difference is $600. The reversing differences in 2011 and 2012 are each $3,000. The related tax effect of each is $900.

Permanent Differences

Some differences between taxable income and pretax financial income are permanent. **Permanent differences** result from items that (1) enter into pretax financial income but **never** into taxable income, or (2) enter into taxable income but **never** into pretax financial income.

Congress has enacted a variety of tax law provisions to attain certain political, economic, and social objectives. Some of these provisions exclude certain revenues from taxation, limit the deductibility of certain expenses, and permit the deduction of certain other expenses in excess of costs incurred. A corporation that has tax-free income, nondeductible expenses, or allowable deductions in excess of cost, has an effective tax rate that differs from its statutory (regular) tax rate.

Since permanent differences affect only the period in which they occur, they do not give rise to future taxable or deductible amounts. As a result, **companies recognize no deferred tax consequences**. Illustration 19-24 shows examples of permanent differences.

ILLUSTRATION 19-24
Examples of Permanent Differences

A. **Items are recognized for financial reporting purposes but not for tax purposes.**
   Examples:
   1. Interest received on state and municipal obligations.
   2. Expenses incurred in obtaining tax-exempt income.
   3. Proceeds from life insurance carried by the company on key officers or employees.
   4. Premiums paid for life insurance carried by the company on key officers or employees (company is beneficiary).
   5. Fines and expenses resulting from a violation of law.
B. **Items are recognized for tax purposes but not for financial reporting purposes.**
   Examples:
   1. "Percentage depletion" of natural resources in excess of their cost.
   2. The deduction for dividends received from U.S. corporations, generally 70% or 80%.

Examples of Temporary and Permanent Differences

To illustrate the computations used when both temporary and permanent differences exist, assume that Bio-Tech Company reports pretax financial income of $200,000 in each of the years 2008, 2009, and 2010. The company is subject to a 30 percent tax rate, and has the following differences between pretax financial income and taxable income.

1. Bio-Tech reports an installment sale of $18,000 in 2008 for tax purposes over an 18-month period at a constant amount per month beginning January 1, 2009. It recognizes the entire sale for book purposes in 2008.
2. It pays life insurance premiums for its key officers of $5,000 in 2009 and 2010. Although not tax-deductible, Bio-Tech expenses the premiums for book purposes.

The installment sale is a temporary difference, whereas the life insurance premium is a permanent difference. Illustration 19-25 shows the reconciliation of Bio-Tech's pretax financial income to taxable income and the computation of income tax payable.

	2008	2009	2010
Pretax financial income	$200,000	$200,000	$200,000
Permanent difference			
Nondeductible expense		5,000	5,000
Temporary difference			
Installment sale	(18,000)	12,000	6,000
Taxable income	182,000	217,000	211,000
Tax rate	30%	30%	30%
Income tax payable	$ 54,600	$ 65,100	$ 63,300

ILLUSTRATION 19-25
Reconciliation and Computation of Income Taxes Payable

Note that Bio-Tech **deducts** the installment sales revenue from pretax financial income to arrive at taxable income. The reason: pretax financial income includes the installment sales revenue; taxable income does not. Conversely, it **adds** the $5,000 insurance premium to pretax financial income to arrive at taxable income. The reason: pretax financial income records an expense for this premium, but for tax purposes the premium is not deductible. As a result, pretax financial income is lower than taxable income. Therefore, the life insurance premium must be added back to pretax financial income to reconcile to taxable income.

Bio-Tech records income taxes for 2008, 2009, and 2010 as follows.

December 31, 2008

Income Tax Expense ($54,600 + $5,400)	60,000	
Deferred Tax Liability ($18,000 × 30%)		5,400
Income Tax Payable ($182,000 × 30%)		54,600

December 31, 2009

Income Tax Expense ($65,100 − $3,600)	61,500	
Deferred Tax Liability ($12,000 × 30%)	3,600	
Income Tax Payable ($217,000 × 30%)		65,100

December 31, 2010

Income Tax Expense ($63,300 − $1,800)	61,500	
Deferred Tax Liability ($6,000 × 30%)	1,800	
Income Tax Payable ($211,000 × 30%)		63,300

Bio-Tech has one temporary difference, which originates in 2008 and reverses in 2009 and 2010. It recognizes a deferred tax liability at the end of 2008 because the temporary difference causes future taxable amounts. As the temporary difference reverses, Bio-Tech reduces the deferred tax liability. There is no deferred tax amount associated with the difference caused by the nondeductible insurance expense because it is a permanent difference.

Although an enacted tax rate of 30 percent applies for all three years, the effective rate differs from the enacted rate in 2009 and 2010. Bio-Tech computes the **effective tax rate** by dividing total income tax expense for the period by pretax financial income. The effective rate is 30 percent for 2008 ($60,000 ÷ $200,000 = 30%) and 30.75 percent for 2009 and 2010 ($61,500 ÷ $200,000 = 30.75%).

Tax Rate Considerations

> **Objective·7**
> Explain the effect of various tax rates and tax rate changes on deferred income taxes.

In our previous illustrations, the enacted tax rate did not change from one year to the next. Thus, to compute the deferred income tax amount to report on the balance sheet, a company simply multiplies the cumulative temporary difference by the current tax rate. Using Bio-Tech as an example, it multiplies the cumulative temporary difference of $18,000 by the enacted tax rate, 30 percent in this case, to arrive at a deferred tax liability of $5,400 ($18,000 × 30%) at the end of 2008.

Future Tax Rates

What happens if tax rates are expected to change in the future? In this case, a company should use the **enacted tax rate** expected to apply. Therefore, a company must consider presently enacted changes in the tax rate that become effective for a particular future year(s) when determining the tax rate to apply to existing temporary differences. For example, assume that Warlen Co. at the end of 2007 has the following cumulative temporary difference of $300,000, computed as shown in Illustration 19-26.

ILLUSTRATION 19-26
Computation of Cumulative Temporary Difference

Book basis of depreciable assets	$1,000,000
Tax basis of depreciable assets	700,000
Cumulative temporary difference	$ 300,000

Furthermore, assume that the $300,000 will reverse and result in taxable amounts in the future, with the enacted tax rates shown in Illustration 19-27.

ILLUSTRATION 19-27
Deferred Tax Liability Based on Future Rates

	2008	2009	2010	2011	2012	Total
Future taxable amounts	$80,000	$70,000	$60,000	$50,000	$40,000	$300,000
Tax rate	40%	40%	35%	30%	30%	
Deferred tax liability	$32,000	$28,000	$21,000	$15,000	$12,000	$108,000

The total deferred tax liability at the end of 2007 is $108,000. Warlen may only use tax rates other than the current rate when the future tax rates have been enacted, as is the case in this example. **If new rates are not yet enacted for future years, Warlen should use the current rate.**

In determining the appropriate enacted tax rate for a given year, companies must use the **average tax rate**. The Internal Revenue Service and other taxing jurisdictions tax income on a graduated tax basis. For a U.S. corporation, the IRS taxes the first $50,000 of taxable income at 15 percent, the next $25,000 at 25 percent, with higher incremental levels of income at rates as high as 39 percent. In computing deferred income taxes, companies for which graduated tax rates are a significant factor must therefore **determine the average tax rate and use that rate**.

Revision of Future Tax Rates

When a change in the tax rate is enacted, companies should record its effect on the existing deferred income tax accounts immediately. **A company reports the effect as an adjustment to income tax expense in the period of the change.**

Assume that on December 10, 2007, a new income tax act is signed into law that lowers the corporate tax rate from 40 percent to 35 percent, effective January 1, 2009.

If Hostel Co. has one temporary difference at the beginning of 2007 related to $3 million of excess tax depreciation, then it has a Deferred Tax Liability account with a balance of $1,200,000 ($3,000,000 × 40%) at January 1, 2007. If taxable amounts related to this difference are scheduled to occur equally in 2008, 2009, and 2010, the deferred tax liability at the end of 2007 is $1,100,000, computed as follows.

	2008	2009	2010	Total
Future taxable amounts	$1,000,000	$1,000,000	$1,000,000	$3,000,000
Tax rate	40%	35%	35%	
Deferred tax liability	$ 400,000	$ 350,000	$ 350,000	$1,100,000

ILLUSTRATION 19-28
Schedule of Future Taxable Amounts and Related Tax Rates

Hostel, therefore, recognizes the decrease of $100,000 ($1,200,000 − $1,100,000) at the end of 2007 in the deferred tax liability as follows.

Deferred Tax Liability	100,000	
Income Tax Expense		100,000

Corporate tax rates do not change often. Therefore, companies usually employ the current rate. However, state and foreign tax rates change more frequently, and they require adjustments in deferred income taxes accordingly.[2]

SHELTERED

As mentioned in the opening story, companies employ various tax strategies to reduce their tax bills and their effective tax rates. The following table reports some high-profile cases in which profitable companies paid little income tax and, in some cases, got tax refunds.

What do the numbers mean?

Company	Pretax Income ($ millions)	Federal Tax Paid (Refund) ($ millions)	Tax Rate (%)
Enron	$ 1,785	$(381)	(21.34)%
El Paso Energy	1,638	(254)	(15.51)
Goodyear	442	(23)	(5.20)
Navistar	1,368	28	2.05
General Motors	12,468	740	5.94

These companies used various tools to lower their tax bills, including off-shore tax shelters, tax deferrals, and hefty use of stock options, the cost of which reduce taxable income but do not affect pretax financial income. Thus, companies can use various provisions in the tax code to reduce their effective tax rate well below the statutory rate of 35 percent.

One IRS provision designed to curb excessive tax avoidance is the **alternative minimum tax (AMT)**. Companies compute their potential tax liability under the AMT, adjusting for various preference items that reduce their tax bills under the regular tax code. (Examples of such preference items are accelerated depreciation methods and the installment method for revenue recognition.) Companies must pay the higher of the two tax obligations computed under the AMT and the regular tax code. But, as indicated by the cases above, some profitable companies avoid high tax bills, even in the presence of the AMT. Indeed, a recent study by the Government Accounting Office found that roughly two-thirds of U.S. and foreign corporations paid no federal income taxes from 1998–2005. Many citizens and public-interest groups cite corporate avoidance of income taxes as a reason for more tax reform.

Source: H. Gleckman, D. Foust, M. Arndt, and K. Kerwin, "Tax Dodging: Enron Isn't Alone," *Business Week* (March 4, 2002), pp. 40–41; and L. Browning, "Study Tallies Corporations Not Paying Income Tax," *New York Times* (August 13, 2008), p. C3.

---

[2]Tax rate changes nearly always will substantially impact income numbers and the reporting of deferred income taxes on the balance sheet. As a result, you can expect to hear an economic consequences argument every time that Congress decides to change the tax rates. For example, when Congress raised the corporate rate from 34 percent to 35 percent in 1993, companies took an additional "hit" to earnings if they were in a deferred tax liability position.

ACCOUNTING FOR NET OPERATING LOSSES

Every management hopes its company will be profitable. But hopes and profits may not materialize. For a start-up company, it is common to accumulate operating losses while expanding its customer base but before realizing economies of scale. For an established company, a major event such as a labor strike, rapidly changing regulatory and competitive forces, or a disaster such as 9/11 or Hurricane Ike can cause expenses to exceed revenues—a net operating loss.

A **net operating loss (NOL)** occurs for tax purposes in a year when tax-deductible expenses exceed taxable revenues. An inequitable tax burden would result if companies were taxed during profitable periods without receiving any tax relief during periods of net operating losses. Under certain circumstances, therefore, the federal tax laws permit taxpayers to use the losses of one year to offset the profits of other years.

Companies accomplish this income-averaging provision through the **carryback and carryforward of net operating losses**. Under this provision, a company pays no income taxes for a year in which it incurs a net operating loss. In addition, it may select one of the two options discussed below and on the following pages.

Loss Carryback

Through use of a **loss carryback**, a company may carry the net operating loss back two years and receive refunds for income taxes paid in those years. The company must apply the loss to the earlier year first and then to the second year. It may **carry forward** any loss remaining after the two-year carryback up to 20 years to offset future taxable income. Illustration 19-29 diagrams the loss carryback procedure, assuming a loss in 2010.

ILLUSTRATION 19-29
Loss Carryback Procedure

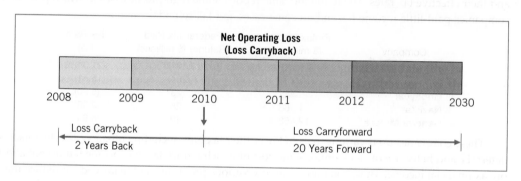

Loss Carryforward

A company may forgo the loss carryback and use only the **loss carryforward** option, offsetting future taxable income for up to 20 years. Illustration 19-30 shows this approach.

ILLUSTRATION 19-30
Loss Carryforward Procedure

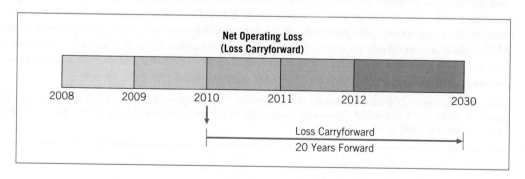

Operating losses can be substantial. For example, **Yahoo!** had net operating losses of approximately $5.4 billion in a recent year. That amount translates into tax savings of $1.4 billion if Yahoo! is able to generate taxable income before the NOLs expire.

Loss Carryback Example

To illustrate the accounting procedures for a net operating loss carryback, assume that Groh Inc. has no temporary or permanent differences. Groh experiences the following.

Year	Taxable Income or Loss	Tax Rate	Tax Paid
2006	$ 50,000	35%	$17,500
2007	100,000	30%	30,000
2008	200,000	40%	80,000
2009	(500,000)	—	–0–

In 2009, Groh incurs a net operating loss that it decides to carry back. Under the law, Groh must apply the carryback first to the **second year preceding the loss year**. Therefore, it carries the loss back first to 2007. Then, Groh carries back any unused loss to 2008. Accordingly, Groh files amended tax returns for 2007 and 2008, receiving refunds for the $110,000 ($30,000 + $80,000) of taxes paid in those years.

For accounting as well as tax purposes, the $110,000 represents the **tax effect (tax benefit)** of the loss carryback. Groh should recognize this tax effect in 2009, the loss year. Since the tax loss gives rise to a refund that is both measurable and currently realizable, Groh should recognize the associated tax benefit in this loss period.

Groh makes the following journal entry for 2009.

Income Tax Refund Receivable	110,000	
Benefit Due to Loss Carryback (Income Tax Expense)		110,000

Groh reports the account debited, **Income Tax Refund Receivable**, on the balance sheet as a current asset at December 31, 2009. It reports the account credited on the income statement for 2009 as shown in Illustration 19-31.

GROH INC.	
INCOME STATEMENT (PARTIAL) FOR 2009	
Operating loss before income taxes	$(500,000)
Income tax benefit	
Benefit due to loss carryback	110,000
Net loss	$(390,000)

ILLUSTRATION 19-31
Recognition of Benefit of the Loss Carryback in the Loss Year

Since the $500,000 net operating loss for 2009 exceeds the $300,000 total taxable income from the 2 preceding years, Groh carries forward the remaining $200,000 loss.

Loss Carryforward Example

If a carryback fails to fully absorb a net operating loss, or if the company decides not to carry the loss back, then it can carry forward the loss for up to 20 years.[3] Because companies use carryforwards to offset future taxable income, the **tax effect of a loss carryforward** represents **future tax savings**. Realization of the future tax benefit depends on future earnings, an uncertain prospect.

The key accounting issue is whether there should be different requirements for recognition of a deferred tax asset for (a) deductible temporary differences, and (b) operating loss carryforwards. The FASB's position is that in substance these items are the same—both are tax-deductible amounts in future years. As a result, the Board concluded that there **should not be different requirements** for recognition of

---

[3]The length of the carryforward period has varied. It has increased from 7 years to 20 years over a period of time.

a deferred tax asset from deductible temporary differences and operating loss carry-forwards.[4]

Carryforward without Valuation Allowance

To illustrate the accounting for an operating loss carryforward, return to the Groh example from the preceding section. In 2009 the company records the tax effect of the $200,000 loss carryforward as a deferred tax asset of $80,000 ($200,000 × 40%), assuming that the enacted future tax rate is 40 percent. Groh records the benefits of the carryback and the carryforward in 2009 as follows.

To recognize benefit of loss carryback

Income Tax Refund Receivable	110,000	
Benefit Due to Loss Carryback (Income Tax Expense)		110,000

To recognize benefit of loss carryforward

Deferred Tax Asset	80,000	
Benefit Due to Loss Carryforward (Income Tax Expense)		80,000

Groh realizes the income tax refund receivable of $110,000 immediately as a refund of taxes paid in the past. It establishes a Deferred Tax Asset for the benefits of future tax savings. The two accounts credited are contra income tax expense items, which Groh presents on the 2009 income statement shown in Illustration 19-32.

ILLUSTRATION 19-32
Recognition of the Benefit of the Loss Carryback and Carryforward in the Loss Year

GROH INC.
INCOME STATEMENT (PARTIAL) FOR 2009

Operating loss before income taxes		$(500,000)
Income tax benefit		
Benefit due to loss carryback	$110,000	
Benefit due to loss carryforward	80,000	190,000
Net loss		$(310,000)

The **current tax benefit** of $110,000 is the income tax refundable for the year. Groh determines this amount by applying the carryback provisions of the tax law to the taxable loss for 2009. The $80,000 is the **deferred tax benefit** for the year, which results from an increase in the deferred tax asset.

For 2010, assume that Groh returns to profitable operations and has taxable income of $250,000 (prior to adjustment for the NOL carryforward), subject to a 40 percent tax rate. Groh then realizes the benefits of the carryforward for tax purposes in 2010, which it recognized for accounting purposes in 2009. Groh computes the income tax payable for 2010 as shown in Illustration 19-33.

ILLUSTRATION 19-33
Computation of Income Tax Payable with Realized Loss Carryforward

Taxable income prior to loss carryforward	$ 250,000
Loss carryforward deduction	(200,000)
Taxable income for 2010	50,000
Tax rate	40%
Income tax payable for 2010	$ 20,000

Groh records income taxes in 2010 as follows.

Income Tax Expense	100,000	
Deferred Tax Asset		80,000
Income Tax Payable		20,000

[4]This requirement is controversial because many believe it is inappropriate to recognize deferred tax assets except when assured beyond a reasonable doubt. Others argue that companies should never recognize deferred tax assets for loss carryforwards until realizing the income in the future.

The benefits of the NOL carryforward, realized in 2010, reduce the Deferred Tax Asset account to zero.

The 2010 income statement that appears in Illustration 19-34 does **not report** the tax effects of either the loss carryback or the loss carryforward, because Groh had reported both previously.

GROH INC. INCOME STATEMENT (PARTIAL) FOR 2010		
Income before income taxes		$250,000
Income tax expense		
Current	$20,000	
Deferred	80,000	100,000
Net income		$150,000

ILLUSTRATION 19-34
Presentation of the Benefit of Loss Carryforward Realized in 2010, Recognized in 2009

Carryforward with Valuation Allowance

Let us return to the Groh example. Assume that it is more likely than not that Groh will *not* realize the entire NOL carryforward in future years. In this situation, Groh records the tax benefits of $110,000 associated with the $300,000 NOL carryback, as we previously described. In addition, it records a Deferred Tax Asset of $80,000 ($200,000 × 40%) for the potential benefits related to the loss carryforward, and an allowance to reduce the deferred tax asset by the same amount. Groh makes the following journal entries in 2009.

To recognize benefit of loss carryback

Income Tax Refund Receivable	110,000	
Benefit Due to Loss Carryback (Income Tax Expense)		110,000

To recognize benefit of loss carryforward

Deferred Tax Asset	80,000	
Benefit Due to Loss Carryforward (Income Tax Expense)		80,000

To record allowance amount

Benefit Due to Loss Carryforward (Income Tax Expense)	80,000	
Allowance to Reduce Deferred Tax Asset to Expected Realizable Value		80,000

The latter entry indicates that because positive evidence of sufficient quality and quantity is unavailable to counteract the negative evidence, Groh needs a valuation allowance. Illustration 19-35 shows Groh's 2009 income statement presentation.

GROH INC. INCOME STATEMENT (PARTIAL) FOR 2009	
Operating loss before income taxes	$(500,000)
Income tax benefit	
Benefit due to loss carryback	110,000
Net loss	$(390,000)

ILLUSTRATION 19-35
Recognition of Benefit of Loss Carryback Only

In 2010, assuming that Groh has taxable income of $250,000 (before considering the carryforward), subject to a tax rate of 40 percent, it realizes the deferred tax asset. It thus no longer needs the allowance. Groh records the following entries.

To record current and deferred income taxes

Income Tax Expense	100,000	
Deferred Tax Asset		80,000
Income Tax Payable		20,000

To eliminate allowance and recognize loss carryforward

Allowance to Reduce Deferred Tax Asset to Expected Realizable Value	80,000	
Benefit Due to Loss Carryforward (Income Tax Expense)		80,000

Groh reports the $80,000 Benefit Due to the Loss Carryforward on the 2010 income statement. The company did not recognize it in 2009 because it was more likely than not that it would not be realized. Assuming that Groh derives the income for 2010 from continuing operations, it prepares the income statement as shown in Illustration 19-36.

ILLUSTRATION 19-36
Recognition of Benefit of
Loss Carryforward When
Realized

GROH INC.		
INCOME STATEMENT (PARTIAL) FOR 2010		
Income before income taxes		$250,000
Income tax expense		
Current	$ 20,000	
Deferred	80,000	
Benefit due to loss carryforward	(80,000)	20,000
Net income		$230,000

Another method is to report only one line for total income tax expense of $20,000 on the face of the income statement and disclose the components of income tax expense in the notes to the financial statements.

Valuation Allowance Revisited

A company should consider all positive and negative information in determining whether it needs a valuation allowance. Whether the company will realize a deferred tax asset depends on whether sufficient taxable income exists or will exist within the carryforward period available under tax law. Illustration 19-37 shows possible sources of taxable income that may be available under the tax law to realize a tax benefit for deductible temporary differences and carryforwards.[5]

ILLUSTRATION 19-37
Possible Sources of
Taxable Income

Taxable Income Sources

a. Future reversals of existing taxable temporary differences

b. Future taxable income exclusive of reversing temporary differences and carryforwards

c. Taxable income in prior carryback year(s) if carryback is permitted under the tax law

d. Tax-planning strategies that would, if necessary, be implemented to:
  (1) Accelerate taxable amounts to utilize expiring carryforwards
  (2) Change the character of taxable or deductible amounts from ordinary income or loss to capital gain or loss
  (3) Switch from tax-exempt to taxable investments. [1]

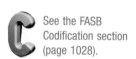

See the FASB
Codification section
(page 1028).

If any one of these sources is sufficient to support a conclusion that a valuation allowance is unnecessary, a company need not consider other sources.

Forming a conclusion that a valuation allowance is not needed is difficult when there is negative evidence such as cumulative losses in recent years. Companies may also cite positive evidence indicating that a valuation allowance is not needed. Illustration 19-38 (on page 1011) presents examples (not prerequisites) of evidence to consider when determining the need for a valuation allowance.[6]

---

[5]Companies implement a tax-planning strategy to realize a tax benefit for an operating loss or tax credit carryforward before it expires. Companies consider tax-planning strategies when assessing the need for and amount of a valuation allowance for deferred tax assets.

[6]General Motors announced that it would record a charge of $39 billion for the third quarter of 2007 related to establishing a valuation allowance against its deferred assets in the U.S., Canada, and Germany. The company noted that this large loss was taken because of the company's three-year historical loss up to the third quarter of 2007, its losses related to its mortgage business in GMAC financial services, and the challenging near-term automotive market conditions in the U.S. and Germany. These all indicate that it will be more likely than not that GM will not realize its deferred tax asset.

ILLUSTRATION 19-38
Evidence to Consider in
Evaluating the Need for a
Valuation Account

Negative Evidence

a. A history of operating loss or tax credit carryforwards expiring unused

b. Losses expected in early future years (by a presently profitable entity)

c. Unsettled circumstances that, if unfavorably resolved, would adversely affect future operations and profit levels on a continuing basis in future years

d. A carryback, carryforward period that is so brief that it would limit realization of tax benefits if (1) a significant deductible temporary difference is expected to reverse in a single year or (2) the enterprise operates in a traditionally cyclical business.

Positive Evidence

a. Existing contracts or firm sales backlog that will produce more than enough taxable income to realize the deferred tax asset based on existing sale prices and cost structures

b. An excess of appreciated asset value over the tax basis of the entity's net assets in an amount sufficient to realize the deferred tax asset

c. A strong earnings history exclusive of the loss that created the future deductible amount (tax loss carryforward or deductible temporary difference) coupled with evidence indicating that the loss is an aberration rather than a continuing condition (for example, the result of an unusual, infrequent, or extraordinary item). [2]

The use of a valuation allowance provides a company with an opportunity to manage its earnings. As one accounting expert notes, "The 'more likely than not' provision is perhaps the most judgmental clause in accounting." Some companies may set up a valuation account and then use it to increase income as needed. Others may take the income immediately to increase capital or to offset large negative charges to income.

INTERNATIONAL INSIGHT

Under international accounting standards *(IAS 12)*, a company may not recognize a deferred tax asset unless realization is "probable." However, "probable" is not defined in the standard, leading to diversity in the recognition of deferred tax assets.

READ THOSE NOTES

A recent study of companies' valuation allowances indicates that the allowances are related to the factors identified as positive and negative evidence. And though there is little evidence that companies use the valuation allowance to manage earnings, the press sometimes understates the impact of reversing the deferred tax valuation allowance.

For example, in one year **Verity, Inc.** eliminated its entire valuation allowance of $18.9 million but focused on a net deferred tax gain of $2.9 million in its press release. Why the difference? As revealed in Verity's financial statement notes, other deferred tax expense amounts totaled over $16 million. Thus, the one-time valuation reversal gave an $18.9 million bump to income, not the net $2.9 million reported in the press.

The lesson: After you read the morning paper, read the financial statement notes.

Source: G. S Miller and D. J. Skinner, "Determinants of the Valuation Allowance for Deferred Tax Assets under *SFAS No. 109*," *The Accounting Review* (April 1998).

What do the numbers mean?

FINANCIAL STATEMENT PRESENTATION

Balance Sheet

Deferred tax accounts are reported on the balance sheet as assets and liabilities. Companies should classify these accounts as a net current amount and a net noncurrent amount. **An individual deferred tax liability or asset is classified as current or noncurrent based on the classification of the related asset or liability for financial reporting purposes.**

A company considers a deferred tax asset or liability to be related to an asset or liability, if reduction of the asset or liability causes the temporary difference to reverse or

Objective·9
Describe the presentation of deferred income taxes in financial statements.

turn around. A company should classify a deferred tax liability or asset that is unrelated to an asset or liability for financial reporting, including a deferred tax asset related to a loss carryforward, according to the expected reversal date of the temporary difference.

To illustrate, assume that Morgan Inc. records bad debt expense using the allowance method for accounting purposes and the direct write-off method for tax purposes. It currently has Accounts Receivable and Allowance for Doubtful Accounts balances of $2 million and $100,000, respectively. In addition, given a 40 percent tax rate, Morgan has a debit balance in the Deferred Tax Asset account of $40,000 (40% × $100,000). It considers the $40,000 debit balance in the Deferred Tax Asset account to be related to the Accounts Receivable and the Allowance for Doubtful Accounts balances because collection or write-off of the receivables will cause the temporary difference to reverse. Therefore, Morgan classifies the Deferred Tax Asset account as current, the same as the Accounts Receivable and Allowance for Doubtful Accounts balances.

In practice, most companies engage in a large number of transactions that give rise to deferred taxes. Companies should classify the balances in the deferred tax accounts on the balance sheet in two categories: one for the **net current amount**, and one for the **net noncurrent amount**. We summarize this procedure as follows.

1. *Classify the amounts as current or noncurrent.* If related to a specific asset or liability, classify the amounts in the same manner as the related asset or liability. If not related, classify them on the basis of the expected reversal date of the temporary difference.
2. *Determine the net current amount* by summing the various deferred tax assets and liabilities classified as current. If the net result is an asset, report it on the balance sheet as a current asset; if a liability, report it as a current liability.
3. *Determine the net noncurrent amount* by summing the various deferred tax assets and liabilities classified as noncurrent. If the net result is an asset, report it on the balance sheet as a noncurrent asset; if a liability, report it as a long-term liability.

To illustrate, assume that K. Scott Company has four deferred tax items at December 31, 2010. Illustration 19-39 shows an analysis of these four temporary differences as current or noncurrent.

ILLUSTRATION 19-39
Classification of Temporary Differences as Current or Noncurrent

Temporary Difference	Resulting Deferred Tax (Asset)	Liability	Related Balance Sheet Account	Classification
1. Rent collected in advance: recognized when earned for accounting purposes and when received for tax purposes.	$(42,000)		Unearned Rent	Current
2. Use of straight-line depreciation for accounting purposes and accelerated depreciation for tax purposes.		$214,000	Equipment	Noncurrent
3. Recognition of profits on installment sales during period of sale for accounting purposes and during period of collection for tax purposes.		45,000	Installment Accounts Receivable	Current
4. Warranty liabilities: recognized for accounting purposes at time of sale; for tax purposes at time paid.	(12,000)		Estimated Liability under Warranties	Current
Totals	$(54,000)	$259,000		

K. Scott classifies as current a deferred tax asset of $9,000 ($42,000 + $12,000 − $45,000). It also reports as noncurrent a deferred tax liability of $214,000. Consequently,

K. Scott's December 31, 2010, balance sheet reports deferred income taxes as shown in Illustration 19-40.

Current assets		
Deferred tax asset	$ 9,000	
Long-term liabilities		
Deferred tax liability	$214,000	

ILLUSTRATION 19-40
Balance Sheet Presentation of Deferred Income Taxes

As we indicated earlier, a deferred tax asset or liability **may not be related** to an asset or liability for financial reporting purposes. One example is an operating loss carryforward. In this case, a company records a deferred tax asset, but there is no related, identifiable asset or liability for financial reporting purposes. In these limited situations, deferred income taxes are classified according to the **expected reversal date** of the temporary difference. That is, a company should report the tax effect of any temporary difference reversing next year as current, and the remainder as noncurrent. If a deferred tax asset is noncurrent, a company should classify it in the "Other assets" section.

The total of all deferred tax liabilities, the total of all deferred tax assets, and the total valuation allowance should be disclosed. In addition, companies should disclose the following: (1) any net change during the year in the total valuation allowance, and (2) the types of temporary differences, carryforwards, or carrybacks that give rise to significant portions of deferred tax liabilities and assets.

Income tax payable is reported as a current liability on the balance sheet. Corporations make estimated tax payments to the Internal Revenue Service quarterly. They record these estimated payments by a debit to Prepaid Income Taxes. As a result, the balance of the Income Tax Payable offsets the balance of the Prepaid Income Taxes account when reporting income taxes on the balance sheet.

> **INTERNATIONAL INSIGHT**
>
> iGAAP requires that deferred tax assets and liabilities be classified as noncurrent, regardless of the classification of the underlying asset or liability.

Income Statement

Companies should allocate income tax expense (or benefit) to continuing operations, discontinued operations, extraordinary items, and prior period adjustments. This approach is referred to as intraperiod tax allocation.

In addition, companies should disclose the significant components of income tax expense attributable to continuing operations:

Expanded Discussion of Intraperiod Tax Allocation

1. Current tax expense or benefit.
2. Deferred tax expense or benefit, exclusive of other components listed below.
3. Investment tax credits.
4. Government grants (if recognized as a reduction of income tax expense).
5. The benefits of operating loss carryforwards (resulting in a reduction of income tax expense).
6. Tax expense that results from allocating tax benefits either directly to paid-in capital or to reduce goodwill or other noncurrent intangible assets of an acquired entity.
7. Adjustments of a deferred tax liability or asset for enacted changes in tax laws or rates or a change in the tax status of a company.
8. Adjustments of the beginning-of-the-year balance of a valuation allowance because of a change in circumstances that causes a change in judgment about the realizability of the related deferred tax asset in future years.

In the notes, companies must also reconcile (using percentages or dollar amounts) income tax expense attributable to continuing operations with the amount that results from applying domestic federal statutory tax rates to pretax income from continuing significant reconciling items. Illustration 19-41 (on page 1014) presents an example from the 2007 annual report of **PepsiCo, Inc.**

ILLUSTRATION 19-41
Disclosure of Income
Taxes—PepsiCo, Inc.

PEPSICO

PepsiCo, Inc.
(in millions)

Note 5—Income Taxes (in part)	2007	2006
Income before income taxes		
U.S.	$4,085	$3,844
Foreign	3,546	3,145
	$7,631	$6,989
Provision for income taxes		
Current: U.S. Federal	$1,422	$ 776
Foreign	489	569
State	104	56
	2,015	1,401
Deferred: U.S. Federal	22	(31)
Foreign	(66)	(16)
State	2	(7)
	(42)	(54)
	$1,973	$1,347
Tax rate reconciliation		
U.S. Federal statutory tax rate	35.0%	35.0%
State income tax, net of U.S. Federal tax benefit	0.9	0.5
Lower taxes on foreign results	(6.5)	(6.5)
Tax settlements	(1.7)	(8.6)
Other, net	(1.8)	(1.1)
Annual tax rate	25.9%	19.3%
Deferred tax liabilities		
Investments in noncontrolled affiliates	$1,163	$1,103
Property, plant and equipment	828	784
Intangible assets other than nondeductible goodwill	280	169
Pension benefits	148	—
Other	136	248
Gross deferred tax liabilities	2,555	2,304
Deferred tax assets		
Net carryforwards	722	667
Stock-based compensation	425	443
Retiree medical benefits	528	541
Other employee-related benefits	447	342
Pension benefits	—	38
Deductible state tax and interest benefits	189	—
Other	618	592
Gross deferred tax assets	2,929	2,623
Valuation allowances	(695)	(624)
Deferred tax assets, net	2,234	1,999
Net deferred tax liabilities	$ 321	$ 305
Deferred taxes included within:		
Assets:		
Prepaid expenses and other current assets	$ 325	$ 223
Liabilities:		
Deferred income taxes	$ 646	$ 528
Analysis of valuation allowances		
Balance, beginning of year	$ 624	$ 532
Provision/(benefit)	39	71
Other additions/(deductions)	32	21
Balance, end of year	$ 695	$ 624

Labels in left margin:

Current and deferred tax expense

Tax rate reconciliation

Deferred tax liabilities and deferred tax assets

Valuation allowance adjustments

Carryforwards and Allowances

Operating loss carryforwards totaling $7.1 billion at year-end 2007 are being carried forward in a number of foreign and state jurisdictions where we are permitted to use tax operating losses from prior periods to reduce future taxable income. These operating losses will expire as follows: $0.5 billion in 2008, $5.6 billion between 2009 and 2027 and $1.0 billion may be carried forward indefinitely. We establish valuation allowances for our deferred tax assets if, based on the available evidence, it is more likely than not that some portion or all of the deferred tax assets will not be realized.

continued on next page

In 2006, the Financial Accounting Standards Board (FASB) issued FASB Interpretation No. 48, *Accounting for Uncertainty in Income Taxes—an Interpretation of FASB Statement No. 109*, (FIN 48), which clarifies the accounting for uncertainty in tax positions. FIN 48 requires that we recognize in our financial statements the impact of a tax position, if that position is more likely than not of being sustained on audit, based on the technical merits of the position. We adopted the provisions of FIN 48 as of the beginning of our 2007 fiscal year. As a result of our adoption of FIN 48, we recognized a $7 million decrease to reserves for income taxes, with a corresponding increase to opening retained earnings.

These income tax disclosures are required for several reasons:

1. *Assessing Quality of Earnings.* Many investors seeking to assess the quality of a company's earnings are interested in the reconciliation of pretax financial income to taxable income. Analysts carefully examine earnings that are enhanced by a favorable tax effect, particularly if the tax effect is nonrecurring. For example, the tax disclosure in Illustration 19-41 indicates that PepsiCo's effective tax rate increased from 19.3 percent in 2006 to 25.9 percent in 2007 (primarily due to less tax settlements in 2007). This increase in the effective tax rate decreased income for 2007.

2. *Making Better Predictions of Future Cash Flows.* Examination of the deferred portion of income tax expense provides information as to whether taxes payable are likely to be higher or lower in the future. In PepsiCo's case, analysts expect future taxable amounts and higher tax payments, due to realization of gains on equity investments, lower deprecation in the future, and higher payments for pension expense. PepsiCo expects future deductible amounts and lower tax payments due to deductions for carryforwards, employee benefits, and state taxes. These deferred tax items indicate that actual tax payments for PepsiCo will be higher than the tax expense reported on the income statement in the future.[7]

3. *Predicting Future Cash Flows for Operating Loss Carryforwards.* Companies should disclose the amounts and expiration dates of any operating loss carryforwards for tax purposes. From this disclosure, analysts determine the amount of income that the company may recognize in the future on which it will pay no income tax. For example, the PepsiCo disclosure in Illustration 19-41 indicates that PepsiCo has $7.1 billion in net operating loss carryforwards that it can use to reduce future taxes. However, the valuation allowance indicates that $695 million of deferred tax assets may not be realized in the future.

Additional Examples of Deferred Tax Disclosures

Loss carryforwards can be valuable to a potential acquirer. For example, as mentioned earlier, **Yahoo!** has a substantial net operating loss carryforward. A potential acquirer would find Yahoo more valuable as a result of these carryforwards. That is, the acquirer may be able to use these carryforwards to shield future income. However the acquiring company has to be careful, because the structure of the deal may lead to a situation where the deductions will be severely limited.

Much the same issue arises in companies emerging from bankruptcy. In many cases these companies have large NOLs, but the value of the losses may be limited. This is because any gains related to the cancellation of liabilities in bankruptcy must be offset against the NOLs. For example, when **Kmart Holding Corp.** emerged from bankruptcy in early 2004, it disclosed NOL carryforwards approximating $3.8 billion. At the same time, Kmart disclosed cancellation of debt gains that reduced the value of the NOL carryforward. These reductions soured the merger between Kmart and **Sears Roebuck** because the cancellation of the indebtedness gains reduced the value of the Kmart carryforwards to the merged company by $3.74 billion.[8]

[7]An article by R. P. Weber and J. E. Wheeler, "Using Income Tax Disclosures to Explore Significant Economic Transactions," *Accounting Horizons* (September 1992), discusses how analysts use deferred tax disclosures to assess the quality of earnings and to predict future cash flows.

[8]P. McConnell, J. Pegg, C. Senyak, and D. Mott, "The ABCs of NOLs," *Accounting Issues*, Bear Stearns Equity Research (June 2005). The IRS frowns on acquisitions done solely to obtain operating loss carryforwards. If it determines that the merger is solely tax-motivated, the IRS disallows the deductions. But because it is very difficult to determine whether a merger is or is not tax-motivated, the "purchase of operating loss carryforwards" continues.

NOLs: GOOD NEWS OR BAD?

What do the numbers mean?

Here are some net operating loss numbers reported by several notable companies.

NOLs ($ in millions)

Company	Income (Loss)	Operating Loss Carryforward	Tax Benefit (Deferred Tax Asset)	Comment
Delta Airlines, Inc.	($5,198.00)	$7,500.00	$2,848.00	Begins to expire in 2022. Valuation allowance recorded.
Goodyear	114.80	1,306.60	457.30	Begins to expire in next year. Full valuation allowance.
Kodak	556.00	509.00	234.00	Begins to expire in next year. Valuation allowance on foreign credits only.
Yahoo Inc.	42.82	5,400.00	1,443.50	State and federal carryforwards. Begins to expire in next year. Valuation allowance recorded.

All of these companies are using the carryforward provisions of the tax code for their NOLs. For many of them, the NOL is an amount far exceeding their reported profits. Why carry forward the loss to get the tax deduction? First, the company may have already used up the carryback provision, which allows only a two-year carryback period. (Carryforwards can be claimed up to 20 years in the future.) In some cases, management expects the tax rates in the future to be higher. This difference in expected rates provides a bigger tax benefit if the losses are carried forward and matched against future income. Is there a downside? To realize the benefits of carryforwards, a company must have future taxable income in the carryforward period in order to claim the NOL deductions. As we learned, if it is more likely than not that a company will not have taxable income, it must record a valuation allowance (and increased tax expense). As the data above indicate, recording a valuation allowance to reflect the uncertainty of realizing the tax benefits has merit. But for some, the NOL benefits begin to expire in the following year, which may be not enough time to generate sufficient taxable income in order to claim the NOL deduction.

Source: Company annual reports.

Uncertain Tax Positions

Whenever there is a contingency, companies determine if the contingency is *probable* and can be reasonably estimated. If both of these criteria are met, the company records the contingency in the financial statements. These guidelines also apply to uncertain tax positions. Uncertain tax positions are tax positions for which the tax authorities may disallow a deduction in whole or in part. Uncertain tax positions often arise when a company takes an aggressive approach in its tax planning. Examples are instances in which the tax law is unclear or the company may believe that the risk of audit is low. Uncertain tax positions give rise to tax benefits either by reducing income tax expense or related payables or by increasing an income tax refund receivable or deferred tax asset.

Unfortunately, companies have not applied these provisions consistently in accounting and reporting of uncertain tax positions. Some companies have not recognized a tax benefit unless it is probable that the benefit will be realized and can be reasonably estimated. Other companies have used a lower threshold, such as that found in the existing authoritative literature. As we have learned, the lower threshold—described as "*more likely than not*"—means that the company believes it has at least a 51 percent chance that the uncertain tax position will pass muster with the taxing authorities. Thus, there has been diversity in practice concerning the accounting and reporting of uncertain tax positions.

As a result, the FASB recently issued rules for companies to follow to determine whether it is "more likely than not" that tax positions will be sustained upon audit. [3] If the probability is more than 50 percent, companies may reduce their liability or increase their assets. If the probability is less that 50 percent, companies may not record the tax benefit. In determining "more likely than not," companies must assume that they will be audited by the tax authorities. If the recognition threshold is passed, companies must then estimate the amount to record as an adjustment to their tax assets and liabilities. (This estimation process is complex and is beyond the scope of this textbook.)

Companies will experience varying financial statement effects upon adoption of these rules. Those with a history of conservative tax strategies may have their tax liabilities decrease or their tax assets increase. Others that followed more aggressive tax planning may have to increase their liabilities or reduce their assets, with a resulting negative effect on net income. For example, as indicated in Illustration 19-41 (on page 1014), PepsiCo recorded a $7 million increase to retained earnings upon adoption of these new guidelines.

REVIEW OF THE ASSET-LIABILITY METHOD

The FASB believes that the **asset-liability method** (sometimes referred to as the **liability approach**) is the most consistent method for accounting for income taxes. One objective of this approach is to recognize the amount of taxes payable or refundable for the current year. A second objective is to recognize **deferred tax liabilities and assets** for the **future tax consequences** of events that have been recognized in the financial statements or tax returns.

> **Objective·10**
> Indicate the basic principles of the asset-liability method.

To implement the objectives, companies apply some basic principles in accounting for income taxes at the date of the financial statements, as listed in Illustration 19-42. [4]

ILLUSTRATION 19-42
Basic Principles of the Asset-Liability Method

> **Basic Principles**
>
> **a.** A current tax liability or asset is recognized for the estimated taxes payable or refundable on the tax return for the current year.
> **b.** A deferred tax liability or asset is recognized for the estimated future tax effects attributable to temporary differences and carryforwards.
> **c.** The measurement of current and deferred tax liabilities and assets is based on provisions of the enacted tax law; the effects of future changes in tax laws or rates are not anticipated.
> **d.** The measurement of deferred tax assets is reduced, if necessary, by the amount of any tax benefits that, based on available evidence, are not expected to be realized.

Illustration 19-43 diagrams the procedures for implementing the asset-liability method.

ILLUSTRATION 19-43
Procedures for Computing and Reporting Deferred Income Taxes

Discussion of Conceptual Approaches to Interperiod Tax Allocation

As an aid to understanding deferred income taxes, we provide the following glossary.

INTERNATIONAL INSIGHT

iGAAP on income taxes is based on the same principles as U.S. GAAP—comprehensive recognition of deferred tax assets and liabilities.

KEY DEFERRED INCOME TAX TERMS

CARRYBACKS. Deductions or credits that cannot be utilized on the tax return during a year and that may be carried back to reduce taxable income or taxes paid in a prior year. An **operating loss carryback** is an excess of tax deductions over gross income in a year. A **tax credit carryback** is the amount by which tax credits available for utilization exceed statutory limitations.

CARRYFORWARDS. Deductions or credits that cannot be utilized on the tax return during a year and that may be carried forward to reduce taxable income or taxes payable in a future year. An **operating loss carryforward** is an excess of tax deductions over gross income in a year. A **tax credit carryforward** is the amount by which tax credits available for utilization exceed statutory limitations.

CURRENT TAX EXPENSE (BENEFIT). The amount of income taxes paid or payable (or refundable) for a year as determined by applying the provisions of the enacted tax law to the taxable income or excess of deductions over revenues for that year.

DEDUCTIBLE TEMPORARY DIFFERENCE. Temporary differences that result in deductible amounts in future years when recovering or settling the related asset or liability, respectively.

DEFERRED TAX ASSET. The deferred tax consequences attributable to deductible temporary differences and carryforwards.

DEFERRED TAX CONSEQUENCES. The future effects on income taxes as measured by the enacted tax rate and provisions of the enacted tax law resulting from temporary differences and carryforwards at the end of the current year.

DEFERRED TAX EXPENSE (BENEFIT). The change during the year in a company's deferred tax liabilities and assets.

DEFERRED TAX LIABILITY. The deferred tax consequences attributable to taxable temporary differences.

INCOME TAXES. Domestic and foreign federal (national), state, and local (including franchise) taxes based on income.

INCOME TAXES CURRENTLY PAYABLE (REFUNDABLE). Refer to current tax expense (benefit).

INCOME TAX EXPENSE (BENEFIT). The sum of current tax expense (benefit) and deferred tax expense (benefit).

TAXABLE INCOME. The excess of taxable revenues over tax deductible expenses and exemptions for the year as defined by the governmental taxing authority.

TAXABLE TEMPORARY DIFFERENCE. Temporary differences that result in taxable amounts in future years when recovering or settling the related asset or liability, respectively.

TAX-PLANNING STRATEGY. An action that meets certain criteria and that a company implements to realize a tax benefit for an operating loss or tax credit carryforward before it expires. Companies consider tax-planning strategies when assessing the need for and amount of a valuation allowance for deferred tax assets.

TEMPORARY DIFFERENCE. A difference between the tax basis of an asset or liability and its reported amount in the financial statements that will result in taxable or deductible amounts in future years when recovering or settling the reported amount of the asset or liability, respectively.

VALUATION ALLOWANCE. The portion of a deferred tax asset for which it is more likely than not that a company will not realize a tax benefit.

You will want to read the **CONVERGENCE CORNER** on page 1019

For discussion of how international convergence efforts relate to income taxes.

CONVERGENCE CORNER

The accounting for income taxes in iGAAP is covered in *IAS 12* ("Income Taxes"). Similar to U.S. GAAP, iGAAP uses the asset and liability approach for recording deferred taxes. The differences between iGAAP and U.S. GAAP involve a few exceptions to the asset-liability approach; some minor differences in the recognition, measurement, and disclosure criteria; and differences in implementation guidance.

RELEVANT FACTS

- The classification of deferred taxes under iGAAP is always noncurrent. As indicated in the chapter, U.S. GAAP classifies deferred taxes based on the classification of the asset or liability to which it relates.

- Under iGAAP, an affirmative judgment approach is used, by which a deferred tax asset is recognized up to the amount that is probable to be realized. U.S. GAAP uses an impairment approach. In this approach, the deferred tax asset is recognized in full. It is then reduced by a valuation account if it is more likely than not that all or a portion of the deferred tax asset will not be realized.

- iGAAP uses the enacted tax rate or substantially enacted tax rate. ("Substantially enacted" means virtually certain.) For U.S. GAAP, the enacted tax rate must be used.

- The tax effects related to certain items are reported in equity under iGAAP. That is not the case under U.S. GAAP, which charges or credits the tax effects to income.

- U.S. GAAP requires companies to assess the likelihood of uncertain tax positions being sustainable upon audit. Potential liabilities must be accrued and disclosed if the position is "more likely than not" to be disallowed. Under iGAAP, *all potential liabilities* must be recognized. With respect to measurement, iGAAP uses an expected-value approach to measure the tax liability, which differs from U.S. GAAP.

ABOUT THE NUMBERS

The following schedule taken from the annual report of Glaxo-SmithKline plc (which uses iGAAP) indicates the impact of differences in iGAAP and U.S. GAAP for deferred taxes.

Reconciliation to U.S. accounting principles

(e) Deferred taxation (in part):

Total tax expense (in millions of British pounds)

IFRS:	2006
Current tax expense	2,710
Deferred tax (credit)/expense	(409)
Total tax expense	2,301
U.S. GAAP:	
Current tax expense	2,735
Deferred tax credit	(685)
Total tax expense	2,050
Total tax expense difference	(251)

Thus, due to the differences highlighted above, Glaxo's income tax expense under iGAAP is 251 million pounds higher than that reported under U.S. GAAP.

ON THE HORIZON

The FASB and the IASB have been working to address some of the differences in the accounting for income taxes. Some of the issues under discussion are the term "probable" under iGAAP for recognition of a deferred tax asset, which might be interpreted to mean "more likely than not." If the term is changed, the reporting for impairments of deferred tax assets will be essentially the same between U.S. GAAP and iGAAP. In addition, the IASB is considering adoption of the classification approach used in U.S. GAAP for deferred assets and liabilities. Also, U.S. GAAP will likely continue to use the enacted tax rate in computing deferred taxes, except in situations where the U.S. taxing jurisdiction is not involved. In that case, companies should use iGAAP, which is based on enacted rates or substantially enacted tax rates. Finally, the issue of allocation of deferred income taxes to equity for certain transactions under iGAAP must be addressed in order to conform to U.S. GAAP, which allocates the effects to income. At the time of this printing, deliberations on the income tax project have been suspended indefinitely. The FASB has no plans to issue an amendment to its literature at this time, but it may revisit this project after the IASB further develops its replacement to *IAS 12*.

SUMMARY OF LEARNING OBJECTIVES

[1] Identify differences between pretax financial income and taxable income. Companies compute pretax financial income (or income for book purposes) in accordance with generally accepted accounting principles. They compute taxable income (or income for tax purposes) in accordance with prescribed tax regulations. Because tax regulations and GAAP differ in many ways, so frequently do pretax financial income and taxable income. Differences may exist, for example, in the timing of revenue recognition and the timing of expense recognition.

[2] Describe a temporary difference that results in future taxable amounts. Revenue recognized for book purposes in the period earned but deferred and reported as revenue for tax purposes when collected results in future taxable amounts. The future taxable amounts will occur in the periods the company recovers the receivable and reports the collections as revenue for tax purposes. This results in a deferred tax liability.

[3] Describe a temporary difference that results in future deductible amounts. An accrued warranty expense that a company pays for and deducts for tax purposes, in a period later than the period in which it incurs and recognizes it for book purposes, results in future deductible amounts. The future deductible amounts will occur in the periods during which the company settles the related liability for book purposes. This results in a deferred tax asset.

[4] Explain the purpose of a deferred tax asset valuation allowance. A deferred tax asset should be reduced by a valuation allowance if, based on all available evidence, it is more likely than not (a level of likelihood that is at least slightly more than 50 percent) that it will not realize some portion or all of the deferred tax asset. The company should carefully consider all available evidence, both positive and negative, to determine whether, based on the weight of available evidence, it needs a valuation allowance.

[5] Describe the presentation of income tax expense in the income statement. Significant components of income tax expense should be disclosed in the income statement or in the notes to the financial statements. The most commonly encountered components are the current expense (or benefit) and the deferred expense (or benefit).

[6] Describe various temporary and permanent differences. Examples of temporary differences are: (1) revenue or gains that are taxable after recognition in financial income; (2) expenses or losses that are deductible after recognition in financial income; (3) revenues or gains that are taxable before recognition in financial income; (4) expenses or losses that are deductible before recognition in financial income. Examples of permanent differences are: (1) items recognized for financial reporting purposes but not for tax purposes, and (2) items recognized for tax purposes but not for financial reporting purposes.

[7] Explain the effect of various tax rates and tax rate changes on deferred income taxes. Companies may use tax rates other than the current rate only after enactment of the future tax rates. When a change in the tax rate is enacted, a company should immediately recognize its effect on the deferred income tax accounts. The company reports the effects as an adjustment to income tax expense in the period of the change.

[8] Apply accounting procedures for a loss carryback and a loss carryforward. A company may carry a net operating loss back two years and receive refunds for income taxes paid in those years. The loss is applied to the earlier year first and then to the second year. Any loss remaining after the two-year carryback may be carried forward up to 20 years to offset future taxable income. A company may forgo the loss carryback and use the loss carryforward, offsetting future taxable income for up to 20 years.

⌐9¬ Describe the presentation of deferred income taxes in financial statements. Companies report deferred tax accounts on the balance sheet as assets and liabilities. These deferred tax accounts are classified as a net current and a net noncurrent amount. Companies classify an individual deferred tax liability or asset as current or noncurrent based on the classification of the related asset or liability for financial reporting. A deferred tax liability or asset that is not related to an asset or liability for financial reporting, including a deferred tax asset related to a loss carryforward, is classified according to the expected reversal date of the temporary difference.

⌐10¬ Indicate the basic principles of the asset-liability method. Companies apply the following basic principles in accounting for income taxes at the date of the financial statements: (1) Recognize a current tax liability or asset for the estimated taxes payable or refundable on the tax return for the current year. (2) Recognize a deferred tax liability or asset for the estimated future tax effects attributable to temporary differences and carryforwards using the enacted tax rate. (3) Base the measurement of current and deferred tax liabilities and assets on provisions of the enacted tax law. (4) Reduce the measurement of deferred tax assets, if necessary, by the amount of any tax benefits that, based on available evidence, companies do not expect to realize.

APPENDIX **19A**	**COMPREHENSIVE EXAMPLE OF INTERPERIOD TAX ALLOCATION**

This appendix presents a comprehensive illustration of a deferred income tax problem with several temporary and permanent differences. The example follows one company through two complete years (2009 and 2010). **Study it carefully.** It should help you understand the concepts and procedures presented in the chapter.

> **Objective·11**
>
> Understand and apply the concepts and procedures of interperiod tax allocation.

FIRST YEAR—2009

Allman Company, which began operations at the beginning of 2009, produces various products on a contract basis. Each contract generates a gross profit of $80,000. Some of Allman's contracts provide for the customer to pay on an installment basis. Under these contracts, Allman collects one-fifth of the contract revenue in each of the following four years. For financial reporting purposes, the company recognizes gross profit in the year of completion (accrual basis); for tax purposes, Allman recognizes gross profit in the year cash is collected (installment basis).

Presented below is information related to Allman's operations for 2009.

1. In 2009, the company completed seven contracts that allow for the customer to pay on an installment basis. Allman recognized the related gross profit of $560,000 for financial reporting purposes. It reported only $112,000 of gross profit on installment sales on the 2009 tax return. The company expects future collections on the related installment receivables to result in taxable amounts of $112,000 in each of the next four years.

2. At the beginning of 2009, Allman Company purchased depreciable assets with a cost of $540,000. For financial reporting purposes, Allman depreciates these assets using the straight-line method over a six-year service life. For tax purposes, the assets fall in the five-year recovery class, and Allman uses the MACRS system. The depreciation schedules for both financial reporting and tax purposes are shown on page 1022.

Year	Depreciation for Financial Reporting Purposes	Depreciation for Tax Purposes	Difference
2009	$ 90,000	$108,000	$(18,000)
2010	90,000	172,800	(82,800)
2011	90,000	103,680	(13,680)
2012	90,000	62,208	27,792
2013	90,000	62,208	27,792
2014	90,000	31,104	58,896
	$540,000	$540,000	$ –0–

3. The company warrants its product for two years from the date of completion of a contract. During 2009, the product warranty liability accrued for financial reporting purposes was $200,000, and the amount paid for the satisfaction of warranty liability was $44,000. Allman expects to settle the remaining $156,000 by expenditures of $56,000 in 2010 and $100,000 in 2011.

4. In 2009 nontaxable municipal bond interest revenue was $28,000.

5. During 2009 nondeductible fines and penalties of $26,000 were paid.

6. Pretax financial income for 2009 amounts to $412,000.

7. Tax rates enacted before the end of 2009 were:

2009	50%
2010 and later years	40%

8. The accounting period is the calendar year.

9. The company is expected to have taxable income in all future years.

Taxable Income and Income Tax Payable—2009

The first step is to determine Allman Company's income tax payable for 2009 by calculating its taxable income. Illustration 19A-1 shows this computation.

ILLUSTRATION 19A-1
Computation of Taxable Income, 2009

Pretax financial income for 2009	$412,000
Permanent differences:	
Nontaxable revenue—municipal bond interest	(28,000)
Nondeductible expenses—fines and penalties	26,000
Temporary differences:	
Excess gross profit per books ($560,000 − $112,000)	(448,000)
Excess depreciation per tax ($108,000 − $90,000)	(18,000)
Excess warranty expense per books ($200,000 − $44,000)	156,000
Taxable income for 2009	$100,000

Allman computes income tax payable on taxable income for $100,000 as follows.

ILLUSTRATION 19A-2
Computation of Income Tax Payable, End of 2009

Taxable income for 2009	$100,000
Tax rate	50%
Income tax payable (current tax expense) for 2009	$ 50,000

Computing Deferred Income Taxes—End of 2009

The schedule in Illustration 19A-3 (on page 1023) summarizes the temporary differences and the resulting future taxable and deductible amounts.

	Future Years					
	2010	2011	2012	2013	2014	Total
Future taxable (deductible) amounts:						
Installment sales	$112,000	$112,000	$112,000	$112,000		$448,000
Depreciation	(82,800)	(13,680)	27,792	27,792	$58,896	18,000
Warranty costs	(56,000)	(100,000)				(156,000)

ILLUSTRATION 19A-3
Schedule of Future Taxable and Deductible Amounts, End of 2009

Allman computes the amounts of deferred income taxes to be reported at the end of 2009 as shown in Illustration 19A-4.

Temporary Difference	Future Taxable (Deductible) Amounts	Tax Rate	Deferred Tax (Asset)	Liability
Installment sales	$448,000	40%		$179,200
Depreciation	18,000	40%		7,200
Warranty costs	(156,000)	40%	$(62,400)	
Totals	$310,000		$(62,400)	$186,400*

*Because only a single tax rate is involved in all relevant years, these totals can be reconciled: $310,000 × 40% = ($62,400) + $186,400.

ILLUSTRATION 19A-4
Computation of Deferred Income Taxes, End of 2009

A temporary difference is caused by the use of the accrual basis for financial reporting purposes and the installment method for tax purposes. This temporary difference will result in future taxable amounts, and hence, a deferred tax liability. Because of the installment contracts completed in 2009, a temporary difference of $448,000 originates that will reverse in equal amounts over the next four years. The company expects to have taxable income in all future years, and there is only one enacted tax rate applicable to all future years. Allman uses that rate (40 percent) to compute the entire deferred tax liability resulting from this temporary difference.

The temporary difference caused by different depreciation policies for books and for tax purposes originates over three years and then reverses over three years. This difference will cause deductible amounts in 2010 and 2011 and taxable amounts in 2012, 2013, and 2014. These amounts sum to a net future taxable amount of $18,000 (which is the cumulative temporary difference at the end of 2009). Because the company expects to have taxable income in all future years and because there is only one tax rate enacted for all of the relevant future years, Allman applies that rate to the net future taxable amount to determine the related net deferred tax liability.

The third temporary difference is caused by different methods of accounting for warranties. This difference will result in deductible amounts in each of the two future years it takes to reverse. Because the company expects to report a positive income on all future tax returns and because there is only one tax rate enacted for each of the relevant future years, Allman uses that 40 percent rate to calculate the resulting deferred tax asset.

Deferred Tax Expense (Benefit) and the Journal Entry to Record Income Taxes—2009

To determine the deferred tax expense (benefit), we need to compare the beginning and ending balances of the deferred income tax accounts. Illustration 19A-5 (on page 1024) shows that computation.

ILLUSTRATION 19A-5
Computation of Deferred
Tax Expense (Benefit),
2009

Deferred tax asset at the end of 2009	$ 62,400
Deferred tax asset at the beginning of 2009	–0–
Deferred tax expense (benefit)	$ (62,400)
Deferred tax liability at the end of 2009	$186,400
Deferred tax liability at the beginning of 2009	–0–
Deferred tax expense (benefit)	$186,400

The $62,400 increase in the deferred tax asset causes a deferred tax benefit to be reported in the income statement. The $186,400 increase in the deferred tax liability during 2009 results in a deferred tax expense. These two amounts **net** to a deferred tax expense of $124,000 for 2009.

ILLUSTRATION 19A-6
Computation of Net
Deferred Tax Expense,
2009

Deferred tax expense (benefit)	$ (62,400)
Deferred tax expense (benefit)	186,400
Net deferred tax expense for 2009	$124,000

Allman then computes the total income tax expense as follows.

ILLUSTRATION 19A-7
Computation of Total
Income Tax Expense, 2009

Current tax expense for 2009	$ 50,000
Deferred tax expense for 2009	124,000
Income tax expense (total) for 2009	$174,000

Allman records income tax payable, deferred income taxes, and income tax expense as follows.

Income Tax Expense	174,000	
Deferred Tax Asset	62,400	
Income Tax Payable		50,000
Deferred Tax Liability		186,400

Financial Statement Presentation—2009

Companies should classify deferred tax assets and liabilities as current and noncurrent on the balance sheet based on the classifications of related assets and liabilities. Multiple categories of deferred taxes are classified into a net current amount and a net noncurrent amount. Illustration 19A-8 shows the classification of Allman's deferred tax accounts at the end of 2009.

ILLUSTRATION 19A-8
Classification of Deferred
Tax Accounts, End of 2009

Temporary Difference	Resulting Deferred Tax (Asset)	Liability	Related Balance Sheet Account	Classification
Installment sales		$179,200	Installment Receivable	Current
Depreciation		7,200	Plant Assets	Noncurrent
Warranty costs	$(62,400)		Warranty Obligation	Current
Totals	$(62,400)	$186,400		

For the first temporary difference, there is a related asset on the balance sheet, installment accounts receivable. Allman classifies that asset as current because it has a trade practice of selling to customers on an installment basis. Allman therefore classifies the resulting deferred tax liability as a current liability.

Certain assets on the balance sheet are related to the depreciation difference—the property, plant, and equipment being depreciated. Allman would classify the plant assets as noncurrent. Therefore, it also classifies the resulting deferred tax liability as noncurrent. Since the company's operating cycle is at least four years in length, Allman classifies the entire $156,000 warranty obligation as a current liability. Thus, it also classifies the related deferred tax asset of $62,400 as current.[9]

The balance sheet at the end of 2009 reports the following amounts.

Current liabilities	
Income tax payable	$ 50,000
Deferred tax liability ($179,200 − $62,400)	116,800
Long-term liabilities	
Deferred tax liability	$ 7,200

ILLUSTRATION 19A-9
Balance Sheet Presentation
of Deferred Taxes, 2009

Allman's income statement for 2009 reports the following.

Income before income taxes		$412,000
Income tax expense		
Current	$ 50,000	
Deferred	124,000	174,000
Net income		$238,000

ILLUSTRATION 19A-10
Income Statement
Presentation of Income
Tax Expense, 2009

SECOND YEAR—2010

1. During 2010 Allman collected $112,000 from customers for the receivables arising from contracts completed in 2009. The company expects recovery of the remaining receivables to result in taxable amounts of $112,000 in each of the following three years.

2. In 2010 the company completed four new contracts that allow for the customer to pay on an installment basis. These installment sales created new installment receivables. Future collections of these receivables will result in reporting gross profit of $64,000 for tax purposes in each of the next four years.

3. During 2010 Allman continued to depreciate the assets acquired in 2009 according to the depreciation schedules appearing on page 1022. Thus, depreciation amounted to $90,000 for financial reporting purposes and $172,800 for tax purposes.

4. An analysis at the end of 2010 of the product warranty liability account showed the following details.

Balance of liability at beginning of 2010	$156,000
Expense for 2010 income statement purposes	180,000
Amount paid for contracts completed in 2009	(56,000)
Amount paid for contracts completed in 2010	(50,000)
Balance of liability at end of 2010	$230,000

[9]If Allman's operating cycle were less than one year in length, the company would expect to settle $56,000 of the warranty obligation within one year of the December 31, 2009, balance sheet and would use current assets to do so. Thus $56,000 of the warranty obligation would be a current liability and the remaining $100,000 warranty obligation would be a long-term (noncurrent) liability. This would mean that Allman would classify $22,400 ($56,000 × 40%) of the related deferred tax asset as a current asset, and $40,000 ($100,000 × 40%) of the deferred tax asset as a noncurrent asset. *In doing homework problems, unless it is evident otherwise, assume a company's operating cycle is not longer than a year.*

The balance of the liability is expected to require expenditures in the future as follows.

> $100,000 in 2011 due to 2009 contracts
> $ 50,000 in 2011 due to 2010 contracts
> $ 80,000 in 2012 due to 2010 contracts
> $230,000

5. During 2010 nontaxable municipal bond interest revenue was $24,000.
6. Allman accrued a loss of $172,000 for financial reporting purposes because of pending litigation. This amount is not tax-deductible until the period the loss is realized, which the company estimates to be 2018.
7. Pretax financial income for 2010 amounts to $504,800.
8. The enacted tax rates still in effect are:

2009	50%
2010 and later years	40%

Taxable Income and Income Tax Payable—2010

Allman computes taxable income for 2010 as follows.

ILLUSTRATION 19A-11
Computation of Taxable Income, 2010

Pretax financial income for 2010	$504,800
Permanent difference:	
Nontaxable revenue—municipal bond interest	(24,000)
Reversing temporary differences:	
Collection on 2009 installment sales	112,000
Payments on warranties from 2009 contracts	(56,000)
Originating temporary differences:	
Excess gross profit per books—2010 contracts	(256,000)
Excess depreciation per tax	(82,800)
Excess warranty expense per books—2010 contracts	130,000
Loss accrual per books	172,000
Taxable income for 2010	$500,000

Income tax payable for 2010 is as follows.

ILLUSTRATION 19A-12
Computation of Income Tax Payable, End of 2010

Taxable income for 2010	$500,000
Tax rate	40%
Income tax payable (current tax expense) for 2010	$200,000

ILLUSTRATION 19A-13
Schedule of Future Taxable and Deductible Amounts, End of 2010

Computing Deferred Income Taxes—End of 2010

The schedule in Illustration 19A-13 summarizes the temporary differences existing at the end of 2010 and the resulting future taxable and deductible amounts.

	Future Years					
	2011	2012	2013	2014	2018	Total
Future taxable (deductible) amounts:						
Installment sales—2009	$112,000	$112,000	$112,000			$336,000
Installment sales—2010	64,000	64,000	64,000	$64,000		256,000
Depreciation	(13,680)	27,792	27,792	58,896		100,800
Warranty costs	(150,000)	(80,000)				(230,000)
Loss accrual					$(172,000)	(172,000)

Allman computes the amounts of deferred income taxes to be reported at the end of 2010 as follows.

ILLUSTRATION 19A-14
Computation of Deferred
Income Taxes, End of 2010

Temporary Difference	Future Taxable (Deductible) Amounts	Tax Rate	Deferred Tax (Asset)	Liability
Installment sales	$592,000*	40%		$236,800
Depreciation	100,800	40%		40,320
Warranty costs	(230,000)	40%	$ (92,000)	
Loss accrual	(172,000)	40%	(68,800)	
Totals	$290,800		$(160,800)	$277,120**

*Cumulative temporary difference = $336,000 + $256,000
**Because of a flat tax rate, these totals can be reconciled: $290,800 × 40% = $(160,800) + $277,120

Deferred Tax Expense (Benefit) and the Journal Entry to Record Income Taxes—2010

To determine the deferred tax expense (benefit), Allman must compare the beginning and ending balances of the deferred income tax accounts, as shown in Illustration 19A-15.

ILLUSTRATION 19A-15
Computation of Deferred
Tax Expense (Benefit),
2010

Deferred tax asset at the end of 2010	$160,800
Deferred tax asset at the beginning of 2010	62,400
Deferred tax expense (benefit)	$ (98,400)
Deferred tax liability at the end of 2010	$277,120
Deferred tax liability at the beginning of 2010	186,400
Deferred tax expense (benefit)	$ 90,720

The deferred tax expense (benefit) and the total income tax expense for 2010 are, therefore, as follows.

ILLUSTRATION 19A-16
Computation of Total
Income Tax Expense, 2010

Deferred tax expense (benefit)	$ (98,400)
Deferred tax expense (benefit)	90,720
Deferred tax benefit for 2010	(7,680)
Current tax expense for 2010	200,000
Income tax expense (total) for 2010	$192,320

The deferred tax expense of $90,720 and the deferred tax benefit of $98,400 net to a deferred tax benefit of $7,680 for 2010.

Allman records income taxes for 2010 with the following journal entry.

Income Tax Expense	192,320	
Deferred Tax Asset	98,400	
Income Tax Payable		200,000
Deferred Tax Liability		90,720

Financial Statement Presentation—2010

Illustration 19A-17 (on the next page) shows the classification of Allman's deferred tax accounts at the end of 2010.

ILLUSTRATION 19A-17
Classification of Deferred
Tax Accounts, End of 2010

Temporary Difference	Resulting Deferred Tax (Asset)	Liability	Related Balance Sheet Account	Classification
Installment sales		$236,800	Installment Receivables	Current
Depreciation		40,320	Plant Assets	Noncurrent
Warranty costs	$ (92,000)		Warranty Obligation	Current
Loss accrual	(68,800)		Litigation Obligation	Noncurrent
Totals	$(160,800)	$277,120		

The new temporary difference introduced in 2010 (due to the litigation loss accrual) results in a litigation obligation that is classified as a long-term liability. Thus, the related deferred tax asset is noncurrent.

Allman's balance sheet at the end of 2010 reports the following amounts.

ILLUSTRATION 19A-18
Balance Sheet Presentation
of Deferred Taxes, End of
2010

Other assets (noncurrent)		
Deferred tax asset ($68,800 − $40,320)	$ 28,480	
Current liabilities		
Income tax payable	$200,000	
Deferred tax liability ($236,800 − $92,000)	144,800	

The income statement for 2010 reports the following.

ILLUSTRATION 19A-19
Income Statement
Presentation of Income
Tax Expense, 2010

Income before income taxes		$504,800
Income tax expense		
Current	$200,000	
Deferred	(7,680)	192,320
Net income		$312,480

SUMMARY OF LEARNING OBJECTIVE FOR APPENDIX 19A

•11 Understand and apply the concepts and procedures of interperiod tax allocation. Accounting for deferred taxes involves the following steps: Calculate taxable income and income tax payable for the year. Compute deferred income taxes at the end of the year. Determine deferred tax expense (benefit) and make the journal entry to record income taxes. Classify deferred tax assets and liabilities as current or noncurrent in the financial statements.

FASB CODIFICATION

FASB Codification References

[1] FASB ASC 740-10-30-18. [Predecessor literature: "Accounting for Income Taxes," *Statement of Financial Accounting Standards No. 109* (Norwalk, Conn.: FASB, 1992).]

[2] FASB ASC 740-10-30-21 & 22. [Predecessor literature: "Accounting for Income Taxes," *Statement of Financial Accounting Standards No. 109* (Norwalk, Conn.: FASB, 1992), pars. 23 and 24.]

[3] FASB ASC 740-10-25-6. [Predecessor literature: "Accounting for Uncertainty in Income Taxes," *FASB Interpretation No. 48* (Norwalk, Conn.: FASB, 2006).]

[4] FASB ASC 740-10-05. [Predecessor literature: "Accounting for Income Taxes," *Statement of Financial Accounting Standards No. 109* (Norwalk, Conn.: FASB, 1992), pars. 6 and 8.]

Exercises

Access the FASB Codification at *http://asc.fasb.org/home* to prepare responses to the following exercises. Provide Codification references for your responses.

CE19-1 Access the glossary ("Master Glossary") to answer the following.

(a) What is a deferred tax asset?
(b) What is taxable income?
(c) What is the definition of valuation allowance?
(d) What is a deferred tax liability?

CE19-2 What are the two basic requirements applied to the measurement of current and deferred income taxes at the date of the financial statements?

CE19-3 A company wishes to conduct business in a foreign country that attracts businesses by granting "holidays" from income taxes for a certain period of time. Would the company have to disclose this "holiday" to the SEC? If so, what information must be disclosed?

CE19-4 When is a company allowed to initially recognize the financial statement effects of a tax position?

An additional Codification case can be found in the Using Your Judgment section, on page 1046.

QUESTIONS

1. Explain the difference between pretax financial income and taxable income.

2. What are the two objectives of accounting for income taxes?

3. Interest on municipal bonds is referred to as a permanent difference when determining the proper amount to report for deferred taxes. Explain the meaning of permanent differences, and give two other examples.

4. Explain the meaning of a temporary difference as it relates to deferred tax computations, and give three examples.

5. Differentiate between an originating temporary difference and a reversing difference.

6. The book basis of depreciable assets for Erwin Co. is $900,000, and the tax basis is $700,000 at the end of 2011. The enacted tax rate is 34% for all periods. Determine the amount of deferred taxes to be reported on the balance sheet at the end of 2011.

7. Roth Inc. has a deferred tax liability of $68,000 at the beginning of 2011. At the end of 2011, it reports accounts receivable on the books at $90,000 and the tax basis at zero (its only temporary difference). If the enacted tax rate is 34% for all periods, and income tax payable for the period is $230,000, determine the amount of total income tax expense to report for 2011.

8. What is the difference between a future taxable amount and a future deductible amount? When is it appropriate to record a valuation account for a deferred tax asset?

9. Pretax financial income for Lake Inc. is $300,000, and its taxable income is $100,000 for 2011. Its only temporary difference at the end of the period relates to a $70,000 difference due to excess depreciation for tax purposes. If the tax rate is 40% for all periods, compute the amount of income tax expense to report in 2011. No deferred income taxes existed at the beginning of the year.

10. How are deferred tax assets and deferred tax liabilities reported on the balance sheet?

11. Describe the procedures involved in segregating various deferred tax amounts into current and noncurrent categories.

12. How is it determined whether deferred tax amounts are considered to be "related" to specific asset or liability amounts?

13. At the end of the year, Falabella Co. has pretax financial income of $550,000. Included in the $550,000 is $70,000 interest income on municipal bonds, $25,000 fine for dumping hazardous waste, and depreciation of $60,000. Depreciation for tax purposes is $45,000. Compute income taxes payable, assuming the tax rate is 30% for all periods.

14. Addison Co. has one temporary difference at the beginning of 2010 of $500,000. The deferred tax liability established for this amount is $150,000, based on a tax rate of 30%. The temporary difference will provide the following taxable amounts: $100,000 in 2011; $200,000 in 2012, and $200,000 in 2013. If a new tax rate for 2013 of 20% is enacted into law at the end of 2010, what is the journal entry necessary in 2010 (if any) to adjust deferred taxes?

15. What are some of the reasons that the components of income tax expense should be disclosed and a reconciliation between the effective tax rate and the statutory tax rate be provided?

16. Differentiate between "loss carryback" and "loss carryforward." Which can be accounted for with the greater certainty when it arises? Why?

17. What are the possible treatments for tax purposes of a net operating loss? What are the circumstances that determine the option to be applied? What is the proper treatment of a net operating loss for financial reporting purposes?

18. What controversy relates to the accounting for net operating loss carryforwards?

19. What is an uncertain tax position, and what are the general guidelines for accounting for uncertain tax positions?

20. Where can authoritative iGAAP related to the accounting for taxes be found?

21. Briefly describe some of the similarities and differences between U.S. GAAP and iGAAP with respect to income tax accounting.

22. Describe the current convergence efforts of the FASB and IASB in the area of accounting for taxes.

BRIEF EXERCISES

BE19-1 In 2010, Amirante Corporation had pretax financial income of $168,000 and taxable income of $120,000. The difference is due to the use of different depreciation methods for tax and accounting purposes. The effective tax rate is 40%. Compute the amount to be reported as income taxes payable at December 31, 2010.

BE19-2 Oxford Corporation began operations in 2010 and reported pretax financial income of $225,000 for the year. Oxford's tax depreciation exceeded its book depreciation by $40,000. Oxford's tax rate for 2010 and years thereafter is 30%. In its December 31, 2010 balance sheet, what amount of deferred tax liability should be reported?

BE19-3 Using the information from BE19-2, assume this is the only difference between Oxford's pretax financial income and taxable income. Prepare the journal entry to record the income tax expense, deferred income taxes, and income tax payable, and show how the deferred tax liability will be classified on the December 31, 2010, balance sheet.

BE19-4 At December 31, 2010, Appaloosa Corporation had a deferred tax liability of $25,000. At December 31, 2011, the deferred tax liability is $42,000. The corporation's 2011 current tax expense is $48,000. What amount should Appaloosa report as total 2011 tax expense?

BE19-5 At December 31, 2010, Suffolk Corporation had an estimated warranty liability of $105,000 for accounting purposes and $0 for tax purposes. (The warranty costs are not deductible until paid.) The effective tax rate is 40%. Compute the amount Suffolk should report as a deferred tax asset at December 31, 2010.

BE19-6 At December 31, 2010, Percheron Inc. had a deferred tax asset of $30,000. At December 31, 2011, the deferred tax asset is $59,000. The corporation's 2011 current tax expense is $61,000. What amount should Percheron report as total 2011 tax expense?

BE19-7 At December 31, 2010, Hillyard Corporation has a deferred tax asset of $200,000. After a careful review of all available evidence, it is determined that it is more likely than not that $60,000 of this deferred tax asset will not be realized. Prepare the necessary journal entry.

BE19-8 Mitchell Corporation had income before income taxes of $195,000 in 2010. Mitchell's current income tax expense is $48,000, and deferred income tax expense is $30,000. Prepare Mitchell's 2010 income statement, beginning with income before income taxes.

BE19-9 Shetland Inc. had pretax financial income of $154,000 in 2010. Included in the computation of that amount is insurance expense of $4,000 which is not deductible for tax purposes. In addition, depreciation for tax purposes exceeds accounting depreciation by $10,000. Prepare Shetland's journal entry to record 2010 taxes, assuming a tax rate of 45%.

BE19-10 Clydesdale Corporation has a cumulative temporary difference related to depreciation of $580,000 at December 31, 2010. This difference will reverse as follows: 2011, $42,000; 2012, $244,000; and 2013, $294,000. Enacted tax rates are 34% for 2011 and 2012, and 40% for 2013. Compute the amount Clydesdale should report as a deferred tax liability at December 31, 2010.

BE19-11 At December 31, 2010, Fell Corporation had a deferred tax liability of $680,000, resulting from future taxable amounts of $2,000,000 and an enacted tax rate of 34%. In May 2011, a new income tax act is signed into law that raises the tax rate to 40% for 2011 and future years. Prepare the journal entry for Fell to adjust the deferred tax liability.

·8 **BE19-12** Conlin Corporation had the following tax information.

Year	Taxable Income	Tax Rate	Taxes Paid
2008	$300,000	35%	$105,000
2009	$325,000	30%	$ 97,500
2010	$400,000	30%	$120,000

In 2011 Conlin suffered a net operating loss of $480,000, which it elected to carry back. The 2011 enacted tax rate is 29%. Prepare Conlin's entry to record the effect of the loss carryback.

·8 **BE19-13** Rode Inc. incurred a net operating loss of $500,000 in 2010. Combined income for 2008 and 2009 was $350,000. The tax rate for all years is 40%. Rode elects the carryback option. Prepare the journal entries to record the benefits of the loss carryback and the loss carryforward.

·4 ·8 **BE19-14** Use the information for Rode Inc. given in BE19-13. Assume that it is more likely than not that the entire net operating loss carryforward will not be realized in future years. Prepare all the journal entries necessary at the end of 2010.

·9 **BE19-15** Youngman Corporation has temporary differences at December 31, 2010, that result in the following deferred taxes.

Deferred tax liability—current	$38,000
Deferred tax asset—current	$(62,000)
Deferred tax liability—noncurrent	$96,000
Deferred tax asset—noncurrent	$(27,000)

Indicate how these balances would be presented in Youngman's December 31, 2010, balance sheet.

· **EXERCISES** · · · · · · · · · · · · · · · ·

·2 ·5 **E19-1** **(One Temporary Difference, Future Taxable Amounts, One Rate, No Beginning Deferred Taxes)** Starfleet Corporation has one temporary difference at the end of 2010 that will reverse and cause taxable amounts of $55,000 in 2011, $60,000 in 2012, and $75,000 in 2013. Starfleet's pretax financial income for 2010 is $400,000, and the tax rate is 30% for all years. There are no deferred taxes at the beginning of 2010.

Instructions
(a) Compute taxable income and income taxes payable for 2010.
(b) Prepare the journal entry to record income tax expense, deferred income taxes, and income taxes payable for 2010.
(c) Prepare the income tax expense section of the income statement for 2010, beginning with the line "Income before income taxes."

·2 **E19-2** **(Two Differences, No Beginning Deferred Taxes, Tracked through 2 Years)** The following information is available for McKee Corporation for 2010.

1. Excess of tax depreciation over book depreciation, $40,000. This $40,000 difference will reverse equally over the years 2011–2014.
2. Deferral, for book purposes, of $25,000 of rent received in advance. The rent will be earned in 2011.
3. Pretax financial income, $350,000.
4. Tax rate for all years, 40%.

Instructions
(a) Compute taxable income for 2010.
(b) Prepare the journal entry to record income tax expense, deferred income taxes, and income taxes payable for 2010.
(c) Prepare the journal entry to record income tax expense, deferred income taxes, and income taxes payable for 2011, assuming taxable income of $325,000.

·2 ·5 **E19-3** **(One Temporary Difference, Future Taxable Amounts, One Rate, Beginning Deferred Taxes)** Brennan Corporation began 2010 with a $90,000 balance in the Deferred Tax Liability account. At the end of 2010, the related cumulative temporary difference amounts to $350,000, and it will reverse evenly over the next 2 years. Pretax accounting income for 2010 is $525,000, the tax rate for all years is 40%, and taxable income for 2010 is $400,000.

Instructions
(a) Compute income taxes payable for 2010.
(b) Prepare the journal entry to record income tax expense, deferred income taxes, and income taxes payable for 2010.
(c) Prepare the income tax expense section of the income statement for 2010 beginning with the line "Income before income taxes."

·2·3·5·6 E19-4 (Three Differences, Compute Taxable Income, Entry for Taxes) Havaci Company reports pretax financial income of $80,000 for 2010. The following items cause taxable income to be different than pretax financial income.

1. Depreciation on the tax return is greater than depreciation on the income statement by $16,000.
2. Rent collected on the tax return is greater than rent earned on the income statement by $27,000.
3. Fines for pollution appear as an expense of $11,000 on the income statement.

Havaci's tax rate is 30% for all years, and the company expects to report taxable income in all future years. There are no deferred taxes at the beginning of 2010.

Instructions
(a) Compute taxable income and income taxes payable for 2010.
(b) Prepare the journal entry to record income tax expense, deferred income taxes, and income taxes payable for 2010.
(c) Prepare the income tax expense section of the income statement for 2010, beginning with the line "Income before income taxes."
(d) Compute the effective income tax rate for 2010.

·2·3·5 E19-5 (Two Temporary Differences, One Rate, Beginning Deferred Taxes) The following facts relate to Alschuler Corporation.

1. Deferred tax liability, January 1, 2010, $40,000.
2. Deferred tax asset, January 1, 2010, $0.
3. Taxable income for 2010, $115,000.
4. Pretax financial income for 2010, $200,000.
5. Cumulative temporary difference at December 31, 2010, giving rise to future taxable amounts, $220,000.
6. Cumulative temporary difference at December 31, 2010, giving rise to future deductible amounts, $35,000.
7. Tax rate for all years, 40%.
8. The company is expected to operate profitably in the future.

Instructions
(a) Compute income taxes payable for 2010.
(b) Prepare the journal entry to record income tax expense, deferred income taxes, and income taxes payable for 2010.
(c) Prepare the income tax expense section of the income statement for 2010, beginning with the line "Income before income taxes."

·6 E19-6 (Identify Temporary or Permanent Differences) Listed below are items that are commonly accounted for differently for financial reporting purposes than they are for tax purposes.

Instructions
For each item below, indicate whether it involves:
(1) A temporary difference that will result in future deductible amounts and, therefore, will usually give rise to a deferred income tax asset.
(2) A temporary difference that will result in future taxable amounts and, therefore, will usually give rise to a deferred income tax liability.
(3) A permanent difference.

Use the appropriate number to indicate your answer for each.

(a) _____ The MACRS depreciation system is used for tax purposes, and the straight-line depreciation method is used for financial reporting purposes for some plant assets.
(b) _____ A landlord collects some rents in advance. Rents received are taxable in the period when they are received.

(c) _____ Expenses are incurred in obtaining tax-exempt income.

(d) _____ Costs of guarantees and warranties are estimated and accrued for financial reporting purposes.

(e) _____ Installment sales of investments are accounted for by the accrual method for financial reporting purposes and the installment method for tax purposes.

(f) _____ Interest is received on an investment in tax-exempt municipal obligations.

(g) _____ For some assets, straight-line depreciation is used for both financial reporting purposes and tax purposes but the assets' lives are shorter for tax purposes.

(h) _____ Proceeds are received from a life insurance company because of the death of a key officer. (The company carries a policy on key officers.)

(i) _____ The tax return reports a deduction for 80% of the dividends received from U.S. corporations. The cost method is used in accounting for the related investments for financial reporting purposes.

(j) _____ Estimated losses on pending lawsuits and claims are accrued for books. These losses are tax deductible in the period(s) when the related liabilities are settled.

(k) _____ Expenses on stock options are accrued for financial reporting purposes.

·2 ·3 ·4
·6

E19-7 (Terminology, Relationships, Computations, Entries)

Instructions
Complete the following statements by filling in the blanks.

(a) In a period in which a taxable temporary difference reverses, the reversal will cause taxable income to be _____ (less than, greater than) pretax financial income.

(b) If a $68,000 balance in Deferred Tax Asset was computed by use of a 40% rate, the underlying cumulative temporary difference amounts to $_____.

(c) Deferred taxes _____ (are, are not) recorded to account for permanent differences.

(d) If a taxable temporary difference originates in 2011, it will cause taxable income for 2011 to be _____ (less than, greater than) pretax financial income for 2011.

(e) If total tax expense is $50,000 and deferred tax expense is $65,000, then the current portion of the expense computation is referred to as current tax _____ (expense, benefit) of $_____.

(f) If a corporation's tax return shows taxable income of $105,000 for Year 2 and a tax rate of 40%, how much will appear on the December 31, Year 2, balance sheet for "Income tax payable" if the company has made estimated tax payments of $36,500 for Year 2? $_____.

(g) An increase in the Deferred Tax Liability account on the balance sheet is recorded by a _____ (debit, credit) to the Income Tax Expense account.

(h) An income statement that reports current tax expense of $82,000 and deferred tax benefit of $23,000 will report total income tax expense of $_____.

(i) A valuation account is needed whenever it is judged to be _____ that a portion of a deferred tax asset _____ (will be, will not be) realized.

(j) If the tax return shows total taxes due for the period of $75,000 but the income statement shows total income tax expense of $55,000, the difference of $20,000 is referred to as deferred tax _____ (expense, benefit).

·2 ·3 ·5
·9

E19-8 (Two Temporary Differences, One Rate, 3 Years) Gordon Company has two temporary differences between its income tax expense and income taxes payable. The information is shown below.

	2010	2011	2012
Pretax financial income	$840,000	$910,000	$945,000
Excess depreciation expense on tax return	(30,000)	(40,000)	(20,000)
Excess warranty expense in financial income	20,000	10,000	8,000
Taxable income	$830,000	$880,000	$933,000

The income tax rate for all years is 40%.

Instructions

(a) Prepare the journal entry to record income tax expense, deferred income taxes, and income tax payable for 2010, 2011, and 2012.

(b) Assuming there were no temporary differences prior to 2010, indicate how deferred taxes will be reported on the 2012 balance sheet. Gordon's product warranty is for 12 months.

(c) Prepare the income tax expense section of the income statement for 2012, beginning with the line "Pretax financial income."

•8 **E19-9** **(Carryback and Carryforward of NOL, No Valuation Account, No Temporary Differences)** The pretax financial income (or loss) figures for Synergetics Company are as follows.

2006	$160,000
2007	250,000
2008	90,000
2009	(160,000)
2010	(350,000)
2011	120,000
2012	100,000

Pretax financial income (or loss) and taxable income (loss) were the same for all years involved. Assume a 45% tax rate for 2006 and 2007 and a 40% tax rate for the remaining years.

Instructions

Prepare the journal entries for the years 2008 to 2012 to record income tax expense and the effects of the net operating loss carrybacks and carryforwards assuming Synergetics Company uses the carryback provision. All income and losses relate to normal operations. (In recording the benefits of a loss carryforward, assume that no valuation account is deemed necessary.)

•8 **E19-10** **(Two NOLs, No Temporary Differences, No Valuation Account, Entries and Income Statement)** Lanier Corporation has pretax financial income (or loss) equal to taxable income (or loss) from 2003 through 2011 as follows.

	Income (Loss)	Tax Rate
2003	$29,000	30%
2004	40,000	30%
2005	22,000	35%
2006	48,000	50%
2007	(150,000)	40%
2008	90,000	40%
2009	30,000	40%
2010	105,000	40%
2011	(50,000)	45%

Pretax financial income (loss) and taxable income (loss) were the same for all years since Lanier has been in business. Assume the carryback provision is employed for net operating losses. In recording the benefits of a loss carryforward, assume that it is more likely than not that the related benefits will be realized.

Instructions

(a) What entry(ies) for income taxes should be recorded for 2007?

(b) Indicate what the income tax expense portion of the income statement for 2007 should look like. Assume all income (loss) relates to continuing operations.

(c) What entry for income taxes should be recorded in 2008?

(d) How should the income tax expense section of the income statement for 2008 appear?

(e) What entry for income taxes should be recorded in 2011?

(f) How should the income tax expense section of the income statement for 2011 appear?

•2 •3 •9 **E19-11** **(Three Differences, Classify Deferred Taxes)** At December 31, 2010, Cascade Company had a net deferred tax liability of $450,000. An explanation of the items that compose this balance is as follows.

Temporary Differences	Resulting Balances in Deferred Taxes
1. Excess of tax depreciation over book depreciation	$200,000
2. Accrual, for book purposes, of estimated loss contingency from pending lawsuit that is expected to be settled in 2011. The loss will be deducted on the tax return when paid.	(50,000)
3. Accrual method used for book purposes and installment method used for tax purposes for an isolated installment sale of an investment.	300,000
	$450,000

In analyzing the temporary differences, you find that $30,000 of the depreciation temporary difference will reverse in 2011, and $120,000 of the temporary difference due to the installment sale will reverse in 2011. The tax rate for all years is 40%.

Instructions
Indicate the manner in which deferred taxes should be presented on Cascade Company's December 31, 2010, balance sheet.

·2·3·5 E19-12 (Two Temporary Differences, One Rate, Beginning Deferred Taxes, Compute Pretax Financial Income) The following facts relate to McKane Corporation.

1. Deferred tax liability, January 1, 2010, $60,000.
2. Deferred tax asset, January 1, 2010, $20,000.
3. Taxable income for 2010, $115,000.
4. Cumulative temporary difference at December 31, 2010, giving rise to future taxable amounts, $210,000.
5. Cumulative temporary difference at December 31, 2010, giving rise to future deductible amounts, $95,000.
6. Tax rate for all years, 40%. No permanent differences exist.
7. The company is expected to operate profitably in the future.

Instructions
(a) Compute the amount of pretax financial income for 2010.
(b) Prepare the journal entry to record income tax expense, deferred income taxes, and income taxes payable for 2010.
(c) Prepare the income tax expense section of the income statement for 2010, beginning with the line "Income before income taxes."
(d) Compute the effective tax rate for 2010.

·2·7 E19-13 (One Difference, Multiple Rates, Effect of Beginning Balance versus No Beginning Deferred Taxes) At the end of 2010, Wasicsko Company has $180,000 of cumulative temporary differences that will result in reporting future taxable amounts as follows.

2011	$ 70,000
2012	50,000
2013	40,000
2014	20,000
	$180,000

Tax rates enacted as of the beginning of 2009 are:

2009 and 2010	40%
2011 and 2012	30%
2013 and later	25%

Wasicsko's taxable income for 2010 is $340,000. Taxable income is expected in all future years.

Instructions
(a) Prepare the journal entry for Wasicsko to record income taxes payable, deferred income taxes, and income tax expense for 2010, assuming that there were no deferred taxes at the end of 2009.
(b) Prepare the journal entry for Wasicsko to record income taxes payable, deferred income taxes, and income tax expense for 2010, assuming that there was a balance of $22,000 in a Deferred Tax Liability account at the end of 2009.

·3·4 E19-14 (Deferred Tax Asset with and without Valuation Account) Callaway Corp. has a deferred tax asset account with a balance of $150,000 at the end of 2010 due to a single cumulative temporary difference of $375,000. At the end of 2011 this same temporary difference has increased to a cumulative amount of $500,000. Taxable income for 2011 is $850,000. The tax rate is 40% for all years. No valuation account related to the deferred tax asset is in existence at the end of 2010.

Instructions
(a) Record income tax expense, deferred income taxes, and income taxes payable for 2011, assuming that it is more likely than not that the deferred tax asset will be realized.
(b) Assuming that it is more likely than not that $30,000 of the deferred tax asset will not be realized, prepare the journal entry at the end of 2011 to record the valuation account.

·3·4·5 E19-15 (Deferred Tax Asset with Previous Valuation Account) Assume the same information as E19-14, except that at the end of 2010, Callaway Corp. had a valuation account related to its deferred tax asset of $40,000.

Instructions

(a) Record income tax expense, deferred income taxes, and income taxes payable for 2011, assuming that it is more likely than not that the deferred tax asset will be realized in full.

(b) Record income tax expense, deferred income taxes, and income taxes payable for 2011, assuming that it is more likely than not that none of the deferred tax asset will be realized.

E19-16 **(Deferred Tax Liability, Change in Tax Rate, Prepare Section of Income Statement)** Sharrer Inc.'s only temporary difference at the beginning and end of 2010 is caused by a $2 million deferred gain for tax purposes for an installment sale of a plant asset, and the related receivable (only one-half of which is classified as a current asset) is due in equal installments in 2011 and 2012. The related deferred tax liability at the beginning of the year is $800,000. In the third quarter of 2010, a new tax rate of 34% is enacted into law and is scheduled to become effective for 2012. Taxable income for 2010 is $5,000,000, and taxable income is expected in all future years.

Instructions

(a) Determine the amount reported as a deferred tax liability at the end of 2010. Indicate proper classification(s).

(b) Prepare the journal entry (if any) necessary to adjust the deferred tax liability when the new tax rate is enacted into law.

(c) Draft the income tax expense portion of the income statement for 2010. Begin with the line "Income before income taxes." Assume no permanent differences exist.

E19-17 **(Two Temporary Differences, Tracked through 3 Years, Multiple Rates)** Taxable income and pretax financial income would be identical for Jones Co. except for its treatments of gross profit on installment sales and estimated costs of warranties. The following income computations have been prepared.

Taxable income	2010	2011	2012
Excess of revenues over expenses (excluding two temporary differences)	$160,000	$210,000	$90,000
Installment gross profit collected	8,000	8,000	8,000
Expenditures for warranties	(5,000)	(5,000)	(5,000)
Taxable income	$163,000	$213,000	$93,000

Pretax financial income	2010	2011	2012
Excess of revenues over expenses (excluding two temporary differences)	$160,000	$210,000	$90,000
Installment gross profit earned	24,000	–0–	–0–
Estimated cost of warranties	(15,000)	–0–	–0–
Income before taxes	$169,000	$210,000	$90,000

The tax rates in effect are: 2010, 45%; 2011 and 2012, 40%. All tax rates were enacted into law on January 1, 2010. No deferred income taxes existed at the beginning of 2010. Taxable income is expected in all future years.

Instructions

Prepare the journal entry to record income tax expense, deferred income taxes, and income tax payable for 2010, 2011, and 2012.

E19-18 **(Three Differences, Multiple Rates, Future Taxable Income)** During 2010, Graham Co.'s first year of operations, the company reports pretax financial income of $250,000. Graham's enacted tax rate is 40% for 2010 and 35% for all later years. Graham expects to have taxable income in each of the next 5 years. The effects on future tax returns of temporary differences existing at December 31, 2010, are summarized below.

	Future Years					
	2011	2012	2013	2014	2015	Total
Future taxable (deductible) amounts:						
Installment sales	$32,000	$32,000	$32,000			$ 96,000
Depreciation	6,000	6,000	6,000	$6,000	$6,000	30,000
Unearned rent	(50,000)	(50,000)				(100,000)

Instructions

(a) Complete the schedule below to compute deferred taxes at December 31, 2010.

(b) Compute taxable income for 2010.

(c) Prepare the journal entry to record income tax payable, deferred taxes, and income tax expense for 2010.

| | Future Taxable | | December 31, 2010 | |
| | (Deductible) | Tax | Deferred Tax | |
Temporary Difference	Amounts	Rate	(Asset)	Liability
Installment sales	$ 96,000			
Depreciation	30,000			
Unearned rent	(100,000)	____	____	____
Totals	$_____			

·2 ·3 ·9 E19-19 (Two Differences, One Rate, Beginning Deferred Balance, Compute Pretax Financial Income) Shamess Co. establishes a $90 million liability at the end of 2010 for the estimated litigation settlement for manufacturing defects. All related costs will be paid and deducted on the tax return in 2011. Also, at the end of 2010, the company has $50 million of temporary differences due to excess depreciation for tax purposes, $7 million of which will reverse in 2011.

The enacted tax rate for all years is 40%, and the company pays taxes of $64 million on $160 million of taxable income in 2010. Shamess expects to have taxable income in 2011.

Instructions

(a) Determine the deferred taxes to be reported at the end of 2010.

(b) Indicate how the deferred taxes computed in (a) are to be reported on the balance sheet.

(c) Assuming that the only deferred tax account at the beginning of 2010 was a deferred tax liability of $10,000,000, draft the income tax expense portion of the income statement for 2010, beginning with the line "Income before income taxes." (*Hint:* You must first compute (1) the amount of temporary difference underlying the beginning $10,000,000 deferred tax liability, then (2) the amount of temporary differences originating or reversing during the year, then (3) the amount of pretax financial income.)

·2 ·3 ·9 E19-20 (Two Differences, No Beginning Deferred Taxes, Multiple Rates) Macinski Inc., in its first year of operations, has the following differences between the book basis and tax basis of its assets and liabilities at the end of 2010.

	Book Basis	Tax Basis
Equipment (net)	$400,000	$340,000
Estimated warranty liability	$150,000	$ –0–

It is estimated that the warranty liability will be settled in 2011. The difference in equipment (net) will result in taxable amounts of $20,000 in 2011, $30,000 in 2012, and $10,000 in 2013. The company has taxable income of $550,000 in 2010. As of the beginning of 2010, the enacted tax rate is 34% for 2010–2012, and 30% for 2013. Macinski expects to report taxable income through 2013.

Instructions

(a) Prepare the journal entry to record income tax expense, deferred income taxes, and income tax payable for 2010.

(b) Indicate how deferred income taxes will be reported on the balance sheet at the end of 2010.

·2 ·3 ·7 E19-21 (Two Temporary Differences, Multiple Rates, Future Taxable Income) Flynn Inc. has two tem-
·9 porary differences at the end of 2010. The first difference stems from installment sales, and the second one results from the accrual of a loss contingency. Flynn's accounting department has developed a schedule of future taxable and deductible amounts related to these temporary differences as follows.

	2011	2012	2013	2014
Taxable amounts	$40,000	$50,000	$60,000	$90,000
Deductible amounts		(15,000)	(19,000)	
	$40,000	$35,000	$41,000	$90,000

As of the beginning of 2010, the enacted tax rate is 34% for 2010 and 2011, and 38% for 2012–2015. At the beginning of 2010, the company had no deferred income taxes on its balance sheet. Taxable income for 2010 is $400,000. Taxable income is expected in all future years.

Instructions

(a) Prepare the journal entry to record income tax expense, deferred income taxes, and income taxes payable for 2010.

(b) Indicate how deferred income taxes would be classified on the balance sheet at the end of 2010.

·2·3·9 **E19-22 (Two Differences, One Rate, First Year)** The differences between the book basis and tax basis of the assets and liabilities of Morgan Corporation at the end of 2010 are presented below.

	Book Basis	Tax Basis
Accounts receivable	$50,000	$-0-
Litigation liability	20,000	-0-

It is estimated that the litigation liability will be settled in 2011. The difference in accounts receivable will result in taxable amounts of $30,000 in 2011 and $20,000 in 2012. The company has taxable income of $300,000 in 2010 and is expected to have taxable income in each of the following 2 years. Its enacted tax rate is 34% for all years. This is the company's first year of operations. The operating cycle of the business is 2 years.

Instructions

(a) Prepare the journal entry to record income tax expense, deferred income taxes, and income tax payable for 2010.

(b) Indicate how deferred income taxes will be reported on the balance sheet at the end of 2010.

·4·7·8 **E19-23 (NOL Carryback and Carryforward, Valuation Account versus No Valuation Account)** Sondgeroth Inc. reports the following pretax income (loss) for both financial reporting purposes and tax purposes. (Assume the carryback provision is used for a net operating loss.)

Year	Pretax Income (Loss)	Tax Rate
2009	$110,000	34%
2010	90,000	34%
2011	(260,000)	38%
2012	220,000	38%

The tax rates listed were all enacted by the beginning of 2009.

Instructions

(a) Prepare the journal entries for the years 2009–2012 to record income tax expense (benefit) and income tax payable (refundable) and the tax effects of the loss carryback and carryforward, assuming that at the end of 2011 the benefits of the loss carryforward are judged more likely than not to be realized in the future.

(b) Using the assumption in (a), prepare the income tax section of the 2011 income statement beginning with the line "Operating loss before income taxes."

(c) Prepare the journal entries for 2011 and 2012, assuming that based on the weight of available evidence, it is more likely than not that one-fourth of the benefits of the loss carryforward will not be realized.

(d) Using the assumption in (c), prepare the income tax section of the 2011 income statement beginning with the line "Operating loss before income taxes."

·4·7·8 **E19-24 (NOL Carryback and Carryforward, Valuation Account Needed)** Nielson Inc. reports the following pretax income (loss) for both book and tax purposes. (Assume the carryback provision is used where possible for a net operating loss.)

Year	Pretax Income (Loss)	Tax Rate
2009	$100,000	40%
2010	90,000	40%
2011	(240,000)	45%
2012	120,000	45%

The tax rates listed were all enacted by the beginning of 2009.

Instructions

(a) Prepare the journal entries for years 2009–2012 to record income tax expense (benefit) and income tax payable (refundable), and the tax effects of the loss carryback and loss carryforward, assuming that based on the weight of available evidence, it is more likely than not that one-half of the benefits of the loss carryforward will not be realized.

(b) Prepare the income tax section of the 2011 income statement beginning with the line "Operating loss before income taxes."

(c) Prepare the income tax section of the 2012 income statement beginning with the line "Income before income taxes."

E19-25 **(NOL Carryback and Carryforward, Valuation Account Needed)** Hayes Co. reported the following pretax financial income (loss) for the years 2009–2013.

2009	$240,000
2010	350,000
2011	90,000
2012	(550,000)
2013	180,000

Pretax financial income (loss) and taxable income (loss) were the same for all years involved. The enacted tax rate was 34% for 2009 and 2010, and 40% for 2011–2013. Assume the carryback provision is used first for net operating losses.

Instructions

(a) Prepare the journal entries for the years 2011–2013 to record income tax expense, income tax payable (refundable), and the tax effects of the loss carryback and loss carryforward, assuming that based on the weight of available evidence, it is more likely than not that one-fifth of the benefits of the loss carryforward will not be realized.

(b) Prepare the income tax section of the 2012 income statement beginning with the line "Income (loss) before income taxes."

See the book's companion website, www.wiley.com/college/kieso, for a set of B Exercises.

PROBLEMS

P19-1 **(Three Differences, No Beginning Deferred Taxes, Multiple Rates)** The following information is available for Remmers Corporation for 2010.

1. Depreciation reported on the tax return exceeded depreciation reported on the income statement by $120,000. This difference will reverse in equal amounts of $30,000 over the years 2011–2014.
2. Interest received on municipal bonds was $10,000.
3. Rent collected in advance on January 1, 2010, totaled $60,000 for a 3-year period. Of this amount, $40,000 was reported as unearned at December 31, for book purposes.
4. The tax rates are 40% for 2010 and 35% for 2011 and subsequent years.
5. Income taxes of $320,000 are due per the tax return for 2010.
6. No deferred taxes existed at the beginning of 2010.

Instructions

(a) Compute taxable income for 2010.
(b) Compute pretax financial income for 2010.
(c) Prepare the journal entries to record income tax expense, deferred income taxes, and income taxes payable for 2010 and 2011. Assume taxable income was $980,000 in 2011.
(d) Prepare the income tax expense section of the income statement for 2010, beginning with "Income before income taxes."

P19-2 **(One Temporary Difference, Tracked for 4 Years, One Permanent Difference, Change in Rate)** The pretax financial income of Truttman Company differs from its taxable income throughout each of 4 years as follows.

Year	Pretax Financial Income	Taxable Income	Tax Rate
2010	$290,000	$180,000	35%
2011	320,000	225,000	40%
2012	350,000	260,000	40%
2013	420,000	560,000	40%

Pretax financial income for each year includes a nondeductible expense of $30,000 (never deductible for tax purposes). The remainder of the difference between pretax financial income and taxable income in each period is due to one depreciation temporary difference. No deferred income taxes existed at the beginning of 2010.

Instructions

(a) Prepare journal entries to record income taxes in all 4 years. Assume that the change in the tax rate to 40% was not enacted until the beginning of 2011.

(b) Prepare the income statement for 2011, beginning with income before income taxes.

 P19-3 (Second Year of Depreciation Difference, Two Differences, Single Rate, Extraordinary Item) The following information has been obtained for the Gocker Corporation.

1. Prior to 2010, taxable income and pretax financial income were identical.
2. Pretax financial income is $1,700,000 in 2010 and $1,400,000 in 2011.
3. On January 1, 2010, equipment costing $1,200,000 is purchased. It is to be depreciated on a straight-line basis over 5 years for tax purposes and over 8 years for financial reporting purposes. (*Hint:* Use the half-year convention for tax purposes, as discussed in Appendix 11A.)
4. Interest of $60,000 was earned on tax-exempt municipal obligations in 2011.
5. Included in 2011 pretax financial income is an extraordinary gain of $200,000, which is fully taxable.
6. The tax rate is 35% for all periods.
7. Taxable income is expected in all future years.

Instructions

(a) Compute taxable income and income tax payable for 2011.

(b) Prepare the journal entry to record 2011 income tax expense, income tax payable, and deferred taxes.

(c) Prepare the bottom portion of Gocker's 2011 income statement, beginning with "Income before income taxes and extraordinary item."

(d) Indicate how deferred income taxes should be presented on the December 31, 2011, balance sheet.

 P19-4 (Permanent and Temporary Differences, One Rate) The accounting records of Shinault Inc. show the following data for 2010.

1. Life insurance expense on officers was $9,000.
2. Equipment was acquired in early January for $300,000. Straight-line depreciation over a 5-year life is used, with no salvage value. For tax purposes, Shinault used a 30% rate to calculate depreciation.
3. Interest revenue on State of New York bonds totaled $4,000.
4. Product warranties were estimated to be $50,000 in 2010. Actual repair and labor costs related to the warranties in 2010 were $10,000. The remainder is estimated to be paid evenly in 2011 and 2012.
5. Sales on an accrual basis were $100,000. For tax purposes, $75,000 was recorded on the installment-sales method.
6. Fines incurred for pollution violations were $4,200.
7. Pretax financial income was $750,000. The tax rate is 30%.

Instructions

(a) Prepare a schedule starting with pretax financial income in 2010 and ending with taxable income in 2010.

(b) Prepare the journal entry for 2010 to record income tax payable, income tax expense, and deferred income taxes.

 P19-5 (NOL without Valuation Account) Jennings Inc. reported the following pretax income (loss) and related tax rates during the years 2006–2012.

	Pretax Income (loss)	Tax Rate
2006	$ 40,000	30%
2007	25,000	30%
2008	50,000	30%
2009	80,000	40%
2010	(180,000)	45%
2011	70,000	40%
2012	100,000	35%

Pretax financial income (loss) and taxable income (loss) were the same for all years since Jennings began business. The tax rates from 2009–2012 were enacted in 2009.

Instructions

(a) Prepare the journal entries for the years 2010–2012 to record income tax payable (refundable), income tax expense (benefit), and the tax effects of the loss carryback and carryforward. Assume that Jennings elects the carryback provision where possible and expects to realize the benefits of any loss carryforward in the year that immediately follows the loss year.

(b) Indicate the effect the 2010 entry(ies) has on the December 31, 2010, balance sheet.

(c) Prepare the portion of the income statement, starting with "Operating loss before income taxes," for 2010.

(d) Prepare the portion of the income statement, starting with "Income before income taxes," for 2011.

  P19-6 **(Two Differences, Two Rates, Future Income Expected)** Presented below are two independent situations related to future taxable and deductible amounts resulting from temporary differences existing at December 31, 2010.

1. Mooney Co. has developed the following schedule of future taxable and deductible amounts.

	2011	2012	2013	2014	2015
Taxable amounts	$300	$300	$300	$ 300	$300
Deductible amount	—	—	—	(1,600)	—

2. Roesch Co. has the following schedule of future taxable and deductible amounts.

	2011	2012	2013	2014
Taxable amounts	$300	$300	$ 300	$300
Deductible amount	—	—	(2,300)	—

Both Mooney Co. and Roesch Co. have taxable income of $4,000 in 2010 and expect to have taxable income in all future years. The tax rates enacted as of the beginning of 2010 are 30% for 2010–2013 and 35% for years thereafter. All of the underlying temporary differences relate to noncurrent assets and liabilities.

Instructions
For each of these two situations, compute the net amount of deferred income taxes to be reported at the end of 2010, and indicate how it should be classified on the balance sheet.

 P19-7 **(One Temporary Difference, Tracked 3 Years, Change in Rates, Income Statement Presentation)** Crosley Corp. sold an investment on an installment basis. The total gain of $60,000 was reported for financial reporting purposes in the period of sale. The company qualifies to use the installment-sales method for tax purposes. The installment period is 3 years; one-third of the sale price is collected in the period of sale. The tax rate was 40% in 2010, and 35% in 2011 and 2012. The 35% tax rate was not enacted in law until 2011. The accounting and tax data for the 3 years is shown below.

	Financial Accounting	Tax Return
2010 (40% tax rate)		
Income before temporary difference	$ 70,000	$70,000
Temporary difference	60,000	20,000
Income	$130,000	$90,000
2011 (35% tax rate)		
Income before temporary difference	$ 70,000	$70,000
Temporary difference	–0–	20,000
Income	$ 70,000	$90,000
2012 (35% tax rate)		
Income before temporary difference	$ 70,000	$70,000
Temporary difference	–0–	20,000
Income	$ 70,000	$90,000

Instructions
(a) Prepare the journal entries to record the income tax expense, deferred income taxes, and the income tax payable at the end of each year. No deferred income taxes existed at the beginning of 2010.

(b) Explain how the deferred taxes will appear on the balance sheet at the end of each year. (Assume the Installment Accounts Receivable is classified as a current asset.)

(c) Draft the income tax expense section of the income statement for each year, beginning with "Income before income taxes."

P19-8 **(Two Differences, 2 Years, Compute Taxable Income and Pretax Financial Income)** The following information was disclosed during the audit of Elbert Inc.

1.

Year	Amount Due per Tax Return
2010	$130,000
2011	104,000

2. On January 1, 2010, equipment costing $600,000 is purchased. For financial reporting purposes, the company uses straight-line depreciation over a 5-year life. For tax purposes, the company uses the elective straight-line method over a 5-year life. (*Hint:* For tax purposes, the half-year convention as discussed in Appendix 11A must be used.)

3. In January 2011, $225,000 is collected in advance rental of a building for a 3-year period. The entire $225,000 is reported as taxable income in 2011, but $150,000 of the $225,000 is reported as unearned revenue in 2011 for financial reporting purposes. The remaining amount of unearned revenue is to be earned equally in 2012 and 2013.

4. The tax rate is 40% in 2010 and all subsequent periods. (*Hint:* To find taxable income in 2010 and 2011, the related income tax payable amounts will have to be "grossed up.")

5. No temporary differences existed at the end of 2009. Elbert expects to report taxable income in each of the next 5 years.

Instructions

(a) Determine the amount to report for deferred income taxes at the end of 2010, and indicate how it should be classified on the balance sheet.

(b) Prepare the journal entry to record income taxes for 2010.

(c) Draft the income tax section of the income statement for 2010 beginning with "Income before income taxes." (*Hint:* You must compute taxable income and then combine that with changes in cumulative temporary differences to arrive at pretax financial income.)

(d) Determine the deferred income taxes at the end of 2011, and indicate how they should be classified on the balance sheet.

(e) Prepare the journal entry to record income taxes for 2011.

(f) Draft the income tax section of the income statement for 2011, beginning with "Income before income taxes."

P19-9 **(Five Differences, Compute Taxable Income and Deferred Taxes, Draft Income Statement)** Wise Company began operations at the beginning of 2011. The following information pertains to this company.

1. Pretax financial income for 2011 is $100,000.

2. The tax rate enacted for 2011 and future years is 40%.

3. Differences between the 2011 income statement and tax return are listed below:

(a) Warranty expense accrued for financial reporting purposes amounts to $7,000. Warranty deductions per the tax return amount to $2,000.

(b) Gross profit on construction contracts using the percentage-of-completion method per books amounts to $92,000. Gross profit on construction contracts for tax purposes amounts to $67,000.

(c) Depreciation of property, plant, and equipment for financial reporting purposes amounts to $60,000. Depreciation of these assets amounts to $80,000 for the tax return.

(d) A $3,500 fine paid for violation of pollution laws was deducted in computing pretax financial income.

(e) Interest revenue earned on an investment in tax-exempt municipal bonds amounts to $1,500. (Assume (a) is short-term in nature; assume (b) and (c) are long-term in nature.)

4. Taxable income is expected for the next few years.

Instructions

(a) Compute taxable income for 2011.

(b) Compute the deferred taxes at December 31, 2011, that relate to the temporary differences described above. Clearly label them as deferred tax asset or liability.

(c) Prepare the journal entry to record income tax expense, deferred taxes, and income taxes payable for 2011.

(d) Draft the income tax expense section of the income statement beginning with "Income before income taxes."

· · · · · · · · · · · · · · · · · · · CONCEPTS FOR ANALYSIS · · · · · · · · · · · · · · · · · · ·

CA19-1 **(Objectives and Principles for Accounting for Income Taxes)** The amount of income taxes due to the government for a period of time is rarely the amount reported on the income statement for that period as income tax expense.

Instructions

(a) Explain the objectives of accounting for income taxes in general purpose financial statements.

(b) Explain the basic principles that are applied in accounting for income taxes at the date of the financial statements to meet the objectives discussed in (a).

(c) List the steps in the annual computation of deferred tax liabilities and assets.

CA19-2 **(Basic Accounting for Temporary Differences)** Dexter Company appropriately uses the asset-liability method to record deferred income taxes. Dexter reports depreciation expense for certain machinery purchased this year using the modified accelerated cost recovery system (MACRS) for income tax purposes and the straight-line basis for financial reporting purposes. The tax deduction is the larger amount this year.

Dexter received rent revenues in advance this year. These revenues are included in this year's taxable income. However, for financial reporting purposes, these revenues are reported as unearned revenues, a current liability.

Instructions
(a) What are the principles of the asset-liability approach?
(b) How would Dexter account for the temporary differences?
(c) How should Dexter classify the deferred tax consequences of the temporary differences on its balance sheet?

CA19-3 **(Identify Temporary Differences and Classification Criteria)** The asset-liability approach for recording deferred income taxes is an integral part of generally accepted accounting principles.

Instructions
(a) Indicate whether each of the following independent situations should be treated as a temporary difference or as a permanent difference, and explain why.
  (1) Estimated warranty costs (covering a 3-year warranty) are expensed for financial reporting purposes at the time of sale but deducted for income tax purposes when paid.
  (2) Depreciation for book and income tax purposes differs because of different bases of carrying the related property, which was acquired in a trade-in. The different bases are a result of different rules used for book and tax purposes to compute the basis of property acquired in a trade-in.
  (3) A company properly uses the equity method to account for its 30% investment in another company. The investee pays dividends that are about 10% of its annual earnings.
  (4) A company reports a gain on an involuntary conversion of a nonmonetary asset to a monetary asset. The company elects to replace the property within the statutory period using the total proceeds so the gain is not reported on the current year's tax return.
(b) Discuss the nature of the deferred income tax accounts and possible classifications in a company's balance sheet. Indicate the manner in which these accounts are to be reported.

CA19-4 **(Accounting and Classification of Deferred Income Taxes)**
Part A
This year Gumowski Company has each of the following items in its income statement.

  1. Gross profits on installment sales.
  2. Revenues on long-term construction contracts.
  3. Estimated costs of product warranty contracts.
  4. Premiums on officers' life insurance policies with Gumowski as beneficiary.

Instructions
(a) Under what conditions would deferred income taxes need to be reported in the financial statements?
(b) Specify when deferred income taxes would need to be recognized for each of the items above, and indicate the rationale for such recognition.

Part B
Gumowski Company's president has heard that deferred income taxes can be classified in different ways in the balance sheet.

Instructions
Identify the conditions under which deferred income taxes would be classified as a noncurrent item in the balance sheet. What justification exists for such classification?

(AICPA adapted)

CA19-5 **(Explain Computation of Deferred Tax Liability for Multiple Tax Rates)** At December 31, 2010, Higley Corporation has one temporary difference which will reverse and cause taxable amounts in 2011. In 2010 a new tax act set taxes equal to 45% for 2010, 40% for 2011, and 34% for 2012 and years thereafter.

Instructions
Explain what circumstances would call for Higley to compute its deferred tax liability at the end of 2010 by multiplying the cumulative temporary difference by:

  (a) 45%.
  (b) 40%.
  (c) 34%.

CA19-6 **(Explain Future Taxable and Deductible Amounts, How Carryback and Carryforward Affects Deferred Taxes)** Maria Rodriquez and Lynette Kingston are discussing accounting for income taxes. They are currently studying a schedule of taxable and deductible amounts that will arise in the future as a result of existing temporary differences. The schedule is as follows.

	Current Year	Future Years			
	2010	2011	2012	2013	2014
Taxable income	$850,000				
Taxable amounts		$375,000	$375,000	$ 375,000	$375,000
Deductible amounts				(2,400,000)	
Enacted tax rate	50%	45%	40%	35%	30%

Instructions

(a) Explain the concept of future taxable amounts and future deductible amounts as illustrated in the schedule.

(b) How do the carryback and carryforward provisions affect the reporting of deferred tax assets and deferred tax liabilities?

CA19-7 **(Deferred Taxes, Income Effects)** Stephanie Delaney, CPA, is the newly hired director of corporate taxation for Acme Incorporated, which is a publicly traded corporation. Ms. Delaney's first job with Acme was the review of the company's accounting practices on deferred income taxes. In doing her review, she noted differences between tax and book depreciation methods that permitted Acme to realize a sizable deferred tax liability on its balance sheet. As a result, Acme paid very little in income taxes at that time.

Delaney also discovered that Acme has an explicit policy of selling off plant assets before they reversed in the deferred tax liability account. This policy, coupled with the rapid expansion of its plant asset base, allowed Acme to "defer" all income taxes payable for several years, even though it always has reported positive earnings and an increasing EPS. Delaney checked with the legal department and found the policy to be legal, but she's uncomfortable with the ethics of it.

Instructions

Answer the following questions.

(a) Why would Acme have an explicit policy of selling plant assets before the temporary differences reversed in the deferred tax liability account?

(b) What are the ethical implications of Acme's "deferral" of income taxes?

(c) Who could be harmed by Acme's ability to "defer" income taxes payable for several years, despite positive earnings?

(d) In a situation such as this, what are Ms. Delaney's professional responsibilities as a CPA?

USING YOUR JUDGMENT

FINANCIAL REPORTING

Financial Reporting Problem

The Procter & Gamble Company (P&G)

The financial statements of **P&G** are presented in Appendix 5B or can be accessed at the book's companion website, **www.wiley.com/college/kieso**.

Instructions

Refer to P&G's financial statements and the accompanying notes to answer the following questions.

(a) What amounts relative to income taxes does P&G report in its:

  (1) 2007 income statement?

  (2) June 30, 2007, balance sheet?

  (3) 2007 statement of cash flows?

(b) P&G's provision for income taxes in 2005, 2006, and 2007 was computed at what effective tax rates? (See the notes to the financial statements.)

(c) How much of P&G's 2007 total provision for income taxes was current tax expense, and how much was deferred tax expense?

(d) What did P&G report as the significant components (the details) of its June 30, 2007, deferred tax assets and liabilities?

Comparative Analysis Case

The Coca-Cola Company and PepsiCo, Inc.

Instructions

Go to the book's companion website and use information found there to answer the following questions related to **The Coca-Cola Company** and **PepsiCo, Inc.**

(a) What are the amounts of Coca-Cola's and PepsiCo's provision for income taxes for the year 2007? Of each company's 2007 provision for income taxes, what portion is current expense and what portion is deferred expense?

(b) What amount of cash was paid in 2007 for income taxes by Coca-Cola and by PepsiCo?

(c) What was the U.S. federal statutory tax rate in 2007? What was the effective tax rate in 2007 for Coca-Cola and PepsiCo? Why might their effective tax rates differ?

(d) For the year-end 2007, what amounts were reported by Coca-Cola and PepsiCo as (a) gross deferred tax assets and (b) gross deferred tax liabilities?

(e) Do either Coca-Cola or PepsiCo disclose any net operating loss carrybacks and/or carryforwards at year-end 2007? What are the amounts, and when do the carryforwards expire?

Financial Statement Analysis Case

Homestake Mining Company

Homestake Mining Company is a 120-year-old international gold mining company with substantial gold mining operations and exploration in the United States, Canada, and Australia. At year-end, Homestake reported the following items related to income taxes (thousands of dollars).

Total current taxes	$ 26,349
Total deferred taxes	(39,436)
Total income and mining taxes (the provision for taxes per its income statement)	(13,087)
Deferred tax liabilities	$303,050
Deferred tax assets, net of valuation allowance of $207,175	95,275
Net deferred tax liability	$207,775

Note 6: The classification of deferred tax assets and liabilities is based on the related asset or liability creating the deferred tax. Deferred taxes not related to a specific asset or liability are classified based on the estimated period of reversal.

Tax loss carryforwards (U.S., Canada, Australia, and Chile)	$71,151
Tax credit carryforwards	$12,007

Instructions

(a) What is the significance of Homestake's disclosure of "Current taxes" of $26,349 and "Deferred taxes" of $(39,436)?

(b) Explain the concept behind Homestake's disclosure of gross deferred tax liabilities (future taxable amounts) and gross deferred tax assets (future deductible amounts).

(c) Homestake reported tax loss carryforwards of $71,151 and tax credit carryforwards of $12,007. How do the carryback and carryforward provisions affect the reporting of deferred tax assets and deferred tax liabilities?

BRIDGE TO THE PROFESSION

Professional Research: FASB Codification

Kleckner Company started operations in 2007, and although it has grown steadily, the company reported accumulated operating losses of $450,000 in its first four years in business. In the most recent year (2011), Kleckner appears to have turned the corner and reported modest taxable income of $30,000. In addition to a deferred tax asset related to its net operating loss, Kleckner has recorded a deferred tax asset related to product warranties and a deferred tax liability related to accelerated depreciation.

Given its past operating results, Kleckner has established a full valuation allowance for its deferred tax assets. However, given its improved performance, Kleckner management wonders whether the company can now reduce or eliminate the valuation allowance. They would like you to conduct some research on the accounting for its valuation allowance.

Instructions

Access the FASB Codification at *http://asc.fasb.org/home* to conduct research using the Codification Research System to prepare responses to the following items. Provide Codification references for your responses.

(a) Briefly explain to Kleckner management the importance of future taxable income as it relates to the valuation allowance for deferred tax assets.

(b) What are the sources of income that may be relied upon to remove the need for a valuation allowance?

(c) What are tax-planning strategies? From the information provided, does it appear that Kleckner could employ a tax-planning strategy to support reducing its valuation allowance?

Professional Simulation

Go to the book's companion website, at **www.wiley.com/college/kieso,** to find an interactive problem that simulates the computerized CPA exam. The professional simulation for this chapter asks you to address questions related to the accounting for taxes.

Remember to check the book's companion website to find additional resources for this chapter.

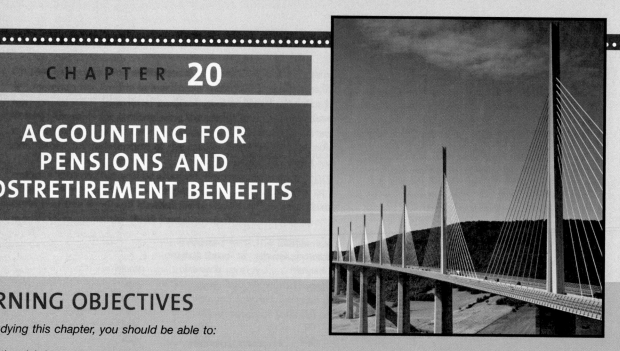

CHAPTER 20

ACCOUNTING FOR PENSIONS AND POSTRETIREMENT BENEFITS

LEARNING OBJECTIVES

After studying this chapter, you should be able to:

•1 Distinguish between accounting for the employer's pension plan and accounting for the pension fund.

•2 Identify types of pension plans and their characteristics.

•3 Explain alternative measures for valuing the pension obligation.

•4 List the components of pension expense.

•5 Use a worksheet for employer's pension plan entries.

•6 Describe the amortization of prior service costs.

•7 Explain the accounting for unexpected gains and losses.

•8 Explain the corridor approach to amortizing gains and losses.

•9 Describe the requirements for reporting pension plans in financial statements.

WHERE HAVE ALL THE PENSIONS GONE?

Many companies have benefit plans that promise income and other benefits to retired employees in exchange for services during their working years. However, a shift is on from traditional defined-benefit plans, in which employers bear the risk of meeting the benefit promises, to plans in which employees bear more of the risk. In some cases, employers are dropping retirement plans altogether. Here are some of the reasons for the shift.

Competition. Newer and foreign competitors do not have the same retiree costs that older U.S. companies do. Southwest Airlines does not offer a traditional pension plan, but Northwest and United both have pension deficits exceeding $100,000 per employee.

Cost. Retirees are living longer, and the costs of retirement are higher. Combined with annual retiree healthcare costs, retirement benefits are costing the S&P 500 companies over $25 billion a year and are rising at double-digit rates.

Insurance. Pensions are backed by premiums paid to the Pension Benefit Guarantee Corporation (PBGC). When a company fails, the PBGC takes over the plan. But due to a number of significant company failures, the PBGC is running a deficit, and healthy companies are subsidizing the weak. For example, steel companies pay just 3 percent of PBGC premiums but account for 56 percent of the claims.

Accounting. To bring U.S. standards in line with international rules, accounting rule makers are considering rules that will require companies to "mark their pensions to market" (value them at market rates). Such a move would increase the reported volatility of the retirement plan and of company financial statements. When Britain made this shift, 25 percent of British companies closed their plans to new entrants.

As a result of such factors, it is not hard to believe that experts can think of no major company that has instituted a traditional pension plan in the past decade.

What does this mean for you as you evaluate job offers and benefit packages in the not-too-distant future? To start, you should begin building *your own* retirement nest egg, rather than relying on your employer to provide postretirement income and healthcare benefits. A look at recent data on retirees' financial position, summarized in the chart to the right, supports a strategy to become more self-reliant.

As indicated, the average person at retirement has about $360,000 in resources to sustain him or her in the retirement years. However, Social Security and traditional pension benefits comprise a substantial share of wealth for typical near-to-retirement households—nearly two-thirds of their $361,000 in total wealth. This wealth snapshot highlights the extraordinary importance of Social Security, traditional pensions, and owner-occupied housing (not very liquid) for typical near-retiree households today. Together, these assets comprise nearly four-fifths of wealth of those on the verge of retirement.

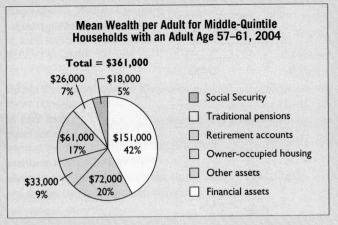

However, these sources of income are in decline and will likely continue to shrink as employers and governments wrestle with financial and other constraints discussed earlier. That means that retirement accounts, including individual retirement accounts and defined-contribution pensions such as 401(k) plans, will need to become a bigger piece of the pie to fill the gap left by smaller government and employer-sponsored benefits. So get started now with a personal savings strategy to ensure an adequate nest egg at your retirement.

Sources: Story adapted from Nanette Byrnes with David Welch, "The Benefits Trap," *BusinessWeek* (July 19, 2004), pp. 54–72. *Source of chart*: G. Mermin, "Typical Wealth Held by Those at the Verge of Retirement," Urban Institute, *http://www.urban.org/url.cfm?ID=411618* (February 22, 2008).

PREVIEW OF CHAPTER 20

As our opening story indicates, the cost of retirement benefits is getting steep. For example, General Motors' pension and healthcare costs for retirees in a recent year totaled $6.2 billion, or approximately $1,784 per vehicle produced. General Motors and many other companies are facing substantial pension and other postretirement expenses and obligations. In this chapter we discuss the accounting issues related to these benefit plans. The content and organization of the chapter are as follows.

ACCOUNTING FOR PENSIONS AND POSTRETIREMENT BENEFITS

NATURE OF PENSION PLANS	ACCOUNTING FOR PENSIONS	USING A PENSION WORKSHEET	REPORTING PENSION PLANS IN FINANCIAL STATEMENTS
• Defined-contribution plan • Defined-benefit plan • Role of actuaries	• Alternative measures of liability • Recognition of net funded status • Components of pension expense	• 2010 entries and worksheet • Amortization of prior service cost • 2011 entries and worksheet • Gain or loss • 2012 entries and worksheet	• Within the financial statements • Within the notes to the financial statements • Pension note disclosure • 2013 entries and worksheet— a comprehensive example • Special issues

NATURE OF PENSION PLANS

A **pension plan** is an arrangement whereby an employer provides benefits (payments) to retired employees for services they provided in their working years. Pension accounting may be divided and separately treated as **accounting for the employer** and **accounting for the pension fund**. The *company* or *employer* is the organization sponsoring the pension plan. It incurs the cost and makes contributions to the pension fund. The *fund* or *plan* is the entity that receives the contributions from the employer, administers the pension assets, and makes the benefit payments to the retired employees (pension recipients). Illustration 20-1 shows the three entities involved in a pension plan and indicates the flow of cash among them.

ILLUSTRATION 20-1
Flow of Cash among
Pension Plan Participants

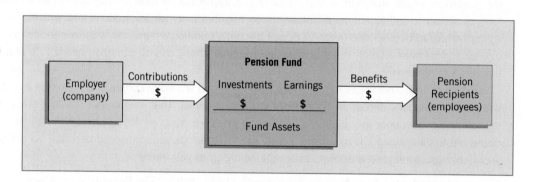

A pension plan is **funded** when the employer makes payments to a funding agency.[1] That agency accumulates the assets of the pension fund and makes payments to the recipients as the benefits come due.

Some pension plans are **contributory**. In these, the employees bear part of the cost of the stated benefits or voluntarily make payments to increase their benefits. Other plans are **noncontributory**. In these plans, the employer bears the entire cost. Companies generally design their pension plans so as to take advantage of federal income tax benefits. Plans that offer tax benefits are called **qualified pension plans**. They permit **deductibility of the employer's contributions to the pension fund and tax-free status of earnings from pension fund assets**.

The pension fund should be a separate legal and accounting entity. The pension fund, as a separate entity, maintains a set of books and prepares financial statements. Maintaining records and preparing financial statements for the fund, an activity known as "accounting for employee benefit plans," is not the subject of this chapter.[2] Instead, this chapter explains the pension accounting and reporting problems **of the employer** as the sponsor of a pension plan.

The need to properly administer and account for pension funds becomes apparent when you understand the size of these funds. Listed in Illustration 20-2 (on page 1051) are the pension fund assets and pension expenses of seven major companies.

---

[1]When used as a verb, **fund** means to pay to a funding agency (as to fund future pension benefits or to fund pension cost). Used as a noun, it refers to assets accumulated in the hands of a funding agency (trustee) for the purpose of meeting pension benefits when they become due.

See the FASB Codification section (page 1092).

[2]The FASB issued a separate standard covering the accounting and reporting for employee benefit plans. [1]

ILLUSTRATION 20-2
Pension Funds and
Pension Expense

Company ($ in millions)	Size of Pension Fund	2007 Pension Expense	Pension Expense as % of Pretax Income
General Motors	$117,378	$1,799	28.77%
Hewlett-Packard	4,258	(81)	0.88
Deere & Company	10,002	99	3.70
Goodyear Tire	6,566	344	74.14
Merck	7,385	447	13.27
The Coca-Cola Company	3,428	113	1.44
Molson Coors Brewing	5,031	21	4.01

As Illustration 20-2 indicates, pension expense is a substantial percentage of total pretax income for many companies.[3] The two most common types of pension plans are **defined-contribution plans** and **defined-benefit plans**, and we look at each of them in the following sections.

Defined-Contribution Plan

In a **defined-contribution plan**, the employer agrees to contribute to a pension trust a certain sum each period, based on a formula. This formula may consider such factors as age, length of employee service, employer's profits, and compensation level. **The plan defines only the employer's contribution.** It makes no promise regarding the ultimate benefits paid out to the employees. A common form of this plan is a **401(k) plan**.

> **Objective·2**
> Identify types of pension plans and their characteristics.

The size of the pension benefits that the employee finally collects under the plan depends on several factors: the amounts originally contributed to the pension trust, the income accumulated in the trust, and the treatment of forfeitures of funds caused by early terminations of other employees. A company usually turns over to an **independent third-party trustee** the amounts originally contributed. The trustee, acting on behalf of the beneficiaries (the participating employees), assumes ownership of the pension assets and is accountable for their investment and distribution. The trust is separate and distinct from the employer.

The accounting for a defined-contribution plan is straightforward. The employee gets the benefit of gain (or the risk of loss) from the assets contributed to the pension plan. The employer simply contributes each year based on the formula established in the plan. As a result, the employer's annual cost (pension expense) is simply the amount that it is obligated to contribute to the pension trust. The employer reports a liability on its balance sheet only if it does not make the contribution in full. The employer reports an asset only if it contributes more than the required amount.

Disclosures for Defined-Contribution Plans

In addition to pension expense, the employer must disclose the following for a defined-contribution plan: a plan description, including employee groups covered; the basis for determining contributions; and the nature and effect of significant matters affecting comparability from period to period. [2]

Defined-Benefit Plan

A **defined-benefit plan** outlines the benefits that employees will receive when they retire. These benefits typically are a function of an employee's years of service and of the compensation level in the years approaching retirement.

To meet the defined-benefit commitments that will arise at retirement, a company must determine what the contribution should be today (a time value of money computation). Companies may use many different contribution approaches. However, the

[3]One study indicated that during the 1990s, pension funds (private and public) held or owned approximately 25 percent of the market value of corporate stock outstanding and accounted for 32 percent of the daily trading volume on the New York Stock Exchange. The enormous size (and the social significance) of these funds is staggering.

INTERNATIONAL
INSIGHT

Outside the U.S., private pension plans are less common because many other nations rely on government-sponsored pension plans. Consequently, accounting for defined-benefit pension plans is typically a less important issue elsewhere in the world.

funding method should provide enough money at retirement to meet the benefits defined by the plan.

The **employees** are the beneficiaries of a defined-**contribution** trust, but the **employer** is the beneficiary of a defined-**benefit** trust. Under a defined-benefit plan, the trust's primary purpose is to safeguard and invest assets so that there will be enough to pay the employer's obligation to the employees. **In form**, the trust is a separate entity. **In substance**, the trust assets and liabilities belong to the employer. That is, **as long as the plan continues, the employer is responsible for the payment of the defined benefits (without regard to what happens in the trust)**. The employer must make up any shortfall in the accumulated assets held by the trust. On the other hand, the employer can recapture any excess accumulated in the trust, either through reduced future funding or through a reversion of funds.

Because a defined-benefit plan specifies benefits in terms of uncertain future variables, a company must establish an appropriate funding pattern to ensure the availability of funds at retirement in order to provide the benefits promised. This funding level depends on a number of factors such as turnover, mortality, length of employee service, compensation levels, and interest earnings.

Employers are at risk with defined-benefit plans because they must contribute enough to meet the cost of benefits that the plan defines. The expense recognized each period is not necessarily equal to the cash contribution. Similarly, the liability is controversial because its measurement and recognition relate to unknown future variables. Thus, the accounting issues related to this type of plan are complex. **Our discussion in the following sections deals primarily with defined-benefit plans.**[4]

WHICH PLAN IS RIGHT FOR YOU?

What do the numbers mean?

Defined-contribution plans have become much more popular with employers than defined-benefit plans. One reason is that they are cheaper. Defined-contribution plans often cost no more than 3 percent of payroll, whereas defined-benefit plans can cost 5 to 6 percent of payroll.

In the late 1970s approximately 15 million individuals had defined-contribution plans; today over 62 million do. The following chart reflects this significant change. It shows the percentage of companies using various types of plans, based on a survey of approximately 150 CFOs and managing corporate directors.

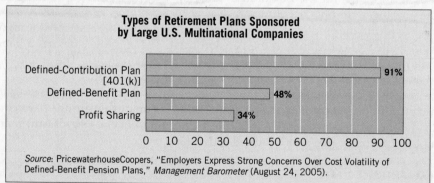

Types of Retirement Plans Sponsored by Large U.S. Multinational Companies

Defined-Contribution Plan [401(k)] — 91%
Defined-Benefit Plan — 48%
Profit Sharing — 34%

Source: PricewaterhouseCoopers, "Employers Express Strong Concerns Over Cost Volatility of Defined-Benefit Pension Plans," *Management Barometer* (August 24, 2005).

Although many companies are changing to defined-contribution plans, over 40 million individuals still are covered under defined-benefit plans.

[4]In terms of total assets, recent Federal Reserve (2005) statistics indicate that assets in private defined-benefit and defined-contribution plans were more than $14.4 trillion. In many cases, companies offer a defined-contribution plan in combination with a defined-benefit plan. A recent federal law requires employees to explicitly opt out of an employer-sponsored defined-contribution plan. This should help employees build their own nest eggs (as suggested in the opening story) and will contribute to further growth in defined-contribution plans. See D. Darlin, "On Making Enrollment in a 401(k) Automatic," *New York Times* (August 19, 2006), p. B1.

The Role of Actuaries in Pension Accounting

The problems associated with pension plans involve complicated mathematical considerations. Therefore, companies engage **actuaries** to ensure that a pension plan is appropriate for the employee group covered.[5] Actuaries are individuals trained through a long and rigorous certification program to assign probabilities to future events and their financial effects. The insurance industry employs actuaries to assess risks and to advise on the setting of premiums and other aspects of insurance policies. Employers rely heavily on actuaries for assistance in developing, implementing, and funding pension funds.

Actuaries make predictions (called *actuarial assumptions*) of mortality rates, employee turnover, interest and earnings rates, early retirement frequency, future salaries, and any other factors necessary to operate a pension plan. They also compute the various pension measures that affect the financial statements, such as the pension obligation, the annual cost of servicing the plan, and the cost of amendments to the plan. In summary, accounting for defined-benefit pension plans relies heavily upon information and measurements provided by actuaries.

ACCOUNTING FOR PENSIONS

In accounting for a company's pension plan, two questions arise: (1) What is the pension obligation that a company should report in the financial statements? (2) What is the pension expense for the period? Attempting to answer the first question has produced much controversy.

> **Objective·3**
> Explain alternative measures for valuing the pension obligation.

Alternative Measures of the Liability

Most agree that an employer's **pension obligation** is the deferred compensation obligation it has to its employees for their service under the terms of the pension plan. Measuring that obligation is not so simple, though, because there are alternative ways of measuring it.[6]

One measure of the pension obligation is to base it only on the benefits vested to the employees. Vested benefits are those that the employee is entitled to receive even if he or she renders no additional services to the company. Most pension plans require a certain minimum number of years of service to the employer before an employee achieves vested benefits status. Companies compute the **vested benefit obligation** using only vested benefits, at current salary levels.

Another way to measure the obligation uses both vested and nonvested years of service. On this basis, the company computes the deferred compensation amount on all years of employees' service—**both vested and nonvested**—using current salary levels. This measurement of the pension obligation is called the **accumulated benefit obligation**.

[5]An actuary's primary purpose is to ensure that the company has established an appropriate funding pattern to meet its pension obligations. This computation involves developing a set of assumptions and continued monitoring of these assumptions to ensure their realism. That the general public has little understanding of what an actuary does is illustrated by the following excerpt from the *Wall Street Journal*: "A polling organization once asked the general public what an actuary was, and received among its more coherent responses the opinion that it was a place where you put dead actors."

[6]One measure of the pension obligation is to determine the amount that the Pension Benefit Guaranty Corporation would require the employer to pay if it defaulted. (This amount is limited to 30 percent of the employer's net worth.) The accounting profession rejected this approach for financial reporting because it is too hypothetical and ignores the going concern concept.

A third measure bases the deferred compensation amount on both vested and non-vested service **using future salaries**. This measurement of the pension obligation is called the **projected benefit obligation**. Because future salaries are expected to be higher than current salaries, this approach results in the largest measurement of the pension obligation.

The choice between these measures is critical. The choice affects the amount of a company's pension liability and the annual pension expense reported. The diagram in Illustration 20-3 presents the differences in these three measurements.

ILLUSTRATION 20-3
Different Measures of the Pension Obligation

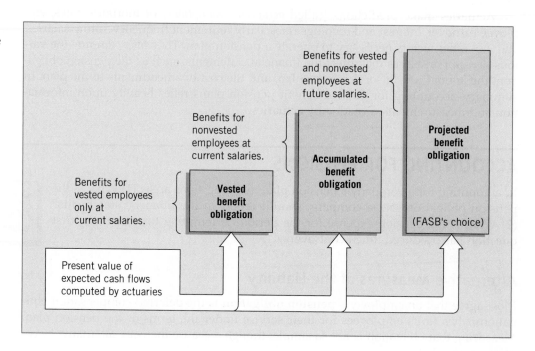

Which of these alternative measures of the pension liability does the profession favor? **The profession adopted the projected benefit obligation—the present value of vested and nonvested benefits accrued to date, based on employees' future salary levels.**[7] Those in favor of the projected benefit obligation contend that a promise by an employer to pay benefits based on a percentage of the employees' future salaries is far greater than a promise to pay a percentage of their current salary, and such a difference should be reflected in the pension liability and pension expense.

Moreover, companies discount to present value the estimated future benefits to be paid. Minor changes in the interest rate used to discount pension benefits can dramatically affect the measurement of the employer's obligation. For example, a 1 percent decrease in the discount rate can increase pension liabilities 15 percent. Accounting rules require that, at each measurement date, a company must determine the appropriate discount rate used to measure the pension liability, based on current interest rates.

Underlying Concepts

The FASB and IASB are studying whether the liability should include estimates of future salaries. This debate will center on whether a company can have a liability today that is based in part on future salaries that have not yet been earned.

---

[7]When we use the term "present value of benefits" throughout this chapter, we really mean the *actuarial* present value of benefits. **Actuarial present value** is the amount payable adjusted to reflect the time value of money *and* the probability of payment (by means of decrements for events such as death, disability, withdrawals, or retirement) between the present date and the expected date of payment. For simplicity, though, we use the term "present value" instead of "actuarial present value" in our discussion.

Recognition of the Net Funded Status of the Pension Plan

Companies must recognize on their balance sheet the full overfunded or underfunded status of their defined-benefit pension plan.[8] [3] The **overfunded** or **underfunded status** is measured as the difference between the fair value of the plan assets and the projected benefit obligation.

INTERNATIONAL INSIGHT

iGAAP differs from U.S. GAAP in that companies have the option to report the funded status of their pension plans on the balance sheet.

To illustrate, assume that Coker Company has a projected benefit obligation of $300,000, and the fair value of its plan assets is $210,000. In this case, Coker Company's pension plan is underfunded, and therefore it reports a pension liability of $90,000 ($300,000 − $210,000) on its balance sheet. If, instead, the fair value of Coker's plan assets were $430,000, it would report a pension asset of $130,000 ($430,000 − $300,000).

As recently as 2004, pension plans for companies in the S&P 500 were underfunded (liabilities exceeded assets) in the aggregate by $158.4 billion. In 2007, by slowing the growth of pension liabilities and increasing contributions to pension funds, the S&P 500 companies reported aggregate overfunding (assets exceeded liabilities) of $61.9 billion.[9]

Components of Pension Expense

There is broad agreement that companies should account for pension cost on the **accrual basis**.[10] The profession recognizes that **accounting for pension plans requires measurement of the cost and its identification with the appropriate time periods**. The determination of pension cost, however, is extremely complicated because it is a function of the following components.

Objective·4
List the components of pension expense.

1. **Service Cost.** Service cost is the expense caused by the increase in pension benefits payable (the **projected benefit obligation**) to employees because of their services rendered during the current year. Actuaries compute **service cost** as the present value of the new benefits earned by employees during the year.

2. **Interest on the Liability.** Because a pension is a deferred compensation arrangement, there is a time value of money factor. As a result, companies record the pension liability on a discounted basis. **Interest expense accrues each year on the projected benefit obligation just as it does on any discounted debt.** The actuary helps to select the interest rate, referred to as the settlement rate.

Underlying Concepts

The expense recognition principle and the definition of a liability justify accounting for pension cost on the accrual basis. This requires recording an expense when employees earn the future benefits, and recognizing an existing obligation to pay pensions later based on current services received.

3. **Actual Return on Plan Assets.** The return earned by the accumulated pension fund assets in a particular year is relevant in measuring the net cost to the employer of sponsoring an employee pension plan. Therefore, **a company should adjust annual pension expense for interest and dividends that accumulate within the fund, as well as increases and decreases in the market value of the fund assets**.

4. **Amortization of Prior Service Cost.** Pension plan amendments (including initiation of a pension plan) often include provisions to increase benefits (or in rare situations, to decrease benefits) for employee service provided in prior years. A company grants plan amendments with the expectation that it will realize economic benefits in future periods. Thus, **it allocates the cost (prior service cost) of providing these**

---

[8]Recognize that GAAP applies to pensions as well as other postretirement benefit plans (OPEBs). Appendix 20A addresses the accounting for OPEBs.

[9]J. Ciesielski, "Benefit Plans 2007: Close To The Edge—And Back," *The Analyst's Accounting Observer* (April 25, 2008).

[10]At one time, companies applied the **cash basis** of accounting to pension plans by recognizing the amount paid in a particular accounting period as the pension expense for the period. The problem was that the amount paid or funded in a fiscal period depended on financial management and was too often discretionary. For example, funding could depend on the availability of cash, the level of earnings, or other factors unrelated to the requirements of the plan. Application of the cash basis made it possible to manipulate the amount of pension expense appearing in the income statement simply by varying the cash paid to the pension fund.

retroactive benefits to pension expense in the future, specifically to the remaining service-years of the affected employees.

5. *Gain or Loss.* Volatility in pension expense can result from sudden and large changes in the market value of plan assets and by changes in the projected benefit obligation (which changes when actuaries modify assumptions or when actual experience differs from expected experience). Two items comprise this gain or loss: (1) the difference between the actual return and the expected return on plan assets, and (2) amortization of the net gain or loss from previous periods. We will discuss this complex computation later in the chapter.

Illustration 20-4 shows the **components of pension expense** and their effect on total pension expense (increase or decrease).

ILLUSTRATION 20-4
Components of Annual
Pension Expense

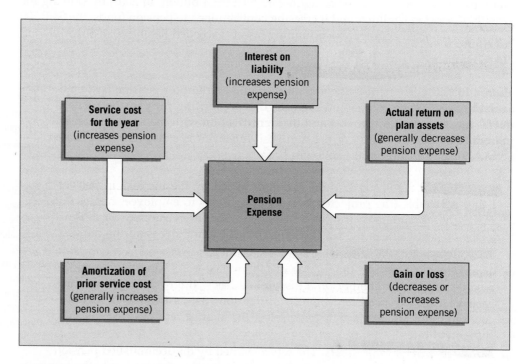

Service Cost

The service cost is the **actuarial present value of benefits attributed by the pension benefit formula to employee service during the period**. That is, the actuary predicts the additional benefits that an employer must pay under the plan's benefit formula as a result of the employees' current year's service, and then discounts the cost of those future benefits back to their present value.

The Board concluded that **companies must consider future compensation levels in measuring the present obligation and periodic pension expense if the plan benefit formula incorporates them**. In other words, the present obligation resulting from a promise to pay a benefit of 1 percent of an employee's **final pay** differs from the promise to pay 1 percent of **current pay**. To overlook this fact is to ignore an important aspect of pension expense. Thus, the FASB adopts the **benefits/years-of-service actuarial method, which determines pension expense based on future salary levels**.

Some object to this determination, arguing that a company should have more freedom to select an expense recognition pattern. Others believe that incorporating future salary increases into current pension expense is accounting for events that have not yet happened. They argue that if a company terminates the plan today, it pays only liabilities for accumulated benefits. **Nevertheless, the FASB indicates that the projected benefit obligation provides a more realistic measure of the employer's obligation under the plan on a going concern basis and, therefore, companies should use it as the basis for determining service cost.**

Interest on the Liability

The second component of pension expense is **interest on the liability**, or **interest expense**. Because a company defers paying the liability until maturity, the company records it on a discounted basis. The liability then accrues interest over the life of the employee. **The interest component is the interest for the period on the projected benefit obligation outstanding during the period.** The FASB did not address the question of how often to compound the interest cost. To simplify our illustrations and problem materials, we use a simple-interest computation, applying it to the beginning-of-the-year balance of the projected benefit liability.

How do companies determine the interest rate to apply to the pension liability? The Board states that the assumed discount rate should **reflect the rates at which companies can effectively settle pension benefits**. In determining these **settlement rates**, companies should look to rates of return on high-quality fixed-income investments currently available, whose cash flows match the timing and amount of the expected benefit payments. The objective of selecting the assumed discount rates is to measure a single amount that, if invested in a portfolio of high-quality debt instruments, would provide the necessary future cash flows to pay the pension benefits when due.

Actual Return on Plan Assets

Pension plan assets are usually investments in stocks, bonds, other securities, and real estate that a company holds to earn a reasonable return, generally at minimum risk. Employer contributions and actual returns on pension plan assets increase pension plan assets. Benefits paid to retired employees decrease them. As we indicated, the actual return earned on these assets increases the fund balance and correspondingly reduces the employer's net cost of providing employees' pension benefits. That is, the higher the actual return on the pension plan assets, the less the employer has to contribute eventually and, therefore, the less pension expense that it needs to report.

The **actual return on the plan assets** is the increase in pension funds from interest, dividends, and realized and unrealized changes in the fair-market value of the plan assets. Companies compute the actual return by adjusting the change in the plan assets for the effects of contributions during the year and benefits paid out during the year. The equation in Illustration 20-5, or a variation thereof, can be used to compute the actual return.

$$\begin{array}{c} \text{Actual} \\ \text{Return} \end{array} = \left(\begin{array}{c} \text{Plan} \\ \text{Assets} \\ \text{Ending} \\ \text{Balance} \end{array} - \begin{array}{c} \text{Plan} \\ \text{Assets} \\ \text{Beginning} \\ \text{Balance} \end{array} \right) - (\text{Contributions} - \text{Benefits Paid})$$

ILLUSTRATION 20-5
Equation for Computing Actual Return

Stated another way, the actual return on plan assets is the difference between the **fair value of the plan assets** at the beginning of the period and at the end of the period, adjusted for contributions and benefit payments. Illustration 20-6 uses the equation above to compute the actual return, using some assumed amounts.

Fair value of plan assets at end of period		$5,000,000
Deduct: Fair value of plan assets at beginning of period		4,200,000
Increase in fair value of plan assets		800,000
Deduct: Contributions to plan during period	$500,000	
Less benefits paid during period	300,000	200,000
Actual return on plan assets		$ 600,000

ILLUSTRATION 20-6
Computation of Actual Return on Plan Assets

If the actual return on the plan assets is positive (a gain) during the period, a company subtracts it when computing pension expense. If the actual return is negative (a loss) during the period, the company adds it when computing pension expense.[11]

---

[11]At this point, we use the actual rate of return. Later, for purposes of computing pension expense, we use the expected rate of return.

USING A PENSION WORKSHEET

We will now illustrate the basic computation of pension expense using the first three components: (1) service cost, (2) interest on the liability, and (3) actual return on plan assets. We discuss the other pension-expense components (amortization of prior service cost, and gains and losses) in later sections.

Objective·5

Use a worksheet for employer's pension plan entries.

Companies often use a worksheet to record pension-related information. As its name suggests, the worksheet is a working tool. A worksheet is **not** a permanent accounting record: it is neither a journal nor part of the general ledger. The worksheet is merely a device to make it easier to prepare entries and the financial statements.[12] Illustration 20-7 shows the format of the **pension worksheet**.

ILLUSTRATION 20-7
Basic Format of Pension Worksheet

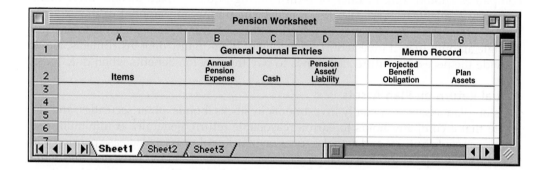

The "General Journal Entries" columns of the worksheet (near the left side) determine the entries to record in the formal general ledger accounts. The "Memo Record" columns (on the right side) maintain balances in the projected benefit obligation and the plan assets. The difference between the projected benefit obligation and the fair value of the plan assets is the **pension asset/liability**, which is shown in the balance sheet. If the projected benefit obligation is greater than the plan assets, a pension liability occurs. If the projected benefit obligation is less than the plan assets, a pension asset occurs.

On the first line of the worksheet, a company records the beginning balances (if any). It then records subsequent transactions and events related to the pension plan using debits and credits, using both sets of columns as if they were one. For each transaction or event, the debits must equal the credits. **The ending balance in the Pension Asset/Liability column should equal the net balance in the memo record.**

2010 Entries and Worksheet

To illustrate the use of a worksheet and how it helps in accounting for a pension plan, assume that on January 1, 2010, Zarle Company provides the following information related to its pension plan for the year 2010.

Plan assets, January 1, 2010, are $100,000.

Projected benefit obligation, January 1, 2010, is $100,000.

Annual service cost is $9,000.

Settlement rate is 10 percent.

Actual return on plan assets is $10,000.

Funding contributions are $8,000.

Benefits paid to retirees during the year are $7,000.

---

[12]The use of a pension entry worksheet is recommended and illustrated by Paul B. W. Miller, "The New Pension Accounting (Part 2)," *Journal of Accountancy* (February 1987), pp. 86–94.

Using the data presented on page 1058, the worksheet in Illustration 20-8 presents the beginning balances and all of the pension entries recorded by Zarle in 2010. Zarle records the beginning balances for the projected benefit obligation and the pension plan assets on the first line of the worksheet in the memo record. Because the projected benefit obligation and the plan assets are the same at January 1, 2010, the Pension Asset/Liability account has a zero balance at January 1, 2010.

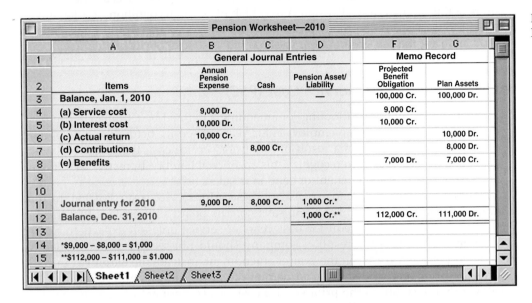

	A	B	C	D	F	G
1		**General Journal Entries**			**Memo Record**	
2	**Items**	Annual Pension Expense	Cash	Pension Asset/ Liability	Projected Benefit Obligation	Plan Assets
3	Balance, Jan. 1, 2010			—	100,000 Cr.	100,000 Dr.
4	(a) Service cost	9,000 Dr.			9,000 Cr.	
5	(b) Interest cost	10,000 Dr.			10,000 Cr.	
6	(c) Actual return	10,000 Cr.				10,000 Dr.
7	(d) Contributions		8,000 Cr.			8,000 Dr.
8	(e) Benefits				7,000 Dr.	7,000 Cr.
9						
10						
11	Journal entry for 2010	9,000 Dr.	8,000 Cr.	1,000 Cr.*		
12	Balance, Dec. 31, 2010			1,000 Cr.**	112,000 Cr.	111,000 Dr.
13						
14	*$9,000 – $8,000 = $1,000					
15	**$112,000 – $111,000 = $1.000					

Pension Worksheet—2010

ILLUSTRATION 20-8
Pension Worksheet—2010

Entry (a) in Illustration 20-8 records the service cost component, which increases pension expense by $9,000 and increases the liability (projected benefit obligation) by $9,000. Entry (b) accrues the interest expense component, which increases both the liability and the pension expense by $10,000 (the beginning projected benefit obligation multiplied by the settlement rate of 10 percent). Entry (c) records the actual return on the plan assets, which increases the plan assets and decreases the pension expense. Entry (d) records Zarle's contribution (funding) of assets to the pension fund, thereby decreasing cash by $8,000 and increasing plan assets by $8,000. Entry (e) records the benefit payments made to retirees, which results in equal $7,000 decreases to the plan assets and the projected benefit obligation.

Zarle makes the "formal journal entry" on December 31, which records the pension expense in 2010, as follows.

2010

Pension Expense	9,000	
Cash		8,000
Pension Asset/Liability		1,000

The credit to Pension Asset/Liability for $1,000 represents the difference between the 2010 pension expense of $9,000 and the amount funded of $8,000. Pension Asset/Liability (credit) is a liability because Zarle underfunds the plan by $1,000. The Pension Asset/Liability account balance of $1,000 also equals the net of the balances in the memo accounts. Illustration 20-9 shows that the projected benefit obligation exceeds the plan assets by $1,000, which reconciles to the pension liability reported in the balance sheet.

Projected benefit obligation (Credit)	$(112,000)
Plan assets at fair value (Debit)	111,000
Pension asset/liability (Credit)	$ (1,000)

ILLUSTRATION 20-9
Pension Reconciliation Schedule—December 31, 2010

If the net of the memo record balances is a credit, the reconciling amount in the pension asset/liability column will be a credit equal in amount. If the net of the memo record balances is a debit, the pension asset/liability amount will be a debit equal in amount. The worksheet is designed to produce this reconciling feature, which is useful later in the preparation of the financial statements and required note disclosure related to pensions.

In this illustration (for 2010), the debit to Pension Expense exceeds the credit to Cash, resulting in a credit to Pension Asset/Liability—the recognition of a liability. If the credit to Cash exceeded the debit to Pension Expense, Zarle would debit Pension Asset/Liability—the recognition of an asset.

Amortization of Prior Service Cost (PSC)

Objective·6

Describe the amortization of prior service costs.

When either initiating (adopting) or amending a defined-benefit plan, a company often provides benefits to employees for years of service before the date of initiation or amendment. As a result of this prior service cost, the projected benefit obligation is increased to recognize this additional liability. In many cases, the increase in the projected benefit obligation is substantial.

Should a company report an expense for these **prior service costs (PSC)** at the time it initiates or amends a plan? The FASB says no. The Board's rationale is that the employer would not provide credit for past years of service unless it expects to receive benefits in the future. As a result, a company should not recognize the **retroactive benefits** as pension expense in the year of amendment. Instead, **the employer initially records the prior service cost as an adjustment to other comprehensive income. The employer then recognizes the prior service cost as a component of pension expense over the remaining service lives of the employees who are expected to benefit from the change in the plan.**

The cost of the retroactive benefits (including any benefits provided to existing retirees) is the increase in the projected benefit obligation at the date of the amendment. An actuary computes the amount of the prior service cost. Amortization of the prior service cost is also an accounting function performed with the assistance of an actuary.

The Board prefers a **years-of-service method** that is similar to a units-of-production computation. First, the company computes the total number of service-years to be worked by all of the participating employees. Second, it divides the prior service cost by the total number of service-years, to obtain a cost per service-year (the unit cost). Third, the company multiplies the number of service-years consumed each year by the cost per service-year, to obtain the annual amortization charge.

To illustrate the amortization of the prior service cost under the years-of-service method, assume that Zarle Company's defined-benefit pension plan covers 170 employees. In its negotiations with the employees, Zarle Company amends its pension plan on January 1, 2011, and grants $80,000 of prior service costs to its employees. The employees are grouped according to expected years of retirement, as shown below.

Group	Number of Employees	Expected Retirement on Dec. 31
A	40	2011
B	20	2012
C	40	2013
D	50	2014
E	20	2015
	170	

Illustration 20-10 shows computation of the service-years per year and the total service-years.

ILLUSTRATION 20-10
Computation of Service-Years

			Service-Years			
Year	A	B	C	D	E	Total
2011	40	20	40	50	20	170
2012		20	40	50	20	130
2013			40	50	20	110
2014				50	20	70
2015					20	20
	40	40	120	200	100	500

Computed on the basis of a prior service cost of $80,000 and a total of 500 service-years for all years, the cost per service-year is $160 ($80,000 ÷ 500). The annual amount of amortization based on a $160 cost per service-year is computed as follows.

ILLUSTRATION 20-11
Computation of Annual Prior Service Cost Amortization

Year	Total Service-Years	×	Cost per Service-Year	=	Annual Amortization
2011	170		$160		$27,200
2012	130		160		20,800
2013	110		160		17,600
2014	70		160		11,200
2015	20		160		3,200
	500				$80,000

An alternative method of computing amortization of **prior service cost is permitted: Employers may use straight-line amortization over the average remaining service life of the employees.** In this case, with 500 service-years and 170 employees, the average would be 2.94 years (500 ÷ 170). The annual expense would be $27,211 ($80,000 ÷ 2.94). Using this method, Zarle Company would charge cost to expense in 2011, 2012, and 2013 as follows.

Year	Expense
2011	$27,211
2012	27,211
2013	25,578*
	$80,000

*.94 × $27,211

2011 Entries and Worksheet

Continuing the Zarle Company illustration into 2011, we note that the company amends the pension plan on January 1, 2011, to grant employees prior service benefits with a present value of $80,000. Zarle uses the annual amortization amounts, as computed in the previous section using the years-of-service approach ($27,200 for 2011). The following additional facts apply to the pension plan for the year 2011.

Annual service cost is $9,500.

Settlement rate is 10 percent.

Actual return on plan assets is $11,100.

Annual funding contributions are $20,000.

Benefits paid to retirees during the year are $8,000.

Amortization of prior service cost (PSC) using the years-of-service method is $27,200.

Accumulated other comprehensive income (hereafter referred to as accumulated OCI) on December 31, 2010, is zero.

Illustration 20-12 presents a worksheet of all the pension entries and information recorded by Zarle in 2011. We now add an additional column to the worksheet to record the prior service cost adjustment to other comprehensive income. In addition, as shown in the last two lines of the "Items" column, the other comprehensive income amount related to prior service cost is added to accumulated other comprehensive income ("Accumulated OCI") to arrive at a debit balance of $52,800 at December 31, 2011.

ILLUSTRATION 20-12
Pension Worksheet—2011

	A	B	C	D	E	G	H
1		General Journal Entries				Memo Record	
2				Other Comprehensive Income			
3	Items	Annual Pension Expense	Cash	Prior Service Cost	Pension Asset/Liability	Projected Benefit Obligation	Plan Assets
4	Balance, Dec. 31, 2010				1,000 Cr.	112,000 Cr.	111,000 Dr.
5	(f) Prior service cost			80,000 Dr.		80,000 Cr.	0
6							
7	Balance, Jan. 1, 2011					192,000 Cr.	111,000 Dr.
8	(g) Service cost	9,500 Dr.				9,500 Cr.	
9	(h) Interest cost	19,200 Dr.				19,200 Cr.	
10	(i) Actual return	11,100 Cr.					11,100 Dr.
11	(j) Amortization of PSC	27,200 Dr.		27,200 Cr.			
12	(k) Contributions		20,000 Cr.				20,000 Dr.
13	(l) Benefits					8,000 Dr.	8,000 Cr.
14							
15	Journal entry for 2011	44,800 Dr.	20,000 Cr.	52,800 Dr.	77,600 Cr.		
16							
17	Accumulated OCI, Dec. 31, 2010			0			
18	Balance, Dec. 31, 2011			52,800 Dr.	78,600 Cr.	212,700 Cr.	134,100 Dr.
19							

The first line of the worksheet shows the beginning balances of the Pension Asset/Liability account and the memo accounts. Entry (f) records Zarle's granting of prior service cost, by adding $80,000 to the projected benefit obligation and decreasing other comprehensive income—prior service cost by the same amount. Entries (g), (h), (i), (k), and (l) are similar to the corresponding entries in 2010. To compute the interest cost on the projected benefit obligation for entry (h), we use the beginning projected benefit balance of $192,000, which has been adjusted for the prior service cost amendment on January 1, 2011. Entry (j) records the 2011 amortization of prior service cost by debiting Pension Expense for $27,200 and crediting **Other Comprehensive Income (PSC)** for the same amount.

Zarle makes the following journal entry on December 31 to formally record the 2011 pension expense (the sum of the annual pension expense column), and related pension information.

2011

Pension Expense	44,800	
Other Comprehensive Income (PSC)	52,800	
Cash		20,000
Pension Asset/Liability		77,600

Because the debits to Pension Expense and to Other Comprehensive Income (PSC) exceed the funding, Zarle credits the Pension Asset/Liability account for the $77,600 difference. That account is a liability. In 2011, as in 2010, the balance of the Pension

Asset/Liability account ($78,600) is equal to the net of the balances in the memo accounts, as shown in Illustration 20-13.

ILLUSTRATION 20-13
Pension Reconciliation
Schedule—December 31,
2011

Projected benefit obligation (Credit)	$(212,700)
Plan assets at fair value (Debit)	134,100
Pension asset/liability (Credit)	$ (78,600)

The reconciliation is the formula that makes the worksheet work. It relates the components of pension accounting, recorded and unrecorded, to one another.

Gain or Loss

Of great concern to companies that have pension plans are the uncontrollable and unexpected swings in pension expense that can result from (1) sudden and large changes in the market value of plan assets, and (2) changes in actuarial assumptions that affect the amount of the projected benefit obligation. If these gains or losses impact fully the financial statements in the period of realization or incurrence, substantial fluctuations in pension expense result.

Objective·7
Explain the accounting for
unexpected gains and losses.

Therefore, the FASB decided to reduce the volatility associated with pension expense by using **smoothing techniques** that dampen and in some cases fully eliminate the fluctuations.

Smoothing Unexpected Gains and Losses on Plan Assets

One component of pension expense, actual return on plan assets, reduces pension expense (assuming the actual return is positive). A large change in the actual return can substantially affect pension expense for a year. Assume a company has a 40 percent return in the stock market for the year. Should this substantial, and perhaps one-time, event affect current pension expense?

Actuaries ignore current fluctuations when they develop a funding pattern to pay expected benefits in the future. They develop an **expected rate of return** and multiply it by an asset value weighted over a reasonable period of time to arrive at an **expected return on plan assets**. They then use this return to determine a company's funding pattern.

The FASB adopted the actuary's approach to dampen wide swings that might occur in the actual return. That is, a company includes the **expected return** on the plan assets as a component of pension expense, not the actual return in a given year. To achieve this goal, the company multiplies the expected rate of return by the market-related value of the plan assets. The **market-related asset value** of the plan assets is either the fair value of plan assets or a calculated value that recognizes changes in fair value in a systematic and rational manner. [4][13]

The difference between the expected return and the actual return is referred to as the **unexpected gain or loss**; the FASB uses the term **asset gains and losses**. **Asset gains** occur when actual return exceeds expected return; **asset losses** occur when actual return is less than expected return.

What happens to unexpected gains or losses in the accounting for pensions? Companies record asset gains and asset losses in an account, **Other Comprehensive Income (G/L)**, combining them with gains and losses accumulated in prior years. This treatment

---

[13]Companies may use different ways of determining the calculated market-related value for different classes of assets. For example, an employer might use fair value for bonds and a five-year-moving-average for equities. But companies should consistently apply the manner of determining market-related value from year to year for each asset class. Throughout our Zarle illustrations, we assume that market-related values based on a calculated value and the fair value of plan assets are equal. *For homework purposes,* use the fair value of plan assets as the measure for the market-related value.

is similar to prior service cost. The Board believes this treatment is consistent with the practice of including in other comprehensive income certain changes in value that have not been recognized in net income (for example, unrealized gains and losses on available-for-sale securities). [5] In addition, the accounting is simple, transparent, and symmetrical.

To illustrate the computation of an unexpected gain or loss and its related accounting, assume that in 2012, Zarle Company has an actual return on plan assets of $12,000 when the expected return is $13,410 (the expected rate of return of 10% on plan assets times the beginning of the year plan assets). The unexpected asset loss of $1,410 ($12,000 − $13,410) is debited to Other Comprehensive Income (G/L) and credited to Pension Expense.

PENSION COSTS UPS AND DOWNS

What do the numbers mean?

For some companies, pension plans generated real profits in the late 1990s. The plans not only paid for themselves but also increased earnings. This happens when the expected return on pension assets exceed the company's annual costs. At **Norfolk Southern**, pension income amounted to 12 percent of operating profit. It tallied 11 percent of operating profit at **Lucent Technologies**, **Coastal Corp.**, and **Unisys Corp.** The issue is important because in these cases management is not driving the operating income—pension income is. And as a result, income can change quickly.

Unfortunately, when the stock market stops booming, pension expense substantially increases for many companies. The reason: Expected return on a smaller asset base no longer offsets pension service costs and interest on the projected benefit obligation. As a result, many companies find it difficult to meet their earnings targets, and at a time when meeting such targets is crucial to maintaining the stock price.

Smoothing Unexpected Gains and Losses on the Pension Liability

In estimating the projected benefit obligation (the liability), actuaries make assumptions about such items as mortality rate, retirement rate, turnover rate, disability rate, and salary amounts. Any change in these actuarial assumptions affects the amount of the projected benefit obligation. Seldom does actual experience coincide exactly with actuarial predictions. These unexpected gains or losses from changes in the projected benefit obligation are called **liability gains and losses**.

Companies report liability gains (resulting from unexpected decreases in the liability balance) and liability losses (resulting from unexpected increases) in Other Comprehensive Income (G/L). Companies combine the liability gains and losses in the same Other Comprehensive Income (G/L) account used for asset gains and losses. They accumulate the asset and liability gains and losses from year to year that are not amortized in Accumulated Other Comprehensive Income. This amount is reported on the balance sheet in the stockholders' equity section.

Corridor Amortization

Objective·8

Explain the corridor approach to amortizing gains and losses.

The asset gains and losses and the liability gains and losses can offset each other. As a result, the Accumulated OCI account related to gains and losses may not grow very large. But, it is possible that no offsetting will occur and that the balance in the Accumulated OCI account related to gains and losses will continue to grow.

To limit the growth of the Accumulated OCI account, the FASB invented the **corridor approach** for amortizing the account's accumulated balance when it gets too large. How large is too large? The FASB set a limit of 10 percent of the larger of the beginning balances of the projected benefit obligation or the market-related value of the plan assets. **Above that size, the Accumulated OCI account related to gains and losses is considered too large and must be amortized.**

To illustrate the corridor approach, data for Callaway Co.'s projected benefit obligation and plan assets over a period of six years are shown in Illustration 20-14.

ILLUSTRATION 20-14
Computation of the Corridor

Beginning-of-the-Year Balances	Projected Benefit Obligation	Market-Related Asset Value	Corridor* +/- 10%
2009	$1,000,000	$ 900,000	$100,000
2010	1,200,000	1,100,000	120,000
2011	1,300,000	1,700,000	170,000
2012	1,500,000	2,250,000	225,000
2013	1,700,000	1,750,000	175,000
2014	1,800,000	1,700,000	180,000

*The corridor becomes 10% of the larger (in colored type) of the projected benefit obligation or the market-related plan asset value.

How the corridor works becomes apparent when we portray the data graphically, as in Illustration 20-15.

ILLUSTRATION 20-15
Graphic Illustration of the Corridor

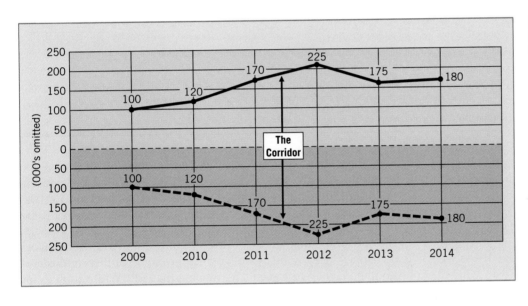

If the balance in the Accumulated OCI account related to gains and losses stays within the upper and lower limits of the corridor, no amortization is required. In that case, Callaway carries forward unchanged the accumulated OCI related to gains and losses.

If amortization is required, the minimum amortization is the excess divided by the average remaining service period of active employees who are expected to receive benefits under the plan. Callaway may use any systematic method of amortization of gains and losses in lieu of the minimum, provided it is greater than the minimum. It must use the method consistently for both gains and losses, and must disclose the amortization method used.

Example of Gains/Losses

In applying the corridor, companies should include amortization of the net gain or loss as a component of pension expense only if, at the **beginning of the year**, the net gain or loss in Accumulated OCI exceeded the corridor. That is, if no net gain or loss exists in Accumulated OCI at the beginning of the period, the company cannot recognize pension expense gains or losses in that period.

To illustrate the amortization of net gains and losses, assume the following information for Soft-White, Inc.

	2010	2011	2012
	(beginning of the year)		
Projected benefit obligation	$2,100,000	$2,600,000	$2,900,000
Market-related asset value	2,600,000	2,800,000	2,700,000

Soft-White recorded in Other Comprehensive Income actuarial losses of $400,000 in 2010 and $300,000 in 2011.

If the average remaining service life of all active employees is 5.5 years, the schedule to amortize the net gain or loss is as shown in Illustration 20-16.

ILLUSTRATION 20-16
Corridor Test and
Gain/Loss Amortization
Schedule

Year	Projected Benefit Obligation[a]	Plan Assets[a]	Corridor[b]	Accumulated OCI (G/L)[a]	Minimum Amortization of Loss (For Current Year)
2010	$2,100,000	$2,600,000	$260,000	$ –0–	$ –0–
2011	2,600,000	2,800,000	280,000	400,000	21,818[c]
2012	2,900,000	2,700,000	290,000	678,182[d]	70,579[d]

[a]All as of the beginning of the period.
[b]10% of the greater of projected benefit obligation or plan assets market-related value.
[c]$400,000 − $280,000 = $120,000; $120,000 ÷ 5.5 = $21,818
[d]$400,000 − $21,818 + $300,000 = $678,182; $678,182 − $290,000 = $388,182; $388,182 ÷ 5.5 = $70,579.

As Illustration 20-16 indicates, the loss recognized in 2011 increased pension expense by $21,818. This amount is small in comparison with the total loss of $400,000. It indicates that the corridor approach dampens the effects (reduces volatility) of these gains and losses on pension expense.

The rationale for the corridor is that gains and losses result from refinements in estimates as well as real changes in economic value; over time, some of these gains and losses will offset one another. It therefore seems reasonable that Soft-White should not fully recognize gains and losses as a component of pension expense in the period in which they arise.

However, Soft-White should immediately recognize in net income certain gains and losses—if they arise from a single occurrence not directly related to the operation of the pension plan and not in the ordinary course of the employer's business. For example, a gain or loss that is directly related to a plant closing, a disposal of a business component, or a similar event that greatly affects the size of the employee work force, should be recognized as a part of the gain or loss associated with that event.

For example, at one time, **Bethlehem Steel** reported a quartererly loss of $477 million. A great deal of this loss was attributable to future estimated benefits payable to workers who were permanently laid off. In this situation, the loss should be treated as an adjustment to the gain or loss on the plant closing and should not affect pension cost for the current or future periods.

Summary of Calculations for Asset Gain or Loss
The difference between the actual return on plan assets and the expected return on plan assets is the **unexpected asset gain or loss** component. This component defers the difference between the actual return and expected return on plan assets in computing

current-year pension expense. Thus, after considering this component, **it is really the expected return on plan assets (not the actual return) that determines current pension expense**.

Companies determine the amortized net gain or loss by amortizing the Accumulated OCI amount related to net gain or loss at the beginning of the year subject to the corridor limitation. In other words, **if the accumulated gain or loss is greater than the corridor, these net gains and losses are subject to amortization**. Soft-White computed this minimum amortization by dividing the net gains or losses subject to amortization by the average remaining service period. When the current-year unexpected gain or loss is combined with the amortized net gain or loss, we determine the current-year gain or loss. Illustration 20-17 summarizes these gain and loss computations.

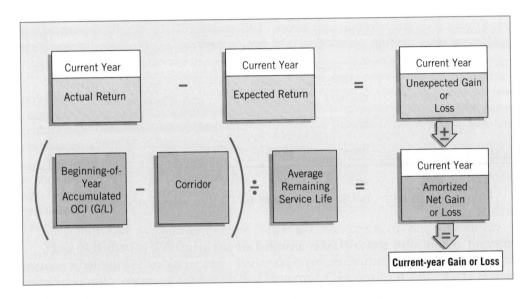

ILLUSTRATION 20-17
Graphic Summary of Gain or Loss Computation

In essence, these gains and losses are subject to *triple* smoothing. That is, companies first smooth the asset gain or loss by using the expected return. Second, they do not amortize the accumulated gain or loss at the beginning of the year unless it is greater than the corridor. Finally, they spread the excess over the remaining service life of existing employees.

2012 Entries and Worksheet

Continuing the Zarle Company illustration, the following facts apply to the pension plan for 2012.

Annual service cost is $13,000.
Settlement rate is 10 percent; expected earnings rate is 10 percent.
Actual return on plan assets is $12,000.
Amortization of prior service cost (PSC) is $20,800.
Annual funding contributions are $24,000.
Benefits paid to retirees during the year are $10,500.
Changes in actuarial assumptions resulted in an end-of-year projected benefit obligation of $265,000.

The worksheet in Illustration 20-18 (on page 1068) presents all of Zarle's 2012 pension entries and related information. The first line of the worksheet records the beginning balances that relate to the pension plan. In this case, Zarle's beginning balances are the ending balances from its 2011 pension worksheet in Illustration 20-12 (page 1062).

	A	B	C	D	E	F	H	I
				Pension Worksheet—2012				
1			**General Journal Entries**				**Memo Record**	
2				**Other Comprehensive Income**				
3	**Items**	**Annual Pension Expense**	**Cash**	**Prior Service Cost**	**Gains/Losses**	**Pension Asset/Liability**	**Projected Benefit Obligation**	**Plan Assets**
4	Balance, Jan. 1, 2012					78,600 Cr.	212,700 Cr.	134,100 Dr.
5	(m) Service cost	13,000 Dr.					13,000 Cr.	
6	(n) Interest cost	21,270 Dr.					21,270 Cr.	
7	(o) Actual return	12,000 Cr.						12,000 Dr.
8	(p) Unexpected loss	1,410 Cr.			1,410 Dr.			
9	(q) Amortization of PSC	20,800 Dr.		20,800 Cr.				
10	(r) Contributions		24,000 Cr.					24,000 Dr.
11	(s) Benefits						10,500 Dr.	10,500 Cr.
12	(t) Liability increase				28,530 Dr.			28,530 Cr.
13								
14	Journal entry for 2012	41,660 Dr.	24,000 Cr.	20,800 Cr.	29,940 Dr.	26,800 Cr.		
15								
16	Accumulated OCI, Dec. 31, 2011			52,800 Dr.	0			
17	Balance, Dec. 31, 2012*			32,000 Dr.	29,940 Dr.	105,400 Cr.	265,000 Cr.	159,600 Dr.
18								
19	*Accumulated OCI (PSC)	$32,000 Dr.						
20	Accumulated OCI (G/L)	29,940 Dr.						
21	Accumulated OCI, Dec. 31, 2012	$61,940 Dr.						

Sheet1 / Sheet2 / Sheet3

ILLUSTRATION 20-18
Pension Worksheet—2012

Entries (m), (n), (o), (q), (r), and (s) are similar to the corresponding entries in 2010 or 2011.

Entries (o) and (p) are related. We explained the recording of the actual return in entry (o) in both 2010 and 2011; it is recorded similarly in 2012. In both 2010 and 2011 Zarle assumed that the actual return on plan assets was equal to the expected return on plan assets. In 2012, the expected return of $13,410 (the expected rate of return of 10 percent times the beginning-of-the-year plan assets balance of $134,100) is higher than the actual return of $12,000. To smooth pension expense, Zarle defers the unexpected loss of $1,410 ($13,410 − $12,000) by debiting the Other Comprehensive Income (G/L) account and crediting Pension Expense. **As a result of this adjustment, the expected return on the plan assets is the amount actually used to compute pension expense.**

Entry (t) records the change in the projected benefit obligation resulting from the change in the actuarial assumptions. As indicated, the actuary has now computed the ending balance to be $265,000. Given the PBO balance at December 31, 2011, and the related transactions during 2012, the PBO balance to date is computed as shown in Illustration 20-19.

ILLUSTRATION 20-19
Projected Benefit
Obligation Balance
(Unadjusted)

December 31, 2011, PBO balance	$212,700
Service cost [entry (m)]	13,000
Interest cost [entry (n)]	21,270
Benefits paid	(10,500)
December 31, 2012, PBO balance (before liability increases)	$236,470

The difference between the ending balance of $265,000 and the balance of $236,470 before the liability increase is $28,530 ($265,000 − $236,470). This $28,530 increase in the employer's liability is an unexpected loss. The journal entry on December 31, 2012, to record the pension information is as follows.

Pension Expense	41,660	
Other Comprehensive Income (G/L)	29,940	
Cash		24,000
Other Comprehensive Income (PSC)		20,800
Pension Asset/Liability		26,800

As the 2012 worksheet indicates, the $105,400 balance in the Pension Asset/Liability account at December 31, 2012, is equal to the net of the balances in the memo accounts. Illustration 20-20 shows this computation.

Projected benefit obligation (Credit)	$(265,000)
Plan assets at fair value (Debit)	159,600
Pension asset/liability	$(105,400)

ILLUSTRATION 20-20
Pension Reconciliation Schedule—December 31, 2012

BOUNCING BACK

The chart below shows what has happened to the financial health of pension plans over the last few years. It is a real roller coaster.

What do the numbers mean?

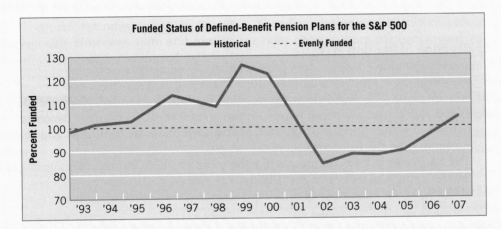

At the turn of the century, when the stock market was strong, pension plans were overfunded. However the bubble burst, and by 2002 companies in the S&P 500 saw their pension plans funded at just 85 percent of reported liabilities. In recent years, plans have bounced back, and by 2007 pension plans were overfunded again. However, due to recent downturns, plans may be soon underfunded again.

A number of factors cause a fund to change from being overfunded to underfunded: First, low interest rates, such as those experienced in the early part of this decade, decimate returns on pension plan assets. As a result, pension fund assets have not grown; in some cases, they have declined in value. Second, using low interest rates to discount the projected benefit payments leads to a higher pension liability. Finally, more individuals are retiring, which leads to a depletion of the pension plan assets. In short, the years 2002 and 2003 produced the perfect pension storm. Since 2003, companies have increased contributions to their plans and curtailed benefits promised to employees, which have helped the plans bounce back.

Sources: David Zion and Bill Carcache, "The Magical World of Pensions: An Update," *CSFB Equity Research: Accounting* (September 8, 2004); and J. Ciesielski, "Benefit Plans 2007: Close To The Edge—And Back," *The Analyst's Accounting Observer* (April 25, 2008).

REPORTING PENSION PLANS IN FINANCIAL STATEMENTS

Objective·9
Describe the requirements for reporting pension plans in financial statements.

As you might suspect, a phenomenon as significant and complex as pensions involves extensive reporting and disclosure requirements. We will cover these requirements in two categories: (1) those within the financial statements, and (2) those within the notes to the financial statements.

Within the Financial Statements

Recognition of the Net Funded Status of the Pension Plan

Companies must recognize on their balance sheet the overfunded (pension asset) or underfunded (pension liability) status of their defined-benefit pension plan. The overfunded or underfunded status is measured as the difference between the fair value of the plan assets and the projected benefit obligation.

Classification of Pension Asset or Pension Liability

No portion of a pension asset is reported as a current asset. The excess of the fair value of the plan assets over the benefit obligation is classified as a noncurrent asset. The rationale for noncurrent classification is that the pension plan assets are restricted. That is, these assets are used to fund the projected benefit obligation, and therefore noncurrent classification is appropriate.

The current portion of a net pension liability represents the amount of benefit payments to be paid in the next 12 months (or operating cycle, if longer), if that amount cannot be funded from existing plan assets. Otherwise, the pension liability is classified as a noncurrent liability.[14]

Aggregation of Pension Plans

Some companies have two or more pension plans. In such instances, a question arises as to whether these multiple plans should be combined and shown as one amount on the balance sheet. The Board takes the position that **all overfunded plans should be combined** and shown as a pension asset on the balance sheet. Similarly, if the company has two or more underfunded plans, the **underfunded plans are combined and shown as one amount** on the balance sheet.

The FASB rejected the alternative of combining *all* plans and representing the net amount as a single net asset or net liability. The rationale: A company does not have the ability to offset excess assets of one plan against underfunded obligations of another plan. Furthermore, netting all plans is inappropriate because offsetting assets and liabilities is not permitted under GAAP unless a right of offset exists.

To illustrate, assume that Cresci Company has three pension plans as shown in Illustration 20-21.

ILLUSTRATION 20-21
Multiple Pension Plans'
Funded Status

	Pension Assets (at Fair Value)	Projected Benefit Obligation	Pension Asset/Liability
Plan A	$400,000	$300,000	$100,000 Asset
Plan B	600,000	720,000	120,000 Liability
Plan C	550,000	700,000	150,000 Liability

In this case, Cresci reports a pension plan asset of $100,000 and a pension plan liability of $270,000 ($120,000 + $150,000).

Actuarial Gains and Losses/Prior Service Cost

Actuarial gains and losses not recognized as part of pension expense are recognized as increases and decreases in other comprehensive income. The same type of accounting is also used for prior service cost. The Board requires that the prior service cost arising in the year of the amendment (which increases the projected benefit obligation) be recognized by an offsetting debit to other comprehensive income. By recognizing both

[14]Recently, the FASB proposed more extensive disclosures related to pension plan assets. At a minimum, companies would have to disclose the amount of assets allocated to equities, government and corporate bonds, mortgage-backed securities, derivatives, and real estate. Also, information on concentrations of risk must be explained. Finally, fair value disclosures would be required, including classification of amounts into levels of the fair value hierarchy. (See *http://www.fasb.org/project/fas132r_disclosures_about_plan_assets.shtml*.)

actuarial gains and losses and prior service cost as part of other comprehensive income, the Board believes that the usefulness of financial statements is enhanced.

To illustrate the presentation of other comprehensive income and related accumulated OCI, assume that Obey Company provides the following information for the year 2010. None of the Accumulated OCI on January 1, 2010, should be amortized in 2010.

Net income for 2010	$100,000
Actuarial liability loss for 2010	60,000
Prior service cost adjustment to provide additional	
benefits in December 2010	15,000
Accumulated OCI, January 1, 2010	40,000

Both the actuarial liability loss and the prior service adjustment decrease the funded status of the plan on the balance sheet. This results because the projected benefit obligation increases. However, neither the actuarial liability loss nor the prior service cost adjustment affects pension expense in 2010. In subsequent periods, these items will impact pension expense through amortization.

For Obey Company, the computation of "Other comprehensive loss" for 2010 is as follows.

Actuarial liability loss	$60,000
Prior service cost benefit adjustment	15,000
Other comprehensive loss	$75,000

ILLUSTRATION 20-22
Computation of Other Comprehensive Income

The computation of "Comprehensive income" for 2010 is as follows.

Net income	$100,000
Other comprehensive loss	75,000
Comprehensive income	$ 25,000

ILLUSTRATION 20-23
Computation of Comprehensive Income

The components of other comprehensive income must be reported in one of three ways: (1) in a second income statement, (2) in a combined statement of comprehensive income, or (3) as a part of the statement of stockholders' equity. Regardless of the format used, net income must be added to other comprehensive income to arrive at comprehensive income. *For homework purposes,* use the second income statement approach unless stated otherwise. Earnings per share information related to comprehensive income is not required.

To illustrate the second income statement approach, assume that Obey Company has reported a traditional income statement. The comprehensive income statement is shown in Illustration 20-24.

ILLUSTRATION 20-24
Comprehensive Income Reporting

OBEY COMPANY COMPREHENSIVE INCOME STATEMENT FOR THE YEAR ENDED DECEMBER 31, 2010		
Net income		$100,000
Other comprehensive loss		
Actuarial liability loss	$60,000	
Prior service cost	15,000	75,000
Comprehensive income		$ 25,000

The computation of "Accumulated other comprehensive income" as reported in stockholders' equity at December 31, 2010, is as follows.

ILLUSTRATION 20-25
Computation of
Accumulated Other
Comprehensive Income

Accumulated other comprehensive income, January 1, 2010	$40,000
Other comprehensive loss	75,000
Accumulated other comprehensive loss, December 31, 2010	$35,000

Regardless of the display format for the income statement, the accumulated other comprehensive loss is reported on the stockholders' equity section of the balance sheet of Obey Company as shown in Illustration 20-26. (Illustration 20-26 uses assumed data for the common stock and retained earnings information.)

ILLUSTRATION 20-26
Reporting of
Accumulated OCI

OBEY COMPANY
BALANCE SHEET
AS OF DECEMBER 31, 2010
(STOCKHOLDERS' EQUITY SECTION)

Stockholders' equity	
Common stock	$100,000
Retained earnings	60,000
Accumulated other comprehensive loss	35,000
Total stockholders' equity	$125,000

By providing information on the components of comprehensive income as well as total accumulated other comprehensive income, the company communicates all changes in net assets.

In this illustration, it is assumed that the accumulated other comprehensive income at January 1, 2010, is not adjusted for the amortization of any prior service cost or actuarial gains and losses that would change pension expense. As discussed in the earlier examples, these items will be amortized into pension expense in future periods.

Within the Notes to the Financial Statements

Pension plans are frequently important to understanding a company's financial position, results of operations, and cash flows. Therefore, a company discloses the following information, either in the body of the financial statements or in the notes. [6]

1. A schedule showing all the major components of pension expense.
Rationale: Information provided about the components of pension expense helps users better understand how a company determines pension expense. It also is useful in forecasting a company's net income.

2. A reconciliation showing how the projected benefit obligation and the fair value of the plan assets changed from the beginning to the end of the period.
Rationale: Disclosing the projected benefit obligation, the fair value of the plan assets, and changes in them should help users understand the economics underlying the obligations and resources of these plans. Explaining the changes in the projected benefit obligation and fair value of plan assets in the form of a reconciliation provides a more complete disclosure and makes the financial statements more understandable.

INTERNATIONAL INSIGHT

The IASB and FASB are studying whether the various components of pension expense, such as interest cost and investment earnings on plan assets, should be presented separately in the income statement along with other interest expense and investment earnings.

3. A disclosure of the rates used in measuring the benefit amounts (discount rate, expected return on plan assets, rate of compensation).

   Rationale: Disclosure of these rates permits users to determine the reasonableness of the assumptions applied in measuring the pension liability and pension expense.

4. A table indicating the allocation of pension plan assets by category (equity securities, debt securities, real estate, and other assets), and showing the percentage of the fair value to total plan assets. In addition, a company must include a narrative description of investment policies and strategies, including the target allocation percentages (if used by the company).

   Rationale: Such information helps financial statement users evaluate the pension plan's exposure to market risk and possible cash flow demands on the company. It also will help users better assess the reasonableness of the company's expected rate of return assumption.

5. The **expected benefit payments** to be paid to current plan participants for each of the next five fiscal years and in the aggregate for the five fiscal years thereafter. Also required is disclosure of a company's best **estimate of expected contributions** to be paid to the plan during the next year.

   Rationale: These disclosures provide information related to the cash outflows of the company. With this information, financial statement users can better understand the potential cash outflows related to the pension plan. They can better assess the liquidity and solvency of the company, which helps in assessing the company's overall financial flexibility.

6. The nature and amount of changes in plan assets and benefit obligations recognized in net income and in other comprehensive income of each period.

   Rationale: This disclosure provides information on pension elements affecting the projected benefit obligation and plan assets and on whether those amounts have been recognized in income or deferred to future periods.

7. The accumulated amount of changes in plan assets and benefit obligations that have been recognized in other comprehensive income and that will be recycled into net income in future periods.

   Rationale: This information indicates the pension-related balances recognized in stockholders' equity, which will affect future income.

8. The amount of estimated net actuarial gains and losses and prior service costs and credits that will be amortized from accumulated other comprehensive income into net income over the next fiscal year.

   Rationale: This information helps users predict the impact of deferred pension expense items on next year's income.

In summary, the disclosure requirements are extensive, and purposely so. One factor that has been a challenge for useful pension reporting has been the lack of consistent terminology. Furthermore, a substantial amount of offsetting is inherent in the measurement of pension expense and the pension liability. These disclosures are designed to address these concerns and take some of the mystery out of pension reporting.

Example of Pension Note Disclosure

In the following sections we provide examples and explain the key pension disclosure elements.

Components of Pension Expense

The FASB requires disclosure of the individual pension expense components (derived from the information in the pension expense worksheet column): (1) service cost,

(2) interest cost, (3) expected return on assets, (4) other gains or losses component, and (5) prior service cost component. The purpose of such disclosure is to clarify to more sophisticated readers how companies determine pension expense. Providing information on the components should also be useful in predicting future pension expense.

Illustration 20-27 presents an example of this part of the disclosure. It uses the information from the Zarle illustration, specifically the expense component information from the worksheets in Illustrations 20-8 (page 1059), 20-12 (page 1062), and 20-18 (page 1068).

ILLUSTRATION 20-27
Summary of Expense Components—2010, 2011, 2012

ZARLE COMPANY			
	2010	2011	2012
Components of Pension Expense			
Service cost	$ 9,000	$ 9,500	$13,000
Interest cost	10,000	19,200	21,270
Expected return on plan assets	(10,000)	(11,100)	(13,410)*
Amortization of prior service cost	–0–	27,200	20,800
Pension expense	$ 9,000	$44,800	$41,660

*Note that the expected return must be disclosed, not the actual return. In 2012, the expected return is $13,410, which is the actual gain ($12,000) adjusted by the unrecognized loss ($1,410).

Underlying Concepts

This represents another compromise between relevance and reliability. Disclosure attempts to balance these objectives.

Funded Status of Plan

Having a reconciliation of the changes in the assets and liabilities from the beginning of the year to the end of the year, statement readers can better understand the underlying economics of the plan. In essence, this disclosure contains the information in the pension worksheet for the projected benefit obligation and plan asset columns. Using the information for Zarle, the schedule in Illustration 20-28 provides an example of the reconciliation.

ILLUSTRATION 20-28
Pension Disclosure for Zarle Company—2010, 2011, 2012

ZARLE COMPANY PENSION DISCLOSURE			
	2010	2011	2012
Change in benefit obligation			
Benefit obligation at beginning of year	$100,000	$112,000	$ 212,700
Service cost	9,000	9,500	13,000
Interest cost	10,000	19,200	21,270
Amendments (Prior service cost)	–0–	80,000	–0–
Actuarial loss	–0–	–0–	28,530
Benefits paid	(7,000)	(8,000)	(10,500)
Benefit obligation at end of year	112,000	212,700	265,000
Change in plan assets			
Fair value of plan assets at beginning of year	100,000	111,000	134,100
Actual return on plan assets	10,000	11,100	12,000
Contributions	8,000	20,000	24,000
Benefits paid	(7,000)	(8,000)	(10,500)
Fair value of plan assets at end of year	111,000	134,100	159,600
Funded status (Pension asset/liability)	$ (1,000)	$ (78,600)	$(105,400)

The 2010 column reveals that Zarle underfunds the projected benefit obligation by $1,000. The 2011 column reveals that Zarle reports the underfunded liability of $78,600 in the balance sheet. Finally, the 2012 column indicates that Zarle recognizes the underfunded liability of $105,400 in the balance sheet.

2013 Entries and Worksheet—A Comprehensive Example

Incorporating the corridor computation and the required disclosures, we continue the Zarle Company pension plan accounting based on the following facts for 2013.

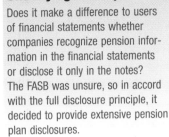

Service cost is $16,000.

Settlement rate is 10 percent; expected rate of return is 10 percent.

Actual return on plan assets is $22,000.

Amortization of prior service cost is $17,600.

Annual funding contributions are $27,000.

Benefits paid to retirees during the year are $18,000.

Average service life of all covered employees is 20 years.

Zarle prepares a worksheet to facilitate accumulation and recording of the components of pension expense and maintenance of amounts related to the pension plan. Illustration 20-29 shows that worksheet, which uses the basic data presented above. Beginning-of-the-year 2013 account balances are the December 31, 2012, balances from Zarle's revised 2012 pension worksheet in Illustration 20-18 (on page 1068).

ILLUSTRATION 20-29
Comprehensive Pension Worksheet—2013

Comprehensive Pension Worksheet—2013

	Annual Pension Expense	Cash	Prior Service Cost	Gains/Losses	Pension Asset/Liability	Projected Benefit Obligation	Plan Assets
	General Journal Entries			Other Comprehensive Income		**Memo Record**	
Items							
Balance, Dec. 31, 2012					105,400 Cr.	265,000 Cr.	159,600 Dr.
(aa) Service cost	16,000 Dr.					16,000 Cr.	
(bb) Interest cost	26,500 Dr.					26,500 Cr.	
(cc) Actual return	22,000 Cr.						22,000 Dr.
(dd) Unexpected gain	6,040 Dr.			6,040 Cr.			
(ee) Amortization of PSC	17,600 Dr.		17,600 Cr.				
(ff) Contributions		27,000 Cr.					27,000 Dr.
(gg) Benefits						18,000 Dr.	18,000 Cr.
(hh) Amortization of loss	172 Dr.			172 Cr.			
Journal entry for 2013	44,312 Dr.	27,000 Cr.	17,600 Cr.	6,212 Cr.	6,500 Dr.		
Accumulated OCI, Dec. 31, 2012			32,000 Dr.	29,940 Dr.			
Balance, Dec. 31, 2013*			14,400 Dr.	23,728 Dr.	98,900 Cr.	289,500 Cr.	190,600 Dr.
*Accumulated OCI (PSC)	$14,400 Dr.						
Accumulated OCI (G/L)	23,728 Dr.						
Accumulated OCI, Dec. 31, 2013	$38,128 Dr.						

Worksheet Explanations and Entries

Entries (aa) through (gg) are similar to the corresponding entries previously explained in the prior years' worksheets, with the exception of entry (dd). In 2012 the expected return on plan assets exceeded the actual return, producing an unexpected loss. In 2013 the actual return of $22,000 exceeds the expected return of $15,960 ($159,600 × 10%), resulting in an unexpected gain of $6,040, entry (dd). By netting the gain of $6,040 against the actual return of $22,000, pension expense is affected only by the expected return of $15,960.

A new entry (hh) in Zarle's worksheet results from application of the corridor test on the accumulated balance of net gain or loss in accumulated other comprehensive income. Zarle Company begins 2013 with a balance in the net loss account of $29,940. The company applies the corridor criterion in 2013 to determine whether the balance is excessive and should be amortized. In 2013 the corridor is 10 percent of the larger of the beginning-of-the-year projected benefit obligation of $265,000 or the plan asset's $159,600 market-related asset value (assumed to be fair value). The corridor for 2013 is $26,500 ($265,000 × 10%). Because the balance in Accumulated OCI is a net loss of $29,940, the excess (outside the corridor) is $3,440 ($29,940 − $26,500). Zarle amortizes the $3,440 excess over the average remaining service life of all employees. Given an average remaining service life of 20 years, the amortization in 2013 is $172 ($3,440 ÷ 20). In the 2013 pension worksheet, Zarle debits Pension Expense for $172 and credits that amount to Other Comprehensive Income (G/L). Illustration 20-30 shows the computation of the $172 amortization charge.

ILLUSTRATION 20-30
Computation of 2013
Amortization Charge
(Corridor Test)

2013 Corridor Test	
Net (gain) or loss at beginning of year in accumulated OCI	$29,940
10% of larger of PBO or market-related asset value of plan assets	26,500
Amortizable amount	$ 3,440
Average service life of all employees	20 years
2013 amortization ($3,440 ÷ 20 years)	$172

Zarle formally records pension expense for 2013 as follows.

2013

Pension Expense	44,312	
Pension Asset/Liability	6,500	
Cash		27,000
Other Comprehensive Income (G/L)		6,212
Other Comprehensive Income (PSC)		17,600

Note Disclosure

Illustration 20-31 (next page) shows the note disclosure of Zarle's pension plan for 2013. Note that this example assumes that the pension liability is noncurrent and that the 2014 adjustment for amortization of the net gain or loss and amortization of prior service cost are the same as 2013.

Underlying Concepts

Many plans are underfunded but still quite viable. For example, at one time **Loews Corp.** had a $159 million shortfall, but also had earnings of $594 million and a good net worth. Thus, the going concern assumption permits us to ignore pension underfundings in some cases because in the long run they are not significant.

Special Issues

The Pension Reform Act of 1974

The Employee Retirement Income Security Act of 1974—ERISA—affects virtually every private retirement plan in the United States. It attempts to safeguard employees' pension rights by mandating many pension plan requirements, including minimum funding, participation, and vesting.

These requirements can influence the employers' cash flows significantly. Under this legislation, annual funding is no longer discretionary. An employer now must fund the plan in accordance with an actuarial funding method that over time will be sufficient to pay for all pension obligations. If companies do not fund their plans in a reasonable manner, they may be subject to fines and/or loss of tax deductions.[15]

---

[15]In 2006, Congress passed the Pension Protection Act. This new law has many provisions. One important aspect of the Act is that it will force many companies to expedite their contributions to their pension plans. One group estimates that companies in the S&P 500 would have had to contribute $47 billion to their pension plans if the new rules were fully phased in for 2006. That amount is about 57 percent more than the $30 billion that companies were expecting to contribute to their plans that year. (*Source*: Credit Suisse, "Pension Protection Act," August 14, 2006, p. 1.)

ZARLE COMPANY
NOTES TO THE FINANCIAL STATEMENTS

ILLUSTRATION 20-31
Minimum Note Disclosure
of Pension Plan, Zarle
Company, 2013

Note D. The company has a pension plan covering substantially all of its employees. The plan is noncontributory and provides pension benefits that are based on the employee's compensation during the three years immediately preceding retirement. The pension plan's assets consist of cash, stocks, and bonds. The company's funding policy is consistent with the relevant government (ERISA) and tax regulations.

Pension expense for 2013 is comprised of the following components of pension cost.

Service cost	$16,000	
Interest on projected benefit obligation	26,500	
Expected return on plan assets	(15,960)	
Amortization of prior service cost	17,600	
Amortization of net loss	172	
Pension expense		$44,312

Components of pension expense

Other changes in plan assets and benefit obligations recognized in other comprehensive income

Net actuarial gain	$ 6,212	
Amortization of prior service cost	17,600	
Total recognized in other comprehensive income		23,812
Total recognized in pension expense and other comprehensive income		$20,500

Amounts recognized in other comprehensive income

The estimated net actuarial loss and prior service cost for the defined-benefit pension plan that will be amortized from accumulated other comprehensive into pension expense over the next year are estimated to be the same as this year.

The amount recognized as a long-term liability in the balance sheet is as follows:

Noncurrent liability	
Pension liability	$98,900

The amounts recognized in accumulated other comprehensive income related to pensions consist of:

Net actuarial loss	$23,728
Prior service cost	14,400
Total	$38,128

Amounts recognized in the balance sheet

Change in benefit obligation	
Benefit obligation at beginning of year	$265,000
Service cost	16,000
Interest cost	26,500
Amendments (Prior service cost)	–0–
Actuarial gain	–0–
Benefits paid	(18,000)
Benefit obligation at end of year	289,500
Change in plan assets	
Fair value of plan assets at beginning of year	159,600
Actual return on plan assets	22,000
Contributions	27,000
Benefits paid	(18,000)
Fair value of plan assets at end of year	190,600
Funded status (liability)	$ 98,900

Reconciliations of pension liability and plan assets

Funded status of plan

The weighted-average discount rate used in determining the 2013 projected benefit obligation was 10 percent. The rate of increase in future compensation levels used in computing the 2013 projected benefit obligation was 4.5 percent. The weighted-average expected long-term rate of return on the plan's assets was 10 percent.

Rates used to estimate plan elements

The law requires plan administrators to publish a comprehensive description and summary of their plans, along with detailed annual reports that include many supplementary schedules and statements.

Another important provision of the Act is the creation of the Pension Benefit Guaranty Corporation (PBGC). **The PBGC's purpose is to administer terminated plans** and to impose liens on an employer's assets for certain unfunded pension liabilities. If a company terminates its pension plan, the PBGC can effectively impose a lien against the employer's assets for the excess of the present value of guaranteed vested benefits over the pension fund assets. This lien generally has had the status of a tax lien; it takes priority over most other creditorship claims. This section of the Act gives the PBGC the power to force an involuntary termination of a pension plan whenever the risks related to nonpayment of the pension obligation seem too great. Because ERISA restricts to 30 percent of net worth the lien that the PBGC can impose, the PBGC must monitor all plans to ensure that net worth is sufficient to meet the pension benefit obligations.[16]

A large number of terminated plans have caused the PBGC to pay out substantial benefits. Currently the PBGC receives its funding from employers, who contribute a certain dollar amount for each employee covered under the plan.[17]

Pension Terminations

A congressman at one time noted, "Employers are simply treating their employee pension plans like company piggy banks, to be raided at will." What this congressman was referring to is the practice of paying off the projected benefit obligation and pocketing any excess. ERISA prevents companies from recapturing excess assets unless they pay participants what is owed to them and then terminate the plan. As a result, companies were buying *annuities* to pay off the pension claimants and then used the excess funds for other corporate purposes.[18]

For example, at one time, pension plan terminations netted $363 million for Occidental Petroleum Corp., $95 million for Stroh's Brewery Co., $58 million for Kellogg Co., and $29 million for Western Airlines. Recently, many large companies have terminated their pension plans and captured billions in surplus assets. The U.S. Treasury also benefits: Federal legislation requires companies to pay an excise tax of anywhere from 20 percent to 50 percent on the gains. All of this is quite legal.[19]

The accounting issue that arises from these terminations is whether a company should recognize a gain when pension plan assets revert back to the company (often called **asset reversion** transactions). The issue is complex: in some cases, a company

---

[16]The major problems in underfunding are occurring in four labor-intensive industries—steel, autos, rubber, and airlines. For example, General Motors' pension plan at one time was 92 percent funded but still had a deficit of over $6 billion.

[17]Pan American Airlines is a good illustration of how difficult it is to assess when to terminate. When Pan Am filed for bankruptcy in 1991, it had a pension liability of $900 million. From 1983 to 1991, the IRS gave it six waivers so it did not have to make contributions. When Pan Am terminated the plan, there was little net worth left upon which to impose a lien. An additional accounting problem relates to the manner of disclosing the possible termination of a plan. For example, should Pan Am have disclosed a contingent liability for its struggling plan? At present this issue is unresolved, and considerable judgment would be needed to analyze a company with these contingent liabilities.

[18]A question exists as to whose money it is. Some argue that the excess funds belong to the employees, not the employer. In addition, given that the funds have been reverting to the employer, critics charge that cost-of-living increases and the possibility of other increased benefits are reduced, because companies will be reluctant to use those remaining funds to pay for such increases.

[19]Another way that companies have reduced their pension obligations is through adoption of cash-balance plans. These are *hybrid* plans combining features of defined-benefit and defined-contribution plans. Although these plans permit employees to transfer their pension benefits when they change employers (like a defined-contribution plan), they are controversial because the change to a cash-balance plan often reduces benefits to older workers.

The accounting for cash-balance plans is similar to that for defined-benefit plans, because employers bear the investment risk in cash-balance plans. When an employer adopts a cash-balance plan, the measurement of the future benefit obligation to employees generally is lower, compared to a traditional defined-benefit plan. See A. T. Arcady and F. Mellors, "Cash-Balance Conversions," *Journal of Accountancy* (February 2000), pp. 22–28.

starts a new defined-benefit plan after it eliminates the old one. Thus, some contend that there has been no change in substance, but merely a change in form. However, the FASB disagrees. It requires recognition in earnings of a gain or loss when the employer settles a pension obligation either by lump-sum cash payments to participants or by purchasing nonparticipating annuity contracts. [7][20]

BAILING OUT

The **Pension Benefit Guaranty Corp.** (PBGC) recently announced that it would take over responsibility for the pilots' pension plan at **United Airlines**, to the tune of $1.4 billion. This federal agency, which acts as an insurer for corporate pension plans, has spent much of the past few years securing pension plans for "Big Steel" (U.S. steel companies), and it looks as if airlines are next.

What do the numbers mean?

For example, the PBGC also became the trustee of **US Airways** pilots' pensions in 2003, and it may soon announce a takeover of that struggling carrier's other three pension plans. The grand total at US Airways? It's $2.8 billion—mere pocket change next to the $6.4 billion the PBGC will owe if it has to bail out all four of United Airlines' plans. To date, the airline industry, which makes up 2 percent of participants in the program, has made 20 percent of the claims. The chart below shows how a $6.4 billion bailout would compare with the PBGC's biggest payouts to date.

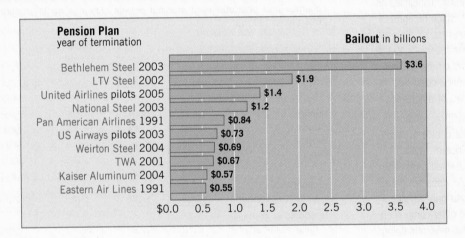

Source: Kate Bonamici, "By the Numbers," *Fortune* (January 24, 2005), p. 24.

Concluding Observations

Hardly a day goes by without the financial press analyzing in depth some issue related to pension plans in the United States. This is not surprising, since U.S. pension funds now hold over $14.4 trillion in assets. As you have seen, the accounting issues related to pension plans are complex. Recent changes to GAAP have clarified many of these issues and should help users understand the financial implications of a company's pension plans on its financial position, results of operations, and cash flows.

You will want to read the **CONVERGENCE CORNER** on page 1080

For discussion of how international convergence efforts relate to pension accounting.

[20]Some companies have established *pension poison pills* as an anti-takeover measure. These plans require asset reversions from termination of a plan to benefit employees and retirees rather than the acquiring company. For a discussion of pension poison pills, see Eugene E. Comiskey and Charles W. Mulford, "Interpreting Pension Disclosures: A Guide for Lending Officers," *Commercial Lending Review* (Winter 1993–94), Vol. 9, No. 1.

CONVERGENCE CORNER

The accounting for various forms of compensation plans under iGAAP is found in *IAS 19* ("Employee Benefits") and *IFRS 2* ("Share-Based Payment"). *IAS 19* addresses the accounting for a wide range of compensation elements—wages, bonuses, postretirement benefits, and compensated absences. Both of these standards were recently amended, resulting in significant convergence between iGAAP and U.S. GAAP in this area.

✳ RELEVANT FACTS

• iGAAP and U.S. GAAP separate pension plans into defined-contribution plans and defined-benefit plans. The accounting for defined-contribution plans is similar.

• For defined-benefit plans, both iGAAP and U.S. GAAP recognize the net of the pension assets and liabilities on the balance sheet. Unlike U.S. GAAP, which recognizes prior service cost on the balance sheet (as an element of "Accumulated other comprehensive income"), iGAAP does not recognize prior service costs on the balance sheet. Both GAAPs amortize prior service costs into income over the expected service lives of employees.

• Another difference in defined-benefit recognition is that under iGAAP companies have the choice of recognizing actuarial gains and losses in income immediately or amortizing them over the expected remaining working lives of employees. U.S. GAAP does not permit choice; actuarial gains and losses (and prior service costs) are recognized in "Accumulated other comprehensive income" and amortized to income over remaining service lives.

• The IASB has recently issued a discussion paper on pensions proposing: (1) elimination of smoothing via the corridor approach, (2) a different presentation of pension costs in the income statement, and (3) a new category of pensions for accounting purposes—so-called "contribution-based promises."

✳ ABOUT THE NUMBERS

The following schedule is taken from the annual report of **Cadbury Schweppes**, which uses iGAAP.

25. Retirement benefit obligations continued (in part)

The market value of the assets and liabilities of the defined-benefit schemes and postretirement medical benefit schemes at 31 December 2006 are as follows:

	UK pension schemes £m	Overseas pension schemes £m	Post-retirement medical benefits £m	Total all schemes £m
Equities	1,002	350	2	1,298
Bonds	763	143	1	907
Property	183	32	—	215
Other	30	34	—	120
	1,978	559	3	2,540
Present value of benefit obligations	(1,988)	(720)	(36)	(2,744)
Recognised in the balance sheet	(10)	(161)	(33)	(204)

The Group's policy is to recognise all actuarial gains and losses immediately. Consequently there are no unrecognized gains or losses.

✳ ON THE HORIZON

The FASB and the IASB are working collaboratively on a postretirement benefit project. As discussed in the chapter, the FASB has issued GAAP rules addressing the recognition of benefit plans in financial statements. The FASB has begun work on the second phase of the project, which will reexamine expense measurement of postretirement benefit plans. The IASB also has added a project in this area, but on a different schedule. The IASB is monitoring the FASB's progress and hopes to issue a converged standard in this area by 2010.

SUMMARY OF LEARNING OBJECTIVES

[·1] Distinguish between accounting for the employer's pension plan and accounting for the pension fund. The company or employer is the organization sponsoring the pension plan. It incurs the cost and makes contributions to the pension fund. The fund or plan is the entity that receives the contributions from the employer, administers the pension assets, and makes the benefit payments to the pension recipients (retired employees). The fund should be a separate legal and accounting entity; it maintains a set of books and prepares financial statements.

[·2] Identify types of pension plans and their characteristics. The two most common types of pension arrangements are: (1) *Defined-contribution plans:* The employer agrees to contribute to a pension trust a certain sum each period based on a formula. This formula may consider such factors as age, length of employee service, employer's profits, and compensation level. Only the employer's contribution is defined; no promise is made regarding the ultimate benefits paid out to the employees. (2) *Defined-benefit plans:* These plans define the benefits that the employee will receive at the time of retirement. The formula typically provides for the benefits to be a function of the employee's years of service and the compensation level when he or she nears retirement.

[·3] Explain alternative measures for valuing the pension obligation. One measure bases the pension obligation only on the benefits vested to the employees. Vested benefits are those that the employee is entitled to receive even if he or she renders no additional services under the plan. Companies compute the *vested benefits pension obligation* using current salary levels; this obligation includes only vested benefits. Another measure of the obligation, called the *accumulated benefit obligation*, computes the deferred compensation amount based on all years of service performed by employees under the plan—both vested and nonvested—using current salary levels. A third measure, called the *projected benefit obligation*, bases the computation of the deferred compensation amount on both vested and nonvested service using future salaries.

[·4] List the components of pension expense. Pension expense is a function of the following components: (1) service cost, (2) interest on the liability, (3) return on plan assets, (4) amortization of prior service cost, and (5) gain or loss.

[·5] Use a worksheet for employer's pension plan entries. Companies may use a worksheet unique to pension accounting. This worksheet records both the formal entries and the memo entries to keep track of all the employer's relevant pension plan items and components.

[·6] Describe the amortization of prior service costs. An actuary computes the amount of the prior service cost and records it as an adjustment to the projected benefit obligation and other comprehensive income. It then amortizes it, generally using a "years-of-service" amortization method, similar to a units-of-production computation. First, the company computes total estimated number of service-years to be worked by all of the participating employees. Second, it divides the accumulated prior service cost by the total number of service-years, to obtain a cost per service-year (the unit cost). Third, the company multiplies the number of service-years consumed each year times the cost per service-year, to obtain the annual amortization charge.

[·7] Explain the accounting for unexpected gains and losses. In estimating the projected benefit obligation (the liability), actuaries make assumptions about such items as mortality rate, retirement rate, turnover rate, disability rate, and salary amounts. Any change in these actuarial assumptions affects the amount of the projected benefit obligation. These unexpected gains or losses from changes in the projected benefit obligation are liability gains and losses. Liability gains result from unexpected decreases in the liability balance; liability losses result from unexpected increases. Companies also incur asset gains or losses. Both types of actuarial gains and losses are recorded in other comprehensive income and adjust either the projected benefit obligation or the plan assets.

KEY TERMS

accumulated benefit obligation, 1053
actual return on plan assets, 1057
actuarial present value, 1054(n)
actuaries, 1053
asset gains and losses, 1063
cash-balance plans, 1078(n)
components of pension expense, 1056
contributory pension plan, 1050
corridor approach, 1064
defined-benefit plan, 1051
defined-contribution plan, 1051
ERISA, 1076
expected rate of return, 1063
expected return on plan assets, 1063
fair value of plan assets, 1057
funded pension plan, 1050
funded status (overfunded or underfunded), 1055
interest on the liability (interest expense), 1057
liability gains and losses, 1064
market-related asset value, 1063
noncontributory pension plan, 1050
other comprehensive income (G/L), 1063
other comprehensive income (PSC), 1062
pension asset/ liability, 1058
pension plan, 1050
pension worksheet, 1058
prior service cost (PSC), 1060
projected benefit obligation, 1054
qualified pension plan, 1050

[•8] **Explain the corridor approach to amortizing gains and losses.** The FASB set a limit for the size of an accumulated net gain or loss balance. That arbitrarily selected limit (called a *corridor*) is 10 percent of the larger of the beginning balances of the projected benefit obligation or the market-related value of the plan assets. Beyond that limit, an accumulated net gain or loss balance is considered too large and must be amortized. If the balance of the accumulated net gain or loss account stays within the upper and lower limits of the corridor, no amortization is required.

[•9] **Describe the requirements for reporting pension plans in financial statements.** Currently, companies must disclose the following pension plan information in their financial statements: (1) The components of pension expense for the period. (2) A schedule showing changes in the benefit obligation and plan assets during the year. (3) The amount of prior service cost and net gains and losses in accumulated OCI, including the estimated prior service cost and gains and losses that will affect net income in the next year. (4) The weighted-average assumed discount rate, the rate of compensation increase used to measure the projected benefit obligation, and the weighted-average expected long-term rate of return on plan assets. (5) A table showing the allocation of pension plan assets by category and the percentage of the fair value to total plan assets. (6) The expected benefit payments for current plan participants for each of the next five fiscal years and for the following five years in aggregate, along with an estimate of expected contributions to the plan during the next year.

APPENDIX 20A | **ACCOUNTING FOR POSTRETIREMENT BENEFITS**

In March 1991 **IBM**'s adoption of a new GAAP requirement on postretirement benefits resulted in a $2.3 billion charge and a historical curiosity—IBM's first-ever quarterly loss. **General Electric** disclosed that its charge for adoption of the same GAAP rules would be $2.7 billion. In the fourth quarter of 1993, **AT&T** absorbed a $2.1 billion pretax hit for postretirement benefits. What is GAAP in this area, and how could its adoption have so grave an impact on companies' earnings?

ACCOUNTING GUIDANCE

After a decade of study, the FASB in December 1990 issued GAAP rules on "Employers' Accounting for Postretirement Benefits Other Than Pensions." [8] It alone was the cause for the large charges to income cited above. These rules cover for healthcare and other "welfare benefits" provided to retirees, their spouses, dependents, and beneficiaries.[21] These other welfare benefits include life insurance offered outside a pension plan; medical, dental, and eye care; legal and tax services; tuition assistance; day care; and housing assistance.[22] Because healthcare benefits are the largest of the other postretirement benefits, we use this item to illustrate accounting for postretirement benefits.

---

[21] *Accounting Trends and Techniques—2007* reports that of its 600 surveyed companies, 317 reported benefit plans that provide postretirement healthcare benefits. In response to rising healthcare costs and higher premiums on healthcare insurance, companies are working to get their postretirement benefit costs under control. For example, a recent study of employer health-benefit plans indicates that employers are limiting or curtailing postretirement health benefits. See Kelly Greene, "Health Benefits for Retirees Continue to Shrink, Study Says," *Wall Street Journal* (September 16, 2002), p. A2.

[22] "OPEB" is the acronym frequently used to describe postretirement benefits other than pensions. This term came into being before the scope of guidance was narrowed from "other postemployment benefits" to "other postretirement benefits," thereby excluding postemployment benefits related to severance pay or wage continuation to disabled, terminated, or laid-off employees.

For many employers (about 95 percent) these GAAP rules required a change from the predominant practice of accounting for postretirement benefits on a pay-as-you-go (cash) basis to an accrual basis. Similar to pension accounting, the accrual basis necessitates measuring the employer's obligation to provide future benefits and accrual of the cost during the years that the employee provides service.

One of the reasons companies had not prefunded these benefit plans was that payments to prefund healthcare costs, unlike excess contributions to a pension trust, are not tax-deductible. Another reason was that postretirement healthcare benefits were once perceived to be a low-cost employee benefit that could be changed or eliminated at will and therefore were not a legal liability. Now, the accounting definition of a liability goes beyond the notion of a legally enforceable claim; the definition now encompasses equitable or constructive obligations as well, making it clear that the postretirement benefit promise is a liability.[23]

DIFFERENCES BETWEEN PENSION BENEFITS AND HEALTHCARE BENEFITS

The FASB used the GAAP rules on pensions as a reference for the accounting prescribed for healthcare and other nonpension postretirement benefits.[24] Why didn't the FASB cover these other types of postretirement benefits in the earlier pension accounting statement? Because the apparent similarities between the two benefits mask some significant differences. Illustration 20A-1 shows these differences.[25]

Objective•10

Identify the differences between pensions and postretirement healthcare benefits.

Item	Pensions	Healthcare Benefits
Funding	Generally funded.	Generally *NOT* funded.
Benefit	Well-defined and level dollar amount.	Generally uncapped and great variability.
Beneficiary	Retiree (maybe some benefit to surviving spouse).	Retiree, spouse, and other dependents.
Benefit payable	Monthly.	As needed and used.
Predictability	Variables are reasonably predictable.	Utilization difficult to predict. Level of cost varies geographically and fluctuates over time.

ILLUSTRATION 20A-1
Differences between Pensions and Postretirement Healthcare Benefits

Two of the differences in Illustration 20A-1 highlight why measuring the future payments for healthcare benefit plans is so much more difficult than for pension plans.

1. Many postretirement plans do not set a limit on healthcare benefits. No matter how serious the illness or how long it lasts, the benefits continue to flow. (Even if the employer uses an insurance company plan, the premiums will escalate according to the increased benefits provided.)
2. The levels of healthcare benefit use and healthcare costs are difficult to predict. Increased longevity, unexpected illnesses (e.g., AIDS, SARS, and avian flu), along with new medical technologies and cures, cause changes in healthcare utilization.

---

[23]"Elements of Financial Statements," *Statement of Financial Accounting Concepts No. 6* (Stamford, Conn.: 1985), p. 13, footnote 21.

[24]Other postemployment (but before retirement) benefits include, but are not limited to, salary continuation, disability-related benefits, severance benefits, and continuance of healthcare benefits and life insurance for inactive or former (e.g., terminated, disabled, or deceased) employees or their beneficiaries. These benefits are accounted for similar to accounting for compensated absences (see Chapter 13). [9]

[25]D. Gerald Searfoss and Naomi Erickson, "The Big Unfunded Liability: Postretirement Health-Care Benefits," *Journal of Accountancy* (November 1988), pp. 28–39.

Additionally, although the fiduciary and reporting standards for employee benefit funds under government regulations generally cover healthcare benefits, the stringent minimum vesting, participation, and funding standards that apply to pensions do not apply to healthcare benefits. Nevertheless, as you will learn, many of the basic concepts of pensions, and much of the related accounting terminology and measurement methodology, do apply to other postretirement benefits. Therefore, in the following discussion and illustrations, we point out the similarities and differences in the accounting and reporting for these two types of postretirement benefits.

OPEBs—HOW BIG ARE THEY?

What do the numbers mean?

For many companies, *other postretirement benefit obligations* (OPEBs) are substantial. Generally, OPEBs are not well funded because companies are not permitted a tax deduction for contributions to the plan assets, as is the case with pensions. That is, the company may not claim a tax deduction until it makes a payment to the participant (pay-as-you-go).

Presented below are companies with the largest OPEB obligations, indicating their relationship with other financial items.

(For year ended 12/31/2007 $ in millions)	Obligation	% Underfunded	Obligation as a % of Stockholders' Equity
General Motors	$64,013	74.53%	172.57%
Ford Motor Company	28,096	86.21%	499.22%
SBC Communications Inc.	40,385	57.91%	35.01%
Verizon Communications Inc.	27,306	84.83%	53.98%
General Electric	12,983	86.10%	11.23%
Boeing Co.	7,662	97.06%	85.10%
Delphi Corp.	8,732	100%	64.82%

So, how big are OPEB obligations? REALLY big.

Source: Company reports.

POSTRETIREMENT BENEFITS ACCOUNTING PROVISIONS

Healthcare and other postretirement benefits for current and future retirees and their dependents are forms of deferred compensation. They are earned through employee service and are subject to accrual during the years an employee is working.

The period of time over which the postretirement benefit cost accrues is called the **attribution period**. It is the period of service during which the employee earns the benefits under the terms of the plan. The attribution period, shown in Illustration 20A-2

ILLUSTRATION 20A-2
Range of Possible
Attribution Periods

for a hypothetical employee, generally begins when an employee is hired and ends on the date the employee is eligible to receive the benefits and ceases to earn additional benefits by performing service, the vesting date.[26]

Obligations Under Postretirement Benefits

In defining the obligation for postretirement benefits, the FASB maintained many concepts similar to pension accounting. It also designed some new and modified terms specifically for postretirement benefits. Two of the most important of these specialized terms are (a) expected postretirement benefit obligation and (b) accumulated postretirement benefit obligation.

The **expected postretirement benefit obligation (EPBO)** is the actuarial present value as of a particular date of **all benefits a company expects to pay after retirement to employees and their dependents**. Companies do not record the EPBO in the financial statements, but they do use it in measuring periodic expense.

The **accumulated postretirement benefit obligation (APBO)** is the actuarial present value of **future benefits attributed to employees' services rendered to a particular date**. The APBO is equal to the EPBO for retirees and active employees fully eligible for benefits. Before the date an employee achieves full eligibility, the APBO is only a portion of the EPBO. Or stated another way, the difference between the APBO and the EPBO is the future service costs of active employees who are not yet fully eligible.

Illustration 20A-3 contrasts the EPBO and the APBO.

ILLUSTRATION 20A-3
APBO and EPBO
Contrasted

At the date an employee is fully eligible (the end of the attribution period), the APBO and the EPBO for that employee are equal.

---

[26]This is a benefit-years-of-service approach (the projected unit credit actuarial cost method). The FASB found no compelling reason to switch from the traditional pension accounting approach. It rejected the employee's full service period (i.e., to the estimated retirement date) because it was unable to identify any approach that would appropriately attribute benefits beyond the date when an employee attains full eligibility for those benefits. Employees attain full eligibility by meeting specified age, service, or age and service requirements of the plan.

Postretirement Expense

Postretirement expense is the employer's annual expense for postretirement benefits. Also called **net periodic postretirement benefit cost**, this expense consists of many of the familiar components used to compute annual pension expense. The components of net periodic postretirement benefit cost are as follows. **[10]**[27]

1. *Service Cost:* The portion of the EPBO attributed to employee service during the period.

2. *Interest Cost:* The increase in the APBO attributable to the passage of time. Companies compute interest cost by applying the beginning-of-the-year discount rate to the beginning-of-the-year APBO, adjusted for benefit payments to be made during the period. The discount rate is based on the rates of return on high-quality, fixed-income investments that are currently available.[28]

3. *Actual Return on Plan Assets:* The change in the fair value of the plan's assets adjusted for contributions and benefit payments made during the period. Because companies charge or credit the postretirement expense for the gain or loss on plan assets (the difference between the actual and the expected return), this component is actually the expected return.

4. *Amortization of Prior Service Cost:* The amortization of the cost of retroactive benefits resulting from plan amendments. The typical amortization period, beginning at the date of the plan amendment, is the remaining service periods through the full eligibility date.

5. *Gains and Losses:* In general, changes in the APBO resulting from changes in assumptions or from experience different from that assumed. For funded plans, this component also includes the difference between actual return and expected return on plan assets.

ILLUSTRATIVE ACCOUNTING ENTRIES

Like pension accounting, the accounting for postretirement plans must recognize in the accounts and in the financial statements effects of several significant items. These items are:

Objective•11

Contrast accounting for pensions to accounting for other postretirement benefits.

1. Expected postretirement benefit obligation (EPBO).
2. Accumulated postretirement benefit obligation (APBO).
3. Postretirement benefit plan assets.
4. Prior service cost.
5. Net gain or loss.

The EPBO is not recognized in the financial statements or disclosed in the notes. Companies recompute it each year, and the actuary uses it in measuring the annual service cost. Because of the numerous assumptions and actuarial complexity involved in measuring annual service cost, we have omitted these computations of the EPBO.

Similar to pensions, companies must recognize in the financial statements items 2 through 5 listed above. In addition, as in pension accounting, companies must know the exact amount of these items in order to compute postretirement expense. Therefore, companies use the worksheet like that for pension accounting to record both the formal general journal entries and the memo entries.

---

[27]See James R. Wilbert and Kenneth E. Dakdduk, "The New FASB 106: How to Account for Postretirement Benefits," *Journal of Accountancy* (August 1991), pp. 36–41.

[28]The FASB concluded that the discount rate for measuring the present value of the postretirement benefit obligation and the service cost component should be the same as that applied to pension measurements. It chose not to label it the *settlement rate*, in order to clarify that the objective of the discount rate is to measure the time value of money.

2010 Entries and Worksheet

To illustrate the use of a worksheet in accounting for a postretirement benefits plan, assume that on January 1, 2010, Quest Company adopts a healthcare benefit plan. The following facts apply to the postretirement benefits plan for the year 2010.

> Plan assets at fair value on January 1, 2010, are zero.
>
> Actual and expected returns on plan assets are zero.
>
> Accumulated postretirement benefit obligation (APBO), January 1, 2010, is zero.
>
> Service cost is $54,000.
>
> No prior service cost exists.
>
> Interest cost on the APBO is zero.
>
> Funding contributions during the year are $38,000.
>
> Benefit payments to employees from plan are $28,000.

Using that data, the worksheet in Illustration 20A-4 presents the postretirement entries for 2010.

ILLUSTRATION 20A-4
Postretirement Worksheet—2010

Postretirement Worksheet—2010

	A	B	C	D		F	G
		General Journal Entries				Memo Record	
	Items	Annual Postretirement Expense	Cash	Postretirement Asset/Liability		APBO	Plan Assets
3	Balance, Jan. 1, 2010						
4	(a) Service cost	54,000 Dr.				54,000 Cr.	
5	(b) Contributions		38,000 Cr.				38,000 Dr.
6	(c) Benefits					28,000 Dr.	28,000 Cr.
7							
8	Journal entry for 2010	54,000 Dr.	38,000 Cr.	16,000 Cr.*			
9	Balance, Dec. 31, 2010			16,000 Cr.**		26,000 Cr.	10,000 Dr.
10							
11	*$54,000 − $38,000 = $16,000						
12	**$26,000 − $10,000 = $16,000						
13							
14							
15							

Sheet1 / Sheet2 / Sheet3

Entry (a) records the service cost component, which increases postretirement expense $54,000 and increases the liability (APBO) $54,000. Entry (b) records Quest's funding of assets to the postretirement fund. The funding decreases cash $38,000 and increases plan assets $38,000. Entry (c) records the benefit payments made to retirees, which results in equal $28,000 decreases to the plan assets and the liability (APBO).

Quest's December 31 adjusting entry formally records the postretirement expense in 2010, as follows.

December 31, 2010

Postretirement Expense	54,000	
Cash		38,000
Postretirement Asset/Liability		16,000

The credit to Postretirement Asset/Liability for $16,000 represents the difference between the APBO and the plan assets. The $16,000 credit balance is a liability because the plan is underfunded. The Postretirement Asset/Liability account balance of $16,000 also equals the net of the balances in the memo accounts.

Illustration 20A-5 shows the funded status reported in the balance sheet. (Notice its similarity to the pension schedule.)

ILLUSTRATION 20A-5
Postretirement
Reconciliation Schedule—
December 31, 2010

Accumulated postretirement benefit obligation (Credit)	$(26,000)
Plan assets at fair value (Debit)	10,000
Postretirement asset/liability (Credit)	$(16,000)

Recognition of Gains and Losses

Gains and losses represent changes in the APBO or the value of plan assets. These changes result either from actual experience different from that expected or from changes in actuarial assumptions. The amortization of these gains and losses follows the approach used for pensions. That is, the gains and losses are recorded in other comprehensive income.

The Corridor Approach

Consistent with pension accounting, companies amortize the gains and losses in accumulated other comprehensive income as a component of postretirement expense if, at the beginning of the period, they exceed a "corridor" limit. The corridor is measured as the greater of 10 percent of the APBO or 10 percent of the market-related value of plan assets.

The intent of the **corridor approach** is to reduce volatility of postretirement expense by providing a reasonable opportunity for gains and losses to offset over time without affecting net periodic expense.

Amortization Methods

If the company must amortize gains and losses (beyond the corridor) on postretirement benefit plans, the **minimum amortization amount** is the excess gain or loss divided by the average remaining service life to expected retirement of all active employees. Companies may use any systematic method of amortization provided that: (1) the amount amortized in any period is equal to or greater than the minimum amount, (2) the company applies the method consistently, and (3) the company applies the method similarly for gains and losses.

The company must recompute the amount of gain or loss in accumulated other comprehensive income each year and amortize the gain or loss over the average remaining service life if the net amount exceeds the "corridor."

2011 Entries and Worksheet

Continuing the Quest Company illustration into 2011, the following facts apply to the postretirement benefits plan for the year 2011.

Actual return on plan assets is $600.

Expected return on plan assets is $800.

Discount rate is 8 percent.

Increase in APBO due to change in actuarial assumptions is $60,000.

Service cost is $26,000.

Funding contributions during the year are $18,000.

Benefit payments to employees during the year are $5,000.

Average remaining service to expected retirement: 25 years.

The worksheet in Illustration 20A-6 (on page 1089) presents all of Quest's postretirement benefit entries and information for 2011. The beginning balances on the first line of the worksheet are the ending balances from Quest's 2010 postretirement benefits worksheet in Illustration 20A-4 (on page 1087).

	Postretirement Benefits Worksheet—2011						
	A	B	C	D	E	G	H
1		General Journal Entries				Memo Record	
2	Items	Annual Postretirement Expense	Cash	Other Comprehensive Income (G/L)	Postretirement Asset/Liability	APBO	Plan Assets
3	Balance, Jan. 1, 2011				16,000 Cr.	26,000 Cr.	10,000 Dr.
4	(d) Service cost	26,000 Dr.				26,000 Cr.	
5	(e) Interest cost	2,080 Dr.				2,080 Cr.	
6	(f) Actual return	600 Cr.					600 Dr.
7	(g) Unexpected loss	200 Cr.		200 Dr.			
8	(h) Contributions		18,000 Cr.				18,000 Dr.
9	(i) Benefits					5,000 Dr.	5,000 Cr.
10	(j) Increase in APBO (Loss)			60,000 Dr.		60,000 Cr.	
11	Journal entry for 2011	27,280 Dr.	18,000 Cr.	60,200 Dr.	69,480 Cr.		
12							
13	Accumulated OCI, Dec. 31, 2010			0			
14	Balance, Dec. 31, 2011			60,200 Dr.	85,480 Cr.	109,080 Cr.	23,600 Dr.
15							

Sheet1 / Sheet2 / Sheet3 /

ILLUSTRATION 20A-6
Postretirement Benefits
Worksheet—2011

Entries (d), (h), and (i) are similar to the corresponding entries previously explained for 2010. Entry (e) accrues the interest expense component, which increases both the liability and the postretirement expense by $2,080 (the beginning APBO multiplied by the discount rate of 8%). Entries (f) and (g) are related. The expected return of $800 is higher than the actual return of $600. To smooth postretirement expense, Quest defers the unexpected loss of $200 ($800 − $600) by debiting Other Comprehensive Income (G/L) and crediting Postretirement Expense. As a result of this adjustment, the expected return on the plan assets is the amount actually used to compute postretirement expense.

Entry (j) records the change in the APBO resulting from a change in actuarial assumptions. This $60,000 increase in the employer's accumulated liability is an unexpected loss. Quest debits this loss to Other Comprehensive Income (G/L).

On December 31 Quest formally records net periodic expense for 2011 as follows.

December 31, 2011

Postretirement Expense	27,280	
Other Comprehensive Income (G/L)	60,200	
Cash		18,000
Postretirement Asset/Liability		69,480

The balance of the Postretirement Asset/Liability account at December 31, 2011, is $85,480. This balance is equal to the net of the balances in the memo accounts as shown in the reconciliation schedule in Illustration 20A-7.

Accumulated Postretirement Benefit Obligation (Credit)	$(109,080)
Plan Assets at Fair Value (Debit)	23,600
Postretirement Asset/Liability (Credit)	$ (85,480)

ILLUSTRATION 20A-7
Postretirement Benefits
Reconciliation Schedule—
December 31, 2011

Amortization of Net Gain or Loss in 2012

Quest has a beginning balance in Accumulated OCI related to losses of $60,200. Therefore, Quest must apply the corridor test for amortization of the balance for 2012. Illustration 20A-8 shows the computation of the amortization charge for the loss.

2012 Corridor Test	
Accumulated OCI at beginning of year	$60,200
10% of greater of APBO or market-related value of plan assets ($109,080 × .10)	10,908
Amortizable amount	$49,292
Average remaining service to expected retirement	25 years
2012 amortization of loss ($49,292 ÷ 25)	$1,972

ILLUSTRATION 20A-8
Computation of
Amortization Charge
(Corridor Test)—2012

DISCLOSURES IN NOTES TO THE FINANCIAL STATEMENTS

The disclosures required for other postretirement benefit plans are similar to and just as detailed and extensive as those required for pensions. The note disclosure for **Tootsie Roll, Inc.** in Illustration 20A-9 provides a good example of the extensive disclosure required for other postretirement benefit plans.

ILLUSTRATION 20A-9
Postretirement Benefit
Disclosure

Tootsie Roll Industries, Inc.

Notes to Financial Statements

Note 7   Employee Benefit Plans (partial)

Postretirement health care and life insurance benefit plans ($000):

The Company provides certain postretirement health care and life insurance benefits for corporate office and management employees. Employees become eligible for these benefits based upon their age and service and if they agree to contribute a portion of the cost. The Company has the right to modify or terminate these benefits. The Company does not fund postretirement health care and life insurance benefits in advance of payments for benefit claims.

Amounts recognized in accumulated other comprehensive loss (pre-tax) at December 31, 2007 are as follows:

Amounts recognized in other comprehensive income

Prior service credit	$(1,127)
Net actuarial loss	1,812
Net amount recognized in accumulated other comprehensive loss	$ 685

The estimated actuarial loss, prior service credit and transition obligation to be amortized from accumulated other comprehensive income into net periodic benefit cost during 2008 are $158, $(125), and $0, respectively.

The changes in the accumulated postretirement benefit obligation at December 31, 2007 and 2006, consist of the following:

Reconciliation of OPEB liability

	December 31, 2007	December 31, 2006
Benefit obligation, beginning of year	$12,582	$ 9,924
Service cost	667	524
Interest cost	694	539
Actuarial (gain)/loss	(550)	2,101
Benefits paid	(179)	(506)
Benefit obligation, end of year	$13,214	$12,582

Net periodic postretirement benefit cost included the following components:

Components of OPEB expense

	2007	2006	2005
Service cost—benefits attributed to service during the period	$ 667	$524	$474
Interest cost on the accumulated postretirement benefit obligation	694	539	519
Net amortization	90	(84)	(74)
Net periodic postretirement benefit cost	$1,451	$979	$919

Rates used to estimate plan elements

For measurement purposes, the 2007 annual rate of increase in the per capita cost of covered health care benefits was assumed to be 8.0% for pre-age 65 retirees, 9.5% for post-age 65 retirees and 11.0% for prescription drugs; these rates were assumed to decrease gradually to 5.0% for 2014 and remain at that level thereafter. The health care cost trend rate assumption has a significant effect on the amounts reported. The weighted-average discount rate used in determining the accumulated postretirement benefit obligation was 5.70% and 5.60% at December 31, 2007 and 2006, respectively.

Increasing or decreasing the health care trend rates by one percentage point in each year would have the following effect on:

	1% Increase	1% Decrease
Postretirement benefit obligation	$1,814	$(1,497)
Total of service and interest cost components	$ 236	$ (190)

The Company estimates future benefit payments will be $453, $483, $569, $598 and $677 in 2008 through 2012, respectively, and a total of $4,723 in 2013 through 2017. The future benefit payments are net of the annual Medicare Part D subsidy of approximately $1,095 beginning in 2008.

As indicated in Illustration 20A-9, Tootsie Roll shows the impact of the postretirement benefit plan on income, the balance sheet, and the cash flow statement, and it provides information on important assumptions used in the measurement of the postretirement benefit obligation. Also note that given no tax incentives for funding, Tootsie Roll (like many companies) does not have any assets set aside for its other postretirement benefit obligations.

While Tootsie Roll has only an other postretirement benefit plan, many companies sponsor both defined-benefit pension and other postretirement plans. Given the similarities in accounting for these plans, companies can combine pension and other postretirement benefit disclosures.

ACTUARIAL ASSUMPTIONS AND CONCEPTUAL ISSUES

Measurement of the EPBO, the APBO, and the net periodic postretirement benefit cost is involved and complex. Due to the uncertainties in forecasting healthcare costs, rates of use, changes in government health programs, and the differences employed in non-medical assumptions (e.g., discount rate, employee turnover, rate of pre-65 retirement, spouse-age difference), estimates of postretirement benefit costs may have a large margin of error. Is the information relevant, reliable, or verifiable? The FASB concluded that "the obligation to provide postretirement benefits meets the definition of a liability, is representationally faithful, is relevant to financial statement users, and can be measured with sufficient reliability at a justifiable cost." [11] Failure to accrue an obligation and an expense prior to payment of benefits would result in an unfaithful representation of what financial statements should represent.

The FASB took a momentous step by requiring recognition of a postretirement liability. Many opposed the requirement, warning that the GAAP rules would devastate earnings. Others argued that putting these numbers on the balance sheet was inappropriate. Others noted that the requirement would force companies to curtail postretirement benefits to employees.

The authors believe that the FASB deserves special praise. Because the Board addressed this issue, companies now recognize the magnitude of these costs. This recognition has led to efforts to control escalating healthcare costs. As John Ruffle, a former president of the Financial Accounting Foundation noted, "The Board has done American industry a gigantic favor. Over the long term, industry will look back and say thanks."

GASB WHO?

What do the numbers mean?

The Governmental Accounting Standards Board (GASB) was organized in 1984 as an operating entity of the Financial Accounting Foundation (FAF) to establish standards of financial accounting and reporting for state and local governmental entities. Similar to the FASB, FAF Trustees are responsible for selecting the members of the GASB and its Advisory Council, funding their activities, and exercising general oversight (with the exception of the GASB's resolution of technical issues). The GASB's function is important because high-quality external financial reporting can demonstrate financial accountability of state and local governments to the public and is the basis for investment, credit, and many legislative and regulatory decisions.

Until recently, the GASB went about its work in relative obscurity. How did the GASB get everyone's attention? It recommended that governmental units recognize other postretirement benefits on their balance sheets on an accrual basis, similar to the accounting required for pensions. Some states do not like that recommendation and have proposed legislation that will allow them to ignore GASB standards. However, the GASB, with the support of users of government reports, has pushed for the change. They are concerned that without the new requirements, governments will continue to misrepresent the true cost of their retirement-related promises to public employees. In their view, the new accounting rules are in the best interests of municipal bondholders and the public in general. Thus, it appears that the FASB is not the only standard-setter subject to political pressure.

Source: R. H. Attmore, "Who Do Texas Elected Officials Think They Are Fooling?" *The Bond Buyer* (June 18, 2007). For more information on the GASB, go to *www.gasb.org/*.

KEY TERMS

accumulated
  postretirement
  benefit obligation
  (APBO), *1085*

attribution period, *1084*

corridor approach, *1088*

expected postretirement
  benefit obligation
  (EPBO), *1085*

SUMMARY OF LEARNING OBJECTIVES FOR APPENDIX 20A

•10 **Identify the differences between pensions and postretirement healthcare benefits.** Pension plans are generally funded, but healthcare benefit plans are not. Pension benefits are generally well-defined and level in amount; healthcare benefits are generally uncapped and variable. Pension benefits are payable monthly; healthcare benefits are paid as needed and used. Pension plan variables are reasonably predictable, whereas healthcare plan variables are difficult to predict.

•11 **Contrast accounting for pensions to accounting for other postretirement benefits.** Many of the basic concepts, accounting terminology, and measurement methodology that apply to pensions also apply to other postretirement benefit accounting. Because other postretirement benefit plans are unfounded, large obligations can occur. Two significant concepts peculiar to accounting for other postretirement benefits are (a) expected postretirement benefit obligation (EPBO), and (b) accumulated postretirement benefit obligation (APBO).

FASB CODIFICATION

FASB Codification References

[1] FASB ASC 960. [Predecessor literature: "Accounting and Reporting by Defined Benefit Pension Plans," *Statement of Financial Accounting Standards No. 35* (Stamford, Conn.: FASB, 1979).]

[2] FASB ASC 715-70-50-1. [Predecessor literature: "Employers' Accounting for Pension Plans," *Statement of Financial Accounting Standards No. 87* (Stamford, Conn.: FASB, 1985), pars. 63–66.]

[3] FASB ASC 715-30-25-1. [Predecessor literature: "Employers' Accounting for Defined Benefit Pension and Other Postretirement Plans: An Amendment to SFAS Nos. 87, 88, 106, and 132(R)," *Statement of Financial Accounting Standards No. 158* (Norwalk, CT: FASB, 2006).]

[4] FASB ASC 715-30-35-22. [Predecessor literature: "Employers' Accounting for Pension Plans," *Statement of Financial Accounting Standards No. 87* (Stamford, Conn.: FASB, 1985), par. 30.]

[5] FASB ASC 220-10-45-13. [Predecessor literature: "Employers' Accounting for Defined Benefit Pension and Other Postretirement Plans: An Amendment of SFAS Nos. 87, 88, 106, and 132(R)," *Statement of Financial Accounting Standards No. 158* (Norwalk, CT: FASB, 2006), par. B41.]

[6] FASB ASC 715-20-50-1. [Predecessor literature: "Employers' Disclosure about Pensions and Other Postretirement Benefits," *Statement of Financial Accounting Standards No. 132* (Stamford, Conn.: FASB, 1998; revised 2003); and "Employers' Accounting for Defined Benefit Pension and Other Postretirement Plans: An Amendment of SFAS Nos. 87, 88, 106, and 132(R)," *Statement of Financial Accounting Standards No. 158* (Norwalk, CT: FASB, 2006).]

[7] FASB ASC 715-30-05-9. [Predecessor literature: "Employers' Accounting for Settlements and Curtailments of Defined Benefit Pension Plans and for Termination Benefits," *Statement of Financial Accounting Standards No. 88* (Stamford, Conn.: FASB, 1985).]

[8] FASB ASC 715-60. [Predecessor literature: "Employers' Accounting for Postretirement Benefits Other Than Pensions," *Statement of Financial Accounting Standards No. 106* (Norwalk, Conn.: FASB, 1990).]

[9] FASB ASC 712-10-05. [Predecessor literature: "Employers' Accounting for Postemployment Benefits," *Statement of Financial Accounting Standards No. 112* (Norwalk, Conn.: FASB, 1992).]

[10] FASB ASC 715-60-35-9. [Predecessor literature: "Employers' Accounting for Postretirement Benefits Other Than Pensions," *Statement of Financial Accounting Standards No. 106* (Norwalk, Conn.: FASB, 1990), pars. 46–66.]

[11] FASB ASC 715-60-25. [Predecessor literature: "Employers' Accounting for Postretirement Benefits Other Than Pensions," *Statement of Financial Accounting Standards No. 106* (Norwalk, Conn.: FASB, 1990), par. 163.]

Exercises

Access the FASB Codification at *http://asc.fasb.org/home* to prepare responses to the following exercises. Provide Codification references for your responses.

CE20-1   Access the glossary ("Master Glossary") to answer the following.

   (a) What is an accumulated benefit obligation?
   (b) What is a defined benefit postretirement plan?
   (c) What is the definition of "actuarial present value"?
   (d) What is a prior service cost?

CE20-2   In general, how can an employer choose an appropriate discount rate for its pension plan? What information could an employer use in choosing a discount rate?

CE20-3   If an employer has a defined-benefit pension plan, what components would make up its net periodic pension cost?

CE20-4   What information about its pension plan must a publicly traded company disclose in its interim financial statements?

An additional Codification case can be found in the Using Your Judgment section, on page 1113.

Be sure to check the companion website for a Review and Analysis Exercise, with solution.

Note: All asterisked Questions, Exercises, and Problems relate to material in the appendix to the chapter.

QUESTIONS

1. What is a private pension plan? How does a contributory pension plan differ from a noncontributory plan?

2. Differentiate between a defined-contribution pension plan and a defined-benefit pension plan. Explain how the employer's obligation differs between the two types of plans.

3. Differentiate between "accounting for the employer" and "accounting for the pension fund."

4. The meaning of the term "fund" depends on the context in which it is used. Explain its meaning when used as a noun. Explain its meaning when it is used as a verb.

5. What is the role of an actuary relative to pension plans? What are actuarial assumptions?

6. What factors must be considered by the actuary in measuring the amount of pension benefits under a defined benefit plan?

7. Name three approaches to measuring benefit obligations from a pension plan and explain how they differ.

8. Explain how cash-basis accounting for pension plans differs from accrual-basis accounting for pension plans. Why is cash-basis accounting generally considered unacceptable for pension plan accounting?

9. Identify the five components that comprise pension expense. Briefly explain the nature of each component.

10. What is service cost, and what is the basis of its measurement?

11. In computing the interest component of pension expense, what interest rates may be used?

12. Explain the difference between service cost and prior service cost.

13. What is meant by "prior service cost"? When is prior service cost recognized as pension expense?

14. What are "liability gains and losses," and how are they accounted for?

15. If pension expense recognized in a period exceeds the current amount funded by the employer, what kind of account arises, and how should it be reported in the financial statements? If the reverse occurs—that is, current funding by the employer exceeds the amount recognized as pension expense—what kind of account arises, and how should it be reported?

16. Given the items and amounts shown on page 1094, compute the actual return on plan assets: fair value of plan

assets at the beginning of the period $9,500,000; benefits paid during the period $1,400,000; contributions made during the period $1,000,000; and fair value of the plan assets at the end of the period $10,150,000.

17. How does an "asset gain or loss" develop in pension accounting? How does a "liability gain or loss" develop in pension accounting?

18. What is the meaning of "corridor amortization"?

19. At the end of the current period, Agler Inc. had a projected benefit obligation of $400,000 and pension plan assets (at fair value) of $350,000. What are the accounts and amounts that will be reported on the company's balance sheet as pension assets or pension liabilities?

20. At the end of the current year, Pociek Co. has prior service cost of $9,150,000. Where should the prior service cost be reported on the balance sheet?

21. Describe the accounting for actuarial gains and losses.

22. Boey Company reported net income of $25,000 in 2011. It had the following amounts related to its pension plan in 2011: Actuarial liability gain $10,000; Unexpected asset loss $14,000; Accumulated other comprehensive income (G/L) (beginning balance), zero. Determine for 2011 (a) Boey's other comprehensive income, and (b) comprehensive income.

23. Describe the reporting of pension plans for a company with multiple plans, some of which are underfunded and some of which are overfunded.

24. Determine the meaning of the following terms.

   (a) Contributory plan.

   (b) Vested benefits.

   (c) Retroactive benefits.

   (d) Years-of-service method.

25. A headline in the *Wall Street Journal* stated, "Firms Increasingly Tap Their Pension Funds to Use Excess Assets." What is the accounting issue related to the use of these "excess assets" by companies?

26. Where can authoritative iGAAP related to the accounting for pensions be found?

27. Briefly describe some of the similarities and differences between U.S. GAAP and iGAAP with respect to the accounting for pensions.

28. **Cadbury Company**, which uses iGAAP, has a postretirement benefit plan. During 2010 Cadbury recognized $30,000 unexpected asset gains in income. Just $10,000 of the gains exceeded the corridor, and the average remaining service lives of Cadbury's employees is 10 years. Discuss how Cadbury's accounting for the unexpected losses would affect comparisons to a U.S. GAAP company with a similar unexpected gain.

29. Briefly discuss the IASB/FASB convergence efforts in the area of postretirement-benefit accounting.

***30.** What are postretirement benefits other than pensions?

***31.** Why didn't the FASB cover both types of postretirement benefits—pensions and healthcare—in the earlier pension accounting rules?

***32.** What are the major differences between postretirement healthcare benefits and pension benefits?

***33.** What is the difference between the APBO and the EPBO? What are the components of postretirement expense?

BRIEF EXERCISES

·4 **BE20-1** **AMR Corporation** (parent company of **American Airlines**) reported the following for 2007 (in millions).

Service cost	$370
Interest on P.B.O.	672
Return on plan assets	747
Amortization of prior service cost	16
Amortization of net loss	25

Compute **AMR Corporation**'s 2007 pension expense.

·4 **BE20-2** For Warren Corporation, year-end plan assets were $2,000,000. At the beginning of the year, plan assets were $1,780,000. During the year, contributions to the pension fund were $120,000, and benefits paid were $200,000. Compute Warren's actual return on plan assets.

·5 **BE20-3** At January 1, 2010, Beaty Company had plan assets of $280,000 and a projected benefit obligation of the same amount. During 2010, service cost was $27,500, the settlement rate was 10%, actual and expected return on plan assets were $25,000, contributions were $20,000, and benefits paid were $17,500. Prepare a pension worksheet for Beaty Company for 2010.

·4 **BE20-4** For 2007, **Campbell Soup Company** had pension expense of $32 million and contributed $32 million to the pension fund. Prepare Campbell Soup Company's journal entry to record pension expense and funding.

•6 **BE20-5** Mancuso Corporation amended its pension plan on January 1, 2010, and granted $160,000 of prior service costs to its employees. The employees are expected to provide 2,000 service years in the future, with 350 service years in 2010. Compute prior service cost amortization for 2010.

•9 **BE20-6** At December 31, 2010, Besler Corporation had a projected benefit obligation of $560,000, plan assets of $322,000, and prior service cost of $127,000 in accumulated other comprehensive income. Determine the pension asset/liability at December 31, 2010.

•8 **BE20-7** Shin Corporation had a projected benefit obligation of $3,100,000 and plan assets of $3,300,000 at January 1, 2010. Shin also had a net actuarial loss of $465,000 in accumulated OCI at January 1, 2010. The average remaining service period of Shin's employees is 7.5 years. Compute Shin's minimum amortization of the actuarial loss.

•9 **BE20-8** Hawkins Corporation has the following balances at December 31, 2010.

Projected benefit obligation	$2,600,000
Plan assets at fair value	2,000,000
Accumulated OCI (PSC)	1,100,000

How should these balances be reported on Hawkins's balance sheet at December 31, 2010?

•9 **BE20-9** Norton Co. had the following amounts related to its pension plan in 2010.

Actuarial liability loss for 2010	$28,000
Unexpected asset gain for 2010	18,000
Accumulated other comprehensive income (G/L) (beginning balance)	7,000 Cr.

Determine for 2010: (a) Norton's other comprehensive income (loss), and (b) comprehensive income. Net income for 2010 is $26,000; no amortization of gain or loss is necessary in 2010.

•9 **BE20-10** Lahey Corp. has three defined-benefit pension plans as follows.

	Pension Assets (at Fair Value)	Projected Benefit Obligation
Plan X	$600,000	$500,000
Plan Y	900,000	720,000
Plan Z	550,000	700,000

How will Lahey report these multiple plans in its financial statements?

•10 **•11** ***BE20-11** Manno Corporation has the following information available concerning its postretirement benefit plan for 2010.

Service cost	$40,000
Interest cost	47,400
Actual and expected return on plan assets	26,900

Compute Manno's 2010 postretirement expense.

•10 **•11** ***BE20-12** For 2010, Sampsell Inc. computed its annual postretirement expense as $240,900. Sampsell's contribution to the plan during 2010 was $180,000. Prepare Sampsell's 2010 entry to record postretirement expense.

· · · · · · · · · · · · · · · · · · ·   **EXERCISES**   · · · · · · · · · · · · · · · ·

•4 **•6** **E20-1** **(Pension Expense, Journal Entries)** The following information is available for the pension plan of Brady Company for the year 2010.

44800 Cr

Actual and expected return on plan assets	$ 15,000
Benefits paid to retirees	40,000
Contributions (funding)	90,000
Interest/discount rate	10%
Prior service cost amortization	8,000
Projected benefit obligation, January 1, 2010	500,000
Service cost	60,000

Instructions
(a) Compute pension expense for the year 2010.
(b) Prepare the journal entry to record pension expense and the employer's contribution to the pension plan in 2010.

`•4` `•6` **E20-2** **(Computation of Pension Expense)** Bickner Company provides the following information about its defined-benefit pension plan for the year 2010.

Service cost	$ 90,000
Contribution to the plan	105,000
Prior service cost amortization	10,000
Actual and expected return on plan assets	64,000
Benefits paid	40,000
Plan assets at January 1, 2010	640,000
Projected benefit obligation at January 1, 2010	700,000
Accumulated OCI (PSC) at January 1, 2010	150,000
Interest/discount (settlement) rate	10%

Instructions

Compute the pension expense for the year 2010.

`•5` **E20-3** **(Preparation of Pension Worksheet)** Using the information in E20-2 prepare a pension worksheet inserting January 1, 2010, balances, showing December 31, 2010, balances, and the journal entry recording pension expense.

`•5` **E20-4** **(Basic Pension Worksheet)** The following facts apply to the pension plan of Boudreau Inc. for the year 2010.

Plan assets, January 1, 2010	$490,000
Projected benefit obligation, January 1, 2010	490,000
Settlement rate	8%
Service cost	40,000
Contributions (funding)	25,000
Actual and expected return on plan assets	49,700
Benefits paid to retirees	33,400

Instructions

Using the preceding data, compute pension expense for the year 2010. As part of your solution, prepare a pension worksheet that shows the journal entry for pension expense for 2010 and the year-end balances in the related pension accounts.

`•6` **E20-5** **(Application of Years-of-Service Method)** Andrews Company has five employees participating in its defined-benefit pension plan. Expected years of future service for these employees at the beginning of 2010 are as follows.

Employee	Future Years of Service
Jim	3
Paul	4
Nancy	5
Dave	6
Kathy	6

On January 1, 2010, the company amended its pension plan increasing its projected benefit obligation by $72,000.

Instructions

Compute the amount of prior service cost amortization for the years 2010 through 2015 using the years-of-service method setting up appropriate schedules.

`•4` **E20-6** **(Computation of Actual Return)** Gingrich Importers provides the following pension plan information.

Fair value of pension plan assets, January 1, 2010	$2,400,000
Fair value of pension plan assets, December 31, 2010	2,725,000
Contributions to the plan in 2010	280,000
Benefits paid retirees in 2010	350,000

Instructions

From the data above, compute the actual return on the plan assets for 2010.

·5 ·6 E20-7 (Basic Pension Worksheet) The following defined pension data of Rydell Corp. apply to the year 2010.

Projected benefit obligation, 1/1/10 (before amendment)	$560,000
Plan assets, 1/1/10	546,200
Pension liability	13,800
On January 1, 2010, Rydell Corp., through plan amendment, grants prior service benefits having a present value of	120,000
Settlement rate	9%
Service cost	58,000
Contributions (funding)	65,000
Actual (expected) return on plan assets	52,280
Benefits paid to retirees	40,000
Prior service cost amortization for 2010	17,000

Instructions
For 2010, prepare a pension worksheet for Rydell Corp. that shows the journal entry for pension expense and the year-end balances in the related pension accounts.

·8 E20-8 (Application of the Corridor Approach) Kenseth Corp. has the following beginning-of-the-year present values for its projected benefit obligation and market-related values for its pension plan assets.

	Projected Benefit Obligation	Plan Assets Value
2009	$2,000,000	$1,900,000
2010	2,400,000	2,500,000
2011	2,950,000	2,600,000
2012	3,600,000	3,000,000

The average remaining service life per employee in 2009 and 2010 is 10 years and in 2011 and 2012 is 12 years. The net gain or loss that occurred during each year is as follows: 2009, $280,000 loss; 2010, $90,000 loss; 2011, $11,000 loss; and 2012, $25,000 gain. (In working the solution the gains and losses must be aggregated to arrive at year-end balances.)

Instructions
Using the corridor approach, compute the amount of net gain or loss amortized and charged to pension expense in each of the four years, setting up an appropriate schedule.

·9 E20-9 (Disclosures: Pension Expense and Other Comprehensive Income) Taveras Enterprises provides the following information relative to its defined benefit pension plan.

Balances or Values at December 31, 2010	
Projected benefit obligation	$2,737,000
Accumulated benefit obligation	1,980,000
Fair value of plan assets	2,278,329
Accumulated OCI (PSC)	210,000
Accumulated OCI—Net loss (1/1/10 balance, –0–)	45,680
Pension liability	458,671
Other pension plan data:	
Service cost for 2010	$ 94,000
Prior service cost amortization for 2010	42,000
Actual return on plan assets in 2010	130,000
Expected return on plan assets in 2010	175,680
Interest on January 1, 2010, projected benefit obligation	253,000
Contributions to plan in 2010	93,329
Benefits paid	140,000

Instructions
(a) Prepare the note disclosing the components of pension expense for the year 2010.
(b) Determine the amounts of other comprehensive income and comprehensive income for 2010. Net income for 2010 is $35,000.
(c) Compute the amount of accumulated other comprehensive income reported at December 31, 2010.

·5 **E20-10** **(Pension Worksheet)** Webb Corp. sponsors a defined-benefit pension plan for its employees. On January 1, 2010, the following balances relate to this plan.

Plan assets	$480,000
Projected benefit obligation	600,000
Pension asset/liability	120,000
Accumulated OCI (PSC)	100,000

As a result of the operation of the plan during 2010, the following additional data are provided by the actuary.

Service cost for 2010	$90,000
Settlement rate, 9%	
Actual return on plan assets in 2010	55,000
Amortization of prior service cost	19,000
Expected return on plan assets	52,000
Unexpected loss from change in projected benefit obligation,	
due to change in actuarial predictions	76,000
Contributions in 2010	99,000
Benefits paid retirees in 2010	85,000

Instructions

(a) Using the data above, compute pension expense for Webb Corp. for the year 2010 by preparing a pension worksheet.

(b) Prepare the journal entry for pension expense for 2010.

 E20-11 **(Pension Expense, Journal Entries, Statement Presentation)** Henning Company sponsors a defined benefit pension plan for its employees. The following data relate to the operation of the plan for the year 2010 in which no benefits were paid.

1. The actuarial present value of future benefits earned by employees for services rendered in 2010 amounted to $56,000.
2. The company's funding policy requires a contribution to the pension trustee amounting to $145,000 for 2010.
3. As of January 1, 2010, the company had a projected benefit obligation of $900,000, an accumulated benefit obligation of $800,000, and a balance of $400,000 in accumulated OCI (PSC). The fair value of pension plan assets amounted to $600,000 at the beginning of the year. The actual and expected return on plan assets was $54,000. The settlement rate was 9%. No gains or losses occurred in 2010 and no benefits were paid.
4. Amortization of prior service cost was $50,000 in 2010. Amortization of net gain or loss was not required in 2010.

Instructions

(a) Determine the amounts of the components of pension expense that should be recognized by the company in 2010.

(b) Prepare the journal entry or entries to record pension expense and the employer's contribution to the pension trustee in 2010.

(c) Indicate the amounts that would be reported on the income statement and the balance sheet for the year 2010.

·4 ·6 ·7 ·8 ·9 **E20-12** **(Pension Expense, Journal Entries, Statement Presentation)** Ferreri Company received the following selected information from its pension plan trustee concerning the operation of the company's defined benefit pension plan for the year ended December 31, 2010.

	January 1, 2010	December 31, 2010
Projected benefit obligation	$1,500,000	$1,527,000
Market-related and fair value of plan assets	800,000	1,130,000
Accumulated benefit obligation	1,600,000	1,720,000
Accumulated OCI (G/L)—Net gain	–0–	(200,000)

The service cost component of pension expense for employee services rendered in the current year amounted to $77,000 and the amortization of prior service cost was $120,000. The company's actual funding (contributions) of the plan in 2010 amounted to $250,000. The expected return on plan assets and the actual rate were both 10%; the interest/discount (settlement) rate was 10%. Accumulated other comprehensive income (PSC) had a balance of $1,200,000 on January 1, 2010. Assume no benefits paid in 2010.

Instructions

(a) Determine the amounts of the components of pension expense that should be recognized by the company in 2010.

(b) Prepare the journal entry to record pension expense and the employer's contribution to the pension plan in 2010.

(c) Indicate the pension-related amounts that would be reported on the income statement and the balance sheet for Ferreri Company for the year 2010.

E20-13 (Computation of Actual Return, Gains and Losses, Corridor Test, and Pension Expense) Erickson Company sponsors a defined benefit pension plan. The corporation's actuary provides the following information about the plan.

	January 1, 2010	December 31, 2010
Vested benefit obligation	$1,500	$1,900
Accumulated benefit obligation	1,900	2,730
Projected benefit obligation	2,500	3,300
Plan assets (fair value)	1,700	2,620
Settlement rate and expected rate of return		10%
Pension asset/liability	800	?
Service cost for the year 2010		400
Contributions (funding in 2010)		700
Benefits paid in 2010		200

Instructions
(a) Compute the actual return on the plan assets in 2010.
(b) Compute the amount of the other comprehensive income (G/L) as of December 31, 2010. (Assume the January 1, 2010, balance was zero.)
(c) Compute the amount of net gain or loss amortization for 2010 (corridor approach).
(d) Compute pension expense for 2010.

E20-14 (Worksheet for E20-13) Using the information in E20-13 about Erickson Company's defined-benefit pension plan, prepare a 2010 pension worksheet with supplementary schedules of computations. Prepare the journal entries at December 31, 2010, to record pension expense and related pension transactions. Also, indicate the pension amounts reported in the balance sheet.

E20-15 (Pension Expense, Journal Entries) Latoya Company provides the following selected information related to its defined-benefit pension plan for 2010.

Pension asset/liability (January 1)	$ 25,000 Cr.
Accumulated benefit obligation (December 31)	400,000
Actual and expected return on plan assets	10,000
Contributions (funding) in 2010	150,000
Fair value of plan assets (December 31)	800,000
Settlement rate	10%
Projected benefit obligation (January 1)	700,000
Service cost	80,000

Instructions
(a) Compute pension expense and prepare the journal entry to record pension expense and the employer's contribution to the pension plan in 2010. Preparation of a pension worksheet is not required. Benefits paid in 2010 were $35,000.
(b) Indicate the pension-related amounts that would be reported in the company's income statement and balance sheet for 2010.

E20-16 (Amortization of Accumulated OCI (G/L), Corridor Approach, Pension Expense Computation) The actuary for the pension plan of Gustafson Inc. calculated the following net gains and losses.

Incurred during the Year	(Gain) or Loss
2010	$300,000
2011	480,000
2012	(210,000)
2013	(290,000)

Other information about the company's pension obligation and plan assets is as follows.

As of January 1,	Projected Benefit Obligation	Plan Assets (market-related asset value)
2010	$4,000,000	$2,400,000
2011	4,520,000	2,200,000
2012	5,000,000	2,600,000
2013	4,240,000	3,040,000

Gustafson Inc. has a stable labor force of 400 employees who are expected to receive benefits under the plan. The total service-years for all participating employees is 5,600. The beginning balance of accumulated OCI (G/L) is zero on January 1, 2010. The market-related value and the fair value of plan assets are the same for the 4-year period. Use the average remaining service life per employee as the basis for amortization.

Instructions

(Round to the nearest dollar)

Prepare a schedule which reflects the minimum amount of accumulated OCI (G/L) amortized as a component of net periodic pension expense for each of the years 2010, 2011, 2012, and 2013. Apply the "corridor" approach in determining the amount to be amortized each year.

•8 E20-17 (Amortization of Accumulated OCI Balances) Keeton Company sponsors a defined-benefit pension plan for its 600 employees. The company's actuary provided the following information about the plan.

	January 1, 2010	December 31, 2010	December 31, 2011
Projected benefit obligation	$2,800,000	$3,650,000	$4,195,000
Accumulated benefit obligation	1,900,000	2,430,000	2,900,000
Plan assets (fair value and market-related asset value)	1,700,000	2,900,000	3,790,000
Accumulated net (gain) or loss (for purposes of the corridor calculation)	–0–	198,000	(24,000)
Discount rate (current settlement rate)		9%	8%
Actual and expected asset return rate		10%	10%
Contributions		1,030,000	660,000

The average remaining service life per employee is 10.5 years. The service cost component of net periodic pension expense for employee services rendered amounted to $400,000 in 2010 and $475,000 in 2011. The accumulated OCI (PSC) on January 1, 2010, was $1,260,000. No benefits have been paid.

Instructions

(Round to the nearest dollar)

(a) Compute the amount of accumulated OCI (PSC) to be amortized as a component of net periodic pension expense for each of the years 2010 and 2011.

(b) Prepare a schedule which reflects the amount of accumulated OCI (G/L) to be amortized as a component of pension expense for 2010 and 2011.

(c) Determine the total amount of pension expense to be recognized by Keeton Company in 2010 and 2011.

•5 •8 E20-18 (Pension Worksheet—Missing Amounts) The accounting staff of Usher Inc. has prepared the following pension worksheet. Unfortunately, several entries in the worksheet are not decipherable. The company has asked your assistance in completing the worksheet and completing the accounting tasks related to the pension plan for 2010.

	Pension Worksheet—Usher Inc.							
	A	B	C	D	E	F	H	I
1				General Journal Entries			Memo Record	
2	Items	Annual Pension Expense	Cash	OCI—Prior Service Cost	OCI— Gain/Losse	Pension Asset/Liability	Projected Benefit Obligation	Plan Assets
3	Balance, Jan. 1, 2010					1,100 Cr.	2,800	1,700
4	Service cost	(1)					500	
5	Interest cost	(2)					280	
6	Actual return	(3)						220
7	Unexpected gain	150			(4)			
8	Amortization of PSC	(5)		55				
9	Contributions		800					800
10	Benefits						200	200
11	Liability increase				(6)		365	
12	Journal entry	(7)	(8)	(9)	(10)	(11)		
13								
14	Accumulated OCI, Dec. 31, 2009			1,100	0			
15	Balance, Dec. 31, 2010			1,045	215	1,225	3,745	2,520
16								

Sheet1 / Sheet2 / Sheet3

Instructions

(a) Determine the missing amounts in the 2010 pension worksheet, indicating whether the amounts are debits or credits.

(b) Prepare the journal entry to record 2010 pension expense for Usher Inc.

(c) The accounting staff has heard of a pension accounting procedure called "corridor amortization." Is Usher required to record any amounts for corridor amortization in (1) 2010? In (2) 2011? Explain.

·10 ·11 *E20-19 (Postretirement Benefit Expense Computation)** Kreter Co. provides the following information about its postretirement benefit plan for the year 2010.

Service cost	$ 45,000
Contribution to the plan	10,000
Actual and expected return on plan assets	11,000
Benefits paid	20,000
Plan assets at January 1, 2010	110,000
Accumulated postretirement benefit obligation at January 1, 2010	330,000
Discount rate	8%

Instructions

Compute the postretirement benefit expense for 2010.

·10 ·11 *E20-20 (Postretirement Benefit Worksheet)** Using the information in *E20-19, prepare a worksheet inserting January 1, 2010, balances, and showing December 31, 2010, balances. Prepare the journal entry recording postretirement benefit expense.

·10 ·11 *E20-21 (Postretirement Benefit Expense Computation)** Garner Inc. provides the following information related to its postretirement benefits for the year 2010.

Accumulated postretirement benefit obligation at January 1, 2010	$710,000
Actual and expected return on plan assets	34,000
Prior service cost amortization	21,000
Discount rate	10%
Service cost	83,000

Instructions

Compute postretirement benefit expense for 2010.

·10 ·11 *E20-22 (Postretirement Benefit Expense Computation)** Englehart Co. provides the following information about its postretirement benefit plan for the year 2010.

Service cost	$ 90,000
Prior service cost amortization	3,000
Contribution to the plan	56,000
Actual and expected return on plan assets	62,000
Benefits paid	40,000
Plan assets at January 1, 2010	710,000
Accumulated postretirement benefit obligation at January 1, 2010	760,000
Accumulated OCI (PSC) at January 1, 2010	100,000 Dr.
Discount rate	9%

Instructions

Compute the postretirement benefit expense for 2010.

·10 ·11 *E20-23 (Postretirement Benefit Worksheet)** Using the information in *E20-22, prepare a worksheet inserting January 1, 2010, balances, showing December 31, 2010, balances, and the journal entry recording postretirement benefit expense.

·10 ·11 *E20-24 (Postretirement Benefit Worksheet—Missing Amounts)** The accounting staff of Holder Inc. has prepared the postretirement benefit worksheet on page 1102. Unfortunately, several entries in the worksheet are not decipherable. The company has asked your assistance in completing the worksheet and completing the accounting tasks related to the pension plan for 2010.

	A	B	C	D	E	G	H
			General Journal Entries			Memo Record	
	Items	Annual Expense	Cash	Other Comprehensive Income—PSC	Postretirement Asset/Liability	APBO	Plan Assets
3	Balance, Jan. 1, 2010				290,000	410,000	120,000
4	Service cost	(1)				56,000	
5	Interest cost	(2)				36,900	
6	Actual/Expected return	(3)					2,000
7	Contributions		66,000				(4)
8	Benefits					5,000	5,000
9	Amortization of PSC	3,000		(5)			
10	Journal entry for 2010	(6)	(7)	(8)	(9)		
11							
12	Accumulated OCI, Dec. 31, 2009			30,000 Dr.			
13	Balance, Dec. 31, 2010			27,000 Dr.	314,900 Cr.	497,900 Cr.	183,000 Dr.
14							

Postretirement Benefit Worksheet—Holder Inc.

Sheet1 / Sheet2 / Sheet3

Instructions

(a) Determine the missing amounts in the 2010 postretirement worksheet, indicating whether the amounts are debits or credits.

(b) Prepare the journal entry to record 2010 postretirement expense for Holder Inc.

(c) What discount rate is Holder using in accounting for the interest on its other postretirement benefit plan? Explain.

See the book's companion website, www.wiley.com/college/kieso, for a set of B Exercises.

PROGRAMS

PROBLEMS

P20-1 (2-Year Worksheet) On January 1, 2010, Cunningham Company has the following defined-benefit pension plan balances.

Projected benefit obligation	$4,500,000
Fair value of plan assets	4,200,000

The interest (settlement) rate applicable to the plan is 10%. On January 1, 2011, the company amends its pension agreement so that prior service costs of $500,000 are created. Other data related to the pension plan are as follows.

	2010	2011
Service cost	$150,000	$180,000
Prior service cost amortization	–0–	90,000
Contributions (funding) to the plan	240,000	285,000
Benefits paid	200,000	280,000
Actual return on plan assets	252,000	260,000
Expected rate of return on assets	6%	8%

Instructions

(a) Prepare a pension worksheet for the pension plan for 2010 and 2011.

(b) For 2011, prepare the journal entry to record pension-related amounts.

P20-2 (3-Year Worksheet, Journal Entries, and Reporting) Jackson Company adopts acceptable accounting for its defined-benefit pension plan on January 1, 2009, with the following beginning balances: plan assets $200,000; projected benefit obligation $250,000. Other data relating to 3 years' operation of the plan are shown on the next page.

	2009	2010	2011
Annual service cost	$16,000	$ 19,000	$ 26,000
Settlement rate and expected rate of return	10%	10%	10%
Actual return on plan assets	18,000	22,000	24,000
Annual funding (contributions)	16,000	40,000	48,000
Benefits paid	14,000	16,400	21,000
Prior service cost (plan amended, 1/1/10)		160,000	
Amortization of prior service cost		54,400	41,600
Change in actuarial assumptions establishes a December 31, 2011, projected benefit obligation of:			520,000

Instructions

(a) Prepare a pension worksheet presenting all 3 years' pension balances and activities.

(b) Prepare the journal entries (from the worksheet) to reflect all pension plan transactions and events at December 31 of each year.

(c) Indicate the pension-related amounts reported in the financial statements for 2011.

P20-3 (Pension Expense, Journal Entries, Amortization of Loss) Gottschalk Company sponsors a defined benefit plan for its 100 employees. On January 1, 2010, the company's actuary provided the following information.

Accumulated other comprehensive loss (PSC)	$150,000
Pension plan assets (fair value and market-related asset value)	200,000
Accumulated benefit obligation	260,000
Projected benefit obligation	380,000

The average remaining service period for the participating employees is 10 years. All employees are expected to receive benefits under the plan. On December 31, 2010, the actuary calculated that the present value of future benefits earned for employee services rendered in the current year amounted to $52,000; the projected benefit obligation was $490,000; fair value of pension assets was $276,000; the accumulated benefit obligation amounted to $365,000. The expected return on plan assets and the discount rate on the projected benefit obligation were both 10%. The actual return on plan assets is $11,000. The company's current year's contribution to the pension plan amounted to $65,000. No benefits were paid during the year.

Instructions

(a) Determine the components of pension expense that the company would recognize in 2010. (With only one year involved, you need not prepare a worksheet.)

(b) Prepare the journal entry to record the pension expense and the company's funding of the pension plan in 2010.

(c) Compute the amount of the 2010 increase/decrease in gains or losses and the amount to be amortized in 2010 and 2011.

(d) Indicate the pension amounts reported in the financial statement as of December 31, 2010.

P20-4 (Pension Expense, Journal Entries for 2 Years) Gordon Company sponsors a defined benefit pension plan. The following information related to the pension plan is available for 2010 and 2011.

	2010	2011
Plan assets (fair value), December 31	$699,000	$849,000
Projected benefit obligation, January 1	700,000	800,000
Pension asset/liability, January 1	140,000 Cr.	?
Prior service cost, January 1	250,000	240,000
Service cost	60,000	90,000
Actual and expected return on plan assets	24,000	30,000
Amortization of prior service cost	10,000	12,000
Contributions (funding)	115,000	120,000
Accumulated benefit obligation, December 31	500,000	550,000
Interest/settlement rate	9%	9%

Instructions

(a) Compute pension expense for 2010 and 2011.

(b) Prepare the journal entries to record the pension expense and the company's funding of the pension plan for both years.

·7 ·8 P20-5 (Computation of Pension Expense, Amortization of Net Gain or Loss–Corridor Approach, Journal Entries for 3 Years) Hiatt Toothpaste Company initiates a defined-benefit pension plan for its 50 employees on January 1, 2010. The insurance company which administers the pension plan provided the following selected information for the years 2010, 2011, and 2012.

	For Year Ended December 31,		
	2010	2011	2012
Plan assets (fair value)	$50,000	$ 85,000	$180,000
Accumulated benefit obligation	45,000	165,000	292,000
Projected benefit obligation	60,000	200,000	324,000
Net (gain) loss (for purposes of corridor calculation)	–0–	78,400	86,121
Employer's funding contribution (made at end of year)	50,000	60,000	105,000

There were no balances as of January 1, 2010, when the plan was initiated. The actual and expected return on plan assets was 10% over the 3-year period but the settlement rate used to discount the company's pension obligation was 13% in 2010, 11% in 2011, and 8% in 2012. The service cost component of net periodic pension expense amounted to the following: 2010, $60,000; 2011, $85,000; and 2012, $119,000. The average remaining service life per employee is 12 years. No benefits were paid in 2010, $30,000 of benefits were paid in 2011, and $18,500 of benefits were paid in 2012 (all benefits paid at end of year).

Instructions
(Round to the nearest dollar.)

(a) Calculate the amount of net periodic pension expense that the company would recognize in 2010, 2011, and 2012.

(b) Prepare the journal entries to record net periodic pension expense, employer's funding contribution, and related pension amounts for the years 2010, 2011, and 2012.

·6 ·7 ·8 P20-6 (Computation of Prior Service Cost Amortization, Pension Expense, Journal Entries, and Net Gain or Loss) Aykroyd Inc. has sponsored a noncontributory-defined benefit pension plan for its employees since 1987. Prior to 2010, cumulative net pension expense recognized equaled cumulative contributions to the plan. Other relevant information about the pension plan on January 1, 2010, is as follows.

1. The company has 200 employees. All these employees are expected to receive benefits under the plan. The average remaining service life per employee is 12 years.
2. The projected benefit obligation amounted to $5,000,000 and the fair value of pension plan assets was $3,000,000. The market-related asset value was also $3,000,000. Unrecognized prior service cost was $2,000,000.

On December 31, 2010, the projected benefit obligation and the accumulated benefit obligation were $4,850,000 and $4,025,000, respectively. The fair value of the pension plan assets amounted to $4,100,000 at the end of the year. A 10% settlement rate and a 10% expected asset return rate were used in the actuarial present value computations in the pension plan. The present value of benefits attributed by the pension benefit formula to employee service in 2010 amounted to $200,000. The employer's contribution to the plan assets amounted to $775,000 in 2010. This problem assumes no payment of pension benefits.

Instructions
(Round all amounts to the nearest dollar.)

(a) Prepare a schedule, based on the average remaining life per employee, showing the prior service cost that would be amortized as a component of pension expense for 2010, 2011, and 2012.
(b) Compute pension expense for the year 2010.
(c) Prepare the journal entries required to report the accounting for the company's pension plan for 2010.
(d) Compute the amount of the 2010 increase/decrease in net gains or losses and the amount to be amortized in 2010 and 2011.

·5 ·6 ·7 P20-7 (Pension Worksheet) Hanson Corp. sponsors a defined-benefit pension plan for its employees. On January 1, 2010, the following balances related to this plan.

Plan assets (market-related value)	$520,000
Projected benefit obligation	700,000
Pension asset/liability	180,000 Cr.
Prior service cost	81,000
Net gain or loss (debit)	91,000

As a result of the operation of the plan during 2010, the actuary provided the following additional data at December 31, 2010.

Service cost for 2010	$108,000
Settlement rate, 9%; expected return rate, 10%	
Actual return on plan assets in 2010	48,000
Amortization of prior service cost	25,000
Contributions in 2010	133,000
Benefits paid retirees in 2010	85,000
Average remaining service life of active employees	10 years

Instructions

Using the preceding data, compute pension expense for Hanson Corp. for the year 2010 by preparing a pension worksheet that shows the journal entry for pension expense. Use the market-related asset value to compute the expected return and for corridor amortization.

P20-8 (Comprehensive 2-Year Worksheet) Lemke Company sponsors a defined-benefit pension plan for its employees. The following data relate to the operation of the plan for the years 2010 and 2011.

	2010	2011
Projected benefit obligation, January 1	$600,000	
Plan assets (fair value and market-related value), January 1	410,000	
Pension asset/liability, January 1	190,000 Cr.	
Prior service cost, January 1	160,000	
Service cost	40,000	$ 59,000
Settlement rate	10%	10%
Expected rate of return	10%	10%
Actual return on plan assets	36,000	61,000
Amortization of prior service cost	70,000	50,000
Annual contributions	97,000	81,000
Benefits paid retirees	31,500	54,000
Increase in projected benefit obligation due to changes in actuarial assumptions	87,000	–0–
Accumulated benefit obligation at December 31	721,800	789,000
Average service life of all employees		20 years
Vested benefit obligation at December 31		464,000

Instructions

(a) Prepare a pension worksheet presenting both years 2010 and 2011 and accompanying computations and amortization of the loss (2011) using the corridor approach.

(b) Prepare the journal entries (from the worksheet) to reflect all pension plan transactions and events at December 31 of each year.

(c) For 2011, indicate the pension amounts reported in the financial statements.

P20-9 (Comprehensive 2-Year Worksheet) Hobbs Co. has the following defined-benefit pension plan balances on January 1, 2010.

Projected benefit obligation	$4,600,000
Fair value of plan assets	4,600,000

The interest (settlement) rate applicable to the plan is 10%. On January 1, 2011, the company amends its pension agreement so that prior service costs of $600,000 are created. Other data related to the pension plan are:

	2010	2011
Service cost	$150,000	$170,000
Prior service cost amortization	–0–	90,000
Contributions (funding) to the plan	200,000	184,658
Benefits paid	220,000	280,000
Actual return on plan assets	252,000	350,000
Expected rate of return on assets	6%	8%

Instructions

(a) Prepare a pension worksheet for the pension plan in 2010.

(b) Prepare any journal entries related to the pension plan that would be needed at December 31, 2010.

(c) Prepare a pension worksheet for 2011 and any journal entries related to the pension plan as of December 31, 2011.

(d) Indicate the pension-related amounts reported in the 2011 financial statements.

•5 •6 •7 **P20-10** **(Pension Worksheet − Missing Amounts)** Kramer Co. has prepared the following pension work-sheet. Unfortunately, several entries in the worksheet are not decipherable. The company has asked your assistance in completing the worksheet and completing the accounting tasks related to the pension plan for 2010.

	Pension Worksheet—Kramer Co.							
	A	**B**		**C**	**D**	**E**	**G**	**H**
1			General Journal Entries				Memo Record	
2	Items	Annual Pension Expense	Cash	OCI—Prior Service Cost	OCI— Gain/Loss	Pension Asset/Liability	Projected Benefit Obligation	Plan Assets
3	Balance, Jan. 1, 2010					120,000	325,000	205,000 Dr.
4	Service cost	(1)					20,000	
5	Interest cost	(2)					26,000	
6	Actual return	(3)						18,000 Dr.
7	Unexpected loss	2,500			(4)			
8	Amortization of PSC	(5)		35,000				
9	Contributions		41,000					41,000 Dr.
10	Benefits						15,000	15,000 Cr.
11	Increase in PBO				(6)		43,500	
12	Journal entry for 2010	(7)	(8)	(9)	(10)	(11)		
13	Accumulated OCI, Dec. 31, 2009			80,000	0			
14	Balance, Dec. 31, 2010			45,000	46,000	150,500 Cr.	399,500 Cr.	249,000 Dr.

Sheet1 / Sheet2 / Sheet3

Instructions

(a) Determine the missing amounts in the 2010 pension worksheet, indicating whether the amounts are debits or credits.

(b) Prepare the journal entry to record 2010 pension expense for Kramer Co.

(c) Determine the following for Kramer for 2010: **(1)** settlement rate used to measure the interest on the liability and **(2)** expected return on plan assets.

•5 •6 •7 **P20-11** **(Pension Worksheet)** The following data relate to the operation of Kramer Co.'s pension plan
•8 •9 in 2011. The pension worksheet for 2010 is provided in P20-10.

Service cost	$59,000
Actual return on plan assets	32,000
Amortization of prior service cost	28,000
Annual contributions	51,000
Benefits paid retirees	27,000
Average service life of all employees	25 years

For 2011, Kramer will use the same assumptions as 2010 for the expected rate of returns on plan assets. The settlement rate for 2011 is 10%.

Instructions

(a) Prepare a pension worksheet for 2011 and accompanying computations and amortization of the loss, if any, in 2011 using the corridor approach.

(b) Prepare the journal entries (from the worksheet) to reflect all pension plan transactions and events at December 31.

(c) Indicate the pension amounts reported in the financial statements.

•5 •6 •7 **P20-12** **(Pension Worksheet)** Larson Corp. sponsors a defined-benefit pension plan for its employees.
•8 •9 On January 1, 2011, the following balances related to this plan.

Plan assets (market-related value)	$270,000
Projected benefit obligation	340,000
Pension asset/liability	70,000 Cr.
Prior service cost	90,000
OCI—Loss	39,000

As a result of the operation of the plan during 2011, the actuary provided the following additional data at December 31, 2011.

Service cost for 2011	$ 45,000
Actual return on plan assets in 2011	27,000
Amortization of prior service cost	12,000
Contributions in 2011	65,000
Benefits paid retirees in 2011	41,000
Settlement rate	7%
Expected return on plan assets	8%
Average remaining service life of active employees	10 years

Instructions

(a) Compute pension expense for Larson Corp. for the year 2011 by preparing a pension worksheet that shows the journal entry for pension expense.

(b) Indicate the pension amounts reported in the financial statements.

·10·11 *P20-13 (Postretirement Benefit Worksheet)** Hollenbeck Foods Inc. sponsors a postretirement medical and dental benefit plan for its employees. The following balances relate to this plan on January 1, 2010.

Plan assets	$200,000
Expected postretirement benefit obligation	820,000
Accumulated postretirement benefit obligation	200,000
No prior service costs exist.	

As a result of the plan's operation during 2010, the following additional data are provided by the actuary.

Service cost for 2010 is $70,000
Discount rate is 10%
Contributions to plan in 2010 are $65,000
Expected return on plan assets is $10,000
Actual return on plan assets is $15,000
Benefits paid to employees are $44,000
Average remaining service to full eligibility: 20 years

Instructions

(a) Using the preceding data, compute the net periodic postretirement benefit cost for 2010 by preparing a worksheet that shows the journal entry for postretirement expense and the year-end balances in the related postretirement benefit memo accounts. (Assume that contributions and benefits are paid at the end of the year.)

(b) Prepare any journal entries related to the postretirement plan for 2010 and indicate the postretirement amounts reported in the financial statements for 2010.

·10·11 *P20-14 (Postretirement Benefit Worksheet—2 Years)** Elton Co. has the following postretirement benefit plan balances on January 1, 2010.

Accumulated postretirement benefit obligation	$2,250,000
Fair value of plan assets	2,250,000

The interest (settlement) rate applicable to the plan is 10%. On January 1, 2011, the company amends the plan so that prior service costs of $175,000 are created. Other data related to the plan are:

	2010	2011
Service costs	$ 75,000	$ 85,000
Prior service costs amortization	–0–	12,000
Contributions (funding) to the plan	45,000	35,000
Benefits paid	40,000	45,000
Actual return on plan assets	140,000	120,000
Expected rate of return on assets	8%	6%

Instructions

(a) Prepare a worksheet for the postretirement plan in 2010.

(b) Prepare any journal entries related to the postretirement plan that would be needed at December 31, 2010.

(c) Prepare a worksheet for 2011 and any journal entries related to the postretirement plan as of December 31, 2011.

(d) Indicate the postretirement-benefit–related amounts reported in the 2011 financial statements.

CA20-1 (Pension Terminology and Theory) Many business organizations have been concerned with providing for the retirement of employees since the late 1800s. During recent decades a marked increase in this concern has resulted in the establishment of private pension plans in most large companies and in many medium- and small-sized ones.

The substantial growth of these plans, both in numbers of employees covered and in amounts of retirement benefits, has increased the significance of pension cost in relation to the financial position, results of operations, and cash flows of many companies. In examining the costs of pension plans, a CPA encounters certain terms. The components of pension costs that the terms represent must be dealt with appropriately if generally accepted accounting principles are to be reflected in the financial statements of entities with pension plans.

Instructions
(a) Define a private pension plan. How does a contributory pension plan differ from a noncontributory plan?
(b) Differentiate between "accounting for the employer" and "accounting for the pension fund."
(c) Explain the terms "funded" and "pension liability" as they relate to:
  (1) The pension fund.
  (2) The employer.
(d) (1) Discuss the theoretical justification for accrual recognition of pension costs.
  (2) Discuss the relative objectivity of the measurement process of accrual versus cash (pay-as-you-go) accounting for annual pension costs.
(e) Distinguish among the following as they relate to pension plans.
  (1) Service cost.
  (2) Prior service costs.
  (3) Vested benefits.

CA20-2 (Pension Terminology) The following items appear on Brueggen Company's financial statements.

1. Under the caption Assets:
   Pension asset/liability.
2. Under the caption Liabilities:
   Pension asset/liability.
3. Under the caption Stockholders' Equity:
   Prior service cost as a component of Accumulated Other Comprehensive Income.
4. On the income statement:
   Pension expense.

Instructions
Explain the significance of each of the items above on corporate financial statements. (*Note:* All items set forth above are not necessarily to be found on the statements of a single company.)

CA20-3 (Basic Terminology) In examining the costs of pension plans, Helen Kaufman, CPA, encounters certain terms. The components of pension costs that the terms represent must be dealt with appropriately if generally accepted accounting principles are to be reflected in the financial statements of entities with pension plans.

Instructions
(a) (1) Discuss the theoretical justification for accrual recognition of pension costs.
  (2) Discuss the relative objectivity of the measurement process of accrual versus cash (pay-as-you-go) accounting for annual pension costs.
(b) Explain the following terms as they apply to accounting for pension plans.
  (1) Market-related asset value.
  (2) Projected benefit obligation.
  (3) Corridor approach.
(c) What information should be disclosed about a company's pension plans in its financial statements and its notes?

(AICPA adapted)

CA20-4 (Major Pension Concepts) Davis Corporation is a medium-sized manufacturer of paperboard containers and boxes. The corporation sponsors a noncontributory, defined-benefit pension plan that covers its 250 employees. Sid Cole has recently been hired as president of Davis Corporation. While reviewing last year's financial statements with Carol Dilbeck, controller, Cole expressed confusion about several of the items in the footnote to the financial statements relating to the pension plan. In part, the footnote reads as follows.

> **Note J.** The company has a defined-benefit pension plan covering substantially all of its employees. The benefits are based on years of service and the employee's compensation during the last four years of employment. The company's funding policy is to contribute annually the maximum amount allowed under the federal tax code. Contributions are intended to provide for benefits expected to be earned in the future as well as those earned to date.

The net periodic pension expense on Davis Corporation's comparative income statement was $72,000 in 2010 and $57,680 in 2009.

The following are selected figures from the plan's funded status and amounts recognized in the Davis Corporation's Statement of Financial Position at December 31, 2010 ($000 omitted).

Actuarial present value of benefit obligations:	
Accumulated benefit obligation	
(including vested benefits of $636)	$ (870)
Projected benefit obligation	$(1,200)
Plan assets at fair value	1,050
Projected benefit obligation in	
excess of plan assets	$ (150)

Given that Davis Corporation's work force has been stable for the last 6 years, Cole could not understand the increase in the net periodic pension expense. Dilbeck explained that the net periodic pension expense consists of several elements, some of which may increase or decrease the net expense.

Instructions
- **(a)** The determination of the net periodic pension expense is a function of five elements. List and briefly describe each of the elements.
- **(b)** Describe the major difference and the major similarity between the accumulated benefit obligation and the projected benefit obligation.
- **(c)** **(1)** Explain why pension gains and losses are not recognized on the income statement in the period in which they arise.
  - **(2)** Briefly describe how pension gains and losses are recognized.

(CMA adapted)

CA20-5 (Implications of GAAP Rules on Pensions) Jill Vogel and Pete Dell have to do a class presentation on GAAP rules for reporting pension information. In developing the class presentation, they decided to provide the class with a series of questions related to pensions and then discuss the answers in class. Given that the class has all read the rules related to pension accounting and reporting, they felt this approach would provide a lively discussion. Here are the questions:

1. In an article in *Business Week* prior to new rules related to pensions, it was reported that the discount rates used by the largest 200 companies for pension reporting ranged from 5% to 11%. How can such a situation exist, and does GAAP alleviate this problem?
2. An article indicated that when new GAAP rules were issued related to pensions, it caused an increase in the liability for pensions for approximately 20% of companies. Why might this situation occur?
3. A recent article noted that while "smoothing" is not necessarily an accounting virtue, pension accounting has long been recognized as an exception—an area of accounting in which at least some dampening of market swings is appropriate. This is because pension funds are managed so that their performance is insulated from the extremes of short-term market swings. A pension expense that reflects the volatility of market swings might, for that reason, convey information of little relevance. Are these statements true?

4. Understanding the impact of the changes required in pension reporting requires detailed information about its pension plan(s) and an analysis of the relationship of many factors, particularly:
    (a) the type of plan(s) and any significant amendments.
    (b) the plan participants.
    (c) the funding status.
    (d) the actuarial funding method and assumptions currently used.
    What impact does each of these items have on financial statement presentation?
5. An article noted "You also need to decide whether to amortize gains and losses using the corridor method, or to use some other systematic method. Under the corridor approach, only gains and losses in excess of 10% of the greater of the projected benefit obligation or the plan assets would have to be amortized." What is the corridor method and what is its purpose?

Instructions
What answers do you believe Jill and Pete gave to each of these questions?

CA20-6 (Gains and Losses, Corridor Amortization) Vickie Plato, accounting clerk in the personnel office of Streisand Corp., has begun to compute pension expense for 2012 but is not sure whether or not she should include the amortization of unrecognized gains/losses. She is currently working with the following beginning-of-the-year present values for the projected benefit obligation and market-related values for the pension plan:

	Projected Benefit Obligation	Plan Assets Value
2009	$2,200,000	$1,900,000
2010	2,400,000	2,500,000
2011	2,900,000	2,600,000
2012	3,900,000	3,000,000

The average remaining service life per employee in 2009 and 2010 is 10 years and in 2011 and 2012 is 12 years. The net gain or loss that occurred during each year is as follows.

2009	$280,000 loss
2010	85,000 loss
2011	12,000 loss
2012	25,000 gain

(In working the solution, you must aggregate the unrecognized gains and losses to arrive at year-end balances.)

Instructions
You are the manager in charge of accounting. Write a memo to Vickie Plato, explaining why in some years she must amortize some of the net gains and losses and in other years she does not need to. In order to explain this situation fully, you must compute the amount of net gain or loss that is amortized and charged to pension expense in each of the 4 years listed above. Include an appropriate amortization schedule, referring to it whenever necessary.

CA20-7 (Nonvested Employees—An Ethical Dilemma) Thinken Technology recently merged with College Electronix (CE), a computer graphics manufacturing firm. In performing a comprehensive audit of CE's accounting system, Gerald Ott, internal audit manager for Thinken Technology, discovered that the new subsidiary did not record pension assets and liabilities, subject to GAAP.

The net present value of CE's pension assets was $15.5 million, the vested benefit obligation was $12.9 million, and the projected benefit obligation was $17.4 million. Ott reported this audit finding to Julie Habbe, the newly appointed controller of CE. A few days later Habbe called Ott for his advice on what to do. Habbe started her conversation by asking, "Can't we eliminate the negative income effect of our pension dilemma simply by terminating the employment of nonvested employees before the end of our fiscal year?"

...uctions
...hould Ott respond to Habbe's remark about firing nonvested employees?

USING YOUR JUDGMENT

FINANCIAL REPORTING

Financial Reporting Problem

The Procter & Gamble Company (P&G)

The financial statements of **P&G** are presented in Appendix 5B or can be accessed at the book's companion website, **www.wiley.com/college/kieso**.

Instructions

Refer to P&G's financial statements and the accompanying notes to answer the following questions.

(a) What kind of pension plan does P&G provide its employees in the United States?

(b) What was P&G's pension expense for 2007, 2006, and 2005 for the United States?

(c) What is the impact of P&G's pension plans for 2007 on its financial statements?

(d) What information does P&G provide on the target allocation of its pension assets? (Compare the asset allocation for "Pensions and Other Retiree Benefits.") How do the allocations relate to the expected returns on these assets?

Comparative Analysis Case

The Coca-Cola Company versus PepsiCo, Inc.

PEPSICO

Instructions

Go to the book's companion website and use information found there to answer the following questions related to **The Coca-Cola Company** and **PepsiCo, Inc.**

(a) What kind of pension plans do Coca-Cola and PepsiCo provide their employees?

(b) What net periodic pension expense (cost) did Coca-Cola and PepsiCo report in 2007?

(c) What is the year-end 2007 funded status of Coca-Cola's and PepsiCo's U.S. plans?

(d) What relevant rates were used by Coca-Cola and PepsiCo in computing their pension amounts?

(e) Compare the expected benefit payments and contributions for Coca-Cola and PepsiCo.

*Financial Statement Analysis Case

General Electric

A *Wall Street Journal* article discussed a $1.8 billion charge to income made by **General Electric** for postretirement benefit costs. It was attributed to previously unrecognized healthcare and life insurance cost. As financial vice president and controller for Peake, Inc., you found this article interesting because the president recently expressed interest in adopting a postemployment benefit program for Peake's employees, to complement the company's existing defined-benefit plan. The president, Martha Beyerlein, wants to know how the expense on the new plan will be determined and what impact the accounting for the plan will have on Peake's financial statements.

Instructions

(a) As financial vice president and controller of Peake, Inc., explain the calculation of postemployment benefit expense under GAAP, and indicate how the accounting for the plan will affect Peake's financial statements.

(b) Discuss the similarities and differences in the accounting for the other postemployment benefit plan relative to the accounting for the defined-benefit plan.

International Reporting Case

Kyowa Hakko Kogyo Co., Ltd., is an R&D–based company with special strengths in biotechnology. The company is dedicated to the creation of new value in the life sciences, especially in its two core business segments of pharmaceuticals and biochemicals, and strives to contribute to the health and well-being of people around the world. The company provided the following disclosures related to its retirement benefits in its 2007 annual report.

Kyowa Hakko Kogyo Co., Ltd.

Note 1. Basis of Presenting Consolidated Financial Statements (partial)

Kyowa Hakko Kogyo Co., Ltd. (the "Company") and its consolidated subsidiaries maintain their accounts and records in accordance with the provisions set forth in the Securities and Exchange Law and in conformity with generally accepted accounting principles and practices prevailing in Japan. . . . The Company's fiscal year is from April 1 to March 31. Therefore, "fiscal 2007" begins on April 1, 2006 and ends on March 31, 2007.

Reserve for Retirement Benefits to Employees

A reserve for retirement benefits to employees is provided at an amount equal to the present value of the projected benefit obligation less fair value of the plan assets at the year-end. Unrecognized prior service costs are amortized on a straight-line basis over five years from the year they occur. Unrecognized actuarial differences are amortized on a straight-line basis over ten years from the year after they occur.

Note 9. Reserve for Retirement Benefits to Employees

The Company and its domestic consolidated subsidiaries operate various defined benefit plans, including a corporate pension plan (the so-called cash-balanced plan), a group contributory plan, a tax-qualified pension plan and a severance payment plan.

(a) The reserve for retirement benefits as of March 31, 2007, is analyzed as follows.

	Millions of Yen 2007	Thousands of U.S. Dollars 2007
Projected benefit obligations	¥(62,221)	$(526,895)
Plan assets	42,888	363,181
Unfunded benefit obligations	(19,333)	(163,714)
Unrecognized actuarial differences	1,660	14,057
Unrecognized prior service costs (Note 2)	(2,350)	(19,900)
Prepaid pension cost	(1,359)	(11,678)
	¥(21,402)	$(181,235)

(b) The net periodic pension expense related to the retirement benefits for fiscal 2007 is as follows.

	Millions of Yen 2007	Thousands of U.S. Dollars 2007
Service cost	¥(2,445)	$(20,705)
Interest cost	1,518	12,855
Expected return on plan assets	(1,136)	(9,620)
Amortization of unrecognized actuarial differences	1,158	9,806
Amortization of unrecognized prior service costs	(1,222)	(10,348)
Special severance payment	202	1,771
	¥ 2,965	$ 25,109

(c) Assumptions used in calculation of the above information are as follows.

	2007
Discount rate	2.5%
Expected rate of return	3.0%

Instructions

Use the information on Kyowa to respond to the following requirements.

(a) What are the key differences in accounting for pensions under U.S. and Japanese standards?

(b) Briefly explain how differences in U.S. and Japanese standards for pensions would affect the amounts reported in the financial statements.

(c) In light of the differences identified above, would Kyowa's income and equity be higher or lower under U.S. GAAP compared to Japanese standards? Explain.

BRIDGE TO THE PROFESSION

Professional Research: FASB Codification

Monat Company has grown rapidly since its founding in 2002. To instill loyalty in its employees, Monat is contemplating establishment of a defined-benefit plan. Monat knows that lenders and potential investors will pay close attention to the impact of the pension plan on the company's financial statements, particularly any gains or losses that develop in the plan. Monat has asked you to conduct some research on the accounting for gains and losses in a defined-benefit plan.

Instructions

Access the FASB Codification at *http://asc.fasb.org/home* to conduct research using the Codification Research System to prepare responses to the following items. Provide Codification references for your responses.

(a) Briefly describe how pension gains and losses are accounted for.

(b) Explain the rationale behind the accounting method described in part (a).

(c) What is the related pension asset or liability that will show up on the balance sheet? When will each of these situations occur?

Professional Simulation

Go to the book's companion website, at **www.wiley.com/college/kieso,** to find an interactive problem that simulates the computerized CPA exam. The professional simulation for this chapter asks you to address questions related to the accounting for pensions.

KWW_Professional _Simulation		
Accounting for Pensions	Time Remaining 2 hours 20 minutes	copy paste calculator sheet standards help splitter done

Remember to check the book's companion website to find additional resources for this chapter.

CHAPTER **21**

ACCOUNTING FOR LEASES

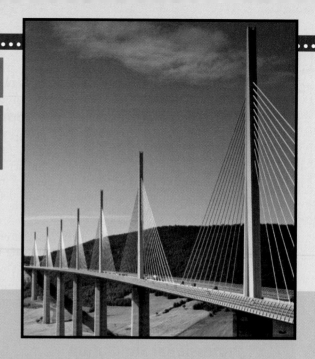

LEARNING OBJECTIVES

After studying this chapter, you should be able to:

- **•1** Explain the nature, economic substance, and advantages of lease transactions.
- **•2** Describe the accounting criteria and procedures for capitalizing leases by the lessee.
- **•3** Contrast the operating and capitalization methods of recording leases.
- **•4** Identify the classifications of leases for the lessor.
- **•5** Describe the lessor's accounting for direct-financing leases.
- **•6** Identify special features of lease arrangements that cause unique accounting problems.
- **•7** Describe the effect of residual values, guaranteed and unguaranteed, on lease accounting.
- **•8** Describe the lessor's accounting for sales-type leases.
- **•9** List the disclosure requirements for leases.

MORE COMPANIES ASK, "WHY BUY?"

Leasing has grown tremendously in popularity. Today it is the fastest growing form of capital investment. Instead of borrowing money to buy an airplane, computer, nuclear core, or satellite, a company makes periodic payments to lease these assets. Even gambling casinos lease their slot machines. Of the 600 companies surveyed by the AICPA in 2007, 591 disclosed lease data.*

A classic example is the airline industry. Many travelers on airlines such as **United**, **Delta**, and **Southwest** believe these airlines own the planes on which they are flying. Often, this is not the case. Airlines lease many of their airplanes due to the favorable accounting treatment they receive if they lease rather than purchase. Presented on the next page are the lease percentages for the major U.S. airlines.

What about other companies? They are also exploiting the existing lease-accounting rules to keep assets and liabilities off the books. For example, **Krispy Kreme**, a chain of 217 doughnut shops, had been showing good growth and profitability, using a relatively small bit

---

*AICPA, *Accounting Trends and Techniques—2007*. Eight out of 10 U.S. companies lease all or some of their equipment. Companies that lease tend to be smaller, are high growth, and are in technology-oriented industries (see *www.techlease.com*).

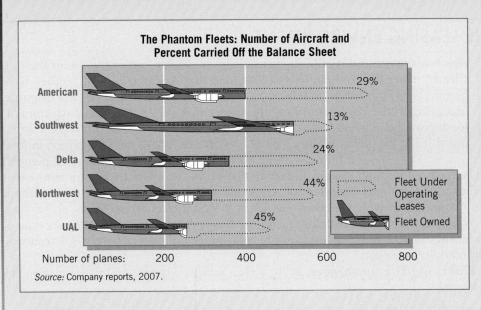

The Phantom Fleets: Number of Aircraft and Percent Carried Off the Balance Sheet

American 29%
Southwest 13%
Delta 24%
Northwest 44%
UAL 45%

Fleet Under Operating Leases
Fleet Owned

Number of planes: 200 400 600 800

Source: Company reports, 2007.

of capital. That's an impressive feat if you care about return on capital. But there's a hole in this doughnut. The company explained that it was building a $30 million new mixing plant and warehouse in Effingham, Illinois. Yet the financial statements failed to disclose the investments and obligations associated with that $30 million.

By financing through a synthetic lease, Krispy Kreme kept the investment and obligation off the books. In a synthetic lease, a financial institution like **Bank of America** sets up a *special purpose entity* (SPE) that borrows money to build the plant and then leases it to Krispy Kreme. For accounting purposes, Krispy Kreme reports only rent expense, but for tax purposes Krispy Kreme can be considered the owner of the asset and gets depreciation tax deductions.

In response to negative publicity about the use of SPEs to get favorable financial reporting and tax benefits, Krispy Kreme announced it would change its method of financing construction of its dough-making plant.

Source: Adapted from Seth Lubore and Elizabeth MacDonald, "Debt? Who, Me?" *Forbes* (February 18, 2002), p. 56.

PREVIEW OF CHAPTER 21

Our opening story indicates the increased significance and prevalence of lease arrangements. As a result, the need for uniform accounting and informative reporting of these transactions has intensified. In this chapter we look at the accounting issues related to leasing. The content and organization of this chapter are as follows.

ACCOUNTING FOR LEASES

LEASING ENVIRONMENT
- Who are players?
- Advantages of leasing
- Conceptual nature of a lease

ACCOUNTING BY LESSEE
- Capitalization criteria
- Accounting differences
- Capital lease method
- Operating method
- Comparison

ACCOUNTING BY LESSOR
- Economics of leasing
- Classification
- Direct-financing method
- Operating method

SPECIAL ACCOUNTING PROBLEMS
- Residual values
- Sales-type leases
- Bargain-purchase option
- Initial direct costs
- Current versus noncurrent
- Disclosure
- Unresolved problems

THE LEASING ENVIRONMENT

Objective·1

Explain the nature, economic substance, and advantages of lease transactions.

Aristotle once said, "Wealth does not lie in ownership but in the use of things"! Clearly, many U.S. companies have decided that Aristotle is right, as they have become heavily involved in leasing assets rather than owning them. For example, according to the Equipment Leasing Association (ELA), the global equipment-leasing market is a $600–$700 billion business, with the U.S. accounting for about one-third of the global market. The ELA estimates that of the $850 billion in total fixed investment expected from domestic businesses in 2006, $229 billion (27 percent) will be financed through leasing. Remember that these statistics are just for equipment leasing; add in real estate leasing, which is probably larger, and we are talking about a very large and growing business, one that is at least in part driven by the accounting.

What types of assets are being leased? As the opening story indicated, any type of equipment can be leased, such as railcars, helicopters, bulldozers, barges, CT scanners, computers, and so on.

Illustration 21-1 summarizes, in their own words, what several major companies are leasing.

ILLUSTRATION 21-1
What Do Companies Lease?

Company	Ticker	Description
Gap	GPS	"We lease most of our store premises and some of our headquarters facilities and distribution centers."
Exxon Mobil Corp.	XOM	"Minimum commitments for operating leases, shown on an undiscounted basis, cover drilling equipment, tankers, service stations, and other properties."
JPMorgan Chase	JPM	"JPMorgan Chase and its subsidiaries were obligated under a number of noncancelable operating leases for premises and equipment used primarily for banking purposes."
Maytag Corp.	MYG	"The Company leases real estate, machinery, equipment, and automobiles under operating leases, some of which have renewal options."
McDonald's Corp.	MCD	"The Company was the lessee at 15,235 restaurant locations through ground leases (the Company leases the land and the Company or franchisee owns the building) and through improved leases (the Company leases land and buildings)."
Starbucks Corp.	SBUX	"Starbucks leases retail stores, roasting and distribution facilities, and office space under operating leases."
TXU Corp.	TXU	"TXU Energy Holdings and TXU Electric Delivery have entered into operating leases covering various facilities and properties including generation plant facilities, combustion turbines, transportation equipment, mining equipment, data processing equipment, and office space."
Viacom Inc.	VIA.B	"The Company has long-term non-cancelable operating lease commitments for office space and equipment, transponders, studio facilities, and vehicles. The Company also enters into capital leases for satellite transponders."

Source: Company 10-K filings; D. Zion, B. Carcache, and A. Varshney, "Bring It On: Off–Balance Sheet Operating Leases," *Credit Suisse Equity Research: Accounting and Tax* (April 19, 2006).

The largest group of leased equipment involves information technology equipment, followed by assets in the transportation area (trucks, aircraft, rail), and then construction and agriculture.

Who Are the Players?

A **lease** is a contractual agreement between a lessor and a lessee. This arrangement gives the **lessee** the right to use specific property, owned by the **lessor**, for a specified period of time. In return for the use of the property, the lessee makes rental payments over the lease term to the lessor.

Who are the lessors that own this property? They generally fall into one of three categories:

1. Banks.
2. Captive leasing companies.
3. Independents.

Banks

Banks are the largest players in the leasing business. They have low-cost funds, which give them the advantage of being able to purchase assets at less cost than their competitors. Banks also have been more aggressive in the leasing markets. They have decided that there is money to be made in leasing, and as a result they have expanded their product lines in this area. Finally, leasing transactions are now more standardized, which gives banks an advantage because they do not have to be as innovative in structuring lease arrangements. Thus banks like Wells Fargo, Chase, Citigroup, and PNC have substantial leasing subsidiaries.

Captive Leasing Companies

Captive leasing companies are subsidiaries whose primary business is to perform leasing operations for the parent company. Companies like Caterpillar Financial Services Corp. (for Caterpillar), Chrysler Financial (for Daimler-Chrysler), and IBM Global Financing (for IBM) facilitate the sale of products to consumers. For example, suppose that Sterling Construction Co. wants to acquire a number of earthmovers from Caterpillar. In this case, Caterpillar Financial Services Corp. will offer to structure the transaction as a lease rather than as a purchase. Thus, Caterpillar Financial provides the financing rather than an outside financial institution.

Captive leasing companies have the point-of-sale advantage in finding leasing customers. That is, as soon as Caterpillar receives a possible order, its leasing subsidiary can quickly develop a lease-financing arrangement. Furthermore, the captive lessor has product knowledge that gives it an advantage when financing the parent's product.

The current trend is for captives to focus primarily on their companies' products rather than do general lease financing. For example, Boeing Capital and UPS Capital are two captives that have left the general finance business to focus exclusively on their parent companies' products.

Independents

Independents are the final category of lessors. Independents have not done well over the last few years. Their market share has dropped fairly dramatically as banks and captive leasing companies have become more aggressive in the lease-financing area. Independents do not have point-of-sale access, nor do they have a low cost of funds advantage. What they *are* often good at is developing innovative contracts for lessees. In addition, they are starting to act as captive finance companies for some companies that do not have a leasing subsidiary.

According to recent data at *www.ficinc.com* on new business volume by lessor type, banks hold about 44 percent of the market, followed by independents at 30 percent. Captives had the remaining 26 percent of new business. Data on changes in market share show that both banks and captives have increased business at the expense of the independents. That is, banks' and captives' market shares had grown by 58 percent and 36 percent respectively, while the independents' market share declined by 44 percent.

Advantages of Leasing

The growth in leasing indicates that it often has some genuine advantages over owning property, such as:

1. *100% Financing at Fixed Rates.* Leases are often signed without requiring any money down from the lessee. This helps the lessee conserve scarce cash—an especially desirable feature for new and developing companies. In addition, lease payments often remain fixed, which protects the lessee against inflation and increases in the cost of money. The following comment explains why companies choose a lease instead of a conventional loan: "Our local bank finally came up to 80 percent of the purchase price but wouldn't go any higher, and they wanted a floating interest rate. We just couldn't afford the down payment, and we needed to lock in a final payment rate we knew we could live with."

2. *Protection Against Obsolescence.* Leasing equipment reduces risk of obsolescence to the lessee, and in many cases passes the risk of residual value to the lessor. For example, **Merck** (a pharmaceutical maker) leases computers. Under the lease agreement, Merck may turn in an old computer for a new model at any time, canceling the old lease and writing a new one. The lessor adds the cost of the new lease to the balance due on the old lease, less the old computer's trade-in value. As one treasurer remarked, "Our instinct is to purchase." But if a new computer is likely to come along in a short time, "then leasing is just a heck of a lot more convenient than purchasing." Naturally, the lessor also protects itself by requiring the lessee to pay higher rental payments or provide additional payments if the lessee does not maintain the asset.

3. *Flexibility.* Lease agreements may contain less restrictive provisions than other debt agreements. Innovative lessors can tailor a lease agreement to the lessee's special needs. For instance, the duration of the lease—the **lease term**—may be anything from a short period of time to the entire expected economic life of the asset. The rental payments may be level from year to year, or they may increase or decrease in amount. The payment amount may be predetermined or may vary with sales, the prime interest rate, the Consumer Price Index, or some other factor. In most cases the rent is set to enable the lessor to recover the cost of the asset plus a fair return over the life of the lease.

4. *Less Costly Financing.* Some companies find leasing cheaper than other forms of financing. For example, start-up companies in depressed industries or companies in low tax brackets may lease to claim tax benefits that they might otherwise lose. Depreciation deductions offer no benefit to companies that have little if any taxable income. Through leasing, the leasing companies or financial institutions use these tax benefits. They can then pass some of these tax benefits back to the user of the asset in the form of lower rental payments.

5. *Tax Advantages.* In some cases, companies can "have their cake and eat it too" with tax advantages that leases offer. That is, for financial reporting purposes companies do not report an asset or a liability for the lease arrangement. For tax purposes, however, companies can capitalize and depreciate the leased asset. As a result, a company takes deductions earlier rather than later and also reduces its taxes. A common vehicle for this type of transaction is a "synthetic lease" arrangement, such as that described in the opening story for **Krispy Kreme**.

6. *Off–Balance-Sheet Financing.* Certain leases do not add debt on a balance sheet or affect financial ratios. In fact, they may add to borrowing capacity.[1] Such **off–balance-sheet financing** is critical to some companies.

---

[1]As demonstrated later in this chapter, certain types of lease arrangements are not capitalized on the balance sheet. The liabilities section is thereby relieved of large future lease commitments that, if recorded, would adversely affect the debt to equity ratio. The reluctance to record lease obligations as liabilities is one of the primary reasons some companies resist capitalized lease accounting.

OFF–BALANCE-SHEET FINANCING

As shown in our opening story, airlines use lease arrangements extensively. This results in a great deal of off–balance-sheet financing. The following chart indicates that many airlines that lease aircraft understate debt levels by a substantial amount.

What do the numbers mean?

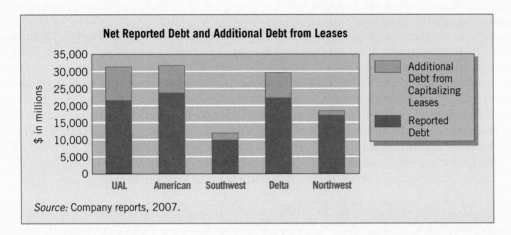

Net Reported Debt and Additional Debt from Leases

Source: Company reports, 2007.

Airlines are not the only ones playing the off–balance-sheet game. A recent SEC study estimates that for SEC registrants, off–balance-sheet lease obligations total more the $1.3 trillion, or 31 times the amount of on–balance-sheet obligations. (See SEC Off–Balance Sheet report at *www.sec.gov/news/studies/soxoffbalancerpt.pdf*.) Thus, analysts must adjust reported debt levels for the effects of non-capitalized leases. A methodology for making this adjustment is discussed in Eugene A. Imhoff, Jr., Robert C. Lipe, and David W. Wright, "Operating Leases: Impact of Constructive Capitalization," *Accounting Horizons* (March 1991).

Conceptual Nature of a Lease

If **Delta** borrows $47 million on a 10-year note from **Bank of America** to purchase a Boeing 737 jet plane, Delta should clearly report an asset and related liability at that amount on its balance sheet. Similarly, if Delta purchases the 737 for $47 million directly from Boeing through an installment purchase over 10 years, it should obviously report an asset and related liability (i.e., it should "capitalize" the installment transaction).

However, what if Delta **leases** the Boeing 737 for 10 years from **International Lease Finance Corp. (ILFC)**—the world's largest lessor of airplanes—through a noncancelable lease transaction with payments of the same amount as the installment purchase transaction? In that case, opinion differs over how to report this transaction. The various views on **capitalization of leases** are as follows.

1. *Do Not Capitalize Any Leased Assets.* This view considers capitalization inappropriate, because Delta does not own the property. Furthermore, a lease is an **"executory" contract** requiring continuing performance by both parties. Because companies do not currently capitalize other executory contracts (such as purchase commitments and employment contracts), they should not capitalize leases either.

2. *Capitalize Leases That Are Similar to Installment Purchases.* This view holds that companies should report transactions in accordance with their economic substance. Therefore, if companies capitalize installment purchases, they should also capitalize leases that have similar characteristics. For example, Delta Airlines makes the same payments over a 10-year period for either a lease or an installment purchase. Lessees make rental payments, whereas owners make mortgage

Underlying Concepts

The issue of how to report leases is the classic case of substance versus form. Although legal title does not technically pass in lease transactions, the benefits from the use of the property do transfer.

payments. Why should the financial statements not report these transactions in the same manner?

3. *Capitalize All Long-Term Leases.* This approach requires only the long-term right to use the property in order to capitalize. This property-rights approach capitalizes all long-term leases.[2]

4. *Capitalize Firm Leases Where the Penalty for Nonperformance Is Substantial.* A final approach advocates capitalizing only "firm" (noncancelable) contractual rights and obligations. "Firm" means that it is unlikely to avoid performance under the lease without a severe penalty.[3]

In short, the various viewpoints range from no capitalization to capitalization of all leases. The FASB apparently agrees with the capitalization approach when the lease is similar to an installment purchase: It notes that Delta **should capitalize a lease that transfers substantially all of the benefits and risks of property ownership, provided the lease is noncancelable.** **Noncancelable** means that Delta can cancel the lease contract only upon the outcome of some remote contingency, or that the cancellation provisions and penalties of the contract are so costly to Delta that cancellation probably will not occur.

This viewpoint leads to three basic conclusions: (1) Companies must identify the characteristics that indicate the transfer of substantially all of the benefits and risks of ownership. (2) The same characteristics should apply consistently to the lessee and the lessor. (3) Those leases that do **not** transfer substantially all the benefits and risks of ownership are operating leases. Companies should not capitalize operating leases. Instead, companies should account for them as rental payments and receipts.

ACCOUNTING BY THE LESSEE

Objective·2

Describe the accounting criteria and procedures for capitalizing leases by the lessee.

If Delta Airlines (the lessee) **capitalizes** a lease, it records an asset and a liability generally equal to the present value of the rental payments. ILFC (the lessor), having transferred substantially all the benefits and risks of ownership, recognizes a sale by removing the asset from the balance sheet and replacing it with a receivable. The typical journal entries for Delta and ILFC, assuming leased and capitalized equipment, appear as shown in Illustration 21-2.

ILLUSTRATION 21-2
Journal Entries for
Capitalized Lease

Delta (Lessee)			ILFC (Lessor)		
Leased Equipment	XXX		Lease Receivable	XXX	
Lease Liability		XXX	Equipment		XXX

Having capitalized the asset, Delta records depreciation on the leased asset. Both ILFC and Delta treat the lease rental payments as consisting of interest and principal.

If Delta does not capitalize the lease, it does not record an asset, nor does ILFC remove one from its books. When Delta makes a lease payment, it records rental expense; ILFC recognizes rental revenue.

---

[2]The property rights approach was originally recommended in a research study by the AICPA: John H. Myers, "Reporting of Leases in Financial Statements," *Accounting Research Study No. 4* (New York: AICPA, 1964), pp. 10–11. Recently, this view has received additional support. See Peter H. Knutson, "Financial Reporting in the 1990s and Beyond," Position Paper (Charlottesville, Va.: AIMR, 1993), and Warren McGregor, "Accounting for Leases: A New Approach," Special Report (Norwalk, Conn.: FASB, 1996).

[3]Yuji Ijiri, *Recognition of Contractual Rights and Obligations,* Research Report (Stamford, Conn.: FASB, 1980).

In order to record a lease as a **capital lease**, the lease must be noncancelable. Further, it must meet one or more of the four criteria listed in Illustration 21-3.

Capitalization Criteria (Lessee)

- The lease transfers ownership of the property to the lessee.
- The lease contains a bargain-purchase option.[4]
- The lease term is equal to 75 percent or more of the estimated economic life of the leased property.
- The present value of the minimum lease payments (excluding executory costs) equals or exceeds 90 percent of the fair value of the leased property. [1]

ILLUSTRATION 21-3
Capitalization Criteria for Lessee

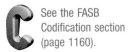

See the FASB Codification section (page 1160).

Delta classifies and accounts for leases that **do not meet any of the four criteria** as **operating leases**. Illustration 21-4 shows that a lease meeting any one of the four criteria results in the lessee having a capital lease.

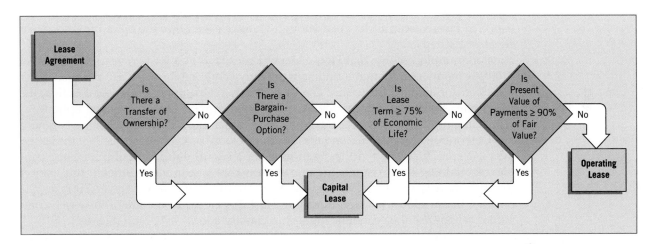

ILLUSTRATION 21-4
Diagram of Lessee's Criteria for Lease Classification

In keeping with the FASB's reasoning that a company consumes a significant portion of the value of the asset in the first 75 percent of its life, the lessee applies neither the third nor the fourth criterion when the inception of the lease occurs during the last 25 percent of the asset's life.

Capitalization Criteria

Three of the four **capitalization criteria** that apply to lessees are controversial and can be difficult to apply in practice. We discuss each of the criteria in detail on the following pages.

Transfer of Ownership Test

If the lease transfers ownership of the asset to the lessee, it is a capital lease. This criterion is not controversial and easily implemented in practice.

Bargain-Purchase Option Test

A **bargain-purchase option** allows the lessee to purchase the leased property for a price that is **significantly lower** than the property's expected fair value at the date the option becomes exercisable. At the inception of the lease, the difference between the option price and the expected fair market value must be large enough to make exercise of the option reasonably assured.

---

[4]We define a bargain-purchase option in the next section.

For example, assume that Brett's Delivery Service was to lease a Honda Accord for $599 per month for 40 months, with an option to purchase for $100 at the end of the 40-month period. If the estimated fair value of the Honda Accord is $3,000 at the end of the 40 months, the $100 option to purchase is clearly a bargain. Therefore, Brett must capitalize the lease. In other cases, the criterion may not be as easy to apply, and determining *now* that a certain *future* price is a bargain can be difficult.

Economic Life Test (75% Test)

If the lease period equals or exceeds 75 percent of the asset's economic life, the lessor transfers most of the risks and rewards of ownership to the lessee. Capitalization is therefore appropriate. However, determining the lease term and the economic life of the asset can be troublesome.

The **lease term** is generally considered to be the fixed, noncancelable term of the lease. However, a bargain-renewal option, if provided in the lease agreement, can extend this period. A **bargain-renewal option** allows the lessee to renew the lease for a rental that is lower than the expected fair rental at the date the option becomes exercisable. At the inception of the lease, the difference between the renewal rental and the expected fair rental must be great enough to make exercise of the option to renew reasonably assured.

For example, assume that **Home Depot** leases **Dell** PCs for two years at a rental of $100 per month per computer and subsequently can lease them for $10 per month per computer for another two years. The lease clearly offers a bargain-renewal option; the lease term is considered to be four years. However, with bargain-renewal options, as with bargain-purchase options, it is sometimes difficult to determine what is a bargain.[5]

Determining estimated economic life can also pose problems, especially if the leased item is a specialized item or has been used for a significant period of time. For example, determining the economic life of a nuclear core is extremely difficult. It is subject to much more than normal "wear and tear." As indicated earlier, the FASB takes the position that if the lease starts during the last 25 percent of the life of the asset, companies cannot use the economic life test to classify a lease as a capital lease.

Recovery of Investment Test (90% Test)

If the present value of the minimum lease payments equals or exceeds 90 percent of the fair market value of the asset, then a lessee like Delta should capitalize the leased asset. Why? If the present value of the minimum lease payments is reasonably close to the market price of the aircraft, Delta is effectively purchasing the asset.

Determining the present value of the minimum lease payments involves three important concepts: (1) minimum lease payments, (2) executory costs, and (3) discount rate.

Minimum Lease Payments. Delta is obligated to make, or expected to make, **minimum lease payments** in connection with the leased property. These payments include the following.

1. *Minimum Rental Payments*—Minimum rental payments are those that Delta must make to ILFC under the lease agreement. In some cases, the minimum rental payments may equal the minimum lease payments. However, the minimum lease payments may also include a guaranteed residual value (if any), penalty for failure to renew, or a bargain-purchase option (if any), as we note on the next page.

[5]The original lease term is also extended for leases having the following: substantial penalties for nonrenewal; periods for which the lessor has the option to renew or extend the lease; renewal periods preceding the date a bargain-purchase option becomes exercisable; and renewal periods in which any lessee guarantees of the lessor's debt are expected to be in effect or in which there will be a loan outstanding from the lessee to the lessor. The lease term, however, can never extend beyond the time a bargain-purchase option becomes exercisable. [2]

2. *Guaranteed Residual Value*—The residual value is the estimated fair (market) value of the leased property at the end of the lease term. ILFC may transfer the risk of loss to Delta or to a third party by obtaining a guarantee of the estimated residual value. The **guaranteed residual value** is either (1) the certain or determinable amount that Delta will pay ILFC at the end of the lease to purchase the aircraft at the end of the lease, or (2) the amount Delta or the third party guarantees that ILFC will realize if the aircraft is returned. (**Third-party guarantors** are, in essence, insurers who for a fee assume the risk of deficiencies in leased asset residual value.) If not guaranteed in full, the **unguaranteed residual value** is the estimated residual value exclusive of any portion guaranteed.[6]

3. *Penalty for Failure to Renew or Extend the Lease*—The amount Delta must pay if the agreement specifies that it must extend or renew the lease, and it fails to do so.

4. *Bargain-Purchase Option*—As we indicated earlier (in item 1), an option given to Delta to purchase the aircraft at the end of the lease term at a price that is fixed sufficiently below the expected fair value, so that, at the inception of the lease, purchase is reasonably assured.

Delta excludes executory costs (defined below) from its computation of the present value of the minimum lease payments.

Executory Costs. Like most assets, leased tangible assets incur insurance, maintenance, and tax expenses—called **executory costs**—during their economic life. If ILFC retains responsibility for the payment of these "ownership-type costs," **it should exclude**, in computing the present value of the minimum lease payments, a portion of each lease payment that represents executory costs. Executory costs do not represent payment on or reduction of the obligation.

Many lease agreements specify that the lessee directly pays executory costs to the appropriate third parties. In these cases, the lessor can use the rental payment **without adjustment** in the present value computation.

Discount Rate. A lessee, like Delta, generally computes the present value of the minimum lease payments using its **incremental borrowing rate**. This rate is defined as: "The rate that, at the inception of the lease, the lessee would have incurred to borrow the funds necessary to buy the leased asset on a secured loan with repayment terms similar to the payment schedule called for in the lease." [4]

To determine whether the present value of these payments is less than 90 percent of the fair market value of the property, Delta discounts the payments using its incremental borrowing rate. Determining the incremental borrowing rate often requires judgment because the lessee bases it on a hypothetical purchase of the property.

However, there is one exception to this rule. If (1) Delta knows the **implicit interest rate computed by ILFC** and (2) it is less than Delta's incremental borrowing rate, then Delta **must use ILFC's implicit rate**. What is the **interest rate implicit in the lease**? It is the discount rate that, when applied to the minimum lease payments and any unguaranteed residual value accruing to the lessor, causes the aggregate present value to equal the fair value of the leased property to the lessor. [5]

The purpose of this exception is twofold. First, **the implicit rate of ILFC is generally a more realistic rate** to use in determining the amount (if any) to report as the asset and related liability for Delta. Second, the guideline ensures that Delta **does not use an artificially high incremental borrowing rate** that would cause the present value of the minimum lease payments to be less than 90 percent of the fair market value of the aircraft. Use of such a rate would thus make it possible to avoid capitalization of the asset and related liability.

---

[6]A lease provision requiring the lessee to make up a residual value deficiency that is attributable to damage, extraordinary wear and tear, or excessive usage is not included in the minimum lease payments. Lessees recognize such costs as period costs when incurred. [3]

Delta may argue that it cannot determine the implicit rate of the lessor and therefore should use the higher rate. However, in most cases, Delta can approximate the implicit rate used by ILFC. The determination of whether or not a reasonable estimate could be made will require judgment, particularly where the result from using the incremental borrowing rate comes close to meeting the 90 percent test. Because Delta **may not capitalize the leased property at more than its fair value** (as we discuss later), it cannot use an excessively low discount rate.

Asset and Liability Accounted for Differently

In a capital lease transaction, Delta uses the lease as a source of financing. ILFC finances the transaction (provides the investment capital) through the leased asset. Delta makes rent payments, which actually are installment payments. Therefore, over the life of the aircraft rented, **the rental payments to ILFC constitute a payment of principal plus interest**.

Asset and Liability Recorded

Under the capital lease method, Delta treats the lease transaction as if it purchases the aircraft in a financing transaction. That is, Delta acquires the aircraft and creates an obligation. Therefore, it records a capital lease as an asset and a liability at the lower of (1) the present value of the minimum lease payments (excluding executory costs) or (2) the fair value of the leased asset at the inception of the lease. The rationale for this approach is that companies should not record a leased asset for more than its fair value.

Depreciation Period

One troublesome aspect of accounting for the depreciation of the capitalized leased asset relates to the period of depreciation. If the lease agreement transfers ownership of the asset to Delta (criterion 1) or contains a bargain-purchase option (criterion 2), Delta depreciates the aircraft consistent with its normal depreciation policy for other aircraft, **using the economic life of the asset**.

On the other hand, if the lease does not transfer ownership or does not contain a bargain purchase option, then Delta depreciates it over the **term of the lease**. In this case, the aircraft reverts to ILFC after a certain period of time.

Effective-Interest Method

Throughout the term of the lease, Delta uses the **effective-interest method** to allocate each lease payment between principal and interest. This method produces a periodic interest expense equal to a constant percentage of the carrying value of the lease obligation. When applying the effective-interest method to capital leases, Delta must use the same discount rate that determines the present value of the minimum lease payments.

Depreciation Concept

Although Delta computes the amounts initially capitalized as an asset and recorded as an obligation at the same present value, the **depreciation of the aircraft and the discharge of the obligation are independent accounting processes** during the term of the lease. It should depreciate the leased asset by applying conventional depreciation methods: straight-line, sum-of-the-years'-digits, declining-balance, units of production, etc. The FASB uses the term "amortization" more frequently than "depreciation" to recognize intangible leased property rights. We prefer "depreciation" to describe the write-off of a tangible asset's expired services.

Capital Lease Method (Lessee)

To illustrate a capital lease, assume that **Caterpillar Financial Services Corp.** (a subsidiary of Caterpillar) and **Sterling Construction Corp.** sign a lease agreement dated

January 1, 2011, that calls for Caterpillar to lease a front-end loader to Sterling beginning January 1, 2011. The terms and provisions of the lease agreement, and other pertinent data, are as follows.

- The term of the lease is five years. The lease agreement is noncancelable, requiring equal rental payments of $25,981.62 at the beginning of each year (annuity due basis).
- The loader has a fair value at the inception of the lease of $100,000, an estimated economic life of five years, and no residual value.
- Sterling pays all of the executory costs directly to third parties except for the property taxes of $2,000 per year, which is included as part of its annual payments to Caterpillar.
- The lease contains no renewal options. The loader reverts to Caterpillar at the termination of the lease.
- Sterling's incremental borrowing rate is 11 percent per year.
- Sterling depreciates, on a straight-line basis, similar equipment that it owns.
- Caterpillar sets the annual rental to earn a rate of return on its investment of 10 percent per year; Sterling knows this fact.

The lease meets the criteria for classification as a capital lease for the following reasons:

1. The lease term of five years, being equal to the equipment's estimated economic life of five years, satisfies the 75 percent test.
2. The present value of the minimum lease payments ($100,000 as computed below) exceeds 90 percent of the fair value of the loader ($100,000).

The minimum lease payments are $119,908.10 ($23,981.62 × 5). Sterling computes the amount capitalized as leased assets as the present value of the minimum lease payments (excluding executory costs—property taxes of $2,000) as shown in Illustration 21-5.

Capitalized amount = ($25,981.62 − $2,000) × Present value of an annuity due of 1 for 5 periods at 10% (Table 6-5)
= $23,981.62 × 4.16986
= $100,000

ILLUSTRATION 21-5
Computation of Capitalized Lease Payments

Sterling uses Caterpillar's implicit interest rate of 10 percent instead of its incremental borrowing rate of 11 percent because (1) it is lower and (2) it knows about it.[7] Sterling records the capital lease on its books on January 1, 2011, as:

Leased Equipment under Capital Leases	100,000	
Lease Liability		100,000

Note that the entry records the obligation at the net amount of $100,000 (the present value of the future rental payments) rather than at the gross amount of $119,908.10 ($23,981.62 × 5).

Sterling records the **first lease payment on January 1, 2011**, as follows:

Property Tax Expense	2,000.00	
Lease Liability	23,981.62	
Cash		25,981.62

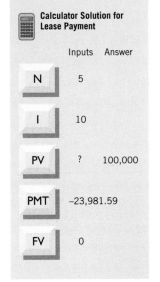

Calculator Solution for Lease Payment

	Inputs	Answer
N	5	
I	10	
PV	?	100,000
PMT	−23,981.59	
FV	0	

[7]If Sterling has an incremental borrowing rate of, say, 9 percent (lower than the 10 percent rate used by Caterpillar) and it did not know the rate used by Caterpillar, the present value computation would yield a capitalized amount of $101,675.35 ($23,981.62 × 4.23972). And, because this amount exceeds the $100,000 fair value of the equipment, Sterling would have to capitalize the $100,000 and use 10 percent as its effective rate for amortization of the lease obligation.

Each lease payment of $25,981.62 consists of three elements: (1) a reduction in the lease liability, (2) a financing cost (interest expense), and (3) executory costs (property taxes). The total financing cost (interest expense) over the term of the lease is $19,908.10. This amount is the difference between the present value of the lease payments ($100,000) and the actual cash disbursed, net of executory costs ($119,908.10). Therefore, the annual interest expense, applying the effective-interest method, is a function of the outstanding liability, as Illustration 21-6 shows.

ILLUSTRATION 21-6
Lease Amortization
Schedule for Lessee—
Annuity-Due Basis

STERLING CONSTRUCTION
LEASE AMORTIZATION SCHEDULE
ANNUITY-DUE BASIS

Date	Annual Lease Payment	Executory Costs	Interest (10%) on Liability	Reduction of Lease Liability	Lease Liability
	(a)	(b)	(c)	(d)	(e)
1/1/11					$100,000.00
1/1/11	$ 25,981.62	$ 2,000	$ –0–	$ 23,981.62	76,018.38
1/1/12	25,981.62	2,000	7,601.84	16,379.78	59,638.60
1/1/13	25,981.62	2,000	5,963.86	18,017.76	41,620.84
1/1/14	25,981.62	2,000	4,162.08	19,819.54	21,801.30
1/1/15	25,981.62	2,000	2,180.32*	21,801.30	–0–
	$129,908.10	$10,000	$19,908.10	$100,000.00	

(a) Lease payment as required by lease.
(b) Executory costs included in rental payment.
(c) Ten percent of the preceding balance of (e) except for 1/1/11; since this is an annuity due, no time has elapsed at the date of the first payment and no interest has accrued.
(d) (a) minus (b) and (c).
(e) Preceding balance minus (d).

*Rounded by 19 cents.

At the end of its fiscal year, December 31, 2011, Sterling records **accrued interest** as follows.

Interest Expense	7,601.84	
Interest Payable		7,601.84

Depreciation of the leased equipment over its five-year lease term, applying Sterling's normal depreciation policy (straight-line method), results in the following entry on December 31, 2011.

Depreciation Expense—Capital Leases	20,000	
Accumulated Depreciation—Capital Leases		20,000
($100,000 ÷ 5 years)		

At December 31, 2011, Sterling separately identifies the assets recorded under capital leases on its balance sheet. Similarly, it separately identifies the related obligations. Sterling classifies the portion due within one year or the operating cycle, whichever is longer, with current liabilities, and the rest with noncurrent liabilities. For example, the current portion of the December 31, 2011, total obligation of $76,018.38 in Sterling's amortization schedule is the amount of the reduction in the obligation in 2012, or $16,379.78. Illustration 21-7 shows the liabilities section as it relates to lease transactions at December 31, 2011.

ILLUSTRATION 21-7
Reporting Current and
Noncurrent Lease
Liabilities

Current liabilities	
Interest payable	$ 7,601.84
Lease liability	16,379.78
Noncurrent liabilities	
Lease liability	$59,638.60

Sterling records the lease payment of January 1, 2012, as follows.

Property Tax Expense	2,000.00	
Interest Payable	7,601.84	
Lease Liability	16,379.78	
Cash		25,981.62

Entries through 2015 would follow the pattern above. Sterling records its other executory costs (insurance and maintenance) in a manner similar to how it records any other operating costs incurred on assets it owns.

Upon expiration of the lease, Sterling has fully amortized the amount capitalized as leased equipment. It also has fully discharged its lease obligation. If Sterling does not purchase the loader, it returns the equipment to Caterpillar. Sterling then removes the leased equipment and related accumulated depreciation accounts from its books.[8]

If Sterling purchases the equipment at termination of the lease, at a price of $5,000 and the estimated life of the equipment changes from five to seven years, it makes the following entry.

Equipment ($100,000 + $5,000)	105,000	
Accumulated Depreciation—Capital Leases	100,000	
Leased Equipment under Capital Leases		100,000
Accumulated Depreciation—Equipment		100,000
Cash		5,000

Operating Method (Lessee)

Under the **operating method,** rent expense (and the associated liability) accrues day by day to the lessee as it uses the property. **The lessee assigns rent to the periods benefiting from the use of the asset and ignores, in the accounting, any commitments to make future payments.** The lessee makes appropriate accruals or deferrals if the accounting period ends between cash payment dates.

For example, assume that the capital lease illustrated in the previous section did not qualify as a capital lease. Sterling therefore accounts for it as an operating lease. The first-year charge to operations is now $25,981.62, the amount of the rental payment. Sterling records this payment on January 1, 2011, as follows.

Rent Expense	25,981.62	
Cash		25,981.62

Sterling does not report the loader, as well as any long-term liability for future rental payments, on the balance sheet. Sterling reports rent expense on the income statement. And, as discussed later in the chapter, **Sterling must disclose all operating leases that have noncancelable lease terms in excess of one year.**

RESTATEMENTS ON THE MENU

Accounting for operating leases would appear routine, so it is unusual for a bevy of companies in a single industry—restaurants—to get caught up in the accounting rules for operating leases. Getting the accounting right is particularly important for restaurant chains, because they make extensive use of leases for their restaurants and equipment.

What do the numbers mean?

The problem stems from the way most property (and equipment) leases cover a specific number of years (the so-called *primary lease term*) as well as renewal periods (sometimes referred to as the *option term*). In some cases, companies were calculating their lease expense for the primary term but depreciating lease-related assets over both the primary and option terms. This practice resulted in understating the total cost of the lease and thus boosted earnings.

[8]If Sterling purchases the front-end loader **during the term of a "capital lease,"** it accounts for it like a renewal or extension of a capital lease. "Any difference between the purchase price and the carrying amount of the lease obligation shall be recorded as an adjustment of the carrying amount of the asset." [6]

**What do the
numbers mean?**

(continued)

For example, the CFO at CKE Restaurants Inc., owner of the Hardee's and Carl's Jr. chains, noted that CKE ran into trouble because it was not consistent in calculating the lease and depreciation expense. Correcting the error at CKE reduced earnings by nine cents a share in fiscal 2002, nine cents a share in fiscal 2003, and 10 cents a share in fiscal 2004. The company now uses the shorter, primary lease terms for calculating both lease expense and depreciation. The change increases depreciation annually, which in turn decreases total assets.

CKE was not alone in improper operating lease accounting. Notable restaurateurs who ran afoul of the lease rules included Brinker International Inc., operator of Chili's; Darden Restaurants Inc., which operates Red Lobster and Olive Garden; and Jack in the Box. To correct their operating lease accounting, these restaurants reported restatements that resulted in lower earnings and assets.

Source: Steven D. Jones and Richard Gibson, *Wall Street Journal* (January 26, 2005), p. C3.

Comparison of Capital Lease with Operating Lease

Objective·3
Contrast the operating and capitalization methods of recording leases.

As we indicated, if accounting for the lease as an operating lease, the first-year charge to operations is $25,981.62, the amount of the rental payment. Treating the transaction as a capital lease, however, results in a first-year charge of $29,601.84: depreciation of $20,000 (assuming straight-line), interest expense of $7,601.84 (per Illustration 21-6), and executory costs of $2,000. Illustration 21-8 shows that **while the total charges to operations are the same over the lease term whether accounting for the lease as a capital lease or as an operating lease, under the capital lease treatment the charges are higher in the earlier years and lower in the later years.**[9]

ILLUSTRATION 21-8
Comparison of Charges to Operations—Capital vs. Operating Leases

STERLING CONSTRUCTION
SCHEDULE OF CHARGES TO OPERATIONS
CAPITAL LEASE VERSUS OPERATING LEASE

| | Capital Lease | | | | Operating Lease | |
Year	Depreciation	Executory Costs	Interest	Total Charge	Lease Charge	Difference
2011	$ 20,000	$ 2,000	$ 7,601.84	$ 29,601.84	$ 25,981.62	$3,620.22
2012	20,000	2,000	5,963.86	27,963.86	25,981.62	1,982.24
2013	20,000	2,000	4,162.08	26,162.08	25,981.62	180.46
2014	20,000	2,000	2,180.32	24,180.32	25,981.62	(1,801.30)
2015	20,000	2,000	—	22,000.00	25,981.62	(3,981.62)
	$100,000	$10,000	$19,908.10	$129,908.10	$129,908.10	$ –0–

If using an accelerated method of depreciation, the differences between the amounts charged to operations under the two methods would be even larger in the earlier and later years.

In addition, using the capital lease approach results in an asset and related liability of $100,000 initially reported on the balance sheet. The lessee would not report any asset or liability under the operating method. Therefore, the following differences occur if using a capital lease instead of an operating lease:

1. An increase in the amount of reported debt (both short-term and long-term).
2. An increase in the amount of total assets (specifically long-lived assets).
3. A lower income early in the life of the lease and, therefore, lower retained earnings.

---

[9]The higher charges in the early years is one reason lessees are reluctant to adopt the capital lease accounting method. Lessees (especially those of real estate) claim that it is really no more costly to operate the leased asset in the early years than in the later years. Thus, they advocate an even charge similar to that provided by the operating method.

Thus, many companies believe that capital leases negatively impact their financial position: Their debt to total equity ratio increases, and their rate of return on total assets decreases. As a result, the business community resists capitalizing leases.

Whether this resistance is well founded is debatable. From a cash flow point of view, the company is in the same position whether accounting for the lease as an operating or a capital lease. Managers often argue against capitalization for several reasons: First is that capitalization can more easily lead to **violation of loan covenants**. It also can affect the **amount of compensation received by owners** (for example, a stock compensation plan tied to earnings). Finally, capitalization can **lower rates of return** and **increase debt to equity relationships**, making the company less attractive to present and potential investors.[10]

ARE YOU LIABLE?

Under current accounting rules, companies can keep the obligations associated with operating leases off the balance sheet. (For example, see the "What Do the Numbers Mean?" box on page 1115 for the effects of this approach for airlines.) This approach may change if the IASB and FASB are able to craft a new lease-accounting rule. The current plans for a new rule in this area should result in many more operating leases on balance sheets. Analysts are beginning to estimate the expected impact of a new rule. As shown in the table below, if the IASB and FASB issue a new rule on operating leases, a company like **Whole Foods** could see its liabilities jump a whopping 374 percent.

What do the numbers mean?

Ring It Up

Rulemakers are debating a change to lease accounting that would have a major impact on the balance sheets of some big-name retailers:

Retailer	Estimated Off–Balance-Sheet Lease Liabilities	Jump in Liabilities If They Were on the Balance Sheet
Whole Foods Market Organic grocer leases all but five of its 175 stores, plus its distribution centers, "bakehouses," and administrative facilities.	$1.96 billion	374%
Walgreen Drugstore has opened 886 stores in the past two years. Of all its stores, 82% are leased, a total of $24 billion in obligations.	15.24	266
Bed Bath & Beyond Home goods retailer leases most of its 809 stores, plus 690,000 square feet of storage space, and 270,000 square feet of offices.	2.24	224
Circuit City Stores Retailer leases 626 U.S. stores, owns 5. Also leases distribution facilities, warehouses, and its headquarters in Richmond, Va.	3.53	208
Starbucks Owns its U.S. roasting and distribution locations, but nearly all of its 6,000 retail coffee bars are leased.	2.45	172
CVS Owns approximately 3% of its 5,471 retail and specialty pharmacy drugstores and leases its mail-order sites.	11.11	160

*as of 5/22/06   Data: Credit Suisse Group, company reports, Bloomberg Financial Markets.

This is not a pretty picture, but investors need to see it if they are to fully understand a company's lease obligations.

Source: Nanette Byrnes, "You May Be Liable for That Lease," *BusinessWeek* (June 5, 2006), p. 76.

---

[10]One study indicates that management's behavior did change as a result of the leasing rules. For example, many companies restructure their leases to avoid capitalization. Others increase their purchases of assets instead of leasing. Still others, faced with capitalization, postpone their debt offerings or issue stock instead. However, note that the study found no significant effect on stock or bond prices as a result of capitalization of leases. A. Rashad Abdel-khalik, "The Economic Effects on Lessees of *FASB Statement No. 13,* Accounting for Leases," Research Report (Stamford, Conn.: FASB, 1981).

ACCOUNTING BY THE LESSOR

Earlier in this chapter we discussed leasing's advantages to the lessee. Three important benefits are available to the lessor:

1. *Interest Revenue.* Leasing is a form of financing. Banks, captives, and independent leasing companies find leasing attractive because it provides competitive interest margins.

2. *Tax Incentives.* In many cases, companies that lease cannot use the tax benefit of the asset, but leasing allows them to transfer such tax benefits to another party (the lessor) in return for a lower rental rate on the leased asset. To illustrate, **Boeing Aircraft** might sell one of its 737 jet planes to a wealthy investor who needed only the tax benefit. The investor then leased the plane to a foreign airline, for whom the tax benefit was of no use. Everyone gained. Boeing sold its airplane, the investor received the tax benefit, and the foreign airline cheaply acquired a 737.[11]

3. *High Residual Value.* Another advantage to the lessor is the return of the property at the end of the lease term. Residual values can produce very large profits. **Citigroup** at one time assumed that the commercial aircraft it was leasing to the airline industry would have a residual value of 5 percent of their purchase price. It turned out that they were worth 150 percent of their cost—a handsome profit. At the same time, if residual values decline, lessors can suffer losses when less-valuable leased assets are returned at the conclusion of the lease. Recently, automaker **Ford** took a $2.1 billion write-down on its lease portfolio, when rising gas prices spurred dramatic declines in the resale values of leased trucks and SUVs. Such residual value losses led **Chrysler** to get out of the leasing business altogether.

Economics of Leasing

A lessor, such as Caterpillar Financial in our earlier example, determines the amount of the rental, basing it on the rate of return—the implicit rate—needed to justify leasing the front-end loader. In establishing the rate of return, Caterpillar considers the credit standing of Sterling Construction, the length of the lease, and the status of the residual value (guaranteed versus unguaranteed).

In the Caterpillar/Sterling example on pages 1124–1127, Caterpillar's implicit rate was 10 percent, the cost of the equipment to Caterpillar was $100,000 (also fair market value), and the estimated residual value was zero. Caterpillar determines the amount of the lease payment as follows.

ILLUSTRATION 21-9
Computation of Lease Payments

Fair market value of leased equipment	$100,000.00
Less: Present value of the residual value	–0–
Amount to be recovered by lessor through lease payments	$100,000.00
Five beginning-of-the-year lease payments to yield a 10% return ($100,000 ÷ 4.16986[a])	$ 23,981.62

[a]PV of an annuity due of 1 for 5 years at 10% (Table 6-5)

If a residual value is involved (whether guaranteed or not), Caterpillar would not have to recover as much from the lease payments. Therefore, the lease payments would be less. (Illustration 21-16, on page 1136, shows this situation.)

---

[11]Some would argue that there is a loser—the U.S. government. The tax benefits enable the profitable investor to reduce or eliminate taxable income.

Classification of Leases by the Lessor

Objective·4
Identify the classifications of leases for the lessor.

For accounting purposes, the **lessor** may classify leases as one of the following:

1. Operating leases.
2. Direct-financing leases.
3. Sales-type leases.

Illustration 21-10 presents two groups of capitalization criteria for the lessor. If at the date of inception, the lessor agrees to a lease that meets **one or more** of the Group I criteria (1, 2, 3, and 4) and **both** of the Group II criteria (1 and 2), the lessor shall classify and account for the arrangement as a direct-financing lease or as a sales-type lease. [7] (Note that the Group I criteria are identical to the criteria that must be met in order for a lessee to classify a lease as a capital lease, as shown in Illustration 21-3 on page 1121.)

ILLUSTRATION 21-10
Capitalization Criteria for Lessor

Capitalization Criteria (Lessor)

Group I
1. The lease transfers ownership of the property to the lessee.
2. The lease contains a bargain-purchase option.
3. The lease term is equal to 75 percent or more of the estimated economic life of the leased property.
4. The present value of the minimum lease payments (excluding executory costs) equals or exceeds 90 percent of the fair value of the leased property.

Group II
1. Collectibility of the payments required from the lessee is reasonably predictable.
2. No important uncertainties surround the amount of unreimbursable costs yet to be incurred by the lessor under the lease (lessor's performance is substantially complete or future costs are reasonably predictable).

Why the Group II requirements? The profession wants to ensure that the lessor has really transferred the risks and benefits of ownership. If collectibility of payments is not predictable or if performance by the lessor is incomplete, then the criteria for revenue recognition have not been met. The lessor should therefore account for the lease as an operating lease.

For example, computer leasing companies at one time used to buy **IBM** equipment, lease the equipment, and remove the leased assets from their balance sheets. In leasing the assets, the computer lessors stated that they would substitute new IBM equipment if obsolescence occurred. However, when IBM introduced a new computer line, IBM refused to sell it to the computer leasing companies. As a result, a number of the lessors could not meet their contracts with their customers and had to take back the old equipment. The computer leasing companies therefore had to reinstate the assets they had taken off the books. Such a case demonstrates one reason for the Group II requirements.

INTERNATIONAL INSIGHT
U.S. GAAP is consistent with *International Standard No. 17* (Accounting for Leases). However, the international standard is a relatively simple statement of basic principles, whereas the U.S. rules on leases are more prescriptive and detailed.

The distinction for the lessor between a direct-financing lease and a sales-type lease is the presence or absence of a manufacturer's or dealer's profit (or loss): A sales-type lease involves a manufacturer's or dealer's profit, and a direct-financing lease does not. The profit (or loss) to the lessor is evidenced by the difference between the fair value of the leased property at the inception of the lease and the lessor's cost or carrying amount (book value).

Normally, sales-type leases arise when manufacturers or dealers use leasing as a means of marketing their products. For example, a computer manufacturer will lease its computer equipment (possibly through a captive) to businesses and institutions. Direct-financing leases generally result from arrangements with lessors that are primarily engaged in financing operations (e.g., banks). However, a lessor need not be a manufacturer or dealer to recognize a profit (or loss) at the inception of a lease that requires application of sales-type lease accounting.

Lessors classify and account for all leases that do not qualify as direct-financing or sales-type leases as operating leases. Illustration 21-11 shows the circumstances under which a lessor classifies a lease as operating, direct-financing, or sales-type.

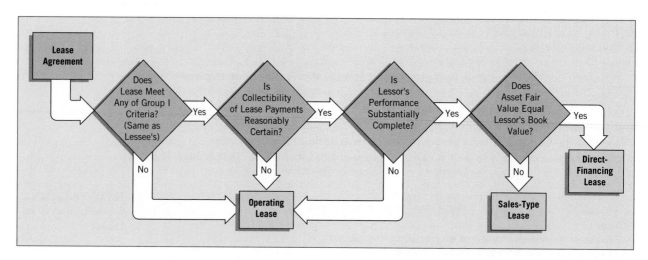

ILLUSTRATION 21-11
Diagram of Lessor's
Criteria for Lease
Classification

As a consequence of the additional Group II criteria for lessors, a lessor may classify a lease as an **operating** lease but the lessee may classify the same lease as a **capital** lease. In such an event, both the lessor and lessee will carry the asset on their books, and both will depreciate the capitalized asset.

For purposes of comparison with the lessee's accounting, we will illustrate only the operating and direct-financing leases in the following section. We will discuss the more complex sales-type lease later in the chapter.

Direct-Financing Method (Lessor)

Direct-financing leases are in substance the financing of an asset purchase by the lessee. In this type of lease, the lessor records a **lease receivable** instead of a leased asset. The lease receivable is the present value of the minimum lease payments. Remember that "minimum lease payments" include:

1. Rental payments (excluding executory costs).
2. Bargain-purchase option (if any).
3. Guaranteed residual value (if any).
4. Penalty for failure to renew (if any).

Thus, the lessor records the residual value, whether guaranteed or not. Also, recall that if the lessor pays any executory costs, then it should reduce the rental payment by that amount in computing minimum lease payments.

The following presentation, using the data from the preceding Caterpillar/Sterling example on pages 1124–1127, illustrates the accounting treatment for a direct-financing lease. We repeat here the information relevant to Caterpillar in accounting for this lease transaction.

1. The term of the lease is five years beginning January 1, 2011, noncancelable, and requires equal rental payments of $25,981.62 at the beginning of each year. Payments include $2,000 of executory costs (property taxes).
2. The equipment (front-end loader) has a cost of $100,000 to Caterpillar, a fair value at the inception of the lease of $100,000, an estimated economic life of five years, and no residual value.

3. Caterpillar incurred no initial direct costs in negotiating and closing the lease transaction.

4. The lease contains no renewal options. The equipment reverts to Caterpillar at the termination of the lease.

5. Collectibility is reasonably assured and Caterpillar incurs no additional costs (with the exception of the property taxes being collected from Sterling).

6. Caterpillar sets the annual lease payments to ensure a rate of return of 10 percent (implicit rate) on its investment as shown in Illustration 21-12.

Fair market value of leased equipment	$100,000.00
Less: Present value of residual value	–0–
Amount to be recovered by lessor through lease payments	$100,000.00
Five beginning-of-the-year lease payments to yield a 10% return ($100,000 ÷ 4.16986ª)	$ 23,981.62
ªPV of an annuity due of 1 for 5 years at 10% (Table 6-5).	

ILLUSTRATION 21-12
Computation of Lease Payments

The lease meets the criteria for classification as a direct-financing lease for several reasons: (1) The lease term exceeds 75 percent of the equipment's estimated economic life. (2) The present value of the minimum lease payments exceeds 90 percent of the equipment's fair value. (3) Collectibility of the payments is reasonably assured. And (4) Caterpillar incurs no further costs. It is not a sales-type lease because there is no difference between the fair value ($100,000) of the loader and Caterpillar's cost ($100,000).

The Lease Receivable is the present value of the minimum lease payments (excluding executory costs which are property taxes of $2,000). Caterpillar computes it as follows.

Lease receivable = ($25,981.62 − $2,000) × Present value of an annuity due of 1 for 5 periods at 10% (Table 6-5)

= $23,981.62 × 4.16986

= $100,000

ILLUSTRATION 21-13
Computation of Lease Receivable

Caterpillar records the lease of the asset and the resulting receivable on January 1, 2011 (the inception of the lease), as follows.

Lease Receivable	100,000	
Equipment		100,000

Companies often **report** the lease receivable in the balance sheet as "Net investment in capital leases." Companies classify it either as current or noncurrent, depending on when they recover the net investment.[12]

Caterpillar replaces its investment (the leased front-end loader, a cost of $100,000), with a lease receivable. In a manner similar to Sterling's treatment of interest, Caterpillar applies the effective-interest method and recognizes interest revenue as a function of the lease receivable balance, as Illustration 21-14 (on page 1134) shows.

---

[12]In the notes to the financial statements (see Illustration 21-32, page 1147), the lease receivable is reported at its gross amount (minimum lease payments plus the unguaranteed residual value). In addition, the lessor also reports total unearned interest related to the lease. As a result, some lessors record lease receivable on a gross basis and record the unearned interest in a separate account. We illustrate the net approach here because it is consistent with the accounting for the lessee.

ILLUSTRATION 21-14
Lease Amortization
Schedule for Lessor—
Annuity-Due Basis

CATERPILLAR FINANCIAL					
LEASE AMORTIZATION SCHEDULE					
ANNUITY-DUE BASIS					
Date	Annual Lease Payment	Executory Costs	Interest (10%) on Lease Receivable	Lease Receivable Recovery	Lease Receivable
	(a)	(b)	(c)	(d)	(e)
1/1/11					$100,000.00
1/1/11	$ 25,981.62	$ 2,000.00	$ –0–	$ 23,981.62	76,018.38
1/1/12	25,981.62	2,000.00	7,601.84	16,379.78	59,638.60
1/1/13	25,981.62	2,000.00	5,963.86	18,017.76	41,620.84
1/1/14	25,981.62	2,000.00	4,162.08	19,819.54	21,801.30
1/1/15	25,981.62	2,000.00	2,180.32*	21,801.30	–0–
	$129,908.10	$10,000.00	$19,908.10	$100,000.00	

(a) Annual rental that provides a 10% return on net investment.
(b) Executory costs included in rental payment.
(c) Ten percent of the preceding balance of (e) except for 1/1/11.
(d) (a) minus (b) and (c).
(e) Preceding balance minus (d).

*Rounded by 19 cents.

On January 1, 2011, Caterpillar records receipt of the first year's lease payment as follows.

Cash	25,981.62	
Lease Receivable		23,981.62
Property Tax Expense/Property Taxes Payable		2,000.00

On December 31, 2011, Caterpillar recognizes the interest revenue earned during the first year through the following entry.

Interest Receivable	7,601.84	
Interest Revenue—Leases		7,601.84

At December 31, 2011, Caterpillar reports the lease receivable in its balance sheet among current assets or noncurrent assets, or both. It classifies the portion due within one year or the operating cycle, whichever is longer, as a current asset, and the rest with noncurrent assets.

Illustration 21-15 shows the assets section as it relates to lease transactions at December 31, 2011.

ILLUSTRATION 21-15
Reporting Lease
Transactions by Lessor

Current assets	
Interest receivable	$ 7,601.84
Lease receivable	16,379.78
Noncurrent assets (investments)	
Lease receivable	$59,638.60

The following entries record receipt of the second year's lease payment and recognition of the interest earned.

January 1, 2012

Cash	25,981.62	
Lease Receivable		16,379.78
Interest Receivable		7,601.84
Property Tax Expense/Property Taxes Payable		2,000.00

December 31, 2012

Interest Receivable	5,963.86	
Interest Revenue—Leases		5,963.86

Journal entries through 2015 follow the same pattern except that Caterpillar records no entry in 2015 (the last year) for earned interest. Because it fully collects the receivable by January 1, 2015, no balance (investment) is outstanding during 2015. Caterpillar **recorded no depreciation**. If Sterling buys the loader for $5,000 upon expiration of the lease, Caterpillar recognizes disposition of the equipment as follows.

Cash	5,000	
Gain on Sale of Leased Equipment		5,000

Operating Method (Lessor)

Under the **operating method**, the lessor records each rental receipt as rental revenue. It **depreciates the leased asset in the normal manner**, with the depreciation expense of the period matched against the rental revenue. The amount of revenue recognized in each accounting period is a level amount (straight-line basis) regardless of the lease provisions, unless another systematic and rational basis better represents the time pattern in which the lessor derives benefit from the leased asset.

In addition to the depreciation charge, the lessor expenses maintenance costs and the cost of any other services rendered under the provisions of the lease that pertain to the current accounting period. The lessor **amortizes over the life of the lease** any costs paid to independent third parties, such as appraisal fees, finder's fees, and costs of credit checks, usually on a straight-line basis.

To illustrate the operating method, assume that the direct-financing lease illustrated in the previous section does not qualify as a capital lease. Therefore, Caterpillar accounts for it as an operating lease. It records the cash rental receipt, assuming the $2,000 was for property tax expense, as follows.

Cash	25,981.62	
Rental Revenue		25,981.62

Caterpillar records depreciation as follows (assuming a straight-line method, a cost basis of $100,000, and a five-year life).

Depreciation Expense—Leased Equipment	20,000	
Accumulated Depreciation—Leased Equipment		20,000

If Caterpillar pays property taxes, insurance, maintenance, and other operating costs during the year, it records them as expenses chargeable against the gross rental revenues.

If Caterpillar owns plant assets that it uses in addition to those leased to others, the company **separately classifies the leased equipment and accompanying accumulated depreciation** as Equipment Leased to Others or Investment in Leased Property. If significant in amount or in terms of activity, Caterpillar separates the rental revenues and accompanying expenses in the income statement from sales revenue and cost of goods sold.

SPECIAL ACCOUNTING PROBLEMS

The features of lease arrangements that cause unique accounting problems are:

Objective·6

Identify special features of lease arrangements that cause unique accounting problems.

1. Residual values.
2. Sales-type leases (lessor).
3. Bargain-purchase options.
4. Initial direct costs.
5. Current versus noncurrent classification.
6. Disclosure.

We discuss each of these features on the following pages.

Residual Values

Up to this point, in order to develop the basic accounting issues related to lessee and lessor accounting, we have generally ignored residual values. Accounting for residual values is complex and will probably provide you with the greatest challenge in understanding lease accounting.

Meaning of Residual Value

The **residual value** is the estimated fair value of the leased asset at the end of the lease term. Frequently, a significant residual value exists at the end of the lease term, especially when the economic life of the leased asset exceeds the lease term. If title does not pass automatically to the lessee (criterion 1) and a bargain-purchase option does not exist (criterion 2), the lessee returns physical custody of the asset to the lessor at the end of the lease term.[13]

Guaranteed versus Unguaranteed

The residual value may be unguaranteed or guaranteed by the lessee. Sometimes the lessee agrees to make up any deficiency below a stated amount that the lessor realizes in residual value at the end of the lease term. In such a case, that stated amount is the **guaranteed residual value**.

The parties to a lease use guaranteed residual value in lease arrangements for two reasons. The first is a business reason: It protects the lessor against any loss in estimated residual value, thereby ensuring the lessor of the desired rate of return on investment. The second reason is an accounting benefit that you will learn from the discussion at the end of this chapter.

Lease Payments

A guaranteed residual value—by definition—has more assurance of realization than does an unguaranteed residual value. As a result, the lessor may adjust lease payments because of the increased certainty of recovery. After the lessor establishes this rate, it makes no difference from an accounting point of view whether the residual value is guaranteed or unguaranteed. The net investment that the lessor records (once the rate is set) will be the same.

Assume the same data as in the Caterpillar/Sterling illustrations except that Caterpillar estimates a residual value of $5,000 at the end of the five-year lease term. In addition, Caterpillar assumes a 10 percent return on investment (ROI),[14] whether the residual value is guaranteed or unguaranteed. Caterpillar would compute the amount of the lease payments as follows.

ILLUSTRATION 21-16
Lessor's Computation of Lease Payments

CATERPILLAR'S COMPUTATION OF LEASE PAYMENTS (10% ROI) GUARANTEED OR UNGUARANTEED RESIDUAL VALUE ANNUITY-DUE BASIS, INCLUDING RESIDUAL VALUE	
Fair market value of leased asset to lessor	$100,000.00
Less: Present value of residual value ($5,000 × .62092, Table 6-2)	3,104.60
Amount to be recovered by lessor through lease payments	$ 96,895.40
Five periodic lease payments ($96,895.40 ÷ 4.16986, Table 6-5)	$ 23,237.09

[13]When the lease term and the economic life are not the same, the residual value and the salvage value of the asset will probably differ. For simplicity, we will assume that residual value and salvage value are the same, even when the economic life and lease term vary.

[14]Technically, the rate of return Caterpillar demands would differ depending upon whether the residual value was guaranteed or unguaranteed. To simplify the illustrations, we are ignoring this difference in subsequent sections.

Contrast the foregoing lease payment amount to the lease payments of $23,981.62 as computed in Illustration 21-9 (on page 1130), where no residual value existed. In the second example, the payments are less, because the present value of the residual value reduces Caterpillar's total recoverable amount from $100,000 to $96,895.40.

Lessee Accounting for Residual Value

Whether the estimated residual value is guaranteed or unguaranteed has both economic and accounting consequence to the lessee. We saw the economic consequence— lower lease payments—in the preceding example. The accounting consequence is that the **minimum lease payments**, the basis for capitalization, include the guaranteed residual value but excludes the unguaranteed residual value.

Guaranteed Residual Value (Lessee Accounting). A guaranteed residual value affects the lessee's computation of minimum lease payments. Therefore it also affects the amounts capitalized as a leased asset and a lease obligation. In effect, the guaranteed residual value **is an additional lease payment that the lessee will pay in property or cash, or both, at the end of the lease term**.

> **Objective·7**
> Describe the effect of residual values, guaranteed and unguaranteed, on lease accounting.

Using the rental payments as computed by the lessor in Illustration 21-16, the minimum lease payments are $121,185.45 ([$23,237.09 × 5] + $5,000). Illustration 21-17 shows the capitalized present value of the minimum lease payments (excluding executory costs) for Sterling Construction.

ILLUSTRATION 21-17
Computation of Lessee's Capitalized Amount— Guaranteed Residual Value

STERLING'S CAPITALIZED AMOUNT (10% RATE) ANNUITY-DUE BASIS, INCLUDING GUARANTEED RESIDUAL VALUE	
Present value of five annual rental payments ($23,237.09 × 4.16986, Table 6-5)	$ 96,895.40
Present value of guaranteed residual value of $5,000 due five years after date of inception: ($5,000 × .62092, Table 6-2)	3,104.60
Lessee's capitalized amount	$100,000.00

Sterling prepares a schedule of interest expense and amortization of the $100,000 lease liability. That schedule, shown in Illustration 21-18, is based on a $5,000 final guaranteed residual value payment at the end of five years.

ILLUSTRATION 21-18
Lease Amortization Schedule for Lessee— Guaranteed Residual Value

	STERLING CONSTRUCTION LEASE AMORTIZATION SCHEDULE ANNUITY-DUE BASIS, GUARANTEED RESIDUAL VALUE—GRV				
Date	Lease Payment Plus GRV	Executory Costs	Interest (10%) on Liability	Reduction of Lease Liability	Lease Liability
	(a)	(b)	(c)	(d)	(e)
1/1/11					$100,000.00
1/1/11	$ 25,237.09	$ 2,000	–0–	$ 23,237.09	76,762.91
1/1/12	25,237.09	2,000	$ 7,676.29	15,560.80	61,202.11
1/1/13	25,237.09	2,000	6,120.21	17,116.88	44,085.23
1/1/14	25,237.09	2,000	4,408.52	18,828.57	25,256.66
1/1/15	25,237.09	2,000	2,525.67	20,711.42	4,545.24
12/31/15	5,000.00*		454.76**	4,545.24	–0–
	$131,185.45	$10,000	$21,185.45	$100,000.00	

(a) Annual lease payment as required by lease.
(b) Executory costs included in rental payment.
(c) Preceding balance of (e) × 10%, except 1/1/11.
(d) (a) minus (b) and (c).
(e) Preceding balance minus (d).

*Represents the guaranteed residual value.
**Rounded by 24 cents.

Sterling records the leased asset (front-end loader) and liability, depreciation, interest, property tax, and lease payments on the basis of a guaranteed residual value. (These journal entries are shown in Illustration 21-23, on page 1140.) The format of these entries is the same as illustrated earlier, although the amounts are different because of the guaranteed residual value. Sterling records the loader at $100,000 and depreciates it over five years. To compute depreciation, it subtracts the guaranteed residual value from the cost of the loader. Assuming that Sterling uses the straight-line method, the depreciation expense each year is $19,000 ([$100,000 − $5,000] ÷ 5 years).

At the end of the lease term, before the lessee transfers the asset to Caterpillar, the lease asset and liability accounts have the following balances.

ILLUSTRATION 21-19
Account Balances on Lessee's Books at End of Lease Term—Guaranteed Residual Value

Leased equipment under capital leases	$100,000.00	Interest payable	$ 454.76
Less: Accumulated depreciation— capital leases	95,000.00	Lease liability	4,545.24
	$ 5,000.00		$5,000.00

If, at the end of the lease, the fair market value of the residual value is less than $5,000, Sterling will have to record a loss. Assume that Sterling depreciated the leased asset down to its residual value of $5,000 but that the fair market value of the residual value at December 31, 2015, was $3,000. In this case, Sterling would have to report a loss of $2,000. Assuming that it pays cash to make up the residual value deficiency, Sterling would make the following journal entry.

Loss on Capital Lease	2,000.00	
Interest Expense (or Interest Payable)	454.76	
Lease Liability	4,545.24	
Accumulated Depreciation—Capital Leases	95,000.00	
Leased Equipment under Capital Leases		100,000.00
Cash		2,000.00

If the fair market value *exceeds* $5,000, a gain may be recognized. Caterpillar and Sterling may apportion gains on guaranteed residual values in whatever ratio the parties initially agree.

When there is a guaranteed residual value, the lessee must be careful not to depreciate the total cost of the asset. For example, if Sterling mistakenly depreciated the total cost of the loader ($100,000), a misstatement would occur. That is, the carrying amount of the asset at the end of the lease term would be zero, but Sterling would show the liability under the capital lease at $5,000. In that case, if the asset was worth $5,000, Sterling would end up reporting a gain of $5,000 when it transferred the asset back to Caterpillar. As a result, Sterling would overstate depreciation and would understate net income in 2011–2014; in the last year (2015) net income would be overstated.

Unguaranteed Residual Value (Lessee Accounting). From the lessee's viewpoint, an **unguaranteed residual value** is the same as no residual value in terms of its effect upon the lessee's method of computing the minimum lease payments and the capitalization of the leased asset and the lease liability.

Assume the same facts as those above except that the $5,000 residual value is **unguaranteed** instead of guaranteed. The amount of the annual lease payments would be the same—$23,237.09. Whether the residual value is guaranteed or unguaranteed, Caterpillar will recover the same amount through lease rentals—that is, $96,895.40. The minimum lease payments are $116,185.45 ($23,237.09 × 5). Lessee Company would capitalize the amount shown in Illustration 21-20.

STERLING'S CAPITALIZED AMOUNT (10% RATE)	
ANNUITY-DUE BASIS, INCLUDING UNGUARANTEED RESIDUAL VALUE	
Present value of 5 annual rental payments of $23,237.09 × 4.16986 (Table 6-5)	$96,895.40
Unguaranteed residual value of $5,000 (not capitalized by lessee)	–0–
Lessee's capitalized amount	$96,895.40

Illustration 21-21 shows Sterling's schedule of interest expense and amortization of the lease liability of $96,895.40, assuming an unguaranteed residual value of $5,000 at the end of five years.

	STERLING CONSTRUCTION				
	LEASE AMORTIZATION SCHEDULE (10%)				
	ANNUITY-DUE BASIS, UNGUARANTEED RESIDUAL VALUE				
Date	Annual Lease Payments	Executory Costs	Interest (10%) on Liability	Reduction of Lease Liability	Lease Liability
	(a)	(b)	(c)	(d)	(e)
1/1/11					$96,895.40
1/1/11	$ 25,237.09	$ 2,000	–0–	$23,237.09	73,658.31
1/1/12	25,237.09	2,000	$ 7,365.83	15,871.26	57,787.05
1/1/13	25,237.09	2,000	5,778.71	17,458.38	40,328.67
1/1/14	25,237.09	2,000	4,032.87	19,204.22	21,124.45
1/1/15	25,237.09	2,000	2,112.64*	21,124.45	–0–
	$126,185.45	$10,000	$19,290.05	$96,895.40	

(a) Annual lease payment as required by lease.
(b) Executory costs included in rental payment.
(c) Preceding balance of (e) × 10%.
(d) (a) minus (b) and (c).
(e) Preceding balance minus (d).

*Rounded by 19 cents.

Sterling records the leased asset and liability, depreciation, interest, property tax, and lease payments on the basis of an unguaranteed residual value. (These journal entries are shown in Illustration 21-23, on page 1140.) The format of these capital lease entries is the same as illustrated earlier. Note that Sterling records the leased asset at $96,895.40 and depreciates it over five years. Assuming that it uses the straight-line method, the depreciation expense each year is $19,379.08 ($96,895.40 ÷ 5 years). At the end of the lease term, before Sterling transfers the asset to Caterpillar, the lease asset and liability accounts have the following balances.

ILLUSTRATION 21-22
Account Balances on
Lessee's Books at
End of Lease Term—
Unguaranteed Residual
Value

		Lease liability	$–0–
Leased equipment under capital leases	$96,895		
Less: Accumulated depreciation— capital leases	96,895		
	$ –0–		

Assuming that Sterling has fully depreciated the leased asset and has fully amortized the lease liability, no entry is required at the end of the lease term, except to remove the asset from the books.

If Sterling depreciated the asset down to its unguaranteed residual value, a misstatement would occur. That is, the carrying amount of the leased asset would be $5,000 at the end of the lease, but the liability under the capital lease would be stated at zero before the transfer of the asset. Thus, Sterling would end up reporting a loss of $5,000 when it transferred the asset back to Caterpillar. Sterling would understate depreciation and would overstate net income in 2011–2014; in the last year (2015) net income would be understated because of the recorded loss.

Lessee Entries Involving Residual Values. Illustration 21-23 shows, in comparative form, Sterling's entries for both a guaranteed and an unguaranteed residual value.

Guaranteed Residual Value			Unguaranteed Residual Value		
Capitalization of lease (January 1, 2011):					
Leased Equipment under Capital Leases	100,000.00		Leased Equipment under Capital Leases	96,895.40	
Lease Liability		100,000.00	Lease Liability		96,895.40
First payment (January 1, 2011):					
Property Tax Expense	2,000.00		Property Tax Expense	2,000.00	
Lease Liability	23,237.09		Lease Liability	23,237.09	
Cash		25,237.09	Cash		25,237.09
Adjusting entry for accrued interest (December 31, 2011):					
Interest Expense	7,676.29		Interest Expense	7,365.83	
Interest Payable		7,676.29	Interest Payable		7,365.83
Entry to record depreciation (December 31, 2011):					
Depreciation Expense— Capital Leases	19,000.00		Depreciation Expense— Capital Leases	19,379.08	
Accumulated Depreciation— Capital Leases ([$100,000 − $5,000] ÷ 5 years)		19,000.00	Accumulated Depreciation— Capital Leases ($96,895.40 ÷ 5 years)		19,379.08
Second payment (January 1, 2012):					
Property Tax Expense	2,000.00		Property Tax Expense	2,000.00	
Lease Liability	15,560.80		Lease Liability	15,871.26	
Interest Expense (or Interest Payable)	7,676.29		Interest Expense (or Interest Payable)	7,365.83	
Cash		25,237.09	Cash		25,237.09

ILLUSTRATION 21-23
Comparative Entries for Guaranteed and Unguaranteed Residual Values, Lessee Company

Lessor Accounting for Residual Value

As we indicated earlier, the lessor will recover the same net investment whether the residual value is guaranteed or unguaranteed. That is, the lessor works on the assumption that it will realize **the residual value at the end of the lease term whether guaranteed or unguaranteed**. The lease payments required in order for the company to earn a certain return on investment are the same (e.g., $23,237.09 in our example) whether the residual value is guaranteed or unguaranteed.

To illustrate, we again use the Caterpillar/Sterling data and assume classification of the lease as a direct-financing lease. With a residual value (either guaranteed or unguaranteed) of $5,000, Caterpillar determines the payments as follows.

Fair market value of leased equipment	$100,000.00
Less: Present value of residual value ($5,000 × .62092, Table 6-2)	3,104.60
Amount to be recovered by lessor through lease payments	$ 96,895.40
Five beginning-of-the-year lease payments to yield a	
10% return ($96,895.40 ÷ 4.16986, Table 6-5)	$ 23,237.09

ILLUSTRATION 21-24
Computation of Direct-
Financing Lease
Payments

The amortization schedule is the same for guaranteed or unguaranteed residual value, as Illustration 21-25 shows.

ILLUSTRATION 21-25
Lease Amortization
Schedule, for Lessor—
Guaranteed or
Unguaranteed Residual
Value

CATERPILLAR FINANCIAL
LEASE AMORTIZATION SCHEDULE
ANNUITY-DUE BASIS, **GUARANTEED OR UNGUARANTEED** RESIDUAL VALUE

Date	Annual Lease Payment Plus Residual Value	Executory Costs	Interest (10%) on Lease Receivable	Lease Receivable Recovery	Lease Receivable
	(a)	(b)	(c)	(d)	(e)
1/1/11					$100,000.00
1/1/11	$ 25,237.09	$ 2,000.00	$ -0-	$ 23,237.09	76,762.91
1/1/12	25,237.09	2,000.00	7,676.29	15,560.80	61,202.11
1/1/13	25,237.09	2,000.00	6,120.21	17,116.88	44,085.23
1/1/14	25,237.09	2,000.00	4,408.52	18,828.57	25,256.66
1/1/15	25,237.09	2,000.00	2,525.67	20,711.42	4,545.24
12/31/15	5,000.00	-0-	454.76*	4,545.24	-0-
	$131,185.45	$10,000.00	$21,185.45	$100,000.00	

(a) Annual lease payment as required by lease.
(b) Executory costs included in rental payment.
(c) Preceding balance of (e) × 10%, except 1/1/11.
(d) (a) minus (b) and (c).
(e) Preceding balance minus (d).

*Rounded by 24 cents.

Using the amounts computed above, Caterpillar would make the following entries for this direct-financing lease in the first year. Note the similarity to Sterling's entries in Illustration 21-23.

ILLUSTRATION 21-26
Entries for Either
Guaranteed or
Unguaranteed Residual
Value, Lessor Company

Inception of lease (January 1, 2011):

| Lease Receivable | 100,000.00 | |
| Equipment | | 100,000.00 |

First payment received (January 1, 2011):

Cash	25,237.09	
Lease Receivable		23,237.09
Property Tax Expense/Property Taxes Payable		2,000.00

Adjusting entry for accrued interest (December 31, 2011):

| Interest Receivable | 7,676.29 | |
| Interest Revenue | | 7,676.29 |

Sales-Type Leases (Lessor)

As already indicated, the primary difference between a direct-financing lease and a **sales-type lease** is the manufacturer's or dealer's gross profit (or loss). The diagram in Illustration 21-27 (on page 1142) presents the distinctions between direct-financing and sales-type leases.

Objective·8
Describe the lessor's accounting for sales-type leases.

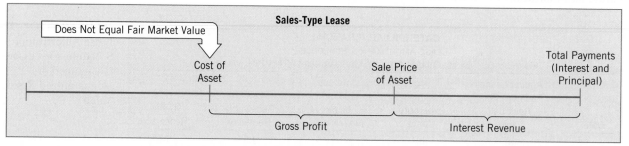

ILLUSTRATION 21-27
Direct-Financing versus
Sales-Type Leases

In a sales-type lease, the lessor records the sale price of the asset, the cost of goods sold and related inventory reduction, and the lease receivable. The information necessary to record the sales-type lease is as follows.

SALES-TYPE LEASE TERMS

LEASE RECEIVABLE (also referred to as **NET INVESTMENT**). The present value of the minimum lease payments plus the present value of any unguaranteed residual value. The lease receivable therefore includes the present value of the residual value, whether guaranteed or not.

SALES PRICE OF THE ASSET. The present value of the minimum lease payments.

COST OF GOODS SOLD. The cost of the asset to the lessor, less the present value of any unguaranteed residual value.

When recording sales revenue and cost of goods sold, there is a difference in the accounting for guaranteed and unguaranteed residual values. The guaranteed residual value can be considered part of sales revenue because the lessor knows that the entire asset has been sold. But there is less certainty that the unguaranteed residual portion of the asset has been "sold" (i.e., will be realized). Therefore, the lessor recognizes sales and cost of goods sold only for the portion of the asset for which realization is assured. However, **the gross profit amount on the sale of the asset is the same whether a guaranteed or unguaranteed residual value is involved**.

To illustrate a sales-type lease with a guaranteed residual value and with an unguaranteed residual value, assume the same facts as in the preceding direct-financing lease situation (pages 1132–1135). The estimated residual value is $5,000 (the present value of which is $3,104.60), and the leased equipment has an $85,000 cost to the dealer, Caterpillar. Assume that the fair market value of the residual value is $3,000 at the end of the lease term.

Illustration 21-28 shows computation of the amounts relevant to a sales-type lease.

Sales-Type Lease		
	Guaranteed Residual Value	Unguaranteed Residual Value
Lease receivable	$100,000 [$23,237.09 × 4.16986 (Table 6-5) + $5,000 × .62092 (Table 6-2)]	Same
Sales price of the asset	$100,000	$96,895.40 ($100,000 − $3,104.60)
Cost of goods sold	$85,000	$81,895.40 ($85,000 − $3,104.60)
Gross profit	$15,000 ($100,000 − $85,000)	$15,000 ($96,895.40 − $81,895.40)

ILLUSTRATION 21-28
Computation of Lease Amounts by Caterpillar Financial—Sales-Type Lease

Caterpillar records the same profit ($15,000) at the point of sale whether the residual value is guaranteed or unguaranteed. The difference between the two is that **the sales revenue and cost of goods sold amounts are different**.

In making this computation, we deduct the present value of the unguaranteed residual value from sales revenue and cost of goods sold for two reasons: (1) The criteria for revenue recognition have not been met. (2) It is improper to match expense against revenue not yet recognized. The revenue recognition criteria have not been met **because of the uncertainty surrounding the realization of the unguaranteed residual value**.

Caterpillar makes the following entries to record this transaction on January 1, 2011, and the receipt of the residual value at the end of the lease term.

ILLUSTRATION 21-29
Entries for Guaranteed and Unguaranteed Residual Values, Lessor Company—Sales-Type Lease

Guaranteed Residual Value			Unguaranteed Residual Value		
To record sales-type lease at inception (January 1, 2011):					
Cost of Goods Sold	85,000.00		Cost of Goods Sold	81,895.40	
Lease Receivable	100,000.00		Lease Receivable	100,000.00	
Sales Revenue		100,000.00	Sales Revenue		96,895.40
Inventory		85,000.00	Inventory		85,000.00
To record receipt of the first lease payment (January 1, 2011):					
Cash	25,237.09		Cash	25,237.09	
Lease Receivable		23,237.09	Lease Receivable		23,237.09
Property Tax Exp./Pay.		2,000.00	Property Tax Exp./Pay.		2,000.00
To recognize interest revenue earned during the first year (December 31, 2011):					
Interest Receivable	7,676.29		Interest Receivable	7,676.29	
Interest Revenue		7,676.29	Interest Revenue		7,676.29
(See lease amortization schedule, Illustration 21-25 on page 1141.)					
To record receipt of the second lease payment (January 1, 2011):					
Cash	25,237.09		Cash	25,237.09	
Interest Receivable		7,676.29	Interest Receivable		7,676.29
Lease Receivable		15,560.80	Lease Receivable		15,560.80
Property Tax Exp./Pay.		2,000.00	Property Tax Exp./Pay.		2,000.00
To recognize interest revenue earned during the second year (December 31, 2012):					
Interest Receivable	6,120.21		Interest Receivable	6,120.21	
Interest Revenue		6,120.21	Interest Revenue		6,120.21
To record receipt of residual value at end of lease term (December 31, 2015):					
Inventory	3,000		Inventory	3,000	
Cash	2,000		Loss on Capital Lease	2,000	
Lease Receivable		5,000	Lease Receivable		5,000

Companies must periodically review the **estimated unguaranteed residual value in a sales-type lease**. If the estimate of the unguaranteed residual value declines, the company must revise the accounting for the transaction using the changed estimate. The decline represents a reduction in the lessor's lease receivable (net investment). The lessor recognizes the decline as a loss in the period in which it reduces the residual estimate. Companies do not recognize upward adjustments in estimated residual value.

XEROX TAKES ON THE SEC

What do the numbers mean?

Xerox derives much of its income from leasing equipment. Reporting such leases as sales leases, Xerox records a lease contract as a sale, therefore recognizing income immediately. One problem is that each lease receipt consists of payments for items such as supplies, services, financing, and equipment.

The SEC *accused* Xerox of inappropriately allocating lease receipts, which affects the timing of income that it reports. If Xerox applied SEC guidelines, it would report income in different time periods. Xerox contended that its methods were correct. It also noted that when the lease term is up, the bottom line is the same using either the SEC's recommended allocation method or its current method.

Although Xerox can refuse to change its method, the SEC has the right to prevent a company from selling stock or bonds to the public if the agency rejects filings of the company.

Apparently, being able to access public markets is very valuable to Xerox. The company agreed to change its accounting according to SEC wishes, and Xerox will pay $670 million to settle a shareholder lawsuit related to its lease transactions. Its former auditor, **KPMG LLP**, will pay $80 million.

Source: Adapted from "Xerox Takes on the SEC," *Accounting Web* (January 9, 2002) (*www.account-ingweb.com*); and K. Shwiff and M. Maremont, "Xerox, KPMG Settle Shareholder Lawsuit," *Wall Street Journal Online* (March 28, 2008), p. B3.

Bargain-Purchase Option (Lessee)

As stated earlier, a bargain-purchase option allows the lessee to purchase the leased property for a future price that is substantially lower than the property's expected future fair value. The price is so favorable at the lease's inception that the future exercise of the option appears to be reasonably assured. If a bargain-purchase option exists, **the lessee must increase the present value of the minimum lease payments by the present value of the option price**.

For example, assume that Sterling Construction in Illustration 21-18 on page 1137 had an option to buy the leased equipment for $5,000 at the end of the five-year lease term. At that point, Sterling and Caterpillar expect the fair value to be $18,000. The significant difference between the option price and the fair value creates a bargain-purchase option, and the exercise of that option is reasonably assured.

A bargain-purchase option affects the accounting for leases in essentially the same way as a guaranteed residual value. In other words, with a guaranteed residual value, the lessee must pay the residual value at the end of the lease. Similarly, a purchase option that is a bargain will almost certainly be paid by the lessee. Therefore, the computations, amortization schedule, and entries that would be prepared for this $5,000 bargain-purchase option are identical to those shown for the $5,000 guaranteed residual value (see Illustrations 21-16, 21-17, and 21-18 on pages 1136 and 1137).

The only difference between the accounting treatment for a bargain-purchase option and a guaranteed residual value of identical amounts and circumstances is in the **computation of the annual depreciation**. In the case of a guaranteed residual value, Sterling depreciates the asset over the lease term; in the case of a bargain-purchase option, it uses the **economic life** of the asset.

Initial Direct Costs (Lessor)

Initial direct costs are of two types: incremental and internal. [8] **Incremental direct costs** are paid to independent third parties for originating a lease arrangement. Examples include the cost of independent appraisal of collateral used to secure a lease, the cost of an outside credit check of the lessee, or a broker's fee for finding the lessee.

Internal direct costs are directly related to specified activities performed **by the lessor** on a given lease. Examples are evaluating the prospective lessee's financial condition; evaluating and recording guarantees, collateral, and other security arrangements; negotiating lease terms and preparing and processing lease documents; and closing the transaction. The costs directly related to an employee's time spent on a specific lease transaction are also considered initial direct costs.

However, initial direct costs should **not** include **internal indirect costs**. Such costs are related to activities the lessor performs for advertising, servicing existing leases, and establishing and monitoring credit policies. Nor should the lessor include the costs for supervision and administration or for expenses such as rent and depreciation.

The accounting for initial direct costs depends on the type of lease:

- For **operating leases**, the lessor should defer initial direct costs and **allocate them over the lease term** in proportion to the recognition of rental revenue.
- For **sales-type leases**, the lessor expenses the initial direct costs **in the period** in which it recognizes the profit on the sale.
- For a **direct-financing lease**, the lessor adds initial direct costs to the net investment in the lease and **amortizes them over the life of the lease as a yield adjustment**.

In a direct-financing lease, the lessor must disclose the unamortized deferred initial direct costs that are part of its investment in the direct-financing lease. For example, if the carrying value of the asset in the lease is $4,000,000 and the lessor incurs initial direct costs of $35,000, then the lease receivable (net investment in the lease) would be $4,035,000. The yield would be lower than the initial rate of return, and the lessor would adjust the yield to ensure proper amortization of the amount over the life of the lease.

Current versus Noncurrent

Earlier in the chapter we presented the classification of the lease liability/receivable in an annuity-due situation. Illustration 21-7 (on page 1126) indicated that Sterling's current liability is the payment of $23,981.62 (excluding $2,000 of executory costs) to be made on January 1 of the next year. Similarly, as shown in Illustration 21-15 (on page 1134), Caterpillar's current asset is the $23,981.62 (excluding $2,000 of executory costs) it will collect on January 1 of the next year. In these annuity-due instances, the balance sheet date is December 31 and the due date of the lease payment is January 1 (less than one year), so the present value ($23,981.62) of the payment due the following January 1 is the same as the rental payment ($23,981.62).

What happens if the situation is an ordinary annuity rather than an annuity due? For example, assume that the rent is due at the **end of the year** (December 31) rather than at the beginning (January 1). *FASB Statement No. 13* does not indicate how to measure the current and noncurrent amounts. It requires that for the lessee the "obligations shall be separately identified on the balance sheet as obligations under capital leases and shall be subject to the same considerations as other obligations in classifying them with current and noncurrent liabilities in classified balance sheets." [9] **The most common method of measuring the current liability portion in ordinary annuity leases is the change-in-the-present-value method.**[15]

---

[15]For additional discussion on this approach and possible alternatives, see R. J. Swieringa, "When Current Is Noncurrent and Vice Versa!" *The Accounting Review* (January 1984), pp. 123–30, and A. W. Richardson, "The Measurement of the Current Portion of the Long-Term Lease Obligations—Some Evidence from Practice," *The Accounting Review* (October 1985), pp. 744–52.

To illustrate the change-in-the-present-value method, assume an ordinary-annuity situation with the same facts as the Caterpillar/Sterling case, excluding the $2,000 of executory costs. Because Sterling pays the rents at the end of the period instead of at the beginning, Caterpillar sets the five rents at $26,379.73, to have an effective interest rate of 10 percent. Illustration 21-30 shows the ordinary-annuity amortization schedule.

ILLUSTRATION 21-30
Lease Amortization
Schedule—Ordinary-
Annuity Basis

	STERLING/CATERPILLAR LEASE AMORTIZATION SCHEDULE ORDINARY-ANNUITY BASIS			
Date	Annual Lease Payment	Interest 10%	Reduction of Lease Liability/Receivable	Balance of Lease Liability/Receivable
1/1/11				$100,000.00
12/31/11	$ 26,379.73	$10,000.00	$ 16,379.73	83,620.27
12/31/12	26,379.73	8,362.03	18,017.70	65,602.57
12/31/13	26,379.73	6,560.26	19,819.47	45,783.10
12/31/14	26,379.73	4,578.31	21,801.42	23,981.68
12/31/15	26,379.73	2,398.05*	23,981.68	–0–
	$131,898.65	$31,898.65	$100,000.00	

*Rounded by 12 cents.

The current portion of the lease liability/receivable under the **change-in-the-present-value method** as of December 31, 2011, would be $18,017.70 ($83,620.27 − $65,602.57). As of December 31, 2012, the current portion would be $19,819.47 ($65,602.57 − $45,783.10). At December 31, 2011, Caterpillar classifies $65,602.57 of the receivable as noncurrent.

Thus, both the annuity-due and the ordinary-annuity situations report the reduction of principal for the next period as a current liability/current asset. In the annuity-due situation, Caterpillar accrues interest during the year but is not paid until the next period. As a result, **a current asset arises for the receivable reduction and for the interest** that was earned in the preceding period.

In the ordinary-annuity situation, the interest accrued during the period is also paid in the same period. Consequently, the lessor shows as a current asset only the principal reduction.

Disclosing Lease Data

Objective·9
List the disclosure requirements for leases.

The FASB requires **lessees** and **lessors** to disclose certain information about leases in their financial statements or in the notes. These requirements vary based upon the type of lease (capital or operating) and whether the issuer is the lessor or lessee. These disclosure requirements provide investors with the following information:

* General description of the nature of leasing arrangements.
* The nature, timing, and amount of cash inflows and outflows associated with leases, including payments to be paid or received for each of the five succeeding years.
* The amount of lease revenues and expenses reported in the income statement each period.
* Description and amounts of leased assets by major balance sheet classification and related liabilities.
* Amounts receivable and unearned revenues under lease agreements. [10]

Illustration 21-31 (on page 1147) presents financial statement excerpts from the 2007 annual report of **Tasty Baking Company**. These excerpts represent the statement and note disclosures typical of a lessee having both capital leases and operating leases.

Tasty Baking Company
(dollar amounts in thousands)

	2007	2006
Current Liabilities		
Current obligations under capital leases	$ 431	$327
Noncurrent Liabilities		
Long-term obligations under capital leases, less current portion	$1,003	$208

Note 8: Commitments and Contingencies

The Company leases certain facilities, machinery, automotive and computer equipment under noncancelable lease agreements. The Company expects that in the normal course of business, leases that expire will be renewed or replaced by other leases. Property, plant and equipment relating to capital leases were $1,618 at December 29, 2007, and $2,234 at December 30, 2006, with accumulated amortization of $116 and $1,881, respectively. Depreciation and amortization of assets recorded under capital leases was $468 in 2007 and $719 in 2006.

The following is a schedule of future minimum lease payments as of December 29, 2007:

	Capital Leases	Noncancelable Operating Leases
2008	$ 565	$1,119
2009	503	947
2010	395	645
2011	193	467
2012	—	180
Later years	—	396
Total minimum lease payments	$1,656	$3,754
Less interest portion of payments	221	
Present value of future minimum lease payments	$1,435	

Rental expense was approximately $2,634 in 2007 and $2,732 in 2006.

ILLUSTRATION 21-31
Disclosure of Leases by Lessee

Description and amount of lease obligations

General description

Description and amounts of leased assets

Nature, timing, and amounts of cash outflows

Amount of lease rental expense

Illustration 21-32 presents the lease note disclosure from the 2007 annual report of **Hewlett-Packard Company**. The disclosure highlights required lessor disclosures.

Hewlett-Packard Company
Notes to Financial Statements
(in millions)

Note 10: Financing Receivables and Operating Leases
Financing receivables represent sales-type and direct-financing leases resulting from the marketing of HP's and third-party products. These receivables typically have terms from two to five years and are usually collateralized by a security interest in the underlying assets. Financing receivables also include billed receivables from operating leases. The components of net financing receivables, which are included in financing receivables and long-term financing receivables and other assets, were as follows for the following fiscal years ended October 31:

	2007	2006
	(In millions)	
Minimum lease payments receivable	$5,568	$5,010
Allowance for doubtful accounts	(84)	(80)
Unguaranteed residual value	291	289
Unearned income	(490)	(439)
Financing receivables, net	$5,285	$4,780
Less current portion	(2,507)	(2,440)
Amounts due after one year, net	$2,778	$2,340

ILLUSTRATION 21-32
Disclosure of Leases by Lessor

General description

Amount receivable and unearned revenues

continued on next page

Nature, timing, and amounts of cash inflows

As of October 31, 2007, scheduled maturities of HP's minimum lease payments receivable were as follows for the following fiscal years ended October 31:

	2008	2009	2010	2011	2012	Thereafter	Total
				(In millions)			
Scheduled maturities of minimum lease payments receivable	$2,706	$1,485	$759	$334	$168	$116	$5,568

Description of leased assets

Equipment leased to customers under operating leases was $2.4 billion at October 31, 2007 and $2.1 billion at October 31, 2006 and is included in machinery and equipment. Accumulated depreciation on equipment under lease was $0.6 billion at both October 31, 2007 and October 31, 2006. As of October 31, 2007, minimum future rentals on non-cancelable operating leases related to leased equipment were as follows for the following fiscal years ended October 31:

	2008	2009	2010	2011	2012	Thereafter	Total
				(In millions)			
Minimum future rentals on non-cancelable operating leases	$882	$430	$196	$85	$31	$25	$1,649

Amount of future rentals

Additional Lease Disclosures

LEASE ACCOUNTING—UNRESOLVED PROBLEMS

As we indicated at the beginning of this chapter, lease accounting is subject to abuse. Companies make strenuous efforts to circumvent GAAP in this area. In practice, the strong desires of lessees to resist capitalization have rendered the accounting rules for capitalizing leases partially ineffective. Leasing generally involves large dollar amounts that, when capitalized, materially increase reported liabilities and adversely affect the debt-to-equity ratio. Lessees also resist lease capitalization because charges to expense made in the early years of the lease term are higher under the capital lease method than under the operating method, frequently without tax benefit. As a consequence, "let's beat the lease standard" is one of the most popular games in town.[16]

To avoid leased asset capitalization, companies design, write, and interpret lease agreements to prevent satisfying any of the four capitalized lease criteria. Companies can easily devise lease agreements in such a way, by meeting the following specifications.

1. Ensure that the lease does not specify the transfer of title of the property to the lessee.

2. Do not write in a bargain-purchase option.

3. Set the lease term at something less than 75 percent of the estimated economic life of the leased property.

4. Arrange for the present value of the minimum lease payments to be less than 90 percent of the fair value of the leased property.

The real challenge lies in disqualifying the lease as a capital lease to the lessee, while having the same lease qualify as a capital (sales or financing) lease to the lessor. Unlike lessees, lessors try to avoid having lease arrangements classified as operating leases.[17]

---

[16]Richard Dieter, "Is Lessee Accounting Working?" *CPA Journal* (August 1979), pp. 13–19. This article provides interesting examples of abuses of GAAP in this area, discusses the circumstances that led to the current situation, and proposes a solution.

[17]The reason is that most lessors are banks, which are not permitted to hold these assets on their balance sheets except for relatively short periods of time. Furthermore, the capital-lease transaction from the lessor's standpoint provides higher income flows in the earlier periods of the lease life.

Avoiding the first three criteria is relatively simple, but it takes a little ingenuity to avoid the "90 percent recovery test" for the lessee while satisfying it for the lessor. Two of the factors involved in this effort are: (1) the use of the incremental borrowing rate by the lessee when it is higher than the implicit interest rate of the lessor, by making information about the implicit rate unavailable to the lessee; and (2) residual value guarantees.

The lessee's use of the higher interest rate is probably the more popular subterfuge. Lessees are knowledgeable about the fair value of the leased property and, of course, the rental payments. However, they generally are unaware of the estimated residual value used by the lessor. Therefore, the lessee who does not know exactly the lessor's implicit interest rate might use a different (higher) incremental borrowing rate.

The residual value guarantee is the other unique, yet popular, device used by lessees and lessors. In fact, a whole new industry has emerged to circumvent symmetry between the lessee and the lessor in accounting for leases. The residual value guarantee has spawned numerous companies whose principal, or even sole, function is to guarantee the residual value of leased assets.

Because the minimum lease payments include the guaranteed residual value for the lessor, this satisfies the 90 percent recovery of fair market value test. The lease is a nonoperating lease to the lessor. **But because a third-party guarantees the residual value, the minimum lease payments of the lessee exclude the guarantee.** Thus, by merely transferring some of the risk to a third party, lessees can alter substantially the accounting treatment by converting what would otherwise be capital leases to operating leases.[18]

The nature of the criteria encourages much of this circumvention, stemming from weaknesses in the basic objective of the lease-accounting guidelines. Accounting rule-makers continue to have poor experience with arbitrary break points or other size and percentage criteria—such as rules like "90 percent of" and "75 percent of." Some believe that a more workable solution is to require capitalization of all leases that have noncancelable payment terms in excess of one year. Under this approach, lessee acquires an asset (a property right) and a corresponding liability, rather than on the basis that the lease transfers substantially all the risks and rewards of ownership.

Three years after it issued a lease-accounting pronouncement, a majority of the FASB expressed "the tentative view that, if the lease-accounting rules were to be reconsidered, they would support a property right approach in which all leases are included as 'rights to use property' and as 'lease obligations' in the lessee's balance sheet."[19] The FASB and other international standard-setters have issued a report on lease accounting that proposes the capitalization of more leases.[20]

> **INTERNATIONAL INSIGHT**
>
> Recently the IASB and the FASB have agreed to jointly undertake a project to reconsider lease-accounting standards.

---

[18]As an aside, third-party guarantors have experienced some difficulty. Lloyd's of London, at one time, insured the fast-growing U.S. computer-leasing industry in the amount of $2 billion against revenue losses, and losses in residual value, for canceled leases. Because of "overnight" technological improvements and the successive introductions of more efficient and less expensive computers, lessees in abundance canceled their leases. As the market for second-hand computers became flooded, residual values plummeted, and third-party guarantor Lloyd's of London projected a loss of $400 million. The lessees' and lessors' desire to circumvent GAAP stimulated much of the third-party guarantee business.

[19]"Is Lessee Accounting Working?" op. cit., p. 19.

[20]H. Nailor and A. Lennard, "Capital Leases: Implementation of a New Approach," *Financial Accounting Series No. 206A* (Norwalk, Conn.: FASB, 2000). See *http://www.fasb.org/project/leases.shtml* for the latest information on the lease-accounting project.

SWAP MEET

*What do the
numbers mean?*

Telecommunication companies have developed one of the more innovative and controversial uses of leases. In order to provide fiber-optic service to their customers in areas where they did not have networks installed, telecommunication companies such as **Global Crossing**, **Qwest Communications International**, and **Cable and Wireless** entered into agreements to swap some of their unused network capacity in exchange for the use of another company's fiber-optic cables. Here's how it works:

Such trades seem like a good way to make efficient use of telecommunication assets. What got some telecommunications companies in trouble, though, was how they did the accounting for the swap.

The most conservative accounting for the capacity trades is to treat the swap as an exchange of assets, which does not affect the income statement. However, Global Crossing got into trouble with the SEC when it structured some of its capacity swaps as leases—the legal right to use capacity. Global Crossing was recognizing as revenue the payments received for the outgoing transfer of capacity, while payments for the incoming cable capacity were treated as capital expenditures, and therefore not expensed. As a result, Global Crossing was showing strong profits from its capacity swaps. However, the company's investors got an unpleasant surprise when the market for bandwidth cooled off and there was no longer demand for its broadband capacity or its long-term leasing arrangements.

Source: Simon Romero and Seth Schiesel, "The Fiber-Optic Fantasy Slips Away," *New York Times on the Web* (February 17, 2002). By permission.

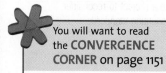

You will want to read the **CONVERGENCE CORNER** on page 1151

For discussion of how international convergence efforts relate to lease accounting.

CONVERGENCE CORNER

LEASE ACCOUNTING

Leasing is a global business. Lessors and lessees enter into arrangements with one another without regard to national boundaries. Although U.S. GAAP and iGAAP for leasing are similar, both the FASB and the IASB have decided that the existing accounting does not provide the most useful, transparent, and complete information about leasing transactions that should be provided in the financial statements.

❈ RELEVANT FACTS

• Leasing was on the FASB's initial agenda in 1973 and *SFAS No. 13* was issued in 1976 (before the conceptual framework was developed). *SFAS No. 13* has been the subject of more than 30 interpretations since its issuance.

• The iGAAP leasing standard is *IAS 17*, first issued in 1982. This standard is the subject of only three interpretations. One reason for this small number of interpretations is that iGAAP does not specifically address a number of leasing transactions that are covered by U.S. GAAP. Examples include lease agreements for natural resources, sale-leasebacks, real estate leases, and leveraged leases.

• Both U.S. GAAP and iGAAP share the same objective of recording leases by lessees and lessors according to their economic substance—that is, according to the definitions of assets and liabilities.

• U.S. GAAP for leases in much more "rule-based" with specific bright-line criteria to determine if a lease arrangement transfers the risks and rewards of ownership; iGAAP is more general in its provisions.

❈ ABOUT THE NUMBERS

One illustration of the differences between U.S. GAAP and iGAAP for leases involves disclosure policy. Under U.S. GAAP, extensive disclosure of future noncancelable lease payments is required for the next five years and the years thereafter. Under iGAAP, not as much detail is required, as shown in the sample disclosure below.

iGAAP Sample Lease Note Disclosure

Note 38 Leasing arrangements (*in part*) Finance leases relate to manufacturing equipment with lease terms of 5 years. The Group has options to purchase the equipment for a nominal amount at the conclusion of the lease agreements. The Group's obligations under finance leases are secured by the lessors' title to the leased assets.

Finance lease liabilities
(euros, 000,000)

	Minimum lease payments, 31/12/08
No later than 1 year	€ 58
Later than 1 year and not later than 5 years	44
Later than 5 years	—
	102
Less: Future finance charges	13
Present value of minimum lease payments	€ 89

Although some international companies (e.g., **Nokia**) provide a year-by-year breakout of payments due in years 1 through 5, iGAAP does not require it.

❈ ON THE HORIZON

Lease accounting is one of the areas identified in the IASB/FASB Memorandum of Understanding and also a topic recommended by the SEC in its off-balance-sheet study for standard-setting attention. It was formally added to the agenda of the FASB and IASB as a joint project in 2006. The joint project will initially focus primarily on lessee accounting. One of the first areas to be studied is, "What are the assets and liabilities to be recognized related to a lease contract?" Should the focus remain on the leased item or the right to use the leased item? This question is tied to the Boards' joint project on the conceptual framework—defining an "asset" and a "liability."

The Boards began deliberations of lease-accounting issues in 2007. Those deliberations will result in issuing a discussion paper for public comment, to be published in 2008, that explores those issues and describes the preliminary views of both Boards. You can follow the lease project at either the FASB (*http://www.fasb.org/project/leases.shtml*) or IASB (*http://www.iasb.org/Current+Projects/IASB+Projects/Leases/Leases.htm*) websites.

SUMMARY OF LEARNING OBJECTIVES

•1 Explain the nature, economic substance, and advantages of lease transactions. A lease is a contractual agreement between a lessor and a lessee that conveys to the lessee the right to use specific property (real or personal), owned by the lessor, for a specified period of time. In return, the lessee periodically pays cash (rent) to the lessor. The advantages of lease transactions are: (1) 100 percent financing; (2) protection against obsolescence, (3) flexibility, (4) less costly financing, (5) possible tax advantages, and (6) off-balance-sheet financing.

•2 Describe the accounting criteria and procedures for capitalizing leases by the lessee. A lease is a capital lease if it meets one or more of the following (Group I) criteria: (1) The lease transfers ownership of the property to the lessee. (2) The lease contains a bargain-purchase option. (3) The lease term is equal to 75 percent or more of the estimated economic life of the leased property. (4) The present value of the minimum lease payments (excluding executory costs) equals or exceeds 90 percent of the fair value of the leased property. For a capital lease, the lessee records an asset and a liability at the lower of (1) the present value of the minimum lease payments, or (2) the fair market value of the leased asset at the inception of the lease.

•3 Contrast the operating and capitalization methods of recording leases. The total charges to operations are the same over the lease term whether accounting for the lease as a capital lease or as an operating lease. Under the capital lease treatment, the charges are higher in the earlier years and lower in the later years. If using an accelerated method of depreciation, the differences between the amounts charged to operations under the two methods would be even larger in the earlier and later years. If using a capital lease instead of an operating lease, the following occurs: (1) an increase in the amount of reported debt (both short-term and long-term), (2) an increase in the amount of total assets (specifically long-lived assets), and (3) lower income early in the life of the lease and, therefore, lower retained earnings.

•4 Identify the classifications of leases for the lessor. A lessor may classify leases for accounting purposes as follows: (1) operating leases, (2) direct-financing leases, (3) sales-type leases. The lessor should classify and account for an arrangement as a direct-financing lease or a sales-type lease if, at the date of the lease agreement, the lease meets one or more of the Group I criteria (as shown in learning objective 2 for lessees) and *both* of the following Group II criteria. *Group II:* (1) Collectibility of the payments required from the lessee is reasonably predictable; and (2) no important uncertainties surround the amount of unreimbursable costs yet to be incurred by the lessor under the lease. The lessor classifies and accounts for all leases that fail to meet the criteria as operating leases.

•5 Describe the lessor's accounting for direct-financing leases. Leases that are in substance the financing of an asset purchase by a lessee require the lessor to substitute a "lease receivable" for the leased asset. "Lease receivable" is the present value of the minimum lease payments plus the present value of the unguaranteed residual value. Therefore lessors include the residual value, whether guaranteed or unguaranteed, as part of lease receivable.

•6 Identify special features of lease arrangements that cause unique accounting problems. The features of lease arrangements that cause unique accounting problems are: (1) residual values; (2) sales-type leases (lessor); (3) bargain-purchase options; (4) initial direct costs; (5) current versus noncurrent; and (6) disclosures.

•7 **Describe the effect of residual values, guaranteed and unguaranteed, on lease accounting.** Whether the estimated residual value is guaranteed or unguaranteed is of both economic and accounting consequence to the lessee. The accounting consequence is that the minimum lease payments, the basis for capitalization, include the guaranteed residual value but exclude the unguaranteed residual value. A guaranteed residual value affects the lessee's computation of minimum lease payments and the amounts capitalized as a leased asset and a lease obligation. In effect, the guaranteed residual value is an additional lease payment that the lessee will pay in property or cash, or both, at the end of the lease term. An unguaranteed residual value from the lessee's viewpoint is the same as no residual value in terms of its effect upon the lessee's method of computing the minimum lease payments and the capitalization of the leased asset and the lease liability.

•8 **Describe the lessor's accounting for sales-type leases.** A sales-type lease recognizes interest revenue like a direct-financing lease. It also recognizes a manufacturer's or dealer's profit. In a sales-type lease, the lessor records at the inception of the lease the sales price of the asset, the cost of goods sold and related inventory reduction, and the lease receivable. Sales-type leases differ from direct-financing leases in terms of the cost and fair value of the leased asset, which results in gross profit. Lease receivable and interest revenue are the same whether a guaranteed or an unguaranteed residual value is involved. The accounting for guaranteed and for unguaranteed residual values requires recording sales revenue and cost of goods sold differently. The guaranteed residual value can be considered part of sales revenue because the lessor knows that the entire asset has been sold. There is less certainty that the unguaranteed residual portion of the asset has been "sold"; therefore, lessors recognize sales and cost of goods sold only for the portion of the asset for which realization is assured. However, the gross profit amount on the sale of the asset is the same whether a guaranteed or unguaranteed residual value is involved.

•9 **List the disclosure requirements for leases.** The disclosure requirements for the lessees and lessors vary based upon the type of lease (capital or operating) and whether the issuer is the lessor or lessee. These disclosure requirements provide investors with the following information: (1) general description of the nature of leasing arrangements, (2) the nature, timing and amount of cash inflows and outflows associated with leases, including payments to be paid or received for each of the five succeeding years, (3) the amount of lease revenues and expenses reported in the income statement each period, (4) description and amounts of leased assets by major balance sheet classification and related liabilities, and (5) amounts receivable and unearned revenues under lease agreements.

Expanded Discussion of Real Estate Leases and Leveraged Leases

---

| APPENDIX **21A** | **EXAMPLES OF LEASE ARRANGEMENTS** |

To illustrate concepts discussed in this chapter, assume that Morgan Bakeries is involved in four different lease situations. Each of these leases is noncancelable, and in no case does Morgan receive title to the properties leased during or at the end of the lease term. All leases start on January 1, 2011, with the first rental due at the beginning of the year. The additional information is shown in Illustration 21A-1 (on page 1154).

> **Objective•10**
> Understand and apply lease-accounting concepts to various lease arrangements.

	Harmon, Inc.	Arden's Oven Co.	Mendota Truck Co.	Appleland Computer
Type of property	Cabinets	Oven	Truck	Computer
Yearly rental	$6,000	$15,000	$5,582.62	$3,557.25
Lease term	20 years	10 years	3 years	3 years
Estimated economic life	30 years	25 years	7 years	5 years
Purchase option	None	$75,000 at end of 10 years $4,000 at end of 15 years	None	$3,000 at end of 3 years, which approximates fair market value
Renewal option	None	5-year renewal option at $15,000 per year	None	1 year at $1,500; no penalty for nonrenewal; standard renewal clause
Fair market value at inception of lease	$60,000	$120,000	$20,000	$10,000
Cost of asset to lessor	$60,000	$120,000	$15,000	$10,000
Residual value				
Guaranteed	–0–	–0–	$7,000	–0–
Unguaranteed	$5,000	–0–	–0–	$3,000
Incremental borrowing rate of lessee	12%	12%	12%	12%
Executory costs paid by	*Lessee* $300 per year	*Lessee* $1,000 per year	*Lessee* $500 per year	*Lessor* Estimated to be $500 per year
Present value of minimum lease payments				
Using incremental borrowing rate of lessee	$50,194.68	$115,153.35	$20,000	$8,224.16
Using implicit rate of lessor	Not known	Not known	Not known	Known by lessee, $8,027.48
Estimated fair market value at end of lease	$5,000	$80,000 at end of 10 years $60,000 at end of 15 years	Not available	$3,000

ILLUSTRATION 21A-1
Illustrative Lease
Situations, Lessors

EXAMPLE 1: HARMON, INC.

The following is an analysis of the Harmon, Inc. lease.

1. **Transfer of title?** No.
2. **Bargain-purchase option?** No.
3. **Economic life test (75% test).** The lease term is 20 years and the estimated economic life is 30 years. Thus it **does not** meet the 75 percent test.
4. **Recovery of investment test (90% test):**

Fair market value	$60,000	Rental payments	$	6,000
Rate	× 90%	PV of annuity due for		
90% of fair market value	$54,000	20 years at 12%		× 8.36578
		PV of rental payments		$50,194.68

Because the present value of the minimum lease payments is less than 90 percent of the fair market value, the lease does not meet the 90 percent test.

Both Morgan and Harmon should account for this lease as an operating lease, as indicated by the January 1, 2011, entries shown in Illustration 21A-2 (on page 1155).

| Morgan Bakeries | | | Harmon, Inc. | | |
(Lessee)			(Lessor)		
Rent Expense	6,000		Cash	6,000	
Cash		6,000	Rental Revenue		6,000

ILLUSTRATION 21A-2
Comparative Entries for
Operating Lease

EXAMPLE 2: ARDEN'S OVEN CO.

The following is an analysis of the Arden's Oven Co. lease.

1. **Transfer of title?** No.
2. **Bargain-purchase option?** The $75,000 option at the end of 10 years does not appear to be sufficiently lower than the expected fair value of $80,000 to make it reasonably assured that it will be exercised. However, the $4,000 at the end of 15 years when the fair value is $60,000 does appear to be a bargain. From the information given, criterion 2 is therefore met. Note that both the guaranteed and the unguaranteed residual values are assigned zero values because the lessor does not expect to repossess the leased asset.
3. **Economic life test (75% test):** Given that a bargain-purchase option exists, the lease term is the initial lease period of 10 years plus the five-year renewal option since it precedes a bargain-purchase option. Even though the lease term is now considered to be 15 years, this test is still not met because 75 percent of the economic life of 25 years is 18.75 years.
4. **Recovery of investment test (90% test):**

Fair market value	$120,000		Rental payments	$ 15,000.00
Rate	× 90%		PV of annuity due for	
90% of fair market value	$108,000		15 years at 12%	× 7.62817
			PV of rental payments	$114,422.55

PV of bargain-purchase option: = $4,000 × (PVF$_{15,12\%}$) = $4,000 × .18270 = $730.80

PV of rental payments	$114,422.55
PV of bargain-purchase option	730.80
PV of minimum lease payments	$115,153.35

The present value of the minimum lease payments is greater than 90 percent of the fair market value; therefore, the lease does meet the 90 percent test.

Morgan Bakeries should account for this as a capital lease because the lease meets both criteria 2 and 4. Assuming that Arden's implicit rate is less than Morgan's incremental borrowing rate, the following entries are made on January 1, 2011.

| Morgan Bakeries | | | Arden's Oven Co. | | |
(Lessee)			(Lessor)		
Leased Asset—Oven	115,153.35		Lease Receivable	120,000	
Lease Liability		115,153.35	Asset—Oven		120,000

ILLUSTRATION 21A-3
Comparative Entries for
Capital Lease—Bargain-
Purchase Option

Morgan Bakeries would depreciate the leased asset over its economic life of 25 years, given the bargain-purchase option. Arden's Oven Co. does not use sales-type accounting because the fair market value and the cost of the asset are the same at the inception of the lease.

EXAMPLE 3: MENDOTA TRUCK CO.

The following is an analysis of the Mendota Truck Co. lease.

1. **Transfer of title?** No.
2. **Bargain-purchase option?** No.

3. **Economic life test (75% test):** The lease term is three years and the estimated economic life is seven years. Thus it **does not** meet the 75 percent test.

4. **Recovery of investment test (90% test):**

Fair market value	$20,000	Rental payments	$ 5,582.62
Rate	× 90%	PV of annuity due for	
90% of fair market value	$18,000	3 years at 12%	× 2.69005
		PV of rental payments	$15,017.54

(Note: Adjusted for $0.01 due to rounding)

PV of guaranteed residual value: = $7,000 × (PVF$_{3,12\%}$) = $7,000 × .71178 = $4,982.46

PV of rental payments	$15,017.54
PV of guaranteed residual value	4,982.46
PV of minimum lease payments	$20,000.00

The present value of the minimum lease payments is greater than 90 percent of the fair market value; therefore, the lease meets the 90 percent test.

Assuming that Mendota's implicit rate is the same as Morgan's incremental borrowing rate, the following entries are made on January 1, 2011.

ILLUSTRATION 21A-4
Comparative Entries for
Capital Lease

Morgan Bakeries (Lessee)			Mendota Truck Co. (Lessor)		
Leased Asset—Truck	20,000		Lease Receivable	20,000	
Lease Liability		20,000	Cost of Goods Sold	15,000	
			Inventory—Truck		15,000
			Sales		20,000

Morgan depreciates the leased asset over three years to its guaranteed residual value.

EXAMPLE 4: APPLELAND COMPUTER

The following is an analysis of the Appleland Computer lease.

1. **Transfer of title?** No.

2. **Bargain-purchase option?** No. The option to purchase at the end of three years at approximate fair market value is clearly not a bargain.

3. **Economic life test (75% test):** The lease term is three years, and no bargain-renewal period exists. Therefore the 75 percent test **is not** met.

4. **Recovery of investment test (90% test):**

Fair market value	$10,000	Rental payments	$3,557.25
Rate	× 90%	Less executory costs	500.00
90% of fair market value	$ 9,000		3,057.25
		PV of annuity-due factor for	
		3 years at 12%	× 2.69005
		PV of minimum lease payments	
		using incremental borrowing rate	$8,224.16

The present value of the minimum lease payments using the incremental borrowing rate is $8,224.16; using the implicit rate, it is $8,027.48 (see Illustration 21A-1 on page 1154). The lessor's implicit rate is therefore higher than the incremental borrowing rate. Given this situation, the lessee uses the $8,224.16 (lower interest rate when discounting) when comparing with the 90 percent of fair market value. Because the present value of the minimum lease payments is lower than 90 percent of the fair market value, the lease does **not** meet the recovery of investment test.

The following entries are made on January 1, 2011, indicating an operating lease.

Morgan Bakeries (Lessee)		Appleland Computer (Lessor)	
Rent Expense	3,557.25	Cash	3,557.25
Cash	3,557.25	Rental Revenue	3,557.25

If the lease payments had been $3,557.25 with no executory costs involved, this lease arrangement would have qualified for capital-lease accounting treatment.

SUMMARY OF LEARNING OBJECTIVE FOR APPENDIX 21A

•10 **Understand and apply lease-accounting concepts to various lease arrangements.** The classification of leases by lessees and lessors is based on criteria that assess whether the lessor has transferred to the lessee substantially all of the risks and benefits of ownership of the asset. In addition, lessors assess two additional criteria to ensure that payment is assured and that there are not uncertainties about lessor's future costs. Lessees capitalize leases that meet any of the criteria, recording a lease asset and related lease liability. For leases that are in substance a financing of an asset purchase, lessors substitute a lease receivable for the leased asset. In a sales-type lease, the fair value of the leased asset is greater than the cost, and lessors record gross profit. Leases that do not meet capitalization criteria are classified as operating leases, on which rent expense (revenue) is recognized by lessees (lessors) for lease payments.

APPENDIX 21B SALE-LEASEBACKS

The term **sale-leaseback** describes a transaction in which the owner of the property (seller-lessee) sells the property to another and simultaneously leases it back from the new owner. The use of the property is generally continued without interruption.

Sale-leasebacks are common. Financial institutions (e.g., **Bank of America** and **First Chicago**) have used this technique for their administrative offices, public utilities (**Ohio Edison** and **Pinnacle West Corporation**) for their generating plants, and airlines (**Continental** and **Alaska Airlines**) for their aircraft. The advantages of a sale-leaseback from the seller's viewpoint usually involve two primary considerations:

> **Objective•11**
> Describe the lessee's accounting for sale-leaseback transactions.

1. *Financing*—If the purchase of equipment has already been financed, a sale-lease-back can allow the seller to refinance at lower rates, assuming rates have dropped. In addition, a sale-leaseback can provide another source of working capital, particularly when liquidity is tight.
2. *Taxes*—At the time a company purchased equipment, it may not have known that it would be subject to an alternative minimum tax and that ownership might increase its minimum tax liability. By selling the property, the seller-lessee may deduct the entire lease payment, which is not subject to alternative minimum tax considerations.

DETERMINING ASSET USE

To the extent the **seller-lessee continues to use** the asset after the sale, the sale-lease-back is really a form of financing. Therefore the lessor **should not recognize a gain or loss** on the transaction. In short, the seller-lessee is simply borrowing funds.

Underlying Concepts

A sale-leaseback is similar in substance to the parking of inventories (discussed in Chapter 8). The ultimate economic benefits remain under the control of the "seller," thus satisfying the definition of an asset.

On the other hand, if the **seller-lessee gives up the right to the use** of the asset, the transaction is in substance a sale. In that case, **gain or loss recognition** is appropriate. Trying to ascertain when the lessee has given up the use of the asset is difficult, however, and the FASB has formulated complex rules to identify this situation.[21] To understand the profession's position in this area, we discuss the basic accounting for the lessee and lessor below.

Lessee

If the lease meets one of the four criteria for treatment as a capital lease (see Illustration 21-3 on page 1121), the **seller-lessee accounts for the transaction as a sale and the lease as a capital lease**. The seller-lessee should defer any profit or loss it experiences from the sale of the assets that are leased back under a capital lease; it should **amortize that profit over the lease term** (or the economic life if either criterion 1 or 2 is satisfied) in proportion to the amortization of the leased assets.

For example, assume **Scott Paper** sells equipment having a book value of $580,000 and a fair value of $623,110 to **General Electric Credit** for $623,110 and leases the equipment back for $50,000 a year for 20 years. Scott should amortize the profit of $43,110 over the 20-year period at the same rate that it depreciates the $623,110. [12] It credits the $43,110 ($623,110 − $580,000) to **Unearned Profit on Sale-Leaseback**.

If none of the capital lease criteria are satisfied, **the seller-lessee accounts for the transaction as a sale and the lease as an operating lease**. Under an operating lease, the lessee defers such profit or loss and amortizes it in proportion to the rental payments over the period when it expects to use the assets.

There are exceptions to these two general rules. They are:

1. *Losses Recognized*—When the fair value of the asset is **less than the book value** (carrying amount), the lessee must recognize a loss immediately, up to the amount of the difference between the book value and fair value. For example, if Lessee, Inc. sells equipment having a book value of $650,000 and a fair value of $623,110, it should charge the difference of $26,890 to a loss account.[22]

2. *Minor Leaseback*—Leasebacks in which the present value of the rental payments are 10 percent or less of the fair value of the asset are **minor leasebacks**. In this case, the seller-lessee gives up most of the rights to the use of the asset sold. Therefore, the transaction is a sale, and full gain or loss recognition is appropriate. It is not a financing transaction because the risks of ownership have been transferred.[23]

Lessor

If the lease meets one of the criteria in Group I and both of the criteria in Group II (see Illustration 21-10 on page 1131), the **purchaser-lessor** records the transaction as a purchase and a direct-financing lease. If the lease does not meet the criteria, the purchaser-lessor records the transaction as a purchase and an operating lease.

SALE-LEASEBACK EXAMPLE

To illustrate the accounting treatment accorded a sale-leaseback transaction, assume that **American Airlines** on January 1, 2011, sells a used Boeing 757 having a carrying

---

[21]Sales and leasebacks of real estate are often accounted for differently. A discussion of the issues related to these transactions is beyond the scope of this textbook. [11]

[22]There can be two types of losses in sale-leaseback arrangements. One is a **real economic loss** that results when the carrying amount of the asset is higher than the fair market value of the asset. In this case, the loss should be recognized. An **artificial loss** results when the sale price is below the carrying amount of the asset but the fair market value is above the carrying amount. In this case the loss is more in the form of prepaid rent, and the lessee should defer the loss and amortize it in the future.

[23]In some cases the seller-lessee retains more than a minor part but less than substantially all. The computations to arrive at these values are complex and beyond the scope of this textbook.

amount on its books of $75,500,000 to **CitiCapital** for $80,000,000. American immediately leases the aircraft back under the following conditions:

1. The term of the lease is 15 years, noncancelable, and requires equal rental payments of $10,487,443 at the beginning of each year.
2. The aircraft has a fair value of $80,000,000 on January 1, 2011, and an estimated economic life of 15 years.
3. American pays all executory costs.
4. American depreciates similar aircraft that it owns on a straight-line basis over 15 years.
5. The annual payments assure the lessor a 12 percent return.
6. American's incremental borrowing rate is 12 percent.

This lease is a capital lease to American because the lease term exceeds 75 percent of the estimated life of the aircraft and because the present value of the lease payments exceeds 90 percent of the fair value of the aircraft to CitiCapital. Assuming that collectibility of the lease payments is reasonably predictable and that no important uncertainties exist in relation to unreimbursable costs yet to be incurred by CitiCapital, it should classify this lease as a direct-financing lease.

Illustration 21B-1 presents the typical journal entries to record the sale-leaseback transactions for American and CitiCapital for the first year.

ILLUSTRATION 21B-1
Comparative Entries for Sale-Leaseback for Lessee and Lessor

American Airlines (Lessee)			CitiCapital (Lessor)		
Sale of Aircraft by American to CitiCapital (January 1, 2011):					
Cash	80,000,000		Aircraft	80,000,000	
Aircraft		75,500,000	Cash		80,000,000
Unearned Profit on Sale-Leaseback		4,500,000	Lease Receivable	80,000,000	
Leased Aircraft under Capital Leases	80,000,000		Aircraft		80,000,000
Lease Liability		80,000,000			
First Lease Payment (January 1, 2011):					
Lease Liability	10,487,443		Cash	10,487,443	
Cash		10,487,443	Lease Receivable		10,487,443
Incurrence and Payment of Executory Costs by American Corp. throughout 2011:					
Insurance, Maintenance, Taxes, etc.	XXX		(No entry)		
Cash or Accounts Payable		XXX			
Depreciation Expense on the Aircraft (December 31, 2011):					
Depreciation Expense	5,333,333		(No entry)		
Accumulated Depr.— Capital Leases ($80,000,000 ÷ 15)		5,333,333			
Amortization of Profit on Sale-Leaseback by American (December 31, 2011):					
Unearned Profit on Sale-Leaseback	300,000		(No entry)		
Depreciation Expense ($4,500,000 ÷ 15)		300,000			

Note: A case might be made for crediting Revenue instead of Depreciation Expense.

Interest for 2011 (December 31, 2011):					
Interest Expense	8,341,507[a]		Interest Receivable	8,341,507	
Interest Payable		8,341,507	Interest Revenue		8,341,507[a]

[a]Partial Lease Amortization Schedule:

Date	Annual Rental Payment	Interest 12%	Reduction of Balance	Balance
1/1/11				$80,000,000
1/1/11	$10,487,443	$ –0–	$10,487,443	69,512,557
1/1/12	10,487,443	8,341,507	2,145,936	67,366,621

SUMMARY OF LEARNING OBJECTIVE FOR APPENDIX 21B

•11 **Describe the lessee's accounting for sale-leaseback transactions.** If the lease meets one of the four criteria for treatment as a capital lease, the seller-lessee accounts for the transaction as a sale and the lease as a capital lease. The seller-lessee defers any profit it experiences from the sale of the assets that are leased back under a capital lease. The seller-lessee amortizes any profit over the lease term (or the economic life if either criterion 1 or 2 is satisfied) in proportion to the amortization of the leased assets. If the lease satisfies none of the capital lease criteria, the seller-lessee accounts for the transaction as a sale and the lease as an operating lease. Under an operating lease, the lessee defers such profit and amortizes it in proportion to the rental payments over the period of time that it expects to use the assets.

FASB CODIFICATION

FASB Codification References

[1] FASB ASC 840-10-25-1. [Predecessor literature: "Accounting for Leases," *FASB Statement No. 13* as amended and interpreted through May 1980 (Stamford, Conn.: FASB, 1980), par. 7.]

[2] FASB ASC 840-10-25. [Predecessor literature: "Accounting for Leases: Sale-Leaseback Transactions Involving Real Estate; Sales-Type Leases of Real Estate; Definition of the Lease Term; Initial Direct Costs of Direct Financing Leases," *Statement of Financial Accounting Standards No. 98* (Stamford, Conn.: FASB, 1988).]

[3] FASB ASC 840-10-25-9. [Predecessor literature: "Lessee Guarantee of the Residual Value of Leased Property," *FASB Interpretation No. 19* (Stamford, Conn.: FASB, 1977), par. 3.]

[4] FASB ASC 840-10-25-22. [Predecessor literature: "Accounting for Leases," *FASB Statement No. 13* as amended and interpreted through May 1980 (Stamford, Conn.: FASB, 1980), par. 5 (l).]

[5] FASB ASC 840-10-25-31. [Predecessor literature: "Accounting for Leases," *FASB Statement No. 13* as amended and interpreted through May 1980 (Stamford, Conn.: FASB, 1980), par. 5 (k).]

[6] FASB ASC 840-30-35-14. [Predecessor literature: "Accounting for Purchase of a Leased Asset by the Lessee During the Term of the Lease," *FASB Interpretation No. 26* (Stamford, Conn.: FASB, 1978), par. 5.]

[7] FASB ASC 840-10-25-43. [Predecessor literature: "Accounting for Leases," *FASB Statement No. 13* as amended and interpreted through May 1980 (Stamford, Conn.: FASB, 1980), pars. 6, 7, and 8.]

[8] FASB ASC 840-30-30-12. [Predecessor literature: "Accounting for Nonrefundable Fees and Costs Associated with Originating or Acquiring Loans and Initial Direct Costs of Leases," *Statement of Financial Accounting Standards No. 91* (Stamford: Conn.: FASB, 1987).]

[9] FASB ASC 840-30-50-1. [Predecessor literature: "Accounting for Leases," *FASB Statement No. 13* as amended and interpreted through May 1980 (Stamford, Conn.: FASB, 1980), par. 16.]

[10] FASB ASC 840-30-50-4. [Predecessor literature: "Accounting for Leases," *FASB Statement No. 13* as amended and interpreted through May 1980 (Stamford, Conn.: FASB, 1980), par. 16; par. 23.]

[11] FASB ASC 840-40. [Predecessor literature: "Accounting for Leases: Sale-Leaseback Transactions Involving Real Estate; Sales-Type Leases of Real Estate; Definition of the Lease Term; Initial Direct Costs of Direct Financing Leases," *Statement of Financial Accounting Standards No. 98* (Stamford, Conn.: FASB, 1988).]

[12] FASB ASC 840-40. [Predecessor literature: *Statement of Financial Accounting Standards No. 28*, "Accounting for Sales with Leasebacks" (Stamford, Conn.: FASB, 1979).]

Exercises

Access the FASB Codification at *http://asc.fasb.org/home* to prepare responses to the following exercises. Provide Codification references for your responses.

CE21-1 Access the glossary ("Master Glossary") to answer the following.

(a) What is a bargain-purchase option?
(b) What is the definition of "incremental borrowing rate"?
(c) What is the definition of "estimated residual value"?
(d) What is an unguaranteed residual value?

CE21-2 What comprises a lessee's minimum lease payments? What is excluded?

CE21-3 What information should a lessee disclose about its capital leases in its financial statements and footnotes?

CE21-4 How should a lessor measure its initial gross investment in either a sales-type lease or a direct-financing lease?

An additional Codification case can be found in the Using Your Judgment section, on page 1179.

Be sure to check the companion website for a Review and Analysis Exercise, with solution.

Note: All asterisked Questions, Exercises, and Problems relate to material in the appendices to the chapter.

QUESTIONS

1. What are the major lessor groups in the United States? What advantage does a captive have in a leasing arrangement?

2. Bradley Co. is expanding its operations and is in the process of selecting the method of financing this program. After some investigation, the company determines that it may (1) issue bonds and with the proceeds purchase the needed assets or (2) lease the assets on a long-term basis. Without knowing the comparative costs involved, answer these questions:

   (a) What might be the advantages of leasing the assets instead of owning them?

   (b) What might be the disadvantages of leasing the assets instead of owning them?

   (c) In what way will the balance sheet be differently affected by leasing the assets as opposed to issuing bonds and purchasing the assets?

3. Identify the two recognized lease-accounting methods for lessees and distinguish between them.

4. Ballard Company rents a warehouse on a month-to-month basis for the storage of its excess inventory. The company periodically must rent space whenever its production greatly exceeds actual sales. For several years the company officials have discussed building their own storage facility, but this enthusiasm wavers when sales increase sufficiently to absorb the excess inventory. What is the nature of this type of lease arrangement, and what accounting treatment should be accorded it?

5. Distinguish between minimum rental payments and minimum lease payments, and indicate what is included in minimum lease payments.

6. Explain the distinction between a direct-financing lease and a sales-type lease for a lessor.

7. Outline the accounting procedures involved in applying the operating method by a lessee.

8. Outline the accounting procedures involved in applying the capital-lease method by a lessee.

9. Identify the lease classifications for lessors and the criteria that must be met for each classification.

10. Outline the accounting procedures involved in applying the direct-financing method.

11. Outline the accounting procedures involved in applying the operating method by a lessor.

12. Walker Company is a manufacturer and lessor of computer equipment. What should be the nature of its lease arrangements with lessees if the company wishes to account for its lease transactions as sales-type leases?

13. Metheny Corporation's lease arrangements qualify as sales-type leases at the time of entering into the transactions. How should the corporation recognize revenues and costs in these situations?

14. Alice Foyle, M.D. (lessee) has a noncancelable 20-year lease with Brownback Realty, Inc. (lessor) for the use of a medical building. Taxes, insurance, and maintenance are paid by the lessee in addition to the fixed annual payments, of which the present value is equal to the fair market value of the leased property. At the end of the lease period, title becomes the lessee's at a nominal price. Considering the terms of the lease described above, comment on the nature of the lease transaction and the accounting treatment that should be accorded it by the lessee.

15. The residual value is the estimated fair value of the leased property at the end of the lease term.

(a) Of what significance is (1) an unguaranteed and (2) a guaranteed residual value in the lessee's accounting for a capitalized-lease transaction?

(b) Of what significance is (1) an unguaranteed and (2) a guaranteed residual value in the lessor's accounting for a direct-financing lease transaction?

16. How should changes in the estimated unguaranteed residual value be handled by the lessor?

17. Describe the effect of a "bargain-purchase option" on accounting for a capital-lease transaction by a lessee.

18. What are "initial direct costs" and how are they accounted for?

19. What disclosures should be made by lessees and lessors related to future lease payments?

20. Where can authoritative iGAAP guidance related to leases be found?

21. Briefly describe some of the similarities and differences between U.S. GAAP and iGAAP with respect to the accounting for leases.

22. Both iGAAP and U.S. GAAP require footnote disclosure of operating lease payments. Are there any differences in the information provided to statement readers in these disclosures? Explain.

23. Briefly discuss the IASB and FASB efforts to converge their accounting guidelines for leases.

*24. What is the nature of a "sale-leaseback" transaction?

BRIEF EXERCISES

·2 BE21-1 **Callaway Golf Co.** leases telecommunication equipment. Assume the following data for equipment leased from Photon Company. The lease term is 5 years and requires equal rental payments of $31,000 at the beginning of each year. The equipment has a fair value at the inception of the lease of $138,000, an estimated useful life of 8 years, and no residual value. Callaway pays all executory costs directly to third parties. Photon set the annual rental to earn a rate of return of 10%, and this fact is known to Callaway. The lease does not transfer title or contain a bargain-purchase option. How should Callaway classify this lease?

·2 BE21-2 Waterworld Company leased equipment from Costner Company. The lease term is 4 years and requires equal rental payments of $43,019 at the beginning of each year. The equipment has a fair value at the inception of the lease of $150,000, an estimated useful life of 4 years, and no salvage value. Waterworld pays all executory costs directly to third parties. The appropriate interest rate is 10%. Prepare Waterworld's January 1, 2011, journal entries at the inception of the lease.

·2 BE21-3 Rick Kleckner Corporation recorded a capital lease at $300,000 on January 1, 2011. The interest rate is 12%. Kleckner Corporation made the first lease payment of $53,920 on January 1, 2011. The lease requires eight annual payments. The equipment has a useful life of 8 years with no salvage value. Prepare Kleckner Corporation's December 31, 2011, adjusting entries.

·2 BE21-4 Use the information for Rick Kleckner Corporation from BE21-3. Assume that at December 31, 2011, Kleckner made an adjusting entry to accrue interest expense of $29,530 on the lease. Prepare Kleckner's January 1, 2012, journal entry to record the second lease payment of $53,920.

·3 BE21-5 Jana Kingston Corporation enters into a lease on January 1, 2011, that does not transfer ownership or contain a bargain-purchase option. It covers 3 years of the equipment's 8-year useful life, and the present value of the minimum lease payments is less than 90% of the fair market value of the asset leased. Prepare Jana Kingston's journal entry to record its January 1, 2011, annual lease payment of $35,000.

·4 ·5 BE21-6 Assume that **IBM** leased equipment that was carried at a cost of $150,000 to Sharon Swander Company. The term of the lease is 6 years beginning January 1, 2011, with equal rental payments of $30,044 at the beginning of each year. All executory costs are paid by Swander directly to third parties. The fair value of the equipment at the inception of the lease is $150,000. The equipment has a useful life of 6 years with no salvage value. The lease has an implicit interest rate of 8%, no bargain-purchase option, and no transfer of title. Collectibility is reasonably assured with no additional cost to be incurred by IBM. Prepare IBM's January 1, 2011, journal entries at the inception of the lease.

BE21-7 Use the information for **IBM** from BE21-6. Assume the direct-financing lease was recorded at a present value of $150,000. Prepare IBM's December 31, 2011, entry to record interest.

BE21-8 Jennifer Brent Corporation owns equipment that cost $80,000 and has a useful life of 8 years with no salvage value. On January 1, 2011, Jennifer Brent leases the equipment to Donna Havaci Inc. for one year with one rental payment of $15,000 on January 1. Prepare Jennifer Brent Corporation's 2011 journal entries.

BE21-9 Indiana Jones Corporation enters into a 6-year lease of equipment on January 1, 2011, which requires 6 annual payments of $40,000 each, beginning January 1, 2011. In addition, Indiana Jones guarantees the lessor a residual value of $20,000 at lease-end. The equipment has a useful life of 6 years. Prepare Indiana Jones' January 1, 2011, journal entries assuming an interest rate of 10%.

BE21-10 Use the information for Indiana Jones Corporation from BE21-9. Assume that for Lost Ark Company, the lessor, collectibility is reasonably predictable, there are no important uncertainties concerning costs, and the carrying amount of the machinery is $202,921. Prepare Lost Ark's January 1, 2011, journal entries.

BE21-11 Geiberger Corporation manufactures replicators. On January 1, 2011, it leased to Althaus Company a replicator that had cost $110,000 to manufacture. The lease agreement covers the 5-year useful life of the replicator and requires 5 equal annual rentals of $40,800 payable each January 1, beginning January 1, 2011. An interest rate of 12% is implicit in the lease agreement. Collectibility of the rentals is reasonably assured, and there are no important uncertainties concerning costs. Prepare Geiberger's January 1, 2011, journal entries.

*BE21-12 On January 1, 2011, Irwin Animation sold a truck to Peete Finance for $33,000 and immediately leased it back. The truck was carried on Irwin's books at $28,000. The term of the lease is 5 years, and title transfers to Irwin at lease-end. The lease requires five equal rental payments of $8,705 at the end of each year. The appropriate rate of interest is 10%, and the truck has a useful life of 5 years with no salvage value. Prepare Irwin's 2011 journal entries.

EXERCISES

E21-1 (Lessee Entries, Capital Lease with Unguaranteed Residual Value) On January 1, 2011, Adams Corporation signed a 5-year noncancelable lease for a machine. The terms of the lease called for Adams to make annual payments of $9,968 at the beginning of each year, starting January 1, 2011. The machine has an estimated useful life of 6 years and a $5,000 unguaranteed residual value. The machine reverts back to the lessor at the end of the lease term. Adams uses the straight-line method of depreciation for all of its plant assets. Adams's incremental borrowing rate is 10%, and the Lessor's implicit rate is unknown.

Instructions
  (a) What type of lease is this? Explain.
  (b) Compute the present value of the minimum lease payments.
  (c) Prepare all necessary journal entries for Adams for this lease through January 1, 2012.

E21-2 (Lessee Computations and Entries, Capital Lease with Guaranteed Residual Value) Brecker Company leases an automobile with a fair value of $10,906 from Emporia Motors, Inc., on the following terms:

  1. Noncancelable term of 50 months.
  2. Rental of $250 per month (at end of each month). (The present value at 1% per month is $9,800.)
  3. Estimated residual value after 50 months is $1,180. (The present value at 1% per month is $715.) Brecker Company guarantees the residual value of $1,180.
  4. Estimated economic life of the automobile is 60 months.
  5. Brecker Company's incremental borrowing rate is 12% a year (1% a month). Emporia's implicit rate is unknown.

Instructions

   (a)   What is the nature of this lease to Brecker Company?
   (b)   What is the present value of the minimum lease payments?
   (c)   Record the lease on Brecker Company's books at the date of inception.
   (d)   Record the first month's depreciation on Brecker Company's books (assume straight-line).
   (e)   Record the first month's lease payment.

E21-3   (Lessee Entries, Capital Lease with Executory Costs and Unguaranteed Residual Value)
Assume that on January 1, 2011, Kimberly-Clark Corp. signs a 10-year noncancelable lease agreement to lease a storage building from Trevino Storage Company. The following information pertains to this lease agreement.

   1.   The agreement requires equal rental payments of $90,000 beginning on January 1, 2011.
   2.   The fair value of the building on January 1, 2011 is $550,000.
   3.   The building has an estimated economic life of 12 years, with an unguaranteed residual value of $10,000. Kimberly-Clark depreciates similar buildings on the straight-line method.
   4.   The lease is nonrenewable. At the termination of the lease, the building reverts to the lessor.
   5.   Kimberly-Clark's incremental borrowing rate is 12% per year. The lessor's implicit rate is not known by Kimberly-Clark.
   6.   The yearly rental payment includes $3,088.14 of executory costs related to taxes on the property.

Instructions

Prepare the journal entries on the lessee's books to reflect the signing of the lease agreement and to record the payments and expenses related to this lease for the years 2011 and 2012. Kimberly-Clark's corporate year end is December 31.

E21-4   (Lessor Entries, Direct-Financing Lease with Option to Purchase)   Krauss Leasing Company signs a lease agreement on January 1, 2011, to lease electronic equipment to Stewart Company. The term of the noncancelable lease is 2 years, and payments are required at the end of each year. The following information relates to this agreement:

   1.   Stewart has the option to purchase the equipment for $16,000 upon termination of the lease.
   2.   The equipment has a cost and fair value of $240,000 to Krauss Leasing Company. The useful economic life is 2 years, with a salvage value of $16,000.
   3.   Stewart Company is required to pay $7,000 each year to the lessor for executory costs.
   4.   Krauss Leasing Company desires to earn a return of 10% on its investment.
   5.   Collectibility of the payments is reasonably predictable, and there are no important uncertainties surrounding the costs yet to be incurred by the lessor.

Instructions

   (a)   Prepare the journal entries on the books of Krauss Leasing to reflect the payments received under the lease and to recognize income for the years 2011 and 2012.
   (b)   Assuming that Stewart Company exercises its option to purchase the equipment on December 31, 2012, prepare the journal entry to reflect the sale on Krauss's books.

E21-5   (Type of Lease, Amortization Schedule)   Jacobsen Leasing Company leases a new machine that has a cost and fair value of $75,000 to Stadler Corporation on a 3-year noncancelable contract. Stadler Corporation agrees to assume all risks of normal ownership including such costs as insurance, taxes, and maintenance. The machine has a 3-year useful life and no residual value. The lease was signed on January 1, 2011. Jacobsen Leasing Company expects to earn a 9% return on its investment. The annual rentals are payable on each December 31.

Instructions

   (a)   Discuss the nature of the lease arrangement and the accounting method that each party to the lease should apply.
   (b)   Prepare an amortization schedule that would be suitable for both the lessor and the lessee and that covers all the years involved.

E21-6   (Lessor Entries, Sales-Type Lease)   Wadkins Company, a machinery dealer, leased a machine to Romero Corporation on January 1, 2011. The lease is for an 8-year period and requires equal annual payments of $38,514 at the beginning of each year. The first payment is received on January 1, 2011. Wadkins had purchased the machine during 2010 for $170,000. Collectibility of lease payments is reasonably predictable, and no important uncertainties surround the amount of costs yet to be incurred by Wadkins. Wadkins set the annual rental to ensure an 11% rate of return. The machine has an economic life of 10 years with no residual value and reverts to Wadkins at the termination of the lease.

Instructions

(a) Compute the amount of the lease receivable.

(b) Prepare all necessary journal entries for Wadkins for 2011.

E21-7 (Lessee-Lessor Entries, Sales-Type Lease) On January 1, 2011, Palmer Company leased equipment to Woods Corporation. The following information pertains to this lease.

1. The term of the noncancelable lease is 6 years, with no renewal option. The equipment reverts to the lessor at the termination of the lease.
2. Equal rental payments are due on January 1 of each year, beginning in 2011.
3. The fair value of the equipment on January 1, 2011, is $200,000, and its cost is $150,000.
4. The equipment has an economic life of 8 years, with an unguaranteed residual value of $10,000. Woods depreciates all of its equipment on a straight-line basis.
5. Palmer sets the annual rental to ensure an 11% rate of return. Woods's incremental borrowing rate is 12%, and the implicit rate of the lessor is unknown.
6. Collectibility of lease payments is reasonably predictable, and no important uncertainties surround the amount of costs yet to be incurred by the lessor.

Instructions

(Both the lessor and the lessee's accounting period ends on December 31.)

(a) Discuss the nature of this lease to Palmer and Woods.

(b) Calculate the amount of the annual rental payment.

(c) Prepare all the necessary journal entries for Woods for 2011.

(d) Prepare all the necessary journal entries for Palmer for 2011.

E21-8 (Lessee Entries with Bargain-Purchase Option) The following facts pertain to a noncancelable lease agreement between Lennox Leasing Company and Gill Company, a lessee.

Inception date:	May 1, 2010
Annual lease payment due at the beginning of each year, beginning with May 1, 2010	$18,829.49
Bargain-purchase option price at end of lease term	$ 4,000.00
Lease term	5 years
Economic life of leased equipment	10 years
Lessor's cost	$65,000.00
Fair value of asset at May 1, 2010	$81,000.00
Lessor's implicit rate	10%
Lessee's incremental borrowing rate	10%

The collectibility of the lease payments is reasonably predictable, and there are no important uncertainties surrounding the costs yet to be incurred by the lessor. The lessee assumes responsibility for all executory costs.

Instructions

(Round all numbers to the nearest cent.)

(a) Discuss the nature of this lease to Gill Company.

(b) Discuss the nature of this lease to Lennox Company.

(c) Prepare a lease amortization schedule for Gill Company for the 5-year lease term.

(d) Prepare the journal entries on the lessee's books to reflect the signing of the lease agreement and to record the payments and expenses related to this lease for the years 2010 and 2011. Gill's annual accounting period ends on December 31. Reversing entries are used by Gill.

E21-9 (Lessor Entries with Bargain-Purchase Option) A lease agreement between Lennox Leasing Company and Gill Company is described in E21-8.

Instructions

(Round all numbers to the nearest cent.)

Refer to the data in E21-8 and do the following for the lessor.

(a) Compute the amount of the lease receivable at the inception of the lease.

(b) Prepare a lease amortization schedule for Lennox Leasing Company for the 5-year lease term.

(c) Prepare the journal entries to reflect the signing of the lease agreement and to record the receipts and income related to this lease for the years 2010, 2011, and 2012. The lessor's accounting period ends on December 31. Reversing entries are not used by Lennox.

·5 **E21-10 (Computation of Rental, Journal Entries for Lessor)** Fieval Leasing Company signs an agreement on January 1, 2010, to lease equipment to Reid Company. The following information relates to this agreement.

1. The term of the noncancelable lease is 6 years with no renewal option. The equipment has an estimated economic life of 6 years.
2. The cost of the asset to the lessor is $343,000. The fair value of the asset at January 1, 2010, is $343,000.
3. The asset will revert to the lessor at the end of the lease term at which time the asset is expected to have a residual value of $61,071, none of which is guaranteed.
4. Reid Company assumes direct responsibility for all executory costs.
5. The agreement requires equal annual rental payments, beginning on January 1, 2010.
6. Collectibility of the lease payments is reasonably predictable. There are no important uncertainties surrounding the amount of costs yet to be incurred by the lessor.

Instructions

(Round all numbers to the nearest cent.)

(a) Assuming the lessor desires a 10% rate of return on its investment, calculate the amount of the annual rental payment required. Round to the nearest dollar.
(b) Prepare an amortization schedule that would be suitable for the lessor for the lease term.
(c) Prepare all of the journal entries for the lessor for 2010 and 2011 to record the lease agreement, the receipt of lease payments, and the recognition of income. Assume the lessor's annual accounting period ends on December 31.

·2 **E21-11 (Amortization Schedule and Journal Entries for Lessee)** Grady Leasing Company signs an agreement on January 1, 2010, to lease equipment to Azure Company. The following information relates to this agreement.

1. The term of the noncancelable lease is 5 years with no renewal option. The equipment has an estimated economic life of 5 years.
2. The fair value of the asset at January 1, 2010, is $90,000.
3. The asset will revert to the lessor at the end of the lease term, at which time the asset is expected to have a residual value of $7,000, none of which is guaranteed.
4. Azure Company assumes direct responsibility for all executory costs, which include the following annual amounts: (1) $900 to Frontier Insurance Company for insurance and (2) $1,600 to Crawford County for property taxes.
5. The agreement requires equal annual rental payments of $20,541.11 to the lessor, beginning on January 1, 2010.
6. The lessee's incremental borrowing rate is 12%. The lessor's implicit rate is 10% and is known to the lessee.
7. Azure Company uses the straight-line depreciation method for all equipment.
8. Azure uses reversing entries when appropriate.

Instructions

(Round all numbers to the nearest cent.)

(a) Prepare an amortization schedule that would be suitable for the lessee for the lease term.
(b) Prepare all of the journal entries for the lessee for 2010 and 2011 to record the lease agreement, the lease payments, and all expenses related to this lease. Assume the lessee's annual accounting period ends on December 31.

·3 ·4 **E21-12 (Accounting for an Operating Lease)** On January 1, 2011, Secada Co. leased a building to Ryker Inc. The relevant information related to the lease is as follows.

1. The lease arrangement is for 10 years.
2. The leased building cost $3,600,000 and was purchased for cash on January 1, 2011.
3. The building is depreciated on a straight-line basis. Its estimated economic life is 50 years with no salvage value.
4. Lease payments are $220,000 per year and are made at the end of the year.
5. Property tax expense of $85,000 and insurance expense of $10,000 on the building were incurred by Secada in the first year. Payment on these two items was made at the end of the year.
6. Both the lessor and the lessee are on a calendar-year basis.

Instructions

(a) Prepare the journal entries that Secada Co. should make in 2011.
(b) Prepare the journal entries that Ryker Inc. should make in 2011.
(c) If Secada paid $30,000 to a real estate broker on January 1, 2011, as a fee for finding the lessee, how much should be reported as an expense for this item in 2011 by Secada Co.?

•3 •4 E21-13 (Accounting for an Operating Lease) On January 1, 2011, a machine was purchased for $900,000 by Floyd Co. The machine is expected to have an 8-year life with no salvage value. It is to be depreciated on a straight-line basis. The machine was leased to Crampton Inc. on January 1, 2011, at an annual rental of $180,000. Other relevant information is as follows.

1. The lease term is for 3 years.
2. Floyd Co. incurred maintenance and other executory costs of $25,000 in 2011 related to this lease.
3. The machine could have been sold by Floyd Co. for $940,000 instead of leasing it.
4. Crampton is required to pay a rent security deposit of $35,000 and to prepay the last month's rent of $15,000.

Instructions

(a) How much should Floyd Co. report as income before income tax on this lease for 2011?
(b) What amount should Crampton Inc. report for rent expense for 2011 on this lease?

•3 •4 E21-14 (Operating Lease for Lessee and Lessor) On February 20, 2011, Hooke Inc., purchased a machine for $1,200,000 for the purpose of leasing it. The machine is expected to have a 10-year life, no residual value, and will be depreciated on the straight-line basis. The machine was leased to Sage Company on March 1, 2011, for a 4-year period at a monthly rental of $15,600. There is no provision for the renewal of the lease or purchase of the machine by the lessee at the expiration of the lease term. Hooke paid $30,000 of commissions associated with negotiating the lease in February 2011:

Instructions

(a) What expense should Sage Company record as a result of the facts above for the year ended December 31, 2011? Show supporting computations in good form.
(b) What income or loss before income taxes should Hooke record as a result of the facts above for the year ended December 31, 2011? (*Hint:* Amortize commissions over the life of the lease.)

(AICPA adapted)

•11 *E21-15 (Sale-Leaseback) Assume that on January 1, 2011, Elmer's Restaurants sells a computer system to Liquidity Finance Co. for $510,000 and immediately leases the computer system back. The relevant information is as follows.

1. The computer was carried on Elmer's books at a value of $450,000.
2. The term of the noncancelable lease is 10 years; title will transfer to Elmer.
3. The lease agreement requires equal rental payments of $83,000.11 at the end of each year.
4. The incremental borrowing rate for Elmer is 12%. Elmer is aware that Liquidity Finance Co. set the annual rental to ensure a rate of return of 10%.
5. The computer has a fair value of $680,000 on January 1, 2011, and an estimated economic life of 10 years.
6. Elmer pays executory costs of $9,000 per year.

Instructions

Prepare the journal entries for both the lessee and the lessor for 2011 to reflect the sale-leaseback agreement. No uncertainties exist, and collectibility is reasonably certain.

•11 *E21-16 (Lessee-Lessor, Sale-Leaseback) Presented below are four independent situations.

(a) On December 31, 2011, Beard Inc. sold computer equipment to Barber Co. and immediately leased it back for 10 years. The sales price of the equipment was $560,000, its carrying amount is $400,000, and its estimated remaining economic life is 12 years. Determine the amount of deferred revenue to be reported from the sale of the computer equipment on December 31, 2011.
(b) On December 31, 2011, Nicklaus Co. sold a machine to Ozaki Co. and simultaneously leased it back for one year. The sale price of the machine was $480,000, the carrying amount is $420,000, and it had an estimated remaining useful life of 14 years. The present value of the rental payments for the one year is $35,000. At December 31, 2011, how much should Nicklaus report as deferred revenue from the sale of the machine?
(c) On January 1, 2011, Barone Corp. sold an airplane with an estimated useful life of 10 years. At the same time, Barone leased back the plane for 10 years. The sales price of the airplane was $500,000,

the carrying amount $401,000, and the annual rental $73,975.22. Barone Corp. intends to depreciate the leased asset using the sum-of-the-years'-digits depreciation method. Discuss how the gain on the sale should be reported at the end of 2011 in the financial statements.

(d) On January 1, 2011, Durocher Co. sold equipment with an estimated useful life of 5 years. At the same time, Durocher leased back the equipment for 2 years under a lease classified as an operating lease. The sales price (fair market value) of the equipment was $212,700, the carrying amount is $300,000, the monthly rental under the lease is $6,000, and the present value of the rental payments is $115,753. For the year ended December 31, 2011, determine which items would be reported on its income statement for the sale-leaseback transaction.

See the book's companion website, www.wiley.com/college/kieso, for a set of B Exercises.

PROBLEMS

 P21-1 (Lessee-Lessor Entries, Sales-Type Lease) Glaus Leasing Company agrees to lease machinery to Jensen Corporation on January 1, 2010. The following information relates to the lease agreement.

1. The term of the lease is 7 years with no renewal option, and the machinery has an estimated economic life of 9 years.
2. The cost of the machinery is $525,000, and the fair value of the asset on January 1, 2010, is $700,000.
3. At the end of the lease term the asset reverts to the lessor. At the end of the lease term the asset has a guaranteed residual value of $100,000. Jensen depreciates all of its equipment on a straight-line basis.
4. The lease agreement requires equal annual rental payments, beginning on January 1, 2010.
5. The collectibility of the lease payments is reasonably predictable, and there are no important uncertainties surrounding the amount of costs yet to be incurred by the lessor.
6. Glaus desires a 10% rate of return on its investments. Jensen's incremental borrowing rate is 11%, and the lessor's implicit rate is unknown.

Instructions
(Assume the accounting period ends on December 31.)

(a) Discuss the nature of this lease for both the lessee and the lessor.
(b) Calculate the amount of the annual rental payment required.
(c) Compute the present value of the minimum lease payments.
(d) Prepare the journal entries Jensen would make in 2010 and 2011 related to the lease arrangement.
(e) Prepare the journal entries Glaus would make in 2010 and 2011.

  P21-2 (Lessee-Lessor Entries, Operating Lease) Cleveland Inc. leased a new crane to Abriendo Construction under a 5-year noncancelable contract starting January 1, 2011. Terms of the lease require payments of $33,000 each January 1, starting January 1, 2011. Cleveland will pay insurance, taxes, and maintenance charges on the crane, which has an estimated life of 12 years, a fair value of $240,000, and a cost to Cleveland of $240,000. The estimated fair value of the crane is expected to be $45,000 at the end of the lease term. No bargain-purchase or renewal options are included in the contract. Both Cleveland and Abriendo adjust and close books annually at December 31. Collectibility of the lease payments is reasonably certain, and no uncertainties exist relative to unreimbursable lessor costs. Abriendo's incremental borrowing rate is 10%, and Cleveland's implicit interest rate of 9% is known to Abriendo.

Instructions
(a) Identify the type of lease involved and give reasons for your classification. Discuss the accounting treatment that should be applied by both the lessee and the lessor.
(b) Prepare all the entries related to the lease contract and leased asset for the year 2011 for the lessee and lessor, assuming the following amounts.
 (1) Insurance $500.
 (2) Taxes $2,000.
 (3) Maintenance $650.
 (4) Straight-line depreciation and salvage value $15,000.
(c) Discuss what should be presented in the balance sheet, the income statement, and the related notes of both the lessee and the lessor at December 31, 2011.

P21-3 **(Lessee-Lessor Entries, Balance Sheet Presentation, Sales-Type Lease)** Winston Industries and Ewing Inc. enter into an agreement that requires Ewing Inc. to build three diesel-electric engines to Winston's specifications. Upon completion of the engines, Winston has agreed to lease them for a period of 10 years and to assume all costs and risks of ownership. The lease is noncancelable, becomes effective on January 1, 2011, and requires annual rental payments of $413,971 each January 1, starting January 1, 2011.

Winston's incremental borrowing rate is 10%. The implicit interest rate used by Ewing Inc. and known to Winston is 8%. The total cost of building the three engines is $2,600,000. The economic life of the engines is estimated to be 10 years, with residual value set at zero. Winston depreciates similar equipment on a straight-line basis. At the end of the lease, Winston assumes title to the engines. Collectibility of the lease payments is reasonably certain; no uncertainties exist relative to unreimbursable lessor costs.

Instructions

(Round all numbers to the nearest dollar.)

(a) Discuss the nature of this lease transaction from the viewpoints of both lessee and lessor.
(b) Prepare the journal entry or entries to record the transaction on January 1, 2011, on the books of Winston Industries.
(c) Prepare the journal entry or entries to record the transaction on January 1, 2011, on the books of Ewing Inc.
(d) Prepare the journal entries for both the lessee and lessor to record the first rental payment on January 1, 2011.
(e) Prepare the journal entries for both the lessee and lessor to record interest expense (revenue) at December 31, 2011. (Prepare a lease amortization schedule for 2 years.)
(f) Show the items and amounts that would be reported on the balance sheet (not notes) at December 31, 2011, for both the lessee and the lessor.

 P21-4 **(Balance Sheet and Income Statement Disclosure—Lessee)** The following facts pertain to a noncancelable lease agreement between Alschuler Leasing Company and McKee Electronics, a lessee, for a computer system.

Inception date	October 1, 2010
Lease term	6 years
Economic life of leased equipment	6 years
Fair value of asset at October 1, 2010	$300,383
Residual value at end of lease term	–0–
Lessor's implicit rate	10%
Lessee's incremental borrowing rate	10%
Annual lease payment due at the beginning of each year, beginning with October 1, 2010	$62,700

The collectibility of the lease payments is reasonably predictable, and there are no important uncertainties surrounding the costs yet to be incurred by the lessor. The lessee assumes responsibility for all executory costs, which amount to $5,500 per year and are to be paid each October 1, beginning October 1, 2010. (This $5,500 is not included in the rental payment of $62,700.) The asset will revert to the lessor at the end of the lease term. The straight-line depreciation method is used for all equipment.

The following amortization schedule has been prepared correctly for use by both the lessor and the lessee in accounting for this lease. The lease is to be accounted for properly as a capital lease by the lessee and as a direct-financing lease by the lessor.

Date	Annual Lease Payment/ Receipt	Interest (10%) on Unpaid Liability/Receivable	Reduction of Lease Liability/Receivable	Balance of Lease Liability/Receivable
10/01/10				$300,383
10/01/10	$ 62,700		$ 62,700	237,683
10/01/11	62,700	$23,768	38,932	198,751
10/01/12	62,700	19,875	42,825	155,926
10/01/13	62,700	15,593	47,107	108,819
10/01/14	62,700	10,822	51,818	57,001
10/01/15	62,700	5,699*	57,001	–0–
	$376,200	$75,817	$300,383	

*Rounding error is $1.

Instructions

(Round all numbers to the nearest cent.)

(a) Assuming the lessee's accounting period ends on September 30, answer the following questions with respect to this lease agreement.

(1) What items and amounts will appear on the lessee's income statement for the year ending September 30, 2011?

(2) What items and amounts will appear on the lessee's balance sheet at September 30, 2011?

(3) What items and amounts will appear on the lessee's income statement for the year ending September 30, 2012?

(4) What items and amounts will appear on the lessee's balance sheet at September 30, 2012?

(b) Assuming the lessee's accounting period ends on December 31, answer the following questions with respect to this lease agreement.

(1) What items and amounts will appear on the lessee's income statement for the year ending December 31, 2010?

(2) What items and amounts will appear on the lessee's balance sheet at December 31, 2010?

(3) What items and amounts will appear on the lessee's income statement for the year ending December 31, 2011?

(4) What items and amounts will appear on the lessee's balance sheet at December 31, 2011?

 P21-5 (Balance Sheet and Income Statement Disclosure—Lessor) Assume the same information as in P21-4.

Instructions

(Round all numbers to the nearest cent.)

(a) Assuming the lessor's accounting period ends on September 30, answer the following questions with respect to this lease agreement.

(1) What items and amounts will appear on the lessor's income statement for the year ending September 30, 2011?

(2) What items and amounts will appear on the lessor's balance sheet at September 30, 2011?

(3) What items and amounts will appear on the lessor's income statement for the year ending September 30, 2012?

(4) What items and amounts will appear on the lessor's balance sheet at September 30, 2012?

(b) Assuming the lessor's accounting period ends on December 31, answer the following questions with respect to this lease agreement.

(1) What items and amounts will appear on the lessor's income statement for the year ending December 31, 2010?

(2) What items and amounts will appear on the lessor's balance sheet at December 31, 2010?

(3) What items and amounts will appear on the lessor's income statement for the year ending December 31, 2011?

(4) What items and amounts will appear on the lessor's balance sheet at December 31, 2011?

P21-6 (Lessee Entries with Residual Value) The following facts pertain to a noncancelable lease agreement between Faldo Leasing Company and Vance Company, a lessee.

Inception date	January 1, 2010
Annual lease payment due at the beginning of each year, beginning with January 1, 2010	$124,798
Residual value of equipment at end of lease term, guaranteed by the lessee	$50,000
Lease term	6 years
Economic life of leased equipment	6 years
Fair value of asset at January 1, 2010	$600,000
Lessor's implicit rate	12%
Lessee's incremental borrowing rate	12%

The lessee assumes responsibility for all executory costs, which are expected to amount to $5,000 per year. The asset will revert to the lessor at the end of the lease term. The lessee has guaranteed the lessor a residual value of $50,000. The lessee uses the straight-line depreciation method for all equipment.

Instructions

(Round all numbers to the nearest cent.)

(a) Prepare an amortization schedule that would be suitable for the lessee for the lease term.

(b) Prepare all of the journal entries for the lessee for 2010 and 2011 to record the lease agreement, the lease payments, and all expenses related to this lease. Assume the lessee's annual accounting period ends on December 31 and reversing entries are used when appropriate.

P21-7 (Lessee Entries and Balance Sheet Presentation, Capital Lease) Ludwick Steel Company as lessee signed a lease agreement for equipment for 5 years, beginning December 31, 2010. Annual rental payments of $40,000 are to be made at the beginning of each lease year (December 31). The taxes, insurance, and the maintenance costs are the obligation of the lessee. The interest rate used by the lessor in setting the payment schedule is 9%; Ludwick's incremental borrowing rate is 10%. Ludwick is unaware of the rate being used by the lessor. At the end of the lease, Ludwick has the option to buy the equipment for $1, considerably below its estimated fair value at that time. The equipment has an estimated useful life of 7 years, with no salvage value. Ludwick uses the straight-line method of depreciation on similar owned equipment.

Instructions
(Round all numbers to the nearest dollar.)

(a) Prepare the journal entry or entries, with explanations, that should be recorded on December 31, 2010, by Ludwick.
(b) Prepare the journal entry or entries, with explanations, that should be recorded on December 31, 2011, by Ludwick. (Prepare the lease amortization schedule for all five payments.)
(c) Prepare the journal entry or entries, with explanations, that should be recorded on December 31, 2012, by Ludwick.
(d) What amounts would appear on Ludwick's December 31, 2012, balance sheet relative to the lease arrangement?

P21-8 (Lessee Entries and Balance Sheet Presentation, Capital Lease) On January 1, 2011, Cage Company contracts to lease equipment for 5 years, agreeing to make a payment of $137,899 (including the executory costs of $6,000) at the beginning of each year, starting January 1, 2011. The taxes, the insurance, and the maintenance, estimated at $6,000 a year, are the obligations of the lessee. The leased equipment is to be capitalized at $550,000. The asset is to be depreciated on a double-declining-balance basis, and the obligation is to be reduced on an effective-interest basis. Cage's incremental borrowing rate is 12%, and the implicit rate in the lease is 10%, which is known by Cage. Title to the equipment transfers to Cage when the lease expires. The asset has an estimated useful life of 5 years and no residual value.

Instructions
(Round all numbers to the nearest dollar.)

(a) Explain the probable relationship of the $550,000 amount to the lease arrangement.
(b) Prepare the journal entry or entries that should be recorded on January 1, 2011, by Cage Company.
(c) Prepare the journal entry to record depreciation of the leased asset for the year 2011.
(d) Prepare the journal entry to record the interest expense for the year 2011.
(e) Prepare the journal entry to record the lease payment of January 1, 2012, assuming reversing entries are not made.
(f) What amounts will appear on the lessee's December 31, 2011, balance sheet relative to the lease contract?

P21-9 (Lessee Entries, Capital Lease with Monthly Payments) Shapiro Inc. was incorporated in 2010 to operate as a computer software service firm with an accounting fiscal year ending August 31. Shapiro's primary product is a sophisticated online inventory-control system; its customers pay a fixed fee plus a usage charge for using the system.

Shapiro has leased a large, Alpha-3 computer system from the manufacturer. The lease calls for a monthly rental of $40,000 for the 144 months (12 years) of the lease term. The estimated useful life of the computer is 15 years.

Each scheduled monthly rental payment includes $3,000 for full-service maintenance on the computer to be performed by the manufacturer. All rentals are payable on the first day of the month beginning with August 1, 2011, the date the computer was installed and the lease agreement was signed. The lease is noncancelable for its 12-year term, and it is secured only by the manufacturer's chattel lien on the Alpha-3 system.

This lease is to be accounted for as a capital lease by Shapiro, and it will be depreciated by the straight-line method with no expected salvage value. Borrowed funds for this type of transaction would cost Shapiro 12% per year (1% per month). Following is a schedule of the present value of $1 for selected periods discounted at 1% per period when payments are made at the beginning of each period.

Periods (months)	Present Value of $1 per Period Discounted at 1% per Period
1	1.000
2	1.990
3	2.970
143	76.658
144	76.899

Instructions

Prepare, in general journal form, all entries Shapiro should have made in its accounting records during August 2011 relating to this lease. Give full explanations and show supporting computations for each entry. Remember, August 31, 2011, is the end of Shapiro's fiscal accounting period and it will be preparing financial statements on that date. Do not prepare closing entries.

(AICPA adapted)

 P21-10 (Lessor Computations and Entries, Sales-Type Lease with Unguaranteed RV) George Company manufactures a computer with an estimated economic life of 12 years and leases it to National Airlines for a period of 10 years. The normal selling price of the equipment is $278,072, and its unguaranteed residual value at the end of the lease term is estimated to be $20,000. National will pay annual payments of $40,000 at the beginning of each year and all maintenance, insurance, and taxes. George incurred costs of $180,000 in manufacturing the equipment and $4,000 in negotiating and closing the lease. George has determined that the collectibility of the lease payments is reasonably predictable, that no additional costs will be incurred, and that the implicit interest rate is 10%.

Instructions

(Round all numbers to the nearest dollar.)

(a) Discuss the nature of this lease in relation to the lessor and compute the amount of each of the following items.
(1) Lease receivable.
(2) Sales price.
(3) Cost of sales.
(b) Prepare a 10-year lease amortization schedule.
(c) Prepare all of the lessor's journal entries for the first year.

P21-11 (Lessee Computations and Entries, Capital Lease with Unguaranteed Residual Value) Assume the same data as in P21-10 with National Airlines Co. having an incremental borrowing rate of 10%.

Instructions

(Round all numbers to the nearest dollar.)

(a) Discuss the nature of this lease in relation to the lessee, and compute the amount of the initial obligation under capital leases.
(b) Prepare a 10-year lease amortization schedule.
(c) Prepare all of the lessee's journal entries for the first year.

P21-12 (Basic Lessee Accounting with Difficult PV Calculation) In 2009 Grishell Trucking Company negotiated and closed a long-term lease contract for newly constructed truck terminals and freight storage facilities. The buildings were erected to the company's specifications on land owned by the company. On January 1, 2010, Grishell Trucking Company took possession of the lease properties. On January 1, 2010 and 2011, the company made cash payments of $948,000 that were recorded as rental expenses.

Although the terminals have a composite useful life of 40 years, the noncancelable lease runs for 20 years from January 1, 2010, with a bargain-purchase option available upon expiration of the lease.

The 20-year lease is effective for the period January 1, 2010, through December 31, 2029. Advance rental payments of $800,000 are payable to the lessor on January 1 of each of the first 10 years of the lease term. Advance rental payments of $320,000 are due on January 1 for each of the last 10 years of the lease. The company has an option to purchase all of these leased facilities for $1 on December 31, 2029. It also must make annual payments to the lessor of $125,000 for property taxes and $23,000 for insurance. The lease was negotiated to assure the lessor a 6% rate of return.

Instructions

(Round all numbers to the nearest dollar.)

(a) Prepare a schedule to compute for Grishell Trucking Company the discounted present value of the terminal facilities and related obligation at January 1, 2010.
(b) Assuming that the discounted present value of terminal facilities and related obligation at January 1, 2010, was $7,600,000, prepare journal entries for Grishell Trucking Company to record the:
(1) Cash payment to the lessor on January 1, 2012.
(2) Amortization of the cost of the leased properties for 2012 using the straight-line method and assuming a zero salvage value.
(3) Accrual of interest expense at December 31, 2012.

Selected present value factors are as follows:

Periods	For an Ordinary Annuity of $1 at 6%	For $1 at 6%
1	.943396	.943396
2	1.833393	.889996
8	6.209794	.627412
9	6.801692	.591898
10	7.360087	.558395
19	11.158117	.330513
20	11.469921	.311805

(AICPA adapted)

·4 ·7 ·8 P21-13 (Lessor Computations and Entries, Sales-Type Lease with Guaranteed Residual Value) Amirante Inc. manufactures an X-ray machine with an estimated life of 12 years and leases it to Chambers Medical Center for a period of 10 years. The normal selling price of the machine is $411,324, and its guaranteed residual value at the end of the noncancelable lease term is estimated to be $15,000. The hospital will pay rents of $60,000 at the beginning of each year and all maintenance, insurance, and taxes. Amirante Inc. incurred costs of $250,000 in manufacturing the machine and $14,000 in negotiating and closing the lease. Amirante Inc. has determined that the collectibility of the lease payments is reasonably predictable, that there will be no additional costs incurred, and that the implicit interest rate is 10%.

Instructions
(Round all numbers to the nearest dollar.)

(a) Discuss the nature of this lease in relation to the lessor and compute the amount of each of the following items.
    (1) Lease receivable at inception of the lease.
    (2) Sales price.
    (3) Cost of sales.

(b) Prepare a 10-year lease amortization schedule.

(c) Prepare all of the lessor's journal entries for the first year.

·2 ·7 P21-14 (Lessee Computations and Entries, Capital Lease with Guaranteed Residual Value) Assume the same data as in P21-13 and that Chambers Medical Center has an incremental borrowing rate of 10%.

Instructions
(Round all numbers to the nearest dollar.)

(a) Discuss the nature of this lease in relation to the lessee, and compute the amount of the initial obligation under capital leases.

(b) Prepare a 10-year lease amortization schedule.

(c) Prepare all of the lessee's journal entries for the first year.

·2 ·3 ·7 P21-15 (Operating Lease vs. Capital Lease) You are auditing the December 31, 2011, financial statements of Hockney, Inc., manufacturer of novelties and party favors. During your inspection of the company garage, you discovered that a 2010 Shirk automobile not listed in the equipment subsidiary ledger is parked in the company garage. You ask Stacy Reeder, plant manager, about the vehicle, and she tells you that the company did not list the automobile because the company was only leasing it. The lease agreement was entered into on January 1, 2011, with Crown New and Used Cars.

You decide to review the lease agreement to ensure that the lease should be afforded operating lease treatment, and you discover the following lease terms.

1. Noncancelable term of 4 years.
2. Rental of $3,240 per year (at the end of each year). (The present value at 8% per year is $10,731.)
3. Estimated residual value after 4 years is $1,100. (The present value at 8% per year is $809.) Hockney guarantees the residual value of $1,100.
4. Estimated economic life of the automobile is 5 years.
5. Hockney's incremental borrowing rate is 8% per year.

Instructions
You are a senior auditor writing a memo to your supervisor, the audit partner in charge of this audit, to discuss the above situation. Be sure to include (a) why you inspected the lease agreement, (b) what you determined about the lease, and (c) how you advised your client to account for this lease. Explain every journal entry that you believe is necessary to record this lease properly on the client's books. (It is also necessary to include the fact that you communicated this information to your client.)

P21-16 (Lessee-Lessor Accounting for Residual Values) Goring Dairy leases its milking equipment from King Finance Company under the following lease terms.

1. The lease term is 10 years, noncancelable, and requires equal rental payments of $30,300 due at the beginning of each year starting January 1, 2011.

2. The equipment has a fair value and cost at the inception of the lease (January 1, 2011) of $220,404, an estimated economic life of 10 years, and a residual value (which is guaranteed by Goring Dairy) of $20,000.

3. The lease contains no renewable options, and the equipment reverts to King Finance Company upon termination of the lease.

4. Goring Dairy's incremental borrowing rate is 9% per year. The implicit rate is also 9%.

5. Goring Dairy depreciates similar equipment that it owns on a straight-line basis.

6. Collectibility of the payments is reasonably predictable, and there are no important uncertainties surrounding the costs yet to be incurred by the lessor.

Instructions

(a) Evaluate the criteria for classification of the lease, and describe the nature of the lease. In general, discuss how the lessee and lessor should account for the lease transaction.

(b) Prepare the journal entries for the lessee and lessor at January 1, 2011, and December 31, 2011 (the lessee's and lessor's year-end). Assume no reversing entries.

(c) What would have been the amount capitalized by the lessee upon the inception of the lease if:
   (1) The residual value of $20,000 had been guaranteed by a third party, not the lessee?
   (2) The residual value of $20,000 had not been guaranteed at all?

(d) On the lessor's books, what would be the amount recorded as the Net Investment (Lease Receivable) at the inception of the lease, assuming:
   (1) The residual value of $20,000 had been guaranteed by a third party?
   (2) The residual value of $20,000 had not been guaranteed at all?

(e) Suppose the useful life of the milking equipment is 20 years. How large would the residual value have to be at the end of 10 years in order for the lessee to qualify for the operating method? (Assume that the residual value would be guaranteed by a third party.) (*Hint*: The lessee's annual payments will be appropriately reduced as the residual value increases.)

CONCEPTS FOR ANALYSIS

CA21-1 (Lessee Accounting and Reporting) On January 1, 2011, Evans Company entered into a noncancelable lease for a machine to be used in its manufacturing operations. The lease transfers ownership of the machine to Evans by the end of the lease term. The term of the lease is 8 years. The minimum lease payment made by Evans on January 1, 2011, was one of eight equal annual payments. At the inception of the lease, the criteria established for classification as a capital lease by the lessee were met.

Instructions

(a) What is the theoretical basis for the accounting standard that requires certain long-term leases to be capitalized by the lessee? Do not discuss the specific criteria for classifying a specific lease as a capital lease.

(b) How should Evans account for this lease at its inception and determine the amount to be recorded?

(c) What expenses related to this lease will Evans incur during the first year of the lease, and how will they be determined?

(d) How should Evans report the lease transaction on its December 31, 2011, balance sheet?

CA21-2 (Lessor and Lessee Accounting and Disclosure) Sylvan Inc. entered into a noncancelable lease arrangement with Breton Leasing Corporation for a certain machine. Breton's primary business is leasing; it is not a manufacturer or dealer. Sylvan will lease the machine for a period of 3 years, which is 50% of the machine's economic life. Breton will take possession of the machine at the end of the initial 3-year lease and lease it to another, smaller company that does not need the most current version of the machine. Sylvan does not guarantee any residual value for the machine and will not purchase the machine at the end of the lease term.

Sylvan's incremental borrowing rate is 10%, and the implicit rate in the lease is 9%. Sylvan has no way of knowing the implicit rate used by Breton. Using either rate, the present value of the minimum lease payments is between 90% and 100% of the fair value of the machine at the date of the lease agreement.

Sylvan has agreed to pay all executory costs directly, and no allowance for these costs is included in the lease payments.

Breton is reasonably certain that Sylvan will pay all lease payments, and because Sylvan has agreed to pay all executory costs, there are no important uncertainties regarding costs to be incurred by Breton. Assume that no indirect costs are involved.

Instructions

(a) With respect to Sylvan (the lessee), answer the following.
  (1) What type of lease has been entered into? Explain the reason for your answer.
  (2) How should Sylvan compute the appropriate amount to be recorded for the lease or asset acquired?
  (3) What accounts will be created or affected by this transaction, and how will the lease or asset and other costs related to the transaction be matched with earnings?
  (4) What disclosures must Sylvan make regarding this leased asset?

(b) With respect to Breton (the lessor), answer the following:
  (1) What type of leasing arrangement has been entered into? Explain the reason for your answer.
  (2) How should this lease be recorded by Breton, and how are the appropriate amounts determined?
  (3) How should Breton determine the appropriate amount of earnings to be recognized from each lease payment?
  (4) What disclosures must Breton make regarding this lease?

(AICPA adapted)

CA21-3 (Lessee Capitalization Criteria) On January 1, Santiago Company, a lessee, entered into three noncancelable leases for brand-new equipment, Lease L, Lease M, and Lease N. None of the three leases transfers ownership of the equipment to Santiago at the end of the lease term. For each of the three leases, the present value at the beginning of the lease term of the minimum lease payments, excluding that portion of the payments representing executory costs such as insurance, maintenance, and taxes to be paid by the lessor, is 75% of the fair value of the equipment.

The following information is peculiar to each lease.

1. Lease L does not contain a bargain-purchase option. The lease term is equal to 80% of the estimated economic life of the equipment.
2. Lease M contains a bargain-purchase option. The lease term is equal to 50% of the estimated economic life of the equipment.
3. Lease N does not contain a bargain-purchase option. The lease term is equal to 50% of the estimated economic life of the equipment.

Instructions

(a) How should Santiago Company classify each of the three leases above, and why? Discuss the rationale for your answer.
(b) What amount, if any, should Santiago record as a liability at the inception of the lease for each of the three leases above?
(c) Assuming that the minimum lease payments are made on a straight-line basis, how should Santiago record each minimum lease payment for each of the three leases above?

(AICPA adapted)

CA21-4 (Comparison of Different Types of Accounting by Lessee and Lessor)

Part 1
Capital leases and operating leases are the two classifications of leases described in FASB pronouncements from the standpoint of the **lessee**.

Instructions

(a) Describe how a capital lease would be accounted for by the lessee both at the inception of the lease and during the first year of the lease, assuming the lease transfers ownership of the property to the lessee by the end of the lease.
(b) Describe how an operating lease would be accounted for by the lessee both at the inception of the lease and during the first year of the lease, assuming equal monthly payments are made by the lessee at the beginning of each month of the lease. Describe the change in accounting, if any, when rental payments are not made on a straight-line basis.

Do **not** discuss the criteria for distinguishing between capital leases and operating leases.

Part 2
Sales-type leases and direct-financing leases are two of the classifications of leases described in FASB pronouncements from the standpoint of the **lessor**.

Instructions

Compare and contrast a sales-type lease with a direct-financing lease as follows.

(a) Lease receivable.
(b) Recognition of interest revenue.
(c) Manufacturer's or dealer's profit.

Do **not** discuss the criteria for distinguishing between the leases described above and operating leases.

(AICPA adapted)

CA21-5 **(Lessee Capitalization of Bargain-Purchase Option)** Albertsen Corporation is a diversified company with nationwide interests in commercial real estate developments, banking, copper mining, and metal fabrication. The company has offices and operating locations in major cities throughout the United States. Corporate headquarters for Albertsen Corporation is located in a metropolitan area of a midwestern state, and executives connected with various phases of company operations travel extensively. Corporate management is currently evaluating the feasibility of acquiring a business aircraft that can be used by company executives to expedite business travel to areas not adequately served by commercial airlines. Proposals for either leasing or purchasing a suitable aircraft have been analyzed, and the leasing proposal was considered to be more desirable.

The proposed lease agreement involves a twin-engine turboprop Viking that has a fair value of $1,000,000. This plane would be leased for a period of 10 years beginning January 1, 2011. The lease agreement is cancelable only upon accidental destruction of the plane. An annual lease payment of $141,780 is due on January 1 of each year; the first payment is to be made on January 1, 2011. Maintenance operations are strictly scheduled by the lessor, and Albertsen Corporation will pay for these services as they are performed. Estimated annual maintenance costs are $6,900. The lessor will pay all insurance premiums and local property taxes, which amount to a combined total of $4,000 annually and are included in the annual lease payment of $141,780. Upon expiration of the 10-year lease, Albertsen Corporation can purchase the Viking for $44,440. The estimated useful life of the plane is 15 years, and its salvage value in the used plane market is estimated to be $100,000 after 10 years. The salvage value probably will never be less than $75,000 if the engines are overhauled and maintained as prescribed by the manufacturer. If the purchase option is not exercised, possession of the plane will revert to the lessor, and there is no provision for renewing the lease agreement beyond its termination on December 31, 2020.

Albertsen Corporation can borrow $1,000,000 under a 10-year term loan agreement at an annual interest rate of 12%. The lessor's implicit interest rate is not expressly stated in the lease agreement, but this rate appears to be approximately 8% based on ten net rental payments of $137,780 per year and the initial market value of $1,000,000 for the plane. On January 1, 2011, the present value of all net rental payments and the purchase option of $44,440 is $888,890 using the 12% interest rate. The present value of all net rental payments and the $44,440 purchase option on January 1, 2011, is $1,022,226 using the 8% interest rate implicit in the lease agreement. The financial vice president of Albertsen Corporation has established that this lease agreement is a capital lease as defined in GAAP.

Instructions

(a) What is the appropriate amount that Albertsen Corporation should recognize for the leased aircraft on its balance sheet after the lease is signed?
(b) Without prejudice to your answer in part (a), assume that the annual lease payment is $141,780 as stated in the question, that the appropriate capitalized amount for the leased aircraft is $1,000,000 on January 1, 2011, and that the interest rate is 9%. How will the lease be reported in the December 31, 2011, balance sheet and related income statement? (Ignore any income tax implications.)

(CMA adapted)

CA21-6 **(Lease Capitalization, Bargain-Purchase Option)** Baden Corporation entered into a lease agreement for 10 photocopy machines for its corporate headquarters. The lease agreement qualifies as an operating lease in all terms except there is a bargain-purchase option. After the 5-year lease term, the corporation can purchase each copier for $1,000, when the anticipated market value is $2,500.

Jerry Suffolk, the financial vice president, thinks the financial statements must recognize the lease agreement as a capital lease because of the bargain-purchase agreement. The controller, Diane Buchanan, disagrees: "Although I don't know much about the copiers themselves, there is a way to avoid recording the lease liability." She argues that the corporation might claim that copier technology advances rapidly and that by the end of the lease term the machines will most likely not be worth the $1,000 bargain price.

Instructions

Answer the following questions.

(a) What ethical issue is at stake?

(b) Should the controller's argument be accepted if she does not really know much about copier technology? Would it make a difference if the controller were knowledgeable about the pace of change in copier technology?

(c) What should Suffolk do?

*CA21-7 (Sale-Leaseback) On January 1, 2011, Perriman Company sold equipment for cash and leased it back. As seller-lessee, Perriman retained the right to substantially all of the remaining use of the equipment.

The term of the lease is 8 years. There is a gain on the sale portion of the transaction. The lease portion of the transaction is classified appropriately as a capital lease.

Instructions

(a) What is the theoretical basis for requiring lessees to capitalize certain long-term leases? **Do not discuss the specific criteria for classifying a lease as a capital lease.**

(b) (1) How should Perriman account for the sale portion of the sale-leaseback transaction at January 1, 2011?

(2) How should Perriman account for the leaseback portion of the sale-leaseback transaction at January 1, 2011?

(c) How should Perriman account for the gain on the sale portion of the sale-leaseback transaction during the first year of the lease? Why?

(AICPA adapted)

*CA21-8 (Sale-Leaseback) On December 31, 2010, Shellhammer Co. sold 6-month old equipment at fair value and leased it back. There was a loss on the sale. Shellhammer pays all insurance, maintenance, and taxes on the equipment. The lease provides for eight equal annual payments, beginning December 31, 2011, with a present value equal to 85% of the equipment's fair value and sales price. The lease's term is equal to 80% of the equipment's useful life. There is no provision for Shellhammer to reacquire ownership of the equipment at the end of the lease term.

Instructions

(a) (1) Why is it important to compare an equipment's fair value to its lease payments' present value and its useful life to the lease term?

(2) Evaluate Shellhammer's leaseback of the equipment in terms of each of the four criteria for determination of a capital lease.

(b) How should Shellhammer account for the sale portion of the sale-leaseback transaction at December 31, 2010?

(c) How should Shellhammer report the leaseback portion of the sale-leaseback transaction on its December 31, 2011, balance sheet?

USING YOUR JUDGMENT

FINANCIAL REPORTING

Financial Reporting Problem

 The Procter & Gamble Company (P&G)

The financial statements of **P&G** are presented in Appendix 5B or can be accessed at the book's companion website, **www.wiley.com/college/kieso.**

Instructions

 Refer to P&G's financial statements, accompanying notes, and management's discussion and analysis to answer the following questions.

(a) What types of leases are used by P&G?

(b) What amount of capital leases was reported by P&G in total and for less than one year?

(c) What minimum annual rental commitments under all noncancelable leases at June 30, 2007, did P&G disclose?

Comparative Analysis Case

UAL, Inc. and Southwest Airlines

Instructions

Go to the book's companion website or the company websites and use information found there to answer the following questions related to **UAL, Inc.** and **Southwest Airlines**.

(a) What types of leases are used by Southwest and on what assets are these leases primarily used?

(b) How long-term are some of Southwest's leases? What are some of the characteristics or provisions of Southwest's (as lessee) leases?

(c) What did Southwest report in 2007 as its future minimum annual rental commitments under non-cancelable leases?

(d) At year-end 2007, what was the present value of the minimum rental payments under Southwest's capital leases? How much imputed interest was deducted from the future minimum annual rental commitments to arrive at the present value?

(e) What were the amounts and details reported by Southwest for rental expense in 2007, 2006, and 2005?

(f) How does UAL's use of leases compare with Southwest's?

Financial Statement Analysis Case

Tasty Baking Company

Presented in Illustration 21-31 are the financial statement disclosures from the 2007 annual report of **Tasty Baking Company**.

Instructions

Answer the following questions related to these disclosures.

(a) What is the total obligation under capital leases at December 29, 2007, for Tasty Baking Company?

(b) What is the book value of the assets under capital lease at December 29, 2007, for Tasty Baking Company? Explain why there is a difference between the amounts reported for assets and liabilities under capital leases.

(c) What is the total rental expense reported for leasing activity for the year ended December 29, 2007, for Tasty Baking Company?

(d) Estimate the off–balance-sheet liability due to Tasty Baking's operating leases at fiscal year-end 2007.

International Reporting Case

As discussed in the chapter, U.S. GAAP accounting for leases allows companies to use off–balance-sheet financing for the purchase of operating assets. International accounting standards are similar to U.S. GAAP in that under these rules, companies can keep leased assets and obligations off their balance sheets. However, under *International Accounting Standard No. 17 (IAS 17)*, leases are capitalized based on the subjective evaluation of whether the risks and rewards of ownership are transferred in the lease. In Japan, virtually all leases are treated as operating leases. Furthermore, unlike U.S. GAAP and iGAAP, the Japanese rules do not require disclosure of future minimum lease payments.

Presented below are financial data for three major airlines that lease some part of their aircraft fleet. **American Airlines** prepares its financial statements under U.S. GAAP and leases approximately 27% of its fleet. **KLM Royal Dutch Airlines** and **Japan Airlines (JAL)** present their statements in accordance with their home country GAAP (Netherlands and Japan, respectively). KLM leases about 22% of its aircraft, and JAL leases approximately 50% of its fleet.

Financial Statement Data	American Airlines (millions of dollars)	KLM Royal Dutch Airlines (millions of guilders)	Japan Airlines (millions of yen)
As-reported			
Assets	20,915	19,205	2,042,761
Liabilities	14,699	13,837	1,857,800
Income	985	606	4,619
Estimated impact of capitalizing operating leases on:[1]			
Assets	5,897	1,812	244,063
Liabilities	6,886	1,776	265,103
Income	(143)	24	(9,598)

[1]Based on *Apples to Apples: Global Airlines: Flight to Quality* (New York: N.Y.: Morgan Stanley Dean Witter).

Instructions

(a) Using the as-reported data for each of the airlines, compute the rate of return on assets and the debt to assets ratio. Compare these companies on the basis of this analysis.

(b) Adjust the as-reported numbers of the three companies for the effects of non-capitalization of leases, and then redo the analysis in part (a).

(c) The following statement was overheard in the library: "Non-capitalization of operating leases is not that big a deal for profitability analysis based on rate of return on assets, since the operating lease payments (under operating lease accounting) are about the same as the sum of the interest and depreciation expense under capital lease treatment." Do you agree? Explain.

(d) Since the accounting for leases worldwide is similar, does your analysis above suggest there is a need for an improved accounting standard for leases? (*Hint:* Reflect on comparability of information about these companies' leasing activities, when leasing is more prevalent in one country than in others.)

BRIDGE TO THE PROFESSION

Professional Research: FASB Codification

Daniel Hardware Co. is considering alternative financing arrangements for equipment used in its warehouses. Besides purchasing the equipment outright, Daniel is also considering a lease. Accounting for the outright purchase is fairly straightforward, but because Daniel has not used equipment leases in the past, the accounting staff is less informed about the specific accounting rules for leases.

The staff is aware of some lease rules related to a "90 percent of fair value," "75 percent of useful life," and "residual value deficiencies," but they are unsure about the meanings of these terms in lease accounting. Daniel has asked you to conduct some research on these items related to lease capitalization criteria.

Instructions

Access the FASB Codification at *http://asc.fasb.org/home* to conduct research using the Codification Research System to prepare responses to the following items. Provide Codification references for your responses.

(a) What is the objective of lease classification criteria?

(b) An important element of evaluating leases is determining whether substantially all of the risks and rewards of ownership are transferred in the lease. How is "substantially all" defined in the authoritative literature?

(c) Besides the noncancelable term of the lease, name at least three other considerations in determining the "lease term."

(d) A common issue in the accounting for leases concerns lease requirements that the lessee make up a residual value deficiency that is attributable to damage, extraordinary wear and tear, or excessive usage (e.g., excessive mileage on a leased vehicle). Do these features constitute a lessee guarantee of the residual value such that the estimated residual value of the leased property at the end of the lease term should be included in minimum lease payments? Explain.

Professional Simulations

Go to the book's companion website, at **www.wiley.com/college/kieso**, to find interactive problems that simulate the computerized CPA exam. The professional simulations for this chapter asks you to address questions related to the accounting for leases.

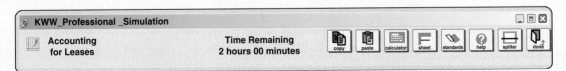

KWW_Professional _Simulation		
Accounting for Leases	Time Remaining 2 hours 00 minutes	copy paste calculator sheet standards help splitter done

Remember to check the book's companion website to find additional resources for this chapter.

CHAPTER **22**

ACCOUNTING CHANGES AND ERROR ANALYSIS

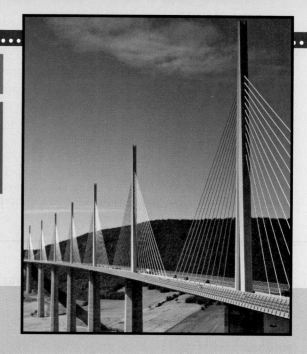

LEARNING OBJECTIVES

After studying this chapter, you should be able to:

•1 Identify the types of accounting changes.

•2 Describe the accounting for changes in accounting principles.

•3 Understand how to account for retrospective accounting changes.

•4 Understand how to account for impracticable changes.

•5 Describe the accounting for changes in estimates.

•6 Identify changes in a reporting entity.

•7 Describe the accounting for correction of errors.

•8 Identify economic motives for changing accounting methods.

•9 Analyze the effect of errors.

IN THE DARK

The FASB's conceptual framework describes comparability (including consistency) as one of the qualitative characteristics that contribute to the usefulness of accounting information. Unfortunately, companies are finding it difficult to maintain comparability and consistency due to the numerous changes in accounting principles mandated by the FASB. In addition, a number of companies have faced restatements due to errors in their financial statements. For example, the table below shows types and numbers of recent accounting changes.

Stock-based compensation	437	Inventories	8
Defined-benefit pension and postretirement plans	305	Goodwill and other intangibles	5
		Lease/rental costs	5
Asset retirement obligations	29	Other (including servicing rights, exchanges	
Prior period financial statement misstatements	18	of nonmonetary assets, and impairments)	34

Although the percentage of companies reporting material changes or errors is small, readers of financial statements still must be careful. The reason: The amounts in the financial statements may have changed due to changing accounting principles and/or restatements. The chart on the next page indicates the recent trends in restatements.

There is some good news in the chart. As indicated, the number of restatements declined in 2007 compared to the high of 2006. However, investors can be in the dark when a company has an error that requires restatement. It may take some time for companies to sort out the source of an error, prepare corrected statements, and get auditor sign-off. Recent data indicate it takes on average about 3 months to resolve a restatement. The following table reports the range of periods when investors are in the dark due to a restatement.

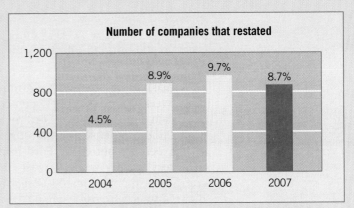

Number of companies that restated

Note: Chart includes all U.S.-listed companies. The total number of companies is based on the number of unique companies that filed at least one annual report, quarterly report, or effective registration statement with the SEC during the year. In 2007, that number was 13,540 and in 2006 it was 13,899.

Time to File Restated Financial Statements	% of All Restatements
Up to 3 Months	77
3–9 Months	11
Greater than 9 Months	12

While most companies (77%) resolve their errors within 3 months, 12% (or over 200 companies) take more than 9 months to file corrected statements.

These lengthy "dark periods" have caught the attention of policy-setters and were a topic of discussion of the Committee for Improvements in Financial Reporting (CIFR). As one member of CIFR noted, "The dark period is bad for users." As a result, the committee is proposing that for some errors, companies might not need to go through the pain of restatement, but enhanced disclosures about errors are needed.

Sources: Accounting change data from *Accounting Trends and Techniques—2007* (New York: AICPA, 2007). Restatement data from M. Grothe, "The Tide is Turning," *Trend Alert* (January 15, 2008), Glass Lewis and Co., p. 2, and M. Leone, "Materiality Debate Emerges from the Dark," *CFO.com* (July 14, 2008).

PREVIEW OF CHAPTER 22

As our opening story indicates, changes in accounting principles and errors in financial information have increased substantially in recent years. When these changes occur, companies must follow specific accounting and reporting requirements. In addition, to ensure comparability among companies, the FASB has standardized reporting of accounting changes, accounting estimates, error corrections, and related earnings per share information. In this chapter, we discuss these reporting standards, which help investors better understand a company's financial condition. The content and organization of the chapter are as follows.

ACCOUNTING CHANGES AND ERROR ANALYSIS

ACCOUNTING CHANGES
- Changes in accounting principle
- Changes in accounting estimate
- Change in reporting entity
- Correction of errors
- Summary
- Motivations for change of method

ERROR ANALYSIS
- Balance sheet errors
- Income statement errors
- Balance sheet and income statement effects
- Comprehensive example
- Preparation of statements with error corrections

SECTION 1 • ACCOUNTING CHANGES

Objective•1

Identify the types of accounting changes.

See the FASB Codification section (page 1218).

Underlying Concepts

While changes in accounting may enhance the qualitative characteristic of *usefulness*, these changes may adversely affect the characteristics of *comparability* and *consistency*.

Accounting alternatives diminish the comparability of financial information between periods and between companies; they also obscure useful historical trend data. For example, if **Ford** revises its estimates for equipment useful lives, depreciation expense for the current year will not be comparable to depreciation expense reported by Ford in prior years. Similarly, if **Best Buy** changes to FIFO inventory pricing while **Circuit City** uses LIFO, it will be difficult to compare these companies' reported results. A reporting framework helps preserve comparability when there is an accounting change.

The FASB has established a reporting framework, which involves three types of accounting changes. **[1]** The three types of accounting changes are:

1. *Change in Accounting Principle.* A change from one generally accepted accounting principle to another one. For example, a company may change its inventory valuation method from LIFO to average cost.

2. *Change in Accounting Estimate.* A change that occurs as the result of new information or additional experience. For example, a company may change its estimate of the useful lives of depreciable assets.

3. *Change in Reporting Entity.* A change from reporting as one type of entity to another type of entity. As an example, a company might change the subsidiaries for which it prepares consolidated financial statements.

A fourth category necessitates changes in accounting, though it is not classified as an accounting change.

4. *Errors in Financial Statements.* Errors result from mathematical mistakes, mistakes in applying accounting principles, or oversight or misuse of facts that existed when preparing the financial statements. For example, a company may incorrectly apply the retail inventory method for determining its final inventory value.

The FASB classifies changes in these categories because each category involves different methods of recognizing changes in the financial statements. In this chapter we discuss these classifications. We also explain how to report each item in the accounts and how to disclose the information in comparative statements.

CHANGES IN ACCOUNTING PRINCIPLE

Objective•2

Describe the accounting for changes in accounting principles.

By definition, a **change in accounting principle involves a change from one generally accepted accounting principle to another**. For example, a company might change the basis of inventory pricing from average cost to LIFO. Or it might change its method of revenue recognition for long-term construction contracts from the completed-contract to the percentage-of-completion method.

Companies must carefully examine each circumstance to ensure that a change in principle has actually occurred. **Adoption of a new principle** in recognition of events that have occurred for the first time or that were previously immaterial is not an accounting change. For example, a change in accounting principle has not occurred when a company adopts an inventory method (e.g., FIFO) for **newly** acquired items of inventory, even if FIFO differs from that used for **previously recorded** inventory. Another example is certain marketing expenditures that were previously immaterial and expensed in the period incurred. It would not be considered a change in accounting principle if they become material and so may be acceptably deferred and amortized.

Finally, what if a company previously followed an accounting principle that was not acceptable? Or what if the company applied a principle incorrectly? In such cases, the profession considers a change to a generally accepted accounting principle **a correction of an error**. For example, a switch from the cash (income tax) basis of accounting to the accrual basis is a correction of an error. Or, if a company deducted salvage value when computing double-declining depreciation on plant assets and later recomputed depreciation without deducting estimated salvage value, it has corrected an error.

There are three possible approaches for reporting changes in accounting principles:

Report changes currently. In this approach, companies report the cumulative effect of the change in the current year's income statement as an irregular item. The **cumulative effect** is the difference in prior years' income between the newly adopted and prior accounting method. Under this approach, the effect of the change on prior years' income appears only in the current-year income statement. The company does not change **prior-year financial statements**.

Advocates of this position argue that changing prior years' financial statements results in a loss of confidence in financial reports. How do investors react when told that the earnings computed three years ago are now entirely different? Changing prior periods, if permitted, also might upset contractual arrangements based on the old figures. For example, profit-sharing arrangements computed on the old basis might have to be recomputed and completely new distributions made, creating numerous legal problems. Many practical difficulties also exist: The cost of changing prior-period financial statements may be excessive, or determining the amount of the prior-period effect may be impossible on the basis of available data.

Report changes retrospectively. Retrospective application refers to the application of a different accounting principle to recast previously issued financial statements—**as if the new principle had always been used**. In other words, the company "goes back" and adjusts **prior years' statements** on a basis consistent with the newly adopted principle. The company shows any cumulative effect of the change as an adjustment to beginning retained earnings of the earliest year presented.

Advocates of this position argue that retrospective application ensures comparability. Think for a moment what happens if this approach is not used: The year *previous* to the change will be on the old method; the year *of the change* will report the entire cumulative adjustment; and the *following* year will present financial statements on the new basis without the cumulative effect of the change. Such lack of consistency fails to provide meaningful earnings-trend data and other financial relationships necessary to evaluate the business.

Report changes prospectively (in the future). In this approach, previously reported results remain. As a result, companies do not adjust opening balances to reflect the change in principle. Advocates of this position argue that once management presents financial statements based on acceptable accounting principles, they are final; management cannot change prior periods by adopting a new principle. According to this line of reasoning, the current-period cumulative adjustment is not appropriate, because that approach includes amounts that have little or no relationship to the current year's income or economic events.

> **INTERNATIONAL INSIGHT**
>
> *IAS 8* generally requires retrospective application to prior years for accounting changes. However, *IAS 8* permits the cumulative-effect method or prospective method if a company cannot reasonably determine the amounts to which to restate prior periods.

Given these three possible approaches, which does the accounting profession prefer? The FASB **requires that companies use the retrospective approach.** Why? Because it provides financial statement users with more useful information than the cumulative-effect or prospective approaches. [2] The rationale is that changing the prior statements to be on the same basis as the newly adopted principle results in greater consistency across accounting periods. Users can then better compare results from one period to the next.[1]

---

[1]Adoption of the retrospective approach contributes to international accounting convergence. The FASB and the IASB are collaborating on a project in which they have agreed to converge around high-quality solutions to resolve differences between U.S. GAAP and International Financial Reporting Standards (IFRS). By adopting the retrospective approach, which is the method used in IFRS, the FASB agreed that this approach is superior to the current approach.

What do the numbers mean?

QUITE A CHANGE

The cumulative-effect approach results in a loss of comparability. Also, reporting the cumulative adjustment in the period of the change can significantly affect net income, resulting in a misleading income figure. For example, at one time Chrysler Corporation changed its inventory accounting from LIFO to FIFO. If Chrysler had used the cumulative-effect approach, it would have reported a $53,500,000 adjustment to net income. That adjustment would have resulted in net income of $45,900,000, instead of a net loss of $7,600,000.

A second case: In the early 1980s the railroad industry switched from the retirement-replacement method of depreciating railroad equipment to more generally used methods such as straight-line depreciation. Using cumulative treatment, railroad companies would have made substantial adjustments to income in the period of change. Many in the industry argued that including such large cumulative-effect adjustments in the current year would distort the information and make it less useful.

Such situations lend support to retrospective application so that comparability is maintained.

Retrospective Accounting Change Approach

Objective·3
Understand how to account for retrospective accounting changes.

A presumption exists that once a company adopts an accounting principle, it should not change. That presumption is understandable, given the idea that consistent use of an accounting principle enhances the usefulness of financial statements. However, the environment continually changes, and companies change in response. Recent standards on such subjects as stock options, exchanges of nonmonetary assets, and derivatives indicate that changes in accounting principle will continue to occur.

When a company changes an accounting principle, it should report the change using retrospective application. In general terms, here is what it must do:

1. It adjusts its financial statements for each prior period presented. Thus, financial statement information about prior periods is on the same basis as the new accounting principle.

2. It adjusts the carrying amounts of assets and liabilities as of the beginning of the first year presented. By doing so, these accounts reflect the cumulative effect on periods prior to those presented of the change to the new accounting principle. The company also makes an offsetting adjustment to the opening balance of retained earnings or other appropriate component of stockholders' equity or net assets as of the beginning of the first year presented.

For example, assume that Target decides to change its inventory valuation method in 2010 from the retail inventory method (FIFO) to the retail inventory (average cost). It provides comparative information for 2008 and 2009 based on the new method. Target would adjust its assets, liabilities, and retained earnings for periods prior to 2008 and report these amounts in the 2008 financial statements, when it prepares comparative financial statements.

Retrospective Accounting Change: Long-Term Contracts

To illustrate the retrospective approach, assume that Denson Company has accounted for its income from long-term construction contracts using the completed-contract method. In 2010 the company changed to the percentage-of-completion method. Management believes this approach provides a more appropriate measure of the income earned. For tax purposes, the company uses the completed-contract method and plans to continue doing so in the future. (We assume a 40 percent enacted tax rate.)

Illustration 22-1 shows portions of three income statements for 2008–2010—for both the completed-contract and percentage-of-completion methods.

COMPLETED-CONTRACT METHOD DENSON COMPANY INCOME STATEMENT (PARTIAL) FOR THE YEARS ENDED DECEMBER 31			
	2008	2009	2010
Income before income tax	$400,000	$160,000	$190,000
Income tax (40%)	160,000	64,000	76,000
Net income	$240,000	$ 96,000	$114,000

PERCENTAGE-OF-COMPLETION METHOD DENSON COMPANY INCOME STATEMENT (PARTIAL) FOR THE YEARS ENDED DECEMBER 31			
	2008	2009	2010
Income before income tax	$600,000	$180,000	$200,000
Income tax (40%)	240,000	72,000	80,000
Net income	$360,000	$108,000	$120,000

ILLUSTRATION 22-1
Comparative Income Statements for Completed-Contract versus Percentage-of-Completion Methods

To record a change from the completed-contract to the percentage-of-completion method, we analyze the various effects, as Illustration 22-2 shows.

	Pretax Income from		Difference in Income		
Year	Percentage-of- Completion	Completed- Contract	Difference	Tax Effect 40%	Income Effect (net of tax)
Prior to 2009	$600,000	$400,000	$200,000	$80,000	$120,000
In 2009	180,000	160,000	20,000	8,000	12,000
Total at beginning of 2010	$780,000	$560,000	$220,000	$88,000	$132,000
Total in 2010	$200,000	$190,000	$ 10,000	$ 4,000	$ 6,000

ILLUSTRATION 22-2
Data for Retrospective Change Example

The entry to record the change at the beginning of 2010 would be:

Construction in Process	220,000	
Deferred Tax Liability		88,000
Retained Earnings		132,000

The Construction in Process account increases by $220,000 (as indicated in the first column under "Difference in Income" in Illustration 22-2). The credit to Retained Earnings of $132,000 reflects the cumulative income effects prior to 2010 (third column under "Difference in Income" in Illustration 22-2). The company credits Retained Earnings because prior years' income is closed to this account each year. The credit to Deferred Tax Liability represents the adjustment to prior years' tax expense. The company now recognizes that amount, $88,000, as a tax liability for future taxable amounts. That is, in future periods, taxable income will be higher than book income as a result of current temporary differences. Therefore, Denson must report a deferred tax liability in the current year.

CHANGE MANAGEMENT

Halliburton offers a case study in the importance of good reporting of an accounting change. Recall from Chapter 18 that Halliburton uses percentage-of-completion accounting for its long-term construction-services contracts. Recently, the SEC questioned the company about its change in accounting for disputed claims.

Prior to 1998 Halliburton took a very conservative approach to its accounting for disputed claims. That is, the company waited until all disputes were resolved before recognizing associated revenues. In contrast, in 1998 the company recognized revenue for disputed claims *before* their resolution, using estimates of amounts expected to be recovered. Such revenue and its related profit are more tentative and subject to possible later adjustment. The accounting method adopted in 1998 is more aggressive than the company's former policy but is within the boundaries of GAAP.

It appears that the problem with Halliburton's accounting stems more from how the company handled its accounting change than from the new method itself. That is, Halliburton did not provide in its 1998 annual report an explicit reference to its change in accounting method. In fact, rather than stating its new policy, the company simply deleted the sentence that described how it accounted for disputed claims. Then later, in its 1999 annual report, the company stated its new accounting policy.

When companies make such changes in accounting, investors need to be informed about the change and about its effects on the financial results. With such information, investors and analysts can compare current results with those of prior periods and can make a more informed assessment about the company's future prospects.

Source: Adapted from "Accounting Ace Charles Mulford Answers Accounting Questions," *Wall Street Journal Online* (June 7, 2002).

Reporting a Change in Principle. The disclosure of accounting changes is particularly important. Users of the financial statements want consistent information from one period to the next. Such consistency ensures the usefulness of financial statements. The major disclosure requirements are as follows.

1. The nature of and reason for the change in accounting principle. This must include an explanation of why the newly adopted accounting principle is preferable.
2. The method of applying the change, and:
   a. A description of the prior-period information that has been retrospectively adjusted, if any.
   b. The effect of the change on income from continuing operations, net income (or other appropriate captions of changes in net assets or performance indicators), any other affected line item, and any affected per-share amounts for the current period and for any prior periods retrospectively adjusted.
   c. The cumulative effect of the change on retained earnings or other components of equity or net assets in the statement of financial position as of the beginning of the earliest period presented.[2]

To illustrate, Denson will prepare comparative financial statements for 2009 and 2010 using the percentage-of-completion method (the new-construction accounting method). Illustration 22-3 (on page 1187) indicates how Denson presents this information.

[2]Presentation of the effect on financial statement subtotals and totals other than income from continuing operations and net income (or other appropriate captions of changes in the applicable net assets or performance indicator) is not required. [3]

DENSON COMPANY
INCOME STATEMENT (PARTIAL)
FOR THE YEAR ENDED

	2010	2009
		As adjusted (Note A)
Income before income tax	$200,000	$180,000
Income tax (40%)	80,000	72,000
Net income	$120,000	$108,000

Note A: Change in Method of Accounting for Long-Term Contracts. The company has accounted for revenue and costs for long-term construction contracts by the percentage-of-completion method in 2010, whereas in all prior years revenue and costs were determined by the completed-contract method. The new method of accounting for long-term contracts was adopted to recognize . . . [state justification for change in accounting principle] . . ., and financial statements of prior years have been restated to apply the new method retrospectively. For income tax purposes, the completed-contract method has been continued. The effect of the accounting change on income of 2010 was an increase of $6,000 net of related taxes and on income of 2009 as previously reported was an increase of $12,000 net of related taxes. The balances of retained earnings for 2009 and 2010 have been adjusted for the effect of applying retroactively the new method of accounting. As a result of the accounting change, retained earnings as of January 1, 2009, increased by $120,000 compared to that reported using the completed-contract method.

ILLUSTRATION 22-3
Comparative Information
Related to Accounting
Change (Percentage-of-
Completion)

As Illustration 22-3 shows, Denson Company reports net income under the newly adopted percentage-of-completion method for both 2009 and 2010. The company retrospectively adjusted the 2009 income statement to report the information on a percentage-of-completion basis. Also, the note to the financial statements indicates the nature of the change, why the company made the change, and the years affected.

In addition, companies are required to provide data on important differences between the amounts reported under percentage-of-completion versus completed-contract. When identifying the significant differences, some companies show the *entire* financial statements and line-by-line differences between percentage-of-completion and completed-contract. However, most companies will show only line-by-line differences. For example, Denson would show the differences in construction in process, retained earnings, gross profit, and net income for 2009 and 2010 under the completed-contract and percentage-of-completion methods.

Retained Earnings Adjustment. As indicated earlier, one of the disclosure requirements is to show the cumulative effect of the change on retained earnings as of the beginning of the earliest period presented. For Denson Company, that date is January 1, 2009. Denson disclosed that information by means of a narrative description (see Note A in Illustration 22-3). Denson also would disclose this information in its retained earnings statement. Assuming a retained earnings balance of $1,360,000 at the beginning of 2008, Illustration 22-4 shows Denson's retained earnings statement under the completed-contract method—that is, before giving effect to the change in accounting principle. (The income information comes from Illustration 22-1 on page 1185.)

DENSON COMPANY
RETAINED EARNINGS STATEMENT
FOR THE YEAR ENDED

	2010	2009	2008
Retained earnings, January 1	$1,696,000	$1,600,000	$1,360,000
Net income	114,000	96,000	240,000
Retained earnings, December 31	$1,810,000	$1,696,000	$1,600,000

ILLUSTRATION 22-4
Retained Earnings
Statement before
Retrospective Change

If Denson presents comparative statements for 2009 and 2010 under percentage-of-completion, then it must change the beginning balance of retained earnings at January 1,

2009. The difference between the retained earnings balances under completed-contract and percentage-of-completion is computed as follows.

Retained earnings, January 1, 2009 (percentage-of-completion)	$1,720,000
Retained earnings, January 1, 2009 (completed-contract)	1,600,000
Cumulative-effect difference	$ 120,000

The $120,000 difference is the cumulative effect. Illustration 22-5 shows a comparative retained earnings statement for 2009 and 2010, giving effect to the change in accounting principle to percentage-of-completion.

ILLUSTRATION 22-5
Retained Earnings
Statement after
Retrospective Application

DENSON COMPANY RETAINED EARNINGS STATEMENT FOR THE YEAR ENDED		
	2010	**2009**
Retained earnings, January 1, as reported	—	$1,600,000
Add: Adjustment for the cumulative effect on prior years of applying retrospectively the new method of accounting for construction contracts		120,000
Retained earnings, January 1, as adjusted	$1,828,000	1,720,000
Net income	120,000	108,000
Retained earnings, December 31	$1,948,000	$1,828,000

Denson adjusted the beginning balance of retained earnings on January 1, 2009, for the excess of percentage-of-completion net income over completed-contract net income in 2008. This comparative presentation indicates the type of adjustment that a company needs to make. It follows that this adjustment would be much larger if a number of prior periods were involved.

Retrospective Accounting Change: Inventory Methods

As a second illustration of the retrospective approach, assume that Lancer Company has accounted for its inventory using the LIFO method. In 2010, the company changes to the FIFO method because management believes this approach provides a more appropriate measure of its inventory costs. Illustration 22-6 provides additional information related to Lancer Company.

ILLUSTRATION 22-6
Lancer Company
Information

1. Lancer Company started its operations on January 1, 2008. At that time stockholders invested $100,000 in the business in exchange for common stock.

2. All sales, purchases, and operating expenses for the period 2008–2010 are cash transactions. Lancer's cash flows over this period are as follows.

	2008	2009	2010
Sales	$300,000	$300,000	$300,000
Purchases	90,000	110,000	125,000
Operating expenses	100,000	100,000	100,000
Cash flow from operations	$110,000	$ 90,000	$ 75,000

3. Lancer has used the LIFO method for financial reporting since its inception.

4. Inventory determined under LIFO and FIFO for the period 2008–2010 is as follows.

	LIFO Method	FIFO Method	Difference
January 1, 2008	$ 0	$ 0	$ 0
December 31, 2008	10,000	12,000	2,000
December 31, 2009	20,000	25,000	5,000
December 31, 2010	32,000	39,000	7,000

continued on next page

5. Cost of goods sold under LIFO and FIFO for the period 2008–2010 are as follows.

	Cost of Goods Sold LIFO	Cost of Goods Sold FIFO	Difference
2008	$ 80,000	$ 78,000	$2,000
2009	100,000	97,000	3,000
2010	113,000	111,000	2,000

6. Earnings per share information is not required on the income statement.
7. All tax effects for this illustration should be ignored.

Given the information about Lancer Company, Illustration 22-7 shows its income statement, retained earnings statement, balance sheet, and statement of cash flows for 2008–2010 under LIFO.

ILLUSTRATION 22-7
Lancer Financial Statements (LIFO)

LANCER COMPANY
INCOME STATEMENT
FOR THE YEAR ENDED DECEMBER 31

	2008	2009	2010
Sales	$300,000	$300,000	$300,000
Cost of goods sold (LIFO)	80,000	100,000	113,000
Operating expenses	100,000	100,000	100,000
Net income	$120,000	$100,000	$ 87,000

LANCER COMPANY
RETAINED EARNINGS STATEMENT
FOR THE YEAR ENDED DECEMBER 31

	2008	2009	2010
Retained earnings (beginning)	$ 0	$120,000	$220,000
Add: Net income	120,000	100,000	87,000
Retained earnings (ending)	$120,000	$220,000	$307,000

LANCER COMPANY
BALANCE SHEET
AT DECEMBER 31

	2008	2009	2010
Cash	$210,000	$300,000	$375,000
Inventory (LIFO)	10,000	20,000	32,000
Total assets	$220,000	$320,000	$407,000
Common stock	$100,000	$100,000	$100,000
Retained earnings	120,000	220,000	307,000
Total liabilities and stockholders' equity	$220,000	$320,000	$407,000

LANCER COMPANY
STATEMENT OF CASH FLOWS
FOR THE YEAR ENDED DECEMBER 31

	2008	2009	2010
Cash flows from operating activities			
Sales	$300,000	$300,000	$300,000
Purchases	90,000	110,000	125,000
Operating expenses	100,000	100,000	100,000
Net cash provided by operating activities	110,000	90,000	75,000
Cash flows from financing activities			
Issuance of common stock	100,000	—	—
Net increase in cash	210,000	90,000	75,000
Cash at beginning of year	0	210,000	300,000
Cash at end of year	$210,000	$300,000	$375,000

As Illustration 22-7 indicates, under LIFO Lancer Company reports $120,000 net income in 2008, $100,000 net income in 2009, and $87,000 net income in 2010. The amount of inventory reported on Lancer's balance sheet reflects LIFO costing.

Illustration 22-8 shows Lancer's income statement, retained earnings statement, balance sheet, and statement of cash flows for 2008–2010 under **FIFO**. You can see that **the cash flow statement under FIFO is the same as under LIFO**. Although the net incomes are different in each period, there is no cash flow effect from these differences in net income. (If we considered income taxes, a cash flow effect would result.)

ILLUSTRATION 22-8
Lancer Financial
Statements (FIFO)

LANCER COMPANY
INCOME STATEMENT
FOR THE YEAR ENDED DECEMBER 31

	2008	2009	2010
Sales	$300,000	$300,000	$300,000
Cost of goods sold (FIFO)	78,000	97,000	111,000
Operating expenses	100,000	100,000	100,000
Net income	$122,000	$103,000	$ 89,000

LANCER COMPANY
RETAINED EARNINGS STATEMENT
FOR THE YEAR ENDED DECEMBER 31

	2008	2009	2010
Retained earnings (beginning)	$ 0	$122,000	$225,000
Add: Net income	122,000	103,000	89,000
Retained earnings (ending)	$122,000	$225,000	$314,000

LANCER COMPANY
BALANCE SHEET
AT DECEMBER 31

	2008	2009	2010
Cash	$210,000	$300,000	$375,000
Inventory (FIFO)	12,000	25,000	39,000
Total assets	$222,000	$325,000	$414,000
Common stock	$100,000	$100,000	$100,000
Retained earnings	122,000	225,000	314,000
Total liabilities and stockholders' equity	$222,000	$325,000	$414,000

LANCER COMPANY
STATEMENT OF CASH FLOWS
FOR THE YEAR ENDED DECEMBER 31

	2008	2009	2010
Cash flows from operating activities			
Sales	$300,000	$300,000	$300,000
Purchases	90,000	110,000	125,000
Operating expenses	100,000	100,000	100,000
Net cash provided by operating activities	110,000	90,000	75,000
Cash flows from financing activities			
Issuance of common stock	100,000	—	—
Net increase in cash	210,000	90,000	75,000
Cast at beginning of year	0	210,000	300,000
Cash at end of year	$210,000	$300,000	$375,000

Compare the financial statements reported in Illustration 22-7 and Illustration 22-8. You can see that, under retrospective application, the change to FIFO inventory valuation affects reported inventories, cost of goods sold, net income, and retained earnings. In the following sections we discuss the accounting and reporting of Lancer's accounting change from LIFO to FIFO.

Given the information provided in Illustrations 22-6, 22-7, and 22-8, we now are ready to account for and report on the accounting change.

Our first step is to adjust the financial records for the change from LIFO to FIFO. To do so, we perform the analysis in Illustration 22-9.

ILLUSTRATION 22-9
Data for Recording
Change in Accounting
Principle

	Net Income		Difference in Income
Year	LIFO	FIFO	
2008	$120,000	$122,000	$2,000
2009	100,000	103,000	3,000
Total at beginning of 2010	$220,000	$225,000	$5,000
Total in 2010	$ 87,000	$ 89,000	$2,000

The entry to record the change to the FIFO method at the beginning of 2010 is as follows.

Inventory	5,000	
Retained Earnings		5,000

The change increases the inventory account by $5,000. This amount represents the difference between the ending inventory at December 31, 2009, under LIFO ($20,000) and the ending inventory under FIFO ($25,000). The credit to Retained Earnings indicates the amount needed to change prior-year's income, assuming that Lancer had used FIFO in previous periods.

Reporting a Change in Principle. Lancer Company will prepare comparative financial statements for 2009 and 2010 using FIFO (the new inventory method). Illustration 22-10 indicates how Lancer might present this information.

ILLUSTRATION 22-10
Comparative Information
Related to Accounting
Change (FIFO)

LANCER COMPANY
INCOME STATEMENT
FOR THE YEAR ENDED DECEMBER 31

	2010	2009
		As adjusted (Note A)
Sales	$300,000	$300,000
Cost of goods sold	111,000	97,000
Operating expenses	100,000	100,000
Net income	$ 89,000	$103,000

Note A
Change in Method of Accounting for Inventory Valuation On January 1, 2010, Lancer Company elected to change its method of valuing its inventory to the FIFO method; in all prior years inventory was valued using the LIFO method. The Company adopted the new method of accounting for inventory to better report cost of goods sold in the year incurred. Comparative financial statements of prior years have been adjusted to apply the new method retrospectively. The following financial statement line items for years 2010 and 2009 were affected by the change in accounting principle.

Nature and reason for change
Description of prior period information adjusted

	2010			2009		
Balance Sheet	LIFO	FIFO	Difference	LIFO	FIFO	Difference
Inventory	$ 32,000	$ 39,000	$7,000	$ 20,000	$ 25,000	$5,000
Retained earnings	307,000	314,000	7,000	220,000	225,000	5,000
Income Statement						
Cost of goods sold	$113,000	$111,000	$2,000	$100,000	$ 97,000	$3,000
Net income	87,000	89,000	2,000	100,000	103,000	3,000
Statement of Cash Flows						
(no effect)						

Effect of change on key performance indicators

As a result of the accounting change, retained earnings as of January 1, 2009, increased from $120,000, as originally reported using the LIFO method, to $122,000 using the FIFO method.

Cumulative effect on retained earnings

As Illustration 22-10 shows, Lancer Company reports net income under the newly adopted FIFO method for both 2009 and 2010. The company retrospectively adjusted the 2009 income statement to report the information on a FIFO basis. In addition, the note to the financial statements indicates the nature of the change, why the company made the change, and the years affected. The note also provides data on important differences between the amounts reported under LIFO versus FIFO. (When identifying the significant differences, some companies show the *entire* financial statements and line-by-line differences between LIFO and FIFO.)

Retained Earnings Adjustment. As indicated earlier, one of the disclosure requirements is to show the cumulative effect of the change on retained earnings as of the beginning of the earliest period presented. For Lancer Company, that date is January 1, 2009. Lancer disclosed that information by means of a narrative description (see Note A in Illustration 22-10). Lancer also would disclose this information in its retained earnings statement. Illustration 22-11 shows Lancer's retained earnings statement under LIFO—that is, before giving effect to the change in accounting principle. (This information comes from Illustration 22-7 on page 1189.)

ILLUSTRATION 22-11
Retained Earnings
Statements (LIFO)

	2010	2009	2008
Retained earnings, January 1	$220,000	$120,000	$ 0
Net income	87,000	100,000	120,000
Retained earnings, December 31	$307,000	$220,000	$120,000

If Lancer presents comparative statements for 2009 and 2010 under FIFO, then it must change the beginning balance of retained earnings at January 1, 2009. The difference between the retained earnings balances under LIFO and FIFO is computed as follows.

Retained earnings, January 1, 2009 (FIFO)	$122,000
Retained earnings, January 1, 2009 (LIFO)	120,000
Cumulative effect difference	$ 2,000

The $2,000 difference is the cumulative effect. Illustration 22-12 shows a comparative retained earnings statement for 2009 and 2010, giving effect to the change in accounting principle to FIFO.

ILLUSTRATION 22-12
Retained Earnings
Statements after
Retrospective Application

	2010	2009
Retained earnings, January 1, as reported		$120,000
Add: Adjustment for the cumulative effect on prior years of applying retrospectively the new method of accounting for inventory		2,000
Retained earnings, January 1, as adjusted	$225,000	122,000
Net income	89,000	103,000
Retained earnings, December 31	$314,000	$225,000

Lancer adjusted the beginning balance of retained earnings on January 1, 2009, for the excess of FIFO net income over LIFO net income in 2008. This comparative presentation indicates the type of adjustment that a company needs to make. It follows that the amount of this adjustment would be much larger if a number of prior periods were involved.

Direct and Indirect Effects of Changes

Are there other effects that a company should report when it makes a change in accounting principle? For example, what happens when a company like Lancer has a bonus plan based on net income and the prior year's net income changes when FIFO is retrospectively applied? Should Lancer also change the reported amount of bonus expense? Or what happens if we had not ignored income taxes in the Lancer example? Should Lancer adjust net income, given that taxes will be different under LIFO and FIFO in prior periods? The answers depend on whether the effects are direct or indirect.

Direct Effects. The FASB takes the position that companies should retrospectively apply the **direct effects of a change in accounting principle.** An example of a **direct effect** is an adjustment to an inventory balance as a result of a change in the inventory valuation method. For example, Lancer Company should change the inventory amounts in prior periods to indicate the change to the FIFO method of inventory valuation. Another inventory-related example would be an impairment adjustment resulting from applying the lower-of-cost-or-market test to the adjusted inventory balance. Related changes, such as deferred income tax effects of the impairment adjustment, are also considered direct effects. This entry was illustrated in the Denson example, in which the change to percentage-of-completion accounting resulted in recording a deferred tax liability.

Indirect Effects. In addition to direct effects, companies can have **indirect effects related to a change in accounting principle.** An **indirect effect** is any change to current or future cash flows of a company that result from making a change in accounting principle that is applied retrospectively. An example of an indirect effect is a change in profit-sharing or royalty payment that is based on a reported amount such as revenue or net income. **Indirect effects do not change prior-period amounts.**

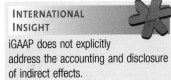

INTERNATIONAL INSIGHT

iGAAP does not explicitly address the accounting and disclosure of indirect effects.

For example, let's assume that Lancer has an employee profit-sharing plan based on net income. As Illustration 22-9 (on page 1191) showed, Lancer would report higher income in 2008 and 2009 if it used the FIFO method. In addition, let's assume that the profit-sharing plan requires that Lancer pay the incremental amount due based on the FIFO income amounts. In this situation, Lancer reports this additional expense **in the current period**; it would not change prior periods for this expense. If the company prepares comparative financial statements, it follows that it does not recast the prior periods for this additional expense.[3]

If the terms of the profit-sharing plan indicate that *no payment is necessary* in the current period due to this change, then the company need not recognize additional profit-sharing expense in the current period. Neither does it change amounts reported for prior periods.

When a company recognizes the indirect effects of a change in accounting principle, it includes in the financial statements a description of the indirect effects. In doing so, it discloses the amounts recognized in the current period and related per share information.

Impracticability

It is not always possible for companies to determine how they would have reported prior periods' financial information under retrospective application of an accounting principle change. Retrospective application is considered **impracticable** if a company cannot determine the prior-period effects using every reasonable effort to do so.

> **Objective·4**
> Understand how to account for impracticable changes.

---

[3]The rationale for this approach is that companies should recognize, in the period the adoption occurs (not the prior period), the effect on the cash flows that is caused by the adoption of the new accounting principle. That is, the accounting change is a necessary "past event" in the definition of an asset or liability that gives rise to the accounting recognition of the indirect effect in the current period. [4]

Companies should not use retrospective application if one of the following conditions exists:

1. The company cannot determine the effects of the retrospective application.
2. Retrospective application requires assumptions about management's intent in a prior period.
3. Retrospective application requires significant estimates for a prior period, and the company cannot objectively verify the necessary information to develop these estimates.

If any of the above conditions exists, it is deemed impracticable to apply the retrospective approach. In this case, the company **prospectively applies** the new accounting principle as of the earliest date it is practicable to do so. [5]

For example, assume that Williams Company changed its inventory method from FIFO to LIFO, effective January 1, 2011. Williams prepares statements on a calendar-year basis and has used the FIFO method since its inception. Williams judges it impracticable to retrospectively apply the new method. Determining prior-period effects would require subjective assumptions about the LIFO layers established in prior periods. These assumptions would ordinarily result in the computation of a number of different earnings figures.

As a result, the only adjustment necessary may be to restate the beginning inventory to a cost basis from a lower-of-cost-or-market approach. Williams must disclose only the effect of the change on the results of operations in the period of change. Also, the company should explain the reasons for omitting the computations of the cumulative effect for prior years. Finally, it should disclose the justification for the change to LIFO. [6][4] Illustration 22-13, from the annual report of **Quaker Oats Company**, shows the type of disclosure needed.

ILLUSTRATION 22-13
Disclosure of Change
to LIFO

The Quaker Oats Company

Note 1 (In Part): Summary of Significant Accounting Policies

Inventories. Inventories are valued at the lower of cost or market, using various cost methods, and include the cost of raw materials, labor and overhead. The percentage of year-end inventories valued using each of the methods is as follows:

June 30	Current Year	Prior Year
Average quarterly cost	21%	54%
Last-in, first-out (LIFO)	65%	29%
First-in, first-out (FIFO)	14%	17%

    Effective July 1, the Company adopted the LIFO cost flow assumption for valuing the majority of remaining U.S. Grocery Products inventories. The Company believes that the use of the LIFO method better matches current costs with current revenues. The cumulative effect of this change on retained earnings at the beginning of the year is not determinable, nor are the pro-forma effects of retroactive application of LIFO to prior years. The effect of this change on current-year fiscal results was to decrease net income by $16.0 million, or $.20 per share.

    If the LIFO method of valuing certain inventories were not used, total inventories would have been $60.1 million higher in the current year, and $24.0 million higher in the prior year.

---

[4]In practice, many companies defer the formal adoption of LIFO until year-end. Management thus has an opportunity to assess the impact that a change to LIFO will have on the financial statements and to evaluate the desirability of a change for tax purposes. As indicated in Chapter 8, many companies use LIFO because of the advantages of this inventory valuation method in a period of inflation.

CHANGES IN ACCOUNTING ESTIMATE

To prepare financial statements, companies must estimate the effects of future conditions and events. For example, the following items require estimates.

> **Objective·5**
> Describe the accounting for changes in estimates.

1. Uncollectible receivables.
2. Inventory obsolescence.
3. Useful lives and salvage values of assets.
4. Periods benefited by deferred costs.
5. Liabilities for warranty costs and income taxes.
6. Recoverable mineral reserves.
7. Change in depreciation methods.

A company cannot perceive future conditions and events and their effects with certainty. Therefore, estimating requires the exercise of judgment. Accounting estimates will change as new events occur, as a company acquires more experience, or as it obtains additional information.

Prospective Reporting

Companies report prospectively changes in accounting estimates. That is, companies should not adjust previously reported results for changes in estimates. Instead, they account for the effects of all changes in estimates in (1) the period of change if the change affects that period only, or (2) the period of change and future periods if the change affects both. The FASB views changes in estimates as **normal recurring corrections and adjustments**, the natural result of the accounting process. It prohibits retrospective treatment.

The circumstances related to a change in estimate differ from those for a change in accounting principle. If companies reported changes in estimates retrospectively, continual adjustments of prior years' income would occur. It seems proper to accept the view that, because new conditions or circumstances exist, the revision fits the new situation (not the old one). Companies should therefore handle such a revision in the current and future periods.

To illustrate, Underwriters Labs Inc. purchased for $300,000 a building that it originally estimated to have a useful life of 15 years and no salvage value. It recorded depreciation for 5 years on a straight-line basis. On January 1, 2010, Underwriters Labs revises the estimate of the useful life. It now considers the asset to have a total life of 25 years. (Assume that the useful life for financial reporting and tax purposes and depreciation method are the same.) Illustration 22-14 shows the accounts at the beginning of the sixth year.

Building	$300,000
Less: Accumulated depreciation—building (5 × $20,000)	100,000
Book value of building	$200,000

ILLUSTRATION 22-14
Book Value after Five Years' Depreciation

Underwriters Labs records depreciation for the year 2010 as follows:

Depreciation Expense	10,000	
Accumulated Depreciation—Building		10,000

The company computes the $10,000 depreciation charge as shown in Illustration 22-15.

$$\text{Depreciation charge} = \frac{\text{Book value of asset}}{\text{Remaining service live}} = \frac{\$200,000}{25 \text{ years} - 5 \text{ years}} = \$10,000$$

ILLUSTRATION 22-15
Depreciation after Change in Estimate

Companies sometimes find it difficult to differentiate between a change in estimate and a change in accounting principle. Is it a change in principle or a change in estimate when a company changes from deferring and amortizing marketing costs to expensing them as incurred because future benefits of these costs have become doubtful? If it is impossible to determine whether a change in principle or a change in estimate has occurred, the rule is this: **Consider the change as a change in estimate.** This is often referred to as a change in estimate effected by a change in accounting principle.

Another example of a change in estimate effected by a change in principle is a change in depreciation (as well as amortization or depletion) methods. Because companies change depreciation methods based on changes in estimates about future benefits from long-lived assets, it is not possible to separate the effect of the accounting principle change from that of the estimates. **As a result, companies account for a change in depreciation methods as a change in estimate effected by a change in accounting principle. [7]**

A similar problem occurs in differentiating between a change in estimate and a correction of an error, although here the answer is more clear-cut. How does a company determine whether it overlooked the information in earlier periods (an error), or whether it obtained new information (a change in estimate)? Proper classification is important because the accounting treatment differs for corrections of errors versus changes in estimates. The general rule is this: **Companies should consider careful estimates that later prove to be incorrect as changes in estimate.** Only when a company obviously computed the estimate incorrectly because of lack of expertise or in bad faith should it consider the adjustment an error. There is no clear demarcation line here. Companies must use good judgment in light of all the circumstances.[5]

Disclosures

Illustration 22-16 shows disclosure of a change in estimated useful lives, which appeared in the annual report of **Ampco–Pittsburgh Corporation.**

ILLUSTRATION 22-16
Disclosure of Change
in Estimated Useful Lives

Ampco–Pittsburgh Corporation

Note 11: Change in Accounting Estimate. The Corporation revised its estimate of the useful lives of certain machinery and equipment. Previously, all machinery and equipment, whether new when placed in use or not, were in one class and depreciated over 15 years. The change principally applies to assets purchased new when placed in use. Those lives are now extended to 20 years. These changes were made to better reflect the estimated periods during which such assets will remain in service. The change had the effect of reducing depreciation expense and increasing net income by approximately $991,000 ($.10 per share).

For the most part, companies need not disclose changes in accounting estimate made as part of normal operations, such as bad debt allowances or inventory obsolescence, unless such changes are material. However, for a change in estimate that affects several periods (such as a change in the service lives of depreciable assets), companies should disclose the effect on income from continuing operations and related per-share

---

[5]In evaluating reasonableness, the auditor should use one or a combination of the following approaches.

(a) Review and test the process used by management to develop the estimate.

(b) Develop an independent expectation of the estimate to corroborate the reasonableness of management's estimate.

(c) Review subsequent events or transactions occurring prior to completion of fieldwork.

"Auditing Accounting Estimates," *Statement on Auditing Standards No. 57* (New York: AICPA, 1988).

amounts of the current period. When a company has a change in estimate effected by a change in accounting principle, it must indicate why the new method is preferable. In addition, companies are subject to all other disclosure guidelines established for changes in accounting principle.

CHANGE IN REPORTING ENTITY

Occasionally companies make changes that result in different reporting entities. In such cases, companies report the change by **changing the financial statements of all prior periods presented**. The revised statements show the financial information for the **new reporting entity** for all periods.

> **Objective·6**
> Identify changes in a reporting entity.

Examples of a change in reporting entity are:

1. Presenting consolidated statements in place of statements of individual companies.
2. Changing specific subsidiaries that constitute the group of companies for which the entity presents consolidated financial statements.
3. Changing the companies included in combined financial statements.
4. Changing the cost, equity, or consolidation method of accounting for subsidiaries and investments.[6] In this case, a change in the reporting entity does not result from creation, cessation, purchase, or disposition of a subsidiary or other business unit.

In the year in which a company changes a reporting entity, it should disclose in the financial statements the nature of the change and the reason for it. It also should report, for all periods presented, the effect of the change on income before extraordinary items, net income, and earnings per share. These disclosures need not be repeated in subsequent periods' financial statements.

Illustration 22-17 shows a note disclosing a change in reporting entity, from the annual report of **Hewlett-Packard Company**.

Hewlett-Packard Company

Note: Accounting and Reporting Changes (In Part)

Consolidation of Hewlett-Packard Finance Company. The company implemented a new accounting pronouncement on consolidations. With the adoption of this new pronouncement, the company consolidated the accounts of Hewlett-Packard Finance Company (HPFC), a wholly owned subsidiary previously accounted for under the equity method, with those of the company. The change resulted in an increase in consolidated assets and liabilities but did not have a material effect on the company's financial position. Since HPFC was previously accounted for under the equity method, the change did not affect net earnings. Prior years' consolidated financial information has been restated to reflect this change for comparative purposes.

ILLUSTRATION 22-17
Disclosure of Change in Reporting Entity

CORRECTION OF ERRORS

No business, large or small, is immune from errors. As the opening story discussed, the number of accounting errors that lead to restatement are beginning to decline. However, without accounting and disclosure guidelines for the reporting of errors, investors can be left in the dark about the effects of errors.

> **Objective·7**
> Describe the accounting for correction of errors.

Certain errors, such as misclassifications of balances within a financial statement, are not as significant to investors as other errors. Significant errors would

---

[6]An exception to retrospective application occurs when changing from the equity method. We provide an expanded illustration of the accounting for a change from or to the equity method in Appendix 22A.

be those resulting in overstating assets or income, for example. However, investors should know the potential impact of all errors. Even "harmless" misclassifications can affect important ratios. Also, some errors could signal important weaknesses in internal controls that could lead to more significant errors.

In general, accounting errors include the following types:

1. A change from an accounting principle that is **not** generally accepted to an accounting principle that is acceptable. The rationale is that the company incorrectly presented prior periods because of the application of an improper accounting principle. For example, a company may change from the cash (income tax) basis of accounting to the accrual basis.

2. Mathematical mistakes, such as incorrectly totaling the inventory count sheets when computing the inventory value.

3. Changes in estimates that occur because a company did not prepare the estimates in good faith. For example, a company may have adopted a clearly unrealistic depreciation rate.

4. An oversight, such as the failure to accrue or defer certain expenses and revenues at the end of the period.

5. A misuse of facts, such as the failure to use salvage value in computing the depreciation base for the straight-line approach.

6. The incorrect classification of a cost as an expense instead of an asset, and vice versa.

ILLUSTRATION 22-18
Accounting-Error Types

Accounting errors occur for a variety of reasons. Illustration 22-18 indicates 11 major categories of accounting errors that drive restatements.

Accounting Category	Type of Restatement
Expense recognition	Recording expenses in the incorrect period or for an incorrect amount
Revenue recognition	Improper revenue accounting. This category includes instances in which revenue was improperly recognized, questionable revenues were recognized, or any other number of related errors that led to misreported revenue.
Misclassification	Misclassifying significant accounting items on the balance sheet, income statement, or statement of cash flows. These include restatements due to misclassification of short- or long-term accounts or those that impact cash flows from operations
Equity—other	Improper accounting for EPS, restricted stock, warrants, and other equity instruments
Reserves/Contingencies	Errors involving accounts receivables bad debts, inventory reserves, income tax allowances, and loss contingencies
Long-lived assets	Asset impairments of property, plant, and equipment, goodwill, or other related items.
Taxes	Errors involving correction of tax provision, improper treatment of tax liabilities, and other tax-related items
Equity—other comprehensive income	Improper accounting for comprehensive income equity transactions including foreign currency items, minimum pension liability adjustments, unrealized gains and losses on certain investments in debt, equity securities, and derivatives.
Inventory	Inventory costing valuations, quantity issues, and cost of sales adjustments
Equity—stock options	Improper accounting for employee stock options
Other	Any restatement not covered by the listed categories including those related to improper accounting for acquisitions or mergers

Source: T. Baldwin and D. Yoo, "Restatements—Traversing Shaky Ground," *Trend Alert*, Glass Lewis & Co. (June 2, 2005), p. 8.

As soon as a company discovers an error, it must correct the error. Companies record **corrections of errors** from prior periods as an adjustment to the beginning balance of retained earnings in the current period. Such corrections are called **prior period adjustments**.[7] [8]

[7]See Mark L. DeFord and James Jiambalvo, "Incidence and Circumstances of Accounting Errors," *The Accounting Review* (July 1991) for examples of different types of errors and why these errors might have occurred.

If it presents comparative statements, a company should restate the prior statements affected, to correct for the error.[8] The company need not repeat the disclosures in the financial statements of subsequent periods.

Example of Error Correction

To illustrate, in 2011 the bookkeeper for Selectro Company discovered an error: In 2010 the company failed to record $20,000 of depreciation expense on a newly constructed building. This building is the only depreciable asset Selectro owns. The company correctly included the depreciation expense in its tax return and correctly reported its income taxes payable. Illustration 22-19 presents Selectro's income statement for 2010 (starting with income before depreciation expense) with and without the error.

SELECTRO COMPANY INCOME STATEMENT FOR THE YEAR ENDED, DECEMBER 31, 2010				
		Without Error		With Error
Income before depreciation expense		$100,000		$100,000
Depreciation expense		20,000		0
Income before income tax		80,000		100,000
Current	$32,000		$ 32,000	
Deferred	–0–	32,000	8,000	40,000
Net income		$ 48,000		$ 60,000

ILLUSTRATION 22-19
Error Correction
Comparison

Illustration 22-20 shows the entries that Selectro should have made and did make for recording depreciation expense and income taxes.

Entries Company Should Have Made (Without Error)			Entries Company Did Make (With Error)		
Depreciation Expense	20,000		No entry made for depreciation		
Accumulated Depreciation —Buildings		20,000			
Income Tax Expense	32,000		Income Tax Expense	40,000	
Income Tax Payable		32,000	Deferred Tax Liability		8,000
			Income Tax Payable		32,000

ILLUSTRATION 22-20
Error Entries

As Illustration 22-20 indicates, the $20,000 omission error in 2010 results in the following effects.

Income Statement Effects

Depreciation expense (2010) is understated $20,000.

Income tax expense (2010) is overstated $8,000 ($20,000 × 40%).

Net income (2010) is overstated $12,000 ($20,000 − $8,000).

Balance Sheet Effects

Accumulated depreciation—buildings is understated $20,000.

Deferred tax liability is overstated $8,000 ($20,000 × 40%).

To make the proper correcting entry in 2011, Selectro should recognize that net income in 2010 is overstated by $12,000, the Deferred Tax Liability is overstated by $8,000,

---

[8]The term **restatement** is used for the process of revising previously issued financial statements to reflect the correction of an error. This distinguishes an error correction from a change in accounting principle. [9]

and Accumulated Depreciation—Buildings is understated by $20,000. The entry to correct this error in 2011 is as follows:

Retained Earnings	12,000	
Deferred Tax Liability	8,000	
Accumulated Depreciation—Buildings		20,000

The debit to Retained Earnings results because net income for 2010 is overstated. The debit to the Deferred Tax Liability is made to remove this account, which was caused by the error. The credit to Accumulated Depreciation—Buildings reduces the book value of the building to its proper amount. Selectro will make the same journal entry to record the correction of the error in 2011 whether it prepares single-period (noncomparative) or comparative financial statements.

Single-Period Statements

To demonstrate how to show this information in a single-period statement, assume that Selectro Company has a beginning retained earnings balance at January 1, 2011, of $350,000. The company reports net income of $400,000 in 2011. Illustration 22-21 shows Selectro's retained earnings statement for 2011.

ILLUSTRATION 22-21
Reporting an Error—
Single-Period Financial
Statement

SELECTRO COMPANY RETAINED EARNINGS STATEMENT FOR THE YEAR ENDED DECEMBER 31, 2011		
Retained earnings, January 1, as reported		$350,000
Correction of an error (depreciation)	$20,000	
Less: Applicable income tax reduction	8,000	(12,000)
Retained earnings, January 1, as adjusted		338,000
Add: Net income		400,000
Retained earnings, December 31		$738,000

The balance sheet in 2011 would not have any deferred tax liability related to the building, and Accumulated Depreciation—Buildings is now restated at a higher amount. The income statement would not be affected.

Comparative Statements

If preparing comparative financial statements, a company should make adjustments to correct the amounts for all affected accounts reported in the statements for **all periods** reported. The company should restate the data to the correct basis for each year presented. It should **show any catch-up adjustment as a prior period adjustment to retained earnings for the earliest period it reported**. These requirements are essentially the same as those for reporting a change in accounting principle.

For example, in the case of Selectro, the error of omitting the depreciation of $20,000 in 2010, discovered in 2011, results in the restatement of the 2010 financial statements. Illustration 22-22 shows the accounts that Selectro restates in the 2010 financial statements.

ILLUSTRATION 22-22
Reporting an Error—
Comparative Financial
Statements

In the balance sheet:	
Accumulated depreciation—buildings	$20,000 increase
Deferred tax liability	$ 8,000 decrease
Retained earnings, ending balance	$12,000 decrease
In the income statement:	
Depreciation expense—buildings	$20,000 increase
Income tax expense	$ 8,000 decrease
Net income	$12,000 decrease
In the retained earnings statement:	
Retained earnings, ending balance (due to lower net income for the period)	$12,000 decrease

Selectro prepares the 2011 financial statements in comparative form with those of 2010 **as if the error had not occurred**. In addition, Selectro must disclose that it has restated its previously issued financial statements, and it describes the nature of the error. Selectro also must disclose the following:

1. The effect of the correction on each financial statement line item and any per-share amounts affected for each prior period presented.

2. The cumulative effect of the change on retained earnings or other appropriate components of equity or net assets in the statement of financial position, as of the beginning of the earliest period presented. [10]

SUMMARY OF ACCOUNTING CHANGES AND CORRECTION OF ERRORS

Having guidelines for reporting accounting changes and corrections has helped resolve several significant and long-standing accounting problems. Yet, because of diversity in situations and characteristics of the items encountered in practice, use of professional judgment is of paramount importance. In applying these guidelines, the primary objective is to serve the users of the financial statements. Achieving this objective requires accuracy, full disclosure, and an absence of misleading inferences.

Illustration 22-23 summarizes the main distinctions and treatments presented in the discussion in this chapter.

ILLUSTRATION 22-23
Summary of Guidelines for Accounting Changes and Errors

- **Changes in accounting principle**
  Employ the retrospective approach by:
  a. Changing the financial statements of all prior periods presented.
  b. Disclosing in the year of the change the effect on net income and earnings per share for all prior periods presented.
  c. Reporting an adjustment to the beginning retained earnings balance in the statement of retained earnings in the earliest year presented.
  If impracticable to determine the prior period effect (e.g., change to LIFO):
  a. Do not change prior years' income.
  b. Use opening inventory in the year the method is adopted as the base-year inventory for all subsequent LIFO computations.
  c. Disclose the effect of the change on the current year, and the reasons for omitting the computation of the cumulative effect and pro forma amounts for prior years.

- **Changes in accounting estimate.**
  Employ the current and prospective approach by:
  a. Reporting current and future financial statements on the new basis.
  b. Presenting prior period financial statements as previously reported.
  c. Making no adjustments to current-period opening balances for the effects in prior periods.

- **Changes in reporting entity.**
  Employ the retrospective approach by:
  a. Restating the financial statements of all prior periods presented.
  b. Disclosing in the year of change the effect on net income and earnings per share data for all prior periods presented.

- **Changes due to error.**
  Employ the restatement approach by:
  a. Correcting all prior period statements presented.
  b. Restating the beginning balance of retained earnings for the first period presented when the error effects occur in a period prior to the first period presented.

Changes in accounting principle are appropriate **only** when a company demonstrates that the newly adopted generally accepted accounting principle is **preferable** to the existing one. Companies and accountants determine preferability on the basis of whether the new principle constitutes an **improvement in financial reporting**, not on the basis of the income tax effect alone.[9]

But it is not always easy to determine an improvement in financial reporting. **How does one measure preferability or improvement?** Such measurement varies from company to company. **Quaker Oats Company**, for example, argued that a change in accounting principle to LIFO inventory valuation "better matches current costs with current revenues" (see Illustration 22-13, page 1194). Conversely, another company might change from LIFO to FIFO because it wishes to report a more realistic ending inventory. How do you determine which is the better of these two arguments? Determining the preferable method requires some "standard" or "objective." Because no universal standard or objective is generally accepted, the problem of determining preferability continues to be difficult.

Initially the SEC took the position that the auditor should indicate whether a change in accounting principle was preferable. The SEC has since modified this approach, noting that greater reliance may be placed on management's judgment in assessing preferability. Even though the preferability criterion is difficult to apply, the general guidelines have acted as a deterrent to capricious changes in accounting principles.[10] **If a FASB rule creates a new principle, expresses preference for, or rejects a specific accounting principle, a change is considered clearly acceptable.**

CAN I GET MY MONEY BACK?

What do the numbers mean?

When companies report restatements, investors usually lose money. What should investors do if a company misleads them by misstating its financial results? Join other investors in a class-action suit against the company and in some cases, the auditor.

Class-action activity has picked up in recent years, and settlements can be large. To find out about class actions, investors can go online to see if they are eligible to join any class actions. Below are some recent examples.

Company	Settlement Amount	Contact for Claim
Xerox	$670 million	*www.gilardi.com*
Transamerica HomeFirst	$ 8 million	*www.gilardi.com*
Tommy Hilfiger Corp.	$ 6 million	*www.gilardi.com*

The amounts reported are *before* attorney's fees, which can range from 15 to 30 percent of the total. Also, investors may owe taxes if the settlement results in a capital gain on the investment. Thus, investors can get back some of the money they lost due to restatements, but they should be prepared to pay an attorney and the government first.

Source: Adapted from C. Coolidge, "Lost and Found," *Forbes* (October 1, 2001), pp. 124–125; data from *www.gilardi.com* as of 8/14/08.

---

[9]A change in accounting principle, a change in the reporting entity (special type of change in accounting principle), and a correction of an error require an explanatory paragraph in the auditor's report discussing lack of consistency from one period to the next. A change in accounting estimate does not affect the auditor's opinion relative to consistency; however, if the change in estimate has a material effect on the financial statements, disclosure may still be required. Error correction not involving a change in accounting principle does not require disclosure relative to consistency.

[10]If management has not provided reasonable justification for the change in accounting principle, the auditor should express a qualified opinion. Or, if the effect of the change is sufficiently material, the auditor should express an adverse opinion on the financial statements. "Reports on Audited Financial Statements," *Statement on Auditing Standards No. 58* (New York: AICPA, 1988).

MOTIVATIONS FOR CHANGE OF ACCOUNTING METHOD

Difficult as it is to determine which accounting standards have the strongest conceptual support, other complications make the process even more complex. These complications stem from the fact that managers have self-interest in how the financial statements make the company look. They naturally wish to show their financial performance in the best light. A **favorable profit picture** can influence investors, and a strong liquidity position can influence creditors. **Too favorable a profit picture**, however, can provide union negotiators and government regulators with ammunition during bargaining talks. Hence, managers might have varying motives for reporting income numbers.

> **Objective·8**
> Identify economic motives for changing accounting methods.

Research has provided additional insight into why companies may prefer certain accounting methods.[11] Some of these reasons are as follows:

1. *Political Costs.* As companies become larger and more politically visible, politicians and regulators devote more attention to them. The larger the firm, the more likely it is to become subject to regulation such as antitrust, and the more likely it is to be required to pay higher taxes. Therefore, companies that are politically visible may seek to report low income numbers, to avoid the scrutiny of regulators. In addition, other constituents, such as labor unions, may be less willing to ask for wage increases if reported income is low. Researchers have found that the larger the company, the more likely it is to adopt income-decreasing approaches in selecting accounting methods.

2. *Capital Structure.* A number of studies have indicated that the capital structure of the company can affect the selection of accounting methods. For example, a company with a high debt-to-equity ratio is more likely to be constrained by debt covenants. The debt covenant may indicate that the company cannot pay dividends if retained earnings fall below a certain level. As a result, such a company is more likely to select accounting methods that will increase net income.

3. *Bonus Payments.* Studies have found that if compensation plans tie managers' bonus payments to income, management will select accounting methods that maximize their bonus payments.

4. *Smooth Earnings.* Substantial earnings increases attract the attention of politicians, regulators, and competitors. In addition, large increases in income are difficult to achieve in following years. Further, executive compensation plans would use these higher numbers as a baseline and make it difficult for managers to earn bonuses in subsequent years. Conversely, investors and competitors might view large decreases in earnings as a signal that the company is in financial trouble. Also, substantial decreases in income raise concerns on the part of stockholders, lenders, and other interested parties about the competency of management. For all these reasons, companies have an incentive to "manage" or "smooth" earnings. In general, management tends to believe that a steady 10 percent growth a year is much better than a 30 percent growth one year and a 10 percent decline the next.[12] In other words, managers usually prefer a gradually increasing income report and sometimes change accounting methods to ensure such a result.

Management pays careful attention to the accounting it follows and often changes accounting methods, not for conceptual reasons, but for economic reasons. As indicated

---

[11]See Ross L. Watts and Jerold L. Zimmerman, "Positive Accounting Theory: A Ten-Year Perspective," *The Accounting Review* (January 1990) for an excellent review of research findings related to management incentives in selecting accounting methods.

[12]O. Douglas Moses, "Income Smoothing and Incentives: Empirical Tests Using Accounting Changes," *The Accounting Review* (April 1987). The findings provide evidence that earnings smoothing is associated with firm size, the existence of bonus plans, and the divergence of actual earnings from expectations.

throughout this textbook, such arguments have come to be known as **economic consequences** arguments. These arguments focus on the supposed impact of the accounting method on the behavior of investors, creditors, competitors, governments, or managers of the reporting companies themselves.[13]

To counter these pressures, standard-setters such as the FASB have declared, as part of their conceptual framework, that they will assess the merits of proposed standards from a position of **neutrality**. That is, they evaluate the soundness of standards on the basis of conceptual soundness, not on the grounds of possible impact on behavior. It is not the FASB's place to choose standards according to the kinds of behavior it wishes to promote and the kinds it wishes to discourage. At the same time, it must be admitted that some standards often **will have** the effect of influencing behavior. Yet their justification should be conceptual, and not viewed in terms of their economic impact.

SECTION 2 · ERROR ANALYSIS

Objective·9
Analyze the effect of errors.

In this section, we show some additional types of accounting errors. Companies generally do not correct for errors that do not have a significant effect on the presentation of the financial statements. For example, should a company with a total annual payroll of $1,750,000 and net income of $940,000 correct its financial statements if it finds it failed to record accrued wages of $5,000? No—it would not consider this error significant.

Obviously, defining materiality is difficult, and managers and auditors must use experience and judgment to determine whether adjustment is necessary for a given error. We assume **all errors discussed in this section to be material and to require adjustment**. (Also, we ignore all tax effects in this section.)

Companies must answer three questions in error analysis:

1. What type of error is involved?
2. What entries are needed to correct for the error?
3. After discovery of the error, how are financial statements to be restated?

As indicated earlier, companies treat errors **as prior-period adjustments and report them in the current year as adjustments to the beginning balance of Retained Earnings**. If a company presents comparative statements, it restates the prior affected statements to correct for the error.

BALANCE SHEET ERRORS

Balance sheet errors affect only the presentation of an asset, liability, or stockholders' equity account. Examples are the classification of a short-term receivable as part of the investment section, the classification of a note payable as an account payable, and the classification of plant assets as inventory.

When the error is discovered, the company reclassifies the item to its proper position. If the company prepares comparative statements that include the error year, it should correctly restate the balance sheet for the error year.

---

[13]Lobbyists use economic consequences arguments—and there are many of them—to put pressure on standard-setters. We have seen examples of these arguments in the oil and gas industry about successful efforts versus full cost, in the technology area with the issue of mandatory expensing of research and developmental costs and stock options.

INCOME STATEMENT ERRORS

Income statement errors involve the improper classification of revenues or expenses. Examples include recording interest revenue as part of sales, purchases as bad debt expense, and depreciation expense as interest expense. An income statement classification error has no effect on the balance sheet and **no effect on net income**.

A company must make a reclassification entry when it discovers the error, if it makes the discovery in the same year in which the error occurs. If the error occurred in prior periods, the company does not need to make a reclassification entry at the date of discovery because the accounts for the current year are correctly stated. (Remember that the company has closed the income statement accounts from the prior period to retained earnings.) If the company prepares comparative statements that include the error year, it restates the income statement for the error year.

BALANCE SHEET AND INCOME STATEMENT ERRORS

The third type of error involves both the balance sheet and income statement. For example, assume that the bookkeeper overlooked accrued wages payable at the end of the accounting period. The effect of this error is to understate expenses, understate liabilities, and overstate net income for that period of time. This type of error affects both the balance sheet and the income statement. We classify this type of error in one of two ways—counterbalancing or noncounterbalancing.

Counterbalancing errors are those that will be offset or corrected over two periods. For example, the failure to record accrued wages is a counterbalancing error because over a two-year period the error will no longer be present. In other words, the failure to record accrued wages in the previous period means: (1) net income for the first period is overstated; (2) accrued wages payable (a liability) is understated, and (3) wages expense is understated. In the next period, net income is understated; accrued wages payable (a liability) is correctly stated; and wages expense is overstated. For the two **years combined**: (1) net income is correct; (2) wages expense is correct; and (3) accrued wages payable at the end of the second year is correct. Most errors in accounting that affect both the balance sheet and income statement are counterbalancing errors.

Noncounterbalancing errors are those that are not offset in the next accounting period. An example would be the failure to capitalize equipment that has a useful life of five years. If we expense this asset immediately, expenses will be overstated in the first period but understated in the next four periods. At the end of the second period, the effect of the error is not fully offset. Net income is correct in the aggregate only at the end of five years, because the asset is fully depreciated at this point. Thus, **noncounterbalancing errors are those that take longer than two periods to correct themselves**.

Only in rare instances is an error never reversed. An example would be if a company initially expenses land. Because land is not depreciable, theoretically the error is never offset, unless the land is sold.

Counterbalancing Errors

We illustrate the usual types of counterbalancing errors on the following pages. In studying these illustrations, keep in mind a couple of points, discussed below.

First, determine whether the company has closed the books for the period in which the error is found:

1. **If the company has closed the books in the current year:**
   (a) If the error is already counterbalanced, no entry is necessary.
   (b) If the error is not yet counterbalanced, make an entry to adjust the present balance of retained earnings.

2. **If the company has not closed the books in the current year:**
  (a) If the error is already counterbalanced, make an entry to correct the error in the current period and to adjust the beginning balance of Retained Earnings.
  (b) If the error is not yet counterbalanced, make an entry to adjust the beginning balance of Retained Earnings.

Second, if the company presents comparative statements, it must restate the amounts for comparative purposes. **Restatement is necessary even if a correcting journal entry is not required.**

To illustrate, assume that Sanford's Cement Co. failed to accrue revenue in 2008 when earned, but recorded the revenue in 2009 when received. The company discovered the error in 2011. It does not need to make an entry to correct for this error because the effects have been counterbalanced by the time Sanford discovered the error in 2011. However, if Sanford presents comparative financial statements for 2008 through 2011, it must **restate the accounts and related amounts for the years 2008 and 2009 for financial reporting purposes**.

The sections that follow demonstrate the accounting for the usual types of counterbalancing errors.

Failure to Record Accrued Wages

On December 31, 2010, Hurley Enterprises did not accrue wages in the amount of $1,500. The entry in 2011 to correct this error, assuming Hurley has not closed the books for 2011, is:

Retained Earnings	1,500	
Wages Expense		1,500

The rationale for this entry is as follows: (1) When Hurley pays the 2010 accrued wages in 2011, it makes an additional debit of $1,500 to 2011 Wages Expense. (2) Wages Expense—2011 is overstated by $1,500. (3) Because the company did not record 2010 accrued wages as Wages Expense in 2010, the net income for 2010 was overstated by $1,500. (4) Because 2010 net income is overstated by $1,500, the Retained Earnings account is overstated by $1,500 (because net income is closed to Retained Earnings).

If Hurley has closed the books for 2011, it makes no entry, because the error is counterbalanced.

Failure to Record Prepaid Expenses

In January 2010 Hurley Enterprises purchased a two-year insurance policy costing $1,000. It debited Insurance Expense, and credited Cash. The company made no adjusting entries at the end of 2010.

The entry on December 31, 2011, to correct this error, assuming Hurley has not closed the books for 2011, is:

Insurance Expense	500	
Retained Earnings		500

If Hurley has closed the books for 2011, it makes no entry, because the error is counterbalanced.

Understatement of Unearned Revenue

On December 31, 2010, Hurley Enterprises received $50,000 as a prepayment for renting certain office space for the following year. At the time of receipt of the rent payment, the company recorded a debit to Cash and a credit to Rent Revenue. It made no adjusting entry as of December 31, 2010. The entry on December 31, 2011, to correct for this error, assuming that Hurley has not closed the books for 2011, is:

Retained Earnings	50,000	
Rent Revenue		50,000

If Hurley has closed the books for 2011, it makes no entry, because the error is counterbalanced.

Overstatement of Accrued Revenue

On December 31, 2010, Hurley Enterprises accrued as interest revenue $8,000 that applied to 2011. On that date, the company recorded a debit to Interest Receivable and a credit to Interest Revenue. The entry on December 31, 2011, to correct for this error, assuming that Hurley has not closed the books for 2011, is:

Retained Earnings	8,000	
Interest Revenue		8,000

If Hurley has closed the books for 2011, it makes no entry, because the error is counterbalanced.

Overstatement of Purchases

Hurley's accountant recorded a purchase of merchandise for $9,000 in 2010 that applied to 2011. The physical inventory for 2010 was correctly stated. The company uses the periodic inventory method. The entry on December 31, 2011, to correct for this error, assuming that Harley has not closed the books for 2011, is:

Purchases	9,000	
Retained Earnings		9,000

If Hurley has closed the books for 2011, it makes no entry, because the error is counterbalanced.

Noncounterbalancing Errors

The entries for noncounterbalancing errors are more complex. Companies must make correcting entries, even if they have closed the books.

Failure to Record Depreciation

Assume that on January 1, 2010, Hurley Enterprises purchased a machine for $10,000 that had an estimated useful life of five years. The accountant incorrectly expensed this machine in 2010, but discovered the error in 2011. If we assume that Hurley uses straight-line depreciation on this asset, the entry on December 31, 2011, to correct for this error, given that Hurley has not closed the books, is:

Machinery	10,000	
Depreciation Expense	2,000	
Retained Earnings		8,000*
Accumulated Depreciation (20% × $10,000 × 2)		4,000

*Computations:
Retained Earnings

Overstatement of expense in 2010	$10,000
Proper depreciation for 2010 (20% × $10,000)	(2,000)
Retained earnings understated as of Dec. 31, 2010	$ 8,000

If Hurley has closed the books for 2011, the entry is:

Machinery	10,000	
Retained Earnings		6,000*
Accumulated Depreciation		4,000

*Computations:
Retained Earnings

Retained earnings understated as of Dec. 31, 2010	$ 8,000
Proper depreciation for 2011 (20% × $10,000)	(2,000)
Retained earnings understated as of Dec. 31, 2011	$ 6,000

Failure to Adjust for Bad Debts

Companies sometimes use a specific charge-off method in accounting for bad debt expense when a percentage of sales is more appropriate. They then make adjustments to change from the specific write-off to some type of allowance method. For example, assume that Hurley Enterprises has recognized bad debt expense when it has the following uncollectible debts.

	2010	2011
From 2010 sales	$550	$690
From 2011 sales		700

Hurley estimates that it will charge off an additional $1,400 in 2012, of which $300 is applicable to 2010 sales and $1,100 to 2011 sales. The entry on December 31, 2011, assuming that Hurley **has not closed the books for 2011**, is:

Bad Debt Expense	410	
Retained Earnings	990	
Allowance for Doubtful Accounts		1,400

Allowance for doubtful accounts: Additional $300 for 2010 sales and $1,100 for 2011 sales.
Bad debts and retained earnings balance:

	2010	2011
Bad debts charged for	$1,240*	$ 700
Additional bad debts anticipated in 2012	300	1,100
Proper bad debt expense	1,540	1,800
Charges currently made to each period	(550)	(1,390)
Bad debt adjustment	$ 990	$ 410

*$550 + $690 = $1,240

If Hurley **has closed the books for 2011**, the entry is:

Retained Earnings	1,400	
Allowance for Doubtful Accounts		1,400

COMPREHENSIVE EXAMPLE: NUMEROUS ERRORS

In some circumstances a combination of errors occurs. The company therefore prepares a worksheet to facilitate the analysis. The following problem demonstrates use of the worksheet. The mechanics of its preparation should be obvious from the solution format. The income statements of Hudson Company for the years ended December 31, 2009, 2010, and 2011 indicate the following net incomes.

2009	$17,400
2010	20,200
2011	11,300

An examination of the accounting records for these years indicates that Hudson Company made several errors in arriving at the net income amounts reported:

1. The company consistently omitted from the records wages earned by workers but not paid at December 31. The amounts omitted were:

December 31, 2009	$1,000
December 31, 2010	$1,400
December 31, 2011	$1,600

When paid in the year following that in which they were earned, Hudson recorded these amounts as expenses.

2. The company overstated merchandise inventory on December 31, 2009, by $1,900 as the result of errors made in the footings and extensions on the inventory sheets.

3. On December 31, 2010, Hudson expensed unexpired insurance of $1,200, applicable to 2011.

4. The company did not record on December 31, 2010, interest receivable in the amount of $240.

5. On January 2, 2010, Hudson sold for $1,800 a piece of equipment costing $3,900. At the date of sale the equipment had accumulated depreciation of $2,400. The company recorded the cash received as Miscellaneous Income in 2010. In addition, the company continued to record depreciation for this equipment in both 2010 and 2011 at the rate of 10 percent of cost.

The first step in preparing the worksheet is to prepare a schedule showing the corrected net income amounts for the years ended December 31, 2009, 2010, and 2011. Each correction of the amount originally reported is clearly labeled. The next step is to indicate the balance sheet accounts affected as of December 31, 2011. Illustration 22-24 shows the completed worksheet for Hudson Company.

ILLUSTRATION 22-24
Worksheet to Correct Income and Balance Sheet Errors

	A	B	C	D	E	F	G	H
		HUDSON COMPANY Worksheet to Correct Income and Balance Sheet Errors						
		Worksheet Analysis of Changes in Net Income				**Balance Sheet Correction at December 31, 2011**		
1								
2		2009	2010	2011	Totals	Debit	Credit	Account
3	Net income as reported	$17,400	$20,200	$11,300	$48,900			
4	Wages unpaid, 12/31/09	(1,000)	1,000		–0–			
5	Wages unpaid, 12/31/10		(1,400)	1,400	–0–			
6	Wages unpaid, 12/31/11			(1,600)	(1,600)		$1,600	Wages Payable
7	Inventory overstatement, 12/31/09	(1,900)	1,900		–0–			
8	Unexpired insurance, 12/31/10		1,200	(1,200)	–0–			
9	Interest receivable, 12/31/10		240	(240)	–0–			
10	Correction for entry made upon sale of equipment, 1/2/10[a]		(1,500)		(1,500)	$2,400	3,900	Accumulated Depreciation Machinery
11	Overcharge of depreciation, 2010		390		390	390		Accumulated Depreciation
12	Overcharge of depreciation, 2011			390	390	390		Accumulated Depreciation
13	Corrected net income	$14,500	$22,030	$10,050	$46,580			
14	[a]Cost	$ 3,900						
15	Accumulated depreciation	2,400						
16	Book value	1,500						
17	Proceeds from sale	1,800						
18	Gain on sale	300						
19	Income reported	(1,800)						
20	Adjustment	$(1,500)						

Sheet1 / Sheet2 / Sheet3

Assuming that Hudson Company **has not closed the books**, correcting entries on December 31, 2011, are:

Retained Earnings	1,400	
Wages Expense		1,400
(To correct improper charge to Wages Expense for 2011)		
Wages Expense	1,600	
Wages Payable		1,600
(To record proper wages expense for 2011)		
Insurance Expense	1,200	
Retained Earnings		1,200
(To record proper insurance expense for 2011)		
Interest Revenue	240	
Retained Earnings		240
(To correct improper credit to Interest Revenue in 2011)		

Retained Earnings	1,500	
Accumulated Depreciation	2,400	
Machinery		3,900
(To record write-off of machinery in 2010 and adjustment of Retained Earnings)		
Accumulated Depreciation	780	
Depreciation Expense		390
Retained Earnings		390
(To correct improper charge for depreciation expense in 2010 and 2011)		

If Hudson Company has closed the books for 2011, the correcting entries are:

Retained Earnings	1,600	
Wages Payable		1,600
(To record proper wage expense for 2011)		
Retained Earnings	1,500	
Accumulated Depreciation	2,400	
Machinery		3,900
(To record write-off of machinery in 2010 and adjustment of Retained Earnings)		
Accumulated Depreciation	780	
Retained Earnings		780
(To correct improper charge for depreciation expense in 2010 and 2011)		

PREPARATION OF FINANCIAL STATEMENTS WITH ERROR CORRECTIONS

Up to now, our discussion of error analysis has focused on identifying the type of error involved and accounting for its correction in the records. We have noted that companies must present the correction of the error on comparative financial statements.

The following example illustrates how a company would restate a typical year's financial statements, given many different errors.

Dick & Wally's Outlet is a small retail outlet in the town of Holiday. Lacking expertise in accounting, the company does not keep adequate records, and numerous errors occurred in recording accounting information.

1. The bookkeeper inadvertently failed to record a cash receipt of $1,000 on the sale of merchandise in 2011.

2. Accrued wages expense at the end of 2010 was $2,500; at the end of 2011, $3,200. The company does not accrue for wages; all wages are charged to Administrative Expenses.

3. The company had not set up an allowance for estimated uncollectible receivables. Dick and Wally decided to set up such an allowance for the estimated probable losses, as of December 31, 2011, for 2010 accounts of $700, and for 2011 accounts of $1,500. They also decided to correct the charge against each year so that it shows the losses (actual and estimated) relating to that year's sales. The company has written off accounts to bad debt expense (selling expense) as follows.

	In 2010	In 2011
2010 accounts	$400	$2,000
2011 accounts		1,600

4. Unexpired insurance not recorded at the end of 2010 was $600, and at the end of 2011, $400. All insurance is charged to Administrative Expenses.

5. An account payable of $6,000 should have been a note payable.

6. During 2010, the company sold for $7,000 an asset that cost $10,000 and had a book value of $4,000. At the time of sale Cash was debited, and Miscellaneous Income was credited for $7,000.

7. As a result of the last transaction, the company overstated depreciation expense (an administrative expense) in 2010 by $800 and in 2011 by $1,200.

Illustration 22-25 presents a worksheet that begins with the unadjusted trial balance of Dick & Wally's Outlet. You can determine the correcting entries and their effect on the financial statements by examining the worksheet.

ILLUSTRATION 22-25
Worksheet to Analyze Effect of Errors in Financial Statements

		Trial Balance Unadjusted		Adjustments				Income Statement Adjusted		Balance Sheet Adjusted	
	A	Debit	Credit		Debit		Credit	Debit	Credit	Debit	Credit
3	Cash	3,100		(1)	1,000					4,100	
4	Accounts Receivable	17,600								17,600	
5	Notes Receivable	8,500								8,500	
6	Inventory	34,000								34,000	
7	Property, Plant, and Equipment	112,000				(6)	10,000[a]			102,000	
8	Accumulated Depreciation		83,500	(6)	6,000[a]						75,500
9				(7)	2,000						
10	Investments	24,300								24,300	
11	Accounts Payable		14,500	(5)	6,000						8,500
12	Notes Payable		10,000			(5)	6,000				16,000
13	Capital Stock		43,500								43,500
14	Retained Earnings		20,000	(3)	2,700[b]						
15				(6)	4,000[a]	(4)	600				
16				(2)	2,500	(7)	800				12,200
17	Sales		94,000			(1)	1,000		95,000		
18	Cost of Goods Sold	21,000						21,000			
19	Selling Expenses	22,000				(3)	500[b]	21,500			
20	Administrative Expenses	23,000		(2)	700	(4)	400	22,700			
21				(4)	600	(7)	1,200				
22	Totals	265,500	265,500								
23	Wages Payable					(2)	3,200				3,200
24	Allowance for Doubtful Accounts					(3)	2,200[b]				2,200
25	Unexpired Insurance			(4)	400					400	
26	Net Income							29,800			29,800
27	Totals				25,900		25,900	95,000	95,000	190,900	190,900

DICK & WALLY'S OUTLET
Worksheet Analysis to Adjust Financial Statements for the Year 2011

Sheet1 / Sheet2 / Sheet3

Computations:

[a]Machinery

Proceeds from sale	$7,000
Book value of machinery	4,000
Gain on sale	3,000
Income credited	7,000
Retained earnings adjustment	$4,000

[b]Bad Debts

	2010	2011
Bad debts charged for	$2,400	$1,600
Additional bad debts anticipated	700	1,500
	3,100	3,100
Charges currently made to each year	(400)	(3,600)
Bad debt adjustment	$2,700	$ (500)

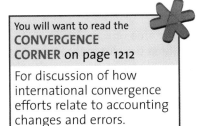

You will want to read the
CONVERGENCE CORNER on page 1212

For discussion of how international convergence efforts relate to accounting changes and errors.

CONVERGENCE CORNER

ACCOUNTING CHANGES AND ERRORS

The iGAAP standard addressing accounting and reporting for changes in accounting principles, changes in estimates, and errors is *IAS 8* ("Accounting Policies, Changes in Accounting Estimates and Errors"). Various presentation issues related to restatements are addressed in *IAS 1* ("Presentation of Financial Statements"). As indicated in the chapter, the FASB has issued guidance on changes in accounting principles, changes in estimates, and corrections of errors, which essentially converges U.S. GAAP to *IAS 8*.

✱ RELEVANT FACTS

• One area in which iGAAP and U.S. GAAP differ is the reporting of error corrections in previously issued financial statements. While both GAAPs require restatement, U.S. GAAP is an absolute standard—that is, there is no exception to this rule.

• The accounting for changes in estimates is similar between U.S. GAAP and iGAAP.

• Under U.S. GAAP and iGAAP, if determining the effect of a change in accounting principle is considered impracticable, then a company should report the effect of the change in the period in which it believes it practicable to do so, which may be the current period.

• Under iGAAP, the impracticality exception applies both to changes in accounting principles and to the correction of errors. Under U.S. GAAP, this exception applies only to changes in accounting principle.

• *IAS 8* does not specifically address the accounting and reporting for indirect effects of changes in accounting principles. As indicated in the chapter, U.S. GAAP has detailed guidance on the accounting and reporting of indirect effects.

✱ ABOUT THE NUMBERS

An interesting sidelight to our discussion of accounting changes involves how companies that follow iGAAP report financial information related to the equity method of accounting. Under the equity method of accounting, the investor increases its investment for the pro-rata share of the net income of the investee (often referred to as an associated company under iGAAP). On the other hand, the investor reduces its investment for any dividends received from the investee. Both iGAAP and U.S. GAAP follow this accounting approach.

However, there is a subtle difference between iGAAP and U.S. GAAP related to how the investor evaluates the accounting policies of the investee. To illustrate, assume that Kirkland Company (the investor company) uses the FIFO inventory method, and Margo Company (the investee company) uses average cost for its inventory valuation. If Kirkland follows iGAAP, Kirkland must conform the accounting policies of Margo to its own accounting policies. Therefore Kirkland adjusts the net income of Margo so its net income is reported on the FIFO basis.

This procedure is not used under U.S. GAAP. Under U.S. GAAP Kirkland ignores the fact that Margo uses a different method of inventory valuation. Kirkland records its pro-rata share of the net income of Margo without adjusting for the fact that Margo uses a different inventory valuation method. As a result, there is a lack of comparability in the inventory methods used to report net income for Kirkland Company under U.S. GAAP.

✱ ON THE HORIZON

For the most part, iGAAP and U.S. GAAP are similar in the area of accounting changes and reporting the effects of errors. Thus, there is no active project in this area. A related development involves the presentation of comparative data. Under iGAAP, when a company prepares financial statements on a new basis, 2 years of comparative data are reported. U.S. GAAP requires comparative information for a 3-year period. Use of the shorter comparative data period must be addressed before U.S. companies can adopt iGAAP.

SUMMARY OF LEARNING OBJECTIVES

•1 Identify the types of accounting changes. The three different types of accounting changes are: (1) *Change in accounting principle:* a change from one generally accepted accounting principle to another generally accepted accounting principle. (2) *Change in accounting estimate:* a change that occurs as the result of new information or as additional experience is acquired. (3) *Change in reporting entity:* a change from reporting as one type of entity to another type of entity.

•2 Describe the accounting for changes in accounting principles. A change in accounting principle involves a change from one generally accepted accounting principle to another. A change in accounting principle is not considered to result from the adoption of a new principle in recognition of events that have occurred for the first time or that were previously immaterial. If the accounting principle previously followed was not acceptable or if the principle was applied incorrectly, a change to a generally accepted accounting principle is considered a correction of an error.

•3 Understand how to account for retrospective accounting changes. The general requirement for changes in accounting principle is retrospective application. Under retrospective application, companies change prior years' financial statements on a basis consistent with the newly adopted principle. They treat any part of the effect attributable to years prior to those presented as an adjustment of the earliest retained earnings presented.

•4 Understand how to account for impracticable changes. Retrospective application is impracticable if the prior period effect cannot be determined using every reasonable effort to do so. For example, in changing to LIFO, the base-year inventory for all subsequent LIFO calculations is generally the opening inventory in the year the company adopts the method. There is no restatement of prior years' income because it is often too impractical to do so.

•5 Describe the accounting for changes in estimates. Companies report changes in estimates prospectively. That is, companies should make no changes in previously reported results. They do not adjust opening balances nor change financial statements of prior periods.

•6 Identify changes in a reporting entity. An accounting change that results in financial statements that are actually the statements of a different entity should be reported by restating the financial statements of all prior periods presented, to show the financial information for the new reporting entity for all periods.

•7 Describe the accounting for correction of errors. Companies must correct errors as soon as they discover them, by proper entries in the accounts, and report them in the financial statements. The profession requires that a company treat corrections of errors as prior-period adjustments, record them in the year in which it discovered the errors, and report them in the financial statements in the proper periods. If presenting comparative statements, a company should restate the prior statements affected to correct for the errors. The company need not repeat the disclosures in the financial statements of subsequent periods.

•8 Identify economic motives for changing accounting methods. Managers might have varying motives for income reporting, depending on economic times and whom they seek to impress. Some of the reasons for changing accounting methods are: (1) political costs, (2) capital structure, (3) bonus payments, and (4) smoothing of earnings.

•9 Analyze the effect of errors. Three types of errors can occur: (1) *Balance sheet errors*, which affect only the presentation of an asset, liability, or stockholders' equity account. (2) *Income statement errors*, which affect only the presentation of revenue, expense, gain, or loss accounts in the income statement. (3) *Balance sheet and income statement errors*, which involve both the balance sheet and income statement. Errors are classified into two types: (1) *Counterbalancing errors* are offset or corrected over two periods. (2) *Non-counterbalancing errors* are not offset in the next accounting period and take longer than two periods to correct themselves.

As an aid to understanding accounting changes, we provide the following glossary.

KEY TERMS RELATED TO ACCOUNTING CHANGES

ACCOUNTING CHANGE. A change in (1) an accounting principle, (2) an accounting estimate, or (3) the reporting entity. The correction of an error in previously issued financial statements is not an accounting change.

CHANGE IN ACCOUNTING PRINCIPLE. A change from one generally accepted accounting principle to another generally accepted accounting principle when two or more generally accepted accounting principles apply or when the accounting principle formerly used is no longer generally accepted.

CHANGE IN ACCOUNTING ESTIMATE. A change that has the effect of adjusting the carrying amount of an existing asset or liability or altering the subsequent accounting for existing or future assets or liabilities. Changes in accounting estimates result from new information.

CHANGE IN ACCOUNTING ESTIMATE EFFECTED BY A CHANGE IN ACCOUNTING PRINCIPLE. A change in accounting estimate that is inseparable from the effect of a related change in accounting principle.

CHANGE IN THE REPORTING ENTITY. A change that results in financial statements that, in effect, are those of a different reporting entity (see page 1197).

DIRECT EFFECTS OF A CHANGE IN ACCOUNTING PRINCIPLE. Those recognized changes in assets or liabilities necessary to effect a change in accounting principle.

ERROR IN PREVIOUSLY ISSUED FINANCIAL STATEMENTS. An error in recognition, measurement, presentation, or disclosure in financial statements resulting from mathematical mistakes, mistakes in the application of GAAP, or oversight or misuse of facts that existed at the time the financial statements were prepared. A change from an accounting principle that is not generally accepted to one that is generally accepted is a correction of an error.

INDIRECT EFFECTS OF A CHANGE IN ACCOUNTING PRINCIPLE. Any changes to current or future cash flows of an entity that result from making a change in accounting principle that is applied retrospectively.

RESTATEMENT. The process of revising previously issued financial statements to reflect the correction of an error in those financial statements.

RETROSPECTIVE APPLICATION. The application of a different accounting principle to one or more previously issued financial statements, or to the statement of financial position at the beginning of the current period, as if that principle had always been used, or a change to financial statements of prior accounting periods to present the financial statements of a new reporting entity as if it had existed in those prior years. [11]

APPENDIX **22A**	**CHANGING FROM OR TO THE EQUITY METHOD**

As noted in the chapter, companies generally should report an accounting change that results in financial statements for a different entity by **changing the financial statements of all prior periods presented**.

An example of a change in reporting entity is when a company's level of ownership or influence changes, such as when it changes from or to the equity method. When changing **to** the equity method, companies use retrospective application. Companies treat a change **from** the equity method prospectively. We present examples of these changes in entity in the following two sections.

CHANGE FROM THE EQUITY METHOD

If the investor level of influence or ownership falls below that necessary for continued use of the equity method, a company must change from the equity method to the fair value method. The earnings or losses that the investor previously recognized under the equity method should **remain as part of the carrying amount** of the investment, with no retrospective application to the new method.

> **Objective•10**
> Make the computations and prepare the entries necessary to record a change from or to the equity method of accounting.

When a company changes **from the equity method to the fair value method, the cost basis for accounting purposes is the carrying amount of the investment at the date of the change**. The investor applies the new method in its entirety once the equity method is no longer appropriate. At the next reporting date, the investor should record the unrealized holding gain or loss to recognize the difference between the carrying amount and fair value.[14]

Dividends in Excess of Earnings

In subsequent periods, dividends received by the investor company may exceed its share of the investee's earnings for such periods (all periods following the change in method). To the extent that they do so, the investor company should account for such dividends as a **reduction of the investment carrying amount**, rather than as revenue. The reason: dividends in excess of earnings are viewed as a liquidating dividend with this excess then accounted for as a reduction of the equity investment.

To illustrate, assume that on January 1, 2009, Investor Company purchased 250,000 shares of Investee Company's 1,000,000 shares of outstanding stock for $8,500,000. Investor correctly accounted for this investment using the equity method. After accounting for dividends received and investee net income, in 2009, Investor reported its investment in Investee Company at $8,780,000 at December 31, 2009. On January 2, 2010, Investee Company sold 1,500,000 additional shares of its own common stock to the public, thereby reducing Investor Company's ownership from 25 percent to 10 percent. Illustration 22A-1 shows the net income (or loss) and dividends of Investee Company for the years 2010 through 2012.

Year	Investor's Share of Investee Income (Loss)	Investee Dividends Received by Investor
2010	$600,000	$ 400,000
2011	350,000	400,000
2012	–0–	210,000
Totals	$950,000	$1,010,000

ILLUSTRATION 22A-1
Income Earned and Dividends Received

[14]A retrospective application for this type of change is impracticable in many cases. Determining fair values on a portfolio basis for securities in previous periods may be quite difficult. As a result, prospective application is used.

Assuming a change from the equity method to the fair value method as of January 2, 2010, Investor Company's reported investment in Investee Company and its reported income would be as shown in Illustration 22A-2.

ILLUSTRATION 22A-2
Impact on Investment
Carrying Amount

Year	Dividend Revenue Recognized	Cumulative Excess of Share of Earnings Over Dividends Received	Investment at December 31
2010	$400,000	$200,000[a]	$8,780,000
2011	400,000	150,000[b]	8,780,000
2012	150,000	(60,000)[c]	$8,780,000 − $60,000 = $8,720,000

[a]$600,000 − $400,000 = $200,000
[b]($350,000 − $400,000) + $200,000 = $150,000
[c]$150,000 − $210,000 = $(60,000)

Investor Company would record the dividends and earnings data for the three years subsequent to the change in methods as shown by the following entries.

2010 and 2011

Cash	400,000	
Dividend Revenue		400,000
(To record dividend received from Investee Company)		

2012

Cash	210,000	
Available-for-Sale Securities		60,000
Dividend Revenue		150,000
(To record dividend revenue from Investee Company in 2012 and to recognize cumulative excess of dividends received over share of Investee earnings in periods subsequent to change from equity method)		

CHANGE TO THE EQUITY METHOD

When converting to the equity method, companies use retrospective application. Such a change involves adjusting the carrying amount of the investment, results of current and prior operations, and retained earnings of the investor **as if the equity method has been in effect during all of the previous periods in which this investment was held.** [12] When changing from the fair value method to the equity method, companies also must eliminate any balances in the Unrealized Holding Gain or Loss—Equity account and the Securities Fair Value Adjustment account. In addition, they eliminate the available-for-sale classification for this investment, and they record the investment under the equity method.

For example, on January 2, 2010, Amsted Corp. purchased, for $500,000 cash, 10 percent of the outstanding shares of Cable Company common stock. On that date, the net identifiable assets of Cable Company had a fair value of $3,000,000. The excess of cost over the underlying equity in the net identifiable assets of Cable Company is goodwill. On January 2, 2012, Amsted Corp. purchased an additional 20 percent of Cable Company's stock for $1,200,000 cash when the fair value of Cable's net identifiable assets was $4,000,000. The excess of cost over fair value related to this additional investment is goodwill. Now having a 30 percent interest, Amsted Corp. must use the equity method.

From January 2, 2010, to January 2, 2012, Amsted Corp. used the fair value method and categorized these securities as available-for-sale. At January 2, 2012, Amsted has a credit balance of $92,000 in its Unrealized Holding Gain or Loss—Equity account and a debit balance in its Securities Fair Value Adjustment account of the same amount. This change in fair value occurred in 2010 (Income tax effects are ignored.) Illustration 22A-3 (page 1217) shows the net income reported by Cable Company and the Cable Company dividends received by Amsted during the period 2010 through 2012.

Year	Cable Company Net Income	Cable Co. Dividends Paid to Amsted
2010	$ 500,000	$ 20,000
2011	1,000,000	30,000
2012	1,200,000	120,000

Amsted makes the following journal entries from January 2, 2010, through December 31, 2012, relative to Amsted Corp.'s investment in Cable Company, reflecting the data above and a change from the fair value method to the equity method.[15]

January 2, 2010

Available-for-Sale Securities	500,000	
Cash		500,000
(To record the purchase of a 10% interest in Cable Company)		

December 31, 2010

Cash	20,000	
Dividend Revenue		20,000
(To record the receipt of cash dividends from Cable Company)		
Securities Fair Value Adjustment (Available-for-Sale)	92,000	
Unrealized Holding Gain or Loss—Equity		92,000
(To record increase in fair value of securities)		

December 31, 2011

Cash	30,000	
Dividend Revenue		30,000
(To record the receipt of cash dividends from Cable Company)		

January 2, 2012

Investment in Cable Stock	1,300,000	
Cash		1,200,000
Retained Earnings		100,000
(To record the purchase of an additional interest in Cable Company and to reflect retrospectively a change from the fair value method to the equity method of accounting for the investment. The $100,000 adjustment is computed as follows:)		

	2010	2011	Total
Amsted Corp. equity in earnings of Cable Company (10%)	$50,000	$100,000	$150,000
Dividend received	(20,000)	(30,000)	(50,000)
Retrospective application	$30,000	$ 70,000	$100,000

January 2, 2012

Investment in Cable Stock	500,000	
Available-for-Sale Securities		500,000
(To reclassify initial 10% interest to equity method)		

January 2, 2012

Unrealized Holding Gain or Loss—Equity	92,000	
Securities Fair Value Adjustment (Available-for-Sale)		92,000
(To eliminate fair value accounts for change to equity method)		

[15]Adapted from Paul A. Pacter, "Applying APB Opinion No. 18—Equity Method," *Journal of Accountancy* (September 1971), pp. 59–60.

December 31, 2012

Investment in Cable Stock	360,000	
Revenue from Investment		360,000
[To record equity in earnings of Cable		
Company (30% of $1,200,000)]		
Cash	120,000	
Investment in Cable Stock		120,000
(To record the receipt of cash dividends from		
Cable Company)		

Companies change to the equity method by placing the accounts related to and affected by the investment on the same basis **as if the equity method had always been the basis of accounting for that investment**. Thus, they report the effects of this accounting change using the retrospective approach.[16]

SUMMARY OF LEARNING OBJECTIVES FOR APPENDIX 22A

•10 Make the computations and prepare the entries necessary to record a change from or to the equity method of accounting. When changing *from* the equity method to the fair value method, the cost basis for accounting purposes is the carrying amount used for the investment at the date of change. The investor company applies the new method in its entirety once the equity method is no longer appropriate. When changing *to* the equity method, the company adjusts the accounts to be on the same basis as if the equity method had always been used for that investment.

FASB CODIFICATION

FASB Codification References

[1] FASB ASC 250-10-05-1. [Predecessor literature: "Accounting Changes and Error Corrections," *Statement of Financial Accounting Standards No. 154* (Stamford, Conn.: FASB, 2005).]

[2] FASB ASC 250-10-05-2. [Predecessor literature: "Accounting Changes and Error Corrections," *Statement of Financial Accounting Standards No. 154* (Stamford, Conn.: FASB, 2005).]

[3] FASB ASC 250-10-50-1. [Predecessor literature: "Accounting Changes and Error Corrections," *Statement of Financial Accounting Standards No. 154* (Stamford, Conn.: FASB, 2005), par. 17.]

[4] FASB ASC 250-10-50-1. [Predecessor literature: "Accounting Changes and Error Corrections," *Statement of Financial Accounting Standards No. 154* (Stamford, Conn.: FASB, 2005), par. B19.]

[5] FASB ASC 250-10-45-6. [Predecessor literature: "Accounting Changes and Error Corrections," *Statement of Financial Accounting Standards No. 154* (Stamford, Conn.: FASB, 2005), pars. 8–11.]

[6] FASB ASC 250-10-50-1. [Predecessor literature: "Accounting Changes and Error Corrections," *Statement of Financial Accounting Standards No. 154* (Stamford, Conn.: FASB, 2005), par. 17.]

[7] FASB ASC 250-10-45-18. [Predecessor literature: "Accounting Changes and Error Corrections," *Statement of Financial Accounting Standards No. 154* (Stamford, Conn.: FASB, 2005), par. 20.]

[8] FASB ASC 250-10-45-24. [Predecessor literature: "Prior Period Adjustments," *Statement of Financial Accounting Standards No. 16* (Stamford, Conn.: FASB, 1977), p. 5.]

---

[16]The change to the equity method illustration assumes that the fair value and the book value of the net identifiable assets of the investee are the same. However, the fair value of the net identifiable assets of the investee may be greater than their book value. In this case, this excess (if depreciable or amortizable) reduces the net income reported by the investor from the investee. For example, assume that the fair value of an investee's building is $1,000,000 and its book value is $800,000 at the time of change to the equity method. In that case, this difference of $200,000 is depreciated over the useful life of the building, thereby reducing the amount of investee's net income reported on the investor's books.

[9] FASB ASC 250-10-50-4. [Predecessor literature: "Accounting Changes and Error Corrections," *Statement of Financial Accounting Standards No. 154* (Stamford, Conn.: FASB, 2005), par. 2.]

[10] FASB ASC 250-10-50-7. [Predecessor literature: "Accounting Changes and Error Corrections," *Statement of Financial Accounting Standards No. 154* (Stamford, Conn.: FASB, 2005), par. 26.]

[11] FASB ASC 250-10-50-1. [Predecessor literature: "Accounting Changes and Error Corrections," *Statement of Financial Accounting Standards No. 154* (Stamford, Conn.: FASB, 2005), par. 2.]

[12] FASB ASC 323-10-35-33. [Predecessor literature: "The Equity Method of Accounting for Investments in Common Stock," *Opinions of the Accounting Principles Board No. 18* (New York: AICPA, 1971), par. 17.]

Exercises

Access the FASB Codification at *http://asc.fasb.org/home* to prepare responses to the following exercises. Provide Codification references for your responses.

CE22-1 Access the glossary ("Master Glossary") to answer the following.

  (a) What is a change in accounting estimate?
  (b) What is a change in accounting principle?
  (c) What is a restatement?
  (d) What is the definition of "retrospective application"?

CE22-2 When a company has to restate its financial statements to correct an error, what information must the company disclose?

CE22-3 What reporting requirements does retrospective application require?

CE22-4 If a company registered with the SEC justifies a change in accounting method as preferable under the circumstances, and the circumstances change, can that company switch back to its prior method of accounting before the change? Why or why not?

An additional Codification case can be found in the Using Your Judgment section, on page 1240.

Be sure to check the companion website for a Review and Analysis Exercise, with solution.

Note: All asterisked Questions, Exercises, and Problems relate to material in the appendix to the chapter.

QUESTIONS

1. In recent years, the *Wall Street Journal* has indicated that many companies have changed their accounting principles. What are the major reasons why companies change accounting methods?

2. State how each of the following items is reflected in the financial statements.

  (a) Change from FIFO to LIFO method for inventory valuation purposes.

  (b) Charge for failure to record depreciation in a previous period.

  (c) Litigation won in current year, related to prior period.

  (d) Change in the realizability of certain receivables.

  (e) Write-off of receivables.

  (f) Change from the percentage-of-completion to the completed-contract method for reporting net income.

3. Discuss briefly the three approaches that have been suggested for reporting changes in accounting principles.

4. Identify and describe the approach the FASB requires for reporting changes in accounting principles.

5. What is the indirect effect of a change in accounting principle? Briefly describe the reporting of the indirect effects of a change in accounting principle.

6. Define a change in estimate and provide an illustration. When is a change in accounting estimate effected by a change in accounting principle?

7. Lenexa State Bank has followed the practice of capitalizing certain marketing costs and amortizing these costs over their expected life. In the current year, the bank determined that the future benefits from these costs were doubtful. Consequently, the bank adopted the policy of expensing these costs as incurred. How should the bank report this accounting change in the comparative financial statements?

8. Indicate how the following items are recorded in the accounting records in the current year of Coronet Co.

   (a) Impairment of goodwill.

   (b) A change in depreciating plant assets from accelerated to the straight-line method.

   (c) Large write-off of inventories because of obsolescence.

   (d) Change from the cash basis to accrual basis of accounting.

   (e) Change from LIFO to FIFO method for inventory valuation purposes.

   (f) Change in the estimate of service lives for plant assets.

9. Whittier Construction Co. had followed the practice of expensing all materials assigned to a construction job without recognizing any salvage inventory. On December 31, 2010, it was determined that salvage inventory should be valued at $52,000. Of this amount, $29,000 arose during the current year. How does this information affect the financial statements to be prepared at the end of 2010?

10. Parsons Inc. wishes to change from the completed-contract to the percentage-of-completion method for financial reporting purposes. The auditor indicates that a change would be permitted only if it is to a preferable method. What difficulties develop in assessing preferability?

11. Discuss how a change to the LIFO method of inventory valuation is handled when it is impracticable to determine previous LIFO inventory amounts.

12. How should consolidated financial statements be reported this year when statements of individual companies were presented last year?

13. Simms Corp. controlled four domestic subsidiaries and one foreign subsidiary. Prior to the current year, Simms Corp. had excluded the foreign subsidiary from consolidation. During the current year, the foreign subsidiary was included in the financial statements. How should this change in accounting entity be reflected in the financial statements?

14. Distinguish between counterbalancing and noncounterbalancing errors. Give an example of each.

15. Discuss and illustrate how a correction of an error in previously issued financial statements should be handled.

16. Prior to 2010, Heberling Inc. excluded manufacturing overhead costs from work in process and finished goods inventory. These costs have been expensed as incurred. In 2010, the company decided to change its accounting methods for manufacturing inventories to full costing by including these costs as product costs. Assuming that these costs are material, how should this change be reflected in the financial statements for 2009 and 2010?

17. Elliott Corp. failed to record accrued salaries for 2009, $2,000; 2010, $2,100; and 2011, $3,900. What is the amount of the overstatement or understatement of Retained Earnings at December 31, 2012?

18. In January 2010, installation costs of $6,000 on new machinery were charged to Repair Expense. Other costs of this machinery of $30,000 were correctly recorded and have been depreciated using the straight-line method with an estimated life of 10 years and no salvage value. At December 31, 2011, it is decided that the machinery has a remaining useful life of 20 years, starting with January 1, 2011. What entry(ies) should be made in 2011 to correctly record transactions related to machinery, assuming the machinery has no salvage value? The books have not been closed for 2011 and depreciation expense has not yet been recorded for 2011.

19. On January 2, 2010, $100,000 of 11%, 10-year bonds were issued for $97,000. The $3,000 discount was charged to Interest Expense. The bookkeeper, Mark Landis, records interest only on the interest payment dates of January 1 and July 1. What is the effect on reported net income for 2010 of this error, assuming straight-line amortization of the discount? What entry is necessary to correct for this error, assuming that the books are not closed for 2010?

20. An entry to record Purchases and related Accounts Payable of $13,000 for merchandise purchased on December 23, 2011, was recorded in January 2012. This merchandise was not included in inventory at December 31, 2011. What effect does this error have on reported net income for 2011? What entry should be made to correct for this error, assuming that the books are not closed for 2011?

21. Equipment was purchased on January 2, 2010, for $24,000, but no portion of the cost has been charged to depreciation. The corporation wishes to use the straight-line method for these assets, which have been estimated to have a life of 10 years and no salvage value. What effect does this error have on net income in 2010? What entry is necessary to correct for this error, assuming that the books are not closed for 2010?

22. Where can authoritative iGAAP related to accounting changes be found?

23. Briefly describe some of the similarities and differences between U.S. GAAP and iGAAP with respect to reporting accounting changes.

24. How might differences in presentation of comparative data under U.S. and iGAAP affect adoption of iGAAP by U.S. companies?

·3 **BE22-1** Wertz Construction Company decided at the beginning of 2010 to change from the completed-contract method to the percentage-of-completion method for financial reporting purposes. The company will continue to use the completed-contract method for tax purposes. For years prior to 2010, pre-tax income under the two methods was as follows: percentage-of-completion $120,000, and completed-contract $80,000. The tax rate is 35%. Prepare Wertz's 2010 journal entry to record the change in accounting principle.

·3 **BE22-2** Refer to the accounting change by Wertz Construction Company in BE22-1. Wertz has a profit-sharing plan, which pays all employees a bonus at year-end based on 1% of pre-tax income. Compute the indirect effect of Wertz's change in accounting principle that will be reported in the 2010 income statement, assuming that the profit-sharing contract explicitly requires adjustment for changes in income numbers.

·3 **BE22-3** Shannon, Inc., changed from the LIFO cost flow assumption to the FIFO cost flow assumption in 2010. The increase in the prior year's income before taxes is $1,200,000. The tax rate is 40%. Prepare Shannon's 2010 journal entry to record the change in accounting principle.

·5 **BE22-4** Tedesco Company changed depreciation methods in 2010 from double-declining-balance to straight-line. Depreciation prior to 2010 under double-declining-balance was $90,000, whereas straight-line depreciation prior to 2010 would have been $50,000. Tedesco's depreciable assets had a cost of $250,000 with a $40,000 salvage value, and an 8-year remaining useful life at the beginning of 2010. Prepare the 2010 journal entries, if any, related to Tedesco's depreciable assets.

·5 **BE22-5** Sesame Company purchased a computer system for $74,000 on January 1, 2009. It was depreciated based on a 7-year life and an $18,000 salvage value. On January 1, 2011, Sesame revised these estimates to a total useful life of 4 years and a salvage value of $10,000. Prepare Sesame's entry to record 2011 depreciation expense.

·7 **BE22-6** In 2010, Bailey Corporation discovered that equipment purchased on January 1, 2008, for $50,000 was expensed at that time. The equipment should have been depreciated over 5 years, with no salvage value. The effective tax rate is 30%. Prepare Bailey's 2010 journal entry to correct the error.

·7 **BE22-7** At January 1, 2010, Beidler Company reported retained earnings of $2,000,000. In 2010, Beidler discovered that 2009 depreciation expense was understated by $400,000. In 2010, net income was $900,000 and dividends declared were $250,000. The tax rate is 40%. Prepare a 2010 retained earnings statement for Beidler Company.

·7 **BE22-8** Indicate the effect—Understate, Overstate, No Effect—that each of the following errors has on 2010 net income and 2011 net income.

	2010	2011
(a) Equipment purchased in 2009 was expensed.	——	——
(b) Wages payable were not recorded at 12/31/10.	——	——
(c) Equipment purchased in 2010 was expensed.	——	——
(d) 2010 ending inventory was overstated.	——	——
(e) Patent amortization was not recorded in 2011.	——	——

·3 ·5 **BE22-9** Roundtree Manufacturing Co. is preparing its year-end financial statements and is considering the accounting for the following items.

   1. The vice president of sales had indicated that one product line has lost its customer appeal and will be phased out over the next 3 years. Therefore, a decision has been made to lower the estimated lives on related production equipment from the remaining 5 years to 3 years.
   2. The Hightone Building was converted from a sales office to offices for the Accounting Department at the beginning of this year. Therefore, the expense related to this building will now appear as an administrative expense rather than a selling expense on the current year's income statement.
   3. Estimating the lives of new products in the Leisure Products Division has become very difficult because of the highly competitive conditions in this market. Therefore, the practice of deferring and amortizing preproduction costs has been abandoned in favor of expensing such costs as they are incurred.

Identify and explain whether each of the above items is a change in principle, a change in estimate, or an error.

·3 ·7 **BE22-10** Palmer Co. is evaluating the appropriate accounting for the following items.

1. Management has decided to switch from the FIFO inventory valuation method to the LIFO inventory valuation method for all inventories.
2. When the year-end physical inventory adjustment was made for the current year, the controller discovered that the prior year's physical inventory sheets for an entire warehouse were mislaid and excluded from last year's count.
3. Palmer's Custom Division manufactures large-scale, custom-designed machinery on a contract basis. Management decided to switch from the completed-contract method to the percentage-of-completion method of accounting for long-term contracts.

Identify and explain whether each of the above items is a change in accounting principle, a change in estimate, or an error.

·10 ***BE22-11** Simmons Corporation owns stock of Armstrong, Inc. Prior to 2010, the investment was accounted for using the equity method. In early 2010, Simmons sold part of its investment in Armstrong, and began using the fair value method. In 2010, Armstrong earned net income of $80,000 and paid dividends of $95,000. Prepare Simmons's entries related to Armstrong's net income and dividends, assuming Simmons now owns 10% of Armstrong's stock.

·10 ***BE22-12** Oliver Corporation has owned stock of Conrad Corporation since 2007. At December 31, 2010, its balances related to this investment were:

Available-for-Sale Securities	$185,000
Securities Fair Value Adj (AFS)	34,000 Dr.
Unrealized Holding Gain or Loss—Equity	34,000 Cr.

On January 1, 2011, Oliver purchased additional stock of Conrad Company for $475,000 and now has significant influence over Conrad. If the equity method had been used in 2007–2010, income would have been $33,000 greater than dividends received. Prepare Oliver's journal entries to record the purchase of the investment and the change to the equity method.

EXERCISES

·3 **E22-1** **(Change in Principle—Long-Term Contracts)** Cherokee Construction Company changed from the completed-contract to the percentage-of-completion method of accounting for long-term construction contracts during 2010. For tax purposes, the company employs the completed-contract method and will continue this approach in the future. (*Hint:* Adjust all tax consequences through the Deferred Tax Liability account.) The appropriate information related to this change is as follows.

	Pretax Income from:		
	Percentage-of-Completion	Completed-Contract	Difference
2009	$780,000	$610,000	$170,000
2010	700,000	480,000	220,000

Instructions

(a) Assuming that the tax rate is 35%, what is the amount of net income that would be reported in 2010?
(b) What entry(ies) are necessary to adjust the accounting records for the change in accounting principle?

·3 **E22-2** **(Change in Principle—Inventory Methods)** Whitman Company began operations on January 1, 2008, and uses the average cost method of pricing inventory. Management is contemplating a change in inventory methods for 2011. The following information is available for the years 2008–2010.

	Net Income Computed Using		
	Average Cost Method	FIFO Method	LIFO Method
2008	$16,000	$19,000	$12,000
2009	18,000	21,000	14,000
2010	20,000	25,000	17,000

Instructions

(Ignore all tax effects.)

(a) Prepare the journal entry necessary to record a change from the average cost method to the FIFO method in 2011.

(b) Determine net income to be reported for 2008, 2009, and 2010, after giving effect to the change in accounting principle.

(c) Assume Whitman Company used the LIFO method instead of the average cost method during the years 2008–2010. In 2011, Whitman changed to the FIFO method. Prepare the journal entry necessary to record the change in principle.

E22-3 (Accounting Change) Ramirez Co. decides at the beginning of 2010 to adopt the FIFO method of inventory valuation. Ramirez had used the LIFO method for financial reporting since its inception on January 1, 2008, and had maintained records adequate to apply the FIFO method retrospectively. Ramirez concluded that FIFO is the preferable inventory method because it reflects the current cost of inventory on the balance sheet. The table presents the effects of the change in accounting principle on inventory and cost of goods sold.

	Inventory Determined by		Cost of Goods Sold Determined by	
Date	LIFO Method	FIFO Method	LIFO Method	FIFO Method
January 1, 2008	$ 0	$ 0	$ 0	$ 0
December 31, 2008	100	80	800	820
December 31, 2009	200	240	1,000	940
December 31, 2010	320	390	1,130	1,100

Retained earnings reported under LIFO are as follows:

	Retained Earnings Balance
December 31, 2008	$2,200
December 31, 2009	4,200
December 31, 2010	6,070

Other information:

1. For each year presented, sales are $4,000 and operating expenses are $1,000.
2. Ramirez provides two years of financial statements. Earnings per share information is not required.

Instructions

(a) Prepare income statements under LIFO and FIFO for 2008, 2009, and 2010.

(b) Prepare income statements reflecting the retrospective application of the accounting change from the LIFO method to the FIFO method for 2010 and 2009.

(c) Prepare the note to the financial statements describing the change in method of inventory valuation. In the note, indicate the income statement line items for 2010 and 2009 that were affected by the change in accounting principle.

(d) Prepare comparative retained earnings statements for 2009 and 2010 under FIFO.

E22-4 (Accounting Change) Linden Company started operations on January 1, 2006, and has used the FIFO method of inventory valuation since its inception. In 2012, it decides to switch to the average cost method. You are provided with the following information.

	Net Income		Retained Earnings (Ending balance)
	Under FIFO	Under Average Cost	Under FIFO
2006	$100,000	$ 92,000	$100,000
2007	70,000	65,000	160,000
2008	90,000	80,000	235,000
2009	120,000	130,000	340,000
2010	300,000	293,000	590,000
2011	305,000	310,000	780,000

Instructions

(a) What is the beginning retained earnings balance at January 1, 2008, if Linden prepares comparative financial statements starting in 2008?

(b) What is the beginning retained earnings balance at January 1, 2011, if Linden prepares comparative financial statements starting in 2011?

(c) What is the beginning retained earnings balance at January 1, 2012, if Linden prepares single-period financial statements for 2012?

(d) What is the net income reported by Linden in the 2011 income statement if it prepares comparative financial statements starting with 2009?

E22-5 (Accounting Change) Presented on page 1224 are income statements prepared on a LIFO and FIFO basis for Carlton Company, which started operations on January 1, 2009. The company presently uses the LIFO method of pricing its inventory and has decided to switch to the FIFO method in 2010. The FIFO income statement is computed in accordance with GAAP requirements. Carlton's profit-sharing agreement with its employees indicates that the company will pay employees 5% of income before profit sharing. Income taxes are ignored.

	LIFO Basis		FIFO Basis	
	2010	2009	2010	2009
Sales	$3,000	$3,000	$3,000	$3,000
Cost of goods sold	1,130	1,000	1,100	940
Operating expenses	1,000	1,000	1,000	1,000
Income before profit sharing	870	1,000	900	1,060
Profit sharing expense	44	50	45	53
Net income	$ 826	$ 950	$ 855	$1,007

Instructions
Answer the following questions.

(a) If comparative income statements are prepared, what net income should Carlton report in 2009 and 2010?

(b) Explain why, under the FIFO basis, Carlton reports $50 in 2009 and $48 in 2010 for its profit-sharing expense.

(c) Assume that Carlton has a beginning balance of retained earnings at January 1, 2010, of $8,000 using the LIFO method. The company declared and paid dividends of $2,500 in 2010. Prepare the retained earnings statement for 2010, assuming that Carlton has switched to the FIFO method.

·5 E22-6 (Accounting Changes—Depreciation) Robillard Inc. acquired the following assets in January of 2007.

Equipment, estimated service life, 5 years; salvage value, $15,000	$465,000
Building, estimated service life, 30 years; no salvage value	$780,000

   The equipment has been depreciated using the sum-of-the-years'-digits method for the first 3 years for financial reporting purposes. In 2010, the company decided to change the method of computing depreciation to the straight-line method for the equipment, but no change was made in the estimated service life or salvage value. It was also decided to change the total estimated service life of the building from 30 years to 40 years, with no change in the estimated salvage value. The building is depreciated on the straight-line method.

Instructions
(a) Prepare the journal entry to record depreciation expense for the equipment in 2010.
(b) Prepare the journal entry to record depreciation expense for the building in 2010. (Round to nearest dollar.)

·5 ·7 E22-7 (Change in Estimate and Error; Financial Statements) Presented below are the comparative income statements for Pannebecker Inc. for the years 2009 and 2010.

	2010	2009
Sales	$340,000	$270,000
Cost of sales	200,000	142,000
Gross profit	140,000	128,000
Expenses	88,000	50,000
Net income	$ 52,000	$ 78,000
Retained earnings (Jan. 1)	$125,000	$ 72,000
Net income	52,000	78,000
Dividends	(30,000)	(25,000)
Retained earnings (Dec. 31)	$147,000	$125,000

The following additional information is provided:

1. In 2010, Pannebecker Inc. decided to switch its depreciation method from sum-of-the-years'-digits to the straight-line method. The assets were purchased at the beginning of 2009 for $90,000 with an estimated useful life of 4 years and no salvage value. (The 2010 income statement contains depreciation expense of $27,000 on the assets purchased at the beginning of 2009.)

2. In 2010, the company discovered that the ending inventory for 2009 was overstated by $20,000; ending inventory for 2010 is correctly stated.

Instructions
Prepare the revised retained earnings statement for 2009 and 2010, assuming comparative statements. (Ignore income taxes.)

·3 ·5 ·7 E22-8 (Accounting for Accounting Changes and Errors) Listed below are various types of accounting changes and errors.

_____ 1. Change from FIFO to average cost inventory method.
_____ 2. Change due to overstatement of inventory.
_____ 3. Change from sum-of-the-years'-digits to straight-line method of depreciation.
_____ 4. Change from presenting unconsolidated to consolidated financial statements.
_____ 5. Change from LIFO to FIFO inventory method.
_____ 6. Change in the rate used to compute warranty costs.
_____ 7. Change from an unacceptable accounting principle to an acceptable accounting principle.
_____ 8. Change in a patent's amortization period.
_____ 9. Change from completed-contract to percentage-of-completion method on construction contracts.
_____ 10. Change in a plant asset's salvage value.

Instructions
For each change or error, indicate how it would be accounted for using the following code letters:

(a) Accounted for prospectively.
(b) Accounted for retrospectively.
(c) Neither of the above.

 ·5 ·7 E22-9 (Error and Change in Estimate—Depreciation) Tarkington Co. purchased a machine on January 1, 2007, for $440,000. At that time it was estimated that the machine would have a 10-year life and no salvage value. On December 31, 2010, the firm's accountant found that the entry for depreciation expense had been omitted in 2008. In addition, management has informed the accountant that the company plans to switch to straight-line depreciation, starting with the year 2010. At present, the company uses the sum-of-the-years'-digits method for depreciating equipment.

Instructions
Prepare the general journal entries that should be made at December 31, 2010 to record these events. (Ignore tax effects.)

·5 E22-10 (Depreciation Changes) On January 1, 2006, McElroy Company purchased a building and equipment that have the following useful lives, salvage values, and costs.

> Building, 40-year estimated useful life, $50,000 salvage value, $1,200,000 cost
> Equipment, 12-year estimated useful life, $10,000 salvage value, $130,000 cost

The building has been depreciated under the double-declining balance method through 2009. In 2010, the company decided to switch to the straight-line method of depreciation. McElroy also decided to change the total useful life of the equipment to 9 years, with a salvage value of $5,000 at the end of that time. The equipment is depreciated using the straight-line method.

Instructions
(a) Prepare the journal entry(ies) necessary to record the depreciation expense on the building in 2010.
(b) Compute depreciation expense on the equipment for 2010.

 ·5 E22-11 (Change in Estimate—Depreciation) Thurber Co. purchased equipment for $710,000 which was estimated to have a useful life of 10 years with a salvage value of $10,000 at the end of that time. Depreciation has been entered for 7 years on a straight-line basis. In 2011, it is determined that the total estimated life should be 15 years with a salvage value of $4,000 at the end of that time.

Instructions
(a) Prepare the entry (if any) to correct the prior years' depreciation.
(b) Prepare the entry to record depreciation for 2011.

·5 E22-12 (Change in Estimate—Depreciation) Frederick Industries changed from the double-declining balance to the straight-line method in 2010 on all its plant assets. There was no change in the assets' salvage values or useful lives. Plant assets, acquired on January 2, 2007, had an original cost of $2,400,000, with a $100,000 salvage value and an 8-year estimated useful life. Income before depreciation expense was $370,000 in 2009 and $300,000 in 2010.

Instructions
(a) Prepare the journal entry(ies) to record the change in depreciation method in 2010.
(b) Starting with income before depreciation expense, prepare the remaining portion of the income statement for 2009 and 2010.

·3 **E22-13** **(Change in Principle—Long-Term Contracts)** Bryant Construction Company changed from the completed-contract to the percentage-of-completion method of accounting for long-term construction contracts during 2010. For tax purposes, the company employs the completed-contract method and will continue this approach in the future. The appropriate information related to this change is as follows.

	Pretax Income from		
	Percentage-of-Completion	Completed-Contract	Difference
2009	$980,000	$730,000	$250,000
2010	900,000	480,000	420,000

Instructions

(a) Assuming that the tax rate is 40%, what is the amount of net income that would be reported in 2010?

(b) What entry(ies) are necessary to adjust the accounting records for the change in accounting principle?

·3 **E22-14** **(Various Changes in Principle—Inventory Methods)** Below is the net income of Benchley Instrument Co., a private corporation, computed under the three inventory methods using a periodic system.

	FIFO	Average Cost	LIFO
2008	$26,000	$23,000	$20,000
2009	30,000	25,000	21,000
2010	29,000	27,000	24,000
2011	34,000	30,000	26,000

Instructions

(Ignore tax considerations.)

(a) Assume that in 2011 Benchley decided to change from the FIFO method to the average cost method of pricing inventories. Prepare the journal entry necessary for the change that took place during 2011, and show net income reported for 2008, 2009, 2010, and 2011.

(b) Assume that in 2011 Benchley, which had been using the LIFO method since incorporation in 2008, changed to the FIFO method of pricing inventories. Prepare the journal entry necessary to record the change in 2011 and show net income reported for 2008, 2009, 2010, and 2011.

·7 **E22-15** **(Error Correction Entries)** The first audit of the books of Fenimore Company was made for the year ended December 31, 2010. In examining the books, the auditor found that certain items had been overlooked or incorrectly handled in the last 3 years. These items are:

1. At the beginning of 2008, the company purchased a machine for $510,000 (salvage value of $51,000) that had a useful life of 5 years. The bookkeeper used straight-line depreciation, but failed to deduct the salvage value in computing the depreciation base for the 3 years.
2. At the end of 2009, the company failed to accrue sales salaries of $45,000.
3. A tax lawsuit that involved the year 2008 was settled late in 2010. It was determined that the company owed an additional $85,000 in taxes related to 2008. The company did not record a liability in 2008 or 2009 because the possibility of loss was considered remote, and debited the $85,000 to a loss account in 2010 and credited Cash for the same amount.
4. Fenimore Company purchased a copyright from another company early in 2008 for $50,000. Fenimore had not amortized the copyright because its value had not diminished. The copyright has a useful life at purchase of 20 years.
5. In 2010, the company wrote off $87,000 of inventory considered to be obsolete; this loss was charged directly to Retained Earnings and credited to Inventory.

Instructions

Prepare the journal entries necessary in 2010 to correct the books, assuming that the books have not been closed. Disregard effects of corrections on income tax.

·7 **E22-16** **(Error Analysis and Correcting Entry)** You have been engaged to review the financial statements of Longfellow Corporation. In the course of your examination you conclude that the bookkeeper hired during the current year is not doing a good job. You notice a number of irregularities as follows.

1. Year-end wages payable of $3,400 were not recorded because the bookkeeper thought that "they were immaterial."
2. Accrued vacation pay for the year of $31,100 was not recorded because the bookkeeper "never heard that you had to do it."
3. Insurance for a 12-month period purchased on November 1 of this year was charged to insurance expense in the amount of $3,300 because "the amount of the check is about the same every year."

4. Reported sales revenue for the year is $1,908,000. This includes all sales taxes collected for the year. The sales tax rate is 6%. Because the sales tax is forwarded to the state's Department of Revenue, the Sales Tax Expense account is debited. The bookkeeper thought that "the sales tax is a selling expense." At the end of the current year, the balance in the Sales Tax Expense account is $103,400.

Instructions

Prepare the necessary correcting entries, assuming that Longfellow uses a calendar-year basis.

•7 E22-17 (Error Analysis and Correcting Entry) The reported net incomes for the first 2 years of Sinclair Products, Inc., were as follows: 2010, $147,000; 2011, $185,000. Early in 2012, the following errors were discovered.

1. Depreciation of equipment for 2010 was overstated $19,000.
2. Depreciation of equipment for 2011 was understated $38,500.
3. December 31, 2010, inventory was understated $50,000.
4. December 31, 2011, inventory was overstated $14,200.

Instructions

Prepare the correcting entry necessary when these errors are discovered. Assume that the books for 2011 are closed. (Ignore income tax considerations.)

•7 •9 E22-18 (Error Analysis) Emerson Tool Company's December 31 year-end financial statements contained the following errors.

	December 31, 2009	December 31, 2010
Ending inventory	$9,600 understated	$7,100 overstated
Depreciation expense	$2,300 understated	—

An insurance premium of $60,000 was prepaid in 2009 covering the years 2009, 2010, and 2011. The entire amount was charged to expense in 2009. In addition, on December 31, 2010, fully depreciated machinery was sold for $15,000 cash, but the entry was not recorded until 2011. There were no other errors during 2009 or 2010, and no corrections have been made for any of the errors. (Ignore income tax considerations.)

Instructions

(a) Compute the total effect of the errors on 2010 net income.
(b) Compute the total effect of the errors on the amount of Emerson's working capital at December 31, 2010.
(c) Compute the total effect of the errors on the balance of Emerson's retained earnings at December 31, 2010.

•7 •9 E22-19 (Error Analysis and Correcting Entries) A partial trial balance of Dickinson Corporation is as follows on December 31, 2010.

	Dr.	Cr.
Supplies on hand	$ 2,500	
Accrued salaries and wages		$ 1,500
Interest receivable	5,100	
Prepaid insurance	90,000	
Unearned rent		–0–
Accrued interest payable		15,000

Additional adjusting data:

1. A physical count of supplies on hand on December 31, 2010, totaled $1,100.
2. Through oversight, the Accrued Salaries and Wages account was not changed during 2010. Accrued salaries and wages on December 31, 2010, amounted to $4,400.
3. The Interest Receivable account was also left unchanged during 2010. Accrued interest on investments amounts to $4,350 on December 31, 2010.
4. The unexpired portions of the insurance policies totaled $65,000 as of December 31, 2010.
5. $24,000 was received on January 1, 2010 for the rent of a building for both 2010 and 2011. The entire amount was credited to rental income.
6. Depreciation for the year was erroneously recorded as $5,000 rather than the correct figure of $50,000.
7. A further review of depreciation calculations of prior years revealed that depreciation of $7,200 was not recorded. It was decided that this oversight should be corrected by a prior period adjustment.

Instructions

(a) Assuming that the books have not been closed, what are the adjusting entries necessary at December 31, 2010? (Ignore income tax considerations.)

(b) Assuming that the books have been closed, what are the adjusting entries necessary at December 31, 2010? (Ignore income tax considerations.)

•7 •9 E22-20 (Error Analysis) The before-tax income for Fitzgerald Co. for 2010 was $101,000 and $77,400 for 2011. However, the accountant noted that the following errors had been made:

1. Sales for 2010 included amounts of $38,200 which had been received in cash during 2010, but for which the related products were delivered in 2011. Title did not pass to the purchaser until 2011.
2. The inventory on December 31, 2010, was understated by $8,640.
3. The bookkeeper in recording interest expense for both 2010 and 2011 on bonds payable made the following entry on an annual basis.

Interest Expense	15,000	
Cash		15,000

The bonds have a face value of $250,000 and pay a stated interest rate of 6%. They were issued at a discount of $10,000 on January 1, 2010, to yield an effective interest rate of 7%. (Assume that the effective-interest method should be used.)

4. Ordinary repairs to equipment had been erroneously charged to the Equipment account during 2010 and 2011. Repairs in the amount of $8,000 in 2010 and $9,400 in 2011 were so charged. The company applies a rate of 10% to the balance in the Equipment account at the end of the year in its determination of depreciation charges.

Instructions

Prepare a schedule showing the determination of corrected income before taxes for 2010 and 2011.

•7 •9 E22-21 (Error Analysis) When the records of Archibald Corporation were reviewed at the close of 2011, the errors listed below were discovered. For each item indicate by a check mark in the appropriate column whether the error resulted in an overstatement, an understatement, or had no effect on net income for the years 2010 and 2011.

	2010			2011		
Item	Over-statement	Under-statement	No Effect	Over-statement	Under-statement	No Effect
1. Failure to reflect supplies on hand on balance sheet at end of 2010.						
2. Failure to record the correct amount of ending 2010 inventory. The amount was understated because of an error in calculation.						
3. Failure to record merchandise purchased in 2010. Merchandise was also omitted from ending inventory in 2010 but was not yet sold.						
4. Failure to record accrued interest on notes payable in 2010; that amount was recorded when paid in 2011.						
5. Failure to record amortization of patent in 2011.						

•10 *E22-22 (Change from Fair Value to Equity)** On January 1, 2010, Sandburg Co. purchased 25,000 shares (a 10% interest) in Yevette Corp. for $1,400,000. At the time, the book value and the fair value of Yevette's net identifiable assets were $13,000,000.

On July 1, 2011, Sandburg paid $3,040,000 for 50,000 additional shares of Yevette common stock, which represented a 20% investment in Yevette. The fair value of Yevette's identifiable assets net of liabilities was equal to their carrying amount of $14,200,000. As a result of this transaction, Sandburg owns 30% of Yevette and can exercise significant influence over Yevette's operating and financial policies. Any excess of the cost over the fair value of the identifiable net assets is attributed to goodwill.

Yevette reported the following net income and declared and paid the following dividends.

	Net Income	Dividend per Share
Year ended 12/31/10	$900,000	None
Six months ended 6/30/11	500,000	None
Six months ended 12/31/11	815,000	$1.40

Instructions
Determine the ending balance that Sandburg Co. should report as its investment in Yevette Corp. at the end of 2011.

•10 *E22-23 (Change from Equity to Fair Value)** Gamble Corp. was a 30% owner of Sabrina Company, holding 210,000 shares of Sabrina's common stock on December 31, 2010. The investment account had the following entries.

Investment in Sabrina

1/1/09 Cost	$3,180,000	12/6/09 Dividend received	$150,000
12/31/09 Share of income	390,000	12/5/10 Dividend received	200,000
12/31/10 Share of income	510,000		

On January 2, 2011, Gamble sold 126,000 shares of Sabrina for $3,440,000, thereby losing its significant influence. During the year 2011 Sabrina experienced the following results of operations and paid the following dividends to Gamble.

	Sabrina Income (Loss)	Dividends Paid to Gamble
2011	$350,000	$50,400

At December 31, 2011, the fair value of Sabrina shares held by Gamble is $1,570,000. This is the first reporting date since the January 2 sale.

Instructions
(a) What effect does the January 2, 2011, transaction have upon Gamble's accounting treatment for its investment in Sabrina?
(b) Compute the carrying amount in Sabrina as of December 31, 2011.
(c) Prepare the adjusting entry on December 31, 2011, applying the fair value method to Gamble's long-term investment in Sabrina Company securities.

See the book's companion website, www.wiley.com/college/kieso, for a set of B Exercises.

PROBLEMS

•2 •5 •7 **P22-1 (Change in Estimate and Error Correction)** Holtzman Company is in the process of preparing its financial statements for 2010. Assume that no entries for depreciation have been recorded in 2010. The following information related to depreciation of fixed assets is provided to you:

1. Holtzman purchased equipment on January 2, 2007, for $85,000. At that time, the equipment had an estimated useful life of 10 years with a $5,000 salvage value. The equipment is depreciated on a straight-line basis. On January 2, 2010, as a result of additional information, the company determined that the equipment has a remaining useful life of 4 years with a $3,000 salvage value.

2. During 2010 Holtzman changed from the double-declining balance method for its building to the straight-line method. The building originally cost $300,000. It had a useful life of 10 years and a

salvage value of $30,000. The following computations present depreciation on both bases for 2008 and 2009.

	2009	2008
Straight-line	$27,000	$27,000
Declining-balance	48,000	60,000

3. Holtzman purchased a machine on July 1, 2008, at a cost of $120,000. The machine has a salvage value of $16,000 and a useful life of 8 years. Holtzman's bookkeeper recorded straight-line depreciation in 2008 and 2009 but failed to consider the salvage value.

Instructions

(a) Prepare the journal entries to record depreciation expense for 2010 and correct any errors made to date related to the information provided.

(b) Show comparative net income for 2009 and 2010. Income before depreciation expense was $300,000 in 2010, and was $310,000 in 2009. Ignore taxes.

·3·5·7 **P22-2** (**Comprehensive Accounting Change and Error Analysis Problem**) Botticelli Inc. was organized in late 2008 to manufacture and sell hosiery. At the end of its fourth year of operation, the company has been fairly successful, as indicated by the following reported net incomes.

2008	$140,000[a]	2010	$205,000
2009	160,000[b]	2011	276,000

[a]Includes a $10,000 increase because of change in bad debt experience rate.
[b]Includes extraordinary gain of $30,000.

The company has decided to expand operations and has applied for a sizable bank loan. The bank officer has indicated that the records should be audited and presented in comparative statements to facilitate analysis by the bank. Botticelli Inc. therefore hired the auditing firm of Check & Doublecheck Co. and has provided the following additional information.

1. In early 2009, Botticelli Inc. changed its estimate from 2% to 1% on the amount of bad debt expense to be charged to operations. Bad debt expense for 2008, if a 1% rate had been used, would have been $10,000. The company therefore restated its net income for 2008.

2. In 2011, the auditor discovered that the company had changed its method of inventory pricing from LIFO to FIFO. The effect on the income statements for the previous years is as follows.

	2008	2009	2010	2011
Net income unadjusted—LIFO basis	$140,000	$160,000	$205,000	$276,000
Net income unadjusted—FIFO basis	155,000	165,000	215,000	260,000
	$ 15,000	$ 5,000	$ 10,000	($ 16,000)

3. In 2011 the auditor discovered that:

a. The company incorrectly overstated the ending inventory by $14,000 in 2010.

b. A dispute developed in 2009 with the Internal Revenue Service over the deductibility of entertainment expenses. In 2008, the company was not permitted these deductions, but a tax settlement was reached in 2011 that allowed these expenses. As a result of the court's finding, tax expenses in 2011 were reduced by $60,000.

Instructions

(a) Indicate how each of these changes or corrections should be handled in the accounting records. Ignore income tax considerations.

(b) Present comparative income statements for the years 2008 to 2011, starting with income before extraordinary items. Ignore income tax considerations.

·3·5·7 **P22-3** (**Error Corrections and Accounting Changes**) Penn Company is in the process of adjusting and correcting its books at the end of 2010. In reviewing its records, the following information is compiled.

1. Penn has failed to accrue sales commissions payable at the end of each of the last 2 years, as follows.

December 31, 2009	$3,500
December 31, 2010	$2,500

2. In reviewing the December 31, 2011, inventory, Penn discovered errors in its inventory-taking procedures that have caused inventories for the last 3 years to be incorrect, as follows.

December 31, 2008	Understated	$16,000
December 31, 2009	Understated	$19,000
December 31, 2010	Overstated	$ 6,700

Penn has already made an entry that established the incorrect December 31, 2010, inventory amount.

3. At December 31, 2010, Penn decided to change the depreciation method on its office equipment from double-declining balance to straight-line. The equipment had an original cost of $100,000 when purchased on January 1, 2008. It has a 10-year useful life and no salvage value. Depreciation expense recorded prior to 2010 under the double-declining balance method was $36,000. Penn has already recorded 2010 depreciation expense of $12,800 using the double-declining balance method.

4. Before 2010, Penn accounted for its income from long-term construction contracts on the completed-contract basis. Early in 2010, Penn changed to the percentage-of-completion basis for accounting purposes. It continues to use the completed-contract method for tax purposes. Income for 2010 has been recorded using the percentage-of-completion method. The following information is available.

	Pretax Income	
	Percentage-of-Completion	Completed-Contract
Prior to 2010	$150,000	$105,000
2010	60,000	20,000

Instructions

Prepare the journal entries necessary at December 31, 2010, to record the above corrections and changes. The books are still open for 2010. The income tax rate is 40%. Penn has not yet recorded its 2010 income tax expense and payable amounts so current-year tax effects may be ignored. Prior-year tax effects must be considered in item 4.

P22-4 (Accounting Changes) Aston Corporation performs year-end planning in November of each year before their calendar year ends in December. The preliminary estimated net income is $3 million. The CFO, Rita Warren, meets with the company president, J. B. Aston, to review the projected numbers. She presents the following projected information.

ASTON CORPORATION
PROJECTED INCOME STATEMENT
FOR THE YEAR ENDED DECEMBER 31, 2010

Sales		$29,000,000
Cost of goods sold	$14,000,000	
Depreciation	2,600,000	
Operating expenses	6,400,000	23,000,000
Income before income tax		6,000,000
Income tax		3,000,000
Net income		$ 3,000,000

ASTON CORPORATION
SELECTED BALANCE SHEET INFORMATION
AT DECEMBER 31, 2010

Estimated cash balance	$ 5,000,000
Available-for-sale securities (at cost)	10,000,000
Security fair value adjustment account (1/1/10)	200,000

Estimated market value at December 31, 2010:

Security	Cost	Estimated Market
A	$ 2,000,000	$ 2,200,000
B	4,000,000	3,900,000
C	3,000,000	3,000,000
D	1,000,000	1,800,000
Total	$10,000,000	$10,900,000

Other information at December 31, 2010:

Equipment	$ 3,000,000
Accumulated depreciation (5-year SL)	1,200,000
New robotic equipment (purchased 1/1/10)	5,000,000
Accumulated depreciation (5-year DDB)	2,000,000

The corporation has never used robotic equipment before, and Warren assumed an accelerated method because of the rapidly changing technology in robotic equipment. The company normally uses straight-line depreciation for production equipment.

Aston explains to Warren that it is important for the corporation to show a $7,000,000 income before taxes because Aston receives a $1,000,000 bonus if the income before taxes and bonus reaches $7,000,000. Aston also does not want the company to pay more than $3,000,000 in income taxes to the government.

Instructions

(a) What can Warren do within GAAP to accommodate the president's wishes to achieve $7,000,000 in income before taxes and bonus? Present the revised income statement based on your decision.

(b) Are the actions ethical? Who are the stakeholders in this decision, and what effect do Warren's actions have on their interests?

·3 **P22-5** **(Change in Principle—Inventory—Periodic)** The management of Utrillo Instrument Company had concluded, with the concurrence of its independent auditors, that results of operations would be more fairly presented if Utrillo changed its method of pricing inventory from last-in, first-out (LIFO) to average cost in 2010. Given below is the 5-year summary of income under LIFO and a schedule of what the inventories would be if stated on the average cost method.

UTRILLO INSTRUMENT COMPANY
STATEMENT OF INCOME AND RETAINED EARNINGS
FOR THE YEARS ENDED MAY 31

	2006	2007	2008	2009	2010
Sales—net	$13,964	$15,506	$16,673	$18,221	$18,898
Cost of goods sold					
Beginning inventory	1,000	1,100	1,000	1,115	1,237
Purchases	13,000	13,900	15,000	15,900	17,100
Ending inventory	(1,100)	(1,000)	(1,115)	(1,237)	(1,369)
Total	12,900	14,000	14,885	15,778	16,968
Gross profit	1,064	1,506	1,788	2,443	1,930
Administrative expenses	700	763	832	907	989
Income before taxes	364	743	956	1,536	941
Income taxes (50%)	182	372	478	768	471
Net income	182	371	478	768	470
Retained earnings—beginning	1,206	1,388	1,759	2,237	3,005
Retained earnings—ending	$ 1,388	$ 1,759	$ 2,237	$ 3,005	$ 3,475
Earnings per share	$1.82	$3.71	$4.78	$7.68	$4.70

SCHEDULE OF INVENTORY BALANCES USING AVERAGE COST METHOD
FOR THE YEARS ENDED MAY 31

2005	2006	2007	2008	2009	2010
$1,010	$1,124	$1,101	$1,270	$1,500	$1,720

Instructions

Prepare comparative statements for the 5 years, assuming that Utrillo changed its method of inventory pricing to average cost. Indicate the effects on net income and earnings per share for the years involved. Utrillo Instruments started business in 2005. (All amounts except EPS are rounded up to the nearest dollar.)

 ·5·7·9 **P22-6** **(Accounting Change and Error Analysis)** On December 31, 2010, before the books were closed, the management and accountants of Madrasa Inc. made the following determinations about three depreciable assets.

1. Depreciable asset A was purchased January 2, 2007. It originally cost $540,000 and, for depreciation purposes, the straight-line method was originally chosen. The asset was originally expected to be useful for 10 years and have a zero salvage value. In 2010, the decision was made to change the depreciation method from straight-line to sum-of-the-years'-digits, and the estimates relating to useful life and salvage value remained unchanged.

2. Depreciable asset B was purchased January 3, 2006. It originally cost $180,000 and, for depreciation purposes, the straight-line method was chosen. The asset was originally expected to be useful for 15 years and have a zero salvage value. In 2010, the decision was made to shorten the total life of this asset to 9 years and to estimate the salvage value at $3,000.

3. Depreciable asset C was purchased January 5, 2006. The asset's original cost was $160,000, and this amount was entirely expensed in 2006. This particular asset has a 10-year useful life and no salvage value. The straight-line method was chosen for depreciation purposes.

Additional data:

1. Income in 2010 before depreciation expense amounted to $400,000.
2. Depreciation expense on assets other than A, B, and C totaled $55,000 in 2010.
3. Income in 2009 was reported at $370,000.
4. Ignore all income tax effects.
5. 100,000 shares of common stock were outstanding in 2009 and 2010.

Instructions

(a) Prepare all necessary entries in 2010 to record these determinations.

(b) Prepare comparative retained earnings statements for Madrasa Inc. for 2009 and 2010. The company had retained earnings of $200,000 at December 31, 2008.

 P22-7 (Error Corrections) You have been assigned to examine the financial statements of Zarle Company for the year ended December 31, 2010. You discover the following situations.

1. Depreciation of $3,200 for 2010 on delivery vehicles was not recorded.
2. The physical inventory count on December 31, 2009, improperly excluded merchandise costing $19,000 that had been temporarily stored in a public warehouse. Zarle uses a periodic inventory system.
3. A collection of $5,600 on account from a customer received on December 31, 2010, was not recorded until January 2, 2011.
4. In 2010, the company sold for $3,700 fully depreciated equipment that originally cost $25,000. The company credited the proceeds from the sale to the Equipment account.
5. During November 2010, a competitor company filed a patent-infringement suit against Zarle claiming damages of $220,000. The company's legal counsel has indicated that an unfavorable verdict is probable and a reasonable estimate of the court's award to the competitor is $125,000. The company has not reflected or disclosed this situation in the financial statements.
6. Zarle has a portfolio of trading securities. No entry has been made to adjust to market. Information on cost and market value is as follows.

	Cost	Market
December 31, 2009	$95,000	$95,000
December 31, 2010	$84,000	$82,000

7. At December 31, 2010, an analysis of payroll information shows accrued salaries of $12,200. The Accrued Salaries Payable account had a balance of $16,000 at December 31, 2010, which was unchanged from its balance at December 31, 2009.
8. A large piece of equipment was purchased on January 3, 2010, for $40,000 and was charged to Repairs Expense. The equipment is estimated to have a service life of 8 years and no residual value. Zarle normally uses the straight-line depreciation method for this type of equipment.
9. A $12,000 insurance premium paid on July 1, 2009, for a policy that expires on June 30, 2012, was charged to insurance expense.
10. A trademark was acquired at the beginning of 2009 for $50,000. No amortization has been recorded since its acquisition. The maximum allowable amortization period is 10 years.

Instructions

Assume the trial balance has been prepared but the books have not been closed for 2010. Assuming all amounts are material, prepare journal entries showing the adjustments that are required. (Ignore income tax considerations.)

P22-8 (Comprehensive Error Analysis) On March 5, 2011, you were hired by Hemingway Inc., a closely held company, as a staff member of its newly created internal auditing department. While reviewing the company's records for 2009 and 2010, you discover that no adjustments have yet been made for the items listed below.

Items

1. Interest income of $14,100 was not accrued at the end of 2009. It was recorded when received in February 2010.

2. A computer costing $4,000 was expensed when purchased on July 1, 2009. It is expected to have a 4-year life with no salvage value. The company typically uses straight-line depreciation for all fixed assets.

3. Research and development costs of $33,000 were incurred early in 2009. They were capitalized and were to be amortized over a 3-year period. Amortization of $11,000 was recorded for 2009 and $11,000 for 2010.

4. On January 2, 2009, Hemingway leased a building for 5 years at a monthly rental of $8,000. On that date, the company paid the following amounts, which were expensed when paid.

Security deposit	$20,000
First month's rent	8,000
Last month's rent	8,000
	$36,000

5. The company received $36,000 from a customer at the beginning of 2009 for services that it is to perform evenly over a 3-year period beginning in 2009. None of the amount received was reported as unearned revenue at the end of 2009.

6. Merchandise inventory costing $18,200 was in the warehouse at December 31, 2009, but was incorrectly omitted from the physical count at that date. The company uses the periodic inventory method.

Instructions

Indicate the effect of any errors on the net income figure reported on the income statement for the year ending December 31, 2009, and the retained earnings figure reported on the balance sheet at December 31, 2010. Assume all amounts are material, and ignore income tax effects. Using the following format, enter the appropriate dollar amounts in the appropriate columns. Consider each item independent of the other items. It is not necessary to total the columns on the grid.

	Net Income for 2009		Retained Earnings at 12/31/10	
Item	Understated	Overstated	Understated	Overstated

(CIA adapted)

·7 ·9 P22-9 (Error Analysis) Lowell Corporation has used the accrual basis of accounting for several years. A review of the records, however, indicates that some expenses and revenues have been handled on a cash basis because of errors made by an inexperienced bookkeeper. Income statements prepared by the bookkeeper reported $29,000 net income for 2009 and $37,000 net income for 2010. Further examination of the records reveals that the following items were handled improperly.

1. Rent was received from a tenant in December 2009. The amount, $1,000, was recorded as income at that time even though the rental pertained to 2010.

2. Wages payable on December 31 have been consistently omitted from the records of that date and have been entered as expenses when paid in the following year. The amounts of the accruals recorded in this manner were:

December 31, 2008	$1,100
December 31, 2009	1,200
December 31, 2010	940

3. Invoices for office supplies purchased have been charged to expense accounts when received. Inventories of supplies on hand at the end of each year have been ignored, and no entry has been made for them.

December 31, 2008	$1,300
December 31, 2009	940
December 31, 2010	1,420

Instructions

Prepare a schedule that will show the corrected net income for the years 2009 and 2010. All items listed should be labeled clearly. (Ignore income tax considerations.)

·7 ·9 P22-10 (Error Analysis and Correcting Entries) You have been asked by a client to review the records of Roberts Company, a small manufacturer of precision tools and machines. Your client is interested in buying the business, and arrangements have been made for you to review the accounting records. Your examination reveals the information shown on page 1235.

1. Roberts Company commenced business on April 1, 2008, and has been reporting on a fiscal year ending March 31. The company has never been audited, but the annual statements prepared by the bookkeeper reflect the following income before closing and before deducting income taxes.

Year Ended March 31	Income Before Taxes
2009	$ 71,600
2010	111,400
2011	103,580

2. A relatively small number of machines have been shipped on consignment. These transactions have been recorded as ordinary sales and billed as such. On March 31 of each year, machines billed and in the hands of consignees amounted to:

2009	$6,500
2010	none
2011	5,590

   Sales price was determined by adding 25% to cost. Assume that the consigned machines are sold the following year.

3. On March 30, 2010, two machines were shipped to a customer on a C.O.D. basis. The sale was not entered until April 5, 2010, when cash was received for $6,100. The machines were not included in the inventory at March 31, 2010. (Title passed on March 30, 2010.)

4. All machines are sold subject to a 5-year warranty. It is estimated that the expense ultimately to be incurred in connection with the warranty will amount to ½ of 1% of sales. The company has charged an expense account for warranty costs incurred.

   Sales per books and warranty costs were as follows.

Year Ended March 31	Sales	Warranty Expense for Sales Made in 2009	2010	2011	Total
2009	$ 940,000	$760			$ 760
2010	1,010,000	360	$1,310		1,670
2011	1,795,000	320	1,620	$1,910	3,850

5. Bad debts have been recorded on a direct write-off basis. Experience of similar enterprises indicates that losses will approximate ¼ of 1% of sales. Bad debts written off were:

	Bad Debts Incurred on Sales Made in 2009	2010	2011	Total
2009	$750			$ 750
2010	800	$ 520		1,320
2011	350	1,800	$1,700	3,850

6. The bank deducts 6% on all contracts financed. Of this amount, ½% is placed in a reserve to the credit of Roberts Company that is refunded to Roberts as finance contracts are paid in full. The reserve established by the bank has not been reflected in the books of Roberts. The excess of credits over debits (net increase) to the reserve account with Roberts on the books of the bank for each fiscal year were as follows.

2009	$ 3,000
2010	3,900
2011	5,100
	$12,000

7. Commissions on sales have been entered when paid. Commissions payable on March 31 of each year were as follows.

2009	$1,400
2010	900
2011	1,120

8. A review of the corporate minutes reveals the manager is entitled to a bonus of 1% of the income before deducting income taxes and the bonus. The bonuses have never been recorded or paid.

Instructions

(a) Present a schedule showing the revised income before income taxes for each of the years ended March 31, 2009, 2010, and 2011. Make computations to the nearest whole dollar.

(b) Prepare the journal entry or entries you would give the bookkeeper to correct the books. Assume the books have not yet been closed for the fiscal year ended March 31, 2011. Disregard correction of income taxes.

(AICPA adapted)

•10 ***P22-11** (Fair Value to Equity Method with Goodwill)* On January 1, 2010, Millay Inc. paid $700,000 for 10,000 shares of Genso Company's voting common stock, which was a 10% interest in Genso. At that date the net assets of Genso totaled $6,000,000. The fair values of all of Genso's identifiable assets and liabilities were equal to their book values. Millay does not have the ability to exercise significant influence over the operating and financial policies of Genso. Millay received dividends of $1.50 per share from Genso on October 1, 2010. Genso reported net income of $550,000 for the year ended December 31, 2010.

On July 1, 2011, Millay paid $2,325,000 for 30,000 additional shares of Genso Company's voting common stock which represents a 30% investment in Genso. The fair values of all of Genso' identifiable assets net of liabilities were equal to their book values of $6,550,000. As a result of this transaction, Millay has the ability to exercise significant influence over the operating and financial policies of Genso. Millay received dividends of $2.00 per share from Genso on April 1, 2011, and $2.50 per share on October 1, 2011. Genso reported net income of $650,000 for the year ended December 31, 2011, and $350,000 for the 6 months ended December 31, 2011.

Instructions

(a) Prepare a schedule showing the income or loss before income taxes for the year ended December 31, 2010, that Millay should report from its investment in Genso in its income statement issued in March 2011.

(b) During March 2012, Millay issues comparative financial statements for 2010 and 2011. Prepare schedules showing the income or loss before income taxes for the years ended December 31, 2010 and 2011, that Millay should report from its investment in Genso.

(AICPA adapted)

•10 ***P22-12** (Change from Fair Value to Equity Method)* On January 3, 2009, Martin Company purchased for $500,000 cash a 10% interest in Renner Corp. On that date the net assets of Renner had a book value of $3,700,000. The excess of cost over the underlying equity in net assets is attributable to undervalued depreciable assets having a remaining life of 10 years from the date of Martin's purchase.

The fair value of Martin's investment in Renner securities is as follows: December 31, 2009, $560,000, and December 31, 2010, $515,000.

On January 2, 2011, Martin purchased an additional 30% of Renner's stock for $1,545,000 cash when the book value of Renner's net assets was $4,150,000. The excess was attributable to depreciable assets having a remaining life of 8 years.

During 2009, 2010, and 2011 the following occurred.

	Renner Net Income	Dividends Paid by Renner to Martin
2009	$350,000	$15,000
2010	450,000	20,000
2011	550,000	70,000

Instructions

On the books of Martin Company prepare all journal entries in 2009, 2010, and 2011 that relate to its investment in Renner Corp., reflecting the data above and a change from the fair value method to the equity method.

CONCEPTS FOR ANALYSIS

CA22-1 (Analysis of Various Accounting Changes and Errors) Joblonsky Inc. has recently hired a new independent auditor, Karen Ogleby, who says she wants "to get everything straightened out." Consequently, she has proposed the accounting changes shown on page 1237 in connection with Joblonsky Inc.'s 2010 financial statements.

1. At December 31, 2009, the client had a receivable of $820,000 from Hendricks Inc. on its balance sheet. Hendricks Inc. has gone bankrupt, and no recovery is expected. The client proposes to write off the receivable as a prior period item.

2. The client proposes the following changes in depreciation policies.

   (a) For office furniture and fixtures it proposes to change from a 10-year useful life to an 8-year life. If this change had been made in prior years, retained earnings at December 31, 2009, would have been $250,000 less. The effect of the change on 2010 income alone is a reduction of $60,000.

   (b) For its equipment in the leasing division the client proposes to adopt the sum-of-the-years'-digits depreciation method. The client had never used SYD before. The first year the client operated a leasing division was 2010. If straight-line depreciation were used, 2010 income would be $110,000 greater.

3. In preparing its 2009 statements, one of the client's bookkeepers overstated ending inventory by $235,000 because of a mathematical error. The client proposes to treat this item as a prior period adjustment.

4. In the past, the client has spread preproduction costs in its furniture division over 5 years. Because its latest furniture is of the "fad" type, it appears that the largest volume of sales will occur during the first 2 years after introduction. Consequently, the client proposes to amortize preproduction costs on a per-unit basis, which will result in expensing most of such costs during the first 2 years after the furniture's introduction. If the new accounting method had been used prior to 2010, retained earnings at December 31, 2009, would have been $375,000 less.

5. For the nursery division the client proposes to switch from FIFO to LIFO inventories because it believes that LIFO will provide a better matching of current costs with revenues. The effect of making this change on 2010 earnings will be an increase of $320,000. The client says that the effect of the change on December 31, 2009, retained earnings cannot be determined.

6. To achieve a better matching of revenues and expenses in its building construction division, the client proposes to switch from the completed-contract method of accounting to the percentage-of-completion method. Had the percentage-of-completion method been employed in all prior years, retained earnings at December 31, 2009, would have been $1,075,000 greater.

Instructions

(a) For each of the changes described above decide whether:

   (1) The change involves an accounting principle, accounting estimate, or correction of an error.

   (2) Restatement of opening retained earnings is required.

(b) What would be the proper adjustment to the December 31, 2009, retained earnings?

CA22-2 (Analysis of Various Accounting Changes and Errors) Various types of accounting changes can affect the financial statements of a business enterprise differently. Assume that the following list describes changes that have a material effect on the financial statements for the current year of your business enterprise.

1. A change from the completed-contract method to the percentage-of-completion method of accounting for long-term construction-type contracts.

2. A change in the estimated useful life of previously recorded fixed assets as a result of newly acquired information.

3. A change from deferring and amortizing preproduction costs to recording such costs as an expense when incurred because future benefits of the costs have become doubtful. The new accounting method was adopted in recognition of the change in estimated future benefits.

4. A change from including the employer share of FICA taxes with payroll tax expenses to including it with "Retirement benefits" on the income statement.

5. Correction of a mathematical error in inventory pricing made in a prior period.

6. A change from presentation of statements of individual companies to presentation of consolidated statements.

7. A change in the method of accounting for leases for tax purposes to conform with the financial accounting method. As a result, both deferred and current taxes payable changed substantially.

8. A change from the FIFO method of inventory pricing to the LIFO method of inventory pricing.

Instructions

Identify the type of change that is described in each item above and indicate whether the prior year's financial statements should be retrospectively applied or restated when presented in comparative form with the current year's financial statements.

CA22-3 **(Analysis of Three Accounting Changes and Errors)** Listed below are three independent, unrelated sets of facts relating to accounting changes.

Situation 1

Sanford Company is in the process of having its first audit. The company has used the cash basis of accounting for revenue recognition. Sanford president, B. J. Jimenez, is willing to change to the accrual method of revenue recognition.

Situation 2

Hopkins Co. decides in January 2011 to change from FIFO to weighted-average pricing for its inventories.

Situation 3

Marshall Co. determined that the depreciable lives of its fixed assets are too long at present to fairly match the cost of the fixed assets with the revenue produced. The company decided at the beginning of the current year to reduce the depreciable lives of all of its existing fixed assets by 5 years.

Instructions

For each of the situations described, provide the information indicated below.

(a) Type of accounting change.
(b) Manner of reporting the change under current generally accepted accounting principles including a discussion, where applicable, of how amounts are computed.
(c) Effect of the change on the balance sheet and income statement.

CA22-4 **(Analysis of Various Accounting Changes and Errors)** Katherine Irving, controller of Lotan Corp., is aware that a pronouncement on accounting changes has been issued. After reading the pronouncement, she is confused about what action should be taken on the following items related to Lotan Corp. for the year 2010.

1. In 2010, Lotan decided to change its policy on accounting for certain marketing costs. Previously, the company had chosen to defer and amortize all marketing costs over at least 5 years because Lotan believed that a return on these expenditures did not occur immediately. Recently, however, the time differential has considerably shortened, and Lotan is now expensing the marketing costs as incurred.

2. In 2010, the company examined its entire policy relating to the depreciation of plant equipment. Plant equipment had normally been depreciated over a 15-year period, but recent experience has indicated that the company was incorrect in its estimates and that the assets should be depreciated over a 20-year period.

3. One division of Lotan Corp., Hawthorne Co., has consistently shown an increasing net income from period to period. On closer examination of their operating statement, it is noted that bad debt expense and inventory obsolescence charges are much lower than in other divisions. In discussing this with the controller of this division, it has been learned that the controller has increased his net income each period by knowingly making low estimates related to the writeoff of receivables and inventory.

4. In 2010, the company purchased new machinery that should increase production dramatically. The company has decided to depreciate this machinery on an accelerated basis, even though other machinery is depreciated on a straight-line basis.

5. All equipment sold by Lotan is subject to a 3-year warranty. It has been estimated that the expense ultimately to be incurred on these machines is 1% of sales. In 2010, because of a production break-through, it is now estimated that ½ of 1% of sales is sufficient. In 2008 and 2009, warranty expense was computed as $64,000 and $70,000, respectively. The company now believes that these warranty costs should be reduced by 50%.

6. In 2010, the company decided to change its method of inventory pricing from average cost to the FIFO method. The effect of this change on prior years is to increase 2008 income by $65,000 and increase 2009 income by $20,000.

Instructions

Katherine Irving has come to you, as her CPA, for advice about the situations above. Prepare a report, indicating the appropriate accounting treatment that should be given each of these situations.

CA22-5 **(Change in Principle, Estimate)** As a certified public accountant, you have been contacted by Toe Davison, CEO of Sports-Pro Athletics, Inc., a manufacturer of a variety of athletic equipment. He has ꞏd you how to account for the following changes.

ꞏrts-Pro appropriately changed its depreciation method for its production machinery from the ꞏouble-declining balance method to the production method effective January 1, 2010.

2. Effective January 1, 2010, Sports-Pro appropriately changed the salvage values used in computing depreciation for its office equipment.

3. On December 31, 2010, Sports-Pro appropriately changed the specific subsidiaries constituting the group of companies for which consolidated financial statements are presented.

Instructions

Write a 1–1.5 page letter to Joe Davison explaining how each of the above changes should be presented in the December 31, 2010, financial statements.

CA22-6 (Change in Estimate) Mike Crane is an audit senior of a large public accounting firm who has just been assigned to the Frost Corporation's annual audit engagement. Frost has been a client of Crane's firm for many years. Frost is a fast-growing business in the commercial construction industry. In reviewing the fixed asset ledger, Crane discovered a series of unusual accounting changes, in which the useful lives of assets, depreciated using the straight-line method, were substantially lowered near the midpoint of the original estimate. For example, the useful life of one dump truck was changed from 10 to 6 years during its fifth year of service. Upon further investigation, Mike was told by Kevin James, Frost's accounting manager, "I don't really see your problem. After all, it's perfectly legal to change an accounting estimate. Besides, our CEO likes to see big earnings!"

Instructions

Answer the following questions.

(a) What are the ethical issues concerning Frost's practice of changing the useful lives of fixed assets?

(b) Who could be harmed by Frost's unusual accounting changes?

(c) What should Crane do in this situation?

USING YOUR JUDGMENT

FINANCIAL REPORTING

Financial Reporting Problem

 The Procter & Gamble Company (P&G)

The financial statements of P&G are provided in Appendix 5B or can be accessed at the book's companion website, **www.wiley.com/college/kieso**.

Instructions

Refer to P&G's financial statements and the accompanying notes to answer the following questions.

(a) Were there changes in accounting principles reported by P&G during the three years covered by its income statements (2004–2007)? If so, describe the nature of the change and the year of change.

(b) What types of estimates did P&G discuss in 2007?

Comparative Analysis Case

The Coca-Cola Company

The Coca-Cola Company and PepsiCo, Inc.

 PEPSICO

Instructions

Go to the book's companion website and use information found there to answer the following questions related to **The Coca-Cola Company** and **PepsiCo Inc.**

(a) Identify the changes in accounting principles reported by Coca-Cola during the 3 years covered by its income statements (2005–2007). Describe the nature of the change and the year of change.

(b) Identify the changes in accounting principles reported by PepsiCo during the 3 years covered by its income statements (2005–2007). Describe the nature of the change and the year of change.

(c) For each change in accounting principle by Coca-Cola and PepsiCo, identify, if possible, the cumulative effect of each change on prior years and the effect on operating results in the year of change.

BRIDGE TO THE PROFESSION

Professional Research: FASB Codification

As part of the year-end accounting process and review of operating policies, Cullen Co. is considering a change in the accounting for its equipment from the straight-line method to an accelerated method. Your supervisor wonders how the company will report this change in principle. He read in a newspaper article that the FASB has issued a standard in this area and has changed GAAP for a "change in estimate that is effected by a change in accounting principle." (Thus, the accounting may be different from that he learned in intermediate accounting.) Your supervisor wants you to research the authoritative guidance on a change in accounting principle related to depreciation methods.

Instructions

Access the FASB Codification at *http://asc.fasb.org/home* to conduct research using the Codification Research System to prepare responses to the following items. Provide Codification references for your responses.

(a) What are the accounting and reporting guidelines for a change in accounting principle related to depreciation methods?

(b) What are the conditions that justify a change in depreciation method, as contemplated by Cullen Co.?

(c) What guidance does the SEC provide concerning the impact that recently issued accounting standards will have on the financial statements in a future period?

Professional Simulation

Go to the book's companion website, at **www.wiley.com/college/kieso,** to find an interactive problem that simulates the computerized CPA exam. The professional simulation for this chapter asks you to address questions related to changes in accounting principles.

Remember to check the book's companion website to find additional resources for this chapter.

CHAPTER 23

STATEMENT OF CASH FLOWS

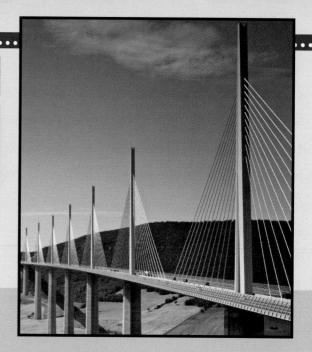

LEARNING OBJECTIVES

After studying this chapter, you should be able to:

•1 Describe the purpose of the statement of cash flows.

•2 Identify the major classifications of cash flows.

•3 Differentiate between net income and net cash flows from operating activities.

•4 Contrast the direct and indirect methods of calculating net cash flow from operating activities.

•5 Determine net cash flows from investing and financing activities.

•6 Prepare a statement of cash flows.

•7 Identify sources of information for a statement of cash flows.

•8 Discuss special problems in preparing a statement of cash flows.

•9 Explain the use of a worksheet in preparing a statement of cash flows.

DON'T TAKE CASH FLOW FOR GRANTED

Investors usually look to net income as a key indicator of a company's financial health and future prospects. The following graph shows the net income of one company over a seven-year period.

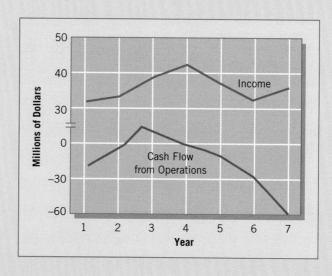

The company showed a pattern of consistent profitability and even some periods of income growth. Between years 1 and 4, net income for this company grew by 32 percent, from $31 million to $41 million. Would you expect its profitability to continue? The company had consistently paid dividends and interest. Would you expect it to continue to do so? Investors answered "yes" to these questions, by buying the company's stock. Eighteen months later, this company—**W. T. Grant**—filed for bankruptcy, in what was then the largest bankruptcy filing in the United States.

How could this happen? As indicated by the second line in the graph, the company had experienced several years of negative cash flow from its operations, even though it reported profits. How can a company have negative cash flows while reporting profits? The answer lay partly in the fact that W. T. Grant was having trouble collecting the receivables from its credit sales, causing cash flow to be less than the net income. Investors who analyzed the cash flows would have been likely to find an early warning signal of W. T. Grant's operating problems.

Source: Adapted from James A. Largay III and Clyde P. Stickney, "Cash Flows, Ratio Analysis, and the W. T. Grant Company Bankruptcy," *Financial Analysts Journal* (July–August 1980), p. 51.

PREVIEW OF CHAPTER 23

As the opening story indicates, examination of **W. T. Grant**'s cash flows from operations would have shown the financial inflexibility that eventually caused the company's bankruptcy. This chapter explains the main components of a statement of cash flows and the types of information it provides. The content and organization of the chapter are as follows.

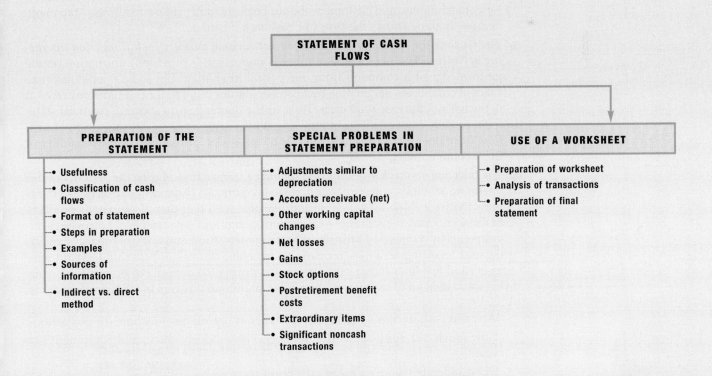

STATEMENT OF CASH FLOWS

PREPARATION OF THE STATEMENT	SPECIAL PROBLEMS IN STATEMENT PREPARATION	USE OF A WORKSHEET
• Usefulness	• Adjustments similar to depreciation	• Preparation of worksheet
• Classification of cash flows	• Accounts receivable (net)	• Analysis of transactions
• Format of statement	• Other working capital changes	• Preparation of final statement
• Steps in preparation	• Net losses	
• Examples	• Gains	
• Sources of information	• Stock options	
• Indirect vs. direct method	• Postretirement benefit costs	
	• Extraordinary items	
	• Significant noncash transactions	

SECTION 1 • PREPARATION OF THE STATEMENT OF CASH FLOWS

Objective•1
Describe the purpose of the statement of cash flows.

The primary purpose of the **statement of cash flows** is to provide information about a company's cash receipts and cash payments during a period. A secondary objective is to provide cash-basis information about the company's operating, investing, and financing activities. The statement of cash flows therefore reports cash receipts, cash payments, and net change in cash resulting from a company's operating, investing, and financing activities during a period. Its format reconciles the beginning and ending cash balances for the period.

USEFULNESS OF THE STATEMENT OF CASH FLOWS

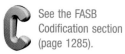

See the FASB Codification section (page 1285).

The statement of cash flows provides information to help investors, creditors, and others assess the following [1]:

1. *The entity's ability to generate future cash flows.* A primary objective of financial reporting is to provide information with which to predict the amounts, timing, and uncertainty of future cash flows. By examining relationships between items such as sales and net cash flow from operating activities, or net cash flow from operating activities and increases or decreases in cash, it is possible to better predict the future cash flows than is possible using accrual-basis data alone.

2. *The entity's ability to pay dividends and meet obligations.* Simply put, cash is essential. Without adequate cash, a company cannot pay employees, settle debts, pay out dividends, or acquire equipment. A statement of cash flows indicates where the company's cash comes from and how the company uses its cash. Employees, creditors, stockholders, and customers should be particularly interested in this statement, because it alone shows the flows of cash in a business.

3. *The reasons for the difference between net income and net cash flow from operating activities.* The net income number is important: It provides information on the performance of a company from one period to another. But some people are critical of accrual-basis net income because companies must make estimates to arrive at it. Such is not the case with cash. Thus, as the opening story showed, financial statement readers can benefit from knowing why a company's net income and net cash flow from operating activities differ, and can assess for themselves the reliability of the income number.

4. *The cash and noncash investing and financing transactions during the period.* Besides operating activities, companies undertake investing and financing transactions. *Investing* activities include the purchase and sale of assets other than a company's products or services. *Financing* activities include borrowings and repayments of borrowings, investments by owners, and distributions to owners. By examining a company's investing and financing activities, a financial statement reader can better understand why assets and liabilities increased or decreased during the period. For example, by reading the statement of cash flows, the reader might find answers to following questions:

   Why did cash decrease for **Toys R Us** when it reported net income for the period?
   How much did **Southwest Airlines** spend on property, plant, and equipment last year?
   Did dividends paid by **Campbell's Soup** increase?
   How much money did **Coca-Cola** borrow last year?
   How much cash did **Hewlett-Packard** use to repurchase its common stock?

CLASSIFICATION OF CASH FLOWS

The statement of cash flows classifies cash receipts and cash payments by operating, investing, and financing activities.[1] Transactions and other events characteristic of each kind of activity is as follows.

Objective·2
Identify the major classifications of cash flows.

1. **Operating activities** involve the cash effects of transactions that enter into the determination of net income, such as cash receipts from sales of goods and services, and cash payments to suppliers and employees for acquisitions of inventory and expenses.
2. **Investing activities** generally involve long-term assets and include (a) making and collecting loans, and (b) acquiring and disposing of investments and productive long-lived assets.
3. **Financing activities** involve liability and stockholders' equity items and include (a) obtaining cash from creditors and repaying the amounts borrowed, and (b) obtaining capital from owners and providing them with a return on, and a return of, their investment.

Illustration 23-1 classifies the typical cash receipts and payments of a company according to operating, investing, and financing activities. The operating activities category is the most important. It shows the cash provided by company operations. This source of cash is generally considered to be the best measure of a company's ability to generate enough cash to continue as a going concern.

ILLUSTRATION 23-1
Classification of Typical Cash Inflows and Outflows

Operating
   Cash inflows
      From sales of goods or services.
      From returns on loans (interest) and on equity
         securities (dividends).
   Cash outflows
      To suppliers for inventory.
      To employees for services.
      To government for taxes.
      To lenders for interest.
      To others for expenses.
	Income
	Statement
	Items

Investing
   Cash inflows
      From sale of property, plant, and equipment.
      From sale of debt or equity securities of other entities.
      From collection of principal on loans to other entities.
   Cash outflows
      To purchase property, plant, and equipment.
      To purchase debt or equity securities of other entities.
      To make loans to other entities.
	Generally
	Long-Term
	Asset Items

Financing
   Cash inflows
      From sale of equity securities.
      From issuance of debt (bonds and notes).
   Cash outflows
      To stockholders as dividends.
      To redeem long-term debt or reacquire capital stock.
	Generally
	Long-Term
	Liability
	and Equity
	Items

INTERNATIONAL INSIGHT

According to International Accounting Standards, companies can define "cash and cash equivalents" as "net monetary assets"—that is, as "cash and demand deposits and highly liquid investments less short-term borrowings."

[1]The basis recommended by the FASB for the statement of cash flows is actually "cash and cash equivalents." **Cash equivalents** are short-term, highly liquid investments that are both: (a) readily convertible to known amounts of cash, and (b) so near their maturity that they present insignificant risk of changes in interest rates. Generally, only investments with original maturities of three months or less qualify under this definition. Examples of cash equivalents are Treasury bills, commercial paper, and money market funds purchased with cash that is in excess of immediate needs.

Although we use the term "cash" throughout our discussion and illustrations, we mean cash and cash equivalents when reporting the cash flows and the net increase or decrease in cash.

Note the following general guidelines about the classification of cash flows.

1. Operating activities involve income statement items.
2. Investing activities involve cash flows resulting from changes in investments and long-term asset items.
3. Financing activities involve cash flows resulting from changes in long-term liability and stockholders' equity items.

Companies classify some cash flows relating to investing or financing activities as operating activities.[2] For example, companies classify receipts of investment income (interest and dividends) and payments of interest to lenders as operating activities. Why are these considered operating activities? Companies report these items in the income statement, where the results of operations are shown.

Conversely, companies classify some cash flows relating to operating activities as investing or financing activities. For example, a company classifies the cash received from the sale of property, plant, and equipment at a gain, although reported in the income statement, as an investing activity. It excludes the effects of the related gain in net cash flow from operating activities. Likewise, a gain or loss on the payment (extinguishment) of debt is generally part of the cash outflow related to the repayment of the amount borrowed. It therefore is a financing activity.

HOW'S MY CASH FLOW?

What do the numbers mean?

To evaluate overall cash flow, it is useful to understand where in the product life cycle a company is. Generally, companies move through several stages of development, which have implications for cash flow. As the graph below shows, the pattern of cash flows from operating, financing, and investing activities will vary depending on the stage of the product life cycle.

In the introductory phase, the product is likely not generating much revenue (operating cash flow is negative). Because the company is making heavy investments to get a product off the ground, cash flow from investment is negative, and financing cash flows are positive.

---

[2]Banks and brokers must classify cash flows from purchases and sales of loans and securities specifically for resale and carried at market value **as operating activities**. This requirement recognizes that for these firms these assets are similar to inventory in other businesses. **[2]**

As the product moves to the growth and maturity phases, these cash flow relationships reverse. The product generates more cash flow from operations, which can be used to cover investments needed to support the product, and less cash is needed from financing. So is a negative operating cash flow bad? Not always. It depends on the product life cycle.

Source: Adapted from Paul D. Kimmel, Jerry J. Weygandt, and Donald E. Kieso, *Financial Accounting: Tools for Business Decision Making*, 5th ed. (New York: John Wiley & Sons, 2009), p. 606.

What do the numbers mean?

(continued)

FORMAT OF THE STATEMENT OF CASH FLOWS

The three activities we discussed above constitute the general format of the statement of cash flows. The operating activities section always appears first. It is followed by the investing activities section and then the financing activities section.

A company reports the individual inflows and outflows from investing and financing activities separately. That is, a company reports them gross, not netted against one another. Thus, a cash outflow from the purchase of property is reported separately from the cash inflow from the sale of property. Similarly, a cash inflow from the issuance of debt is reported separately from the cash outflow from its retirement.

The net increase or decrease in cash reported during the period should reconcile the beginning and ending cash balances as reported in the comparative balance sheets. The general format of the statement of cash flows presents the results of the three activities discussed previously–operating, investing, and financing. Illustration 23-2 shows a widely used form of the statement of cash flows.

ILLUSTRATION 23-2
Format of the Statement of Cash Flows

COMPANY NAME STATEMENT OF CASH FLOWS PERIOD COVERED		
Cash flows from operating activities		
Net income		XXX
Adjustments to reconcile net income to net cash provided (used) by operating activities:		
(List of individual items)	XX	XX
Net cash provided (used) by operating activities		XXX
Cash flows from investing activities		
(List of individual inflows and outflows)	XX	
Net cash provided (used) by investing activities		XXX
Cash flows from financing activities		
(List of individual inflows and outflows)	XX	
Net cash provided (used) by financing activities		XXX
Net increase (decrease) in cash		XXX
Cash at beginning of period		XXX
Cash at end of period		XXX

INTERNATIONAL INSIGHT

Both iGAAP and U.S. GAAP specify that companies must classify cash flows as operating, investing, or financing.

STEPS IN PREPARATION

Companies prepare the statement of cash flows differently from the three other basic financial statements. For one thing, it is not prepared from an adjusted trial balance. The cash flow statement requires detailed information concerning the changes in account balances that occurred between two points in time. An adjusted trial balance will not provide the necessary data. Second, the statement of cash flows deals with cash receipts and payments. As a result, the company must adjust the effects of the use of accrual accounting to determine cash flows. The information to prepare this statement usually comes from three sources:

1. **Comparative balance sheets** provide the amount of the changes in assets, liabilities, and equities from the beginning to the end of the period.
2. **Current income statement** data help determine the amount of cash provided by or used by operations during the period.
3. **Selected transaction data** from the general ledger provide additional detailed information needed to determine how the company provided or used cash during the period.

Preparing the statement of cash flows from the data sources above involves three major steps:

Step 1. *Determine the change in cash.* This procedure is straightforward. A company can easily compute the difference between the beginning and the ending cash balance from examining its comparative balance sheets.

Step 2. *Determine the net cash flow from operating activities.* This procedure is complex. It involves analyzing not only the current year's income statement but also comparative balance sheets as well as selected transaction data.

Step 3. *Determine net cash flows from investing and financing activities.* A company must analyze all other changes in the balance sheet accounts to determine their effects on cash.

On the following pages we work through these three steps in the process of preparing the statement of cash flows for Tax Consultants Inc. over several years.

FIRST EXAMPLE—2009

To illustrate a statement of cash flows, we use the **first year of operations** for Tax Consultants Inc. The company started on January 1, 2009, when it issued 60,000 shares of $1 par value common stock for $60,000 cash. The company rented its office space, furniture, and equipment, and performed tax consulting services throughout the first year. The comparative balance sheets at the beginning and end of the year 2009 appear in Illustration 23-3.

ILLUSTRATION 23-3
Comparative Balance Sheets, Tax Consultants Inc., Year 1

TAX CONSULTANTS INC. COMPARATIVE BALANCE SHEETS			
Assets	Dec. 31, 2009	Jan. 1, 2009	Change Increase/Decrease
Cash	$49,000	$-0-	$49,000 Increase
Accounts receivable	36,000	-0-	36,000 Increase
Total	$85,000	$-0-	
Liabilities and Stockholders' Equity			
Accounts payable	$ 5,000	$-0-	$ 5,000 Increase
Common stock ($1 par)	60,000	-0-	60,000 Increase
Retained earnings	20,000	-0-	20,000 Increase
Total	$85,000	$-0-	

Illustration 23-4 (on page 1249) shows the income statement and additional information for Tax Consultants.

ILLUSTRATION 23-4
Income Statement, Tax
Consultants Inc., Year 1

TAX CONSULTANTS INC.
INCOME STATEMENT
FOR THE YEAR ENDED DECEMBER 31, 2009

Revenues	$125,000
Operating expenses	85,000
Income before income taxes	40,000
Income tax expense	6,000
Net income	$ 34,000

Additional Information
Examination of selected data indicates that a dividend of $14,000 was declared and paid during the year.

Step 1: Determine the Change in Cash

To prepare a statement of cash flows, the first step is to **determine the change in cash**. This is a simple computation. Tax Consultants had no cash on hand at the beginning of the year 2009. It had $49,000 on hand at the end of 2009. Thus, cash changed (increased) in 2009 by $49,000.

Step 2: Determine Net Cash Flow from Operating Activities

To determine net cash flow from operating activities,[3] companies adjust net income in numerous ways. A useful starting point is to understand why net income must be converted to net cash provided by operating activities.

Objective·3
Differentiate between net income and net cash flows from operating activities.

Under generally accepted accounting principles, most companies use the accrual basis of accounting. As you have learned, this basis requires that companies record revenue when earned and record expenses when incurred. Earned revenues may include credit sales for which the company has not yet collected cash. Expenses incurred may include some items that the company has not yet paid in cash. Thus, under the accrual basis of accounting, net income is not the same as net cash flow from operating activities.

To arrive at net cash flow from operating activities, a company must determine revenues and expenses on a **cash basis**. **It does this by eliminating the effects of income statement transactions that do not result in an increase or decrease in cash.** Illustration 23-5 shows the relationship between net income and net cash flow from operating activities.

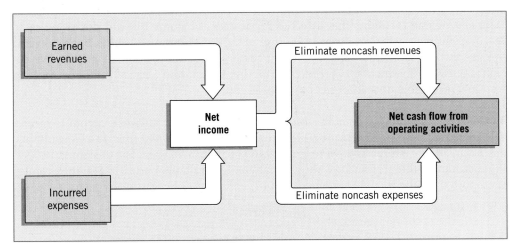

ILLUSTRATION 23-5
Net Income versus Net
Cash Flow from
Operating Activities

[3]"Net cash flow from operating activities" is a generic phrase, replaced in the statement of cash flows with either "Net cash **provided by** operating activities" if operations increase cash, or "Net cash **used by** operating activities" if operations decrease cash.

In this chapter, we use the term net income to refer to accrual-based net income. A company may convert net income to net cash flow from operating activities through either a direct method or an indirect method. We explain both methods in the following sections. The advantages and disadvantages of these two methods are discussed later in the chapter.

Direct Method

The **direct method** (also called the **income statement method**) reports cash receipts and cash disbursements from operating activities. The difference between these two amounts is the net cash flow from operating activities. In other words, the direct method deducts operating cash disbursements from operating cash receipts. The direct method results in the presentation of a condensed cash receipts and cash disbursements statement.

As indicated from the accrual-based income statement, Tax Consultants reported revenues of $125,000. However, because the company's accounts receivable increased during 2009 by $36,000, the company collected only $89,000 ($125,000 − $36,000) in cash from these revenues. Similarly, Tax Consultants reported operating expenses of $85,000. However, accounts payable increased during the period by $5,000. Assuming that these payables relate to operating expenses, cash operating expenses were $80,000 ($85,000 − $5,000). Because no taxes payable exist at the end of the year, the company must have paid $6,000 income tax expense for 2009 in cash during the year. Tax Consultants computes net cash flow from operating activities as shown in Illustration 23-6.

ILLUSTRATION 23-6
Computation of Net Cash Flow from Operating Activities, Year 1—Direct Method

Cash collected from revenues	$89,000
Cash payments for expenses	80,000
Income before income taxes	9,000
Cash payments for income taxes	6,000
Net cash provided by operating activities	$ 3,000

"Net cash provided by operating activities" is the equivalent of cash basis net income. ("Net cash used by operating activities" is equivalent to cash basis net loss.)

Indirect Method

The **indirect method** (or **reconciliation method**) starts with net income and converts it to net cash flow from operating activities. In other words, **the indirect method adjusts net income for items that affected reported net income but did not affect cash**. To compute net cash flow from operating activities, a company adds back noncash charges in the income statement to net income and deducts noncash credits. We explain the two adjustments to net income for Tax Consultants, namely, the increases in accounts receivable and accounts payable, as follows.

Increase in Accounts Receivable—Indirect Method. Tax Consultant's accounts receivable increased by $36,000 (from $0 to $36,000) during the year. For Tax Consultants, this means that cash receipts were $36,000 lower than revenues. The Accounts Receivable account in Illustration 23-7 shows that Tax Consultants had $125,000 in revenues (as reported on the income statement), but it collected only $89,000 in cash.

ILLUSTRATION 23-7
Analysis of Accounts Receivable

Accounts Receivable				
1/1/09	Balance	–0–	Receipts from customer	89,000
	Revenues	125,000		
12/31/09	Balance	36,000		

As shown in Illustration 23-8, to adjust net income to net cash provided by operating activities, Tax Consultants must deduct the increase of $36,000 in accounts receivable from net income. When the Accounts Receivable balance *decreases*, cash receipts are higher than revenue earned under the accrual basis. Therefore, the company adds to net income the amount of the decrease in accounts receivable to arrive at net cash provided by operating activities.

Increase in Accounts Payable—Indirect Method. When accounts payable increase during the year, expenses on an accrual basis exceed those on a cash basis. Why? Because Tax Consultants incurred expenses, but some of the expenses are not yet paid. To convert net income to net cash flow from operating activities, Tax Consultants must add back the increase of $5,000 in accounts payable to net income.

As a result of the accounts receivable and accounts payable adjustments, Tax Consultants determines net cash provided by operating activities is $3,000 for the year 2009. Illustration 23-8 shows this computation.

Net income		$34,000
Adjustments to reconcile net income to net cash provided by operating activities:		
Increase in accounts receivable	$(36,000)	
Increase in accounts payable	5,000	(31,000)
Net cash provided by operating activities		$ 3,000

ILLUSTRATION 23-8
Computation of Net Cash Flow from Operating Activities, Year 1—Indirect Method

Note that net cash provided by operating activities is the same whether using the direct (Illustration 23-6) or the indirect method (Illustration 23-8).

PUMPING UP CASH

Due to recent concerns about a decline in the quality of earnings, some investors have been focusing on cash flow. Management has an incentive to make operating cash flow look good because Wall Street has paid a premium for companies that generate a lot of cash from operations, rather than through borrowings. However, similar to earnings, companies have ways to pump up cash flow from operations.

What do the numbers mean?

One way that companies can boost their operating cash flow is by "securitizing" receivables. That is, companies can speed up cash collections by selling their receivables. For example, Federated Department Stores reported a $2.2 billion increase in cash flow from operations. This seems impressive until you read the fine print, which indicates that a big part of the increase was due to the sale of receivables. As discussed in this section, decreases in accounts receivable increase cash flow from operations. So while it appeared that Federated's core operations had improved, the company really did little more than accelerate collections of its receivables. In fact, the cash flow from the securitizations represented more than half of Federated's operating cash flow. Thus, just like earnings, cash flow can be of high or low quality.

Source: Adapted from Ann Tergesen, "Cash Flow Hocus Pocus," *Business Week* (July 16, 2002), pp. 130–131. *See also* Bear Stearns Equity Research, *Accounting Issues: Cash Flow Metrics* (June 2006).

Step 3: Determine Net Cash Flows from Investing and Financing Activities

After Tax Consultants has computed the net cash provided by operating activities, the next step is to determine whether any other changes in balance sheet accounts caused an increase or decrease in cash.

For example, an examination of the remaining balance sheet accounts for Tax Consultants shows increases in both common stock and retained earnings. The

Objective·5
Determine net cash flows from investing and financing activities.

common stock increase of $60,000 resulted from the issuance of common stock for cash. The issuance of common stock is reported in the statement of cash flows as a receipt of cash from a financing activity.

Two items caused the retained earnings increase of $20,000:

1. Net income of $34,000 increased retained earnings.
2. Declaration of $14,000 of dividends decreased retained earnings.

Tax Consultants has converted net income into net cash flow from operating activities, as explained earlier. The additional data indicate that it paid the dividend. Thus, the company reports the dividend payment as a cash outflow, classified as a financing activity.

Statement of Cash Flows—2009

Objective·6
Prepare a statement of cash flows.

We are now ready to prepare the statement of cash flows. The statement starts with the operating activities section. Tax Consultants may use either the direct or indirect method to report net cash flow from operating activities.

The FASB **encourages** the use of the direct method over the indirect method. If a company uses the direct method of reporting net cash flow from operating activities, the FASB **requires** that the company provide in a separate schedule a reconciliation of net income to net cash flow from operating activities. If a company uses the indirect method, it can either report the reconciliation within the statement of cash flows or can provide it in a separate schedule, with the statement of cash flows reporting only the **net** cash flow from operating activities. [3] Throughout this chapter we use the indirect method, which is also used more extensively in practice.[4] *In doing homework assignments, you should follow instructions for use of either the direct or indirect method.*

Illustration 23-9 shows the statement of cash flows for Tax Consultants Inc., for year 1 (2009).

ILLUSTRATION 23-9
Statement of Cash Flows,
Tax Consultants Inc.,
Year 1

TAX CONSULTANTS INC. STATEMENT OF CASH FLOWS FOR THE YEAR ENDED DECEMBER 31, 2009 INCREASE (DECREASE) IN CASH		
Cash flows from operating activities		
Net income		$34,000
Adjustments to reconcile net income to net cash provided by operating activities:		
Increase in accounts receivable	$(36,000)	
Increase in accounts payable	5,000	(31,000)
Net cash provided by operating activities		3,000
Cash flows from financing activities		
Issuance of common stock	60,000	
Payment of cash dividends	(14,000)	
Net cash provided by financing activities		46,000
Net increase in cash		49,000
Cash, January 1, 2009		–0–
Cash, December 31, 2009		$49,000

As indicated, the $60,000 increase in common stock results in a financing-activity cash inflow. The payment of $14,000 in cash dividends is a financing-activity outflow of cash. The $49,000 increase in cash reported in the statement of cash flows agrees with the increase of $49,000 shown in the comparative balance sheets as the change in the cash account.

---

[4]*Accounting Trends and Techniques—2007* reports that out of its 600 surveyed companies, 594 (approximately 99 percent) used the indirect method, and only 6 used the direct method.

SECOND EXAMPLE—2010

Tax Consultants Inc. continued to grow and prosper in its second year of operations. The company purchased land, building, and equipment, and revenues and net income increased substantially over the first year. Illustrations 23-10 and 23-11 present information related to the second year of operations for Tax Consultants Inc.

TAX CONSULTANTS INC.
COMPARATIVE BALANCE SHEETS
AS OF DECEMBER 31

Assets	2010	2009	Change Increase/Decrease
Cash	$ 37,000	$49,000	$ 12,000 Decrease
Accounts receivable	26,000	36,000	10,000 Decrease
Prepaid expenses	6,000	–0–	6,000 Increase
Land	70,000	–0–	70,000 Increase
Building	200,000	–0–	200,000 Increase
Accumulated depreciation—building	(11,000)	–0–	11,000 Increase
Equipment	68,000	–0–	68,000 Increase
Accumulated depreciation—equipment	(10,000)	–0–	10,000 Increase
Total	$386,000	$85,000	
Liabilities and Stockholders' Equity			
Accounts payable	$ 40,000	$ 5,000	$ 35,000 Increase
Bonds payable	150,000	–0–	150,000 Increase
Common stock ($1 par)	60,000	60,000	–0–
Retained earnings	136,000	20,000	116,000 Increase
Total	$386,000	$85,000	

ILLUSTRATION 23-10
Comparative Balance Sheets, Tax Consultants Inc., Year 2

TAX CONSULTANTS INC.
INCOME STATEMENT
FOR THE YEAR ENDED DECEMBER 31, 2010

Revenues		$492,000
Operating expenses (excluding depreciation)	$269,000	
Depreciation expense	21,000	290,000
Income from operations		202,000
Income tax expense		68,000
Net income		$134,000

Additional Information
(a) The company declared and paid an $18,000 cash dividend.
(b) The company obtained $150,000 cash through the issuance of long-term bonds.
(c) Land, building, and equipment were acquired for cash.

ILLUSTRATION 23-11
Income Statement, Tax Consultants Inc., Year 2

Step 1: Determine the Change in Cash

To prepare a statement of cash flows from the available information, the first step is to determine the change in cash. As indicated from the information presented, cash decreased $12,000 ($49,000 − $37,000).

Step 2: Determine Net Cash Flow from Operating Activities—Indirect Method

Using the indirect method, we adjust net income of $134,000 on an accrual basis to arrive at net cash flow from operating activities. Explanations for the adjustments to net income follow.

Decrease in Accounts Receivable. Accounts receivable decreased during the period, because cash receipts (cash-basis revenues) are higher than revenues reported on an accrual basis. To convert net income to net cash flow from operating activities, the decrease of $10,000 in accounts receivable must be added to net income.

Increase in Prepaid Expenses. When prepaid expenses (assets) increase during a period, expenses on an accrual-basis income statement are lower than they are on a cash-basis income statement. The reason: Tax Consultants has made cash payments in the current period, but expenses (as charges to the income statement) have been deferred to future periods. To convert net income to net cash flow from operating activities, the company must deduct from net income the increase of $6,000 in prepaid expenses. An increase in prepaid expenses results in a decrease in cash during the period.

Increase in Accounts Payable. Like the increase in 2009, Tax Consultants must add the 2010 increase of $35,000 in accounts payable to net income, to convert to net cash flow from operating activities. The company incurred a greater amount of expense than the amount of cash it disbursed.

Depreciation Expense (Increase in Accumulated Depreciation). The purchase of depreciable assets is a use of cash, shown in the investing section in the year of acquisition. Tax Consultant's depreciation expense of $21,000 (also represented by the increase in accumulated depreciation) is a noncash charge; the company adds it back to net income, to arrive at net cash flow from operating activities. The $21,000 is the sum of the $11,000 depreciation on the building plus the $10,000 depreciation on the equipment.

Certain other periodic charges to expense do not require the use of cash. Examples are the amortization of intangible assets and depletion expense. Such charges are treated in the same manner as depreciation. Companies frequently list depreciation and similar noncash charges as the first adjustments to net income in the statement of cash flows.

As a result of the foregoing items, net cash provided by operating activities is $194,000 as shown in Illustration 23-12.

ILLUSTRATION 23-12
Computation of Net Cash Flow from Operating Activities, Year 2—Indirect Method

Net income		$134,000
Adjustments to reconcile net income to		
net cash provided by operating activities:		
Depreciation expense	$21,000	
Decrease in accounts receivable	10,000	
Increase in prepaid expenses	(6,000)	
Increase in accounts payable	35,000	60,000
Net cash provided by operating activities		$194,000

Step 3: Determine Net Cash Flows from Investing and Financing Activities

After you have determined the items affecting net cash provided by operating activities, the next step involves analyzing the remaining changes in balance sheet accounts. Tax Consultants Inc. analyzed the following accounts.

Increase in Land. As indicated from the change in the land account, the company purchased land of $70,000 during the period. This transaction is an investing activity, reported as a use of cash.

Increase in Building and Related Accumulated Depreciation. As indicated in the additional data, and from the change in the building account, Tax Consultants acquired an office building using $200,000 cash. This transaction is a cash outflow, reported in the investing section. The $11,000 increase in accumulated depreciation results from recording depreciation expense on the building. As indicated earlier, the reported depreciation expense has no effect on the amount of cash.

Increase in Equipment and Related Accumulated Depreciation. An increase in equipment of $68,000 resulted because the company used cash to purchase equipment. This transaction is an outflow of cash from an investing activity. The depreciation expense entry for the period explains the increase in Accumulated Depreciation—Equipment.

Increase in Bonds Payable. The bonds payable account increased $150,000. Cash received from the issuance of these bonds represents an inflow of cash from a financing activity.

Increase in Retained Earnings. Retained earnings increased $116,000 during the year. Two factors explain this increase: (1) Net income of $134,000 increased retained earnings, and (2) dividends of $18,000 decreased retained earnings. As indicated earlier, the company adjusts net income to net cash provided by operating activities in the operating activities section. Payment of the dividends is a financing activity that involves a cash outflow.

Statement of Cash Flows—2010

Combining the foregoing items, we get a statement of cash flows for 2010 for Tax Consultants Inc., using the indirect method to compute net cash flow from operating activities.

ILLUSTRATION 23-13
Statement of Cash Flows,
Tax Consultants Inc.,
Year 2

TAX CONSULTANTS INC. STATEMENT OF CASH FLOWS FOR THE YEAR ENDED DECEMBER 31, 2010 INCREASE (DECREASE) IN CASH		
Cash flows from operating activities		
Net income		$134,000
Adjustments to reconcile net income to		
net cash provided by operating activities:		
Depreciation expense	$ 21,000	
Decrease in accounts receivable	10,000	
Increase in prepaid expenses	(6,000)	
Increase in accounts payable	35,000	60,000
Net cash provided by operating activities		194,000
Cash flows from investing activities		
Purchase of land	(70,000)	
Purchase of building	(200,000)	
Purchase of equipment	(68,000)	
Net cash used by investing activities		(338,000)
Cash flows from financing activities		
Issuance of bonds	150,000	
Payment of cash dividends	(18,000)	
Net cash provided by financing activities		132,000
Net decrease in cash		(12,000)
Cash, January 1, 2010		49,000
Cash, December 31, 2010		$ 37,000

THIRD EXAMPLE—2011

Our third example, covering the 2011 operations of Tax Consultants Inc., is more complex. It again uses the indirect method to compute and present net cash flow from operating activities.

Tax Consultants Inc. experienced continued success in 2011 and expanded its operations to include the sale of computer software used in tax-return preparation and tax planning. Thus, inventory is a new asset appearing in the company's December 31, 2011, balance sheet. Illustrations 23-14 and 23-15 (on page 1256) show the comparative balance sheets, income statements, and selected data for 2011.

ILLUSTRATION 23-14
Comparative Balance
Sheets, Tax Consultants
Inc., Year 3

TAX CONSULTANTS INC.
COMPARATIVE BALANCE SHEETS
AS OF DECEMBER 31

Assets	2011	2010	Change Increase/Decrease
Cash	$ 54,000	$ 37,000	$ 17,000 Increase
Accounts receivable	68,000	26,000	42,000 Increase
Inventories	54,000	–0–	54,000 Increase
Prepaid expenses	4,000	6,000	2,000 Decrease
Land	45,000	70,000	25,000 Decrease
Buildings	200,000	200,000	–0–
Accumulated depreciation—buildings	(21,000)	(11,000)	10,000 Increase
Equipment	193,000	68,000	125,000 Increase
Accumulated depreciation—equipment	(28,000)	(10,000)	18,000 Increase
Totals	$569,000	$386,000	
Liabilities and Stockholders' Equity			
Accounts payable	$ 33,000	$ 40,000	$ 7,000 Decrease
Bonds payable	110,000	150,000	40,000 Decrease
Common stock ($1 par)	220,000	60,000	160,000 Increase
Retained earnings	206,000	136,000	70,000 Increase
Totals	$569,000	$386,000	

ILLUSTRATION 23-15
Income Statement, Tax
Consultants Inc., Year 3

TAX CONSULTANTS INC.
INCOME STATEMENT
FOR THE YEAR ENDED DECEMBER 31, 2011

Revenues		$890,000
Cost of goods sold	$465,000	
Operating expenses	221,000	
Interest expense	12,000	
Loss on sale of equipment	2,000	700,000
Income from operations		190,000
Income tax expense		65,000
Net income		$125,000

Additional Information
(a) Operating expenses include depreciation expense of $33,000 and expiration of prepaid expenses of $2,000.
(b) Land was sold at its book value for cash.
(c) Cash dividends of $55,000 were declared and paid.
(d) Interest expense of $12,000 was paid in cash.
(e) Equipment with a cost of $166,000 was purchased for cash. Equipment with a cost of $41,000 and a book value of $36,000 was sold for $34,000 cash.
(f) Bonds were redeemed at their book value for cash.
(g) Common stock ($1 par) was issued for cash.

Step 1: Determine the Change in Cash

The first step in the preparation of the statement of cash flows is to determine the change in cash. As the comparative balance sheets show, cash increased $17,000 in 2011.

Step 2: Determine Net Cash Flow from Operating Activities—Indirect Method

We explain the adjustments to net income of $125,000 as follows.

Increase in Accounts Receivable. The increase in accounts receivable of $42,000 represents recorded accrual-basis revenues in excess of cash collections in 2011. The company deducts this increase from net income to convert from the accrual basis to the cash basis.

Increase in Inventories. The $54,000 increase in inventories represents an operating use of cash, not an expense. Tax Consultants therefore deducts this amount from net income, to arrive at net cash flow from operations. In other words, when inventory purchased exceeds inventory sold during a period, cost of goods sold on an accrual basis is lower than on a cash basis.

Decrease in Prepaid Expenses. The $2,000 decrease in prepaid expenses represents a charge to the income statement for which Tax Consultants made no cash payment in the current period. The company adds back the decrease to net income, to arrive at net cash flow from operating activities.

Decrease in Accounts Payable. When accounts payable decrease during the year, cost of goods sold and expenses on a cash basis are higher than they are on an accrual basis. To convert net income to net cash flow from operating activities, the company must deduct the $7,000 in accounts payable from net income.

Depreciation Expense (Increase in Accumulated Depreciation). Accumulated Depreciation—Buildings increased $10,000 ($21,000 − $11,000). The Buildings account did not change during the period, which means that Tax Consultants recorded depreciation expense of $10,000 in 2011.

Accumulated Depreciation—Equipment increased by $18,000 ($28,000 − $10,000) during the year. But Accumulated Depreciation—Equipment decreased by $5,000 as a result of the sale during the year. Thus, depreciation for the year was $23,000. The company reconciled Accumulated Depreciation—Equipment as follows.

Beginning balance	$10,000
Add: Depreciation for 2011	23,000
	33,000
Deduct: Sale of equipment	5,000
Ending balance	$28,000

The company must add back to net income the total depreciation of $33,000 ($10,000 + $23,000) charged to the income statement, to determine net cash flow from operating activities.

Loss on Sale of Equipment. Tax Consultants Inc. sold for $34,000 equipment that cost $41,000 and had a book value of $36,000. As a result, the company reported a loss of $2,000 on its sale. To arrive at net cash flow from operating activities, it must add back to net income the loss on the sale of the equipment. The reason is that the loss is a noncash charge to the income statement. The loss did not reduce cash, but it did reduce net income.[5]

From the foregoing items, the company prepares the operating activities section of the statement of cash flows, as shown in Illustration 23-16.

Cash flows from operating activities		
Net income		$125,000
Adjustments to reconcile net income to		
net cash provided by operating activities:		
Depreciation expense	$33,000	
Loss on sale of equipment	2,000	
Increase in accounts receivable	(42,000)	
Increase in inventories	(54,000)	
Decrease in prepaid expenses	2,000	
Decrease in accounts payable	(7,000)	(66,000)
Net cash provided by operating activities		59,000

ILLUSTRATION 23-16
Operating Activities Section of Cash Flows Statement

Step 3: Determine Net Cash Flows from Investing and Financing Activities

By analyzing the remaining changes in the balance sheet accounts, Tax Consultants identifies cash flows from investing and financing activities.

[5]A similar adjustment is required for unrealized gains or losses recorded on trading security investments or other financial assets and liabilities accounted for under the fair value option. Marking these assets and liabilities to fair value results in an increase or decrease in income, but there is no effect on cash flows.

Land. Land decreased $25,000 during the period. As indicated from the information presented, the company sold land for cash at its book value. This transaction is an investing activity, reported as a $25,000 source of cash.

Equipment. An analysis of the equipment account indicates the following.

Beginning balance	$ 68,000
Purchase of equipment	166,000
	234,000
Sale of equipment	41,000
Ending balance	$193,000

The company used cash to purchase equipment with a fair value of $166,000—an investing transaction reported as a cash outflow. The sale of the equipment for $34,000 is also an investing activity, but one that generates a cash inflow.

Bonds Payable. Bonds payable decreased $40,000 during the year. As indicated from the additional information, the company redeemed the bonds at their book value. This financing transaction used $40,000 of cash.

Common Stock. The common stock account increased $160,000 during the year. As indicated from the additional information, Tax Consultants issued common stock of $160,000 at par. This financing transaction provided cash of $160,000.

Retained Earnings. Retained earnings changed $70,000 ($206,000 − $136,000) during the year. The $70,000 change in retained earnings results from net income of $125,000 from operations and the financing activity of paying cash dividends of $55,000.

Statement of Cash Flows—2011

Tax Consultants Inc. combines the foregoing items to prepare the statement of cash flows shown in Illustration 23-17.

ILLUSTRATION 23-17
Statement of Cash Flows,
Tax Consultants Inc.,
Year 3

TAX CONSULTANTS INC.
STATEMENT OF CASH FLOWS
FOR THE YEAR ENDED DECEMBER 31, 2011
INCREASE (DECREASE) IN CASH

Cash flows from operating activities		
Net income		$125,000
Adjustments to reconcile net income to		
net cash provided by operating activities:		
Depreciation expense	$ 33,000	
Loss on sale of equipment	2,000	
Increase in accounts receivable	(42,000)	
Increase in inventories	(54,000)	
Decrease in prepaid expenses	2,000	
Decrease in accounts payable	(7,000)	(66,000)
Net cash provided by operating activities		59,000
Cash flows from investing activities		
Sale of land	25,000	
Sale of equipment	34,000	
Purchase of equipment	(166,000)	
Net cash used by investing activities		(107,000)
Cash flows from financing activities		
Redemption of bonds	(40,000)	
Sale of common stock	160,000	
Payment of dividends	(55,000)	
Net cash provided by financing activities		65,000
Net increase in cash		17,000
Cash, January 1, 2011		37,000
Cash, December 31, 2011		$ 54,000

SOURCES OF INFORMATION FOR THE STATEMENT OF CASH FLOWS

Objective·7
Identify sources of information for a statement of cash flows.

Important points to remember in the preparation of the statement of cash flows are these:

1. Comparative balance sheets provide the basic information from which to prepare the report. Additional information obtained from analyses of specific accounts is also included.

2. An analysis of the Retained Earnings account is necessary. The net increase or decrease in Retained Earnings without any explanation is a meaningless amount in the statement. Without explanation, it might represent the effect of net income, dividends declared, or prior period adjustments.

3. The statement includes all changes that have passed through cash or have resulted in an increase or decrease in cash.

4. Write-downs, amortization charges, and similar "book" entries, such as depreciation of plant assets, represent neither inflows nor outflows of cash, because they have no effect on cash. To the extent that they have entered into the determination of net income, however, the company must add them back to or subtract them from net income, to arrive at net cash provided (used) by operating activities.

NET CASH FLOW FROM OPERATING ACTIVITIES—INDIRECT VERSUS DIRECT METHOD

As we discussed previously, the two different methods available to adjust income from operations on an accrual basis to net cash flow from operating activities are the indirect (reconciliation) method and the direct (income statement) method.

The FASB encourages use of the direct method and permits use of the indirect method. Yet, if the direct method is used, the Board requires that companies provide in a separate schedule a reconciliation of net income to net cash flow from operating activities. Therefore, under either method, companies must prepare and report information from the indirect (reconciliation) method.

Indirect Method

For consistency and comparability and because it is the most widely used method in practice, we used the indirect method in the examples just presented. We determined net cash flows from operating activities by adding back to or deducting from net income those items that had no effect on cash. Illustration 23-18 presents more completely

ILLUSTRATION 23-18
Adjustments Needed to Determine Net Cash Flow from Operating Activities—Indirect Method

the common types of adjustments that companies make to net income to arrive at net cash flow from operating activities.

The additions and deductions in Illustration 23-18 reconcile net income to net cash flow from operating activities, illustrating why the indirect method is also called the reconciliation method.

Direct Method—An Example

Under the direct method the statement of cash flows reports net cash flow from operating activities as major classes of *operating cash receipts* (e.g., cash collected from customers and cash received from interest and dividends) and *cash disbursements* (e.g., cash paid to suppliers for goods, to employees for services, to creditors for interest, and to government authorities for taxes).

We illustrate the direct method here in more detail to help you understand the difference between accrual-based income and net cash flow from operating activities. This example also illustrates the data needed to apply the direct method. Emig Company, which began business on January 1, 2010, has the following selected balance sheet information.

ILLUSTRATION 23-19
Balance Sheet Accounts, Emig Co.

	December 31, 2010	January 1, 2010
Cash	$159,000	–0–
Accounts receivable	15,000	–0–
Inventory	160,000	–0–
Prepaid expenses	8,000	–0–
Property, plant, and equipment (net)	90,000	–0–
Accounts payable	60,000	–0–
Accrued expenses payable	20,000	–0–

Emig Company's December 31, 2010, income statement and additional information are as follows.

ILLUSTRATION 23-20
Income Statement, Emig Co.

Revenues from sales		$780,000
Cost of goods sold		450,000
Gross profit		330,000
Operating expenses	$160,000	
Depreciation	10,000	170,000
Income before income taxes		160,000
Income tax expense		48,000
Net income		$112,000

Additional Information:
(a) Dividends of $70,000 were declared and paid in cash.
(b) The accounts payable increase resulted from the purchase of merchandise.
(c) Prepaid expenses and accrued expenses payable relate to operating expenses.

Under the **direct method**, companies compute net cash provided by operating activities by **adjusting each item in the income statement** from the accrual basis to the cash basis. To simplify and condense the operating activities section, only major classes of operating cash receipts and cash payments are reported. As Illustration 23-21 shows, the difference between these major classes of cash receipts and cash payments is the net cash provided by operating activities.

ILLUSTRATION 23-21
Major Classes of Cash
Receipts and Payments

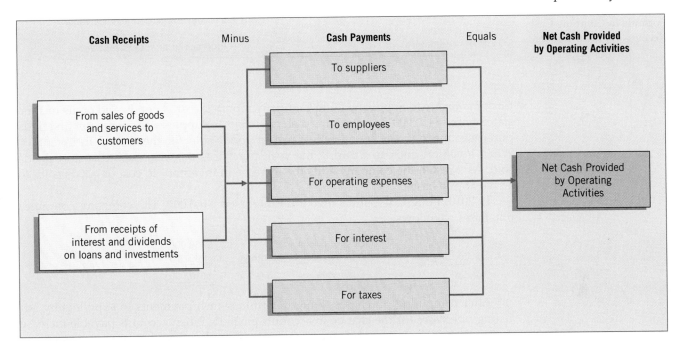

An efficient way to apply the direct method is to analyze the revenues and expenses reported in the income statement in the order in which they are listed. The company then determines cash receipts and cash payments related to these revenues and expenses. In the following sections, we present the direct method adjustments for Emig Company in 2010, to determine net cash provided by operating activities.

Cash Receipts from Customers. The income statement for Emig Company reported revenues from customers of $780,000. To determine cash receipts from customers, the company considers the change in accounts receivable during the year.

When accounts receivable increase during the year, revenues on an accrual basis are higher than cash receipts from customers. In other words, operations led to increased revenues, but not all of these revenues resulted in cash receipts. To determine the amount of increase in cash receipts, deduct the amount of the increase in accounts receivable from the total sales revenues. Conversely, a decrease in accounts receivable is added to sales revenues, because cash receipts from customers then exceed sales revenues.

For Emig Company, accounts receivable increased $15,000. Thus, cash receipts from customers were $765,000, computed as follows.

Revenues from sales	$780,000
Deduct: Increase in accounts receivable	15,000
Cash receipts from customers	$765,000

Emig could also determine cash receipts from customers by analyzing the Accounts Receivable account as shown below.

Accounts Receivable

1/1/10	Balance	–0–	Receipts from customers	765,000
	Revenue from sales	780,000		
12/31/10	Balance	15,000		

Illustration 23-22 shows the relationships between cash receipts from customers, revenues from sales, and changes in accounts receivable.

ILLUSTRATION 23-22
Formula to Compute Cash
Receipts from Customers

Cash receipts from customers	=	Revenues from sales	{ + **Decrease in accounts receivable** **or** − **Increase in accounts receivable**

Cash Payments to Suppliers. Emig Company reported cost of goods sold on its income statement of $450,000. To determine cash payments to suppliers, the company first finds purchases for the year, by adjusting cost of goods sold for the change in inventory. When inventory increases during the year, purchases this year exceed cost of goods sold. As a result, the company adds the increase in inventory to cost of goods sold, to arrive at purchases.

In 2010, Emig Company's inventory increased $160,000. The company computes purchases as follows.

Cost of goods sold	$450,000
Add: Increase in inventory	160,000
Purchases	$610,000

After computing purchases, Emig determines cash payments to suppliers by adjusting purchases for the change in accounts payable. When accounts payable increase during the year, purchases on an accrual basis are higher than they are on a cash basis. As a result, it deducts from purchases the increase in accounts payable to arrive at cash payments to suppliers. Conversely, if cash payments to suppliers exceed purchases, Emig adds to purchases the decrease in accounts payable. Cash payments to suppliers were $550,000, computed as follows.

Purchases	$610,000
Deduct: Increase in accounts payable	60,000
Cash payments to suppliers	$550,000

Emig also can determine cash payments to suppliers by analyzing Accounts Payable, as shown below.

Accounts Payable				
Payments to suppliers	550,000	1/1/10	Balance	–0–
			Purchases	610,000
		12/31/10	Balance	60,000

Illustration 23-23 shows the relationships between cash payments to suppliers, cost of goods sold, changes in inventory, and changes in accounts payable.

ILLUSTRATION 23-23
Formula to Compute Cash
Payments to Suppliers

Cash Payments for Operating Expenses. Emig reported operating expenses of $160,000 on its income statement. To determine the cash paid for operating expenses, it must adjust this amount for any changes in prepaid expenses and accrued expenses payable.

For example, when prepaid expenses increased $8,000 during the year, cash paid for operating expenses was $8,000 higher than operating expenses reported on the income statement. To convert operating expenses to cash payments for operating expenses, the company adds to operating expenses the increase of $8,000. Conversely, if prepaid expenses decrease during the year, it deducts from operating expenses the amount of the decrease.

Emig also must adjust operating expenses for changes in accrued expenses payable. When accrued expenses payable increase during the year, operating expenses on an accrual basis are higher than they are on a cash basis. As a result, the company deducts from operating expenses an increase in accrued expenses payable, to arrive at cash payments for operating expenses. Conversely, it adds to operating expenses a decrease in accrued expenses payable, because cash payments exceed operating expenses.

Emig Company's cash payments for operating expenses were $148,000, computed as follows.

Operating expenses	$160,000
Add: Increase in prepaid expenses	8,000
Deduct: Increase in accrued expenses payable	(20,000)
Cash payments for operating expenses	$148,000

The relationships among cash payments for operating expenses, changes in prepaid expenses, and changes in accrued expenses payable are shown in Illustration 23-24.

Cash payments for operating expenses	=	Operating expenses	+ Increase in prepaid expense or − Decrease in prepaid expense	+ Decrease in accrued expenses payable or − Increase in accrued expenses payable

ILLUSTRATION 23-24
Formula to Compute Cash Payments for Operating Expenses

Note that the company did not consider depreciation expense, because it is a non-cash charge.

Cash Payments for Income Taxes. The income statement for Emig shows income tax expense of $48,000. This amount equals the cash paid. How do we know that? Because the comparative balance sheet indicated no income taxes payable at either the beginning or end of the year.

Summary of Net Cash Flow from Operating Activities—Direct Method
The following schedule summarizes the computations illustrated above.

ILLUSTRATION 23-25
Accrual Basis to Cash Basis

Accrual Basis			Adjustment	Add (Subtract)	Cash Basis
Revenues from sales	$780,000	−	Increase in accounts receivable	$(15,000)	$765,000
Cost of goods sold	450,000	+	Increase in inventory	160,000	
		−	Increase in accounts payable	(60,000)	550,000
Operating expenses	160,000	+	Increase in prepaid expenses	8,000	
		−	Increase in accrued expenses payable	(20,000)	148,000
Depreciation expense	10,000	−	Depreciation expense	(10,000)	–0–
Income tax expense	48,000				48,000
Total expense	668,000				746,000
Net income	$112,000		Net cash provided by operating activities		$ 19,000

Illustration 23-26 shows the presentation of the direct method for reporting net cash flow from operating activities for the Emig Company illustration.

ILLUSTRATION 23-26
Operating Activities
Section—Direct Method,
2010

EMIG COMPANY		
STATEMENT OF CASH FLOWS (PARTIAL)		
Cash flows from operating activities		
Cash received from customers		$765,000
Cash payments:		
To suppliers	$550,000	
For operating expenses	148,000	
For income taxes	48,000	746,000
Net cash provided by operating activities		$ 19,000

If Emig Company uses the direct method to present the net cash flows from operating activities, it must provide in a separate schedule the reconciliation of net income to net cash provided by operating activities. The reconciliation assumes the identical form and content of the indirect method of presentation, as shown below.

ILLUSTRATION 23-27
Reconciliation of Net
Income to Net Cash
Provided by Operating
Activities

EMIG COMPANY		
RECONCILIATION		
Net income		$112,000
Adjustments to reconcile net income to net cash		
provided by operating activities:		
Depreciation expense	$ 10,000	
Increase in accounts receivable	(15,000)	
Increase in inventory	(160,000)	
Increase in prepaid expenses	(8,000)	
Increase in accounts payable	60,000	
Increase in accrued expense payable	20,000	(93,000)
Net cash provided by operating activities		$ 19,000

When the direct method is used, the company may present this reconciliation at the bottom of the statement of cash flows or in a separate schedule.

Direct versus Indirect Controversy

The most contentious decision that the FASB faced related to cash flow reporting was choosing between the direct method and the indirect method of determining net cash flow from operating activities. Companies lobbied *against* the direct method, urging adoption of the indirect method. Commercial lending officers expressed to the FASB a strong preference in favor of the direct method. In the next two sections, we consider the arguments in favor of each of the methods.

In Favor of the Direct Method

The principal advantage of the direct method is that **it shows operating cash receipts and payments**. Thus, it is more consistent with the objective of a statement of cash flows—to provide information about cash receipts and cash payments—than the indirect method, which does not report operating cash receipts and payments.

Supporters of the direct method contend that knowledge of the specific sources of operating cash receipts and the purposes for which operating cash payments were made in past periods is useful in estimating future operating cash flows. Furthermore, information about amounts of major classes of operating cash receipts and payments is more useful than information only about their arithmetic sum (the net cash flow from operating activities). Such information is more revealing of a company's ability (1) to generate sufficient cash from operating activities to pay its debts, (2) to reinvest in its operations, and (3) to make distributions to its owners. [4]

Many companies indicate that they do not currently collect information in a manner that allows them to determine amounts such as cash received from customers or cash paid to suppliers directly from their accounting systems. But supporters of the direct method contend that the incremental cost of determining operating cash receipts and payments is not significant.

In Favor of the Indirect Method

The principal advantage of the indirect method is that **it focuses on the differences between net income and net cash flow from operating activities**. That is, it provides a useful link between the statement of cash flows and the income statement and balance sheet.

Many companies contend that it is less costly to adjust net income to net cash flow from operating activities (indirect) than it is to report gross operating cash receipts and payments (direct). Supporters of the indirect method also state that the direct method, which effectively reports income statement information on a cash rather than an accrual basis, may erroneously suggest that net cash flow from operating activities is as good as, or better than, net income as a measure of performance.

Special Rules Applying to Direct and Indirect Methods

Companies that use the direct method are required, at a minimum, to report separately the following classes of operating cash receipts and payments:

Receipts

1. Cash collected from customers (including lessees, licensees, etc.).
2. Interest and dividends received.
3. Other operating cash receipts, if any.

Payments

1. Cash paid to employees and suppliers of goods or services (including suppliers of insurance, advertising, etc.).
2. Interest paid.
3. Income taxes paid.
4. Other operating cash payments, if any.

> **INTERNATIONAL INSIGHT**
>
> Consolidated statements of cash flows may be of limited use to analysts evaluating multinational companies. Without disaggregation, users of such statements are not able to determine "where in the world" the funds are sourced and used.

The FASB encourages companies to provide further breakdowns of operating cash receipts and payments that they consider meaningful.

Companies using the indirect method must disclose separately changes in inventory, receivables, and payables in order to reconcile net income to net cash flow from operating activities. In addition, they must disclose, elsewhere in the financial statements or in accompanying notes, interest paid (net of amount capitalized) and income taxes paid.[6] The FASB requires these separate and additional disclosures so that users may approximate the direct method. Also, an acceptable alternative presentation of the indirect method is to report net cash flow from operating activities as a single line item in the statement of cash flows and to present the reconciliation details elsewhere in the financial statements.

---

[6]*Accounting Trends and Techniques—2007* reports that of the 600 companies surveyed, 298 disclosed interest paid in notes to the financial statements, 282 disclosed interest paid at the bottom of the statement of cash flows, 6 disclosed interest paid within the statement of cash flows, and 14 reported no separate amount. Income taxes paid during the year were disclosed in a manner similar to interest payments.

NOT WHAT IT SEEMS

The controversy over direct and indirect methods highlights the importance that the market attributes to operating cash flow. By showing an improving cash flow, a company can give a favorable impression of its ongoing operations. For example, WorldCom concealed declines in its operations by capitalizing certain operating expenses—to the tune of $3.8 billion! This practice not only "juiced up" income but also made it possible to report the cash payments in the investing section of the cash flow statement rather than as a deduction from operating cash flow.

The SEC recently addressed a similar cash flow classification issue with automakers like Ford, GM, and Chrysler. For years, automakers classified lease receivables and other dealer-financing arrangements as investment cash flows. Thus, they reported an increase in lease or loan receivables from cars sold as a use of cash in the investing section of the statement of cash flows. The SEC objected and now requires automakers to report these receivables as operating cash flows, since the leases and loans are used to facilitate car sales. At GM, these reclassifications reduced its operating cash flows from $7.6 billion to $3 billion in the year before the change. So while the overall cash flow—from operations, investing, and financing—remained the same, operating cash flow at these companies looked better than it really was.

Source: Peter Elstrom, "How to Hide $3.8 Billion in Expenses," *BusinessWeek Online* (July 8, 2002); and Judith Burns, "SEC Tells US Automakers to Retool Cash-Flow Accounting," *Wall Street Journal Online* (February 28, 2005).

SECTION 2 • SPECIAL PROBLEMS IN STATEMENT PREPARATION

Objective•8

Discuss special problems in preparing a statement of cash flows.

We discussed some of the special problems related to preparing the statement of cash flows in connection with the preceding illustrations. Other problems that arise with some frequency in the preparation of this statement include the following.

1. Adjustments similar to depreciation.
2. Accounts receivable (net).
3. Other working capital changes.
4. Net losses.
5. Gains.
6. Stock options.
7. Postretirement benefit cost.
8. Extraordinary items.
9. Significant noncash transactions.

ADJUSTMENTS SIMILAR TO DEPRECIATION

Depreciation expense is the most common adjustment to net income that companies make to arrive at net cash flow from operating activities. But there are numerous other noncash expense or revenue items. Examples of expense items that companies must add back to net income are the **amortization of limited-life intangible assets** such as patents, and the **amortization of deferred costs** such as bond issue costs. These charges to expense involve expenditures made in prior periods that a company amortizes currently. These charges reduce net income without affecting cash in the current period.

Also, **amortization of bond discount or premium** on long-term bonds payable affects the amount of interest expense. However, neither changes cash. As a result, a company should add back discount amortization and subtract premium amortization from net income to arrive at net cash flow from operating activities.

In a similar manner, **changes in deferred income taxes** affect net income but have no effect on cash. For example, Delta Airlines reported an increase in its liability for deferred taxes of approximately $1.2 billion. This change in the liability increased tax expense and decreased net income, but did not affect cash. Therefore, Delta added back $1.2 billion to net income on its statement of cash flows.

Another common adjustment to net income is **a change related to an investment in common stock** when recording income or loss under the equity method. Recall that under the equity method, the investor (1) debits the investment account and credits revenue for its share of the investee's net income, and (2) credits dividends received to the investment account. Therefore, the net increase in the investment account does not affect cash flow. A company must deduct the net increase from net income to arrive at net cash flow from operating activities.

Assume that Victor Co. owns 40 percent of Milo Inc. During the year Milo reports net income of $100,000 and pays a cash dividend of $30,000. Victor reports this in its statement of cash flows as a deduction from net income in the following manner— Equity in earnings of Milo, net of dividends, $28,000 [($100,000 − $30,000) × 40%].

If Victor Co. does not exercise significant influence over Milo, it cannot use the equity method. Instead, it uses the fair value method. Under the fair value method, Victor does not recognize any of Milo's net income. Further, it records any cash dividend received as revenue. As a result, the company makes no adjustment to net income in the statement of cash flows because cash dividends received are included in income.

ACCOUNTS RECEIVABLE (NET)

Up to this point, we assumed no allowance for doubtful accounts—a contra account— to offset accounts receivable. However, if a company needs an allowance for doubtful accounts, how does that allowance affect the company's determination of net cash flow from operating activities? For example, assume that Redmark Co. reports net income of $40,000. It has the accounts receivable balances as shown in Illustration 23-28.

	2010	2009	Change Increase/Decrease
Accounts receivable	$105,000	$90,000	$15,000 Increase
Allowance for doubtful accounts	(10,000)	(4,000)	6,000 Increase
Accounts receivable (net)	$ 95,000	$86,000	9,000 Increase

ILLUSTRATION 23-28
Accounts Receivable
Balances, Redmark Co.

Indirect Method

Because an increase in the Allowance for Doubtful Accounts results from a charge to bad debt expense, a company should add back an increase in the Allowance for Doubtful Accounts to net income to arrive at net cash flow from operating activities. Illustration 23-29 shows one method for presenting this information in a statement of cash flows.

REDMARK CO.
STATEMENT OF CASH FLOWS (PARTIAL)
FOR THE YEAR 2010

Cash flows from operating activities		
Net income		$40,000
Adjustments to reconcile net income to net cash provided by operating activities:		
Increase in accounts receivable	$(15,000)	
Increase in allowance for doubtful accounts	6,000	(9,000)
		$31,000

ILLUSTRATION 23-29
Presentation of Allowance
for Doubtful Accounts—
Indirect Method

As we indicated, the increase in the Allowance for Doubtful Accounts balance results from a charge to bad debt expense for the year. Because bad debt expense is a noncash charge, a company must add it back to net income in arriving at net cash flow from operating activities.

Instead of separately analyzing the allowance account, a short-cut approach is to net the allowance balance against the receivable balance and compare the change in accounts receivable on a net basis. Illustration 23-30 shows this presentation.

ILLUSTRATION 23-30
Net Approach to
Allowance for Doubtful
Accounts—Indirect
Method

REDMARK CO. STATEMENT OF CASH FLOWS (PARTIAL) FOR THE YEAR 2010	
Cash flows from operating activities	
Net income	$40,000
Adjustments to reconcile net income to	
net cash provided by operating activities:	
Increase in accounts receivable (net)	(9,000)
	$31,000

This short-cut procedure works also if the change in the allowance account results from a write-off of accounts receivable. This reduces both the Accounts Receivable and the Allowance for Doubtful Accounts. No effect on cash flows occurs. Because of its simplicity, *use the net approach for your homework assignments.*

Direct Method

If using the direct method, a company **should not net** the Allowance for Doubtful Accounts against Accounts Receivable. To illustrate, assume that Redmark Co.'s net income of $40,000 consisted of the following items.

ILLUSTRATION 23-31
Income Statement,
Redmark Co.

REDMARK CO. INCOME STATEMENT FOR THE YEAR 2010		
Sales		$100,000
Expenses		
Salaries	$46,000	
Utilities	8,000	
Bad debts	6,000	60,000
Net income		$ 40,000

If Redmark deducts the $9,000 increase in accounts receivable (net) from sales for the year, it would report cash sales at $91,000 ($100,000 − $9,000) and cash payments for operating expenses at $60,000. Both items would be misstated: Cash sales should be reported at $85,000 ($100,000 − $15,000), and total cash payments for operating expenses should be reported at $54,000 ($60,000 − $6,000). Illustration 23-32 shows the proper presentation.

ILLUSTRATION 23-32
Bad Debts—Direct
Method

REDMARK CO. STATEMENT OF CASH FLOWS (PARTIAL) FOR THE YEAR 2010		
Cash flows from operating activities		
Cash received from customers		$85,000
Salaries paid	$46,000	
Utilities paid	8,000	54,000
Net cash provided by operating activities		$31,000

An added complication develops when a company writes off accounts receivable. Simply adjusting sales for the change in accounts receivable will not provide the proper amount of cash sales. The reason is that the write-off of the accounts receivable is not a cash collection. Thus an additional adjustment is necessary.

OTHER WORKING CAPITAL CHANGES

Up to this point, we showed how companies handled all of the changes in working capital items (current asset and current liability items) as adjustments to net income in determining net cash flow from operating activities. You must be careful, however, because **some changes in working capital, although they affect cash, do not affect net income**. Generally, these are investing or financing activities of a current nature.

One activity is the purchase of **short-term available-for-sale securities**. For example, the purchase of short-term available-for-sale securities for $50,000 cash has no effect on net income but it does cause a $50,000 decrease in cash.[7] A company reports this transaction as a cash flow from investing activities as follows. [5]

Cash flows from investing activities	
Purchase of short-term available-for-sale securities	$(50,000)

What about **trading securities**? Because companies hold these investments principally for the purpose of selling them in the near term, companies should classify the cash flows from purchases and sales of trading securities as cash flows from **operating activities**. [6]

Another example is the issuance of a **short-term nontrade note payable** for cash. This change in a working capital item has no effect on income from operations but it increases cash by the amount of the note payable. For example, a company reports the issuance of a $10,000 short-term note payable for cash in the statement of cash flows as follows.

Cash flows from financing activities	
Issuance of short-term note	$10,000

Another change in a working capital item that has no effect on income from operations or on cash is a **cash dividend payable**. Although a company will report the cash dividends when paid as a financing activity, it does not report the declared but unpaid dividend on the statement of cash flows.

NET LOSSES

If a company reports a net loss instead of a net income, it must adjust the net loss for those items that do not result in a cash inflow or outflow. The net loss, after adjusting for the charges or credits not affecting cash, may result in a negative or a positive cash flow from operating activities.

For example, if the net loss is $50,000 and the total amount of charges to add back is $60,000, then net cash provided by operating activities is $10,000. Illustration 23-33 (on page 1270) shows this computation.

---

[7]If the basis of the statement of cash flows is **cash and cash equivalents** and the short-term investment is considered a cash equivalent, then a company reports nothing in the statement because the transaction does not affect the balance of cash and cash equivalents. The Board notes that cash purchases of short term investments generally are part of the company's cash management activities rather than part of its operating, investing, or financing activities.

ILLUSTRATION 23-33
Computation of Net Cash
Flow from Operating
Activities—Cash Inflow

Net loss		$(50,000)
Adjustments to reconcile net income to net		
cash provided by operating activities:		
Depreciation of plant assets	$55,000	
Amortization of patents	5,000	60,000
Net cash provided by operating activities		$ 10,000

If the company experiences a net loss of $80,000 and the total amount of the charges to add back is $25,000, the presentation appears as follows.

ILLUSTRATION 23-34
Computation of Net Cash
Flow from Operating
Activities—Cash Outflow

Net loss	$(80,000)
Adjustments to reconcile net income to	
net cash used by operating activities:	
Depreciation of plant assets	25,000
Net cash used by operating activities	$(55,000)

Although not illustrated in this chapter, a negative cash flow may result even if the company reports a net income.

GAINS

In the illustration for Tax Consultants, the company experienced a loss of $2,000 from the sale of equipment. The company added this loss to net income to compute net cash flow from operating activities because **the loss is a noncash charge in the income statement**.

If Tax Consultants experiences a **gain** from a sale of equipment it too requires an adjustment to net income. Because a company reports the gain in the statement of cash flows as part of the cash proceeds from the sale of equipment under investing activities, **it deducts the gain from net income to avoid double counting**—once as part of net income, and again as part of the cash proceeds from the sale.

STOCK OPTIONS

Recall for share-based compensation plans that companies are required to use the fair value method to determine total compensation cost. The compensation cost is then recognized as an expense in the periods in which the employee provides services. When Compensation Expense is debited, Paid-in Capital—Stock Options is often credited. Cash is not affected by recording the expense. **Therefore, the company must increase net income by the amount of compensation expense from stock options in computing net cash flow from operating activities.**

To illustrate how this information should be reported on a statement of cash flows, assume that First Wave Inc. grants 5,000 options to its CEO, Ann Johnson. Each option entitles Johnson to purchase one share of First Wave's $1 par value common stock at $50 per share at any time in the next two years (the service period). The fair value of the options is $200,000. First Wave records compensation expense in the first year as follows:

Compensation Expense ($200,000 ÷ 2)	100,000	
Paid-in Capital—Stock Options		100,000

In addition, if we assume that First Wave has a 35 percent tax rate, it would recognize a deferred tax asset of $35,000 ($100,000 × 35%) in the first year as follows:

Deferred Tax Asset	35,000	
Income Tax Expense		35,000

Therefore, on the statement of cash flows for the first year, First Wave reports the following (assuming a net income of $600,000).

Net income	$600,000
Adjustments to reconcile net income to net cash provided by operating activities:	
Share-based compensation expense	100,000
Increase in deferred tax asset	(35,000)

As shown in First Wave's statement of cash flows, it adds the share-based compensation expense to net income because it is a noncash expense. The increase in the deferred tax asset and the related reduction in income tax expense increase net income. Although the negative income tax expense increases net income, it does not increase cash. Therefore it should be deducted.

Subsequently, if Ann Johnson exercises her options, Third Wave reports "Cash provided by exercise of stock options" in the financing section of the statement of cash flows.[8]

POSTRETIREMENT BENEFIT COSTS

If a company has postretirement costs such as an employee pension plan, chances are that the pension expense recorded during a period will either be higher or lower than the cash funded. It will be higher when there is an unfunded liability and will be lower when there is a prepaid pension cost. When the expense is higher or lower than the cash paid, **the company must adjust net income by the difference between cash paid and the expense reported** in computing net cash flow from operating activities.

EXTRAORDINARY ITEMS

Companies should report **either as investing activities or as financing activities** cash flows from extraordinary transactions and other events whose effects are included in net income, but which are not related to operations.

For example, assume that Tax Consultants had land with a carrying value of $200,000, which was condemned by the state of Maine for a highway project. The condemnation proceeds received were $205,000, resulting in a gain of $5,000 less $2,000 of taxes. In the statement of cash flows (indirect method), the company would deduct the $5,000 gain from net income in the operating activities section. It would report the $205,000 cash inflow from the condemnation as an investing activity, as follows.

Cash flows from investing activities	
Condemnation of land	$205,000

Underlying Concepts

By rejecting the requirement to allocate taxes to the various activities, the Board invoked the cost-benefit constraint. The information would be beneficial, but the cost of providing such information would exceed the benefits of providing it.

Note that Tax Consultants handles the gain at its **gross** amount ($5,000), not net of tax. The company reports the cash received in the condemnation as an investing activity at $205,000, also exclusive of the tax effect.

The FASB requires companies to classify **all income taxes paid as operating cash outflows**. Some suggested that income taxes paid be allocated to investing and financing transactions. But the Board decided that allocation of income taxes paid to operating, investing, and financing activities would be so complex and

---

[8]Companies receive a tax deduction related to share-based compensation plans at the time employees exercise their options. The amount of the deduction is equal to the difference between the market price of the stock and the exercise price at the date the employee purchases the stock, which in most cases, is much larger than the total compensation expense recorded. When the tax deduction exceeds the total compensation recorded, this provides an additional cash inflow to the company. For example, in a recent year Cisco Systems reported an additional cash inflow related to its stock option plans equal to $537 million. Under GAAP, this tax-related cash inflow is reported in the financing section of the statement of cash flows. [7]

arbitrary that the benefits, if any, would not justify the costs involved. Under both the direct method and the indirect method, companies must disclose the total amount of income taxes paid.[9]

SIGNIFICANT NONCASH TRANSACTIONS

Because the statement of cash flows reports only the effects of operating, investing, and financing activities in terms of cash flows, it omits some **significant noncash transactions** and other events that are investing or financing activities. Among the more common of these noncash transactions that a company should report or disclose in some manner are the following.

Examples of Cash Flow Statements

1. Acquisition of assets by assuming liabilities (including capital lease obligations) or by issuing equity securities.
2. Exchanges of nonmonetary assets.
3. Refinancing of long-term debt.
4. Conversion of debt or preferred stock to common stock.
5. Issuance of equity securities to retire debt.

A company does not incorporate these noncash items in the statement of cash flows. If material in amount, these disclosures may be either narrative or summarized in a separate schedule at the bottom of the statement, or they may appear in a separate note or supplementary schedule to the financial statements.[10] Illustration 23-35 shows the presentation of these significant noncash transactions or other events in a separate schedule at the bottom of the statement of cash flows.

ILLUSTRATION 23-35
Schedule Presentation of Noncash Investing and Financing Activities

Net increase in cash	$3,717,000
Cash at beginning of year	5,208,000
Cash at end of year	$8,925,000
Noncash investing and financing activities	
Purchase of land and building through issuance of 250,000 shares of common stock	$1,750,000
Exchange of Steadfast, NY, land for Bedford, PA, land	$2,000,000
Conversion of 12% bonds to 50,000 shares of common stock	$500,000

Or, companies may present these noncash transactions in a separate note, as shown in Illustration 23-36.

ILLUSTRATION 23-36
Note Presentation of Noncash Investing and Financing Activities

Note G: Significant noncash transactions. During the year the company engaged in the following significant noncash investing and financing transactions:	
Issued 250,000 shares of common stock to purchase land and building	$1,750,000
Exchanged land in Steadfast, NY, for land in Bedford, PA	$2,000,000
Converted 12% bonds to 50,000 shares of common stock	$500,000

[9]For an insightful article on some weaknesses and limitations in the statement of cash flows, see Hugo Nurnberg, "Inconsistencies and Ambiguities in Cash Flow Statements Under *FASB Statement No. 95*," *Accounting Horizons* (June 1993), pp. 60–73. Nurnberg identifies the inconsistencies caused by the three-way classification of all cash receipts and cash payments, gross versus net of tax, the ambiguous disclosure requirements for noncash investing and financing transactions, and the ambiguous presentation of third-party financing transactions. See also Paul B. W. Miller, and Bruce P. Budge, "Nonarticulation in Cash Flow Statements and Implications for Education, Research, and Practice," *Accounting Horizons* (December 1996), pp. 1–15; and Charles Mulford and Michael Ely, "Calculating Sustainable Cash Flow: A Study of the S&P 100," *Georgia Tech Financial Analysis Lab* (October 2004).

[10]Some noncash investing and financing activities are part cash and part noncash. Companies should report only the cash portion on the statement of cash flows. The noncash component should be reported at the bottom of the statement or in a separate note.

Companies do not generally report certain other significant noncash transactions or other events in conjunction with the statement of cash flows. Examples of these types of transactions are **stock dividends**, **stock splits**, **and restrictions on retained earnings**. Companies generally report these items, neither financing nor investing activities, in conjunction with the statement of stockholders' equity or schedules and notes pertaining to changes in capital accounts.

CASH FLOW TOOL

By understanding the relationship between cash flow and income measures, analysts can gain better insights into company performance. Because earnings altered through creative accounting practices generally do not change operating cash flows, analysts can use the relationship between earnings and operating cash flow to detect suspicious accounting practices. Also, by monitoring the ratio between cash flow from operations and operating income, they can get a clearer picture of developing problems in a company.

For example, the chart below plots the ratio of operating cash flows to earnings for Xerox Corp. in the years leading up to the SEC singling it out in 2000 for aggressive revenue recognition practices on its leases.

What do the numbers mean?

Ratio of Cash Flow to Operating Income

Similar to W. T. Grant in the chapter opening story, Xerox was reporting earnings growth in the years leading up to its financial breakdown in 2000 but teetering near bankruptcy in 2001. However, Xerox's ratio of cash flow to earnings showed a declining trend and became negative well before its revenue recognition practices were revealed. The trend revealed in the graph should have given any analyst reason to investigate Xerox further. As one analyst noted, "Earnings growth that exceeds the growth in operating cash flow cannot continue for extended periods and should be investigated."

Source: Adapted from Charles Mulford and Eugene Comiskey, *The Financial Numbers Game: Detecting Creative Accounting Practices* (New York: John Wiley & Sons, 2002), Chapter 11, by permission.

SECTION 3 • USE OF A WORKSHEET

When numerous adjustments are necessary or other complicating factors are present, companies often use **a worksheet to assemble and classify the data that will appear on the statement of cash flows**. The worksheet (a **spreadsheet** when using computer software) is merely a device that aids in the preparation of the

Objective•9
Explain the use of a worksheet in preparing a statement of cash flows.

statement. Its use is optional. Illustration 23-37 shows the skeleton format of the worksheet for preparation of the statement of cash flows using the indirect method.

XYZ COMPANY
Statement of Cash Flows For the Year Ended...

	A	B	C	D	E
		End of Prior Year Balances	Reconciling Items		End of Current Year Balances
			Debits	Credits	
1	Balance Sheet Accounts				
2	Debit balance accounts	XX	XX	XX	XX
3		XX	XX	XX	XX
4	Totals	XXX			XXX
5	Credit balance accounts	XX	XX	XX	XX
6		XX	XX	XX	XX
7	Totals	XXX			XXX
8	Statement of Cash Flows Effects				
9	Operating activities				
10	Net income		XX		
11	Adjustments		XX	XX	
12	Investing activities				
13	Receipts and payments		XX	XX	
14	Financing activities				
15	Receipts and payments		XX	XX	
16	Totals		XXX	XXX	
17	Increase (decrease) in cash		(XX)	XX	
18	Totals		XXX	XXX	

Sheet1 / Sheet2 / Sheet3

ILLUSTRATION 23-37
Format of Worksheet for
Preparation of Statement
of Cash Flows

The following guidelines are important in using a worksheet.

1. In the balance sheet accounts section, **list accounts with debit balances separately from those with credit balances**. This means, for example, that Accumulated Depreciation is listed under credit balances and not as a contra account under debit balances. Enter the beginning and ending balances of each account in the appropriate columns. Then, enter the transactions that caused the change in the account balance during the year as reconciling items in the two middle columns.

   After all reconciling items have been entered, each line pertaining to a balance sheet account should foot across. That is, the beginning balance plus or minus the reconciling item(s) must equal the ending balance. When this agreement exists for all balance sheet accounts, all changes in account balances have been reconciled.

2. The bottom portion of the worksheet consists of the operating, investing, and financing activities sections. Accordingly, it provides the information necessary to prepare the formal statement of cash flows. **Enter inflows of cash as debits in the reconciling columns, and outflows of cash as credits in the reconciling columns.** Thus, in this section, a company would enter the sale of equipment for cash at book value as a debit under inflows of cash from investing activities. Similarly, it would enter the purchase of land for cash as a credit under outflows of cash from investing activities.

3. **Do not enter in any journal or post to any account the reconciling items shown in the worksheet.** These items do not represent either adjustments or corrections of the balance sheet accounts. They are used only to facilitate the preparation of the statement of cash flows.

PREPARATION OF THE WORKSHEET

The preparation of a worksheet involves the following steps.

Step 1. Enter the balance sheet accounts and their beginning and ending balances in the balance sheet accounts section.

Step 2. Enter the data that explain the changes in the balance sheet accounts (other than cash) and their effects on the statement of cash flows in the reconciling columns of the worksheet.

Step 3. Enter the increase or decrease in cash on the cash line and at the bottom of the worksheet. This entry should enable the totals of the reconciling columns to be in agreement.

To illustrate the preparation and use of a worksheet and to illustrate the reporting of some of the special problems discussed in the prior section, we present a comprehensive example for Satellite Corporation. Again, the indirect method serves as the basis for the computation of net cash provided by operating activities. Illustrations 23-38 and 23-39 (on page 1276) present the balance sheet, combined statement of income and retained

ILLUSTRATION 23-38
Comparative Balance Sheet, Satellite Corporation

SATELLITE CORPORATION
Comparative Balance Sheet–December 31, 2010 and 2009

	A	B 2010	C 2009	D Increase or (Decrease)
2	Assets			
3	Cash	$ 59,000	$ 66,000	$ (7,000)
4	Accounts receivable (net)	104,000	51,000	53,000
5	Inventories	493,000	341,000	152,000
6	Prepaid expenses	16,500	17,000	(500)
7	Investments in stock of Porter Co. (equity method)	18,500	15,000	3,500
8	Land	131,500	82,000	49,500
9	Equipment	187,000	142,000	45,000
10	Accumulated depreciation—equipment	(29,000)	(31,000)	(2,000)
11	Buildings	262,000	262,000	—
12	Accumulated depreciation—buildings	(74,100)	(71,000)	3,100
13	Trademark	7,600	10,000	(2,400)
14	Total assets	$1,176,000	$884,000	
15	Liabilities			
16	Accounts payable	$ 132,000	$ 131,000	1,000
17	Accrued liabilities	43,000	39,000	4,000
18	Income tax payable	3,000	16,000	(13,000)
19	Notes payable (long-term)	60,000	—	60,000
20	Bonds payable	100,000	100,000	—
21	Premium on bonds payable	7,000	8,000	(1,000)
22	Deferred tax liability (long-term)	9,000	6,000	3,000
23	Total liabilities	354,000	300,000	
24	Stockholders' Equity			
25	Common stock ($1 par)	60,000	50,000	10,000
26	Additional paid-in capital	187,000	38,000	149,000
27	Retained earnings	592,000	496,000	96,000
28	Treasury stock	(17,000)	—	17,000
29	Total stockholders' equity	822,000	584,000	
30	Total liabilities and stockholders' equity	$1,176,000	$884,000	

Sheet1 / Sheet2 / Sheet3

ILLUSTRATION 23-39
Income and Retained
Earnings Statements,
Satellite Corporation

SATELLITE CORPORATION
COMBINED STATEMENT OF INCOME AND RETAINED EARNINGS
FOR THE YEAR ENDED DECEMBER 31, 2010

Net sales		$526,500
Other revenue		3,500
Total revenues		530,000
Expense		
Cost of goods sold		310,000
Selling and administrative expenses		47,000
Other expenses and losses		12,000
Total expenses		369,000
Income before income tax and extraordinary item		161,000
Income tax		
Current	$47,000	
Deferred	3,000	50,000
Income before extraordinary item		111,000
Gain on condemnation of land (net of $2,000 tax)		6,000
Net income		117,000
Retained earnings, January 1		496,000
Less:		
Cash dividends	6,000	
Stock dividend	15,000	21,000
Retained earnings, December 31		$592,000
Per share:		
Income before extraordinary item		$2.02
Extraordinary item		.11
Net income		$2.13

Additional Information

(a) Other income of $3,500 represents Satellite's equity share in the net income of Porter Co., an equity investee. Satellite owns 22% of Porter Co.

(b) An analysis of the equipment account and related accumulated depreciation indicates the following:

	Equipment Dr./(Cr.)	Accum. Dep. Dr./(Cr.)	Gain or (Loss)
Balance at end of 2009	$142,000	$(31,000)	
Purchases of equipment	53,000		
Sale of equipment	(8,000)	2,500	$(1,500)
Depreciation for the period		(11,500)	
Major repair charged to accumulated depreciation		11,000	
Balance at end of 2010	$187,000	$(29,000)	

(c) Land in the amount of $60,000 was purchased through the issuance of a long-term note; in addition, certain parcels of land costing $10,500 were condemned. The state government paid Satellite $18,500, resulting in an $8,000 gain which has a $2,000 tax effect.

(d) The change in the accumulated depreciation—buildings, trademark, and premium on bonds payable accounts resulted from depreciation and amortization entries.

(e) An analysis of the paid-in capital accounts in stockholders' equity discloses the following:

	Common Stock	Additional Paid-In Capital
Balance at end of 2009	$50,000	$ 38,000
Issuance of 2% stock dividend	1,000	14,000
Sale of stock for cash	9,000	135,000
Balance at end of 2010	$60,000	$187,000

(f) Interest paid (net of amount capitalized) is $9,000; income taxes paid is $62,000.

earnings, and additional information for Satellite Corporation. The discussion that follows these financial statements provides additional explanations related to the preparation of the worksheet.

ANALYSIS OF TRANSACTIONS

The following discussion explains the individual adjustments that appear on the worksheet in Illustration 23-40 (page 1281). Because cash is the basis for the analysis, Satellite reconciles the cash account last. Because income is the first item that appears on the statement of cash flows, it is handled first.

Change in Retained Earnings

Net income for the period is $117,000. The entry for it on the worksheet is as follows.

(1)

Operating—Net Income	117,000	
Retained Earnings		117,000

Satellite reports net income on the bottom section of the worksheet. This **is the starting point for preparation of the statement of cash flows (under the indirect method)**.

A stock dividend and a cash dividend also affected retained earnings. The retained earnings statement reports a stock dividend of $15,000. The worksheet entry for this transaction is as follows.

(2)

Retained Earnings	15,000	
Common Stock		1,000
Additional Paid-in Capital		14,000

The issuance of stock dividends is not a cash operating, investing, or financing item. Therefore, **although the company enters this transaction on the worksheet for reconciling purposes, it does not report it in the statement of cash flows**.

The $6,000 cash dividend paid represents a financing activity cash outflow. Satellite makes the following worksheet entry:

(3)

Retained Earnings	6,000	
Financing—Cash Dividends		6,000

The company reconciles the beginning and ending balances of retained earnings by entry of the three items above.

Accounts Receivable (Net)

The increase in accounts receivable (net) of $53,000 represents adjustments that did not result in cash inflows during 2010. As a result, the company would deduct from net income the increase of $53,000. Satellite makes the following worksheet entry.

(4)

Accounts Receivable (net)	53,000	
Operating—Increase in Accounts Receivable (net)		53,000

Inventories

The increase in inventories of $152,000 represents an operating use of cash. The incremental investment in inventories during the year reduces cash without increasing the cost of goods sold. Satellite makes the following worksheet entry.

(5)

Inventories	152,000	
Operating—Increase in Inventories		152,000

Prepaid Expense

The decrease in prepaid expenses of $500 represents a charge in the income statement for which there was no cash outflow in the current period. Satellite should add that amount back to net income through the following entry.

(6)

Operating—Decrease in Prepaid Expenses	500	
Prepaid Expenses		500

Investment in Stock

Satellite's investment in the stock of Porter Co. increased $3,500. This amount reflects Satellite's share of net income earned by Porter (its equity investee) during the current year. Although Satellite's revenue, and therefore its net income increased $3,500 by recording Satellite's share of Porter Co.'s net income, no cash (dividend) was provided. Satellite makes the following worksheet entry.

(7)

Investment in Stock of Porter Co.	3,500	
Operating—Equity in Earnings of Porter Co.		3,500

Land

Satellite purchased land in the amount of $60,000 through the issuance of a long-term note payable. This transaction did not affect cash. It is a significant noncash investing/financing transaction that the company would disclose either in a separate schedule below the statement of cash flows or in the accompanying notes. Satellite makes the following entry to reconcile the worksheet.

(8)

Land	60,000	
Notes Payable		60,000

In addition to the noncash transaction involving the issuance of a note to purchase land, the Land account was decreased by the condemnation proceedings. The following worksheet entry records the receipt of $18,500 for land having a book value of $10,500.

(9)

Investing—Proceeds from Condemnation of Land	18,500	
Land		10,500
Operating—Gain on Condemnation of Land		8,000

In reconciling net income to net cash flow from operating activities, Satellite deducts from net income the extraordinary gain of $8,000. The reason is that the transaction that gave rise to the gain is an item whose cash effect is already classified as an investing cash inflow. The Land account is now reconciled.

Equipment and Accumulated Depreciation

An analysis of Equipment and Accumulated Depreciation shows that a number of transactions have affected these accounts. The company purchased equipment in the amount of $53,000 during the year. Satellite records this transaction on the worksheet as follows.

(10)

Equipment	53,000	
Investing—Purchase of Equipment		53,000

In addition, Satellite sold at a loss of $1,500 equipment with a book value of $5,500. It records this transaction as follows.

(11)

Investing—Sale of Equipment	4,000	
Operating—Loss on Sale of Equipment	1,500	
Accumulated Depreciation—Equipment	2,500	
Equipment		8,000

The proceeds from the sale of the equipment provided cash of $4,000. In addition, the loss on the sale of the equipment has reduced net income, but did not affect cash. Therefore, the company adds back to net income the amount of the loss, in order to accurately report cash provided by operating activities.

Satellite reported depreciation on the equipment at $11,500 and recorded it on the worksheet as follows.

(12)

Operating—Depreciation Expense—Equipment	11,500	
Accumulated Depreciation—Equipment		11,500

The company adds depreciation expense back to net income because that expense reduced income but did not affect cash.

Finally, the company made a major repair to the equipment. It charged this expenditure, in the amount of $11,000, to Accumulated Depreciation—Equipment. This expenditure required cash, and so Satellite makes the following worksheet entry.

(13)

Accumulated Depreciation—Equipment	11,000	
Investing—Major Repairs of Equipment		11,000

After adjusting for the foregoing items, Satellite has reconciled the balances in the Equipment and related Accumulated Depreciation accounts.

Building Depreciation and Amortization of Trademark

Depreciation expense on the buildings of $3,100 and amortization of trademark of $2,400 are both expenses in the income statement that reduced net income but did not require cash outflows in the current period. Satellite makes the following worksheet entry.

(14)

Operating—Depreciation Expense—Buildings	3,100	
Operating—Amortization of Trademark	2,400	
Accumulated Depreciation—Buildings		3,100
Trademark		2,400

Other Noncash Charges or Credits

Analysis of the remaining accounts indicates that changes in the Accounts Payable, Accrued Liabilities, Income Tax Payable, Premium on Bonds Payable, and Deferred Tax Liability balances resulted from charges or credits to net income that did not affect cash. The company should individually analyze each of these items and enter them in the worksheet. The following compound entry summarizes these noncash, income-related items.

(15)

Income Tax Payable	13,000	
Premium on Bonds Payable	1,000	
Operating—Increase in Accounts Payable	1,000	
Operating—Increase in Accrued Liabilities	4,000	
Operating—Increase in Deferred Tax Liability	3,000	
Operating—Decrease in Income Tax Payable		13,000
Operating—Amortization of Bond Premium		1,000
Accounts Payable		1,000
Accrued Liabilities		4,000
Deferred Tax Liability		3,000

Common Stock and Related Accounts

Comparison of the common stock balances and the additional paid-in capital balances shows that transactions during the year affected these accounts. First, Satellite issues a stock dividend of 2 percent to stockholders. As the discussion of worksheet entry (2) indicated, no cash was provided or used by the stock dividend transaction. In addition to the shares issued via the stock dividend, Satellite sold shares of common stock at $16 per share. The company records this transaction as follows.

(16)

Financing—Sale of Common Stock	144,000	
Common Stock		9,000
Additional Paid-in Capital		135,000

Also, the company purchased shares of its common stock in the amount of $17,000. It records this transaction on the worksheet as follows.

(17)

Treasury Stock	17,000	
Financing—Purchase of Treasury Stock		17,000

Final Reconciling Entry

The final entry to reconcile the change in cash and to balance the worksheet is shown below. The $7,000 amount is the difference between the beginning and ending cash balance.

(18)

Decrease in Cash	7,000	
Cash		7,000

Once the company has determined that the differences between the beginning and ending balances per the worksheet columns have been accounted for, it can total the reconciling transactions columns, and they should balance. Satellite can prepare the statement of cash flows entirely from the items and amounts that appear at the bottom of the worksheet under "Statement of Cash Flows Effects," as shown in Illustration 23-40 (on page 1281).

SATELLITE CORPORATION
Worksheet for Preparation of Statement of Cash Flows For the Year Ended December 31, 2010

	A	B	Debits		Credits		G
		Balance 12/31/09	Reconciling Items–2010 Debits		Credits		Balance 12/31/10
2	Debits						
3	Cash	$ 66,000			(18)	7,000	$ 59,000
4	Accounts receivable (net)	51,000	(4)	$ 53,000			104,000
5	Inventories	341,000	(5)	152,000			493,000
6	Prepaid expenses	17,000			(6)	500	16,500
7	Investment (equity method)	15,000	(7)	3,500			18,500
8	Land	82,000	(8)	60,000	(9)	10,500	131,500
9	Equipment	142,000	(10)	53,000	(11)	8,000	187,000
10	Building	262,000					262,000
11	Trademark	10,000			(14)	2,400	7,600
12	Treasury stock		(17)	17,000			17,000
13	Total debits	$986,000					$1,296,100
14	Credits						
15	Accum. depr.–equipment	$ 31,000	(11)	2,500	(12)	11,500	
16			(13)	11,000			$ 29,000
17	Accum. depr.–building	71,000			(14)	3,100	74,100
18	Accounts payable	131,000			(15)	1,000	132,000
19	Accrued liabilities	39,000			(15)	4,000	43,000
20	Income tax payable	16,000	(15)	13,000			3,000
21	Notes payable	-0-			(8)	60,000	60,000
22	Bonds payable	100,000					100,000
23	Premium on bonds payable	8,000	(15)	1,000			7,000
24	Deferred tax liability	6,000			(15)	3,000	9,000
25	Common stock	50,000			(2)	1,000	
26					(16)	9,000	60,000
27	Additional paid-in capital	38,000			(2)	14,000	
28					(16)	135,000	187,000
29	Retained earnings	496,000	(2)	15,000	(1)	117,000	
30			(3)	6,000			592,000
31	Total credits	$986,000					$1,296,100
32	Statement of Cash Flows Effects						
33	Operating activities						
34	Net income		(1)	117,000			
35	Increase in accounts receivable (net)				(4)	53,000	
36	Increase in inventories				(5)	152,000	
37	Decrease in prepaid expenses		(6)	500			
38	Equity in earnings of Porter Co.				(7)	3,500	
39	Gain on condemnation of land				(9)	8,000	
40	Loss on sale of equipment		(11)	1,500			
41	Depr. expense–equipment		(12)	11,500			
42	Depr. expense–building		(14)	3,100			
43	Amortization of trademark		(14)	2,400			
44	Increase in accounts payable		(15)	1,000			
45	Increase in accrued liabilities		(15)	4,000			
46	Increase in deferred tax liability		(15)	3,000			
47	Decrease in income tax payable				(15)	13,000	
48	Amortization of bond premium				(15)	1,000	
49	Investing activities						
50	Proceeds from condemnation of land		(9)	18,500			
51	Purchase of equipment				(10)	53,000	
52	Sale of equipment		(11)	4,000			
53	Major repairs of equipment				(13)	11,000	
54	Financing activities						
55	Payment of cash dividend				(3)	6,000	
56	Issuance of common stock		(16)	144,000			
57	Purchase of treasury stock				(17)	17,000	
58	Totals			697,500		704,500	
59	Decrease in cash		(18)	7,000			
60	Totals			$704,500		$704,500	

ILLUSTRATION 23-40
Completed Worksheet for Preparation of Statement of Cash Flows, Satellite Corporation

PREPARATION OF FINAL STATEMENT

Illustration 23-41 presents a formal statement of cash flows prepared from the data compiled in the lower portion of the worksheet.

ILLUSTRATION 23-41
Statement of Cash Flows, Satellite Corporation

Discussion of the T-Account Approach to Preparation of the Statement of Cash Flows

SATELLITE CORPORATION		
STATEMENT OF CASH FLOWS		
FOR THE YEAR ENDED DECEMBER 31, 2010		
INCREASE (DECREASE) IN CASH		
Cash flows from operating activities		
Net income		$117,000
Adjustments to reconcile net income to net		
cash used by operating activities:		
Depreciation expense	$ 14,600	
Amortization of trademark	2,400	
Amortization of bond premium	(1,000)	
Equity in earnings of Porter Co.	(3,500)	
Gain on condemnation of land	(8,000)	
Loss on sale of equipment	1,500	
Increase in deferred tax liability	3,000	
Increase in accounts receivable (net)	(53,000)	
Increase in inventories	(152,000)	
Decrease in prepaid expenses	500	
Increase in accounts payable	1,000	
Increase in accrued liabilities	4,000	
Decrease in income tax payable	(13,000)	(203,500)
Net cash used by operating activities		(86,500)
Cash flows from investing activities		
Proceeds from condemnation of land	18,500	
Purchase of equipment	(53,000)	
Sale of equipment	4,000	
Major repairs of equipment	(11,000)	
Net cash used by investing activities		(41,500)
Cash flows from financing activities		
Payment of cash dividend	(6,000)	
Issuance of common stock	144,000	
Purchase of treasury stock	(17,000)	
Net cash provided by financing activities		121,000
Net decrease in cash		(7,000)
Cash, January 1, 2010		66,000
Cash, December 31, 2010		$ 59,000
Supplemental Disclosures of Cash Flow Information:		
Cash paid during the year for:		
Interest (net of amount capitalized)		$ 9,000
Income taxes		$ 62,000
Supplemental Schedule of Noncash Investing and Financing Activities:		
Purchase of land for $60,000 in exchange for a $60,000 long-term note.		

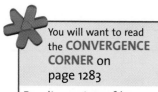

You will want to read the **CONVERGENCE CORNER** on page 1283

For discussion of how international convergence efforts relate to the statement of cash flows.

CONVERGENCE CORNER

STATEMENT OF CASH FLOWS

As in U.S. GAAP, the statement of cash flows is a required statement for iGAAP. In addition, the content and presentation of an iGAAP balance sheet is similar to one used for U.S. GAAP. However, the disclosure requirements related to the statement of cash flows are more extensive under U.S. GAAP. *IAS 7* ("Cash Flow Statements") provides the overall iGAAP requirements for cash flow information.

RELEVANT FACTS

* Companies preparing financial statements under iGAAP must prepare a statement of cash flows as an integral part of the financial statements.

* Both iGAAP and U.S. GAAP require that the statement of cash flows should have three major sections—operating, investing, and financing—along with changes in cash and cash equivalents.

* Similar to U.S. GAAP, the cash flow statement can be prepared using either the indirect or direct method under iGAAP. In both U.S. and international settings, companies choose for the most part to use the indirect method for reporting net cash flows from operating activities.

* iGAAP encourages companies to disclose the aggregate amount of cash flows that are attributable to the increase in operating capacity separately from those cash flows that are required to maintain operating capacity.

* The definition of cash equivalents used in iGAAP is similar to that used in U.S. GAAP. A major difference is that in certain situations bank overdrafts are considered part of cash and cash equivalents under iGAAP (which is not the case in U.S. GAAP). Under U.S. GAAP, bank overdrafts are classified as financing activities.

* iGAAP requires that noncash investing and financing activities be excluded from the statement of cash flows. Instead, these noncash activities should be reported elsewhere. This requirement is interpreted to mean that noncash investing and financing activities should be disclosed in the notes to the financial statements instead of in the financial statements. Under U.S. GAAP, companies may present this information in the cash flow statement.

ABOUT THE NUMBERS

One area where there can be substantive differences between iGAAP and U.S. GAAP relates to the classification of interest, dividends, and taxes. The following table indicates the differences between the two approaches.

Item	iGAAP	U.S. GAAP
Interest paid	Operating or financing	Operating
Interest received	Operating or investing	Operating
Dividends paid	Operating or financing	Financing
Dividends received	Operating or investing	Operating
Taxes paid	Operating—unless specific identification with financing or investing	Operating[1,2]

[1]U.S. GAAP has additional disclosure rules
[2]U.S. GAAP has specific rules regarding the classification of the benefit associated with share-based compensation arrangements and the classification of derivatives that contain a financing element

Source: PricewaterhouseCoopers, *Similarities and Difference–A Comparison of IFRS and U.S. GAAP* (October 2007).

As indicated, the major difference is that iGAAP provides more alternatives for disclosing certain items.

ON THE HORIZON

Presently, the FASB and the IASB are involved in a joint project on the presentation and organization of information in the financial statements. With respect to the cash flow statement specifically, the notion of *cash equivalents* will probably not be retained. The definition of cash in the existing literature would be retained, and the statement of cash flows would present information on changes in cash only. In addition, the FASB favors presentation of operating cash flows using the direct method only. However, the majority of IASB members express a preference for not requiring use of the direct method of reporting operating cash flows. So the two Boards will have to resolve their differences in this area in order to issue a converged standard for the statement of cash flows.

SUMMARY OF LEARNING OBJECTIVES

•1 **Describe the purpose of the statement of cash flows.** The primary purpose of the statement of cash flows is to provide information about cash receipts and cash payments of an entity during a period. A secondary objective is to report the entity's operating, investing, and financing activities during the period.

•2 **Identify the major classifications of cash flows.** Companies classify cash flows as: (1) *Operating activities*—transactions that result in the revenues, expenses, gains, and losses that determine net income. (2) *Investing activities*—lending money and collecting on those loans, and acquiring and disposing of investments, plant assets, and intangible assets. (3) *Financing activities*—obtaining cash from creditors and repaying loans, issuing and reacquiring capital stock, and paying cash dividends.

•3 **Differentiate between net income and net cash flows from operating activities.** Companies must adjust net income on an accrual basis to determine net cash flow from operating activities because some expenses and losses do not cause cash outflows, and some revenues and gains do not provide cash inflows.

•4 **Contrast the direct and indirect methods of calculating net cash flow from operating activities.** Under the direct approach, companies calculate the major classes of operating cash receipts and cash disbursements. Companies summarize the computations in a schedule of changes from the accrual to the cash basis income statement. Presentation of the direct approach of reporting net cash flow from operating activities takes the form of a condensed cash-basis income statement. The indirect method adds back to net income the noncash expenses and losses and subtracts the noncash revenues and gains.

•5 **Determine net cash flows from investing and financing activities.** Once a company has computed the net cash flow from operating activities, the next step is to determine whether any other changes in balance sheet accounts caused an increase or decrease in cash. Net cash flows from investing and financing activities can be determined by examining the changes in noncurrent balance sheet accounts.

•6 **Prepare a statement of cash flows.** Preparing the statement involves three major steps: (1) *Determine the change in cash*. This is the difference between the beginning and the ending cash balance shown on the comparative balance sheets. (2) *Determine the net cash flow from operating activities*. This procedure is complex; it involves analyzing not only the current year's income statement but also the comparative balance sheets and the selected transaction data. (3) *Determine cash flows from investing and financing activities*. Analyze all other changes in the balance sheet accounts to determine the effects on cash.

•7 **Identify sources of information for a statement of cash flows.** The information to prepare the statement usually comes from three sources: (1) *Comparative balance sheets*. Information in these statements indicates the amount of the changes in assets, liabilities, and equities during the period. (2) *Current income statement*. Information in this statement is used in determining the cash provided by operations during the period. (3) *Selected transaction data*. These data from the general ledger provide additional detailed information needed to determine how cash was provided or used during the period.

•8 **Discuss special problems in preparing a statement of cash flows.** These special problems are: (1) adjustments similar to depreciation; (2) accounts receivable (net); (3) other working capital changes; (4) net losses; (5) gains; (6) stock options; (7) postretirement benefit costs; (8) extraordinary items; and (9) significant noncash transactions.

•9 Explain the use of a worksheet in preparing a statement of cash flows. When numerous adjustments are necessary, or other complicating factors are present, companies often use a worksheet to assemble and classify the data that will appear on the statement of cash flows. The worksheet is merely a device that aids in the preparation of the statement. Its use is optional.

FASB CODIFICATION

FASB Codification References

[1] FASB ASC 230-10-10-2. [Predecessor literature: "The Statement of Cash Flows," *Statement of Financial Accounting Standards No. 95* (Stamford, Conn.: FASB, 1987), pars. 4 and 5.]

[2] FASB ASC 230-10-45-18 through 21. [Predecessor literature: "Statement of Cash Flows—Exemption of Certain Enterprises and Classification of Cash Flows from Certain Securities Acquired for Resale (amended)," *Statement of Financial Accounting Standards No. 102* (February 1989).]

[3] FASB ASC 230-10-45-31. [Predecessor literature: "The Statement of Cash Flows," *Statement of Financial Accounting Standards No. 95* (Stamford, Conn.: FASB, 1987), pars. 27 and 30.]

[4] FASB ASC 230-10-45-25. [Predecessor literature: "Statement of Cash Flows," *Statement of Financial Accounting Standards No. 95* (Stamford, Conn.: FASB, 1987), pars. 107 and 111.]

[5] FASB ASC 320-10-45-11. [Predecessor literature: "Accounting for Certain Investments in Debt and Equity Securities," *Statement of Financial Accounting Standards No. 115* (Norwalk, Conn.: 1993), par. 118.]

[6] FASB ASC 320-10-45-11. [Predecessor literature: "Accounting for Certain Investments in Debt and Equity Securities," *Statement of Financial Accounting Standards No. 115* (Norwalk, Conn.: 1993), par. 118.]

[7] FASB ASC 230-10-45-14. [Predecessor literature: "Share-Based Payment," *Statement of Financial Accounting Standard No. 123(R)* (Norwalk, Conn.: FASB, 2004), par. 68.]

Exercises

Access the FASB Codification at *http://asc.fasb.org/home* to prepare responses to the following exercises. Provide Codification references for your responses.

CE23-1 Access the glossary ("Master Glossary") to answer the following.

    (a) What are cash equivalents?
    (b) What are financing activities?
    (c) What are investing activities?
    (d) What are operating activities?

CE23-2 Name five cash inflows that would qualify as a "financing activity."

CE23-3 How should cash flows from purchases, sales, and maturities of available-for-sale securities be classified and reported in the statement of cash flows?

CE23-4 Do companies need to disclose information about investing and financing activities that do not affect cash receipts or cash payments? If so, how should such information be disclosed?

An additional codification case can be found in the Using Your Judgment section, on page 1311.

Be sure to check the companion website for a Review and Analysis Exercise, with solution.

QUESTIONS

1. What is the purpose of the statement of cash flows? What information does it provide?

2. Of what use is the statement of cash flows?

3. Differentiate between investing activities, financing activities, and operating activities.

4. What are the major sources of cash (inflows) in a statement of cash flows? What are the major uses (outflows) of cash?

5. Identify and explain the major steps involved in preparing the statement of cash flows.

6. Identify the following items as (1) operating, (2) investing, or (3) financing activities: purchase of land; payment of dividends; cash sales; and purchase of treasury stock.

7. Unlike the other major financial statements, the statement of cash flows is not prepared from the adjusted trial balance. From what sources does the information to prepare this statement come, and what information does each source provide?

8. Why is it necessary to convert accrual-based net income to a cash basis when preparing a statement of cash flows?

9. Differentiate between the direct method and the indirect method by discussing each method.

10. Broussard Company reported net income of $3.5 million in 2010. Depreciation for the year was $520,000; accounts receivable increased $500,000; and accounts payable increased $300,000. Compute net cash flow from operating activities using the indirect method.

11. Collinsworth Co. reported sales on an accrual basis of $100,000. If accounts receivable increased $30,000, and the allowance for doubtful accounts increased $9,000 after a write-off of $2,000, compute cash sales.

12. Your roommate is puzzled. During the last year, the company in which she is a stockholder reported a net loss of $675,000, yet its cash increased $321,000 during the same period of time. Explain to your roommate how this situation could occur.

13. The board of directors of Gifford Corp. declared cash dividends of $260,000 during the current year. If dividends payable was $85,000 at the beginning of the year and $90,000 at the end of the year, how much cash was paid in dividends during the year?

14. Explain how the amount of cash payments to suppliers is computed under the direct method.

15. The net income for Letterman Company for 2010 was $320,000. During 2010, depreciation on plant assets was $124,000, amortization of patent was $40,000, and the company incurred a loss on sale of plant assets of $21,000. Compute net cash flow from operating activities.

16. Each of the following items must be considered in preparing a statement of cash flows for Blackwell Inc. for the year ended December 31, 2010. State where each item is to be shown in the statement, if at all.

(a) Plant assets that had cost $18,000 6½ years before and were being depreciated on a straight-line basis over 10 years with no estimated scrap value were sold for $4,000.

(b) During the year, 10,000 shares of common stock with a stated value of $20 a share were issued for $41 a share.

(c) Uncollectible accounts receivable in the amount of $22,000 were written off against the Allowance for Doubtful Accounts.

(d) The company sustained a net loss for the year of $50,000. Depreciation amounted to $22,000, and a gain of $9,000 was realized on the sale of available-for-sale securities for $38,000 cash.

17. Classify the following items as (1) operating, (2) investing, (3) financing, or (4) significant noncash investing and financing activities, using the direct method.

(a) Cash payments to employees.

(b) Redemption of bonds payable.

(c) Sale of building at book value.

(d) Cash payments to suppliers.

(e) Exchange of equipment for furniture.

(f) Issuance of preferred stock.

(g) Cash received from customers.

(h) Purchase of treasury stock.

(i) Issuance of bonds for land.

(j) Payment of dividends.

(k) Purchase of equipment.

(l) Cash payments for operating expenses.

18. Stan Conner and Mark Stein were discussing the presentation format of the statement of cash flows of Bombeck Co. At the bottom of Bombeck's statement of cash flows was a separate section entitled "Noncash investing and financing activities." Give three examples of significant noncash transactions that would be reported in this section.

19. During 2010, Simms Company redeemed $2,000,000 of bonds payable for $1,880,000 cash. Indicate how this transaction would be reported on a statement of cash flows, if at all.

20. What are some of the arguments in favor of using the indirect (reconciliation) method as opposed to the direct method for reporting a statement of cash flows?

21. Why is it desirable to use a worksheet when preparing a statement of cash flows? Is a worksheet required to prepare a statement of cash flows?

22. Where can authoritative iGAAP related to the statement of cash flows be found?

23. Briefly describe some of the similarities and differences between U.S. GAAP and iGAAP with respect to cash flow reporting.

24. Some believe that iGAAP provides too many choices within its accounting guidance. Is this a possible concern in the area of cash flow reporting? Explain.

25. What are some of the key obstacles for the FASB and IASB in their convergence project for the statement of cash flows?

BRIEF EXERCISES

•5 **BE23-1** Wainwright Corporation had the following activities in 2010.

1. Sale of land $180,000
2. Purchase of inventory $845,000
3. Purchase of treasury stock $72,000
4. Purchase of equipment $415,000
5. Issuance of common stock $320,000
6. Purchase of available-for-sale securities $59,000

Compute the amount Wainwright should report as net cash provided (used) by investing activities in its statement of cash flows.

•5 **BE23-2** Stansfield Corporation had the following activities in 2010.

1. Payment of accounts payable $770,000
2. Issuance of common stock $250,000
3. Payment of dividends $350,000
4. Collection of note receivable $100,000
5. Issuance of bonds payable $510,000
6. Purchase of treasury stock $46,000

Compute the amount Stansfield should report as net cash provided (used) by financing activities in its 2010 statement of cash flows.

•2 **BE23-3** Novak Corporation is preparing its 2010 statement of cash flows, using the indirect method. Presented below is a list of items that may affect the statement. Using the code below, indicate how each item will affect Novak's 2010 statement of cash flows.

Code Letter	Effect
A	Added to net income in the operating section
D	Deducted from net income in the operating section
R-I	Cash receipt in investing section
P-I	Cash payment in investing section
R-F	Cash receipt in financing section
P-F	Cash payment in financing section
N	Noncash investing and/or financing activity

Items

_____ **(a)** Purchase of land and building.
_____ **(b)** Decrease in accounts receivable.
_____ **(c)** Issuance of stock.
_____ **(d)** Depreciation expense.
_____ **(e)** Sale of land at book value.
_____ **(f)** Sale of land at a gain.
_____ **(g)** Payment of dividends.
_____ **(h)** Increase in accounts receivable.
_____ **(i)** Purchase of available-for-sale investment.

_____ **(j)** Increase in accounts payable.
_____ **(k)** Decrease in accounts payable.
_____ **(l)** Loan from bank by signing note.
_____ **(m)** Purchase of equipment using a note.
_____ **(n)** Increase in inventory.
_____ **(o)** Issuance of bonds.
_____ **(p)** Retirement of bonds payable.
_____ **(q)** Sale of equipment at a loss.
_____ **(r)** Purchase of treasury stock.

•3 •4 **BE23-4** Bloom Corporation had the following 2010 income statement.

Sales	$200,000
Cost of goods sold	120,000
Gross profit	80,000
Operating expenses (includes depreciation of $21,000)	50,000
Net income	$ 30,000

The following accounts increased during 2010: accounts receivable $12,000; inventory $11,000; accounts payable $13,000. Prepare the cash flows from operating activities section of Bloom's 2010 statement of cash flows using the direct method.

•3 •4 **BE23-5** Use the information from BE23-4 for Bloom Corporation. Prepare the cash flows from operating activities section of Bloom's 2010 statement of cash flows using the indirect method.

•4 **BE23-6** At January 1, 2010, Eikenberry Inc. had accounts receivable of $72,000. At December 31, 2010, accounts receivable is $54,000. Sales for 2010 total $420,000. Compute Eikenberry's 2010 cash receipts from customers.

·4 **BE23-7** Moxley Corporation had January 1 and December 31 balances as follows.

	1/1/10	12/31/10
Inventory	$95,000	$113,000
Accounts payable	61,000	69,000

For 2010, cost of goods sold was $500,000. Compute Moxley's 2010 cash payments to suppliers.

·6 **BE23-8** In 2010, Elbert Corporation had net cash provided by operating activities of $531,000; net cash used by investing activities of $963,000; and net cash provided by financing activities of $585,000. At January 1, 2010, the cash balance was $333,000. Compute December 31, 2010, cash.

·3 ·4 **BE23-9** Loveless Corporation had the following 2010 income statement.

Revenues	$100,000
Expenses	60,000
	$ 40,000

In 2010, Loveless had the following activity in selected accounts.

Accounts Receivable					Allowance for Doubtful Accounts		
1/1/10	20,000					1,200	1/1/10
Revenues	100,000	1,000	Write-offs	Write-offs	1,000	1,840	Bad debt expense
		90,000	Collections				
12/31/10	29,000					2,040	12/31/10

Prepare Loveless's cash flows from operating activities section of the statement of cash flows using (a) the direct method and (b) the indirect method.

·3 **BE23-10** Hendrickson Corporation reported net income of $50,000 in 2010. Depreciation expense was $17,000. The following working capital accounts changed.

Accounts receivable	$11,000 increase
Available-for-sale securities	16,000 increase
Inventory	7,400 increase
Nontrade note payable	15,000 decrease
Accounts payable	12,300 increase

Compute net cash provided by operating activities.

·3 **BE23-11** In 2010, Wild Corporation reported a net loss of $70,000. Wild's only net income adjustments were depreciation expense $81,000, and increase in accounts receivable $8,100. Compute Wild's net cash provided (used) by operating activities.

·8 **BE23-12** In 2010, Leppard Inc. issued 1,000 shares of $10 par value common stock for land worth $40,000.
   (a) Prepare Leppard's journal entry to record the transaction.
   (b) Indicate the effect the transaction has on cash.
   (c) Indicate how the transaction is reported on the statement of cash flows.

·9 **BE23-13** Indicate in general journal form how the items below would be entered in a worksheet for the preparation of the statement of cash flows.

   (a) Net income is $317,000.
   (b) Cash dividends declared and paid totaled $120,000.
   (c) Equipment was purchased for $114,000.
   (d) Equipment that originally cost $40,000 and had accumulated depreciation of $32,000 was sold for $10,000.

EXERCISES

·2 **E23-1** **(Classification of Transactions)** Springsteen Co. had the following activity in its most recent year of operations.

   (a) Pension expense exceeds amount funded.
   (b) Redemption of bonds payable.
   (c) Sale of building at book value.
   (d) Depreciation.
   (e) Exchange of equipment for furniture.
   (f) Issuance of capital stock.
   (g) Amortization of intangible assets.
   (h) Purchase of treasury stock.

(i) Issuance of bonds for land.

(j) Payment of dividends.

(k) Increase in interest receivable on notes receivable.

(l) Purchase of equipment.

Instructions
Classify the items as (1) operating—add to net income; (2) operating—deduct from net income; (3) investing; (4) financing; or (5) significant noncash investing and financing activities. Use the indirect method.

 E23-2 **(Statement Presentation of Transactions—Indirect Method)** Each of the following items must be considered in preparing a statement of cash flows (indirect method) for Granderson Inc. for the year ended December 31, 2010.

(a) Plant assets that had cost $25,000 6 years before and were being depreciated on a straight-line basis over 10 years with no estimated scrap value were sold at the beginning of the year for $5,300.

(b) During the year, 10,000 shares of common stock with a stated value of $10 a share were issued for $33 a share.

(c) Uncollectible accounts receivable in the amount of $27,000 were written off against the Allowance for Doubtful Accounts.

(d) The company sustained a net loss for the year of $50,000. Depreciation amounted to $22,000, and a gain of $9,000 was realized on the sale of land for $39,000 cash.

(e) A 3-month U.S. Treasury bill was purchased for $100,000. The company uses a cash and cash-equivalent basis for its cash flow statement.

(f) Patent amortization for the year was $20,000.

(g) The company exchanged common stock for a 70% interest in Plumlee Co. for $900,000.

(h) During the year, treasury stock costing $47,000 was purchased.

Instructions
State where each item is to be shown in the statement of cash flows, if at all.

  E23-3 **(Preparation of Operating Activities Section—Indirect Method, Periodic Inventory)** The income statement of Rodriquez Company is shown below.

RODRIQUEZ COMPANY INCOME STATEMENT FOR THE YEAR ENDED DECEMBER 31, 2010		
Sales		$6,900,000
Cost of goods sold		
Beginning inventory	$1,900,000	
Purchases	4,400,000	
Goods available for sale	6,300,000	
Ending inventory	1,600,000	
Cost of goods sold		4,700,000
Gross profit		2,200,000
Operating expenses		
Selling expenses	450,000	
Administrative expenses	700,000	1,150,000
Net income		$1,050,000

Additional information:
1. Accounts receivable decreased $310,000 during the year.
2. Prepaid expenses increased $170,000 during the year.
3. Accounts payable to suppliers of merchandise decreased $275,000 during the year.
4. Accrued expenses payable decreased $120,000 during the year.
5. Administrative expenses include depreciation expense of $60,000.

Instructions
Prepare the operating activities section of the statement of cash flows for the year ended December 31, 2010, for Rodriquez Company, using the indirect method.

 E23-4 **(Preparation of Operating Activities Section—Direct Method)** Data for the Rodriquez Company are presented in E23-3.

Instructions
Prepare the operating activities section of the statement of cash flows using the direct method.

·3·4 **E23-5** **(Preparation of Operating Activities Section—Direct Method)** Norman Company's income statement for the year ended December 31, 2010, contained the following condensed information.

Revenue from fees		$840,000
Operating expenses (excluding depreciation)	$624,000	
Depreciation expense	60,000	
Loss on sale of equipment	26,000	710,000
Income before income taxes		130,000
Income tax expense		40,000
Net income		$ 90,000

Norman's balance sheet contained the following comparative data at December 31.

	2010	2009
Accounts receivable	$37,000	$59,000
Accounts payable	46,000	31,000
Income taxes payable	4,000	8,500

(Accounts payable pertains to operating expenses.)

Instructions
Prepare the operating activities section of the statement of cash flows using the direct method.

·3·4 **E23-6** **(Preparation of Operating Activities Section—Indirect Method)** Data for Norman Company are presented in E23-5.

Instructions
Prepare the operating activities section of the statement of cash flows using the indirect method.

·3·4 **E23-7** **(Computation of Operating Activities—Direct Method)** Presented below are two independent situations.

Situation A:

Chenowith Co. reports revenues of $200,000 and operating expenses of $110,000 in its first year of operations, 2010. Accounts receivable and accounts payable at year-end were $71,000 and $39,000, respectively. Assume that the accounts payable related to operating expenses. Ignore income taxes.

Instructions
Using the direct method, compute net cash provided (used) by operating activities.

Situation B:

The income statement for Edgebrook Company shows cost of goods sold $310,000 and operating expenses (exclusive of depreciation) $230,000. The comparative balance sheet for the year shows that inventory increased $21,000, prepaid expenses decreased $8,000, accounts payable (related to merchandise) decreased $17,000, and accrued expenses payable increased $11,000.

Instructions
Compute (a) cash payments to suppliers and (b) cash payments for operating expenses.

·3·4 **E23-8** **(Schedule of Net Cash Flow from Operating Activities—Indirect Method)** Messner Co. reported $145,000 of net income for 2010. The accountant, in preparing the statement of cash flows, noted several items occurring during 2010 that might affect cash flows from operating activities. These items are listed below and on page 1291.

1. Messner purchased 100 shares of treasury stock at a cost of $20 per share. These shares were then resold at $25 per share.
2. Messner sold 100 shares of IBM common at $200 per share. The acquisition cost of these shares was $165 per share. This investment was shown on Messner's December 31, 2009, balance sheet as an available-for-sale security.
3. Messner revised its estimate for bad debts. Before 2010, Messner's bad debt expense was 1% of its net sales. In 2010, this percentage was increased to 2%. Net sales for 2010 were $500,000, and net accounts receivable decreased by $12,000 during 2010.
4. Messner issued 500 shares of its $10 par common stock for a patent. The market value of the shares on the date of the transaction was $23 per share.
5. Depreciation expense is $39,000.
6. Messner Co. holds 30% of the Sanchez Company's common stock as a long-term investment. Sanchez Company reported $27,000 of net income for 2010.

7. Sanchez Company paid a total of $2,000 of cash dividends to all investees in 2010.
8. Messner declared a 10% stock dividend. One thousand shares of $10 par common stock were distributed. The market price at date of issuance was $20 per share.

Instructions
Prepare a schedule that shows the net cash flow from operating activities using the indirect method. Assume no items other than those listed above affected the computation of 2010 net cash flow from operating activities.

•6 **E23-9 (SCF—Direct Method)** Waubansee Corp. uses the direct method to prepare its statement of cash flows. Waubansee's trial balances at December 31, 2010 and 2009, are as follows.

	December 31	
	2010	2009
Debits		
Cash	$ 35,000	$ 32,000
Accounts receivable	33,000	30,000
Inventory	31,000	47,000
Property, plant, & equipment	100,000	95,000
Unamortized bond discount	4,500	5,000
Cost of goods sold	250,000	380,000
Selling expenses	141,500	172,000
General and administrative expenses	137,000	151,300
Interest expense	4,300	2,600
Income tax expense	20,400	61,200
	$756,700	$976,100
Credits		
Allowance for doubtful accounts	$ 1,300	$ 1,100
Accumulated depreciation	16,500	13,500
Trade accounts payable	25,000	17,000
Income taxes payable	21,000	29,100
Deferred income taxes	5,300	4,600
8% callable bonds payable	45,000	20,000
Common stock	50,000	40,000
Additional paid-in capital	9,100	7,500
Retained earnings	44,700	64,600
Sales	538,800	778,700
	$756,700	$976,100

Additional information:

1. Waubansee purchased $5,000 in equipment during 2010.
2. Waubansee allocated one-third of its depreciation expense to selling expenses and the remainder to general and administrative expenses.
3. Bad debt expense for 2010 was $5,000, and writeoffs of uncollectible accounts totaled $3,800.

Instructions
Determine what amounts Waubansee should report in its statement of cash flows for the year ended December 31, 2010, for the following items.

1. Cash collected from customers.   4. Cash paid for income taxes.
2. Cash paid to suppliers.   5. Cash paid for selling expenses.
3. Cash paid for interest.

•2 •8 **E23-10 (Classification of Transactions)** Following are selected balance sheet accounts of Sander Bros. Corp. at December 31, 2010 and 2009, and the increases or decreases in each account from 2009 to 2010. Also presented is selected income statement information for the year ended December 31, 2010, and additional information.

Selected balance sheet accounts	2010	2009	Increase (Decrease)
Assets			
Accounts receivable	$ 34,000	$ 24,000	$ 10,000
Property, plant, and equipment	277,000	247,000	30,000
Accumulated depreciation	(178,000)	(167,000)	(11,000)

	2010	2009	Increase
Liabilities and stockholders' equity			
Bonds payable	$ 49,000	$46,000	$ 3,000
Dividends payable	8,000	5,000	3,000
Common stock, $1 par	22,000	19,000	3,000
Additional paid-in capital	9,000	3,000	6,000
Retained earnings	104,000	91,000	13,000

Selected income statement information for the year ended December 31, 2010

Sales revenue	$155,000
Depreciation	38,000
Gain on sale of equipment	14,500
Net income	31,000

Additional information:

1. During 2010, equipment costing $45,000 was sold for cash.
2. Accounts receivable relate to sales of merchandise.
3. During 2010, $25,000 of bonds payable were issued in exchange for property, plant, and equipment. There was no amortization of bond discount or premium.

Instructions

Determine the category (operating, investing, or financing) and the amount that should be reported in the statement of cash flows for the following items.

1. Payments for purchase of property, plant, and equipment.
2. Proceeds from the sale of equipment.
3. Cash dividends paid.
4. Redemption of bonds payable.

•6 E23-11 (SCF—Indirect Method) Condensed financial data of Fairchild Company for 2010 and 2009 are presented below.

FAIRCHILD COMPANY
COMPARATIVE BALANCE SHEET
AS OF DECEMBER 31, 2010 AND 2009

	2011	2010
Cash	$1,800	$1,100
Receivables	1,750	1,300
Inventory	1,600	1,900
Plant assets	1,900	1,700
Accumulated depreciation	(1,200)	(1,170)
Long-term investments (Held-to-maturity)	1,300	1,470
	$7,150	$6,300
Accounts payable	$1,200	$ 800
Accrued liabilities	200	250
Bonds payable	1,400	1,650
Capital stock	1,900	1,700
Retained earnings	2,450	1,900
	$7,150	$6,300

FAIRCHILD COMPANY
INCOME STATEMENT
FOR THE YEAR ENDED DECEMBER 31, 2010

Sales	$6,900
Cost of goods sold	4,700
Gross margin	2,200
Selling and administrative expense	930
Income from operations	1,270
Other revenues and gains	
Gain on sale of investments	80
Income before tax	1,350
Income tax expense	540
Net income	$ 810

Additional information:

During the year, $70 of common stock was issued in exchange for plant assets. No plant assets were sold in 2010. Cash dividends were $260.

Instructions

Prepare a statement of cash flows using the indirect method.

•6 **E23-12 (SCF—Direct Method)** Data for Fairchild Company are presented in E23-11.

Instructions

Prepare a statement of cash flows using the direct method. (Do not prepare a reconciliation schedule.)

•6 **E23-13 (SCF—Direct Method)** Andrews Inc., a greeting card company, had the following statements prepared as of December 31, 2010.

ANDREWS INC.
COMPARATIVE BALANCE SHEET
AS OF DECEMBER 31, 2010 AND 2009

	12/31/10	12/31/09
Cash	$ 6,000	$ 9,000
Accounts receivable	62,000	49,000
Short-term investments (Available-for-sale)	35,000	18,000
Inventories	40,000	60,000
Prepaid rent	5,000	4,000
Printing equipment	154,000	130,000
Accumulated depr.—equipment	(35,000)	(25,000)
Copyrights	46,000	50,000
Total assets	$313,000	$295,000
Accounts payable	$ 46,000	$ 42,000
Income taxes payable	4,000	6,000
Wages payable	8,000	4,000
Short-term loans payable	8,000	10,000
Long-term loans payable	60,000	67,000
Common stock, $10 par	100,000	100,000
Contributed capital, common stock	30,000	30,000
Retained earnings	57,000	36,000
Total liabilities & stockholders' equity	$313,000	$295,000

ANDREWS INC.
INCOME STATEMENT
FOR THE YEAR ENDING DECEMBER 31, 2010

Sales		$338,150
Cost of goods sold		175,000
Gross margin		163,150
Operating expenses		120,000
Operating income		43,150
Interest expense	$11,400	
Gain on sale of equipment	2,000	9,400
Income before tax		33,750
Income tax expense		6,750
Net income		$ 27,000

Additional information:

1. Dividends in the amount of $6,000 were declared and paid during 2010.
2. Depreciation expense and amortization expense are included in operating expenses.
3. No unrealized gains or losses have occurred on the investments during the year.
4. Equipment that had a cost of $30,000 and was 70% depreciated was sold during 2010.

Instructions

Prepare a statement of cash flows using the direct method. (Do not prepare a reconciliation schedule.)

·6 E23-14 (SCF—Indirect Method) Data for Andrews Inc. are presented in E23-13.

Instructions
Prepare a statement of cash flows using the indirect method.

·6 E23-15 (SCF—Indirect Method) Presented below are data taken from the records of Morganstern Company.

	December 31, 2010	December 31, 2009
Cash	$ 15,000	$ 10,000
Current assets other than cash	85,000	58,000
Long-term investments	10,000	53,000
Plant assets	335,000	215,000
	$445,000	$336,000
Accumulated depreciation	$ 20,000	$ 40,000
Current liabilities	40,000	22,000
Bonds payable	75,000	–0–
Capital stock	254,000	254,000
Retained earnings	56,000	20,000
	$445,000	$336,000

Additional information:

1. Held-to-maturity securities carried at a cost of $43,000 on December 31, 2009, were sold in 2010 for $34,000. The loss (not extraordinary) was incorrectly charged directly to Retained Earnings.
2. Plant assets that cost $60,000 and were 80% depreciated were sold during 2010 for $8,000. The loss (not extraordinary) was incorrectly charged directly to Retained Earnings.
3. Net income as reported on the income statement for the year was $59,000.
4. Dividends paid amounted to $10,000.
5. Depreciation charged for the year was $28,000.

Instructions
Prepare a statement of cash flows for the year 2010 using the indirect method.

·2 ·3 ·5 E23-16 (Cash Provided by Operating, Investing, and Financing Activities) The balance sheet data of Wyeth Company at the end of 2010 and 2009 follow.

	2010	2009
Cash	$ 30,000	$ 35,000
Accounts receivable (net)	55,000	45,000
Merchandise inventory	65,000	45,000
Prepaid expenses	15,000	25,000
Equipment	90,000	75,000
Accumulated depreciation—equipment	(18,000)	(8,000)
Land	70,000	40,000
	$307,000	$257,000
Accounts payable	$ 65,000	$ 52,000
Accrued expenses	15,000	18,000
Notes payable—bank, long-term	–0–	23,000
Bonds payable	30,000	–0–
Common stock, $10 par	189,000	159,000
Retained earnings	8,000	5,000
	$307,000	$257,000

Land was acquired for $30,000 in exchange for common stock, par $30,000, during the year; all equipment purchased was for cash. Equipment costing $13,000 was sold for $3,000; book value of the equipment was $6,000. Cash dividends of $9,000 were declared and paid during the year.

Instructions
Compute net cash provided (used) by:

(a) Operating activities.
(b) Investing activities.
(c) Financing activities.

·6 **E23-17** **(SCF—Indirect Method and Balance Sheet)** Ochoa Inc., had the following condensed balance sheet at the end of operations for 2009.

OCHOA INC. BALANCE SHEET DECEMBER 31, 2009			
Cash	$ 8,500	Current liabilities	$ 15,000
Current assets other than cash	29,000	Long-term notes payable	25,500
Investments	20,000	Bonds payable	25,000
Plant assets (net)	67,500	Capital stock	75,000
Land	40,000	Retained earnings	24,500
	$165,000		$165,000

During 2010 the following occurred.

1. A tract of land was purchased for $11,000.
2. Bonds payable in the amount of $20,000 were retired at par.
3. An additional $10,000 in capital stock was issued at par.
4. Dividends totaling $9,375 were paid to stockholders.
5. Net income was $30,250 after deducting depreciation of $13,500.
6. Land was purchased through the issuance of $22,500 in bonds.
7. Ochoa Inc. sold part of its investment portfolio for $12,875. This transaction resulted in a gain of $2,000 for the company. The company classifies the investments as available-for-sale.
8. Both current assets (other than cash) and current liabilities remained at the same amount.

Instructions
(a) Prepare a statement of cash flows for 2010 using the indirect method.
(b) Prepare the condensed balance sheet for Ochoa Inc. as it would appear at December 31, 2010.

·6 ·8 **E23-18** **(Partial SCF—Indirect Method)** The accounts below appear in the ledger of Popovich Company.

Retained Earnings		Dr.	Cr.	Bal.
Jan. 1, 2010	Credit Balance			$ 42,000
Aug. 15	Dividends (cash)	$15,000		27,000
Dec. 31	Net Income for 2010		$50,000	77,000

Machinery		Dr.	Cr.	Bal.
Jan. 1, 2010	Debit Balance			$140,000
Aug. 3	Purchase of Machinery	$62,000		202,000
Sept. 10	Cost of Machinery Constructed	48,000		250,000
Nov. 15	Machinery Sold		$66,000	184,000

Accumulated Depreciation— Machinery		Dr.	Cr.	Bal.
Jan. 1, 2010	Credit Balance			$ 84,000
Apr. 8	Extraordinary Repairs	$21,000		63,000
Nov. 15	Accum. Depreciation on Machinery Sold	25,200		37,800
Dec. 31	Depreciation for 2010		$16,800	54,600

Instructions
From the postings in the accounts above, indicate how the information is reported on a statement of cash flows by preparing a partial statement of cash flows using the indirect method. The loss on sale of equipment (November 15) was $5,800.

·9 **E23-19** **(Worksheet Analysis of Selected Accounts)** Data for Popovich Company are presented in E23-18.

Instructions
Prepare entries in journal form for all adjustments that should be made on a worksheet for a statement of cash flows.

·9 **E23-20** **(Worksheet Analysis of Selected Transactions)** The transactions below took place during the year 2010.

1. Convertible bonds payable with a par value of $300,000 were exchanged for unissued common stock with a par value of $300,000. The market price of both types of securities was par.
2. The net income for the year was $360,000.
3. Depreciation expense for the building was $90,000.
4. Some old office equipment was traded in on the purchase of some newer office equipment and the following entry was made. (The exchange has commercial substance.)

Office Equipment	45,000	
Accum. Depreciation—Office Equipment	30,000	
Office Equipment		40,000
Cash		34,000
Gain on Disposal of Plant Assets		1,000

The Gain on Disposal of Plant Assets was credited to current operations as ordinary income.
5. Dividends in the amount of $123,000 were declared. They are payable in January of next year.

Instructions
Show by journal entries the adjustments that would be made on a worksheet for a statement of cash flows.

·9 **E23-21** **(Worksheet Preparation)** Below is the comparative balance sheet for Lowenstein Corporation.

	Dec. 31, 2010	Dec. 31, 2009
Cash	$ 16,500	$ 24,000
Short-term investments	25,000	19,000
Accounts receivable	43,000	45,000
Allowance for doubtful accounts	(1,800)	(2,000)
Prepaid expenses	4,200	2,500
Inventories	81,500	57,000
Land	50,000	50,000
Buildings	125,000	78,500
Accumulated depreciation—buildings	(30,000)	(23,000)
Equipment	53,000	46,000
Accumulated depreciation—equipment	(19,000)	(15,500)
Delivery equipment	39,000	39,000
Accumulated depreciation—delivery equipment	(22,000)	(20,500)
Patents	15,000	–0–
	$379,400	$300,000
Accounts payable	$ 26,000	$ 16,000
Short-term notes payable (trade)	4,000	6,000
Accrued payables	3,000	4,600
Mortgage payable	73,000	53,400
Bonds payable	50,000	62,500
Capital stock	140,000	102,000
Additional paid-in capital	10,000	4,000
Retained earnings	73,400	51,500
	$379,400	$300,000

Dividends in the amount of $10,000 were declared and paid in 2010.

Instructions

From this information, prepare a worksheet for a statement of cash flows. Make reasonable assumptions as appropriate. The short-term investments are considered available-for-sale, and no unrealized gains or losses have occurred on these securities.

See the book's companion website, www.wiley.com/college/kieso, for a set of B Exercises.

PROBLEMS

·6 ·7 ·8 P23-1 (SCF—Indirect Method)   The following is Sullivan Corp.'s comparative balance sheet accounts at December 31, 2010 and 2009, with a column showing the increase (decrease) from 2009 to 2010.

COMPARATIVE BALANCE SHEETS			
	2010	2009	Increase (Decrease)
Cash	$ 815,000	$ 700,000	$115,000
Accounts receivable	1,128,000	1,168,000	(40,000)
Inventories	1,850,000	1,715,000	135,000
Property, plant and equipment	3,307,000	2,967,000	340,000
Accumulated depreciation	(1,165,000)	(1,040,000)	(125,000)
Investment in Myers Co.	310,000	275,000	35,000
Loan receivable	250,000	—	250,000
Total assets	$6,495,000	$5,785,000	$710,000
Accounts payable	$1,015,000	$ 955,000	$ 60,000
Income taxes payable	30,000	50,000	(20,000)
Dividends payable	80,000	100,000	(20,000)
Capital lease obligation	400,000	—	400,000
Capital stock, common, $1 par	500,000	500,000	—
Additional paid-in capital	1,500,000	1,500,000	—
Retained earnings	2,970,000	2,680,000	290,000
Total liabilities and stockholders' equity	$6,495,000	$5,785,000	$710,000

Additional information:

1. On December 31, 2009, Sullivan acquired 25% of Myers Co.'s common stock for $275,000. On that date, the carrying value of Myers's assets and liabilities, which approximated their fair values, was $1,100,000. Myers reported income of $140,000 for the year ended December 31, 2010. No dividend was paid on Myers's common stock during the year.
2. During 2010, Sullivan loaned $300,000 to TLC Co., an unrelated company. TLC made the first semi-annual principal repayment of $50,000, plus interest at 10%, on December 31, 2010.
3. On January 2, 2010, Sullivan sold equipment costing $60,000, with a carrying amount of $38,000, for $40,000 cash.
4. On December 31, 2010, Sullivan entered into a capital lease for an office building. The present value of the annual rental payments is $400,000, which equals the fair value of the building. Sullivan made the first rental payment of $60,000 when due on January 2, 2011.
5. Net income for 2010 was $370,000.
6. Sullivan declared and paid cash dividends for 2010 and 2009 as shown below.

	2010	2009
Declared	December 15, 2010	December 15, 2009
Paid	February 28, 2011	February 28, 2010
Amount	$80,000	$100,000

Instructions

Prepare a statement of cash flows for Sullivan Corp. for the year ended December 31, 2010, using the indirect method.

(AICPA adapted)

·6 ·7 ·8 P23-2 (SCF—Indirect Method) The comparative balance sheets for Hinckley Corporation show the following information.

	December 31	
	2010	**2009**
Cash	$ 33,500	$13,000
Accounts receivable	12,250	10,000
Inventory	12,000	9,000
Investments	–0–	3,000
Building	–0–	29,750
Equipment	45,000	20,000
Patent	5,000	6,250
	$107,750	$91,000
Allowance for doubtful accounts	$ 3,000	$ 4,500
Accumulated depreciation on equipment	2,000	4,500
Accumulated depreciation on building	–0–	6,000
Accounts payable	5,000	3,000
Dividends payable	–0–	5,000
Notes payable, short-term (nontrade)	3,000	4,000
Long-term notes payable	31,000	25,000
Common stock	43,000	33,000
Retained earnings	20,750	6,000
	$107,750	$91,000

Additional data related to 2010 are as follows.

1. Equipment that had cost $11,000 and was 40% depreciated at time of disposal was sold for $2,500.
2. $10,000 of the long-term note payable was paid by issuing common stock.
3. Cash dividends paid were $5,000.
4. On January 1, 2010, the building was completely destroyed by a flood. Insurance proceeds on the building were $30,000 (net of $2,000 taxes).
5. Investments (available-for-sale) were sold at $1,700 above their cost. The company has made similar sales and investments in the past.
6. Cash was paid for the acquisition of equipment.
7. A long-term note for $16,000 was issued for the acquisition of equipment.
8. Interest of $2,000 and income taxes of $6,500 were paid in cash.

Instructions

Prepare a statement of cash flows using the indirect method. Flood damage is unusual and infrequent in that part of the country.

·6 P23-3 (SCF—Direct Method) Mortonson Company has not yet prepared a formal statement of cash flows for the 2010 fiscal year. Comparative balance sheets as of December 31, 2009 and 2010, and a statement of income and retained earnings for the year ended December 31, 2010, are presented below.

MORTONSON COMPANY
STATEMENT OF INCOME AND RETAINED EARNINGS
FOR THE YEAR ENDED DECEMBER 31, 2010
($000 OMITTED)

Sales		$3,800
Expenses		
Cost of goods sold	$1,200	
Salaries and benefits	725	
Heat, light, and power	75	
Depreciation	80	
Property taxes	19	
Patent amortization	25	
Miscellaneous expenses	10	
Interest	30	2,164

MORTONSON COMPANY
STATEMENT OF INCOME AND RETAINED EARNINGS
FOR THE YEAR ENDED DECEMBER 31, 2010
(CONTINUED)

Income before income taxes	1,636
Income taxes	818
Net income	818
Retained earnings—Jan. 1, 2010	310
	1,128
Stock dividend declared and issued	600
Retained earnings—Dec. 31, 2010	$ 528

MORTONSON COMPANY
COMPARATIVE BALANCE SHEETS
AS OF DECEMBER 31
($000 OMITTED)

Assets	2010	2009
Current assets		
Cash	$ 333	$ 100
U.S. Treasury notes (Available-for-sale)	10	50
Accounts receivable	780	500
Inventory	720	560
Total current assets	1,843	1,210
Long-term assets		
Land	150	70
Buildings and equipment	910	600
Accumulated depreciation	(200)	(120)
Patents (less amortization)	105	130
Total long-term assets	965	680
Total assets	$2,808	$1,890
Liabilities and Stockholders' Equity		
Current liabilities		
Accounts payable	$ 420	$ 330
Income taxes payable	40	30
Notes payable	320	320
Total current liabilities	780	680
Long-term notes payable—due 2012	200	200
Total liabilities	980	880
Stockholders' equity		
Common stock	1,300	700
Retained earnings	528	310
Total stockholders' equity	1,828	1,010
Total liabilities and stockholders' equity	$2,808	$1,890

Instructions

Prepare a statement of cash flows using the direct method. Changes in accounts receivable and accounts payable relate to sales and cost of goods sold. Do not prepare a reconciliation schedule.

(CMA adapted)

•6 •7 •8   **P23-4   (SCF—Direct Method)**   Michaels Company had available at the end of 2010 the information on page 1300.

MICHAELS COMPANY
COMPARATIVE BALANCE SHEETS
AS OF DECEMBER 31, 2010 AND 2009

	2010	2009
Cash	$ 10,000	$ 4,000
Accounts receivable	20,500	12,950
Short-term investments	22,000	30,000
Inventory	42,000	35,000
Prepaid rent	3,000	12,000
Prepaid insurance	2,100	900
Office supplies	1,000	750
Land	125,000	175,000
Building	350,000	350,000
Accumulated depreciation	(105,000)	(87,500)
Equipment	525,000	400,000
Accumulated depreciation	(130,000)	(112,000)
Patent	45,000	50,000
Total assets	$910,600	$871,100
Accounts payable	$ 22,000	$ 32,000
Income taxes payable	5,000	4,000
Wages payable	5,000	3,000
Short-term notes payable	10,000	10,000
Long-term notes payable	60,000	70,000
Bonds payable	400,000	400,000
Premium on bonds payable	20,303	25,853
Common stock	240,000	220,000
Paid-in capital in excess of par	25,000	17,500
Retained earnings	123,297	88,747
Total liabilities and stockholders' equity	$910,600	$871,100

MICHAELS COMPANY
INCOME STATEMENT
FOR THE YEAR ENDED DECEMBER 31, 2010

Sales revenue		$1,160,000
Cost of goods sold		(748,000)
		412,000
Gross margin		
Operating expenses		
Selling expenses	$ 79,200	
Administrative expenses	156,700	
Depreciation/Amortization expense	40,500	
Total operating expenses		(276,400)
Income from operations		135,600
Other revenues/expenses		
Gain on sale of land	8,000	
Gain on sale of short-term investment	4,000	
Dividend revenue	2,400	
Interest expense	(51,750)	(37,350)
Income before taxes		98,250
Income tax expense		(39,400)
Net income		58,850
Dividends to common stockholders		(24,300)
To retained earnings		$ 34,550

Instructions

Prepare a statement of cash flows for Michaels Company using the direct method accompanied by a reconciliation schedule. Assume the short-term investments are available-for-sale securities.

·6·7·8 **P23-5 (SCF—Indirect Method)** You have completed the field work in connection with your audit of Alexander Corporation for the year ended December 31, 2010. The balance sheet accounts at the beginning and end of the year are shown on the next page.

	Dec. 31, 2010	Dec. 31, 2009	Increase or (Decrease)
Cash	$ 277,900	$ 298,000	($20,100)
Accounts receivable	469,424	353,000	116,424
Inventory	741,700	610,000	131,700
Prepaid expenses	12,000	8,000	4,000
Investment in subsidiary	110,500	–0–	110,500
Cash surrender value of life insurance	2,304	1,800	504
Machinery	207,000	190,000	17,000
Buildings	535,200	407,900	127,300
Land	52,500	52,500	–0–
Patents	69,000	64,000	5,000
Copyright	40,000	50,000	(10,000)
Bond discount and issue cost	4,502	–0–	4,502
	$2,522,030	$2,035,200	$486,830
Accrued taxes payable	$ 90,250	$ 79,600	$ 10,650
Accounts payable	299,280	280,000	19,280
Dividends payable	70,000	–0–	70,000
Bonds payable—8%	125,000	–0–	125,000
Bonds payable—12%	–0–	100,000	(100,000)
Allowance for doubtful accounts	35,300	40,000	(4,700)
Accumulated depreciation—buildings	424,000	400,000	24,000
Accumulated depreciation—machinery	173,000	130,000	43,000
Premium on bonds payable	–0–	2,400	(2,400)
Capital stock—no par	1,176,200	1,453,200	(277,000)
Additional paid-in capital	109,000	–0–	109,000
Retained earnings—unappropriated	20,000	(450,000)	470,000
	$2,522,030	$2,035,200	$486,830

STATEMENT OF RETAINED EARNINGS
FOR THE YEAR ENDED DECEMBER 31, 2010

January	1, 2010	Balance (deficit)	$(450,000)
March	31, 2010	Net income for first quarter of 2010	25,000
April	1, 2010	Transfer from paid-in capital	425,000
		Balance	–0–
December 31, 2010		Net income for last three quarters of 2010	90,000
		Dividend declared—payable January 21, 2011	(70,000)
		Balance	$ 20,000

Your working papers from the audit contain the following information:

1. On April 1, 2010, the existing deficit was written off against paid-in capital created by reducing the stated value of the no-par stock.
2. On November 1, 2010, 29,600 shares of no-par stock were sold for $257,000. The board of directors voted to regard $5 per share as stated capital.
3. A patent was purchased for $15,000.
4. During the year, machinery that had a cost basis of $16,400 and on which there was accumulated depreciation of $5,200 was sold for $9,000. No other plant assets were sold during the year.
5. The 12%, 20-year bonds were dated and issued on January 2, 1998. Interest was payable on June 30 and December 31. They were sold originally at 106. These bonds were retired at 100.9 plus accrued interest on March 31, 2010.
6. The 8%, 40-year bonds were dated January 1, 2010, and were sold on March 31 at 97 plus accrued interest. Interest is payable semiannually on June 30 and December 31. Expense of issuance was $839.
7. Alexander Corporation acquired 70% control in Crimson Company on January 2, 2010, for $100,000. The income statement of Crimson Company for 2010 shows a net income of $15,000.
8. Extraordinary repairs to buildings of $7,200 were charged to Accumulated Depreciation—Buildings.
9. Interest paid in 2010 was $10,500 and income taxes paid were $34,000.

Instructions

From the information given, prepare a statement of cash flows using the indirect method. A worksheet is not necessary, but the principal computations should be supported by schedules or skeleton ledger accounts. The company uses straight-line amortization for bond interest.

 P23-6 (SCF—Indirect Method, and Net Cash Flow from Operating Activities, Direct Method) Comparative balance sheet accounts of Marcus Inc. are presented below.

MARCUS INC.
COMPARATIVE BALANCE SHEET ACCOUNTS
AS OF DECEMBER 31, 2010 AND 2009

	December 31	
Debit Accounts	2010	2009
Cash	$ 42,000	$ 33,750
Accounts Receivable	70,500	60,000
Merchandise Inventory	30,000	24,000
Investments (available-for-sale)	22,250	38,500
Machinery	30,000	18,750
Buildings	67,500	56,250
Land	7,500	7,500
	$269,750	$238,750
Credit Accounts		
Allowance for Doubtful Accounts	$ 2,250	$ 1,500
Accumulated Depreciation—Machinery	5,625	2,250
Accumulated Depreciation—Buildings	13,500	9,000
Accounts Payable	35,000	24,750
Accrued Payables	3,375	2,625
Long-Term Note Payable	21,000	31,000
Common Stock, no par	150,000	125,000
Retained Earnings	39,000	42,625
	$269,750	$238,750

Additional data (ignoring taxes):

1. Net income for the year was $42,500.
2. Cash dividends declared and paid during the year were $21,125.
3. A 20% stock dividend was declared during the year. $25,000 of retained earnings was capitalized.
4. Investments that cost $25,000 were sold during the year for $28,750.
5. Machinery that cost $3,750, on which $750 of depreciation had accumulated, was sold for $2,200.

Marcus's 2010 income statement follows (ignoring taxes).

Sales		$540,000
Less: Cost of goods sold		380,000
Gross margin		160,000
Less: Operating expenses (includes $8,625 depreciation and $5,400 bad debts)		120,450
Income from operations		39,550
Other: Gain on sale of investments	$3,750	
Loss on sale of machinery	(800)	2,950
Net income		$ 42,500

Instructions

(a) Compute net cash flow from operating activities using the direct method.
(b) Prepare a statement of cash flows using the indirect method.

 P23-7 (SCF—Direct and Indirect Methods from Comparative Financial Statements) Chapman Company, a major retailer of bicycles and accessories, operates several stores and is a publicly traded company. The comparative statement of financial position and income statement for Chapman as of May 31, 2010, are shown on the next page. The company is preparing its statement of cash flows.

CHAPMAN COMPANY
COMPARATIVE STATEMENT OF FINANCIAL POSITION
AS OF MAY 31

	2010	2009
Current assets		
Cash	$ 28,250	$ 20,000
Accounts receivable	75,000	58,000
Merchandise inventory	220,000	250,000
Prepaid expenses	9,000	7,000
Total current assets	332,250	335,000
Plant assets		
Plant assets	600,000	502,000
Less: Accumulated depreciation	150,000	125,000
Net plant assets	450,000	377,000
Total assets	$782,250	$712,000
Current liabilities		
Accounts payable	$123,000	$115,000
Salaries payable	47,250	72,000
Interest payable	27,000	25,000
Total current liabilities	197,250	212,000
Long-term debt		
Bonds payable	70,000	100,000
Total liabilities	267,250	312,000
Shareholders' equity		
Common stock, $10 par	370,000	280,000
Retained earnings	145,000	120,000
Total shareholders' equity	515,000	400,000
Total liabilities and shareholders' equity	$782,250	$712,000

CHAPMAN COMPANY
INCOME STATEMENT
FOR THE YEAR ENDED MAY 31, 2010

Sales	$1,255,250
Cost of merchandise sold	722,000
Gross profit	533,250
Expenses	
Salary expense	252,100
Interest expense	75,000
Other expenses	8,150
Depreciation expense	25,000
Total expenses	360,250
Operating income	173,000
Income tax expense	43,000
Net income	$ 130,000

The following is additional information concerning Chapman's transactions during the year ended May 31, 2010.

1. All sales during the year were made on account.
2. All merchandise was purchased on account, comprising the total accounts payable account.
3. Plant assets costing $98,000 were purchased by paying $28,000 in cash and issuing 7,000 shares of stock.
4. The "other expenses" are related to prepaid items.
5. All income taxes incurred during the year were paid during the year.
6. In order to supplement its cash, Chapman issued 2,000 shares of common stock at par value.
7. There were no penalties assessed for the retirement of bonds.
8. Cash dividends of $105,000 were declared and paid at the end of the fiscal year.

Instructions

(a) Compare and contrast the direct method and the indirect method for reporting cash flows from operating activities.

(b) Prepare a statement of cash flows for Chapman Company for the year ended May 31, 2010, using the direct method. Be sure to support the statement with appropriate calculations. (A reconciliation of net income to net cash provided is not required.)

(c) Using the indirect method, calculate only the net cash flow from operating activities for Chapman Company for the year ended May 31, 2010.

·6 ·7 ·8 P23-8 (SCF—Direct and Indirect Methods) Comparative balance sheet accounts of Sharpe Company are presented below.

SHARPE COMPANY
COMPARATIVE BALANCE SHEET ACCOUNTS
AS OF DECEMBER 31

Debit Balances	2010	2009
Cash	$ 70,000	$ 51,000
Accounts Receivable	155,000	130,000
Merchandise Inventory	75,000	61,000
Investments (Available-for-sale)	55,000	85,000
Equipment	70,000	48,000
Buildings	145,000	145,000
Land	40,000	25,000
Totals	$610,000	$545,000

Credit Balances		
Allowance for Doubtful Accounts	$ 10,000	$ 8,000
Accumulated Depreciation—Equipment	21,000	14,000
Accumulated Depreciation—Building	37,000	28,000
Accounts Payable	66,000	60,000
Income Taxes Payable	12,000	10,000
Long-Term Notes Payable	62,000	70,000
Common Stock	310,000	260,000
Retained Earnings	92,000	95,000
Totals	$610,000	$545,000

Additional data:

1. Equipment that cost $10,000 and was 60% depreciated was sold in 2010.
2. Cash dividends were declared and paid during the year.
3. Common stock was issued in exchange for land.
4. Investments that cost $35,000 were sold during the year.
5. There were no write-offs of uncollectible accounts during the year.

Sharpe's 2010 income statement is as follows.

Sales		$950,000
Less: Cost of goods sold		600,000
Gross profit		350,000
Less: Operating expenses (includes depreciation expense and bad debt expense)		250,000
Income from operations		100,000
Other revenues and expenses		
Gain on sale of investments	$15,000	
Loss on sale of equipment	(3,000)	12,000
Income before taxes		112,000
Income taxes		45,000
Net income		$ 67,000

Instructions

(a) Compute net cash provided by operating activities under the direct method.

(b) Prepare a statement of cash flows using the indirect method.

P23-9 (Indirect SCF) Dingel Corporation has contracted with you to prepare a statement of cash flows. The controller has provided the following information.

	December 31	
	2010	2009
Cash	$ 38,500	$13,000
Accounts receivable	12,250	10,000
Inventory	12,000	10,000
Investments	–0–	3,000
Building	–0–	29,750
Equipment	40,000	20,000
Copyright	5,000	5,250
Totals	$107,750	$91,000
Allowance for doubtful accounts	$ 3,000	$ 4,500
Accumulated depreciation on equipment	2,000	4,500
Accumulated depreciation on building	–0–	6,000
Accounts payable	5,000	4,000
Dividends payable	–0–	5,000
Notes payable, short-term (nontrade)	3,000	4,000
Long-term notes payable	36,000	25,000
Common stock	38,000	33,000
Retained earnings	20,750	5,000
	$107,750	$91,000

Additional data related to 2010 are as follows.

1. Equipment that had cost $11,000 and was 30% depreciated at time of disposal was sold for $2,500.
2. $5,000 of the long-term note payable was paid by issuing common stock.
3. Cash dividends paid were $5,000.
4. On January 1, 2010, the building was completely destroyed by a flood. Insurance proceeds on the building were $33,000 (net of $4,000 taxes).
5. Investments (available-for-sale) were sold at $1,500 above their cost. The company has made similar sales and investments in the past.
6. Cash and long-term note for $16,000 were given for the acquisition of equipment.
7. Interest of $2,000 and income taxes of $5,000 were paid in cash.

Instructions
(a) Use the indirect method to analyze the above information and prepare a statement of cash flows for Dingel. Flood damage is unusual and infrequent in that part of the country.
(b) What would you expect to observe in the operating, investing, and financing sections of a statement of cash flows of:
(1) A severely financially troubled firm?
(2) A recently formed firm that is experiencing rapid growth?

CONCEPTS FOR ANALYSIS

CA23-1 (Analysis of Improper SCF) The following statement was prepared by Maloney Corporation's accountant.

MALONEY CORPORATION
STATEMENT OF SOURCES AND APPLICATION OF CASH
FOR THE YEAR ENDED SEPTEMBER 30, 2010

Sources of cash	
Net income	$111,000
Depreciation and depletion	70,000
Increase in long-term debt	179,000
Changes in current receivables and inventories, less current liabilities (excluding current maturities of long-term debt)	14,000
	$374,000

Application of cash	
Cash dividends	$ 60,000
Expenditure for property, plant, and equipment	214,000
Investments and other uses	20,000
Change in cash	80,000
	$374,000

The following additional information relating to Maloney Corporation is available for the year ended September 30, 2010.

1. Wage and salary expense attributable to stock option plans was $25,000 for the year.

2. Expenditures for property, plant, and equipment $250,000
   Proceeds from retirements of property, plant, and equipment   36,000

   Net expenditures $214,000

3. A stock dividend of 10,000 shares of Maloney Corporation common stock was distributed to common stockholders on April 1, 2010, when the per share market price was $7 and par value was $1.

4. On July 1, 2010, when its market price was $6 per share, 16,000 shares of Maloney Corporation common stock were issued in exchange for 4,000 shares of preferred stock.

5. Depreciation expense $ 65,000
   Depletion expense   5,000

        $ 70,000

6. Increase in long-term debt $620,000
   Retirement of debt   441,000

   Net increase $179,000

Instructions

(a) In general, what are the objectives of a statement of the type shown above for Maloney Corporation? Explain.

(b) Identify the weaknesses in the form and format of Maloney Corporation's statement of cash flows without reference to the additional information. (Assume adoption of the indirect method.)

(c) For each of the six items of additional information for the statement of cash flows, indicate the preferable treatment and explain why the suggested treatment is preferable.

(AICPA adapted)

 CA23-2 **(SCF Theory and Analysis of Improper SCF)** Teresa Ramirez and Lenny Traylor are examining the following statement of cash flows for Pacific Clothing Store's first year of operations.

PACIFIC CLOTHING STORE
STATEMENT OF CASH FLOWS
FOR THE YEAR ENDED JANUARY 31, 2010

Sources of cash	
From sales of merchandise	$ 382,000
From sale of capital stock	380,000
From sale of investment	120,000
From depreciation	80,000
From issuance of note for truck	30,000
From interest on investments	8,000
Total sources of cash	1,000,000
Uses of cash	
For purchase of fixtures and equipment	330,000
For merchandise purchased for resale	253,000
For operating expenses (including depreciation)	170,000
For purchase of investment	95,000
For purchase of truck by issuance of note	30,000
For purchase of treasury stock	10,000
For interest on note	3,000
Total uses of cash	891,000
Net increase in cash	$ 109,000

Teresa claims that Pacific's statement of cash flows is an excellent portrayal of a superb first year, with cash increasing $109,000. Lenny replies that it was not a superb first year—that the year was an operating failure, the statement was incorrectly presented, and $109,000 is not the actual increase in cash.

Instructions

(a) With whom do you agree, Teresa or Lenny? Explain your position.

(b) Using the data provided, prepare a statement of cash flows in proper indirect method form. The only noncash items in income are depreciation and the gain from the sale of the investment (purchase and sale are related).

CA23-3 **(SCF Theory and Analysis of Transactions)** Ashley Company is a young and growing producer of electronic measuring instruments and technical equipment. You have been retained by Ashley to advise it in the preparation of a statement of cash flows using the indirect method. For the fiscal year ended October 31, 2010, you have obtained the following information concerning certain events and transactions of Ashley.

1. The amount of reported earnings for the fiscal year was $700,000, which included a deduction for an extraordinary loss of $110,000 (see item 5 below).
2. Depreciation expense of $315,000 was included in the income statement.
3. Uncollectible accounts receivable of $40,000 were written off against the allowance for doubtful accounts. Also, $51,000 of bad debt expense was included in determining income for the fiscal year, and the same amount was added to the allowance for doubtful accounts.
4. A gain of $6,000 was realized on the sale of a machine. It originally cost $75,000, of which $30,000 was undepreciated on the date of sale.
5. On April 1, 2010, lightning caused an uninsured building loss of $110,000 ($180,000 loss, less reduction in income taxes of $70,000). This extraordinary loss was included in determining income as indicated in 1 above.
6. On July 3, 2010, building and land were purchased for $700,000. Ashley gave in payment $75,000 cash, $200,000 market value of its unissued common stock, and signed a $425,000 mortgage note payable.
7. On August 3, 2010, $800,000 face value of Ashley's 10% convertible debentures was converted into $150,000 par value of its common stock. The bonds were originally issued at face value.

Instructions

Explain whether each of the seven numbered items above is a source or use of cash, and explain how it should be disclosed in Ashley's statement of cash flows for the fiscal year ended October 31, 2010. If any item is neither a source nor a use of cash, explain why it is not, and indicate the disclosure, if any, that should be made of the item in Ashley's statement of cash flows for the fiscal year ended October 31, 2010.

CA23-4 **(Analysis of Transactions' Effect on SCF)** Each of the following items must be considered in preparing a statement of cash flows for Cruz Fashions Inc. for the year ended December 31, 2010.

1. Fixed assets that had cost $20,000 6½ years before and were being depreciated on a 10-year basis, with no estimated scrap value, were sold for $4,750.
2. During the year, goodwill of $15,000 was considered impaired and was completely written off to expense.
3. During the year, 500 shares of common stock with a stated value of $25 a share were issued for $32 a share.
4. The company sustained a net loss for the year of $2,100. Depreciation amounted to $2,000 and patent amortization was $400.
5. Uncollectible accounts receivable in the amount of $2,000 were written off against the Allowance for Doubtful Accounts.
6. Investments (available-for-sale) that cost $12,000 when purchased 4 years earlier were sold for $10,600. The loss was considered ordinary.
7. Bonds payable with a par value of $24,000 on which there was an unamortized bond premium of $2,000 were redeemed at 101. The gain was credited to ordinary income.

Instructions

For each item, state where it is to be shown in the statement and then how you would present the necessary information, including the amount. Consider each item to be independent of the others. Assume that correct entries were made for all transactions as they took place.

CA23-5 **(Purpose and Elements of SCF)** GAAP requires the statement of cash flows be presented when financial statements are prepared.

Instructions

(a) Explain the purposes of the statement of cash flows.

(b) List and describe the three categories of activities that must be reported in the statement of cash flows.

(c) Identify and describe the two methods that are allowed for reporting cash flows from operations.

(d) Describe the financial statement presentation of noncash investing and financing transactions. Include in your description an example of a noncash investing and financing transaction.

CA23-6 **(Cash Flow Reporting)** Brockman Guitar Company is in the business of manufacturing top-quality, steel-string folk guitars. In recent years the company has experienced working capital problems resulting from the procurement of factory equipment, the unanticipated buildup of receivables and inventories, and the payoff of a balloon mortgage on a new manufacturing facility. The founder and president of the company, Barbara Brockman, has attempted to raise cash from various financial institutions, but to no avail because of the company's poor performance in recent years. In particular, the company's lead bank, First Financial, is especially concerned about Brockman's inability to maintain a positive cash position. The commercial loan officer from First Financial told Barbara, "I can't even consider your request for capital financing unless I see that your company is able to generate positive cash flows from operations."

Thinking about the banker's comment, Barbara came up with what she believes is a good plan: With a more attractive statement of cash flows, the bank might be willing to provide long-term financing. To "window dress" cash flows, the company can sell its accounts receivables to factors and liquidate its raw materials inventories. These rather costly transactions would generate lots of cash. As the chief accountant for Brockman Guitar, it is your job to tell Barbara what you think of her plan.

Instructions
Answer the following questions.

   (a) What are the ethical issues related to Barbara Brockman's idea?
   (b) What would you tell Barbara Brockman?

USING YOUR JUDGMENT

FINANCIAL REPORTING

Financial Reporting Problem

P&G The Procter & Gamble Company (P&G)

The financial statements of **P&G** are presented in Appendix 5B or can be accessed at the book's companion website, **www.wiley.com/college/kieso.**

Instructions

Refer to P&G's financial statements and the accompanying notes to answer the following questions.

   (a) Which method of computing net cash provided by operating activities does P&G use? What were the amounts of net cash provided by operating activities for the years 2005, 2006, and 2007? Which two items were most responsible for the increase in net cash provided by operating activities in 2007?

   (b) What was the most significant item in the cash flows used for investing activities section in 2007? What was the most significant item in the cash flows used for financing activities section in 2007?

   (c) Where is "deferred income taxes" reported in P&G's statement of cash flows? Why does it appear in that section of the statement of cash flows?

   (d) Where is depreciation reported in P&G's statement of cash flows? Why is depreciation added to net income in the statement of cash flows?

Comparative Analysis Case

The Coca-Cola Company and PepsiCo, Inc.

Instructions

Go to the book's companion website and use information found there to answer the following questions related to **The Coca-Cola Company** and **PepsiCo, Inc.**

   (a) What method of computing net cash provided by operating activities does Coca-Cola use? What method does PepsiCo use? What were the amounts of cash provided by operating activities reported by Coca-Cola and PepsiCo in 2007?

   (b) What was the most significant item reported by Coca-Cola and PepsiCo in 2007 in their investing activities sections? What is the most significant item reported by Coca-Cola and PepsiCo in 2007 in their financing activities sections?

   (c) What were these two companies' trends in net cash provided by operating activities over the period 2005 to 2007?

(d) Where is "depreciation and amortization" reported by Coca-Cola and PepsiCo in their statements of cash flows? What is the amount and why does it appear in that section of the statement of cash flows?

(e) Based on the information contained in Coca-Cola's and PepsiCo's financial statements, compute the following 2007 ratios for each company. These ratios require the use of statement of cash flows data. (These ratios were covered in Chapter 5.)

    (1) Current cash debt coverage ratio.

    (2) Cash debt coverage ratio.

(f) What conclusions concerning the management of cash can be drawn from the ratios computed in (e)?

Financial Statement Analysis Case

Vermont Teddy Bear Co.

Founded in the early 1980s, the **Vermont Teddy Bear Co.** designs and manufactures American-made teddy bears and markets them primarily as gifts called Bear-Grams or Teddy Bear-Grams. Bear-Grams are personalized teddy bears delivered directly to the recipient for special occasions such as birthdays and anniversaries. The Shelburne, Vermont, company's primary markets are New York, Boston, and Chicago. Sales have jumped dramatically in recent years. Such dramatic growth has significant implications for cash flows. Provided below are the cash flow statements for two recent years for the company.

	Current Year	Prior Year
Cash flows from operating activities:		
Net income	$ 17,523	$ 838,955
Adjustments to reconcile net income to net cash provided by operating activities		
Deferred income taxes	(69,524)	(146,590)
Depreciation and amortization	316,416	181,348
Changes in assets and liabilities:		
Accounts receivable, trade	(38,267)	(25,947)
Inventories	(1,599,014)	(1,289,293)
Prepaid and other current assets	(444,794)	(113,205)
Deposits and other assets	(24,240)	(83,044)
Accounts payable	2,017,059	(284,567)
Accrued expenses	61,321	170,755
Accrued interest payable, debentures	—	(58,219)
Other	—	(8,960)
Income taxes payable	—	117,810
Net cash provided by (used for) operating activities	236,480	(700,957)
Net cash used for investing activities	(2,102,892)	(4,422,953)
Net cash (used for) provided by financing activities	(315,353)	9,685,435
Net change in cash and cash equivalents	(2,181,765)	4,561,525

Other information:

Current liabilities	$ 4,055,465	$ 1,995,600
Total liabilities	4,620,085	2,184,386
Net sales	20,560,566	17,025,856

Instructions

(a) Note that net income in the current year was only $17,523 compared to prior-year income of $838,955, but cash flow from operations was $236,480 in the current year and a negative $700,957 in the prior year. Explain the causes of this apparent paradox.

(b) Evaluate Vermont Teddy Bear's liquidity, solvency, and profitability for the current year using cash flow-based ratios.

International Reporting Case

As noted in the chapter, there is international diversity in the preparation of the statement of cash flows. For example, under International Accounting Standards companies may choose how to classify dividends and interest in the cash flow statement. In some countries, like Brazil, a cash flow statement is not required. **Embraer**, a Brazilian aircraft manufacturer, prepared a statement of changes in financial position, rather than a statement of cash flows.

Instructions

Refer to Embraer's recent statement of changes in financial position below, to answer the following questions.

(a) Briefly discuss at least two similarities between Embraer's statement of changes in financial position and a statement of cash flows prepared according to U.S. GAAP.

(b) Briefly discuss at least two differences between Embraer's statement of changes in financial position and a statement of cash flows prepared according to U.S. GAAP.

Embraer
Consolidated Statement of Changes in Financial Position
(in thousands of Brazilian reals)

Sources of Funds	
Provided from operations	
Net income	1,255,833
Items not affecting working capital	
Equity in unconsolidated subsidiary	
Translation losses on foreign investments	19,613
Minority interest	8,618
Depreciation and amortization	221,554
Net book value of permanent asset disposal	799
Interest on long-term items added to principal, net	(25,759)
Net monetary and exchange variations on long-term items	(201,030)
Provision for losses	34,268
Long-term deferred income and social contribution taxes	(47,765)
Provisions for contingencies	57,930
Funds provided from operations	1,324,061
From shareholders	
Capital increase	9,524
From third parties	
Increase in long-term liabilities	
Customers' advances	257,528
Loans	1,317,535
Accounts payable and other liabilities	964,260
Tax incentives	5,672
Transfers to current asset	1,042,182
Increase in minority interest	17,997
Funds provided from third parties	3,605,174
Total sources	4,938,759
Applications of Funds	
Increase in noncurrent assets	1,390,520
Investments	41,219
Property plant and equipment	109,656
Deferred charges	415,954
Transfers to current liabilities	731,098
Interest on capital	585,173
Total applications	3,273,620
Increase in working capital	1,665,139
Working capital—end of year	
Current assets	10,329,032
Current liabilities	5,420,966
	4,908,066
Working capital—beginning of year	3,242,927
Increase in working capital	1,665,139

BRIDGE TO THE PROFESSION

Professional Research: FASB Codification

As part of the year-end accounting process for your company, you are preparing the statement of cash flows according to GAAP. One of your team, a finance major, believes the statement should be prepared to report the change in working capital, because analysts many times use working capital in ratio analysis. Your supervisor would like research conducted to verify the basis for preparing the statement of cash flows.

Instructions

Access the FASB Codification at *http://asc.fasb.org/home* to conduct research using the Codification Research System to prepare responses to the following items. Provide Codification references for your responses.

(a) What is the primary objective for the statement of cash flows? Is working capital the basis for meeting this objective?

(b) What information is provided in a statement of cash flows?

(c) List some of the typical cash inflows and outflows from operations.

Professional Simulation

Go to the book's companion website, at **www.wiley.com/college/kieso,** to find an interactive problem that simulates the computerized CPA exam. The professional simulation for this chapter asks you to address questions related to the accounting for the statement of cash flows.

Remember to check the book's companion website to find additional resources for this chapter.

CHAPTER 24

FULL DISCLOSURE IN FINANCIAL REPORTING

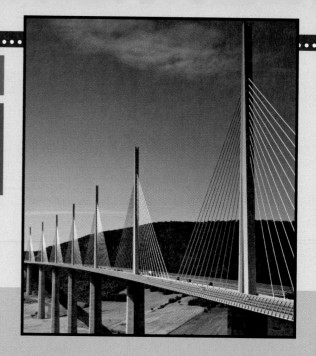

LEARNING OBJECTIVES

After studying this chapter, you should be able to:

- **•1** Review the full disclosure principle and describe implementation problems.
- **•2** Explain the use of notes in financial statement preparation.
- **•3** Discuss the disclosure requirements for major business segments.
- **•4** Describe the accounting problems associated with interim reporting.
- **•5** Identify the major disclosures in the auditor's report.
- **•6** Understand management's responsibilities for financials.
- **•7** Identify issues related to financial forecasts and projections.
- **•8** Describe the profession's response to fraudulent financial reporting.

HIGH-QUALITY FINANCIAL REPORTING—ALWAYS IN FASHION

Here are excerpts from leading experts regarding the importance of high-quality financial reporting:

Warren E. Buffett, Chairman and Chief Executive Officer, **Berkshire Hathaway Inc.**:

Financial reporting for Berkshire Hathaway, and for me personally, is the beginning of every decision that we make around here in terms of capital. I'm punching out 10-Ks and 10-Qs every single day. We look at the numbers and try to evaluate the quality of the financial reporting, and then we try to figure out what that means for the bonds and stocks that we're looking at, and thinking of either buying or selling.

Judy Lewent, Executive Vice President and Chief Financial Officer, **Merck & Co., Inc.**

. . . Higher standards, when properly implemented, drive excellence. I can make a parallel to the pharmaceutical industry. If you look around the world at where innovations come from, economists have studied and seen that where regulatory standards are the highest is where innovation is also the highest.

Floyd Norris, Chief Financial Correspondent, the **New York Times**:

We are in a situation now in our society where the temptations to provide "bad" financial reporting are probably greater than they used to be. The need to get the stock price up, or to keep it up, is intense. So, the temptation to play games, the temptation to manage earnings—some of which can be legitimate and some of which cannot be—is probably greater than it used to be.

Abby Joseph Cohen, Chair, Investment Policy Committee, **Goldman, Sachs & Co.**:

High-quality financial reporting is perhaps the most important thing we can expect from companies. For investors to make good decisions—whether those investors are buying stocks or bonds or making private investments—they need to know the truth. And we think that when information is as clear as possible and is reported as frequently as makes sense, investors can do their jobs as best they can.

We can also get insight into the importance of high-quality reporting based on the market assessment of companies perceived to have poor-quality reporting. In a recent quarter, **Coach, Inc.** stopped reporting as separate items sales from regular stores (full price) and factory outlets. As a result, readers of its financial statements have a hard time determining the source of Coach's sales growth. Analysts are especially concerned that the less-transparent reporting may obscure slowing sales at its regular stores, as consumers cut down on luxury goods in the sluggish economy. Did Coach's stock price suffer as a result of this lower-quality reporting? You bet, as shown in the price graph on the right.

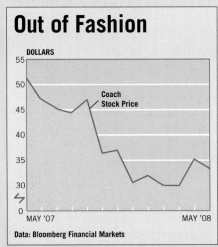

Since the change in reporting in 2007, Coach's stock price has been down 34 percent. As one analyst noted, "It's never a good sign when you reduce transparency . . . It's a sign of weakness."

In short, the analysts' comments above illustrate why high-quality reporting is always in fashion—for companies, investors, and the capital markets. And, as the Coach example illustrates, full disclosure is at the heart of high-quality reporting.

Sources: Excerpts taken from video entitled "Financially Correct with Ben Stein," Financial Accounting Standards Board (Norwalk, Conn.: FASB, 2002). By permission. See also J. Porter, "As Belts Tighten, Coach Feels the Pinch," *BusinessWeek* (May 29, 2008), p. 66.

PREVIEW OF CHAPTER 24

As the opening story indicates, our markets will not function properly without transparent, complete, and truthful reporting of financial performance. Investors and other interested parties need to read and understand all aspects of financial reporting—the financial statements, the notes, the president's letter, and management's discussion and analysis. In this chapter, we cover the full disclosure principle in more detail and examine disclosures that must accompany financial statements so that they are not misleading. The content and organization of this chapter are as follows.

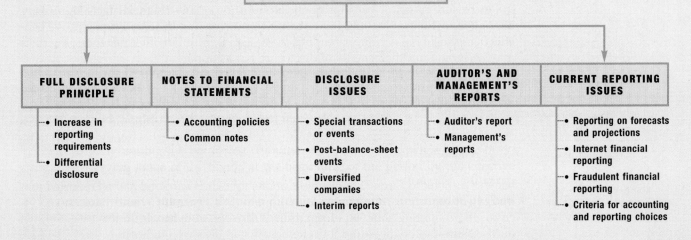

FULL DISCLOSURE PRINCIPLE

FASB Concepts Statement No. 1 notes that some useful information is best provided in the financial statements, and some is best provided by means other than in financial statements. For example, earnings and cash flows are readily available in financial statements—but investors might do better to look at comparisons to other companies in the same industry, found in news articles or brokerage house reports.

Objective·1
Review the full disclosure principle and describe implementation problems.

FASB rules directly affect financial statements, notes to the financial statements, and supplementary information. Other types of information found in the annual report, such as management's discussion and analysis, are not subject to FASB rules. Illustration 24-1 indicates the various types of financial information.

All Information Useful for Investment, Credit, and Similar Decisions				
Financial Reporting				
Area Directly Affected by Existing FASB Rules				
Basic Financial Statements				
Financial Statements	**Notes to the Financial Statements**	**Supplementary Information**	**Other Means of Financial Reporting**	**Other Information**
• Balance Sheet • Income Statement • Statement of Cash Flows • Statement of Changes in Stockholders' Equity	Examples: • Accounting Policies • Contingencies • Inventory Methods • Number of Shares of Stock Outstanding • Alternative Measures (fair values of items carried at historical cost)	Examples: • Changing Prices Disclosures • Oil and Gas Reserves Information	Examples: • Management's Discussion and Analysis • Letters to Stockholders	Examples: • Discussion of Competition and Order Backlog in SEC Forms • Analysts' Reports • Economic Statistics • News Articles about Company

ILLUSTRATION 24-1
Types of Financial Information

As Chapter 2 indicated, the profession has adopted a **full disclosure principle**. The full disclosure principle calls for financial reporting of **any financial facts significant enough to influence the judgment of an informed reader**. In some situations, the benefits of disclosure may be apparent but the costs uncertain. In other instances, the costs may be certain but the benefits of disclosure not as apparent.

Underlying Concepts

Here is a good example of the trade-off between cost considerations and the benefits of full disclosure.

For example, recently, the SEC required companies to provide expanded disclosures about their contractual obligations. In light of the off-balance-sheet accounting frauds at companies like **Enron**, the benefits of these expanded disclosures seem fairly obvious to the investing public. While no one has documented the exact costs of disclosure in these situations, they would appear to be relatively small.

On the other hand, the cost of disclosure can be substantial in some cases and the benefits difficult to assess. For example, at one time the *Wall Street Journal* reported that if segment reporting were adopted, a company like **Fruehauf** would have had to increase its accounting staff 50 percent, from 300 to 450 individuals. In this case, the cost of disclosure can be measured, but the benefits are less well defined.

Some even argue that the reporting requirements are so detailed and substantial that users have a difficult time absorbing the information. These critics charge the profession with engaging in **information overload**.

Financial disasters at **Microstrategy**, **PharMor**, **WorldCom**, and **AIG** highlight the difficulty of implementing the full disclosure principle. They raise the issue of why investors were not aware of potential problems: Was the information these companies presented not comprehensible? Was it buried? Was it too technical? Was it properly presented and fully disclosed as of the financial statement date, but the situation later deteriorated? Or was it simply not there? In the following sections, we describe the elements of high-quality disclosure that will enable companies to avoid these disclosure pitfalls.

Underlying Concepts

The AICPA's Special Committee on Financial Reporting notes that business reporting is not free, and improving it requires considering the relative costs and benefits of information. Undisciplined expansion of mandated reporting could result in large and needless costs.

Increase in Reporting Requirements

Disclosure requirements have increased substantially. One survey showed that the size of many companies' annual reports is growing in response to demands for increased transparency. For example, annual report page counts ranged from 70 pages for **Gateway** up to a whopping 244 pages in **Eastman Kodak**'s annual report. Compared to prior years' reports, the percentage increase in pages ranged from 17 percent at **IBM** to over 80 percent at **Siebel Systems**.[1] This result is not surprising; as illustrated throughout this textbook, the FASB has issued many pronouncements in the last 10 years that have substantial disclosure provisions.

The reasons for this increase in disclosure requirements are varied. Some of them are:

Complexity of the Business Environment. The increasing complexity of business operations magnifies the difficulty of distilling economic events into summarized reports. Such areas as derivatives, leasing, business combinations, pensions, financing arrangements, revenue recognition, and deferred taxes are complex. As a result, companies extensively use **notes to the financial statements** to explain these transactions and their future effects.

Underlying Concepts

The AICPA's Special Committee on Financial Reporting states that to meet users' changing needs, business reporting must: (1) Provide more forward-looking information. (2) Focus more on the factors that create longer-term value, including nonfinancial measures. (3) Better align information reported externally with the information reported internally.

Necessity for Timely Information. Today, more than ever before, users are demanding information that is current and predictive. For example, users want more complete **interim data**. Also, the SEC recommends published financial forecasts, long avoided and even feared by management.

Accounting as a Control and Monitoring Device. The government has recently sought public disclosure of such phenomena as management compensation, off-balance-sheet financing arrangements, and related party transactions. An "Enronitis" concern is expressed in many of these newer disclosure requirements, and the SEC has selected accountants and auditors as the agents to assist in controlling and monitoring these concerns.

Differential Disclosure

A trend toward **differential disclosure** is also occurring. For example, the SEC requires that companies report to it certain substantive information that is not found in annual reports to stockholders. Likewise, the FASB, recognizing that certain disclosure requirements are costly and unnecessary for certain companies, has eliminated reporting requirements for nonpublic enterprises in such areas as fair value of financial instruments and segment reporting.[2]

[1]Aliya Sternstein, "Heavy Lifting Required," *Forbes* (October 13, 2003) p. 58.

[2]The FASB has had a disclosure-effectiveness project. The revised pension and postretirement benefit disclosures discussed in Chapter 20 are one example of how disclosures can be streamlined and made more useful. However, as noted by one FASB member, the usefulness of expanded required disclosure also depends on users' ability to distinguish between disclosed versus recognized items in financial statements. Research to date is inconclusive on this matter. See Katherine Schipper, "Required Disclosures in Financial Reports," Presidential Address to the American Accounting Association Annual Meeting; San Francisco, CA (August 2005).

"THE HEART OF THE MATTER"

What do the numbers mean?

As we discussed in the opening story, financial disclosure is one of a number of institutional features that contribute to vibrant security markets. In fact, a recent study of disclosure and other mechanisms (such as civil lawsuits and criminal sanctions) found that good disclosure is the most important contributor to a vibrant market.

The study, which compared disclosure and other legal and regulatory elements across 49 countries, found that countries with the best disclosure laws have the biggest stock markets. Countries with more successful market environments also tend to have regulations that make it relatively easy for private investors to sue corporations that provide bad information. That is, while criminal sanctions can be effective in some circumstances, disclosure and other legal and regulatory elements encouraging good disclosure are the most important determinants of highly liquid and deep securities markets.

These findings hold for nations in all stages of economic development, with particular importance for nations that are in the early stages of securities regulation. The lesson: Disclosure is good for your market.

Source: Rebecca Christie, "Study: Disclosure at Heart of Effective Securities Laws," *Wall Street Journal Online* (August 11, 2003).

Underlying Concepts

The AICPA Special Committee on Financial Reporting indicated that users differ in their needs for information and that not all companies should report all elements of information. Rather, companies should report only information that users and preparers agree is needed in the particular circumstances.

Objective·2

Explain the use of notes in financial statement preparation.

Some still complain that the FASB has not gone far enough. They note that certain types of companies (small or nonpublic) should not have to follow complex GAAP requirements such as those for deferred income taxes, leases, or pensions. This issue, often referred to as "**big GAAP versus little GAAP**," continues to be controversial. The FASB takes the position that there should be one set of GAAP, except in unusual situations.[3]

NOTES TO THE FINANCIAL STATEMENTS

As you know from your study of this textbook, notes are an integral part of the financial statements of a business enterprise. However, readers of financial statements often overlook them because they are highly technical and often appear in small print. **Notes are the means of amplifying or explaining the items presented in the main body of the statements.** They can explain in qualitative terms information pertinent to specific financial statement items. In addition, they can provide supplementary data of a quantitative nature to expand the information in the financial statements. Notes also can explain restrictions imposed by financial arrangements or basic contractual agreements. Although notes may be technical and difficult to understand, they provide meaningful information for the user of the financial statements.

Accounting Policies

Accounting policies are the specific accounting principles and methods a company currently uses and considers most appropriate to present fairly its financial statements. GAAP

---

[3]In response to cost-benefit concerns, the SEC has exempted some small public companies from certain rules implemented in response to the Sarbanes-Oxley Act of 2002. For example, smaller companies have more time to comply with the internal control rules required by the Sarbanes-Oxley law and have more time to file annual and interim reports. Both the FASB and the AICPA are studying the big GAAP/little GAAP issue to ensure that any kind of differential reporting is conceptually sound and meets the needs of users. See Remarks of Robert H. Herz, Chairman, Financial Accounting Standards Board, 2004 AICPA National Conference on Current SEC and PCAOB Reporting Developments (December 7, 2004).

states that information about the accounting policies adopted by a reporting entity is essential for financial statement users in making economic decisions. It recommended that companies should present **as an integral part of the financial statements a statement identifying the accounting policies adopted and followed by the reporting entity**. Companies should present the disclosure as the first note or in a separate Summary of Significant Accounting Policies section preceding the notes to the financial statements.

The Summary of Significant Accounting Policies answers such questions as: What method of depreciation is used on plant assets? What valuation method is employed on inventories? What amortization policy is followed in regard to intangible assets? How are marketing costs handled for financial reporting purposes?

Refer to Appendix 5B, pages 210–238, for an illustration of note disclosure of accounting policies (Note 1) and other notes accompanying the audited financial statements of **The Procter & Gamble Company**. Illustration 24-2 shows another example, from **Tootsie Roll Industries**.

INTERNATIONAL INSIGHT

iGAAP has a project that is considering different accounting rules for small- and medium-sized enterprises.

ILLUSTRATION 24-2
Note Disclosure of Accounting Policies

Tootsie Roll Industries, Inc. and Subsidiaries
(Dollars in thousands, except per share amounts)

Note 1—Significant Accounting Policies (in part)

Basis of consolidation

The consolidated financial statements include the accounts of Tootsie Roll Industries, Inc. and its wholly-owned subsidiaries (the Company), which are primarily engaged in the manufacture and sale of candy products. All significant intercompany transactions have been eliminated.

The preparation of financial statements in conformity with generally accepted accounting principles in the United States of America requires management to make estimates and assumptions that affect the reported amounts of assets and liabilities and disclosure of contingent assets and liabilities at the date of the financial statements and the reported amounts of revenues and expense during the reporting period. Actual results could differ from those estimates.

Certain reclassifications have been made to the prior year financial statements to conform to the current year presentation.

Revenue recognition

Products are sold to customers based on accepted purchase orders which include quantity, sales price and other relevant term of sale. Revenue, net of applicable provisions for discounts, returns, allowances, and certain advertising and promotional costs, is recognized when products are delivered to customers and collectibility is reasonably assured. Shipping and handling costs of $41,775, $40,353 and $37,836 in 2007, 2006 and 2005, respectively, are included in selling, marketing and administrative expenses. Accounts receivable are unsecured. Revenues from a major customer aggregated approximately 22.4%, 23.7% and 24.0% of net product sales during the years ended December 31, 2007, 2006 and 2005, respectively. . . .

Cash and cash equivalents

The Company considers temporary cash investments with an original maturity of three months or less to be cash equivalents.

Investments

Investments consist of various marketable securities with maturities of generally up to four years. The Company classifies debt and equity securities as either available for sale or trading. Available for sale are not actively traded and are carried at fair value. Unrealized gains and losses on these securities are excluded from earnings and are reported as a separate component of shareholders' equity, net of applicable taxes, until realized. Trading securities relate to deferred compensation arrangements and are carried at fair value. The Company invests in trading securities to hedge changes in its deferred compensation liabilities.

Hedging activities

From time to time, the Company enters into commodities futures contracts that are intended and effective as hedges of market price risks associated with the anticipated purchase of certain raw materials (primarily sugar). To qualify as a hedge, the Company evaluates a variety of characteristics of these transactions, including the probability that the anticipated transaction will occur. If the anticipated transaction were not to occur, the gain or loss would then be recognized in current earnings. The Company does not engage in trading or other speculative use of derivative instruments. The Company does assume the risk that counter parties may not be able to meet the terms of their contracts. The Company does not expect any losses as a result of counter party defaults.

The Company's commodities futures contracts are being accounted for as cash flow hedges and are recorded on the balance sheet at fair value. Changes therein are recorded in other comprehensive earnings and are reclassified to earnings in the periods in which earnings are affected by the hedged item. Substantially all amounts reported in accumulated other comprehensive earnings (loss) are expected to be reclassified to cost of goods sold.

Inventories

Inventories are stated at cost, not to exceed market. The cost of substantially all of the Company's inventories ($54,367 and $61,092 at December 31, 2007 and 2006, respectively) has been determined by the last-in, first-out (LIFO) method. The excess of current cost over LIFO cost of inventories approximates $11,284 and $7,350 at December 31, 2007 and 2006, respectively. The cost of certain foreign inventories ($3,036 and $2,865 at December 31, 2007 and 2006, respectively) has been determined by the first-in, first-out (FIFO) method. Rebates, discounts and other cash consideration received from a vendor related to inventory purchases is reflected as a reduction in the cost of the related inventory item, and is therefore reflected in cost of sales when the related inventory item is sold.

Property, plant and equipment

Depreciation is computed for financial reporting purposes by use of the straight-line method based on useful lives of 20 to 35 years for buildings and 5 to 20 years for machinery and equipment. Depreciation expense was $15,859, $15,816, and $14,687 in 2007, 2006 and 2005, respectively.

Carrying value of long-lived assets

The Company reviews long-lived assets to determine if there are events or circumstances indicating that the amount of the asset reflected in the Company's balance sheet may not be recoverable. When such indicators are present, the Company compares the carrying value of the long-lived asset, or asset group, to the future undiscounted cash flows of the underlying assets to determine if an impairment exists. If applicable, an impairment charge would be recorded to write down the carrying value to its fair value. The determination of fair value involves the use of estimates of future cash flows that involve considerable management judgment and are based upon assumptions about expected future operating performance. The actual cash flows could differ from management's estimates due to changes in business conditions, operating performance, and economic conditions. No impairment charges were recorded by the Company during 2007, 2006 or 2005.

Postretirement health care and life insurance benefits

The Company provides certain postretirement health care and life insurance benefits. The cost of these postretirement benefits is accrued during employees' working careers. The Company also provides split dollar life insurance benefits to certain executive officers. The Company records an asset equal to the cumulative insurance premiums that will be recovered upon the death of a covered employee(s) or earlier under the terms of the plan. Split dollar premiums paid were $1,586, $3,002, and $3,678 in 2007, 2006 and 2005, respectively.

Goodwill and intangible assets

The Company accounts for intangible assets in accordance with SFAS No. 142, "Goodwill and Other Intangible Assets." In accordance with this statement, goodwill and intangible assets with indefinite lives are not amortized, but rather tested for impairment at least annually. All trademarks have been assessed by management to have indefinite lives because they are expected to generate cash flows indefinitely. The Company has completed its annual impairment testing of its goodwill and trademarks during the fourth quarter of each of the years presented, and recorded an impairment of $4,743 in the fourth quarter of 2005 relating to a minor trademark and related goodwill. No impairments were recorded in either 2007 or 2006.

Income taxes

Deferred income taxes are recorded and recognized for future tax effects of temporary differences between financial and income tax reporting. The Company records valuation allowances in situations where the realization of deferred tax assets is not likely. Federal income taxes are provided on the portion of income of foreign subsidiaries that is expected to be remitted to the U.S. and become taxable, but not on the portion that is considered to be permanently invested in the foreign subsidiary.

Foreign currency translation

The Company has determined the functional currency for each foreign subsidiary. The U.S. dollar is used as the functional currency where a substantial portion of the subsidiary's business is indexed to the U.S. dollar or where its manufactured products are principally sold in the U.S. All other foreign subsidiaries use the local currency as their functional currency. Where the U.S. dollar is used as the functional currency, foreign currency translation adjustments are recorded as a charge or credit to other income in the statement of earnings. Where the foreign currency is used as the functional currency, translation adjustments are recorded as a separate component of comprehensive earnings (loss).

Joint venture

The Company's 50% interest in two companies is accounted for using the equity method. The Company records an increase in its investment in the joint venture to the extent of its share of the joint venture's earnings, and reduces its investment to the extent of dividends received. Dividends of $861, $1,946 and

$651 were paid in 2007, 2006 and 2005, respectively, by the joint venture. The $1,946 dividend declared in 2006 was not received by the Company until after December 31, 2006; this amount is included in other receivables at December 31, 2006.

Comprehensive earnings
Comprehensive earnings includes net earnings, foreign currency translation adjustments and unrealized gains/losses on commodity hedging contracts, available for sale securities and certain postretirement benefit obligations.

Earnings per share
A dual presentation of basic and diluted earnings per share is not required due to the lack of potentially dilutive securities under the Company's simple capital structure. Therefore, all earnings per share amounts represent basic earnings per share.

Analysts examine carefully the summary of accounting policies to determine whether a company is using conservative or liberal accounting practices. For example, depreciating plant assets over an unusually long period of time is considered liberal. Using LIFO inventory valuation in a period of inflation is generally viewed as conservative.

Companies that fail to adopt high-quality reporting policies may be heavily penalized by the market. For example, when **Microstrategy** disclosed that it would restate prior-year results due to use of aggressive revenue recognition policies, its share price dropped over 60 percent in one day. Investors viewed Microstrategy's quality of earnings as low.

Common Notes

We have discussed many of the **notes to the financial statements** throughout this textbook, and will discuss others more fully in this chapter. The more common are as follows.

MAJOR DISCLOSURES

INVENTORY. Companies should report the basis upon which inventory amounts are stated (lower-of-cost-or-market) and the method used in determining cost (LIFO, FIFO, average cost, etc.). Manufacturers should report, either in the balance sheet or in a separate schedule in the notes, the inventory composition (finished goods, work in process, raw materials). Unusual or significant financing arrangements relating to inventories that may require disclosure include transactions with related parties, product financing arrangements, firm purchase commitments, involuntary liquidation of LIFO inventories, and pledging of inventories as collateral. Chapter 9 (pages 457–459) illustrates these disclosures.

PROPERTY, PLANT, AND EQUIPMENT. Companies should state the basis of valuation for property, plant, and equipment. It is usually historical cost. Companies also should disclose pledges, liens, and other commitments related to these assets. In the presentation of depreciation, companies should disclose the following in the financial statements or in the notes: (1) depreciation expense for the period; (2) balances of major classes of depreciable assets, by nature and function, at the balance sheet date; (3) accumulated depreciation, either by major classes of depreciable assets or in total, at the balance sheet date; and (4) a general description of the method or methods used in computing depreciation with respect to major classes of depreciable assets. Finally, companies should explain any major impairments. Chapter 11 (pages 559–560) illustrates these disclosures.

CREDITOR CLAIMS. Investors normally find it extremely useful to understand the nature and cost of creditor claims. However, the liabilities section in the balance sheet can provide the major types of liabilities only in the aggregate. Note schedules regarding such obligations provide additional information about how a company is financing its operations, the costs that it will bear in future periods, and the timing of future cash outflows. Financial statements must disclose for each of the five years following the date of the statements the aggregate amount of maturities and sinking fund requirements for all long-term borrowings. Chapter 14 (pages 711–712) illustrates these disclosures.

EQUITY HOLDERS' CLAIMS. Many companies present in the body of the balance sheet information about equity securities: the number of shares authorized, issued, and outstanding and the par value for each type of security. Or, companies may present such data in a note. Beyond that, a common equity note disclosure relates to contracts and senior securities outstanding that might affect the various claims of the residual equity holders. An example would be the existence of outstanding stock options, outstanding convertible debt, redeemable preferred stock, and convertible preferred stock. In addition, it is necessary to disclose certain types of restrictions currently in force. Generally, these types of restrictions involve the amount of earnings available for dividend distribution. Examples of these types of disclosures are illustrated in Chapter 15 (pages 765–766) and Chapter 16 (pages 821–822).

CONTINGENCIES AND COMMITMENTS. A company may have gain or loss contingencies that are not disclosed in the body of the financial statements. These contingencies include litigation, debt and other guarantees, possible tax assessments, renegotiation of government contracts, and sales of receivables with recourse. In addition, companies should disclose in the notes commitments that relate to dividend restrictions, purchase agreements (through-put and take-or-pay), hedge contracts, and employment contracts. Disclosures of such items are illustrated in Chapter 7 (page 343), Chapter 9 (pages 446–447), and Chapter 13 (pages 662–665).

FAIR VALUES. Companies that have assets or liabilities measured at fair value must disclose both the cost and the fair value of all financial instruments in the notes to the financial statements. Fair value measurements may be used for many financial assets and liabilities, investments, impairments of long-lived assets, and some contingencies. Companies also provide disclosure of information that enables users to determine the extent of usage of fair value and the inputs used to implement fair value measurement. This fair value hierarchy identifies three broad levels related to the measurement of fair values (Levels 1, 2, and 3). The levels indicate the reliability of the measurement of fair value information. An appendix to Chapter 17 (pages 905–908) discusses in detail fair value disclosures.

Underlying Concepts

The AICPA Special Committee on Financial Reporting notes that standard-setters should address disclosures and accounting requirements for off-balance-sheet financial arrangements. The goal should be to report the risks, opportunities, resources, and obligations that result from those arrangements, consistent with users' needs for information.

DEFERRED TAXES, PENSIONS, AND LEASES. The FASB also requires extensive disclosure in the areas of deferred taxes, pensions, and leases. Chapter 19 (pages 1011–1015), Chapter 20 (pages 1069–1074), and Chapter 21 (pages 1146–1148) discuss in detail each of these disclosures. Users of financial statements should carefully read notes to the financial statements for information about off-balance-sheet commitments, future financing needs, and the quality of a company's earnings.

CHANGES IN ACCOUNTING PRINCIPLES. The profession defines various types of accounting changes and establishes guides for reporting each type. Companies discuss, either in the summary of significant accounting policies or in the other notes, changes in accounting principles (as well as material changes in estimates and corrections of errors). See Chapter 22 (pages 1191–1196).

In earlier chapters we discussed the disclosures listed above. The following sections of this chapter illustrate four additional disclosures of significance—special transactions or events, subsequent events, segment reporting, and interim reporting.

Additional Examples of Major Disclosures

FOOTNOTE SECRETS

What do the numbers mean?

Often, note disclosures are needed to give a complete picture of a company's financial position. A good example of such disclosures is the required disclosure of debt triggers that may be buried in financing arrangements. These triggers can require a company to pay off a loan immediately if the debt rating collapses; they are one of the reasons **Enron** crumbled so quickly. But few Enron stockholders knew about the debt triggers until the gun had gone off. Companies are also disclosing more about their bank credit lines, liquidity, and any special purpose entities. (The latter were major villains in the Enron drama.)

How can you get better informed about note disclosures that may contain important information related to your investments? Beyond your study in this class, a good web resource for understanding the contents of note disclosures is *http://www.footnoted.org/*. This site highlights "the things companies bury in their SEC filings." It notes that company reports are more complete of late, but only the largest companies are preparing documents that are readable. As the editor of the site noted, "[some companies] are being dragged kicking and screaming into plain English."

Source: Gretchen Morgenson, "Annual Reports: More Pages, But Better?" *New York Times* (March 17, 2002), and D. Stead, "The Secrets in SEC Filings," *BusinessWeek* (August 25, 2008), p. 12.

DISCLOSURE ISSUES

Disclosure of Special Transactions or Events

Related-party transactions, errors and fraud, and illegal acts pose especially sensitive and difficult problems. The accountant/auditor who has responsibility for reporting on these types of transactions must take care to properly balance the rights of the reporting company and the needs of users of the financial statements.

Related-party transactions arise when a company engages in transactions in which one of the parties has the ability to significantly influence the policies of the other. They may also occur when a nontransacting party has the ability to influence the policies of the two transacting parties.[4] Competitive, free-market dealings may not exist in related-party transactions, and so an "arm's-length" basis cannot be assumed. Transactions such as borrowing or lending money at abnormally low or high interest rates, real estate sales at amounts that differ significantly from appraised value, exchanges of nonmonetary assets, and transactions involving enterprises that have no economic substance ("shell corporations") suggest that related parties may be involved.

In order to make adequate disclosure, companies should report the economic substance, rather than the legal form, of these transactions. GAAP requires the following disclosures of material related-party transactions. [1]

 See the FASB Codification section (page 1361).

1. The nature of the relationship(s) involved.
2. A description of the transactions (including transactions to which no amounts or nominal amounts were ascribed) for each of the periods for which income statements are presented.

---

[4]Examples of related-party transactions include transactions between (a) a parent company and its subsidiaries; (b) subsidiaries of a common parent; (c) a company and trusts for the benefit of employees (controlled or managed by the enterprise); and (d) a company and its principal owners, management, or members of immediate families, and affiliates. Two classic cases of related-party transactions were **Enron,** with its misuse of special purpose entities, and **Tyco International,** which forgave loans to its management team.

3. The dollar amounts of transactions for each of the periods for which income statements are presented.

4. Amounts due from or to related parties as of the date of each balance sheet presented.

Illustration 24-3, from the annual report of **Harley-Davidson, Inc.**, shows disclosure of related-party transactions.

ILLUSTRATION 24-3
Disclosure of Related-
Party Transactions

Harley-Davidson, Inc.

Note 12. Related Party Transactions
The Company has the following material related party transactions. A director of the Company is Chairman and Chief Executive Officer and an equity owner of Fred Deeley Imports Ltd. (Deeley Imports), the exclusive distributor of the Company's motorcycles in Canada. During 2007, 2006 and 2005, the Company recorded revenue and financial services income from Deeley Imports of $231.9 million, $187.7 million and $145.1 million, respectively, and had accounts receivables balances due from Deeley Imports of $42.6 million and $21.0 million at December 31, 2007 and 2006, respectively. All such products were provided in the ordinary course of business at prices and on terms and conditions that the Company believes are the same as those that would result from arm's-length negotiations between unrelated parties.

Many companies are involved in related-party transactions. Errors, fraud (sometimes referred to as irregularities), and illegal acts, however, are the exception rather than the rule. Accounting **errors** are **unintentional** mistakes, whereas **fraud** (misappropriation of assets and fraudulent financial reporting) involves **intentional** distortions of financial statements.[5] As indicated earlier, companies should correct the financial statements when they discover errors. The same treatment should be given fraud. The discovery of fraud, however, gives rise to a different set of procedures and responsibilities for the accountant/auditor.[6]

Illegal acts encompass such items as illegal political contributions, bribes, kickbacks, and other violations of laws and regulations.[7] In these situations, the accountant/auditor must evaluate the adequacy of disclosure in the financial statements. For example, if a company derives revenue from an illegal act that is considered material in relation to the financial statements, this information should be disclosed. The Sarbanes-Oxley Act of 2002 is intended to deter these illegal acts. This law adds significant fines and longer jail time for those who improperly sign off on the correctness of financial statements that include willing and knowing misstatements.

Disclosure plays a very important role in these types of transactions because the events are more qualitative than quantitative and involve more subjective than objective evaluation. Users of the financial statements need some indication of the existence and nature of these transactions, through disclosures, modifications in the auditor's report, or reports of changes in auditors.

---

[5]"Consideration of Fraud in a Financial Statement Audit," *Statement on Auditing Standards No. 99* (New York, AICPA, 2002). We have an expanded discussion of fraudulent financial reporting later in this chapter. Since passage of the Sarbanes-Oxley Act of 2002, auditors of public companies are regulated by the Public Company Accounting Oversight Board (PCAOB). The PCAOB is now the audit standard-setter for auditors of public companies. It has adopted much of the prior auditing standards issued by the Auditing Standards Board of the AICPA.

[6]The profession became so concerned with certain management frauds that affect financial statements that it established a National Commission on Fraudulent Financial Reporting. The major purpose of this organization was to determine how fraudulent reporting practices could be constrained. Fraudulent financial reporting is discussed later in this chapter.

[7]"Illegal Acts by Clients," *Statement on Auditing Standards No. 54* (New York, AICPA, 1988).

Post-Balance-Sheet Events (Subsequent Events)

Notes to the financial statements should explain any significant financial events that took place after the formal balance sheet date, but before the statement is issued. These events are referred to as **post-balance-sheet events**, or just plain **subsequent events**. Illustration 24-4 shows a time diagram of the subsequent events period.

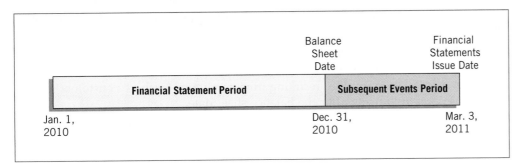

ILLUSTRATION 24-4
Time Periods for
Subsequent Events

A period of several weeks, and sometimes months, may elapse after the end of the fiscal year but before the company issues financial statements. Various activities involved in closing the books for the period and issuing the statements all take time: taking and pricing the inventory, reconciling subsidiary ledgers with controlling accounts, preparing necessary adjusting entries, ensuring that all transactions for the period have been entered, obtaining an audit of the financial statements by independent certified public accountants, and printing the annual report. During the period between the balance sheet date and its distribution to stockholders and creditors, important transactions or other events may occur that materially affect the company's financial position or operating situation.

Many who read a balance sheet believe the balance sheet condition is constant, and they project it into the future. However, readers must be told if the company has experienced a significant change—e.g., sold one of its plants, acquired a subsidiary, suffered extraordinary losses, settled significant litigation, or experienced any other important event in the post-balance-sheet period. Without an explanation in a note, the reader might be misled and draw inappropriate conclusions.

Two types of events or transactions occurring after the balance sheet date may have a material effect on the financial statements or may need disclosure so that readers interpret these statements accurately:

Underlying Concepts

The periodicity or time period assumption implies that economic activities of an enterprise can be divided into artificial time periods for purpose of analysis.

1. Events that provide additional evidence about conditions **that existed** at the balance sheet date, including the estimates inherent in the process of preparing financial statements. These events are referred to as **recognized subsequent events** and require adjustments to the financial statements. All information available prior to the issuance of the financial statements helps investors and creditors evaluate estimates previously made. To ignore these subsequent events is to pass up an opportunity to improve the accuracy of the financial statements. This first type of event encompasses information that an accountant would have recorded in the accounts had the information been known at the balance sheet date.

   For example, if a loss on an account receivable results from a customer's bankruptcy subsequent to the balance sheet date, the company adjusts the financial statements before their issuance. The bankruptcy stems from the customer's poor financial health existing at the balance sheet date.

   The same criterion applies to settlements of litigation. The company must adjust the financial statements if the events that gave rise to the litigation, such as personal injury or patent infringement, took place prior to the balance sheet date.

2. Events that provide evidence about conditions that **did not exist** at the balance sheet date but arise subsequent to that date. These events are referred as **nonrecognized subsequent events** and do not require adjustment of the financial statements. To illustrate, a loss resulting from a customer's fire or flood *after* the balance sheet date does not reflect conditions existing at that date. Thus, adjustment of the financial

statements is not necessary. A company should not recognize subsequent events that provide evidence about conditions that did not exist at the date of the balance sheet but that arose after the balance sheet date.

The following are examples of nonrecognized subsequent events:

(a) Sale of a bond or capital stock issued after the balance sheet date.

(b) A business combination that occurs after the balance sheet date.

(c) Settlement of litigation when the event giving rise to the claim took place after the balance sheet date.

(d) Loss of plant or inventories as a result of fire or natural disaster that occurred after the balance sheet date.

(e) Losses on receivables resulting from conditions (such as a customer's major casualty) arising after the balance sheet date.

(f) Changes in the quoted market prices of securities or foreign exchange rates after the balance sheet date.

(g) Entering into significant commitments or contingent liabilities, for example, by issuing significant guarantees after the balance sheet date. [2][8]

> **Underlying Concepts**
>
> A company also should consider supplementing the historical financial statements with pro forma financial data. Occasionally, a nonrecognized subsequent event may be so significant that disclosure can best be made by means of pro forma financial data.

Some nonrecognized subsequent events may have to be disclosed to keep the financial statements from being misleading. For such events, a company discloses the nature of the event and an estimate of its financial effect.

Illustration 24-5 presents an example of subsequent events disclosure, excerpted from the annual report of **Masco Corporation**.

ILLUSTRATION 24-5
Disclosure of
Subsequent Events

Masco Corporation

Note K (In Part): Debt

Subsequent Event

On January 20, 2007, holders of $1.8 billion (94 percent) principal amount at maturity of the Zero Coupon Convertible Senior Notes ("Notes") required the Company to repurchase their Notes at a cash value of $825 million. As a result of this repurchase, a $93 million deferred income tax liability will be payable in June 2007. Subsequent to the repurchase, there were outstanding $108 million principal amount at maturity of such Notes, with an accreted value of $51 million, which has been included in long-term debt at December 31, 2006, as the next put option date is July 20, 2011. The Company may, at any time on or after January 25, 2007, redeem all or part of the Notes at their accreted value.

Many subsequent events or developments do not require adjustment of or disclosure in the financial statements. Typically, these are nonaccounting events or conditions that management normally communicates by other means. These events include legislation, product changes, management changes, strikes, unionization, marketing agreements, and loss of important customers.

> **Objective·3**
>
> Discuss the disclosure requirements for major business segments.

Reporting for Diversified (Conglomerate) Companies

In certain business climates, companies have a tendency to diversify their operations. Take the case of conglomerate **General Electric (GE)**, whose products include locomotives and jet engines, credit card services, and water purification

---

[8]The effects from natural disasters, like hurricanes Katrina and Rita, which occurred after the year-end for companies with August fiscal years, require disclosure in order to keep the statements from being misleading. Some companies may have to consider whether these disasters affect their ability to continue as going concerns. *Accounting Trends and Techniques—2007* listed the following types of subsequent events and their frequency of occurrence among the 600 companies surveyed: business combinations pending or effected, 94; debt incurred, reduced or refinanced, 63; discontinued operations or asset disposals, 60; litigation, 42; restructuring/bankruptcy, 28; capital stock issued or purchased, 27; stock splits or dividends, 18; and employee benefits, 12.

systems. Its **NBC Universal** subsidiary owns **NBC TV**, **Vivendi Universal Entertainment**, and **Universal Pictures**. When businesses are so diversified, investors and investment analysts want more information about the details behind conglomerate financial statements. Particularly, they want income statement, balance sheet, and cash flow information on the **individual segments** that compose the total income figure.

Illustration 24-6 shows **segmented** (disaggregated) financial information of an office equipment and auto parts company.

OFFICE EQUIPMENT AND AUTO PARTS COMPANY INCOME STATEMENT DATA (IN MILLIONS)			
	Consolidated	Office Equipment	Auto Parts
Net sales	$78.8	$18.0	$60.8
Manufacturing costs			
Inventories, beginning	12.3	4.0	8.3
Materials and services	38.9	10.8	28.1
Wages	12.9	3.8	9.1
Inventories, ending	(13.3)	(3.9)	(9.4)
	50.8	14.7	36.1
Selling and administrative expenses	12.1	1.6	10.5
Total operating expenses	62.9	16.3	46.6
Income before taxes	15.9	1.7	14.2
Income taxes	(9.3)	(1.0)	(8.3)
Net income	$ 6.6	$ 0.7	$ 5.9

ILLUSTRATION 24-6
Segmented Income Statement

Much information is hidden in the aggregated totals. If the analyst has only the consolidated figures, he/she cannot tell the extent to which the differing product lines **contribute to the company's profitability, risk, and growth potential**. For example, in Illustration 24-6, the office equipment segment looks like a risky venture. Segmented reporting would provide useful information about the two business segments and would be useful for making an informed investment decision regarding the whole company.

In addition to the example of **Coach, Inc.** in the opening story, a classic situation that demonstrates the need for segmented data involved **Caterpillar, Inc.** The SEC cited Caterpillar because it failed to tell investors that nearly a quarter of its income in one year came from a Brazilian unit and was nonrecurring in nature. The company knew that different economic policies in the next year would probably greatly affect earnings of the Brazilian unit. But Caterpillar presented its financial results on a consolidated basis, not disclosing the Brazilian operations. The SEC found that Caterpillar's failure to include information about Brazil left investors with an incomplete picture of the company's financial results and denied investors the opportunity to see the company "through the eyes of management."

Companies have always been somewhat hesitant to disclose segmented data for various reasons:

1. Without a thorough knowledge of the business and an understanding of such important factors as the competitive environment and capital investment requirements, the investor may find the segmented information meaningless or may even draw improper conclusions about the reported earnings of the segments.

2. Additional disclosure may be helpful to competitors, labor unions, suppliers, and certain government regulatory agencies, and thus harm the reporting company.

3. Additional disclosure may discourage management from taking intelligent business risks because segments reporting losses or unsatisfactory earnings may cause stockholder dissatisfaction with management.

4. The wide variation among companies in the choice of segments, cost allocation, and other accounting problems limits the usefulness of segmented information.

5. The investor is investing in the company as a whole and not in the particular segments, and it should not matter how any single segment is performing if the overall performance is satisfactory.

6. Certain technical problems, such as classification of segments and allocation of segment revenues and costs (especially "common costs"), are formidable.

On the other hand, the advocates of segmented disclosures offer these reasons in support of the practice:

1. Investors need segmented information to make an intelligent investment decision regarding a diversified company.
   (a) Sales and earnings of individual segments enable investors to evaluate the differences between segments in growth rate, risk, and profitability, and to forecast consolidated profits.
   (b) Segmented reports help investors evaluate the company's investment worth by disclosing the nature of a company's businesses and the relative size of the components.

2. The absence of segmented reporting by a diversified company may put its unsegmented, single product-line competitors at a competitive disadvantage because the conglomerate may obscure information that its competitors must disclose.

The advocates of segmented disclosures appear to have a much stronger case. Many users indicate that segmented data are the most useful financial information provided, aside from the basic financial statements. As a result, the FASB has issued extensive reporting guidelines in this area.

Objective of Reporting Segmented Information

The objective of reporting segmented financial data is to provide information about the **different types of business activities** in which an enterprise engages and the **different economic environments** in which it operates. Meeting this objective will help users of financial statements do the following.

(a) Better understand the enterprise's performance.
(b) Better assess its prospects for future net cash flows.
(c) Make more informed judgments about the enterprise as a whole.

Basic Principles

Financial statements can be disaggregated in several ways. For example, they can be disaggregated by products or services, by geography, by legal entity, or by type of customer. However, it is not feasible to provide all of that information in every set of financial statements. GAAP requires that general-purpose financial statements include selected information on a single basis of segmentation. Thus, a company can meet the segmented reporting objective by providing financial statements segmented based on how the company's operations are managed. The method chosen is referred to as the **management approach**. [3] **The management approach reflects how management segments the company for making operating decisions.** The segments are evident from the components of the company's organization structure. These components are called **operating segments**.

Identifying Operating Segments

An **operating segment** is a component of an enterprise:

(a) That engages in business activities from which it earns revenues and incurs expenses.
(b) Whose operating results are regularly reviewed by the company's chief operating decision maker to assess segment performance and allocate resources to the segment.
(c) For which discrete financial information is available that is generated by or based on the internal financial reporting system.

Companies may aggregate information about two or more operating segments only if the segments have the same basic characteristics in each of the following areas.

(a) The nature of the products and services provided.

(b) The nature of the production process.

(c) The type or class of customer.

(d) The methods of product or service distribution.

(e) If applicable, the nature of the regulatory environment.

After the company decides on the possible segments for disclosure, it makes a quantitative materiality test. This test determines whether the segment is significant enough to warrant actual disclosure. An operating segment is deemed significant, and therefore a reportable segment, if it satisfies **one or more** of the following quantitative thresholds.

1. Its **revenue** (including both sales to external customers and intersegment sales or transfers) is 10 percent or more of the combined revenue of all the company's operating segments.

2. The absolute amount of its **profit or loss** is 10 percent or more of the greater, in absolute amount, of **(a)** the combined operating profit of all operating segments that did not incur a loss, or **(b)** the combined loss of all operating segments that did report a loss.

3. Its **identifiable assets** are 10 percent or more of the combined assets of all operating segments.

In applying these tests, the company must consider two additional factors. First, segment data must explain a significant portion of the company's business. Specifically, the segmented results must equal or exceed 75 percent of the combined sales to unaffiliated customers for the entire company. This test prevents a company from providing limited information on only a few segments and lumping all the rest into one category.

Second, the profession recognizes that reporting too many segments may overwhelm users with detailed information. The FASB decided that 10 is a reasonable upper limit for the number of segments that a company must disclose.

To illustrate these requirements, assume a company has identified six possible reporting segments, as shown in Illustration 24-7 (000s omitted).

Segments	Total Revenue (Unaffiliated)	Operating Profit (Loss)	Identifiable Assets
A	$ 100	$10	$ 60
B	50	2	30
C	700	40	390
D	300	20	160
E	900	18	280
F	100	(5)	50
	$2,150	$85	$970

ILLUSTRATION 24-7
Data for Different Possible Reporting Segments

The company would apply the respective tests as follows:

Revenue test: 10% × $2,150 = $215; C, D, and E meet this test.

Operating profit (loss) test: 10% × $90 = $9 (note that the $5 loss is ignored, because the test is based on non-loss segments); A, C, D, and E meet this test.

Identifiable assets tests: 10% × $970 = $97; C, D, and E meet this test.

The reporting segments are therefore A, C, D, and E, assuming that these four segments have enough sales to meet the 75 percent of combined sales test. The 75 percent test is computed as follows.

75% of combined sales test: 75% × \$2,150 = \$1,612.50. The sales of A, C, D, and E total \$2,000 (\$100 + \$700 + \$300 + \$900); therefore, the 75 percent test is met.

Measurement Principles

The accounting principles that companies use for segment disclosure need not be the same as the principles they use to prepare the consolidated statements. This flexibility may at first appear inconsistent. But, preparing segment information in accordance with generally accepted accounting principles would be difficult because some principles are not expected to apply at a segment level. Examples are accounting for the cost of company-wide employee benefit plans, accounting for income taxes in a company that files a consolidated tax return, and accounting for inventory on a LIFO basis if the pool includes items in more than one segment.

The FASB does not require allocations of joint, common, or company-wide costs solely for external reporting purposes. **Common costs** are those incurred for the benefit of more than one segment and whose interrelated nature prevents a completely objective division of costs among segments. For example, the company president's salary is difficult to allocate to various segments. Allocations of common costs are inherently arbitrary and may not be meaningful. There is a presumption that if companies allocate common costs to segments, these allocations are either directly attributable or reasonably allocable.

Segmented Information Reported

The FASB requires that an enterprise report the following.

1. *General information about its operating segments.* This includes factors that management considers most significant in determining the company's operating segments, and the types of products and services from which each operating segment derives its revenues.

2. *Segment profit and loss and related information.* Specifically, companies must report the following information about each operating segment if the amounts are included in determining segment profit or loss.

   (a) Revenues from transactions with external customers.

   (b) Revenues from transactions with other operating segments of the same enterprise.

   (c) Interest revenue.

   (d) Interest expense.

   (e) Depreciation, depletion, and amortization expense.

   (f) Unusual items.

   (g) Equity in the net income of investees accounted for by the equity method.

   (h) Income tax expense or benefit.

   (i) Extraordinary items.

   (j) Significant noncash items other than depreciation, depletion, and amortization expense.

3. *Segment assets.* A company must report each operating segment's total assets.

4. *Reconciliations.* A company must provide a reconciliation of the total of the segments' revenues to total revenues, a reconciliation of the total of the operating segments' profits and losses to its income before income taxes, and a reconciliation of the total of the operating segments' assets to total assets.

5. *Information about products and services and geographic areas.* For each operating segment not based on geography, the company must report (unless it is impracticable): (1) revenues from external customers, (2) long-lived assets, and (3) expenditures during the period for long-lived assets. This information, if material, must be reported (a) in the enterprise's country of domicile and (b) in each other country.

6. *Major customers.* If 10 percent or more of company revenue is derived from a single customer, the company must disclose the total amount of revenue from each such customer by segment.

Illustration of Disaggregated Information

Illustration 24-8 shows the segment disclosure for Johnson & Johnson.

ILLUSTRATION 24-8
Segment Disclosure

Johnson & Johnson
(Notes excluded)

Segments of Business and Geographic Areas

	Sales to Customers		
(Dollars in Millions)	2007	2006	2005
Consumer—United States	$ 6,408	$ 4,573	$ 4,405
International	8,085	5,201	4,691
Total	14,493	9,774	9,096
Pharmaceutical—United States	15,603	15,092	14,478
International	9,263	8,175	7,844
Total	24,866	23,267	22,322
Medical Devices and Diagnostics—United States	10,433	10,110	9,494
International	11,303	10,173	9,602
Total	21,736	20,283	19,096
Worldwide total	$61,095	$53,324	$50,514

	Operating Profit			Identifiable Assets		
(Dollars in Millions)	2007	2006	2005	2007	2006	2005
Consumer	$ 2,277	$ 1,374	$ 1,592	$26,550	$25,380	$ 6,275
Pharmaceutical	6,540	6,894	6,365	19,780	18,799	16,091
Medical Devices and Diagnostics	4,846	6,126	5,240	19,978	18,601	16,540
Total	13,663	14,394	13,197	66,308	62,780	38,906
Less: (Income)/Expenses not allocated to segments	380	(193)	81			
General corporate				14,646	7,776	19,958
Worldwide total	$13,283	$14,587	$13,116	$80,954	$70,556	$58,864

	Additions to Property, Plant & Equipment			Depreciation and Amortization		
(Dollars in Millions)	2007	2006	2005	2007	2006	2005
Consumer	$ 504	$ 344	$ 321	$ 472	$ 255	$ 232
Pharmaceutical	1,137	1,246	1,388	1,033	929	918
Medical Devices and Diagnostics	919	823	785	1,080	861	821
Segments total	2,560	2,413	2,494	2,585	2,045	1,971
General corporate	382	253	138	192	132	122
Worldwide total	$2,942	$2,666	$2,632	$2,777	$2,177	$2,093

	Sales to Customers			Long-Lived Assets		
(Dollars in Millions)	2007	2006	2005	2007	2006	2005
United States	$32,444	$29,775	$28,377	$21,685	$22,432	$15,355
Europe	15,644	12,786	12,187	15,578	14,443	5,646
Western Hemisphere excluding U.S.	4,681	3,542	3,087	3,722	3,108	957
Asia-Pacific, Africa	8,326	7,221	6,863	1,261	1,206	596
Segments total	61,095	53,324	50,514	42,246	41,189	22,554
General corporate				702	543	451
Other non long-lived assets				38,006	28,824	35,859
Worldwide total	$61,095	$53,324	$50,514	$80,954	$70,556	$58,864

Interim Reports

Another source of information for the investor is interim reports. As noted earlier, **interim reports** cover periods of less than one year. The stock exchanges, the SEC, and the accounting profession have an active interest in the presentation of interim information.

The SEC mandates that certain companies file a **Form 10-Q**, in which a company discloses quarterly data similar to that disclosed in the annual report. It also requires those companies to disclose selected quarterly information in notes to the annual financial statements. Illustration 24-9 presents the selected quarterly disclosure of **Tootsie Roll Industries, Inc.** In addition to Form 10-Q, GAAP narrows the reporting alternatives related to interim reports. [4]

ILLUSTRATION 24-9
Disclosure of Selected
Quarterly Data

Tootsie Roll Industries, Inc.
For the Year Ended December 31, 2007

(Thousands of dollars except per share data)

	First	Second	Third	Fourth	Total
Net product sales	$92,914	$101,901	$182,917	$115,010	$492,742
Gross product margin	33,178	34,425	60,659	36,785	165,047
Net earnings	9,811	10,226	23,432	8,156	51,625
Net earnings per share	.18	.19	.43	.15	.94

	Stock Prices		Dividends
	2007		2007
	High	Low	
1st Qtr	$32.69	$28.19	$.08
2nd Qtr	$30.50	$27.65	$.08
3rd Qtr	$30.85	$25.03	$.08
4th Qtr	$27.44	$23.55	$.08

Because of the short-term nature of the information in these reports, there is considerable controversy as to the general approach companies should employ. One group, which favors the **discrete approach**, believes that companies should treat each interim period as a separate accounting period. Using that treatment, companies would follow the principles for deferrals and accruals used for annual reports. In this view, companies should report accounting transactions as they occur, and expense recognition should not change with the period of time covered.

Another group, which favors the **integral approach**, believes that the interim report is an integral part of the annual report and that deferrals and accruals should take into consideration what will happen for the entire year. In this approach, companies should assign estimated expenses to parts of a year on the basis of sales volume or some other activity base.

At present, many companies follow the discrete approach for certain types of expenses and the integral approach for others, because the standards currently employed in practice are vague and lead to differing interpretations.

Interim Reporting Requirements

Generally, companies should use the same accounting principles for interim reports and for annual reports. They should recognize revenues in interim periods on the same basis as they are for annual periods. For example, if Cedars Corp. uses the installment-sales method as the basis for recognizing revenue on an annual basis, then it should use the installment basis for interim reports as well. Also, Cedars should treat costs directly associated with revenues (product costs, such as materials, labor and related fringe benefits, and manufacturing overhead) in the same manner for interim reports as for annual reports.

Companies should use the same inventory pricing methods (FIFO, LIFO, etc.) for interim reports and for annual reports. However, the following exceptions are appropriate at interim reporting periods.

1. Companies may use the gross profit method for interim inventory pricing. But they must disclose the method and adjustments to reconcile with annual inventory.

2. When a company liquidates LIFO inventories at an interim date and expects to replace them by year-end, cost of goods sold should include the expected cost of replacing the liquidated LIFO base, rather than give effect to the interim liquidation.

3. Companies should not defer inventory market declines beyond the interim period unless they are temporary and no loss is expected for the fiscal year.

4. Companies ordinarily should defer planned variances under a standard cost system; such variances are expected to be absorbed by year-end.

Companies often charge to the interim period, as incurred, costs and expenses other than product costs (often referred to as **period costs**). But companies may allocate these costs among interim periods on the basis of an estimate of time expired, benefit received, or activity associated with the periods. Companies display considerable latitude in accounting for these costs in interim periods, and many believe more definitive guidelines are needed.

Regarding disclosure, companies should report the following interim data at a minimum.

1. Sales or gross revenues, provision for income taxes, extraordinary items, and net income.

2. Basic and diluted earnings per share where appropriate.

3. Seasonal revenue, cost, or expenses.

4. Significant changes in estimates or provisions for income taxes.

5. Disposal of a component of a business and extraordinary, unusual, or infrequently occurring items.

6. Contingent items.

7. Changes in accounting principles or estimates.

8. Significant changes in financial position.

The FASB encourages, but does not require, companies to publish an interim balance sheet and statement of cash flows. If a company does not present this information, it should disclose significant changes in such items as liquid assets, net working capital, long-term liabilities, and stockholders' equity.

Unique Problems of Interim Reporting

GAAP reflects a preference for the integral approach. However, within this broad guideline, a number of unique reporting problems develop related to the following items.

Advertising and Similar Costs. The general guidelines are that companies should defer in an interim period costs such as advertising if the benefits extend beyond that period; otherwise the company should expense those costs as incurred. But such a determination is difficult, and even if the company defers the costs, how should it allocate them between quarters?

Because of the vague guidelines in this area, accounting for advertising varies widely. At one time, some companies in the food industry, such as **RJR Nabisco** and

Pillsbury, charged advertising costs as a percentage of sales and adjusted to actual at year-end, whereas **General Foods** and **Kellogg** expensed these costs as incurred.

The same type of problem relates to such items as Social Security taxes, research and development costs, and major repairs. For example, should the company expense Social Security costs (payroll taxes) on highly paid personnel early in the year, or allocate and spread them to subsequent quarters? Should a major repair that occurs later in the year be anticipated and allocated proportionately to earlier periods?

Expenses Subject to Year-End Adjustment. Companies often do not know with a great deal of certainty amounts of bad debts, executive bonuses, pension costs, and inventory shrinkage until year-end. **They should estimate these costs and allocate them to interim periods as best they can.** Companies use a variety of allocation techniques to accomplish this objective.

Income Taxes. Not every dollar of corporate taxable income is taxed at the same rate; the tax rate is progressive. This aspect of business income taxes poses a problem in preparing interim financial statements. Should the company use the **annualized approach,** which is to annualize income to date and accrue the proportionate income tax for the period to date? Or should it follow the **marginal principle approach,** which is to apply the lower rate of tax to the first amount of income earned? At one time, companies generally followed the latter approach and accrued the tax applicable to each additional dollar of income.

The profession now, however, uses the annualized approach. This requires that "at the end of each interim period the company should make its best estimate of the effective tax rate expected to be applicable for the full fiscal year. The rate so determined should be used in providing for income taxes on income for the quarter." [5][9]

Because businesses did not uniformly apply this guideline in accounting for similar situations, the FASB issued authoritative guidance. GAAP now requires companies, when computing the year-to-date tax, to apply the **estimated annual effective tax rate** to the year-to-date "ordinary" income at the end of each interim period. Further, the **interim period tax** related to "ordinary" income shall be the difference between the amount so computed and the amounts reported for previous interim periods of the fiscal period. [6][10]

Extraordinary Items. Extraordinary items consist of unusual and nonrecurring material gains and losses. In the past, companies handled them in interim reports in one of three ways: (1) absorbed them entirely in the quarter in which they occurred; (2) prorated them over four quarters; or (3) disclosed them only by note. **The required approach now is to charge or credit the loss or gain in the quarter in which it occurs,** instead of attempting some arbitrary multiple-period allocation. This approach is consistent with the way in which companies must handle extraordinary items on an annual basis. No attempt is made to prorate the extraordinary items over several years.

Some favor the omission of extraordinary items from the quarterly net income. They believe that inclusion of extraordinary items that may be large in proportion to interim results distorts the predictive value of interim reports. Many, however, consider such an omission inappropriate because it deviates from actual results.

Earnings per Share. Interim reporting of earnings per share has all the problems inherent in computing and presenting annual earnings per share, and then some. If a company issues shares in the third period, EPS for the first two periods will not reflect year-end

---

[9]The estimated annual effective tax rate should reflect anticipated tax credits, foreign tax rates, percentage depletion, capital gains rates, and other available tax-planning alternatives.

[10]"Ordinary" income (or loss) refers to "income (or loss) from continuing operations before income taxes (or benefits)" excluding extraordinary items and discontinued operations.

EPS. If an extraordinary item is present in one period and the company sells new equity shares in another period, the EPS figure for the extraordinary item will change for the year. On an annual basis only one EPS figure can be associated with an extraordinary item and that figure does not change; the interim figure is subject to change.

For purposes of computing earnings per share and making the required disclosure determinations, each interim period should stand alone. That is, all applicable tests should be made for that single period.

Seasonality. **Seasonality** occurs when most of a company's sales occur in one short period of the year while certain costs are fairly evenly spread throughout the year. For example, the natural gas industry has its heavy sales in the winter months. In contrast, the beverage industry has its heavy sales in the summer months.

The problem of seasonality is related to the expense recognition principle in accounting. Generally, expenses are associated with the revenues they create. In a seasonal business, wide fluctuations in profits occur because off-season sales do not absorb the company's fixed costs (for example, manufacturing, selling, and administrative costs that tend to remain fairly constant regardless of sales or production).

To illustrate why seasonality is a problem, assume the following information.

Selling price per unit	$1
Annual sales for the period (projected and actual)	
100,000 units @ $1	$100,000
Manufacturing costs	
Variable	10¢ per unit
Fixed	20¢ per unit or $20,000 for the year
Nonmanufacturing costs	
Variable	10¢ per unit
Fixed	30¢ per unit or $30,000 for the year

ILLUSTRATION 24-10
Data for Seasonality Example

Sales for four quarters and the year (projected and actual) were:

		Percent of Sales
1st Quarter	$ 20,000	20%
2nd Quarter	5,000	5
3rd Quarter	10,000	10
4th Quarter	65,000	65
Total for the year	$100,000	100%

ILLUSTRATION 24-11
Sales Data for Seasonality Example

Under the present accounting framework, the income statements for the quarters might be as shown in Illustration 24-12.

	1st Qtr	2nd Qtr	3rd Qtr	4th Qtr	Year
Sales	$20,000	$ 5,000	$10,000	$65,000	$100,000
Manufacturing costs					
Variable	(2,000)	(500)	(1,000)	(6,500)	(10,000)
Fixed[a]	(4,000)	(1,000)	(2,000)	(13,000)	(20,000)
	14,000	3,500	7,000	45,500	70,000
Nonmanufacturing costs					
Variable	(2,000)	(500)	(1,000)	(6,500)	(10,000)
Fixed[b]	(7,500)	(7,500)	(7,500)	(7,500)	(30,000)
Net income	$ 4,500	$(4,500)	$ (1,500)	$31,500	$ 30,000

[a]The fixed manufacturing costs are inventoried, so that equal amounts of fixed costs do not appear during each quarter.
[b]The fixed nonmanufacturing costs are not inventoried, so equal amounts of fixed costs appear during each quarter.

ILLUSTRATION 24-12
Interim Net Income for Seasonal Business—Discrete Approach

An investor who uses the first quarter's results might be misled. If the first quarter's earnings are $4,500, should this figure be multiplied by four to predict annual earnings of $18,000? Or, if first-quarter sales of $20,000 are 20 percent of the predicted sales for the year, would the net income for the year be $22,500 ($4,500 × 5)? Both figures are obviously wrong, and after the second quarter's results occur, the investor may become even more confused.

The problem with the conventional approach is that the fixed nonmanufacturing costs are not charged in proportion to sales. Some enterprises have adopted a way of avoiding this problem by making all fixed nonmanufacturing costs follow the sales pattern, as shown in Illustration 24-13.

ILLUSTRATION 24-13
Interim Net Income for
Seasonal Business—
Integral Approach

	1st Qtr	2nd Qtr	3rd Qtr	4th Qtr	Year
Sales	$20,000	$ 5,000	$10,000	$65,000	$100,000
Manufacturing costs					
Variable	(2,000)	(500)	(1,000)	(6,500)	(10,000)
Fixed	(4,000)	(1,000)	(2,000)	(13,000)	(20,000)
	14,000	3,500	7,000	45,500	70,000
Nonmanufacturing costs					
Variable	(2,000)	(500)	(1,000)	(6,500)	(10,000)
Fixed	(6,000)	(1,500)	(3,000)	(19,500)	(30,000)
Net income	$ 6,000	$ 1,500	$ 3,000	$19,500	$ 30,000

This approach solves some of the problems of interim reporting: Sales in the first quarter are 20 percent of total sales for the year, and net income in the first quarter is 20 percent of total income. In this case, as in the previous example, the investor cannot rely on multiplying any given quarter by four, but can use comparative data or rely on some estimate of sales in relation to income for a given period.

The greater the degree of seasonality experienced by a company, the greater the possibility of distortion. Because there are no definitive guidelines for handling such items as the fixed nonmanufacturing costs, variability in income can be substantial. To alleviate this problem, the profession recommends that companies subject to material seasonal variations disclose the seasonal nature of their business and consider supplementing their interim reports with information for 12-month periods ended at the interim date for the current and preceding years.

The two illustrations highlight the difference between the **discrete** and **integral** approaches. Illustration 24-12 represents the discrete approach, in which the fixed nonmanufacturing expenses are expensed as incurred. Illustration 24-13 shows the integral approach, in which expenses are charged to expense on the basis of some measure of activity.

INTERNATIONAL INSIGHT

iGAAP requires that interim financial statements use the discrete method, except for tax expenses.

Underlying Concepts

The AICPA Special Committee on Financial Reporting indicates that users would benefit from separate fourth-quarter reporting, including management's analysis of fourth-quarter activities and events. Also, the Committee recommended quarterly segment reporting, which companies now provide.

Continuing Controversy. The profession has developed some rules for interim reporting, but much still has to be done. As yet, it is unclear whether the discrete or the integral method, or some combination of the two, will be settled on.

Discussion also persists about the independent auditor's involvement in interim reports. Many auditors are reluctant to express an opinion on interim financial information, arguing that the data are too tentative and subjective. On the other hand, more people are advocating some examination of interim reports. As a compromise, the SEC currently requires that auditors perform a review of interim financial information. Such a review, which is much more limited in its procedures than the annual audit, provides some assurance that the interim information appears to be in accord with GAAP.[11]

Analysts and investors want financial information as soon as possible, before it's old news. We may not be far from a continuous database system in which corporate financial records can be accessed via the Internet. Investors might be able to access a company's financial records whenever they wish and put the information in the format they need. Thus, they could learn about sales slippage, cost increases, or earnings changes as they happen, rather than waiting until after the quarter has ended.[12]

A steady stream of information from the company to the investor could be very positive because it might alleviate management's continual concern with short-run interim numbers. Today many contend that U.S. management is too oriented to the short-term. The truth of this statement is echoed by the words of the president of a large company who decided to retire early: "I wanted to look forward to a year made up of four seasons rather than four quarters."

"I WANT IT FASTER"

The SEC has decided that timeliness of information is of extreme importance. First, the SEC has said that large public companies will have only 60 days to complete their annual reports, down from 90 days. Quarterly reports must be done within 40 days of the close of the quarter, instead of 45. In addition, corporate executives and shareholders with more than 10 percent of a company's outstanding stock now have two days to disclose their sale or purchase of stock.

What do the numbers mean?

Also, in a bid to increase Internet disclosure, the SEC encourages companies to post current, quarterly, and annual reports on their websites—or explain why they don't. The Internet postings would have to be made by the day the company submits the information to the SEC, rather than within 24 hours as current rules allow.

AUDITOR'S AND MANAGEMENT'S REPORTS

Auditor's Report

Another important source of information, which is often overlooked, is the **auditor's report**. An **auditor** is an accounting professional who conducts an independent examination of a company's accounting data.

If satisfied that the financial statements present the financial position, results of operations, and cash flows fairly in accordance with generally accepted accounting principles, the auditor expresses an **unqualified opinion**. An example is shown in Illustration 24-14 (on page 1336).[13]

Objective·5
Identify the major disclosures in the auditor's report.

---

[11]"Interim Financial Information," *Statement on Auditing Standards No. 101* (New York, AICPA, 2002).

[12]A step in this direction is the SEC's mandate for companies to file their financial statements electronically with the SEC. The system, called EDGAR (electronic data gathering and retrieval) provides interested parties with computer access to financial information such as periodic filings, corporate prospectuses, and proxy materials.

[13]This auditor's report is in exact conformance with the specifications contained in "Reports on Audited Financial Statements," *Statement on Auditing Standards No. 58* (New York: AICPA, 1988). The last paragraph refers to the assessment of the company's internal controls, as required by the PCAOB.

ILLUSTRATION 24-14
Auditor's Report

Best Buy Co., Inc.

Report of Independent Registered Public Accounting Firm

To the Board of Directors and Shareholders of Best Buy Co., Inc.
We have audited the accompanying consolidated balance sheets of Best Buy Co., Inc. and subsidiaries (the "Company") as of March 1, 2008 and March 3, 2007, and the related consolidated statements of earnings, shareholders' equity, and cash flows for each of the three years in the period ended March 1, 2008, March 3, 2007 and February 25, 2006. Our audits also included the financial statement schedule listed in the index at Item 15(a). These financial statements and financial statement schedule are the responsibility of the Company's management. Our responsibility is to express an opinion on the financial statements and financial statement schedule based on our audits.

We conducted our audits in accordance with the standards of the Public Company Accounting Oversight Board (United States). Those standards require that we plan and perform the audit to obtain reasonable assurance about whether the financial statements are free of material misstatement. An audit includes examining, on a test basis, evidence supporting the amounts and disclosures in the financial statements. An audit also includes assessing the accounting principles used and significant estimates made by management, as well as evaluating the overall financial statement presentation. We believe that our audits provide a reasonable basis for our opinion.

In our opinion, such consolidated financial statements present fairly, in all material respects, the financial position of Best Buy Co., Inc. and subsidiaries as of March 1, 2008 and March 3, 2007, and the results of their operations and their cash flows for each of the three years in the period ended March 1, 2008, in conformity with accounting principles generally accepted in the United States of America. Also, in our opinion, such financial statement schedule, when considered in relation to the basic consolidated financial statements taken as a whole, presents fairly, in all material respects, the information set forth therein.

As discussed in Note 1 to the consolidated financial statements, effective March 4, 2007, Best Buy Co., Inc. and subsidiaries changed their method of accounting for uncertain tax benefits upon adoption of Financial Accounting Standards Board Interpretation No. 48. *Accounting for Uncertainty in Income Taxes—an Interpretation of FASB Statement No. 109.*

We have also audited, in accordance with the standards of the Public Company Accounting Oversight Board (United States), the Company's internal control over financial reporting as of March 1, 2008, based on the criteria established in *Internal Control—Integrated Framework* issued by the Committee of Sponsoring Organizations of the Treadway Commission and our report dated April 25, 2008 expressed an unqualified opinion on the Company's internal control over financial reporting.

Deloitte & Touche LLP

Minneapolis, Minnesota
April 25, 2008

In preparing the report, the auditor follows these reporting standards.

1. The report states whether the financial statements are in accordance with generally accepted accounting principles.
2. The report identifies those circumstances in which the company has not consistently observed such principles in the current period in relation to the preceding period.
3. Users are to regard the informative disclosures in the financial statements as reasonably adequate unless the report states otherwise.
4. The report contains either an expression of opinion regarding the financial statements taken as a whole or an assertion to the effect that an opinion cannot be expressed. When the auditor cannot express an overall opinion, the report should state the reasons. In all cases where an auditor's name is associated with financial statements, the report should contain a clear-cut indication of the character of the auditor's examination, if any, and the degree of responsibility being taken.

In most cases, the auditor issues a standard **unqualified** or **clean opinion**. That is, the auditor expresses the opinion that the financial statements present fairly, in all material respects, the financial position, results of operations, and cash flows of the entity in conformity with generally accepted accounting principles.

Certain circumstances, although they do not affect the auditor's unqualified opinion, may require the auditor to add an explanatory paragraph to the audit report. Some of the more important circumstances are as follows.

1. *Going Concern.* The auditor must evaluate whether there is substantial doubt about the entity's **ability to continue as a going concern** for a reasonable period of time, taking into consideration all available information about the future. (The future is at least, but not limited to, 12 months from the end of the reporting period.) If substantial doubt exists about the company continuing as a going concern, the auditor adds to the report an explanatory note describing the potential problem. [7]

2. *Lack of Consistency.* If a company has changed accounting principles or the method of their application in a way that has a material effect on the comparability of its financial statements, the auditor should refer to the change in an explanatory paragraph of the report. Such an explanatory paragraph should identify the nature of the change and refer readers to the note in the financial statements that discusses the change in detail. The auditor's concurrence with a change is implicit unless the auditor takes exception to the change in expressing an opinion as to fair presentation in conformity with generally accepted accounting principles.

3. *Emphasis of a Matter.* The auditor may wish to emphasize a matter regarding the financial statements, but nevertheless intends to express an unqualified opinion. For example, the auditor may wish to emphasize that the entity is a component of a larger business enterprise or that it has had significant transactions with related parties. The auditor presents such explanatory information in a separate paragraph of the report.

In some situations, however, the auditor is required to express (1) a **qualified** opinion or (2) an **adverse** opinion, or (3) to **disclaim** an opinion.

A **qualified opinion** contains an exception to the standard opinion. Ordinarily the exception is not of sufficient magnitude to invalidate the statements as a whole; if it were, an adverse opinion would be rendered. The usual circumstances in which the auditor may deviate from the standard unqualified short-form report on financial statements are as follows.

1. The scope of the examination is limited or affected by conditions or restrictions.
2. The statements do not fairly present financial position or results of operations because of:
   (a) Lack of conformity with generally accepted accounting principles and standards.
   (b) Inadequate disclosure.

If confronted with one of the situations noted above, the auditor must offer a qualified opinion. A qualified opinion states that, except for the effects of the matter to which the qualification relates, the financial statements present fairly, in all material respects, the financial position, results of operations, and cash flows in conformity with generally accepted accounting principles.

Illustration 24-15 (page 1338) shows an example of an auditor's report with a qualified opinion. The auditor qualified the opinion because the company used an accounting principle at variance with generally accepted accounting principles.

Helio Company

Independent Auditor's Report

(Same first and second paragraphs as the standard report)

Helio Company has excluded, from property and debt in the accompanying balance sheets, certain lease obligations that, in our opinion, should be capitalized in order to conform with generally accepted accounting principles. If these lease obligations were capitalized, property would be increased by $1,500,000 and $1,300,000, long-term debt by $1,400,000 and $1,200,000, and retained earnings by $100,000 and $50,000 as of December 31, in the current and prior year, respectively. Additionally, net income would be decreased by $40,000 and $30,000 and earnings per share would be decreased by $.06 and $.04, respectively, for the years then ended.

In our opinion, except for the effects of not capitalizing certain lease obligations as discussed in the preceding paragraph, the financial statements referred to above present fairly, in all material respects, the financial position of Helio Company, and the results of its operations and its cash flows for the years then ended in conformity with generally accepted accounting principles.

An **adverse opinion** is required in any report in which the exceptions to fair presentation are so material that in the independent auditor's judgment, a qualified opinion is not justified. In such a case, the financial statements taken as a whole are not presented in accordance with generally accepted accounting principles. Adverse opinions are rare, because most companies change their accounting to conform with GAAP. The SEC will not permit a company listed on an exchange to have an adverse opinion.

A **disclaimer of an opinion** is appropriate when the auditor has gathered so little information on the financial statements that no opinion can be expressed.

The audit report should provide useful information to the investor. One investment banker noted, "Probably the first item to check is the auditor's opinion to see whether or not it is a clean one—'in conformity with generally accepted accounting principles'—or is qualified in regard to differences between the auditor and company management in the accounting treatment of some major item, or in the outcome of some major litigation."

Management's Reports

Management's Discussion and Analysis

The SEC mandates inclusion of **management's discussion and analysis (MD&A)**. This section covers three financial aspects of an enterprise's business—liquidity, capital resources, and results of operations. In it, management highlights favorable or unfavorable trends and identifies significant events and uncertainties that affect these three factors. This approach obviously involves subjective estimates, opinions, and soft data. However, the SEC believes that the relevance of this information exceeds the potential lack of reliability.

Illustration 24-16 presents an excerpt from the MD&A section (2007 "Business Risks" only) of **PepsiCo's** annual report.

PEPSICO

PepsiCo, Inc.

Our Business Risks
We are subject to risks in the normal course of business. We manage our risks through an integrated risk management framework.

Risk Management Framework
The achievement of our strategic and operating objectives will necessarily involve taking risks. Our risk management process is intended to ensure that risks are taken knowingly and purposefully. As such, we leverage an integrated risk management framework to identify, assess, prioritize, manage, monitor and communicate risks across the Company. This framework includes:

• The PepsiCo Executive Council (PEC), comprised of a cross-functional, geographically diverse, senior management group which identifies, assesses, prioritizes and addresses strategic and reputational risks;

• Division Risk Committees (DRCs), comprised of cross-functional senior management teams which meet regularly each year to identify, assess, prioritize and address division-specific operating risks;

ILLUSTRATION 24-16
(*continued*)

- PepsiCo's Risk Management Office, which manages the overall risk management process, provides ongoing guidance, tools and analytical support to the PEC and the DRCs, identifies and assesses potential risks, and facilitates ongoing communication between the parties, as well as to PepsiCo's Audit Committee and Board of Directors;
- PepsiCo Corporate Audit, which evaluates the ongoing effectiveness of our key internal controls through periodic audit and review procedures; and
- PepsiCo's Compliance Office, which leads and coordinates our compliance policies and practices.

Market Risks

We are exposed to market risks arising from adverse changes in:

- commodity prices, affecting the cost of our raw materials and energy.
- foreign exchange rates, and
- interest rates.

In the normal course of business, we manage these risks through a variety of strategies, including productivity initiatives, global purchasing programs and hedging strategies. Ongoing productivity initiatives involve the identification and effective implementation of meaningful cost saving opportunities or efficiencies. Our global purchasing programs include fixed-price purchase orders and pricing agreements. Our hedging strategies include the use of derivatives. Certain derivatives are designated as either cash flow or fair value hedges and qualify for hedge accounting treatment, while others do not qualify and are marked to market through earnings. We do not use derivative instruments for trading or speculative purposes, and we limit our exposure to individual counterparties to manage credit risk. The fair value of our derivatives fluctuates based on market rates and prices. The sensitivity of our derivatives to these market fluctuations is discussed below. See Note 10 for further discussion of these derivatives and our hedging policies. See "Our Critical Accounting Policies" for a discussion of the exposure of our pension plan assets and pension and retiree medical liabilities to risks related to stock prices and discount rates.

Inflationary, deflationary and recessionary conditions impacting these market risks also impact the demand for and pricing of our products.

Commodity Prices

Our open commodity derivative contracts that qualify for hedge accounting had a face value of $5 million at December 29, 2007 and $55 million at December 30, 2006. . . .

Our open commodity derivative contracts that do not qualify for hedge accounting had a face value of $105 million at December 29, 2007 and $196 million at December 30, 2006. . . .

We expect to be able to continue to reduce the impact of increases in our raw material and energy costs through our hedging strategies and ongoing productivity initiatives.

Foreign Exchange

Financial statements of foreign subsidiaries are translated into U.S. dollars using period-end exchange rates for assets and liabilities and weighted-average exchange rates for revenues and expenses. Adjustments resulting from translating net assets are reported as a separate component of accumulated other comprehensive loss within shareholders' equity under the caption currency translation adjustment.

Our operations outside of the U.S. generate 44% of our net revenue with Mexico, the United Kingdom and Canada comprising 19% of our net revenue. As a result, we are exposed to foreign currency risks. During 2007, net favorable foreign currency, primarily due to appreciation in the euro. British pound, Canadian dollar and Brazilian real, contributed 2 percentage points to net revenue growth. Currency declines which are not offset could adversely impact our future results. . . .

Interest Rates

We centrally manage our debt and investment portfolios considering investment opportunities and risks, tax consequences and overall financing strategies. We may use interest rate and cross currency interest rate swaps to manage our overall interest expense and foreign exchange risk. These instruments effectively change the interest rate and currency of specific debt issuances. These swaps are entered into concurrently with the issuance of the debt that they are intended to modify. The notional amount, interest payment and maturity date of the swaps match the principal, interest payment and maturity date of the related debt. Our counterparty credit risk is considered low because these swaps are entered into only with strong creditworthy counterparties and are generally settled on a net basis.

Assuming year-end 2007 variable rate debt and investment levels, a 1-percentage-point increase in interest rates would have decreased net interest expense by $1 million in 2007.

Underlying Concepts

FASB Concepts Statement No. 1 notes that management knows more about the company than users and therefore can increase the usefulness of financial information by identifying significant transactions that affect the company and by explaining their financial impact.

The MD&A section also must provide information about the effects of inflation and changing prices, if they are material to financial statement trends. The SEC has not required specific numerical computations, and companies have provided little analysis on changing prices.

An additional voluntary disclosure provided in the MD&A of many companies is discussion of the company's critical accounting policies. This disclosure identifies

Expanded Discussion of Accounting for Changing Prices

accounting policies that require management to make subjective judgments regarding uncertainties, resulting in potentially significant effects on the financial results.[14] For example, in its critical accounting policy disclosure, **PepsiCo** showed the impact on stock-based compensation expense in response to changes in estimated interest rates and stock return volatility. Through this voluntary disclosure, companies can expand on the information contained in the notes to the financial statements to indicate the sensitivity of the financial results to accounting policy judgments.

Management's Responsibilities for Financial Statements

The Sarbanes-Oxley Act requires the SEC to develop guidelines for *all* publicly traded companies to report on management's responsibilities for, and assessment of, the internal control system. An example of the type of disclosure that public companies are now making is shown in Illustration 24-17.[15]

Objective•6
Understand management's responsibilities for financials.

ILLUSTRATION 24-17
Report on Management's Responsibilities

Home Depot

Management's Responsibility for Financial Statements

The financial statements presented in this Annual Report have been prepared with integrity and objectivity and are the responsibility of the management of The Home Depot, Inc. These financial statements have been prepared in conformity with U.S. generally accepted accounting principles and properly reflect certain estimates and judgments based upon the best available information.

The financial statements of the Company have been audited by KPMG LLP, an independent registered public accounting firm. Their accompanying report is based upon an audit conducted in accordance with the standards of the Public Company Accounting Oversight Board (United States).

The Audit Committee of the Board of Directors, consisting solely of outside directors, meets five times a year with the independent registered public accounting firm, the internal auditors and representatives of management to discuss auditing and financial reporting matters. In addition, a telephonic meeting is held prior to each quarterly earnings release. The Audit Committee retains the independent registered public accounting firm and regularly reviews the internal accounting controls, the activities of the independent registered public accounting firm and internal auditors and the financial condition of the Company. Both the Company's independent registered public accounting firm and the internal auditors have free access to the Audit Committee.

Management's Report an Internal Control over Financial Reporting

Our management is responsible for establishing and maintaining adequate internal control over financial reporting, as such term is defined in Rules 13a-15(f) promulgated under the Securities Exchange Act of 1934, as amended. Under the supervision and with the participation of our management, including our chief executive officer and chief financial officer, we conducted an evaluation of the effectiveness of our internal control over financial reporting as of February 3, 2008 based on the framework in *Internal Control—Integrated Framework* issued by the Committee of Sponsoring Organizations of the Treadway Commission (COSO). Based on our evaluation, our management concluded that our internal control over financial reporting was effective as of February 3, 2008 in providing reasonable assurance regarding the reliability of financial reporting and the preparation of financial statements for external purposes in accordance with generally accepted accounting principles. The effectiveness of our internal control over financial reporting as of February 3, 2008 has been audited by KPMG LLP, an independent registered public accounting firm, as stated in their report which is included on page 32 in this Form 10-K.

Francis S. Blake
Chairman & Chief Executive Officer

Carol B. Tomé
Chief Financial Officer &
Executive Vice President—Corporate Services

[14]See *Cautionary Advice Regarding Disclosure about Critical Accounting Policies,* Release Nos. 33-8040; 34-45149; FR-60 (Washington, D.C.: SEC); and *Proposed Rule: Disclosure in Management's Discussion and Analysis about the Application of Critical Accounting Policies,* Release Nos. 33-8098; 34-45907; International Series Release No. 1258; File No. S7-16-02 (Washington, D.C.: SEC).

[15]As indicated in this disclosure, management is responsible for preparing the financial statements and establishing and maintaining an effective system of internal controls. The auditor provides an independent assessment of whether the financial statements are prepared in accordance with GAAP, and for public companies, whether the internal controls are effective (see the audit opinion in Illustration 24-14 on page 1336).

CURRENT REPORTING ISSUES

Reporting on Financial Forecasts and Projections

Objective·7
Identify issues related to financial forecasts and projections.

In recent years, the investing public's demand for more and better information has focused on disclosure of corporate expectations for the future.[16] These disclosures take one of two forms:[17]

> *Financial forecasts.* A **financial forecast** is a set of prospective financial statements that present, to the best of the responsible party's knowledge and belief, a company's expected financial position, results of operations, and cash flows. The responsible party bases a financial forecast on conditions it expects to exist and the course of action it expects to take.
>
> *Financial projections.* **Financial projections** are prospective financial statements that present, to the best of the responsible party's knowledge and belief, given one or more *hypothetical assumptions*, an entity's expected financial position, results of operations, and cash flows. The responsible party bases a financial projection on conditions it expects *would* exist and the course of action it expects *would* be taken, given one or more hypothetical assumptions.

The difference between a financial forecast and a financial projection is clear-cut: A forecast provides information on what is **expected** to happen, whereas a projection provides information on what **might** take place, but is not necessarily expected to happen.

Whether companies should be required to provide financial forecasts is the subject of intensive discussion with journalists, corporate executives, the SEC, financial analysts, accountants, and others. Predictably, there are strong arguments on either side. Listed below are some of the arguments.

Arguments for requiring published forecasts:

1. Investment decisions are based on future expectations. Therefore information about the future facilitates better decisions.

2. Companies already circulate forecasts informally. This situation should be regulated to ensure that the forecasts are available to all investors.

3. Circumstances now change so rapidly that historical information is no longer adequate for prediction.

Arguments against requiring published forecasts:

1. No one can foretell the future. Therefore forecasts will inevitably be wrong. Worse, they may mislead, if they convey an impression of precision about the future,.

2. Companies may strive only to meet their published forecasts, thereby failing to produce results that are in the stockholders' best interest.

3. If forecasts prove inaccurate, there will be recriminations and probably legal actions.[18]

---

[16]Some areas in which companies are using financial information about the future are equipment lease-versus-buy analysis, analysis of a company's ability to successfully enter new markets, and examination of merger and acquisition opportunities. In addition, companies also prepare forecasts and projections for use by third parties in public offering documents (requiring financial forecasts), tax-oriented investments, and financial feasibility studies. Use of forward-looking data has been enhanced by the increased capability of microcomputers to analyze, compare, and manipulate large quantities of data.

[17]"Financial Forecasts and Projections," and "Guide for Prospective Financial Information," *Codification of Statements on Standards for Attestation Engagements* (New York: AICPA 2006), pars. 3.04 and 3.05.

[18]The issue is serious. Over a recent three-year period, 8 percent of the companies on the NYSE were sued because of an alleged lack of financial disclosure. Companies complain that they are subject to lawsuits whenever the stock price drops. And as one executive noted, "You can even be sued if the stock price goes up—because you did not disclose the good news fast enough."

4. Disclosure of forecasts will be detrimental to organizations, because forecasts will inform competitors (foreign and domestic), as well as investors.

The AICPA has issued a statement on standards for accountants' services on prospective financial information. This statement establishes guidelines for the preparation and presentation of financial forecasts and projections.[19] It requires accountants to provide (1) a summary of significant assumptions used in the forecast or projection and (2) guidelines for minimum presentation.

To encourage management to disclose prospective financial information, the SEC has a **safe harbor rule**. It provides protection to a company that presents an erroneous forecast, as long as the company prepared the forecast on a reasonable basis and disclosed it in good faith.[20] However, many companies note that the safe harbor rule does not work in practice, since it does not cover oral statements, nor has it kept them from investor lawsuits.

Experience in Great Britain

Great Britain permits financial forecasts, and the results have been fairly successful. Some significant differences do exist between the English and the U.S. business and legal environments.[21] But such differences probably could be overcome if influential interests in this country cooperated to produce an atmosphere conducive to quality forecasting. A typical British forecast adapted from a construction company's report to support a public offering of stock is as follows.

ILLUSTRATION 24-18
Financial Forecast of a British Company

> Profits have grown substantially over the past 10 years and directors are confident of being able to continue this expansion. . . . While the rate of expansion will be dependent on the level of economic activity in Ireland and England, the group is well structured to avail itself of opportunities as they arise, particularly in the field of property development, which is expected to play an increasingly important role in the group's future expansion.
>
> Profits before taxation for the half year ended 30th June were 402,000 pounds. On the basis of trading experiences since that date and the present level of sales and completions, the directors expect that in the absence of unforeseen circumstances, the group's profits before taxation for the year to 31st December will be not less than 960,000 pounds.
>
> No dividends will be paid in respect of the current year. In a full financial year, on the basis of above forecasts (not including full year profits) it would be the intention of the board, assuming current rates of tax, to recommend dividends totaling 40% (of after-tax profits), which will be payable in the next two years.

A general narrative-type forecast issued by a U.S. corporation might appear as follows.

ILLUSTRATION 24-19
Financial Forecast for an American Company

> On the basis of promotions planned by the company for the second half of the fiscal year, net earnings for that period are expected to be approximately the same as those for the first half of the fiscal year, with net earnings for the third quarter expected to make the predominant contribution to net earnings for the second half of the year.

---

[19]Op cit., par. 1.02.

[20]"Safe-Harbor Rule for Projections," *Release No. 5993* (Washington: SEC, 1979). The Private Securities Litigation Reform Act of 1995 recognizes that some information that is useful to investors is inherently subject to less certainty or reliability than other information. By providing safe harbor for forward-looking statements, Congress has sought to facilitate access to this information by investors.

[21]The British system, for example, does not permit litigation on forecasted information, and the solicitor (lawyer) is not permitted to work on a contingent fee basis. See "A Case for Forecasting—The British Have Tried It and Find That It Works," *World* (New York: Peat, Marwick, Mitchell & Co., Autumn 1978), pp. 10–13.

Questions of Liability

What happens if a company does not meet its forecasts? Can the company and the auditor be sued? If a company, for example, projects an earnings increase of 15 percent and achieves only 5 percent, should stockholders be permitted to have some judicial recourse against the company?

One court case involving **Monsanto Chemical Corporation** set a precedent. In this case, Monsanto predicted that sales would increase 8 to 9 percent and that earnings would rise 4 to 5 percent. In the last part of the year, the demand for Monsanto's products dropped as a result of a business turndown. Instead of increasing, the company's earnings declined. Investors sued the company because the projected earnings figure was erroneous, but a judge dismissed the suit because the forecasts were the best estimates of qualified people whose intents were honest.

As indicated earlier, the SEC's safe harbor rules are intended to protect companies that provide good-faith projections. However, much concern exists as to how the SEC and the courts will interpret such terms as "good faith" and "reasonable assumptions" when erroneous forecasts mislead users of this information.

Internet Financial Reporting

Most companies now use the power and reach of the Internet to provide more useful information to financial statement readers. All large companies have Internet sites, and a large proportion of companies' websites contain links to their financial statements and other disclosures. The popularity of such reporting is not surprising, since companies can reduce the costs of printing and disseminating paper reports with the use of Internet reporting.

Does Internet financial reporting improve the usefulness of a company's financial reports? Yes, in several ways: First, dissemination of reports via the Web allows firms **to communicate more easily and quickly with users** than do traditional paper reports. In addition, **Internet reporting allows users to take advantage of tools** such as search engines and hyperlinks to quickly find information about the firm and, sometimes, to download the information for analysis, perhaps in computer spreadsheets. Finally, **Internet reporting can help make financial reports more relevant** by allowing companies to report expanded disaggregated data and more timely data than is possible through paper-based reporting. For example, some companies voluntarily report weekly sales data and segment operating data on their websites.

Given the widespread use of the Internet by investors and creditors, it is not surprising that organizations are developing new technologies and standards to further enable Internet financial reporting. An example is the increasing use of extensible business reporting language (XBRL). **XBRL** is a computer language adapted from the code of the Internet. It "tags" accounting data to correspond to financial reporting items that are reported in the balance sheet, income statement, and the cash flow statement. Once tagged, any company's XBRL data can be easily processed using spreadsheets and other computer programs. In fact, the SEC is planning to require all companies and mutual funds to prepare their financial reports using XBRL, thereby allowing users to more easily search a company's reports, extract and analyze data, and perform financial comparisons within industries.[22]

---

[22]C. Twarowski, "Financial Data 'on Steroids'," *Washington Post* (August 19, 2008), p. D01. Also, see *www.xbrl.org/us/us/BusinessCaseForXBRL.pdf* for additional information on XBRL. The FASB has issued a report on electronic dissemination of financial reports. This report summarizes current practice and research conducted on Internet financial reporting. See Business Reporting Research Project, "Electronic Distribution of Business Reporting Information" (Norwalk, Conn.: FASB, 2000).

To complement the implementation of XBRL use, the SEC has also announced a major upgrade to its EDGAR database. The new system is called IDEA (short for Interactive Data Electronic Applications). This replacement of EDGAR marks the SEC's transition from collecting forms and documents to making the information itself freely available to investors in a timely form they can readily use. With IDEA, investors will be able to quickly collate information from thousands of companies and forms and create reports and analysis on the fly, in any way they choose. It is hoped that IDEA will open the door for both the SEC and investors to the new world of financial disclosure in interactive data (XBRL) format.[23]

NEW FORMATS, NEW DISCLOSURE

What do the numbers mean?

As indicated earlier in the Convergence Corner discussions, the FASB and the IASB are exploring better ways to present information in the financial statements. Recently, these two standard-setters have issued a discussion paper that requests input on a proposed reformatting of the financial statements. The table below provides a "snapshot" of the proposed changes (go to *http://www.fasb.org/ project/financial_statement_presentation.shtml* to learn more about this joint international project).

Statement of Financial Position	Statement of Comprehensive Income	Statement of Cash Flows
Business	Business	Business
• Operating assets and liabilities	• Operating income and expenses	• Operating cash flows
• Investing assets and liabilities	• Investing income and expenses	• Investing cash flows
Financing	Financing	Financing
• Financing assets	• Financing asset income	• Financing asset cash flows
• Financing liabilities	• Financing liability expenses	• Financing liability cash flows
Income Taxes	Income Taxes	Income Taxes

As indicated, each statement will use the same format. While the proposed changes will not affect the measurement of individual financial statement elements, the use of a consistent format (e.g., Business, Financing, Income Taxes), will help users understand the interrelationships in the financial statements. In addition, a new schedule reconciling cash flows to comprehensive income will be provided. As part of this schedule, changes in fair value will be included. It is a good thing the timeline for the project is lengthy, as these changes in presentation are significant.

Fraudulent Financial Reporting

Objective·8
Describe the profession's response to fraudulent financial reporting.

Fraudulent financial reporting is defined as "intentional or reckless conduct, whether act or omission, that results in materially misleading financial statements."[24] Fraudulent reporting can involve gross and deliberate distortion of corporate records (such as inventory count tags), or misapplication of accounting

---

[23]See "SEC Announces Successor to EDGAR Database," *http://www.sec.gov/news/press/2008/ 2008-179.htm.* The SEC has implemented other regulations to ensure that investors get high-quality disclosures. For example, as discussed in Chapter 4, the SEC was concerned that companies may use pro forma reporting to deflect investor attention from bad news. In response, the SEC issued Regulation G, which requires companies to reconcile non-GAAP financial measures to GAAP. This regulation provides investors with a roadmap to analyze adjustments companies make to their GAAP numbers to arrive at pro forma results. [See SEC Regulation G, "Conditions for Use of Non-GAAP Financial Measures," Release No. 33-8176 (March 28, 2003).] Regulation FD (Release Nos. 33-7881) was issued in 2000 to address the concern that some analysts were receiving information sooner than the general public (e.g., during conference calls with analysts when earnings releases were discussed). Regulation FD requires that when relevant information is released, all have equal access to it.

[24]"Report of the National Commission on Fraudulent Financial Reporting" (Washington, D.C., 1987), page 2. Unintentional errors as well as corporate improprieties (such as tax fraud, employee embezzlements, and so on) which do not cause the financial statements to be misleading are excluded from the definition of fraudulent financial reporting.

principles (failure to disclose material transactions). Although frauds are unusual, recent events involving such well-known companies as Enron, WorldCom, Adelphia, and Tyco indicate that more must be done to address this issue.

Causes of Fraudulent Financial Reporting

Fraudulent financial reporting usually occurs because of conditions in a company's internal or external environment. Influences in the **internal environment** relate to poor internal control systems, management's poor attitude toward ethics, or perhaps a company's liquidity or profitability. Those in the **external environment** may relate to industry conditions, overall business environment, or legal and regulatory considerations.

General incentives for fraudulent financial reporting vary. Common ones are the desire to obtain a higher stock price, to avoid default on a loan covenant, or to make a personal gain of some type (additional compensation, promotion). Situational pressures on the company or an individual manager also may lead to fraudulent financial reporting. Examples of these situational pressures include the following.

- *Sudden decreases in revenue or market share* for a single company or an entire industry.
- *Unrealistic budget pressures* may occur when headquarters arbitrarily determines profit objectives (particularly for short-term results) and budgets without taking actual conditions into account.
- *Financial pressure resulting from bonus plans* that depend on short-term economic performance. This pressure is particularly acute when the bonus is a significant component of the individual's total compensation.

Opportunities for fraudulent financial reporting are present in circumstances when the fraud is easy to commit and when detection is difficult. Frequently these opportunities arise from:

1. *The absence of a board of directors or audit committee* that vigilantly oversees the financial reporting process.
2. *Weak or nonexistent internal accounting controls.* This situation can occur, for example, when a company's revenue system is overloaded as a result of a rapid expansion of sales, an acquisition of a new division, or the entry into a new, unfamiliar line of business.
3. *Unusual or complex transactions* such as the consolidation of two companies, the divestiture or closing of a specific operation, and the purchase and sale of derivative instruments.
4. *Accounting estimates requiring significant subjective judgment* by company management, such as the allowance for loan losses and the estimated liability for warranty expense.
5. *Ineffective internal audit staffs* resulting from inadequate staff size and severely limited audit scope.

A weak corporate ethical climate contributes to these situations. Opportunities for fraudulent financial reporting also increase dramatically when the accounting principles followed in reporting transactions are nonexistent, evolving, or subject to varying interpretations.[25]

---

[25]The discussion in this section is based on the Report of the National Commission on Fraudulent Financial Reporting, pp. 23–24. See "2004 Report to the Nation on Occupational Fraud and Abuse, Association of Certified Fraud Examiners," (*www.cfenet.com/pdfs/2004RttN.pdf*) for fraudulent financial reporting causes and consequences.

The AICPA has issued numerous auditing standards in response to concerns of the accounting profession, the media, and the public.[26] For example, the recent standard on fraudulent financial reporting "raises the bar" on the performance of financial statement audits by explicitly requiring auditors to assess the risk of material financial misstatement due to fraud.[27] As indicated earlier, the Sarbanes-Oxley Act now raises the penalty substantially for executives who are involved in fraudulent financial reporting.

What do the numbers mean?

HERE'S A FRAUD

ESM Government Securities, Inc. (ESM) is a classic case exemplifying the seriousness of financial reporting frauds. ESM was a Fort Lauderdale securities dealer entrusted with monies to invest by municipalities from Toledo, Ohio, to Beaumont, Texas. The cities that provided funds thought, based on the company name, that ESM was collateralized with government securities.

Examination of ESM's balance sheet indicated that the company owed about as much as it expected to collect. Unfortunately, the amount it expected to collect was from insolvent affiliates which, in effect, meant that ESM was bankrupt. In fact, ESM had been bankrupt for more than six years, and the fraud was discovered only because a customer questioned a note to the balance sheet! ESM had disguised more than $300 million of losses.

Source: For an expanded discussion of this case, see Robert J. Sack and Robert Tangreti, "ESM: Implications for the Profession," *Journal of Accountancy* (April 1987).

Criteria for Making Accounting and Reporting Choices

Throughout this textbook, we have stressed the need to provide information that is useful to predict the amounts, timing, and uncertainty of future cash flows. To achieve this objective, companies must make judicious choices between alternative accounting concepts, methods, and means of disclosure. You are probably surprised by the large number of choices that exist among acceptable alternatives.

You should recognize, however, as indicated in Chapter 1, that accounting is greatly influenced by its environment. It does not exist in a vacuum. Therefore, it is unrealistic to assume that the profession can entirely eliminate alternative presentations of certain transactions and events. Nevertheless, we are hopeful that the profession, by adhering to the conceptual framework, will be able to focus on the needs of financial statement users and eliminate diversity where appropriate. The SEC's and FASB's projects on principle-based standards are directed at these very issues. They seek to develop guidance that will result in accounting and financial reporting that reflects the economic substance of the transactions, not the desired financial result of management. The profession must continue its efforts to develop a sound foundation upon which to build financial standards and practice. As Aristotle said, "The correct beginning is more than half the whole."

Underlying Concepts

The FASB concept statements on objectives of financial reporting, elements of financial statements, qualitative characteristics of accounting information, and recognition and measurement are important steps in the right direction.

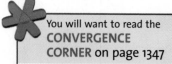

You will want to read the **CONVERGENCE CORNER on page 1347**

For discussion of how international convergence efforts relate to disclosure.

[26]Because the profession believes that the role of the auditor is not well understood outside the profession, much attention has been focused on the expectation gap. The **expectation gap** is the gap between (1) the expectation of financial statement users concerning the level of assurance they believe the independent auditor provides, and (2) the assurance that the independent auditor actually does provide under generally accepted auditing standards.

[27]"Consideration of Fraud in a Financial Statement Audit," *Statement on Auditing Standards No. 99* (New York: AICPA, 2002).

CONVERGENCE CORNER

DISCLOSURE

iGAAP and U.S. GAAP disclosure requirements are similar in many regards. The iGAAP standards addressing related-party disclosures are: *IAS 1* ("First Time Adoption of IFRS"); *IAS 24* ("Related Party Disclosures"); disclosure and recognition of post-balance-sheet events in *IAS 10* ("Events after the Balance Sheet Date); segment reporting iGAAP provisions in *IFRS 8* ("Operating Segments"); and interim reporting requirements in *IAS 34* ("Interim Financial Reporting").

RELEVANT FACTS

- Due to the broader range of judgments allowed in more principle-based iGAAP, note disclosures generally are more expansive under iGAAP compared to U.S. GAAP.

- Like U.S. GAAP, iGAAP requires that for transactions with related parties, companies disclose the amounts involved in a transaction, the amount, terms and nature of the outstanding balances, and any doubtful amounts related to those outstanding balances for each major category of related parties. There is no specific requirement to disclose the name of the related party.

- iGAAP and U.S. GAAP have similar standards on post-balance-sheet events. That is, under both sets of GAAP, events that occurred after the balance sheet date that provide additional evidence of conditions that existed at the balance sheet date are recognized in the financial statements.

- Following the recent issuance of *IFRS 8*, "Operating Segments," the requirements under iGAAP and U.S. GAAP are very similar. That is, both GAAPs use the management approach to identify reportable segments, and similar segment disclosures are required.

- Neither U.S. GAAP nor iGAAP requires interim reports. Rather the SEC and stock exchanges outside the U.S. establish the rules. In the U.S., interim reports generally are provided on a quarterly basis; outside the U.S., 6-month interim reports are common.

ABOUT THE NUMBERS

Because iGAAP and U.S. GAAP are quite similar in their disclosure provisions, we provide some observations on the application of iGAAP by foreign companies listing securities in the United States. Recently the staff of the SEC reviewed the financial statements filed with the SEC by 100 foreign issuers, prepared for the first time using iGAAP. The staff did not make any statements regarding the overall *quality* of the reports but did identify areas where additional questions might be asked. Here are some of the items that warranted staff comment:

1. Revenue recognition, especially where a company provided generic policy disclosure but did not provide disclosure specific to its circumstances.
2. Intangible assets and goodwill, including the factors that led a company to recognize them in a business combination.
3. Companies' policies for identifying and evaluating impairment, the circumstances resulting in impairment recognition, or the circumstances surrounding impairment reversals of long-lived assets including goodwill.
4. Leases, including their terms and the future minimum payments under operating and financial leases.
5. Contingent liabilities, including their nature and estimated financial effects.
6. The significant terms of financial instruments, including derivatives, their effects on future cash flow, and the recognition and measurement criteria the company applied in accounting for financial instruments.
7. Additional issues related to income statement and cash flow statement formats and related notes.

ON THE HORIZON

Sir David Tweedie, chair of the IASB, recently stated, "By 2011–2012, U.S. and international accounting should be pretty much the same." There is no question that iGAAP and U.S. GAAP are converging quickly. We have provided the Convergence Corner discussions to help you understand the issues surrounding convergence as they relate to intermediate accounting. After reading these discussions, you should realize that iGAAP and U.S. GAAP are very similar in many areas, with differences in those areas revolving around some minor technical points. In other situations, the differences are major; for example, iGAAP does not permit LIFO inventory accounting. Our hope is that the FASB and IASB can quickly complete their convergence efforts, resulting in a single set of high-quality accounting standards for use by companies around the world.

SUMMARY OF LEARNING OBJECTIVES

•1 Review the full disclosure principle and describe implementation problems. The full disclosure principle calls for financial reporting of any financial facts significant enough to influence the judgment of an informed reader. Implementing the full disclosure principle is difficult, because the cost of disclosure can be substantial and the benefits difficult to assess. Disclosure requirements have increased because of (1) the growing complexity of the business environment, (2) the necessity for timely information, and (3) the use of accounting as a control and monitoring device.

•2 Explain the use of notes in financial statement preparation. Notes are the accountant's means of amplifying or explaining the items presented in the main body of the statements. Notes can explain in qualitative terms information pertinent to specific financial statement items, and can provide supplementary data of a quantitative nature. Common note disclosures relate to such items as: accounting policies; inventories; property, plant, and equipment; creditor claims; contingencies and commitments; and subsequent events.

•3 Discuss the disclosure requirements for major business segments. Aggregated figures hide much information about the composition of these consolidated figures. There is no way to tell from the consolidated data the extent to which the differing product lines contribute to the company's profitability, risk, and growth potential. As a result, the profession requires segment information in certain situations.

•4 Describe the accounting problems associated with interim reporting. Interim reports cover periods of less than one year. Two viewpoints exist regarding interim reports. The discrete approach holds that each interim period should be treated as a separate accounting period. The integral approach is that the interim report is an integral part of the annual report and that deferrals and accruals should take into consideration what will happen for the entire year.

Companies should use the same accounting principles for interim reports that they use for annual reports. A number of unique reporting problems develop related to the following items: (1) advertising and similar costs, (2) expenses subject to year-end adjustment, (3) income taxes, (4) extraordinary items, (5) earnings per share, and (6) seasonality.

•5 Identify the major disclosures in the auditor's report. The auditor expresses an unqualified opinion if satisfied that the financial statements present the financial position, results of operations, and cash flows fairly in accordance with generally accepted accounting principles. A qualified opinion contains an exception to the standard opinion; ordinarily the exception is not of sufficient magnitude to invalidate the statements as a whole.

An adverse opinion is required when the exceptions to fair presentation are so material that a qualified opinion is not justified. A disclaimer of an opinion is appropriate when the auditor has so little information on the financial statements that no opinion can be expressed.

•6 Understand management's responsibilities for financials. Management's discussion and analysis (MD&A) section covers three financial aspects of an enterprise's business: liquidity, capital resources, and results of operations. Management's responsibility for the financial statements is often indicated in a letter to stockholders in the annual report.

•7 Identify issues related to financial forecasts and projections. The SEC has indicated that companies are permitted (not required) to include profit forecasts in their reports. To encourage management to disclose such information, the SEC issued a safe harbor rule. The rule provides protection to a company that presents an erroneous forecast, as long as it prepared the projection on a reasonable basis and disclosed it in good faith. However, the safe harbor rule has not worked well in practice.

•8 **Describe the profession's response to fraudulent financial reporting.** Fraudulent financial reporting is intentional or reckless conduct, whether through act or omission, that results in materially misleading financial statements. Fraudulent financial reporting usually occurs because of poor internal control, management's poor attitude toward ethics, poor performance, and so on. The Sarbanes-Oxley Act has numerous provisions intended to help prevent fraudulent financial reporting.

| APPENDIX **24A** | **BASIC FINANCIAL STATEMENT ANALYSIS** |

What would be important to you in studying a company's financial statements? The answer depends on your particular interest—whether you are a creditor, stockholder, potential investor, manager, government agency, or labor leader. For example, **short-term creditors** such as banks are primarily interested in the ability of the firm to pay its currently maturing obligations. In that case, you would examine the current assets and their relation to short-term liabilities to evaluate the short-run solvency of the firm.

Bondholders, on the other hand, look more to long-term indicators, such as the enterprise's capital structure, past and projected earnings, and changes in financial position. **Stockholders**, present or prospective, also are interested in many of the features considered by a long-term creditor. As a stockholder, you would focus on the earnings picture, because changes in it greatly affect the market price of your investment. You also would be concerned with the financial position of the company, because it affects indirectly the stability of earnings.

The **managers** of a company are concerned about the composition of its capital structure and about the changes and trends in earnings. This financial information has a direct influence on the type, amount, and cost of external financing that the company can obtain. In addition, the company managers find financial information useful on a day-to-day operating basis in such areas as capital budgeting, breakeven analysis, variance analysis, gross margin analysis, and for internal control purposes.

PERSPECTIVE ON FINANCIAL STATEMENT ANALYSIS

Readers of financial statements can gather information by examining relationships between items on the statements and identifying trends in these relationships. The relationships are expressed numerically in ratios and percentages, and trends are identified through comparative analysis.

A problem with learning how to analyze statements is that the means may become an end in itself. Analysts could identify and calculate thousands of possible relationships and trends. If one knows only how to calculate ratios and trends without understanding how such information can be used, little is accomplished. Therefore, a logical approach to financial statement analysis is necessary, consisting of the following steps.

Objective•9
Understand the approach to financial statement analysis.

Underlying Concepts
Because financial statements report on the past, they emphasize the *qualitative characteristic of feedback value*. This feedback value is useful because it can be used to better achieve the *qualitative characteristic of predictive value*.

1. *Know the questions for which you want to find answers.* As indicated earlier, various groups have different types of interest in a company.

2. *Know the questions that particular ratios and comparisons are able to help answer.* These will be discussed in this appendix.

3. *Match 1 and 2 above.* By such a matching, the statement analysis will have a logical direction and purpose.

Several caveats must be mentioned. **Financial statements report on the past.** Thus, analysis of these data is an examination of the past. When using such information in a decision-making (future-oriented) process, analysts assume that the past is a reasonable basis for predicting the future. This is usually a reasonable approach, but its limitations should be recognized.

Also, ratio and trend analyses will help identify a company's present strengths and weaknesses. They may serve as "red flags" indicating problem areas. In many cases, however, such analyses will not reveal **why** things are as they are. Finding answers about "why" usually requires an in-depth analysis and an awareness of many factors about a company that are not reported in the financial statements.

Another caveat is that a **single ratio by itself is not likely to be very useful**. For example, analysts may generally view a current ratio of 2 to 1 (current assets are twice current liabilities) as satisfactory. However, if the industry average is 3 to 1, such a conclusion may be invalid. Even given this industry average, one may conclude that the particular company is doing well if one knows the previous year's ratio was 1.5 to 1. Consequently, to derive meaning from ratios, analysts need some standard against which to compare them. Such a standard may come from industry averages, past years' amounts, a particular competitor, or planned levels.

Finally, **awareness of the limitations of accounting numbers used in an analysis** is important. We will discuss some of these limitations and their consequences later in this appendix.

RATIO ANALYSIS

Objective·10

Identify major analytic ratios and describe their calculation.

In analyzing financial statement data, analysts use various devices to bring out the comparative and relative significance of the financial information presented. These devices include ratio analysis, comparative analysis, percentage analysis, and examination of related data. No one device is more useful than another. Every situation is different, and analysts often obtain the needed answers only upon close examination of the interrelationships among all the data provided. Ratio analysis is the starting point. Ratios can be classified as follows.

MAJOR TYPES OF RATIOS

LIQUIDITY RATIOS. Measures of the company's short-run ability to pay its maturing obligations.

ACTIVITY RATIOS. Measures of how effectively the company is using the assets employed.

PROFITABILITY RATIOS. Measures of the degree of success or failure of a given company or division for a given period of time.

COVERAGE RATIOS. Measures of the degree of protection for long-term creditors and investors.[28]

We have integrated discussions and illustrations about the computation and use of these financial ratios throughout this book. Illustration 24A-1 (on page 1351) summarizes all of the ratios presented in the book and identifies the specific chapters that presented that material.

---

[28]Some analysts use other terms to categorize these ratios. For example, liquidity ratios are sometimes referred to as *solvency* ratios; activity ratios as *turnover* or *efficiency* ratios; and coverage ratios as *leverage* or *capital structure* ratios.

ILLUSTRATION 24A-1
Summary of Financial Ratios

Ratio	Formula for Computation	Reference
I. Liquidity		
1. **Current ratio**	$\dfrac{\text{Current assets}}{\text{Current liabilities}}$	Chapter 13, p. 665
2. **Quick or acid-test ratio**	$\dfrac{\text{Cash, marketable securities, and net receivables}}{\text{Current liabilities}}$	Chapter 13, p. 666
3. **Current cash debt coverage ratio**	$\dfrac{\text{Net cash provided by operating activities}}{\text{Average current liabilities}}$	Chapter 5, p. 204
II. Activity		
4. **Receivables turnover**	$\dfrac{\text{Net sales}}{\text{Average trade receivables (net)}}$	Chapter 7, p. 344
5. **Inventory turnover**	$\dfrac{\text{Cost of goods sold}}{\text{Average inventory}}$	Chapter 9, p. 459
6. **Asset turnover**	$\dfrac{\text{Net sales}}{\text{Average total assets}}$	Chapter 11, p. 560
III. Profitability		
7. **Profit margin on sales**	$\dfrac{\text{Net income}}{\text{Net sales}}$	Chapter 11, p. 561
8. **Rate of return on assets**	$\dfrac{\text{Net income}}{\text{Average total assets}}$	Chapter 11, p. 561
9. **Rate of return on common stock equity**	$\dfrac{\text{Net income minus preferred dividends}}{\text{Average common stockholders' equity}}$	Chapter 15, p. 767
10. **Earnings per share**	$\dfrac{\text{Net income minus preferred dividends}}{\text{Weighted shares outstanding}}$	Chapter 16, p. 812
11. **Payout ratio**	$\dfrac{\text{Cash dividends}}{\text{Net income}}$	Chapter 15, p. 767
IV. Coverage		
12. **Debt to total assets ratio**	$\dfrac{\text{Debt}}{\text{Total assets}}$	Chapter 14, p. 713
13. **Times interest earned**	$\dfrac{\text{Income before interest expense and taxes}}{\text{Interest expense}}$	Chapter 14, p. 713
14. **Cash debt coverage ratio**	$\dfrac{\text{Net cash provided by operating activities}}{\text{Average total liabilities}}$	Chapter 5, p. 204
15. **Book value per share**	$\dfrac{\text{Common stockholders' equity}}{\text{Outstanding shares}}$	Chapter 15, p. 768

SUMMARY OF RATIOS PRESENTED IN EARLIER CHAPTERS

Financial Analysis Primer

You can find additional coverage of these ratios, accompanied by assignment material, at the book's website, at **www.wiley.com/college/kieso**. This supplemental coverage takes the form of a comprehensive case adapted from the annual report of a large international chemical company that we have disguised under the name of Anetek Chemical Corporation.

Limitations of Ratio Analysis

The reader of financial statements must understand the basic limitations associated with ratio analysis. As analytical tools, ratios are attractive because they are simple and convenient. But too frequently, decision makers base their decisions

Objective•11
Explain the limitations of ratio analysis.

on only these simple computations. The ratios are only as good as the data upon which they are based and the information with which they are compared.

One important limitation of ratios is that they generally are **based on historical cost, which can lead to distortions in measuring performance**. Inaccurate assessments of the enterprise's financial condition and performance can result from failing to incorporate fair value information.

Also, investors must remember that **where estimated items (such as depreciation and amortization) are significant, income ratios lose some of their credibility**. For example, income recognized before the termination of a company's life is an approximation. In analyzing the income statement, users should be aware of the uncertainty surrounding the computation of net income. As one writer aptly noted, "The physicist has long since conceded that the location of an electron is best expressed by a probability curve. Surely an abstraction like earnings per share is even more subject to the rules of probability and risk."[29]

Underlying Concepts

Consistency and comparability are important concepts for financial statement analysis. If the principles and assumptions used to prepare the financial statements are continually changing, accurate assessments of a company's progress become difficult.

Probably the greatest limitation of ratio analysis is the **difficult problem of achieving comparability among firms in a given industry**. Achieving comparability requires that the analyst (1) identify basic differences in companies' accounting principles and procedures, and (2) adjust the balances to achieve comparability. Basic differences in accounting usually involve one of the following areas.

1. Inventory valuation (FIFO, LIFO, average cost).
2. Depreciation methods, particularly the use of straight-line versus accelerated depreciation.
3. Capitalization versus expensing of certain costs.
4. Capitalization of leases versus noncapitalization.
5. Investments in common stock carried at equity versus fair value.
6. Differing treatments of postretirement benefit costs.
7. Questionable practices of defining discontinued operations, impairments, and extraordinary items.

The use of these different alternatives can make a significant difference in the ratios computed. For example, at one time Anheuser-Busch noted that if it had used average cost for inventory valuation instead of LIFO, inventories would have increased approximately $33,000,000. Such an increase would have a substantive impact on the current ratio. Several studies have analyzed the impact of different accounting methods on financial statement analysis. The differences in income that can develop are staggering in some cases. Investors must be aware of the potential pitfalls if they are to be able to make the proper adjustments.[30]

Finally, analysts should recognize that a **substantial amount of important information** is not included in a company's financial statements. Events involving such things as industry changes, management changes, competitors' actions, technological developments, government actions, and union activities are often critical to a company's successful operation. These events occur continuously, and information about them must come from careful analysis of financial reports in the media and other sources. Indeed many argue, in what is known as the **efficient-market hypothesis**, that financial statements contain "no surprises" to those engaged in market activities. They contend that the effect of these events is known in the marketplace—and the price of the company's stock adjusts accordingly—well before the issuance of such reports.

---

[29]Richard E. Cheney, "How Dependable Is the Bottom Line?" *The Financial Executive* (January 1971), p. 12.

[30]See for example, Eugene A. Imhoff, Jr., Robert C. Lipe, and David W. Wright, "Operating Leases: Impact of Constructive Capitalization," *Accounting Horizons* (March 1991).

COMPARATIVE ANALYSIS

Comparative analysis presents the same information for two or more different dates or periods, so that like items may be compared. Ratio analysis provides only a single snapshot, for one given point or period in time. In a comparative analysis, an investment analyst can concentrate on a given item and determine whether it appears to be growing or diminishing year by year and the proportion of such change to related items. Generally, companies present comparative financial statements.[31] They typically include two years of balance sheet information and three years of income statement information.

> **Objective·12**
> Describe techniques of comparative analysis.

In addition, many companies include in their annual reports five- or ten-year summaries of pertinent data that permit readers to examine and analyze trends. As indicated in GAAP, "the presentation of comparative financial statements in annual and other reports enhances the usefulness of such reports and brings out more clearly the nature and trends of current changes affecting the enterprise." Illustration 24A-2 presents a five-year condensed statement, with additional supporting data, of Anetek Chemical Corporation.

ILLUSTRATION 24A-2
Condensed Comparative Financial Information

ANETEK CHEMICAL CORPORATION
CONDENSED COMPARATIVE STATEMENTS
(000,000 OMITTED)

	2010	2009	2008	2007	2006	10 Years Ago 2000	20 Years Ago 1990
Sales and other revenue:							
Net sales	$1,600.0	$1,350.0	$1,309.7	$1,176.2	$1,077.5	$636.2	$170.7
Other revenue	75.0	50.0	39.4	34.1	24.6	9.0	3.7
Total	1,675.0	1,400.0	1,349.1	1,210.3	1,102.1	645.2	174.4
Costs and other charges:							
Cost of sales	1,000.0	850.0	827.4	737.6	684.2	386.8	111.0
Depreciation and amortization	150.0	150.0	122.6	115.6	98.7	82.4	14.2
Selling and administrative expenses	225.0	150.0	144.2	133.7	126.7	66.7	10.7
Interest expense	50.0	25.0	28.5	20.7	9.4	8.9	1.8
Income taxes	100.0	75.0	79.5	73.5	68.3	42.4	12.4
Total	1,525.0	1,250.0	1,202.2	1,081.1	987.3	587.2	150.1
Net income for the year	$ 150.0	$ 150.0	$ 146.9	$ 129.2	$ 114.8	$ 58.0	$ 24.3
Other Statistics							
Earnings per share on common stock (in dollars)[a]	$ 5.00	$ 5.00	$ 4.90	$ 3.58	$ 3.11	$ 1.66	$ 1.06
Cash dividends per share on common stock (in dollars)[a]	2.25	2.15	1.95	1.79	1.71	1.11	0.25
Cash dividends declared on common stock	67.5	64.5	58.5	64.6	63.1	38.8	5.7
Stock dividend at approximate market value				46.8		27.3	
Taxes (major)	144.5	125.9	116.5	105.6	97.8	59.8	17.0
Wages paid	389.3	325.6	302.1	279.6	263.2	183.2	48.6
Cost of employee benefits	50.8	36.2	32.9	28.7	27.2	18.4	4.4
Number of employees at year end (thousands)	47.4	36.4	35.0	33.8	33.2	26.6	14.6
Additions to property	306.3	192.3	241.5	248.3	166.1	185.0	49.0

[a]Adjusted for stock splits and stock dividends.

[31]All 600 companies surveyed in *Accounting Trends and Techniques—2007* presented comparative 2005 amounts in their 2006 balance sheets and presented comparative 2004 and 2005 amounts in their 2006 income statements.

PERCENTAGE (COMMON-SIZE) ANALYSIS

Objective·13
Describe techniques of percentage analysis.

Analysts also use percentage analysis to help them evaluate and compare companies. **Percentage analysis** consists of reducing a series of related amounts to a series of percentages of a given base. For example, analysts frequently express all items in an income statement as a percentage of sales or sometimes as a percentage of cost of goods sold. They may analyze a balance sheet on the basis of total assets. Percentage analysis facilitates comparison and is helpful in evaluating the relative size of items or the relative change in items. A conversion of absolute dollar amounts to percentages may also facilitate comparison between companies of different size.

Illustration 24A-3 shows a comparative analysis of the expense section of Anetek for the last two years.

ILLUSTRATION 24A-3
Horizontal Percentage
Analysis

ANETEK CHEMICAL CORPORATION HORIZONTAL COMPARATIVE ANALYSIS (000,000 OMITTED)				
	2010	2009	Difference	% Change Inc. (Dec.)
Cost of sales	$1,000.0	$850.0	$150.0	17.6%
Depreciation and amortization	150.0	150.0	0	0
Selling and administrative expenses	225.0	150.0	75.0	50.0
Interest expense	50.0	25.0	25.0	100.0
Income taxes	100.0	75.0	25.0	33.3

This approach, normally called **horizontal analysis**, indicates the proportionate change over a period of time. It is especially useful in evaluating trends, because absolute changes are often deceiving.

Another comparative approach, called **vertical analysis**, is the proportional expression of each financial statement item in a given period to a base figure. For example, Anetek Chemical's income statement using this approach appears in Illustration 24A-4.

ILLUSTRATION 24A-4
Vertical Percentage
Analysis

ANETEK CHEMICAL CORPORATION INCOME STATEMENT (000,000 OMITTED)		
	Amount	Percentage of Total Revenue
Net sales	$1,600.0	96%
Other revenue	75.0	4
Total revenue	1,675.0	100
Less:		
Cost of sales	1,000.0	60
Depreciation and amortization	150.0	9
Selling and administrative expenses	225.0	13
Interest expense	50.0	3
Income taxes	100.0	6
Total expenses	1,525.0	91
Net income	$ 150.0	9%

Vertical analysis is frequently called **common-size analysis** because it reduces all of the statement items to a "common size." That is, all of the elements within each statement are expressed in percentages of some common number and always add up to 100 percent. Common-size (percentage) analysis reveals the composition of each of the financial statements.

In the analysis of the balance sheet, common-size analysis answers such questions as: What percentage of the capital structure is stockholders' equity, current liabilities, and long-term debt? What is the mix of assets (percentage-wise) with which the company has chosen to conduct business? What percentage of current assets is in inventory, receivables, and so forth?

Common-size analysis of the income statement typically relates each item to sales. It is instructive to know what proportion of each sales dollar is absorbed by various costs and expenses incurred by the enterprise.

Analysts may use common-size statements to compare one company's statements from different years, to detect trends not evident from comparing absolute amounts. Also, common-size statements provide intercompany comparisons regardless of size because they recast financial statements into a comparable common-size format.

SUMMARY OF LEARNING OBJECTIVES FOR APPENDIX 24A

•9 Understand the approach to financial statement analysis. Basic financial statement analysis involves examining relationships between items on the statements (ratio and percentage analysis) and identifying trends in these relationships (comparative analysis). Analysis is used to predict the future, but ratio analysis is limited because the data are from the past. Also, ratio analysis identifies present strengths and weaknesses of a company, but it may not reveal *why* they are as they are. Although single ratios are helpful, they are not conclusive; for maximum usefulness, analysts must compare them with industry averages, past years, planned amounts, and the like.

•10 Identify major analytic ratios and describe their calculation. Ratios are classified as liquidity ratios, activity ratios, profitability ratios, and coverage ratios: (1) *Liquidity ratio analysis* measures the short-run ability of a company to pay its currently maturing obligations. (2) *Activity ratio analysis* measures how effectively a company is using its assets. (3) *Profitability ratio analysis* measures the degree of success or failure of a company to generate revenues adequate to cover its costs of operation and provide a return to the owners. (4) *Coverage ratio analysis* measures the degree of protection afforded long-term creditors and investors.

•11 Explain the limitations of ratio analysis. Ratios are based on historical cost, which can lead to distortions in measuring performance. Also, where estimated items are significant, income ratios lose some of their credibility. In addition, comparability problems exist because companies use different accounting principles and procedures. Finally, analysts must recognize that a substantial amount of important information is not included in a company's financial statements.

•12 Describe techniques of comparative analysis. Companies present comparative data, which generally includes two years of balance sheet information and three years of income statement information. In addition, many companies include in their annual reports five- to ten-year summaries of pertinent data that permit the reader to analyze trends.

•13 Describe techniques of percentage analysis. Percentage analysis consists of reducing a series of related amounts to a series of percentages of a given base. Analysts use two approaches: *Horizontal analysis* indicates the proportionate change in financial statement items over a period of time; such analysis is most helpful in evaluating trends. *Vertical analysis* (common-size analysis) is a proportional expression of each item on the financial statements in a given period to a base amount. It analyzes the composition of each of the financial statements from different years (a) to detect trends not evident from the comparison of absolute amounts and (b) to make intercompany comparisons of different-sized enterprises.

Objective•14
Describe the current international accounting environment.

In Chapter 1, we noted that the former U.S. Secretary of the Treasury judged the single most important innovation shaping the capital markets to be the idea of generally accepted accounting principles. He went on to say that we need something similar internationally.

We believe the secretary is right. We also believe that environmental forces are in place to achieve a worldwide set of accounting standards in the not-too-distant future. Currently, many companies find it costly to comply with different reporting standards in different countries. Likewise, investors, attempting to diversify their holdings and manage their risks, have become very interested in investing overseas. Having one common set of accounting rules will make it easier for international investors to compare the financial results of companies from different countries.

The purpose of this appendix is to provide additional insight into the movement toward one set of accounting standards to be used by all companies.

THE PRESENT ENVIRONMENT

Most agree that, for the following reasons, there is a need for one set of globalized accounting standards.

Multinational corporations. Today companies view the entire world as their market. Some of the best-known corporations, such as **Coca-Cola**, **Intel**, and **McDonald's**, generate more than 50 percent of their sales outside the United States. These organizations no longer think of themselves as simply U.S. companies. The same situation is occurring overseas as many foreign companies find their largest market to be the United States.

Mergers and acquisitions. All you have to do is look in the *Wall Street Journal* to quickly understand the merger activity taking place between companies from different countries. The merger of such an international giant as **Vodafone/Mannesmann** suggest that we will see even more of this type of merger in the future.

Information technology. We have witnessed an incredible transformation in the speed and scale of communications among companies and individuals across borders. As communication barriers continue to drop, companies and individuals in different countries and markets are becoming comfortable buying and selling goods and services from one another.

Financial markets. Financial markets are some of the most significant international markets today. Whether it is currency, equity securities (stocks), bonds, or derivatives, there are active markets throughout the world trading these types of instruments. With the touch of a computer key, billions of dollars are transferred from one market to another.

REASONS TO UNDERSTAND INTERNATIONAL ACCOUNTING STANDARDS

As we discuss more fully below, the FASB and international accounting standard-setters are working diligently to narrow the differences between U.S. GAAP and international accounting standards (iGAAP). As a result, U.S. investors, regulators, and preparers who have vested interests in the reporting practices of multinational companies should be familiar with iGAAP. Here is why.

Convergence. International accounting standards converge when differences between international and U.S. standards are eliminated. Such convergence is illustrated if U.S. GAAP changes to international standards. For example, a recent IASB exposure draft requires companies to record all liability contingencies at fair value, no matter the likelihood of occurrence. If this standard passes, no doubt the FASB will also consider the change. This change could affect the financial reporting practices of U.S. companies.

Investors' expectations. To attract foreign investors, U.S. companies may need to provide additional information regarding how iGAAP would affect their financial statements. As investors gain a better understanding of iGAAP, they may demand this additional information from U.S. companies.

Competitive factors. There is some concern that iGAAP may provide certain companies with a competitive advantage. For example, international standards that are more permissive for revenue recognition may lead to an income number that is more favorable but in reality is misleading. Conversely, the U.S. standards may force a U.S. company to report lower income. Understanding this difference may be important in judging the competing companies.

Given these forces, it is no wonder that many are working to establish a set of accounting principles that can be used worldwide.

THE CHALLENGE OF INTERNATIONAL ACCOUNTING

The only way that international standards will work is if they are of high quality. High-quality standards must have the following characteristics.[32]

- They must permit *few alternative practices*.
- They must be *clearly stated*, to allow for easy interpretation and consistent application.
- They must be *comprehensive*, covering the major transactions facing companies, and must provide an *effective system* for responding to new transactions.
- They must provide *transparency of information* (full disclosure, understandability), to make that information relevant for making effective decisions.

Developing high-quality international standards is not easy. Accounting for transactions in the United States sometimes differs significantly from practices in other countries. We have highlighted these differences throughout the text within the Convergence Corner pages. These differences in some cases are quite fundamental; they involve issues such as when companies should recognize and measure assets, liabilities, revenues, and expenses.

Here are some examples of such differences:

- iGAAP permits companies to value assets at fair value using appraisals. In the United States this practice is not allowed.
- iGAAP prohibits use of LIFO costing for inventories. In the United States, a significant number of companies use LIFO to cost some, or their entire, inventory.
- iGAAP gives companies the option of reporting the funded position of postretirement benefit plans in the balance sheet. U.S. GAAP requires recognition.
- iGAAP requires use of the cost-recovery method instead of completed-contract revenue recognition for long-term contracts.

The FASB and international accounting standard-setters have already eliminated some differences between U.S. GAAP and iGAAP.[33] Discussions in this book have highlighted a number of the remaining differences between them. The fact that there *are* differences should not be surprising, because standard-setters worldwide have developed standards in response to different user needs. In some countries, the primary users of financial statements are private investors; in others, the primary users are tax authorities or central government planners. In the United States, capital market participants (investors and creditors) have driven accounting standard formulation.

[32]Adapted from Edmund L. Jenkins, "Global Financial Reporting and the Global Financial Markets," 1999 Financial Executive Summit (Vancouver, B.C., May 28, 1999).

[33]Notable examples are exchanges of nonmonetary assets (discussed in Chapter 10) and accounting changes (discussed in Chapter 22.)

WHO ARE THE KEY PLAYERS IN DEVELOPING INTERNATIONAL STANDARDS?

Throughout this book, we have discussed the FASB and its role in establishing accounting rules. We have also explained the role the SEC plays in ensuring that companies follow these standards appropriately. Both of these organizations have strongly supported the movement toward one set of international standards.

In the international arena, the primary organization involved in developing iGAAP is the International Accounting Standards Board (IASB).

IASB

Ed Jenkins, former chair of the FASB, noted, "We have reached a historic milestone for the future of financial reporting that will benefit investors around the world. The FASB is pleased that the IASC—a standard-setting organization based in London—has accepted the recommendations of its Strategy Working Party to restructure the IASC. When it is in place, the proposed restructuring would provide an independent, objective international standard-setter whose standards could meet the needs of the global capital markets."[34]

The independent objective standard-setting body now in place is called the **International Accounting Standards Board (IASB)**. The IASB is a privately funded accounting standard-setter based in London, UK. Its members currently come from nine countries and have a variety of functional backgrounds; twelve of the fourteen IASB's members have full-time positions on the Board. The Board is committed to developing, in the public interest, a single set of high-quality, understandable, and enforceable global accounting standards that require transparent and comparable information in general-purpose financial statements. In addition, the Board cooperates with national accounting standard-setters to achieve convergence in accounting standards around the world.[35]

The standard-setting structure internationally is now very similar to the standard-setting structure in the United States. That is, the structure is comprised of two main bodies: The International Accounting Standards Committee Foundation (IASCF) provides oversight. The International Accounting Standards Board (IASB) develops the standards, which are referred to as **International Financial Reporting Standards (IFRS)** or **iGAAP**. In addition, the IASB has an interpretations committee (similar to the U.S. Emerging Issues Task Force) and an advisory council (similar to the FASB's Financial Accounting Standards Advisory Committee). The structure is depicted in Illustration 24B-1 (on page 1359).

Because it is a private organization, the IASB has no regulatory mandate and therefore no enforcement mechanism in place. In other words, unlike the U.S. setting, there is no SEC to enforce the use of IASB standards. Their use is completely voluntary.[36]

Other Organizations

National Standard-Setters. Some countries have domestic accounting standard-setting organizations. For example, Canada and the United Kingdom have Accounting Standards Boards that develop accounting standards to be used by companies that do not list their securities on international exchanges. These national standard-setters often consult with the IASB in establishing accounting rules.

IOSCO. IOSCO stands for **International Organization of Securities Commissions**. IOSCO does not set accounting standards. This organization is dedicated to ensuring that the global markets can operate in an efficient and effective basis. The SEC, for example, is a member of IOSCO.

---

[34]Edmund L. Jenkins, "Global Financial Reporting and the Global Financial Markets," 1999 Financial Executive Summit (Vancouver, B.C., May 28, 1999). See also SEC Concept Release, "International Accounting Standards" (Washington, D.C.: SEC, 2000).

[35]See *www.iasb.org/about/constitution.asp.*

[36]Effective January 1, 2005, the European Union (EU) required member country companies that list on EU securities exchanges to use IASB standards.

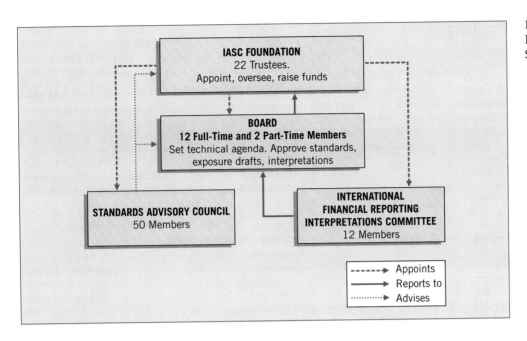

ILLUSTRATION 24B-1
International Standard-
Setting Structure

ACCOUNTING STANDARD-SETTING AND INTERNATIONAL CONVERGENCE

The FASB and the IASB are working together toward the goal of a single set of high-quality accounting standards that will be used both domestically and internationally. To achieve this goal, the FASB and IASB are undertaking several joint projects. One joint project is development of a common conceptual framework for financial accounting and reporting. The goal of this project is to build a framework that both the FASB and the IASB can use when developing new and revised accounting standards.

Other joint efforts involve developing new standards on major topics. Presently, the FASB and IASB are working on such major projects as lease accounting, revenue recognition, and financial statement presentation. When these issues are ultimately settled, there should be little, if any, difference between the FASB and IASB standards.

The FASB and IASB are also attempting to eliminate or narrow differences through short-term convergence projects. This approach has been quite successful so far. For example, the FASB has issued standards that mirror present IASB standards on such reporting issues as exchanges of nonmonetary assets and accounting changes. The goal of this collaboration is to select the better standard and move forward with it.

Finally, the two Boards are also coordinating interpretive activity. As often stated, "the devil is in the details." Both groups are working hard to ensure that not only are the broad conceptual approaches the same, but also the methods of applying them are the same. The Boards are not looking for mutual recognition of each other's standards. Rather, they want the **same** standards, interpretations, and language.

Regarding the FASB and convergence, Bob Herz, present chair of the FASB, has taken a position he calls "killing three birds with one stone." That is, he hopes that new standards will accomplish the following: (1) improve U.S. reporting, (2) simplify U.S. standards and standard-setting, and (3) provide international convergence.

To illustrate what the FASB is trying to accomplish, consider leasing. As you learned in your study of leases, there are many rules and interpretations related to the accounting for leasing transactions. Most agree that the reporting results achieved in applying the present standard often do not reflect the substance of the transaction. Recently, the IASB and the FASB started a joint project that will revisit the questions related to accounting and reporting of leases. When this project is completed, the parties hope that it will (1) improve U.S. reporting, (2) simplify U.S. standards, and (3) lead to international convergence.

Challenges to Convergence

There are many challenges to convergence. Presently, domestic and international accounting parties are often starting from different places. Not only are the FASB and the IASB involved, but also numerous national standard-setters are in the mix, as indicated in Illustration 24B-2.

ILLUSTRATION 24B-2
International Standard-Setters

Country(ies)	Standard-Setter
Australia	Australian Accounting Standards Board (AASB)
Canada	Accounting Standards Board (AcSB)
France	Conseil Nationale de la Comptabilité (CNC)
Germany	German Accounting Standards Committee (DRSC)
Japan	Accounting Standards Board of Japan (ASBJ)
United Kingdom	Accounting Standards Board (ASB)
United States	Financial Accounting Standards Board (FASB)

It follows that there are significant cultural differences among countries and regions of the world. For example, Europe sometimes seems more interested in developing a **representative** IASB than an **independent** IASB. In the United States, the FASB is faced with a very litigious society, and therefore is often encouraged to write very detailed standards.

In addition, there are often institutional or legal barriers to change. For example, any time a standard is issued that affects debt versus equity classifications, loan covenants may have to be changed. In some countries, changing loan covenants is often very difficult to implement.

And there are the political issues. On both sides of the Atlantic, companies that do not want change are pleading with politicians to stop standards from being issued. In the United States, high-tech companies have fought bitterly to derail the stock-option standard issued by the FASB. In Europe, the IASB issued a similar option standard and met little opposition. Conversely, bankers in Europe were up in arms regarding an IASB standard to record derivatives at fair value; U.S. GAAP requires fair value for derivatives in most situations. Although there was much opposition in the United States, the FASB passed the rule and companies now report derivatives at fair values.

CONCLUDING REMARKS

Financial statements prepared according to U.S. GAAP have been the standard for communicating financial information to the world. Regulators from around the world have readily accepted these financial statements when a company has chosen to list on an exchange. However, the IASB standards have become the common financial-statement language for over 12,000 companies in almost a hundred countries.

For many years, companies that report on a basis other than U.S. GAAP were required by the SEC to provide a **reconciliation** of their earnings and stockholders' equity to U.S. GAAP. This reconciliation imposed a cost on foreign filers: They essentially had to prepare two sets of financial statements, one under iGAAP (or their national GAAP) and one under U.S. GAAP. In 2007, the SEC eliminated this reconciliation in the name of convergence. In addition, the SEC has now proposed that U.S. companies be allowed to choose between using U.S. GAAP or iGAAP. While this proposal has not passed, it will be difficult for the SEC to permit foreign companies to file using iGAAP but not permit U.S. companies to do so as well.

It does make sense to have one set of international standards, but many are questioning the fast pace of change that is taking place. As we have indicated, in certain areas significant differences between iGAAP and U.S. GAAP need to be resolved. Until these issues are resolved, comparability among companies using iGAAP versus U.S. GAAP may be difficult. In summary, there are still many bumps in the road to the establishment of one set of worldwide standards, but the progress to date is remarkable.

SUMMARY OF LEARNING OBJECTIVE FOR APPENDIX 24B

KEY TERMS

converge, convergence,
1356

iGAAP, *1358*

IASC, *1358*

International Accounting
Standards Board
(IASB), *1358*

International Financial
Reporting Standards
(IFRS), *1358*

·14 **Describe the current international accounting environment.** Investors and creditors increasingly demand international accounting reports. The growth of multinational corporations, increased international mergers and acquisitions, and financial markets, all facilitated by technology, contribute to the demand for international accounting standards. Given these forces, many are working to establish a set of accounting principles that can be used worldwide. High-quality international standards: (1) permit *few alternative practices*, (2) are *clearly stated* to allow for easy interpretation and consistent application, (3) are *comprehensive*, covering the major transactions facing companies, (4) provide an *effective system* for responding to new transactions, and (5) provide *transparency of information* (full disclosure, understandability), to make that information relevant for making effective decisions.

The leading international accounting standard-setter, the IASB, is working with the FASB to develop common, high-quality accounting standards. The U.S. SEC may allow U.S. companies to use iGAAP.

FASB CODIFICATION

FASB Codification References

[1] FASB ASC 850-10-05 [Predecessor literature: "Related Party Disclosures," *Statement of Financial Accounting Standards No. 57* (Stamford, Conn.: FASB, 1982).]

[2] FASB ASC 855-10-05 [Predecessor literature: "Subsequent Events," *Statement on Auditing Standards No. 1* (New York: AICPA, 1973), pp. 123–124.]

[3] FASB ASC 280-10-05-3. [Predecessor literature: "Disclosures about Segments of an Enterprise and Related Information," *Statement of Financial Accounting Standards No. 131* (Norwalk, Conn.: FASB, 1997).]

[4] FASB ASC 270-10. [Predecessor literature: "Interim Financial Reporting," *Opinions of the Accounting Principles Board No. 28* (New York: AICPA, 1973).]

[5] FASB ASC 740-270-30-2 through 3. [Predecessor literature: "Interim Financial Reporting," *Opinions of the Accounting Principles Board No. 28* (New York: AICPA, 1973), par. 19.]

[6] FASB ASC 740-270-35-4. [Predecessor literature: "Accounting for Income Taxes in Interim Periods," *FASB Interpretation No. 18* (Stamford, Conn.: FASB, March 1977), par. 9.]

[7] FASB ASC 205-30 [Predecessor literature: "The Auditor's Consideration of an Entity's Ability to Continue as a Going Concern," *Statement on Auditing Standards No. 59* (New York: AICPA, 1988).]

Exercises

Access the FASB Codification at *http://asc.fasb.org/home* to prepare responses to the following exercises. Provide Codification references for your responses.

CE24-1 Access the glossary ("Master Glossary") to answer the following.

(a) What is the definition of "ordinary income" (loss)?

(b) What is an error in previously issued financial statements?

(c) What is the definition of "earnings per share"?

(d) What is a publicly traded company?

CE24-2 What are some examples of related parties?

CE24-3 What are the quantitative thresholds that would require a public company to report separately information about an operating segment?

CE24-4 If an SEC-registered company uses the gross profit method to determine cost of goods sold for interim periods, would it be acceptable for the company to state that it's not practicable to determine components of inventory at interim periods? Why or why not?

An additional Codification case can be found in the Using Your Judgment section, on page 1379.

Be sure to check the companion website for a Review and Analysis Exercise, with solution.

Note: All asterisked Questions, Exercises, and Problems relate to material in the appendices to the chapter.

QUESTIONS

1. What are the major advantages of notes to the financial statements? What types of items are usually reported in notes?

2. What is the full disclosure principle in accounting? Why has disclosure increased substantially in the last 10 years?

3. The FASB requires a reconciliation between the effective tax rate and the federal government's statutory rate. Of what benefit is such a disclosure requirement?

4. What type of disclosure or accounting do you believe is necessary for the following items?

  (a) Because of a general increase in the number of labor disputes and strikes, both within and outside the industry, there is an increased likelihood that a company will suffer a costly strike in the near future.

  (b) A company reports an extraordinary item (net of tax) correctly on the income statement. No other mention is made of this item in the annual report.

  (c) A company expects to recover a substantial amount in connection with a pending refund claim for a prior year's taxes. Although the claim is being contested, counsel for the company has confirmed the client's expectation of recovery.

5. The following information was described in a note of Canon Packing Co.

  "During August, Holland Products Corporation purchased 311,003 shares of the Company's common stock which constitutes approximately 35% of the stock outstanding. Holland has since obtained representation on the Board of Directors."

  "An affiliate of Holland Products Corporation acts as a food broker for Canon Packing in the greater New York City marketing area. The commissions for such services after August amounted to approximately $20,000."

Why is this information disclosed?

6. What are the major types of subsequent events? Indicate how each of the following "subsequent events" would be reported.

  (a) Collection of a note written off in a prior period.

  (b) Issuance of a large preferred stock offering.

  (c) Acquisition of a company in a different industry.

  (d) Destruction of a major plant in a flood.

  (e) Death of the company's chief executive officer (CEO).

  (f) Additional wage costs associated with settlement of a four-week strike.

  (g) Settlement of a federal income tax case at considerably more tax than anticipated at year-end.

  (h) Change in the product mix from consumer goods to industrial goods.

7. What are diversified companies? What accounting problems are related to diversified companies?

8. What quantitative materiality test is applied to determine whether a segment is significant enough to warrant separate disclosure?

9. Identify the segment information that is required to be disclosed by GAAP.

10. What is an operating segment, and when can information about two operating segments be aggregated?

11. The controller for Lafayette Inc. recently commented, "If I have to disclose our segments individually, the only people who will gain are our competitors and the only people that will lose are our present stockholders." Evaluate this comment.

12. An article in the financial press entitled "Important Information in Annual Reports This Year" noted that annual reports include a management's discussion and analysis section. What would this section contain?

13. "The financial statements of a company are management's, not the accountant's." Discuss the implications of this statement.

14. Olga Conrad, a financial writer, noted recently, "There are substantial arguments for including earnings projections in annual reports and the like. The most compelling is that it would give anyone interested something now available to only a relatively select few—like large stockholders, creditors, and attentive bartenders." Identify some arguments against providing earnings projections.

15. The following comment appeared in the financial press: "Inadequate financial disclosure, particularly with respect to how management views the future and its role in the marketplace, has always been a stone in the shoe. After all, if you don't know how a company views the future, how can you judge the worth of its corporate strategy?" What are some arguments for reporting earnings forecasts?

16. What are interim reports? Why are balance sheets often not provided with interim data?

17. What are the accounting problems related to the presentation of interim data?

18. Dierdorf Inc., a closely held corporation, has decided to go public. The controller, Ed Floyd, is concerned with presenting interim data when a LIFO inventory valuation is used. What problems are encountered with LIFO inventories when quarterly data are presented?

19. What approaches have been suggested to overcome the seasonality problem related to interim reporting?

20. What is the difference between a CPA's unqualified opinion or "clean" opinion and a qualified one?

21. Jane Ellerby and Sam Callison are discussing the recent fraud that occurred at LowRental Leasing, Inc. The fraud involved the improper reporting of revenue to ensure that the company would have income in excess of $1 million. What is fraudulent financial reporting, and how does it differ from an embezzlement of company funds?

22. Where can authoritative iGAAP be found related to the various disclosure issues discussed in the chapter?

23. Bill Novak is working on an audit of an iGAAP client. In his review of the client's interim reports, he notes that the reports are prepared on a discrete basis. That is, each interim report is viewed as a distinct period. Is this acceptable under iGAAP? If so, explain how that treatment could affect comparisons to a U.S. GAAP company.

*24. "The significance of financial statement data is not in the amount alone." Discuss the meaning of this statement.

*25. A close friend of yours, who is a history major and who has not had any college courses or any experience in business, is receiving the financial statements from companies in which he has minor investments (acquired for him by his now-deceased father). He asks you what he needs to know to interpret and to evaluate the financial statement data that he is receiving. What would you tell him?

*26. Distinguish between ratio analysis and percentage analysis relative to the interpretation of financial statements. What is the value of these two types of analyses?

*27. In calculating inventory turnover, why is cost of goods sold used as the numerator? As the inventory turnover increases, what increasing risk does the business assume?

*28. What is the relationship of the asset turnover ratio to the rate of return on assets?

*29. Explain the meaning of the following terms: (a) common-size analysis, (b) vertical analysis, (c) horizontal analysis, (d) percentage analysis.

*30. Presently, the profession requires that earnings per share be disclosed on the face of the income statement. What are some disadvantages of reporting ratios on the financial statements?

*31. Why is it important to understand international accounting standards?

*32. Describe some of the similarities between U.S. and international standard-setting structures.

BRIEF EXERCISES

•2 BE24-1 An annual report of Crestwood Industries states, "The company and its subsidiaries have long-term leases expiring on various dates after December 31, 2010. Amounts payable under such commitments, without reduction for related rental income, are expected to average approximately $5,711,000 annually for the next 3 years. Related rental income from certain subleases to others is estimated to average $3,094,000 annually for the next 3 years." What information is provided by this note?

•2 BE24-2 An annual report of **Ford Motor Corporation** states, "Net income a share is computed based upon the average number of shares of capital stock of all classes outstanding. Additional shares of common stock may be issued or delivered in the future on conversion of outstanding convertible debentures, exercise of outstanding employee stock options, and for payment of defined supplemental compensation. Had such additional shares been outstanding, net income a share would have been reduced by 10¢ in the current year and 3¢ in the previous year. . . . As a result of capital stock transactions by the company during the current year (primarily the purchase of Class A Stock from Ford Foundation), net income a share was increased by 6¢." What information is provided by this note?

•2 BE24-3 Morlan Corporation is preparing its December 31, 2010, financial statements. Two events that occurred between December 31, 2010, and March 10, 2011, when the statements were issued, are described below.

1. A liability, estimated at $160,000 at December 31, 2010, was settled on February 26, 2011, at $170,000.
2. A flood loss of $80,000 occurred on March 1, 2011.

What effect do these subsequent events have on 2010 net income?

·3 **BE24-4** Tina Bailey, a student of intermediate accounting, was heard to remark after a class discussion on segment reporting, "All this is very confusing to me. First we are told that there is merit in presenting the consolidated results, and now we are told that it is better to show segmental results. I wish they would make up their minds." Evaluate this comment.

·3 **BE24-5** Foley Corporation has seven industry segments with total revenues as follows.

Penley	$600	Cheng	$225
Konami	650	Takuhi	200
KSC	250	Molina	700
Red Moon	275		

Based only on the revenues test, which industry segments are reportable?

·3 **BE24-6** Operating profits and losses for the seven industry segments of Foley Corporation are:

Penley	$ 90	Cheng	$ (20)
Konami	(40)	Takuhi	34
KSC	25	Molina	150
Red Moon	50		

Based only on the operating profit (loss) test, which industry segments are reportable?

·3 **BE24-7** Identifiable assets for the seven industry segments of Foley Corporation are:

Penley	$500	Cheng	$200
Konami	550	Takuhi	150
KSC	250	Molina	475
Red Moon	400		

Based only on the identifiable assets test, which industry segments are reportable?

·10 ***BE24-8** Answer each of the questions in the following unrelated situations.

(a) The current ratio of a company is 5:1 and its acid-test ratio is 1:1. If the inventories and prepaid items amount to $500,000, what is the amount of current liabilities?

(b) A company had an average inventory last year of $200,000 and its inventory turnover was 5. If sales volume and unit cost remain the same this year as last and inventory turnover is 8 this year, what will average inventory have to be during the current year?

(c) A company has current assets of $90,000 (of which $40,000 is inventory and prepaid items) and current liabilities of $40,000. What is the current ratio? What is the acid-test ratio? If the company borrows $15,000 cash from a bank on a 120-day loan, what will its current ratio be? What will the acid-test ratio be?

(d) A company has current assets of $600,000 and current liabilities of $240,000. The board of directors declares a cash dividend of $180,000. What is the current ratio after the declaration but before payment? What is the current ratio after the payment of the dividend?

·10 ***BE24-9** Heartland Company's budgeted sales and budgeted cost of goods sold for the coming year are $144,000,000 and $99,000,000 respectively. Short-term interest rates are expected to average 10%. If Heartland can increase inventory turnover from its present level of 9 times a year to a level of 12 times per year, compute its expected cost savings for the coming year.

EXERCISES

·2 **E24-1** **(Post-Balance-Sheet Events)** Keystone Corporation issued its financial statements for the year ended December 31, 2010, on March 10, 2011. The following events took place early in 2011.

(a) On January 10, 10,000 shares of $5 par value common stock were issued at $66 per share.

(b) On March 1, Keystone determined after negotiations with the Internal Revenue Service that income taxes payable for 2010 should be $1,320,000. At December 31, 2010, income taxes payable were recorded at $1,100,000.

Instructions
Discuss how the preceding post-balance-sheet events should be reflected in the 2010 financial statements.

·2 **E24-2** **(Post-Balance-Sheet Events)** For each of the following subsequent (post-balance-sheet) events, indicate whether a company should (a) adjust the financial statements, (b) disclose in notes to the financial statements, or (c) neither adjust nor disclose.

_____ **1.** Settlement of federal tax case at a cost considerably in excess of the amount expected at year-end.
_____ **2.** Introduction of a new product line.
_____ **3.** Loss of assembly plant due to fire.
_____ **4.** Sale of a significant portion of the company's assets.
_____ **5.** Retirement of the company president.
_____ **6.** Issuance of a significant number of shares of common stock.
_____ **7.** Loss of a significant customer.
_____ **8.** Prolonged employee strike.
_____ **9.** Material loss on a year-end receivable because of a customer's bankruptcy.
_____ **10.** Hiring of a new president.
_____ **11.** Settlement of prior year's litigation against the company.
_____ **12.** Merger with another company of comparable size.

•3 **E24-3** **(Segmented Reporting)** LaGreca Company is involved in four separate industries. The following information is available for each of the four industries.

Operating Segment	Total Revenue	Operating Profit (Loss)	Identifiable Assets
W	$ 60,000	$15,000	$167,000
X	10,000	1,500	83,000
Y	23,000	(2,000)	21,000
Z	9,000	1,000	19,000
	$102,000	$15,500	$290,000

Instructions
Determine which of the operating segments are reportable based on the:

(a) Revenue test.
(b) Operating profit (loss) test.
(c) Identifiable assets test.

•10 *E24-4** **(Ratio Computation and Analysis; Liquidity)** As loan analyst for Madison Bank, you have been presented the following information.

	Plunkett Co.	Herring Co.
Assets		
Cash	$ 120,000	$ 320,000
Receivables	220,000	302,000
Inventories	570,000	518,000
Total current assets	910,000	1,140,000
Other assets	500,000	612,000
Total assets	$1,410,000	$1,752,000
Liabilities and Stockholders' Equity		
Current liabilities	$ 300,000	$ 350,000
Long-term liabilities	400,000	500,000
Capital stock and retained earnings	710,000	902,000
Total liabilities and stockholders' equity	$1,410,000	$1,752,000
Annual sales	$ 930,000	$1,500,000
Rate of gross profit on sales	30%	40%

Each of these companies has requested a loan of $50,000 for 6 months with no collateral offered. Inasmuch as your bank has reached its quota for loans of this type, only one of these requests is to be granted.

Instructions
Which of the two companies, as judged by the information given above, would you recommend as the better risk and why? Assume that the ending account balances are representative of the entire year.

•10 *E24-5** **(Analysis of Given Ratios)** Robbins Company is a wholesale distributor of professional equipment and supplies. The company's sales have averaged about $900,000 annually for the 3-year period 2009–2011. The firm's total assets at the end of 2011 amounted to $850,000.

The president of Robbins Company has asked the controller to prepare a report that summarizes the financial aspects of the company's operations for the past 3 years. This report will be presented to the board of directors at their next meeting.

In addition to comparative financial statements, the controller has decided to present a number of relevant financial ratios which can assist in the identification and interpretation of trends. At the request of the controller, the accounting staff has calculated the following ratios for the 3-year period 2009–2011.

	2009	2010	2011
Current ratio	1.80	1.89	1.96
Acid-test (quick) ratio	1.04	0.99	0.87
Accounts receivable turnover	8.75	7.71	6.42
Inventory turnover	4.91	4.32	3.72
Total debt to total assets	51.0%	46.0%	41.0%
Long-term debt to total assets	31.0%	27.0%	24.0%
Sales to fixed assets (fixed asset turnover)	1.58	1.69	1.79
Sales as a percent of 2009 sales	1.00	1.03	1.05
Gross margin percentage	36.0%	35.1%	34.6%
Net income to sales	6.9%	7.0%	7.2%
Return on total assets	7.7%	7.7%	7.8%
Return on stockholders' equity	13.6%	13.1%	12.7%

In preparation of the report, the controller has decided first to examine the financial ratios independent of any other data to determine if the ratios themselves reveal any significant trends over the 3-year period.

Instructions

(a) The current ratio is increasing while the acid-test (quick) ratio is decreasing. Using the ratios provided, identify and explain the contributing factor(s) for this apparently divergent trend.

(b) In terms of the ratios provided, what conclusion(s) can be drawn regarding the company's use of financial leverage during the 2009–2011 period?

(c) Using the ratios provided, what conclusion(s) can be drawn regarding the company's net investment in plant and equipment?

·10 ***E24-6 (Ratio Analysis)** Howser Inc. is a manufacturer of electronic components and accessories with total assets of $20,000,000. Selected financial ratios for Howser and the industry averages for firms of similar size are presented below.

	Howser			2011 Industry Average
	2009	2010	2011	
Current ratio	2.09	2.27	2.51	2.24
Quick ratio	1.15	1.12	1.19	1.22
Inventory turnover	2.40	2.18	2.02	3.50
Net sales to stockholders' equity	2.75	2.80	2.95	2.85
Net income to stockholders' equity	0.14	0.15	0.17	0.11
Total liabilities to stockholders' equity	1.41	1.37	1.44	0.95

Howser is being reviewed by several entities whose interests vary, and the company's financial ratios are a part of the data being considered. Each of the parties listed below must recommend an action based on its evaluation of Howser's financial position.

Citizens National Bank. The bank is processing Howser's application for a new 5-year term note. Citizens National has been Howser's banker for several years but must reevaluate the company's financial position for each major transaction.

Charleston Company. Charleston is a new supplier to Howser and must decide on the appropriate credit terms to extend to the company.

Shannon Financial. A brokerage firm specializing in the stock of electronics firms that are sold over-the-counter, Shannon Financial must decide if it will include Howser in a new fund being established for sale to Shannon Financial's clients.

Working Capital Management Committee. This is a committee of Howser's management personnel chaired by the chief operating officer. The committee is charged with the responsibility of periodically reviewing the company's working capital position, comparing actual data against budgets, and recommending changes in strategy as needed.

Instructions

(a) Describe the analytical use of each of the six ratios presented above.

(b) For each of the four entities described above, identify two financial ratios, from those ratios presented in Illustration 24A-1 (on page 1351), that would be most valuable as a basis for its decision regarding Howser.

(c) Discuss what the financial ratios presented in the question reveal about Howser. Support your answer by citing specific ratio levels and trends as well as the interrelationships between these ratios.

(CMA adapted)

See the book's companion website, www.wiley.com/college/kieso, for a set of B Exercises.

PROBLEMS

·2 **P24-1** **(Subsequent Events)** Your firm has been engaged to examine the financial statements of Almaden Corporation for the year 2010. The bookkeeper who maintains the financial records has prepared all the unaudited financial statements for the corporation since its organization on January 2, 2005. The client provides you with the information below.

ALMADEN CORPORATION
BALANCE SHEET
DECEMBER 31, 2010

Assets		**Liabilities**	
Current assets	$1,881,100	Current liabilities	$ 962,400
Other assets	5,171,400	Long-term liabilities	1,439,500
		Capital	4,650,600
	$7,052,500		$7,052,500

An analysis of current assets discloses the following.

Cash (restricted in the amount of $300,000 for plant expansion)	$ 571,000
Investments in land	185,000
Accounts receivable less allowance of $30,000	480,000
Inventories (LIFO flow assumption)	645,100
	$1,881,100

Other assets include:

Prepaid expenses	$ 62,400
Plant and equipment less accumulated depreciation of $1,430,000	4,130,000
Cash surrender value of life insurance policy	84,000
Unamortized bond discount	34,500
Notes receivable (short-term)	162,300
Goodwill	252,000
Land	446,200
	$5,171,400

Current liabilities include:

Accounts payable	$ 510,000
Notes payable (due 2013)	157,400
Estimated income taxes payable	145,000
Premium on common stock	150,000
	$ 962,400

Long-term liabilities include:

Unearned revenue	$ 489,500
Dividends payable (cash)	200,000
8% bonds payable (due May 1, 2015)	750,000
	$1,439,500

Capital includes:

Retained earnings	$2,810,600
Capital stock, par value $10; authorized 200,000 shares, 184,000 shares issued	1,840,000
	$4,650,600

The supplementary information below is also provided.

1. On May 1, 2010, the corporation issued at 95.4, $750,000 of bonds to finance plant expansion. The long-term bond agreement provided for the annual payment of interest every May 1. The existing plant was pledged as security for the loan. Use the straight-line method for discount amortization.

2. The bookkeeper made the following mistakes.
   (a) In 2008, the ending inventory was overstated by $183,000. The ending inventories for 2009 and 2010 were correctly computed.
   (b) In 2010, accrued wages in the amount of $225,000 were omitted from the balance sheet, and these expenses were not charged on the income statement.
   (c) In 2010, a gain of $175,000 (net of tax) on the sale of certain plant assets was credited directly to retained earnings.

3. A major competitor has introduced a line of products that will compete directly with Almaden's primary line, now being produced in a specially designed new plant. Because of manufacturing innovations, the competitor's line will be of comparable quality but priced 50% below Almaden's line. The competitor announced its new line on January 14, 2011. Almaden indicates that the company will meet the lower prices that are high enough to cover variable manufacturing and selling expenses, but permit recovery of only a portion of fixed costs.

4. You learned on January 28, 2011, prior to completion of the audit, of heavy damage because of a recent fire to one of Almaden's two plants; the loss will not be reimbursed by insurance. The newspapers described the event in detail.

Instructions

Analyze the above information to prepare a corrected balance sheet for Almaden in accordance with proper accounting and reporting principles. Prepare a description of any notes that might need to be prepared. The books are closed and adjustments to income are to be made through retained earnings.

·3 P24-2 (Segmented Reporting) Cineplex Corporation is a diversified company that operates in five different industries: A, B, C, D, and E. The following information relating to each segment is available for 2011.

	A	B	C	D	E
Sales	$40,000	$ 75,000	$580,000	$35,000	$55,000
Cost of goods sold	19,000	50,000	270,000	19,000	30,000
Operating expenses	10,000	40,000	235,000	12,000	18,000
Total expenses	29,000	90,000	505,000	31,000	48,000
Operating profit (loss)	$11,000	$(15,000)	$ 75,000	$ 4,000	$ 7,000
Identifiable assets	$35,000	$ 80,000	$500,000	$65,000	$50,000

Sales of segments B and C included intersegment sales of $20,000 and $100,000, respectively.

Instructions

(a) Determine which of the segments are reportable based on the:
   (1) Revenue test.
   (2) Operating profit (loss) test.
   (3) Identifiable assets test.
(b) Prepare the necessary disclosures required by GAAP.

·10 ·12 *P24-3 (Ratio Computations and Additional Analysis) Bradburn Corporation was formed 5 years ago through a public subscription of common stock. Daniel Brown, who owns 15% of the common stock, was one of the organizers of Bradburn and is its current president. The company has been successful, but it currently is experiencing a shortage of funds. On June 10, Daniel Brown approached the Topeka National Bank, asking for a 24-month extension on two $35,000 notes, which are due on June 30, 2011, and September 30, 2011. Another note of $6,000 is due on March 31, 2012, but he expects no difficulty in paying this note on its due date. Brown explained that Bradburn's cash flow problems are due primarily to the company's desire to finance a $300,000 plant expansion over the next 2 fiscal years through internally generated funds.

The commercial loan officer of Topeka National Bank requested financial reports for the last 2 fiscal years. These reports are reproduced on page 1369.

BRADBURN CORPORATION
STATEMENT OF FINANCIAL POSITION
MARCH 31

Assets	2011	2010
Cash	$ 18,200	$ 12,500
Notes receivable	148,000	132,000
Accounts receivable (net)	131,800	125,500
Inventories (at cost)	105,000	50,000
Plant & equipment (net of depreciation)	1,449,000	1,420,500
Total assets	$1,852,000	$1,740,500
Liabilities and Owners' Equity		
Accounts payable	$ 79,000	$ 91,000
Notes payable	76,000	61,500
Accrued liabilities	9,000	6,000
Common stock (130,000 shares, $10 par)	1,300,000	1,300,000
Retained earnings[a]	388,000	282,000
Total liabilities and owners' equity	$1,852,000	$1,740,500

[a]Cash dividends were paid at the rate of $1 per share in fiscal year 2010 and $2 per share in fiscal year 2011.

BRADBURN CORPORATION
INCOME STATEMENT
FOR THE FISCAL YEARS ENDED MARCH 31

	2011	2010
Sales	$3,000,000	$2,700,000
Cost of goods sold[a]	1,530,000	1,425,000
Gross margin	$1,470,000	$1,275,000
Operating expenses	860,000	780,000
Income before income taxes	$ 610,000	$ 495,000
Income taxes (40%)	244,000	198,000
Net income	$ 366,000	$ 297,000

[a]Depreciation charges on the plant and equipment of $100,000 and $102,500 for fiscal years ended March 31, 2010 and 2011, respectively, are included in cost of goods sold.

Instructions

(a) Compute the following items for Bradburn Corporation.
  (1) Current ratio for fiscal years 2010 and 2011.
  (2) Acid-test (quick) ratio for fiscal years 2010 and 2011.
  (3) Inventory turnover for fiscal year 2011.
  (4) Return on assets for fiscal years 2010 and 2011. (Assume total assets were $1,688,500 at 3/31/09.)
  (5) Percentage change in sales, cost of goods sold, gross margin, and net income after taxes from fiscal year 2010 to 2011.
(b) Identify and explain what other financial reports and/or financial analyses might be helpful to the commercial loan officer of Topeka National Bank in evaluating Daniel Brown's request for a time extension on Bradburn's notes.
(c) Assume that the percentage changes experienced in fiscal year 2011 as compared with fiscal year 2010 for sales and cost of goods sold will be repeated in each of the next 2 years. Is Bradburn's desire to finance the plant expansion from internally generated funds realistic? Discuss.
(d) Should Topeka National Bank grant the extension on Bradburn's notes considering Daniel Brown's statement about financing the plant expansion through internally generated funds? Discuss.

•13 *P24-4 (Horizontal and Vertical Analysis) Presented on page 1370 are comparative balance sheets for the Gilmour Company.

GILMOUR COMPANY
COMPARATIVE BALANCE SHEET
AS OF DECEMBER 31, 2011 AND 2010

	December 31	
	2011	2010
Assets		
Cash	$ 180,000	$ 275,000
Accounts receivable (net)	220,000	155,000
Short-term investments	270,000	150,000
Inventories	1,060,000	980,000
Prepaid expenses	25,000	25,000
Fixed assets	2,585,000	1,950,000
Accumulated depreciation	(1,000,000)	(750,000)
	$3,340,000	$2,785,000
Liabilities and Stockholders' Equity		
Accounts payable	$ 50,000	$ 75,000
Accrued expenses	170,000	200,000
Bonds payable	450,000	190,000
Capital stock	2,100,000	1,770,000
Retained earnings	570,000	550,000
	$3,340,000	$2,785,000

Instructions

(Round to two decimal places.)

(a) Prepare a comparative balance sheet of Gilmour Company showing the percent each item is of the total assets or total liabilities and stockholders' equity.

(b) Prepare a comparative balance sheet of Gilmour Company showing the dollar change and the percent change for each item.

(c) Of what value is the additional information provided in part (a)?

(d) Of what value is the additional information provided in part (b)?

·10 ***P24-5** **(Dividend Policy Analysis)** Matheny Inc. went public 3 years ago. The board of directors will be meeting shortly after the end of the year to decide on a dividend policy. In the past, growth has been financed primarily through the retention of earnings. A stock or a cash dividend has never been declared. Presented below is a brief financial summary of Matheny Inc. operations.

			($000 omitted)		
	2011	2010	2009	2008	2007
Sales	$20,000	$16,000	$14,000	$6,000	$4,000
Net income	2,400	1,400	800	700	250
Average total assets	22,000	19,000	11,500	4,200	3,000
Current assets	8,000	6,000	3,000	1,200	1,000
Working capital	3,600	3,200	1,200	500	400
Common shares:					
Number of shares					
outstanding (000)	2,000	2,000	2,000	20	20
Average market price	$9	$6	$4	—	—

Instructions

(a) Suggest factors to be considered by the board of directors in establishing a dividend policy.

(b) Compute the rate of return on assets, profit margin on sales, earnings per share, price-earnings ratio, and current ratio for each of the 5 years for Matheny Inc.

(c) Comment on the appropriateness of declaring a cash dividend at this time, using the ratios computed in part (b) as a major factor in your analysis.

CONCEPTS FOR ANALYSIS

CA24-1 (General Disclosures; Inventories; Property, Plant, and Equipment) Koch Corporation is in the process of preparing its annual financial statements for the fiscal year ended April 30, 2011. Because all of Koch's shares are traded intrastate, the company does not have to file any reports with the Securities and Exchange Commission. The company manufactures plastic, glass, and paper containers for sale to food and drink manufacturers and distributors.

Koch Corporation maintains separate control accounts for its raw materials, work-in-process, and finished goods inventories for each of the three types of containers. The inventories are valued at the lower-of-cost-or-market.

The company's property, plant, and equipment are classified in the following major categories: land, office buildings, furniture and fixtures, manufacturing facilities, manufacturing equipment, and leasehold improvements. All fixed assets are carried at cost. The depreciation methods employed depend on the type of asset (its classification) and when it was acquired.

Koch Corporation plans to present the inventory and fixed asset amounts in its April 30, 2011, balance sheet as shown below.

Inventories	$4,814,200
Property, plant, and equipment (net of depreciation)	6,310,000

Instructions
What information regarding inventories and property, plant, and equipment must be disclosed by Koch Corporation in the audited financial statements issued to stockholders, either in the body or the notes, for the 2010–2011 fiscal year?

(CMA adapted)

CA24-2 (Disclosures Required in Various Situations) Ace Inc. produces electronic components for sale to manufacturers of radios, television sets, and digital sound systems. In connection with her examination of Ace's financial statements for the year ended December 31, 2011, Gloria Rodd, CPA, completed field work 2 weeks ago. Ms. Rodd now is evaluating the significance of the following items prior to preparing her auditor's report. Except as noted, none of these items have been disclosed in the financial statements or notes.

Item 1
A 10-year loan agreement, which the company entered into 3 years ago, provides that dividend payments may not exceed net income earned after taxes subsequent to the date of the agreement. The balance of retained earnings at the date of the loan agreement was $420,000. From that date through December 31, 2011, net income after taxes has totaled $570,000 and cash dividends have totaled $320,000. On the basis of these data, the staff auditor assigned to this review concluded that there was no retained earnings restriction at December 31, 2011.

Item 2
Recently Ace interrupted its policy of paying cash dividends quarterly to its stockholders. Dividends were paid regularly through 2010, discontinued for all of 2011 to finance purchase of equipment for the company's new plant, and resumed in the first quarter of 2012. In the annual report dividend policy is to be discussed in the president's letter to stockholders.

Item 3
A major electronics firm has introduced a line of products that will compete directly with Ace's primary line, now being produced in the specially designed new plant. Because of manufacturing innovations, the competitor's line will be of comparable quality but priced 50% below Ace's line. The competitor announced its new line during the week following completion of field work. Ms. Rodd read the announcement in the newspaper and discussed the situation by telephone with Ace executives. Ace will meet the lower prices that are high enough to cover variable manufacturing and selling expenses but will permit recovery of only a portion of fixed costs.

Item 4
The company's new manufacturing plant building, which cost $2,400,000 and has an estimated life of 25 years, is leased from Wichita National Bank at an annual rental of $600,000. The company is obligated to pay property taxes, insurance, and maintenance. At the conclusion of its 10-year noncancellable lease, the company has the option of purchasing the property for $1. In Ace's income statement, the rental payment is reported on a separate line.

Instructions

For each of the items on page 1371, discuss any additional disclosures in the financial statements and notes that the auditor should recommend to her client. (The cumulative effect of the four items should not be considered.)

CA24-3 (Disclosures, Conditional and Contingent Liabilities)   Presented below are three independent situations.

Situation 1

A company offers a one-year warranty for the product that it manufactures. A history of warranty claims has been compiled, and the probable amounts of claims related to sales for a given period can be determined.

Situation 2

Subsequent to the date of a set of financial statements, but prior to the issuance of the financial statements, a company enters into a contract that will probably result in a significant loss to the company. The amount of the loss can be reasonably estimated.

Situation 3

A company has adopted a policy of recording self-insurance for any possible losses resulting from injury to others by the company's vehicles. The premium for an insurance policy for the same risk from an independent insurance company would have an annual cost of $4,000. During the period covered by the financial statements, there were no accidents involving the company's vehicles that resulted in injury to others.

Instructions

Discuss the accrual or type of disclosure necessary (if any) and the reason(s) why such disclosure is appropriate for each of the three independent sets of facts above.

(AICPA adapted)

CA24-4 (Post-Balance-Sheet Events)   At December 31, 2010, Coburn Corp. has assets of $10,000,000, liabilities of $6,000,000, common stock of $2,000,000 (representing 2,000,000 shares of $1 par common stock), and retained earnings of $2,000,000. Net sales for the year 2010 were $18,000,000, and net income was $800,000. As auditors of this company, you are making a review of subsequent events on February 13, 2011, and you find the following.

1. On February 3, 2011, one of Coburn's customers declared bankruptcy. At December 31, 2010, this company owed Coburn $300,000, of which $60,000 was paid in January, 2011.
2. On January 18, 2011, one of the three major plants of the client burned.
3. On January 23, 2011, a strike was called at one of Coburn's largest plants, which halted 30% of its production. As of today (February 13) the strike has not been settled.
4. A major electronics enterprise has introduced a line of products that would compete directly with Coburn's primary line, now being produced in a specially designed new plant. Because of manufacturing innovations, the competitor has been able to achieve quality similar to that of Coburn's products, but at a price 50% lower. Coburn officials say they will meet the lower prices, which are high enough to cover variable manufacturing and selling costs but which permit recovery of only a portion of fixed costs.
5. Merchandise traded in the open market is recorded in the company's records at $1.40 per unit on December 31, 2010. This price had prevailed for 2 weeks, after release of an official market report that predicted vastly enlarged supplies; however, no purchases were made at $1.40. The price throughout the preceding year had been about $2, which was the level experienced over several years. On January 18, 2011, the price returned to $2, after public disclosure of an error in the official calculations of the prior December, correction of which destroyed the expectations of excessive supplies. Inventory at December 31, 2010, was on a lower-of-cost-or-market basis.
6. On February 1, 2011, the board of directors adopted a resolution accepting the offer of an investment banker to guarantee the marketing of $1,200,000 of preferred stock.

Instructions

State in each case how the 2010 financial statements would be affected, if at all.

CA24-5 (Segment Reporting)   You are compiling the consolidated financial statements for Winsor Corporation International. The corporation's accountant, Anthony Reese, has provided you with the segment information shown on page 1373.

Note 7: Major Segments of Business

WCI conducts funeral service and cemetery operations in the United States and Canada. Substantially all revenues of WCI's major segments of business are from unaffiliated customers. Segment information for fiscal 2011, 2010, and 2009 follows.

	Funeral	Floral	Cemetery	Real Estate	Dried Whey	Limousine	Consolidated
				(thousands)			
Revenues							
2011	$302,000	$10,000	$ 73,000	$ 2,000	$7,000	$12,000	$406,000
2010	245,000	6,000	61,000	4,000	4,000	4,000	324,000
2009	208,000	3,000	42,000	3,000	1,000	3,000	260,000
Operating Income							
2011	74,000	1,500	18,000	(36,000)	500	2,000	60,000
2010	64,000	200	12,000	(28,000)	200	400	48,800
2009	54,000	150	6,000	(21,000)	100	350	39,600
Capital Expenditures							
2011	26,000	1,000	9,000	400	300	1,000	37,700
2010	28,000	2,000	60,000	1,500	100	700	92,300
2009	14,000	25	8,000	600	25	50	22,700
Depreciation and Amortization							
2011	13,000	100	2,400	1,400	100	200	17,200
2010	10,000	50	1,400	700	50	100	12,300
2009	8,000	25	1,000	600	25	50	9,700
Identifiable Assets							
2011	334,000	1,500	162,000	114,000	500	8,000	620,000
2010	322,000	1,000	144,000	52,000	1,000	6,000	526,000
2009	223,000	500	78,000	34,000	500	3,500	339,500

Instructions

Determine which of the above segments must be reported separately and which can be combined under the category "Other." Then, write a one-page memo to the company's accountant, Anthony Reese, explaining the following.

  (a) What segments must be reported separately and what segments can be combined.
  (b) What criteria you used to determine reportable segments.
  (c) What major items for each must be disclosed.

CA24-6 (Segment Reporting—Theory) Presented below is an excerpt from the financial statements of **H. J. Heinz Company**.

Segment and Geographic Data

The company is engaged principally in one line of business—processed food products—which represents over 90% of consolidated sales. Information about the business of the company by geographic area is presented in the table below.

There were no material amounts of sales or transfers between geographic areas or between affiliates, and no material amounts of United States export sales.

(in thousands of U.S. dollars)	Domestic	United Kingdom	Canada	Western Europe	Other	Total	Worldwide
				Foreign			
Sales	$2,381,054	$547,527	$216,726	$383,784	$209,354	$1,357,391	$3,738,445
Operating income	246,780	61,282	34,146	29,146	25,111	149,685	396,465
Identifiable assets	1,362,152	265,218	112,620	294,732	143,971	816,541	2,178,693
Capital expenditures	72,712	12,262	13,790	8,253	4,368	38,673	111,385
Depreciation expense	42,279	8,364	3,592	6,355	3,606	21,917	64,196

Instructions

  (a) Why does H. J. Heinz not prepare segment information on its products or services?
  (b) What are export sales, and when should they be disclosed?
  (c) Why are sales by geographical area important to disclose?

CA24-7 (Segment Reporting—Theory) The following article appeared in the *Wall Street Journal*.

WASHINGTON—The Securities and Exchange Commission staff issued guidelines for companies grappling with the problem of dividing up their business into industry segments for their annual reports.

An industry segment is defined by the Financial Accounting Standards Board as a part of an enterprise engaged in providing a product or service or a group of related products or services primarily to unaffiliated customers for a profit.

Although conceding that the process is a "subjective task" that "to a considerable extent, depends on the judgment of management," the SEC staff said companies should consider . . . various factors . . . to determine whether products and services should be grouped together or reported as segments.

Instructions
- **(a)** What does financial reporting for segments of a business enterprise involve?
- **(b)** Identify the reasons for requiring financial data to be reported by segments.
- **(c)** Identify the possible disadvantages of requiring financial data to be reported by segments.
- **(d)** Identify the accounting difficulties inherent in segment reporting.

CA24-8 (Interim Reporting) Snider Corporation, a publicly traded company, is preparing the interim financial data which it will issue to its stockholders and the Securities and Exchange Commission (SEC) at the end of the first quarter of the 2010–2011 fiscal year. Snider's financial accounting department has compiled the following summarized revenue and expense data for the first quarter of the year.

Sales	$60,000,000
Cost of goods sold	36,000,000
Variable selling expenses	1,000,000
Fixed selling expenses	3,000,000

Included in the fixed selling expenses was the single lump-sum payment of $2,000,000 for television advertisements for the entire year.

Instructions
- **(a)** Snider Corporation must issue its quarterly financial statements in accordance with generally accepted accounting principles regarding interim financial reporting.
  - **(1)** Explain whether Snider should report its operating results for the quarter as if the quarter were a separate reporting period in and of itself, or as if the quarter were an integral part of the annual reporting period.
  - **(2)** State how the sales, cost of goods sold, and fixed selling expenses would be reflected in Snider Corporation's quarterly report prepared for the first quarter of the 2010–2011 fiscal year. Briefly justify your presentation.
- **(b)** What financial information, as a minimum, must Snider Corporation disclose to its stockholders in its quarterly reports?

(CMA adapted)

 CA24-9 (Treatment of Various Interim Reporting Situations) The following statement is an excerpt from the FASB pronouncement related to interim reporting.

Interim financial information is essential to provide investors and others with timely information as to the progress of the enterprise. The usefulness of such information rests on the relationship that it has to the annual results of operations. Accordingly, the Board has concluded that each interim period should be viewed primarily as an integral part of an annual period.

In general, the results for each interim period should be based on the accounting principles and practices used by an enterprise in the preparation of its latest annual financial statements unless a change in an accounting practice or policy has been adopted in the current year. The Board has concluded, however, that certain accounting principles and practices followed for annual reporting purposes may require modification at interim reporting dates so that the reported results for the interim period may better relate to the results of operations for the annual period.

Instructions
Listed on page 1375 are six independent cases on how accounting facts might be reported on an individual company's interim financial reports. For each of these cases, state whether the method proposed to be used for interim reporting would be acceptable under generally accepted accounting principles applicable to interim financial data. Support each answer with a brief explanation.

(a) J. D. Long Company takes a physical inventory at year-end for annual financial statement purposes. Inventory and cost of sales reported in the interim quarterly statements are based on estimated gross profit rates, because a physical inventory would result in a cessation of operations. Long Company does have reliable perpetual inventory records.

(b) Rockford Company is planning to report one-fourth of its pension expense each quarter.

(c) Republic Company wrote inventory down to reflect lower-of-cost-or-market in the first quarter. At year-end the market exceeds the original acquisition cost of this inventory. Consequently, management plans to write the inventory back up to its original cost as a year-end adjustment.

(d) Gansner Company realized a large gain on the sale of investments at the beginning of the second quarter. The company wants to report one-third of the gain in each of the remaining quarters.

(e) Fredonia Company has estimated its annual audit fee. It plans to pro rate this expense equally over all four quarters.

(f) LaBrava Company was reasonably certain it would have an employee strike in the third quarter. As a result, it shipped heavily during the second quarter but plans to defer the recognition of the sales in excess of the normal sales volume. The deferred sales will be recognized as sales in the third quarter when the strike is in progress. LaBrava Company management thinks this is more representative of normal second- and third-quarter operations.

CA24-10 (Financial Forecasts) An article in *Barron's* noted the following.

Okay. Last fall, someone with a long memory and an even longer arm reached into that bureau drawer and came out with a moldy cheese sandwich and the equally moldy notion of corporate forecasts. We tried to find out what happened to the cheese sandwich—but, rats!, even recourse to the Freedom of Information Act didn't help. However, the forecast proposal was dusted off, polished up and found quite serviceable. The SEC, indeed, lost no time in running it up the old flagpole—but no one was very eager to salute. Even after some of the more objectionable features—compulsory corrections and detailed explanations of why the estimates went awry—were peeled off the original proposal.

Seemingly, despite the Commission's smiles and sweet talk, those craven corporations were still afraid that an honest mistake would lead them down the primrose path to consent decrees and class action suits. To lay to rest such qualms, the Commission last week approved a "Safe Harbor" rule that, providing the forecasts were made on a reasonable basis and in good faith, protected corporations from litigation should the projections prove wide of the mark (as only about 99% are apt to do).

Instructions
(a) What are the arguments for preparing profit forecasts?
(b) What is the purpose of the "safe harbor" rule?
(c) Why are corporations concerned about presenting profit forecasts?

CA24-11 (Disclosure of Estimates) Nancy Tercek, the financial vice president, and Margaret Lilly, the controller, of Romine Manufacturing Company are reviewing the financial ratios of the company for the years 2010 and 2011. The financial vice president notes that the profit margin on sales ratio has increased from 6% to 12%, a hefty gain for the 2-year period. Tercek is in the process of issuing a media release that emphasizes the efficiency of Romine Manufacturing in controlling cost. Margaret Lilly knows that the difference in ratios is due primarily to an earlier company decision to reduce the estimates of warranty and bad debt expense for 2011. The controller, not sure of her supervisor's motives, hesitates to suggest to Tercek that the company's improvement is unrelated to efficiency in controlling cost. To complicate matters, the media release is scheduled in a few days.

Instructions
(a) What, if any, is the ethical dilemma in this situation?
(b) Should Lilly, the controller, remain silent? Give reasons.
(c) What stakeholders might be affected by Tercek's media release?
(d) Give your opinion on the following statement and cite reasons: "Because Tercek, the vice president, is most directly responsible for the media release, Lilly has no real responsibility in this matter."

CA24-12 (Reporting of Subsequent Events) In June 2010, the board of directors for McElroy Enterprises Inc. authorized the sale of $10,000,000 of corporate bonds. Jennifer Grayson, treasurer for McElroy Enterprises Inc., is concerned about the date when the bonds are issued. The company really needs the

cash, but she is worried that if the bonds are issued before the company's year-end (December 31, 2010) the additional liability will have an adverse effect on a number of important ratios. In July, she explains to company president William McElroy that if they delay issuing the bonds until after December 31 the bonds will not affect the ratios until December 31, 2011. They will have to report the issuance as a subsequent event which requires only footnote disclosure. Grayson expects that with expected improved financial performance in 2011 ratios should be better.

Instructions

(a) What are the ethical issues involved?

(b) Should McElroy agree to the delay?

*CA24-13 (Effect of Transactions on Financial Statements and Ratios) The transactions listed below relate to Wainwright Inc. You are to assume that on the date on which each of the transactions occurred the corporation's accounts showed only common stock ($100 par) outstanding, a current ratio of 2.7:1, and a substantial net income for the year to date (before giving effect to the transaction concerned). On that date the book value per share of stock was $151.53.

Each numbered transaction is to be considered completely independent of the others, and its related answer should be based on the effect(s) of that transaction alone. Assume that all numbered transactions occurred during 2011 and that the amount involved in each case is sufficiently material to distort reported net income if improperly included in the determination of net income. Assume further that each transaction was recorded in accordance with generally accepted accounting principles and, where applicable, in conformity with the all-inclusive concept of the income statement.

For each of the numbered transactions you are to decide whether it:

a. Increased the corporation's 2011 net income.
b. Decreased the corporation's 2011 net income.
c. Increased the corporation's total retained earnings directly (i.e., not via net income).
d. Decreased the corporation's total retained earnings directly.
e. Increased the corporation's current ratio.
f. Decreased the corporation's current ratio.
g. Increased each stockholder's proportionate share of total stockholders' equity.
h. Decreased each stockholder's proportionate share of total stockholders' equity.
i. Increased each stockholder's equity per share of stock (book value).
j. Decreased each stockholder's equity per share of stock (book value).
k. Had none of the foregoing effects.

Instructions

List the numbers 1 through 9. Select as many letters as you deem appropriate to reflect the effect(s) of each transaction as of the date of the transaction by printing beside the transaction number the letter(s) that identifies that transaction's effect(s).

Transactions

_____ 1. In January the board directed the write-off of certain patent rights that had suddenly and unexpectedly become worthless.

_____ 2. The corporation sold at a profit land and a building that had been idle for some time. Under the terms of the sale, the corporation received a portion of the sales price in cash immediately, the balance maturing at 6-month intervals.

_____ 3. Treasury stock originally repurchased and carried at $127 per share was sold for cash at $153 per share.

_____ 4. The corporation wrote off all of the unamortized discount and issue expense applicable to bonds that it refinanced in 2011.

_____ 5. The corporation called in all its outstanding shares of stock and exchanged them for new shares on a 2-for-1 basis, reducing the par value at the same time to $50 per share.

_____ 6. The corporation paid a cash dividend that had been recorded in the accounts at time of declaration.

_____ 7. Litigation involving Wainwright Inc. as defendant was settled in the corporation's favor, with the plaintiff paying all court costs and legal fees. In 2008 the corporation had appropriately established a special contingency for this court action. (Indicate the effect of reversing the contingency only.)

_____ 8. The corporation received a check for the proceeds of an insurance policy from the company with which it is insured against theft of trucks. No entries concerning the theft had been made previously, and the proceeds reduce but do not cover completely the loss.

_____ 9. Treasury stock, which had been repurchased at and carried at $127 per share, was issued as a stock dividend. In connection with this distribution, the board of directors of Wainwright Inc. had authorized a transfer from retained earnings to permanent capital of an amount equal to the aggregate market value ($153 per share) of the shares issued. No entries relating to this dividend had been made previously.

(AICPA adapted)

*Additional Financial
Statement Analysis
Problems*

USING YOUR JUDGMENT

FINANCIAL REPORTING

Financial Reporting Problem

The Procter & Gamble Company (P&G)

As stated in the chapter, notes to the financial statements are the means of explaining the items presented in the main body of the statements. Common note disclosures relate to such items as accounting policies, segmented information, and interim reporting. The financial statements of **P&G** are provided in Appendix 5B or can be accessed at the book's companion website, **www.wiley.com/college/kieso.**

Instructions

Refer to **P&G**'s financial statements and the accompanying notes to answer the following questions.

(a) What specific items does P&G discuss in its Note 1—Summary of Significant Accounting Policies? (List the headings only.)

(b) For what segments did P&G report segmented information? Which segment is the largest? Who is P&G largest customer?

(c) What interim information was reported by P&G?

Comparative Analysis Case

The Coca-Cola Company versus PepsiCo, Inc.

Instructions

Go to the book's companion website and use information found there to answer the following questions related to **The Coca-Cola Company** and **PepsiCo, Inc.**

(a) (1) What specific items does Coca-Cola discuss in its **Note 1—Accounting Policies**? (Prepare a list of the headings only.)

(2) What specific items does PepsiCo discuss in its **Note 2—Our Summary of Significant Accounting Policies**? (Prepare a list of the headings only.)

(b) For what lines of business or segments do Coca-Cola and PepsiCo present segmented information?

(c) Note and comment on the similarities and differences between the auditors' reports submitted by the independent auditors of Coca-Cola and PepsiCo for the year 2007.

*Financial Statement Analysis Case

RNA Inc. manufactures a variety of consumer products. The company's founders have run the company for 30 years and are now interested in retiring. Consequently, they are seeking a purchaser who will continue its operations, and a group of investors, Morgan Inc., is looking into the acquisition of RNA. To evaluate its financial stability and operating efficiency, RNA was requested to provide the latest financial statements and selected financial ratios. Summary information provided by RNA is presented on the next page.

RNA
INCOME STATEMENT
FOR THE YEAR ENDED NOVEMBER 30, 2011
(IN THOUSANDS)

Sales (net)	$30,500
Interest income	500
Total revenue	31,000
Costs and expenses	
Cost of goods sold	17,600
Selling and administrative expenses	3,550
Depreciation and amortization expense	1,890
Interest expense	900
Total costs and expenses	23,940
Income before taxes	7,060
Income taxes	2,800
Net income	$ 4,260

RNA
STATEMENT OF FINANCIAL POSITION
AS OF NOVEMBER 30
(IN THOUSANDS)

	2011	2010
Cash	$ 400	$ 500
Marketable securities (at cost)	300	200
Accounts receivable (net)	3,200	2,900
Inventory	6,000	5,400
Total current assets	9,900	9,000
Property, plant, & equipment (net)	7,100	7,000
Total assets	$17,000	$16,000
Accounts payable	$ 3,700	$ 3,400
Income taxes payable	900	800
Accrued expenses	1,700	1,400
Total current liabilities	6,300	5,600
Long-term debt	2,000	1,800
Total liabilities	8,300	7,400
Common stock ($1 par value)	2,700	2,700
Paid-in capital in excess of par	1,000	1,000
Retained earnings	5,000	4,900
Total shareholders' equity	8,700	8,600
Total liabilities and shareholders' equity	$17,000	$16,000

SELECTED FINANCIAL RATIOS

	RNA 2010	RNA 2009	Current Industry Average
Current ratio	1.61	1.62	1.63
Acid-test ratio	.64	.63	.68
Times interest earned	8.55	8.50	8.45
Profit margin on sales	13.2%	12.1%	13.0%
Asset turnover	1.84	1.83	1.84
Inventory turnover	3.17	3.21	3.18

Instructions

(a) Calculate a new set of ratios for the fiscal year 2011 for RNA based on the financial statements presented.
(b) Explain the analytical use of each of the seven ratios presented, describing what the investors can learn about RNA's financial stability and operating efficiency.
(c) Identify two limitations of ratio analysis.

(CMA adapted)

BRIDGE TO THE PROFESSION

Professional Research: FASB Codification

As part of the year-end audit, you are discussing the disclosure checklist with your client. The checklist identifies the items that must be disclosed in a set of GAAP financial statements. The client is surprised by the disclosure item related to accounting policies. Specifically, since the audit report will attest to the statements being prepared in accordance with GAAP, the client questions the accounting policy checklist item. The client has asked you to conduct some research to verify the accounting policy disclosures.

Instructions

Access the FASB Codification at *http://asc.fasb.org/home* to conduct research using the Codification Research System to prepare responses to the following items. Provide Codification references for your responses.

(a) In general, what should disclosures of accounting policies encompass?

(b) List some examples of the most commonly required disclosures.

*Professional Simulation

Go to the book's companion website, at **www.wiley.com/college/kieso,** to find an interactive problem that simulates the computerized CPA exam. The professional simulation for this chapter asks you to address questions related to financial ratio analysis.

KWW_Professional _Simulation		
Financial Ratio Analysis	Time Remaining 0 hours 40 minutes	copy paste calculator sheet standards help splitter done

Remember to check the book's companion website to find additional resources for this chapter.

FASB CODIFICATION—THE NEW VIEW OF GENERALLY ACCEPTED ACCOUNTING PRINCIPLES

Learning Generally Accepted Accounting Principles (GAAP) used to be a daunting task, as the documents that comprise it vary in format, completeness, and structure. In some cases, these documents are inconsistent and difficult to interpret. As a result, financial statement preparers sometimes are unsure whether they have the right GAAP, which makes determining what is authoritative, and what is not, difficult. In response to these concerns, the FASB **developed the Financial Accounting Standards Board Accounting Standards Codification** (or simply, the Codification). The Codification provides in one place all the authoritative literature related to a given topic. It explains what GAAP is and eliminates nonessential information, such as redundant document summaries, basis for conclusions sections, and historical content. This greatly simplifies user access to GAAP.

USING THE FASB CODIFICATION

The Codification – accessible at **http://asc.fasb.org/home** — is available as an online, real-time database. Presently, the Codification is available to use at no cost. You simply need to register by clicking on the Registration link, which is located in the **area marked "D"** on the Codification screenshot shown below.

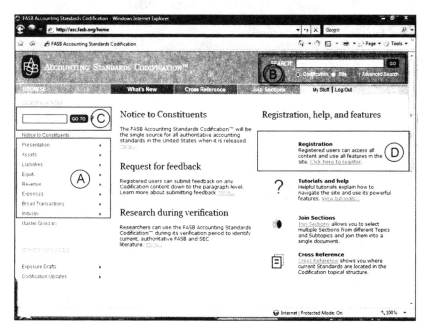

In order to use the Codification effectively, you need to understand its structure. Four major categories of topics are used to structure all of the topics:

- ● Presentation—topics related to financial statement presentation, such as the Balance Sheet and Earnings per Share
- ● Financial Statement Accounts—topics related to specific Assets, Liabilities, Equity, Revenue and Expenses
- ● Broad Transactions: topics related to multiple financial statement accounts, such as Leasing
- ● Industries—all industry-specific guidance

For example, suppose you had a question related to the proper accounting for the intangible asset Goodwill. You could directly access this information by drilling down into the Codification as follows: Assets>Intangible Assets>Goodwill. To navigate in this manner, go to the **area marked "A"** on the screenshot.

However, understanding the overall structure of the Codification is only one of three methods used for accessing its contents. A second method is to use the Codification search tool, which works much like common Internet search engines. As with most search engines, the more often you use it, the more efficient and effective you will be at locating the information. The **area to input your search terms is marked "B"** in the Codification screenshot.

The third method to access specific material in the Codification is through the Codification's numbering system. If you know specific Topic, Subtopic, and Section numbers, you can access them directly. For example, if you wanted to review all of the Codification material related to disclosures for operating leases, you could go directly to Topic 840 (Leases), Subtopic 320 (Operating Leases), and Section 50 (Disclosure). This numbering system also provides a way to efficiently reference material in the Codification. For example, FASB ASC 840-20-50 would be the reference for the operating lease disclosure material. To use this method, enter the information in the boxed **area marked "C"** in the screenshot.

USING THE FASB CODIFICATION IN THIS TEXTBOOK

For individuals (like you) attempting to learn GAAP, the Codification will be invaluable. It is an outstanding effort by the profession to streamline and simplify how to determine what GAAP is, which will lead to better financial accounting and reporting. We provide references to the Codification throughout this textbook using a numbering system. For example, a bracket with a number, such as **[1]**, indicates that the citation to the FASB Codification can be found in the FASB Codification section at the end of the chapter (immediately before the assignment materials). FASB Codification Exercises have been included at the end of each chapter, to help familiarize you with this useful tool.

See the FASB Codification section at the end of each chapter for Codification references and exercises.